Contents at a Glance

Table of Contents

About the Author

John Ray is currently serving as the Interim Director of the Office of Research Information Systems for the Ohio State University. He has written numerous books for Macmillan/Sams/ Que, including *Using TCP/IP: Special Edition, Teach Yourself Dreamweaver MX in 21 Days, Mac OS X Unleashed, My Mountain Lion MacBook,* and *Teach Yourself iOS 5 Development in 24 Hours.* As a Macintosh user since 1984, he strives to ensure that each project presents the Macintosh with the equality and depth it deserves. Even technical titles such as *Using TCP/IP* contain extensive information about the Macintosh and its applications and have garnered numerous positive reviews for their straightforward approach and accessibility to beginner and intermediate users.

You can visit his website at http://teachyourselfios.com or follow him on Twitter at @johnemeryray or #iOSIn24.

Dedication

This edition of iOS 6 is dedicated to the memory
of iOS 5 and the upcoming birth of iOS 7.

Acknowledgments

Thank you to the group at Sams Publishing—Laura Norman, Keith Cline, Anne Groves—for slowly nudging me toward the finish line. As I read and re-read these chapters, I'm amazed at how you can see the intention behind the seemingly random words that I type. The team has performed pure magic in transforming the files I've submitted into clean, well-styled, content.

As always, thanks to everyone who puts up with me over the months of writing. I'm grateful for your support.

We Want to Hear from You!

As the reader of this book, *you* are our most important critic and commentator. We value your opinion and want to know what we're doing right, what we could do better, what areas you'd like to see us publish in, and any other words of wisdom you're willing to pass our way.

We welcome your comments. You can email or write to let us know what you did or didn't like about this book—as well as what we can do to make our books better.

Please note that we cannot help you with technical problems related to the topic of this book.

When you write, please be sure to include this book's title and author as well as your name and email address. We will carefully review your comments and share them with the author and editors who worked on the book.

Email: consumer@samspublishing.com

Mail: Sams Publishing
         ATTN: Reader Feedback
         800 East 96th Street
         Indianapolis, IN 46240 USA

Reader Services

Visit our website and register this book at informit.com/register for convenient access to any updates, downloads, or errata that might be available for this book.

Introduction

When you pick up an iOS device and use it, you feel connected. Whether it be an iPad, an iPhone, or an iPod, the interface acts as an extension to your fingers; it is smooth, comfortable, and invites exploration. Other competing devices offer similar features, and even sport gadgets such as styluses and trackpads, but they cannot match the user experience that is iOS.

When creating iOS and the Xcode tools used to develop for it, Apple considered everything from interface to application performance and battery life. There is always the expectation that, no matter what, the device will remain responsive and usable. As a developer, does this mean that there are rules to follow? Absolutely. But, by following these rules, you can create applications that are interactive works of art for your users to love—not software they will load and forget.

Through the App Store, Apple has created the ultimate digital distribution system for iOS applications. Programmers of any age or affiliation can submit their applications to the App Store for just the cost of a modest yearly Developer Membership fee. Games, utilities, and full-feature applications have been built for everything from pre-K education to retirement living. No matter what the content, with a user base as large as the iPhone, iPod Touch, and iPad, an audience exists.

Each year, Apple introduces new devices—bringing larger, faster, and higher-resolution capabilities to the iOS family. With each new hardware refresh come new development opportunities and new ways to explore the boundaries between software and art.

My hope is that this book brings iOS development to a new generation of developers. *Teach Yourself iOS 6 Development in 24 Hours* provides a clear and natural progression of skills development, from installing developer tools and registering your device with Apple, to submitting an application to the App Store. It's everything you need to get started in 24 one-hour lessons.

Who Can Become an iOS Developer?

If you have an interest in learning, time to invest in exploring and practicing with Apple's developer tools, and an Intel Macintosh computer running Mountain Lion, you have everything you need to begin creating software for iOS.

Developing an app won't happen overnight, but with dedication and practice, you can be writing your first applications in a matter of days. The more time you spend working with the Apple developer tools, the more opportunities you'll discover for creating new and exciting projects.

You should approach iOS application development as creating software that *you* want to use, not what you think others want. If you're solely interested in getting rich quick, you're likely to be disappointed. (The App Store is a crowded marketplace—albeit one with a lot of room—and competition for top sales is fierce.) However, if you focus on building useful and unique apps, you're much more likely to find an appreciative audience.

Who Should Use This Book?

This book targets individuals who are new to development for iOS and have experience using the Macintosh platform. No previous experience with Objective-C, Cocoa, or the Apple developer tools is required. Of course, if you do have development experience, some of the tools and techniques may be easier to master, but the author does not assume that you've coded before.

That said, some things are expected of you, the reader. Specifically, you must be willing to invest in the learning process. If you just read each hour's lesson without working through the tutorials, you will likely miss some fundamental concepts. In addition, you need to spend time reading the Apple developer documentation and researching the topics presented in this book. A vast amount of information on iOS development is available, but only limited space in this book. Therefore, this book covers what you need to forge your own path forward.

What Is (and Isn't) in This Book?

The material in this book specifically targets iOS release 6 and later on Xcode 4.5 and later. Much of what you'll learn is common to all the iOS releases, but this book also covers several important areas that have only come about in recent iOS releases, such as gesture recognizers, embedded video playback with AirPlay, Core Image, social networking, multitasking, universal (iPhone/iPad) applications, and more!

Unfortunately, this is not a complete reference for the iOS application programming interfaces (APIs); some topics just require much more space than this book allows. Thankfully, the Apple developer documentation is available directly within the free tools you install in Hour 1, "Preparing Your System and iDevice for Development." In many hours, you'll find a section titled "Further Exploration." This identifies additional related topics of interest. Again, a willingness to explore is an important quality in becoming a successful developer.

Each coding lesson is accompanied by project files that include everything you need to compile and test an example or, preferably, follow along and build the application yourself. Be sure to download the project files from this book's website at http://teachyourselfios.com. If you have issues with any projects, view the posts on this site to see whether a solution has been identified.

In addition to the support website, you can follow along on Twitter! Search for #iOSIn24 on Twitter to receive official updates and tweets from other readers. Use the hashtag #iOSIn24 in your tweets to join the conversation. To send me messages via Twitter, begin each tweet with @johnemeryray.

HOUR 1
Preparing Your System and iDevice for Development

What You'll Learn in This Hour:

▶ The iOS hardware limitations you face

▶ Where to get the tools you need to develop for iOS devices

▶ How to join the iOS Developer Program

▶ The need for (and use of) provisioning profiles

▶ What to expect during the first few hours of this book

The iOS device family opens up a whole realm of possibilities for developers: Multitouch interfaces, always-on Internet access, video, and a whole range of built-in sensors can be used to create everything from games to serious productivity applications. Believe it or not, as a new developer, you have an advantage. You are starting fresh, free from any preconceived notions of what is possible in a mobile application. Your next big idea may well become the next big thing on Apple's App Store.

This hour prepares you for your first development project. You're about to embark on the road to becoming an iOS developer, but you need to do a bit of prep work before you start coding.

Welcome to the iOS Platform

If you're reading this book, you probably already have an iOS device, and that means you already understand how to interact with its interface. Crisp graphics, amazing responsiveness, multitouch, and hundreds of thousands of apps—this just begins to scratch the surface. As a developer, however, you need to get accustomed to dealing with a platform that, to borrow a phrase from Apple, forces you to "think different."

iOS Devices

The iOS platform family currently consists of the iPhone, iPad, iPod touch, and Apple TV; but at present, the Apple TV is not open for development. As you work on the tutorials in this book, you'll notice that in many screenshots that I focus on iPhone-centric projects. This isn't because I'm lacking iPad love; it's because iPad interfaces are so large, it's difficult to capture them in a screenshot. The good news is that if you want to develop a project on the iPad, you develop it on the iPad. If you want to develop it for the iPhone, you develop it for the iPhone. In almost all cases, the coding process is identical. In the few cases where it isn't, I make sure you understand what is different between the devices (and why). You'll also find that each tutorial is available in an iPad and iPhone version on this book's website (http://teachyourselfios.com), so you can follow along with a working application on whatever device you choose.

NOTE

Like Apple's developer tools and documentation, I do not differentiate between the iPhone and iPod touch in the lessons. For all intents and purposes, developing for these devices is identical, although some capabilities aren't available in earlier versions of the iPod touch (but the same can be said for earlier versions of the iPhone and iPad, as well).

Display and Graphics

The iOS devices offer a variety of different resolutions, but iOS provides a simple way of thinking about them. The traditional iPhone screen (before the iPhone 5), for example, is 320×480 points. Notice that I said *points*, not pixels. Before the release of the iPhone 4's Retina display, the iPhone was 320×480 pixels. Now, the actual resolution of an iOS device is abstracted behind a scaling factor. This means that although you may be working with the numbers like 320×480 for positioning elements, your device may have more pixels than that. The iPhone 4 and 4(s), for example, have a scaling factor of 2, which means that they are really (320×2) × (480×2) or 640×960 pixel resolution devices. The iPhone 5 changes things a bit by using a longer 320×568 point (640×1136 pixel) screen (see Figure 1.1). Although that might seem like quite a bit of screen real estate, remember that all these pixels are displayed on a screen that is roughly 4 inches diagonal.

The iPad family follows a similar pattern. The iPad 2 and iPad mini use screens with 768×1024 points and a scaling factor of 1. The latest generation full-sized iPad with a Retina display, still has a 768×1024-point screen but with a scaling factor of 2 and a resolution of 1536×2048 pixels.

We take a closer look at how scaling factors work when we position objects on the screen throughout this book. The important thing to know is that when you're building your applications, iOS automatically takes the scaling factor into play to display your apps and their interfaces at the highest possible resolution (with rarely any additional work on your part).

320 points

568 points

FIGURE 1.1
The iPhone 5 screen is measured in points—320x568 (portrait), 568x320 (landscape)—but each point may be made up of more than 1 pixel.

If you have a 27-inch cinema display on your desk, these handheld resolutions may seem limiting. Keep in mind, however, that desktop computers only recently exceeded this size, and many websites are still designed for 800×600. In addition, an iOS device's display is dedicated to the currently running application. You have one window to work in. You can change the content within that window, but the desktop and multiwindow application metaphors are gone.

The screen limits aren't a bad thing. As you'll learn, the iOS development tools give you plenty of opportunities to create applications with just as much depth as your desktop software—albeit with a more structured and efficient interface design.

The graphics that you display on your screen can include complex animated 2D and 3D displays thanks to the OpenGL ES implementation available on all iOS devices. OpenGL is an industry standard for defining and manipulating graphic images that is widely used when creating games. Each year's device revisions improve these capabilities with more advanced 3D chipsets and rendering abilities, but even the original iPhone has very respectable imaging abilities.

What About the iPhone 5? Doesn't Its Odd Screen Size Make Life Difficult?

When the iPhone 4 introduced the Retina display, Apple made it remarkably simple to deal with. Without writing any additional code, developers could add Retina-ready resources to their applications that would be loaded automatically as needed. This was possible because even though the resolution of the screen changed, the aspect ratio didn't; there were still the same number of horizontal and vertical points on the screen.

The iPhone 5, however, adds a new wrinkle. The screen is now longer, meaning that, for the first time in the iPhone's lifetime, the number of points on the screen has changed—from 320x480 to 320x568. Although this might seem problematic at first, Apple has updated their interface tools so that interfaces can now smoothly scale to accommodate different screen sizes. Later in this book, you learn how to accommodate the new iPhone 5 screen (and any future displays that Apple may add to their iDevices).

Application Resource Constraints

As with the HD displays on our desktops and laptops, we've grown accustomed to processors that can work faster than we can click. The iOS devices use a range of processors, from a ~400MHz ARM in the early iPhones to the multicore A5, A5X, and A6X in the currently selling iPhone and iPad devices. The "A" chips are a "system on a chip" that provide central processing unit (CPU), graphics processing unit (GPU), and other capabilities to the device, and this series is the first Apple-designed CPU series to be used in quite awhile.

Because Apple has gone to great lengths to keep the iOS devices responsive, your device's capability to multitask is limited. Starting in iOS 4, Apple created a limited set of multitasking application programming interfaces (APIs) for very specific situations. These enable you to perform some tasks in the background, but your application can never assume that it will remain running. iOS preserves the user experience above all else.

Another constraint that you need to be mindful of is the available memory. In the original iPhone, 128MB of RAM is available for the entire system, including your application. There is no virtual memory (slower storage space used as RAM), so you must carefully manage the objects that your application creates. In the latest models of the iPhone and iPad, Apple has graciously provided 1GB. This is great for us, but keep in mind that there are no RAM upgrades for earlier models.

Connectivity

The iPhone and iPad can always be connected to the Internet via a cellular provider (such as AT&T, Verizon, and Sprint in the United States). This wide-area access is supplemented with built-in WiFi and Bluetooth. WiFi can provide desktop-like browsing speeds within the range of a wireless hot spot. Bluetooth, in contrast, can be used to connect a variety of peripheral devices to your device, including a keyboard.

As a developer, you can make use of the Internet connectivity to update the content in your application, display web pages, and create multiplayer games. The only drawback is that applications that rely heavily on 3G or LTE data usage stand a greater chance of being rejected from the App Store. These restrictions have been lessened as time goes by, but what is and isn't permissible on a cell network is still a point of frustration among developers.

Input and Feedback

iOS devices shine when it comes to input and feedback mechanisms and your ability to work with them. You can read the input values from the capacitive multitouch (up to 11 fingers on the iPad) screen, sense motion and tilt via the accelerometer and gyroscope (iPhone 4, iPad 2, and later), determine where you are using the global positioning system (GPS) (cellular service required), see which way you're facing with the digital compass (iPhone 4, iPad 2, and later), and understand how a device is being used with the proximity and light sensors. iOS can provide so much data to your application about how and where it is being used that the device itself truly becomes a controller of sorts—much like (but surpassing) devices such as the Nintendo Wii and PlayStation Move.

iOS devices also support capturing pictures and video (iPhone, iPad 2, and later) directly into your applications, opening a realm of possibilities for interacting with the real world. Already applications are available that identify objects you've taken pictures of and that find references to them online (such as the Amazon Mobile app) or perform real-time translation of printed text (Word Lens).

Finally, for each action your user takes when interacting with your application, you can provide feedback. This, obviously, can be visible feedback on the screen, or it can be high-quality audio and force feedback via vibration (iPhone only). As a developer, you can leverage all these capabilities (as you'll learn in this book).

That wraps up our quick tour of the iOS platform. Never before has a single device defined and provided so many capabilities for a developer. As long as you think through the resource limitations and plan accordingly, a wealth of development opportunities await you.

Becoming an iOS Developer

Being an iOS developer requires more than just sitting down and writing a program. You need a modern Intel Macintosh desktop or laptop running Lion or Mountain Lion and at least 6GB of free space on your hard drive. The more screen space you have on your development system, the easier it is to create an effective workspace. You can even take Xcode into fullscreen mode, removing all distractions. That said, I've worked perfectly happily on a 13-inch MacBook Air, so an ultra-HD multimonitor setup certainly isn't necessary.

So assuming you already have a Mac, what else do you need? The good news is that there isn't *much* more, and it won't cost you a cent to write your first application.

Joining the Apple Developer Program

Despite somewhat confusing messages on the Apple website, there really is no fee associated with joining the Apple Developer Program, downloading the iOS SDK (software development kit), writing iOS applications, and running them on Apple's iOS Simulator.

Limitations do apply, however, to what you can do for free. If you want to have early access to beta versions of the iOS and SDK, you must be a paid member. If you want to load the applications you write on a physical device or distribute them via the App Store, you also need to pay the membership fee. Most applications in this book work just fine on the Simulator provided with the free tools, so the decision on how to proceed is up to you.

Perhaps you aren't yet sure whether the paid program is right for you. Don't worry; you can upgrade at any time. I recommend that you start with the free program and upgrade after you've written a few sample applications and run them in the Simulator.

NOTE
> Obviously, things such as motion sensor input and GPS readings can't be accurately presented in the Simulator, but these are special cases and aren't needed until later in this book.

If you choose to pay, the paid Developer Program offers two levels: a standard program ($99) for those who will be creating applications that they want to distribute from the App Store, and an enterprise program ($299) for large (500+ employee) companies that want to develop and distribute applications in-house but not through the App Store. Most likely, the standard program is what you want.

The standard program is available for both companies and individuals. If you want to publish to the App Store with a business name, you are given the option of choosing a standard "individual" or "company" program during the registration.

Registering as a Developer

Big or small, free or paid, your venture into iOS development begins on Apple's website. To start, visit the Apple Developer Registration Center (https://developer.apple.com/programs/register/), shown in Figure 1.2. If you have an existing Apple ID from using iTunes, iCloud, or other Apple services, you can use that ID for your developer account. If not, or if you want a new ID to use solely for development, you can create a new Apple ID from the registration site as well.

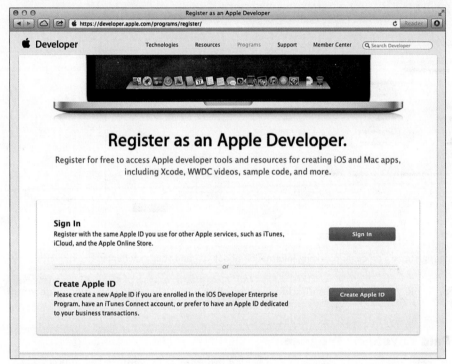

FIGURE 1.2
Visit the Developer Registration site to register or create a new Apple ID.

Assuming you have an ID, click the Sign In button, and then log in using your credentials.

The registration process walks you through the process of collecting information about you or your company, development interests, and experience, as shown in Figure 1.3.

FIGURE 1.3
Walk through the registration process, providing information about you and your experience.

As a final step, Apple verifies your email address by sending you a clickable link to activate your account.

Joining a Paid Developer Program

After you have registered, you can decide to join a paid program or to continue using the free resources. If you choose to join a paid program, point your browser to the iOS Developer enrollment page (http://developer.apple.com/programs/ios/) and click Enroll Now, as shown in Figure 1.4.

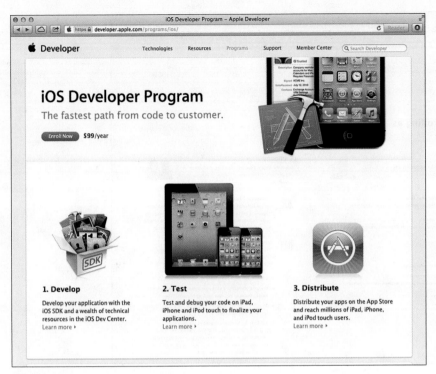

FIGURE 1.4
Choose Enroll Now to join a paid Developer Program.

After reading the introductory text, click Continue to begin the enrollment process. When prompted, choose Sign In with your Apple ID, and then click Continue again.

The registration tool now asks you for your Apple ID and then guides you through applying for the paid programs, including choosing between the individual and company options, as shown in Figure 1.5.

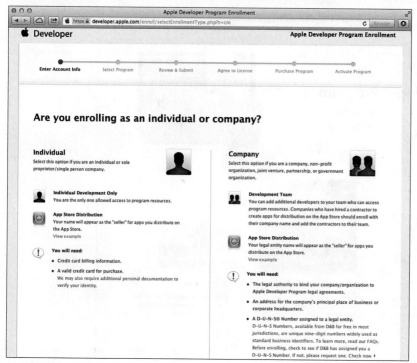

FIGURE 1.5
Choose which paid program you want.

Unlike the free developer membership, the paid Developer Program does not take effect immediately. When the App Store first launched, it took months for new developers to join and be
approved into the program. Today, however, it might take hours or a few days. Just be patient.

Installing Xcode

Thanks to the Mac App Store, downloading Xcode (the iOS development suite) is as easy as point
and click. Open the App Store from your Dock, search for Xcode, and download it for free, as
shown in Figure 1.6. Sit back while your Mac downloads the large (~3GB) application.

FIGURE 1.6
Download the release version of Xcode from the App Store.

If you're interested in the cutting-edge beta releases of Xcode, you can download preview versions directly from the iOS Dev Center (http://developer.apple.com/ios).

TIP

If you have the free developer membership and log in to the iOS Dev Center, you'll likely see just a single installer for Xcode and the iOS SDK (the current-release version of the development tools). If you've become a paid program member, you may see additional links for different versions of the SDK (6.1, 7.0, and so on). The examples in this book are based on the 6.0+ series of iOS SDKs, so be sure to choose that option if presented.

When the download completes, you have either a disk image (if you downloaded a preview release from the iOS Developer site) or an application (if you downloaded from the Mac App Store). Open the disk image, if necessary, and copy the application to your Mac's Applications folder. You can have multiple copies of Xcode installed, so feel free to install both the beta from the dev center and the current stable release from the Mac App Store.

Xcode is interesting in that it is both an application that provides a development environment *and* a wrapper around a collection of standalone tools (such as the iOS Simulator). These additional tools are launched from within Xcode. Xcode, itself, is started like any other application using the Finder or Launchpad (see Figure 1.7).

Mac App Store Release
Developer Preview Release

FIGURE 1.7
Your work will start with Xcode (which you can find in the Applications folder or Launchpad).

Adding Device Support Components

Once the Xcode application itself is installed, you may still need to install some additional software before it can be used. Launch Xcode from the Finder or Launchpad, and then wait for it to start. If it's your first time using the application, you'll likely be prompted to install an additional component (see Figure 1.8) to support mobile development. Click Install to continue.

When the installation completes, you can exit out of Xcode by choosing Quit from the Xcode menu. Your development environment is now ready to go. Although we do not get into real development for a few more hours, we will be configuring a few options in Xcode in the next section, so make sure you've properly prepared your system before proceeding.

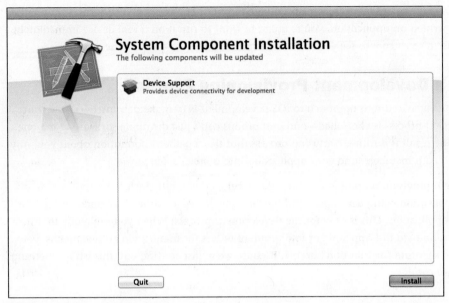

FIGURE 1.8
Xcode requires the installation of additional components before you can use it.

Creating and Installing a Development Provisioning Profile

Even after you've obtained an Apple developer membership, joined a paid Developer Program, and downloaded and installed the iOS development tools, you still cannot run any applications that you write on your actual device. Why? Because you haven't created a development provisioning profile.

CAUTION
___

Only paid developer accounts can complete the following steps. If you have a free developer account, don't fret; you can use the iOS Simulator to test your apps until you're ready for a paid membership. Skip ahead to "Running Your First iOS App," later in this hour.
___

In many development guides, this step isn't covered until after development begins. In my mind, once you've written an application, you're going to want to run it on a real device immediately. Why? Because it's just cool to see your own code running on your own iPhone or iPad.

What's a Development Provisioning Profile?

Like it or not, Apple's current approach to iOS development is to make absolutely certain that the development process is controlled—and that groups can't just distribute software to anyone they want. The result is a rather confusing process that ties together information about you, any development team members, and your application into a *provisioning profile*.

A development provisioning profile identifies the developer who may install an application, an ID for the application being developed, and the "unique device identifiers" for each device that will run the application. This is only for the development process. When you are ready to distribute an application via the App Store or to a group of testers (or friends) via ad hoc means, you must create a separate "distribution" profile. Because we're just starting out, this isn't something you need right away.

Configuring a Device for Development

In the past, creating a provisioning profile for the sole purpose of development was a frustrating and time-consuming activity that took place in an area of the iOS developer site called the Provisioning Portal. Apple has dramatically streamlined the process in recent versions of Xcode, making provisioning as simple as connecting your device and clicking a button.

To install the development profile, first make sure that your device is connected to your computer, and then launch Xcode. When Xcode first launches, dismiss any "welcome" windows that appear, and then immediately choose Window, Organizer from the menu. The Organizer utility slightly resembles iTunes in its layout. You should see your iOS device listed in the leftmost column of the Organizer under the Devices section, as shown in Figure 1.9.

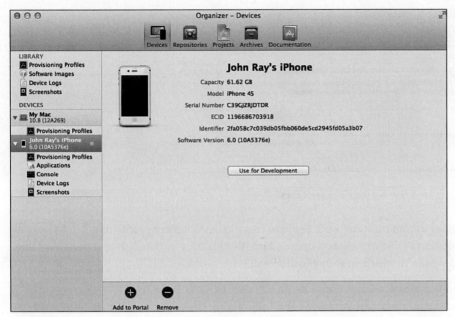

FIGURE 1.9
Open the Xcode Organizer and select your device.

Click the device icon to select it, and then click the Use for Development button (visible in Figure 1.9). When prompted, provide the Apple ID login associated with your paid developer membership. Be sure to click the Remember Password in Keychain check box so that you can access online developer resources through Xcode without encountering additional prompts.

In the background, Xcode is adding a unique identity to the iOS developer portal that identifies you and will be used to digitally sign any applications you generate. It also registers your device with Apple so that it can run the software you create (and beta releases of iOS). If this is the first time you've been through the process, you are asked whether a development certificate should be generated, as shown in Figure 1.10. Click Submit Request to continue.

FIGURE 1.10
Submit a request for a new development certificate.

Xcode continues to communicate with Apple to create a development profile that will be named Team Provisioning Profile as well as a unique App ID. This ID identifies a shared portion of the iOS device keychain to which your application will have access.

The keychain is a secure information store on iOS devices that can be used to save passwords and other critical information. Most apps don't share a keychain space (and therefore cannot share protected information). If you use the same App ID for multiple applications, however, those applications can share keychain data.

For the purposes of this book, there's no reason the tutorial apps can't share a single App ID, so letting Xcode generate an ID for us is just fine. Xcode will, in fact, create a "wildcard" App ID that will be applied to any application you create using the Team Provisioning Profile.

Finally, Apple's servers use all of this information, along with the unique identifier of your connected iOS device, to provide Xcode with a completed provisioning profile. Xcode then transparently uploads the profile to your device.

To view the details of the profile (and verify its installation), make sure the disclosure arrow beside your device name in the Organizer is expanded, and then click the Provisioning Profiles line. You should see the Team Provisioning Profile, date of creation, the automatically generated App ID, and the devices using the profile, as demonstrated in Figure 1.11. Congratulations! You're ready to run an application on your device.

FIGURE 1.11
The profile should now be listed in the Xcode Organizer.

But Wait... I Have More Than One iOS Device

We've discussed provisioning a single device for development. But what if you have multiple devices that you want to install onto? No problem. Just connect the additional devices and use the Use for Development button to add them to your account and provision them.

Apple allows a total of 100 unique devices to be used on your account within the span of 1 year, so be judicious in registering devices if you plan to do extensive in-house development testing.

After you have a development machine configured, you can easily configure other computers using the Provisioning Profile item in the Xcode Organizer's Library section. The Export and Import buttons export (and subsequently import) all your developer profiles/certificates in a single package.

Running Your First iOS App

It seems wrong to go through a whole hour about getting ready for iOS development without any payoff, right? For a real-world test of your efforts, let's actually try to run an application on your iOS device. If you haven't downloaded the project files to your computer, now is a good time to visit http://teachyourselfiOS.com and download the archives.

Within the Hour 1 Projects folder, choose between iPhone and iPad versions of the project, and then open the Welcome folder. Double-click Welcome.xcodeproj to open a simple application in Xcode. After the project opens, your display should be similar to Figure 1.12.

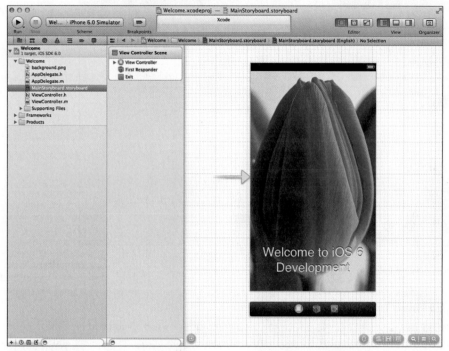

FIGURE 1.12
The opened project should look a bit like this—don't worry if it isn't exactly the same.

Next, make sure that your iOS Device is plugged into your computer. Using the right-hand side of the Scheme pop-up menu in the upper-left corner of the Xcode window, choose the name of your device, as shown in Figure 1.12. This tells Xcode that when the project is built, it should be installed on your device, not run in the Simulator. If you don't have a paid developer membership, choose either the iPhone Simulator or iPad Simulator option, depending on which version of the project you're using.

Typically, you see just one option for running an application on either the iPhone Simulator or the iPad Simulator. In Figure 1.13, you see both. This occurs when you are using an iPhone-targeted app (because they run on both iPhones and iPads) or when an app is a universal application (more on that later in the book). In this case, the screenshot was captured using the iPhone version of the project so that both options could be seen.

FIGURE 1.13
Choose where you want the app to run (on a device or in the Simulator).

Finally, click the Run button in the upper-left corner of the window. After a few seconds, the application should be installed and launched on your device. Because I can't actually show you my device running the app, Figure 1.14 demonstrates what it looks like in the iPhone Simulator.

FIGURE 1.14
Congratulations! You've just installed your first homegrown iOS application.

Click Stop in the Xcode toolbar to exit the application. You can now quit Xcode—we're done with it for the day.

When you clicked Run, the Welcome application was installed and started on your iOS device. It remains there until you remove it manually. Just touch and hold the Welcome icon until it starts wiggling, and then delete the application as you would any other. Applications installed with your development certificate stop working when the certificate expires (120 days after issuance).

Developer Technology Overview

Over the course of the next few hours, you are introduced to the technologies that you'll be using to create iOS applications. The goal is to get you up to speed on the tools and technology, and then you can start actively developing. This means you're still a few hours away from writing your first app, but when you start coding, you'll have the necessary background skills and knowledge to successfully create a wide variety of applications.

The Apple Developer Tools

In this hour, you downloaded and worked with the Xcode application. This, coupled with the iOS Simulator, will be your home for the duration of the book. These two applications are so critical and feature packed that we spend a couple more hours (Hour 2, "Introduction to Xcode and the iOS Simulator," and Hour 5, "Exploring Interface Builder") covering their capabilities and use.

It's worth mentioning that almost every iPhone, iPad, iPod, and Macintosh application you run, whether created by a single developer at home or by a huge company, is built using the Apple developer tools. This means that you have everything you need to create software as powerful as any you've ever run.

Objective-C

Objective-C is the language that you'll be using to write your applications. It provides the structure for our applications and controls the logic and decision making that goes on when an application is running.

If you've never worked with a programming language before, don't worry. Hour 3, "Discovering Objective-C: The Language of Apple Platforms," covers everything you need to get started. Developing for iOS in Objective-C is a unique programming experience, even if you've used other programming languages in the past. The language is unobtrusive and structured in a way that makes it easy to follow. After your first few projects, Objective-C will fade into the background, letting you concentrate on the specifics of your application.

Cocoa Touch

While Objective-C defines the structure for iOS applications, Cocoa Touch defines the functional building blocks, called *classes*, that can make iOS devices perform certain actions. Cocoa Touch isn't a "thing," per se, but a collection of interface elements, data storage elements, and other handy tools that you can access from your applications.

As you'll learn in Hour 4, "Inside Cocoa Touch," you can access literally hundreds of different Cocoa Touch classes and do thousands of things with them. This book covers quite a few of the most useful classes and gives you the pointers necessary to explore even more on your own.

Model-View-Controller

The iOS platform and Macintosh use a development approach called Model-View-Controller (MVC) to structure applications. Understanding why MVC is used and the benefits it provides will help you make good decisions in structuring your most complex applications. Despite the complicated-sounding name, MVC is really just a way to keep your application projects arranged so that you can easily update and extend them in the future. You learn more about MVC in Hour 6, "Model-View-Controller Application Design."

Further Exploration

Xcode is the cornerstone of your iOS development experience. You will design, code, and test your apps in Xcode. You'll provision your devices and even submit apps to the App Store, all through Xcode. Noticing my emphasis yet? Xcode. Xcode. Xcode. Although we'll be spending time going through the Xcode features now, take a moment to watch Apple's introductory videos to get a sense for what you'll be seeing. To do this, open Xcode, and then choose Xcode Help from the Help menu.

The more you familiarize yourself with the tools, the quicker you'll be able to use them to build production-ready applications.

Summary

This hour introduced you to the iOS platform, its capabilities, and its limitations. You learned about the different iOS devices' graphic features, RAM sizes, and the various sensors that you can use in your applications to create uniquely "aware" experiences. We also discussed the Apple iOS developer tools, how to download and install them, and the differences between the various paid Developer Programs. To prepare you for actual on-phone development, you explored the process of creating and installing a development provisioning profile in Xcode and even installed an application on your device.

The hour wrapped up with a quick discussion about the development technologies that make up the first part of this book and form the basis for all the iOS development you'll be doing.

Q&A

Q. I thought that iOS devices ranged from a minimum of 16GB of RAM in the low-end iPad and iPhone to 64GB on the high-end models. Don't they?

A. The "memory" capabilities of devices that are advertised to the public are the storage sizes available for applications, songs, and so forth. It is separate from the RAM that can be used for executing programs. If Apple implements virtual memory in a future version of iOS, it is possible that the larger storage could be used for increasing available RAM.

Q. What platform should I target for development?

A. That depends on your goals. If you want to reach the largest audience, consider a universal application that works on the iPhone, iPad, and iPod touch. We explore this in a few projects later in this book. If you want to make use of the most-capable hardware, you can certainly target the unique capabilities of a specific device, but by doing so you might be limiting the size of your customer base.

Q. Why isn't the iOS platform open?

A. Great question. Apple has long sought to control the user experience so that it remains "positive" regardless of how users have set up their device, be it a Mac, an iPad, or an iPhone. By ensuring that applications can be tied to a developer and by enforcing an approval process, Apple attempts to limit the potential for a harmful application to cause damage to data or otherwise negatively impact the user. Whether this is an appropriate approach, however, is open to debate.

Workshop

Quiz

1. What is the pixel resolution of the iPhone screen?

2. What is the cost of joining an individual iOS Developer Program?

3. What language will you use when creating iOS applications?

Answers

1. Trick question. The iPhone screen is measured in points, not pixels. The iPhone 4 and 4(s) have a 320×480 points, whereas the iPhone 5 is 320×568 points. To get the true resolution, you must multiply by the device's scaling factor. For the iPhone 4/4(s)/5, this is 2. Therefore, the pixel resolution of the iPhone 4/4(s) is 640×960, whereas the iPhone 5 is 640×1136.

2. The Developer Program costs $99 a year for the individual option.

3. Objective-C is used for iOS development.

Activities

1. Establish an Apple developer membership and download and install the developer tools. This is an important activity that you should complete before starting the next hour's lesson (if you didn't do so while following along in this hour).

2. Review the resources available in the iOS Dev Center. Apple has published several introductory videos and tutorials that supplement what you'll learn in this book.

HOUR 2

Introduction to Xcode and the iOS Simulator

What You'll Learn in This Hour:

▶ How to create new projects in Xcode
▶ Code editing and navigation features
▶ Where to add classes and resources to a project
▶ How to modify project properties
▶ Compiling for iOS devices and the iOS Simulator
▶ How to interpret error messages
▶ Features and limitations of the iOS Simulator

The core of your development work will be spent in two applications: Xcode and the iOS Simulator. These apps provide the core tools that you need to design, program, and test applications for the iPhone and iPad. And, unlike other platforms, they're entirely free.

This hour walks you through the basics you need to work with Xcode's code-editing tools and the iOS Simulator, and you get some hands-on practice working with each. We cover Xcode's interface-creation tools in Hour 5, "Exploring Interface Builder."

Using Xcode

When you think of coding—actually typing the statements that will make your iDevice meet Apple's "magical" mantra—think Xcode. Xcode is the IDE, or integrated development environment, that manages your application's resources and lets you edit the code and user interface (UI) that ties the different pieces together.

After you install Xcode, as described in Hour 1, "Preparing Your System and iDevice for Development," you should be able to find it in the Application folder located at the root level of your hard drive or in Launchpad. We walk through the day-to-day use of Xcode's tools in this hour. If you haven't finished the installation, do so now.

Launch Xcode now. After a few moments, the Welcome to Xcode screen displays, as shown in Figure 2.1.

FIGURE 2.1
Explore Apple's developer resources, right from the Xcode Welcome screen.

You can choose to disable this screen by unchecking the Show This Window When Xcode Launches check box, but it does provide a convenient jumping-off point for sample code, tutorials, and documentation. In Hour 4, "Inside Cocoa Touch," we take a detailed look at the documentation system included in Xcode, which is quite extensive. For now, click Cancel to exit the Welcome screen.

Creating and Managing Projects

Most of your development work will start with an Xcode project. A *project* is a collection of all the files associated with an application, along with the settings needed to "build" a working piece of software from the files. This includes images, source code, and a file that describes the appearance and objects that make up the interface.

Choosing a Project Type

To create a new project, choose File, New Project (Shift-Command-N) from the Xcode menu. Do this now. Xcode prompts you to choose a template for your application, as shown in Figure 2.2. The Xcode templates contain the files you need to quickly start a new development effort.

FIGURE 2.2
To create a new project, start by choosing an appropriate template.

Although it is possible to build an application completely from scratch, the time saved by using a template is significant. We use several templates throughout this book, depending on what type of application we're building.

Along the left side of the Template window are the categories of templates available. Our focus is on the iOS Application category, so be sure that it is selected.

On the right side of the display are the templates within the category, with a description of the currently highlighted template. For this tutorial, click the Empty Application template, and then click Next.

After choosing the template, you are prompted for a product name, organization name, and a company identifier. The product name is the name of your application, and the organization name can be anything you want, such as your name or your company name. The Company Identifier field is a bit different. This is typically the domain name of the organization or individual producing the app, but in reverse order. Together, the product name and the company identifier make up something called the *bundle identifier*, which uniquely identifies your application among all other iOS apps.

For example, in this hour, we create an app called HelloXcode. This becomes the product name. I own the domain teachyourselfios.com, so I enter **com.teachyourselfios** as the Company Identifier field. If you do not own a domain name, you can just use the default identifier for your initial development.

Go ahead and enter **HelloXcode** as your product name, and then provide an organization name and a company identifier of your choice. Leave the Class Prefix field empty. Choose which device (iPad or iPhone) you are using from the Device Family pop-up, and make sure that the Use Automatic Reference Counting check box is selected. The Use Core Data and Include Unit Tests check boxes should be unchecked. Your screen will look similar to mine, as shown in Figure 2.3.

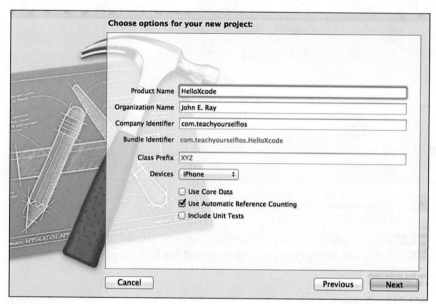

FIGURE 2.3
Choose a product name, company name, and company identifier for your app.

NOTE

The class prefix is an arbitrary string that is appended onto the start of the filenames in an Xcode application template. Apple has traditionally automatically assigned the product name as the prefix but has changed this in recent versions of Xcode.

Core data is an advanced means of storing application data that may be of interest as your projects needs grow.

Finally, unit testing is a process for defining automated tests for functional units of your code. These topics are beyond the scope of this book, but you can read more about them using the Xcode documentation system discussed in the next hour.

When satisfied with your settings, click Next. Xcode prompts for a save location for the project. Navigate to an appropriate location on your drive, make sure the Source Control option is unchecked, and then click Create. Xcode makes a folder with the name of the project and places all the associated template files within that folder.

TIP

Within your project folder, you'll find a file with the extension .xcodeproj. This is the file you need to open to return to your project workspace after exiting Xcode.

Getting Your Bearings

After you've created or opened a project in Xcode, the interface displays an iTunes-like window that will be used for everything from writing code to designing your application interfaces. If this is your first time in Xcode, the assortment of buttons and menus and icons can be more than a little intimidating. To help get a feel for what all of this is, let's start by defining the major functional areas of the interface, shown in Figure 2.4.

FIGURE 2.4
Finding your way around the Xcode interface can be intimidating at first.

Toolbar: Displays project status and provides easy access to common functions.

Navigator: Manages files, groups, and other information related to your project.

Editor: Edits project content (code, interfaces, and more).

Utility: Provides quick access to object inspectors, help, and project components.

Debug: If something goes wrong with your code during execution, this is where you'll find it.

NOTE

By default, the debug and utility areas are usually hidden. You can toggle the debug visibility using the second button in the View area of the toolbar and the utility area using the third. Likewise, you can hide and show the navigator using the first view button. You'll get accustomed to the features offered within each of these areas as we work through the book. For now, we focus on the navigator and editor.

If you ever find that your display seems completely different from what you're expecting, use the View menu on the Xcode menu bar to show the toolbar, navigator, or any other pieces that have gone missing.

Navigating Your Project

The navigator can operate in many different modes, from navigating your project files to searching results and error messages. The modes are changed using the icons immediately above the navigator area. The folder icon shows the project navigator and is where you'll spend most of your time.

The project navigator displays a top-level icon representing (and named after) your project; this is the project group. You can use the disclosure arrow in front of the project group to open and show the files and groups that make up your application. Let's take a look at the HelloXcode project we created a few minutes ago.

In Xcode, expand the HelloXcode project group in the project navigator. You'll see three folders associated with the application, as highlighted in Figure 2.5.

Project Navigator

FIGURE 2.5
Use the project navigator to browse your project resources.

NOTE

The folders you see in Xcode are logical groupings. You won't find all these files in your project directory, nor will you find the same folder structure. The Xcode layout is designed to help you find what you're looking for easily, not to mirror a file system structure.

Within the project group are three subgroups that you'll find useful:

▶ **Project Code:** Named after the project, this group contains the code for the class files and resources that you add to your project. As you'll learn in the next hour, classes group together application features that complement one another. Most of your development will be within a file located here.

▶ **Frameworks:** Frameworks are the core code libraries that give your application a certain level of functionality. By default, Xcode includes the basic frameworks for you, but if you want to add special features, such as sound or vibration, you may need an additional framework. We walk through the process of adding frameworks in Hour 10, "Getting the User's Attention."

▶ **Products:** Anything produced by Xcode is included here (typically, the executable application).

If you dig a bit further, you'll find a Supporting Files group within the Project Code folder. This contains files that, although necessary for your application to work correctly, are rarely edited by hand.

TIP
_____

If you find that you want additional logical groupings of files, you can define your own groups via File, New, New Group. Some people, for example, like to keep images, icons, and other files grouped in a Resources group.

_____

Finding Your Way with Filtering

At the bottom of the navigator area is a small toolbar that you can use to filter or adjust what is currently being displayed. In the project navigator, for example, you can enter text in the search field to only display project resources (groups or files) that match. You can also use the icons to the right of the field to limit the results to recent files or files that haven't been saved (the clock and pen/paper icons, respectively).

The filtering options are contextual; they change based on what is currently being displayed in the navigator. Be sure to take advantage of Xcode's extensive tooltips to explore the interface as you encounter new areas and features.

Adding New Code Files to a Project

Even though the Apple iOS application templates give you a great starting point for your development, you'll find, especially in more advanced projects, that you need to add additional code files to supplement the base project. To add a new file to a project, first highlight the group you want to add the file to (usually the project code group). Next, choose File, New or click the +

button located at the bottom-left corner of the navigator. In an interface similar to the project templates, Xcode prompts you, as shown in Figure 2.6, for the category and type of file that you want to add to the project. You are fully guided throughout this book, so don't worry if the options in the figure look alien at first.

Add Files

FIGURE 2.6
Use Xcode to add new files to a project.

Can I Add Empty Files Manually?

Yes, you could drag your own files into one of the Xcode groups and copy them into the project. However, just as a project template gives you a head start on implementation, Xcode's file templates do the same thing. They often include an outline for the different features that you must implement to make the code functional.

Adding Resources to a Project

Many applications will require sound or image files that you'll integrate into your development. Obviously, Xcode can't help you "create" these files, so you'll have to add them by hand. To do this, just click and drag the file from its location into the project code group in Xcode. You are prompted to copy the files. Always make sure the Copy check box is selected so that Xcode can put the files where they need to go within your project directory.

In the provided HelloXcode project folder that corresponds with what you're building this hour, you'll find an Images folder containing the file Background.png. Drag this file into your project code group within the Xcode navigator. Choose to copy if needed, as shown in Figure 2.7. Copying the files ensures that they are correctly placed within your project and accessible by your code.

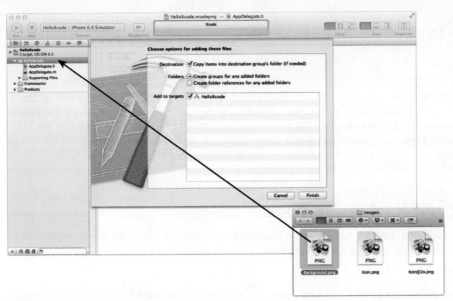

FIGURE 2.7
Drag the Background.png file into the project code folder and choose to copy if needed.

TIP

If you drag a folder with multiple files into your project, Xcode, by default, automatically creates a group containing all the files. In the tutorials, I will usually add multiple files by dragging the whole folder (and thus creating a group) into the project.

Removing Files and Resources

If you've added something to Xcode that you decide you don't want, you can delete it easily. To remove a file or resource from your project, simply select it within the Project Navigator and press the Delete key. Xcode gives you the option to move the file to the Trash or just to delete the project's reference to the file (see Figure 2.8).

If you choose to delete references, the file itself will remain but will no longer be visible in the project.

FIGURE 2.8
Deleting a file's reference leaves the actual file untouched.

NOTE

If Xcode can't find a file that it expects to be part of a project, that file is highlighted in red in the Xcode interface. This might happen if you accidentally use the Finder to delete a file from the project folder. It also occurs when Xcode knows that an application file will be created by a project but the application hasn't been generated yet. In this case, you can safely ignore the red .app file within the Products group.

Editing and Navigating Code

To edit code in Xcode, just use the Project Navigator to find the file you want to edit, and then click the filename. The editable contents of the file are shown in the editor area of the Xcode interface (see Figure 2.9).

The Xcode editor works just like any text editor, with a few nice additions. To get a feel for how it works, open the project code group within the HelloXcode project, and then click AppDelegate.m to begin editing the source code. Notice that above the editor is a visual path to the file you are editing. Clicking any portion of the path reveals a pop-up menu for quickly jumping to other files in same location. To the left of the path are forward and back arrows that move back and forth between files that you've been editing, just like pages you visit in a web browser.

File

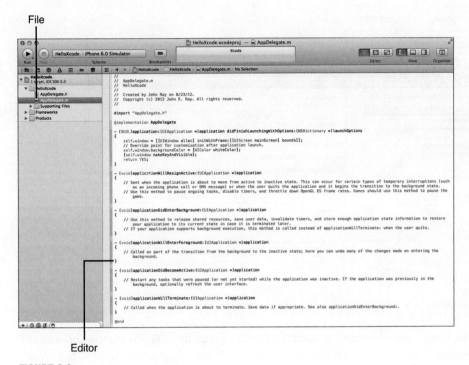

Editor

FIGURE 2.9
Choose the group, then the file, and then edit.

For this project, we use an interface element called a label to display the text Hello Xcode on your device's screen. This application, like most that you write, uses a method to show our greeting. A method is just a block of code that executes when some thing needs to happen. In this example, we use an existing method called `application:didFinishLaunchingWithOptions` that runs as soon as the application starts.

Jumping Through Code with the Symbol Navigator

The easiest way to find a method or property within a source code file is to use the symbol navigator, opened by clicking the icon to the immediate right of the project navigator. This view, shown in Figure 2.10, enables you to expand your project classes to show all the methods, properties, and variables that are defined. Choosing an item from the list jumps to and highlights the relevant line in your source code.

Symbol Navigator   Symbol

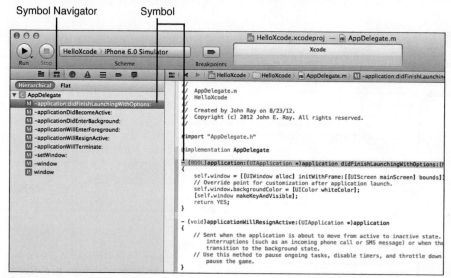

FIGURE 2.10
The symbol navigator is a quick way to jump between methods and properties.

Switch to the symbol navigator and expand the `AppDelegate` item. This is the only object used in this application. Next, find and select `application:didFinishLaunchingWithOptions` from the list that is displayed. Xcode jumps to the line where the method begins. Let's start coding.

TIP
_____

When you are editing a file, the visual path above the editor ends in the symbol label where your cursor is currently located (if any). Clicking this label displays a list of the symbols defined in code you are working on, and choosing one jumps to that section of code.

Using Code Completion

Using the Xcode editor, type the following text to implement the `application:didFinish LaunchingWithOptions` method. Start a new line immediately following the line with text `//Override point for customization after application launch` (a comment). You need to enter just the bolded code lines shown in Listing 2.1.

LISTING 2.1   Your First Code Exercise

```
- (BOOL)application:(UIApplication *)application didFinishLaunchingWithOptions:
                    (NSDictionary *)launchOptions
{
    self.window = [[UIWindow alloc] initWithFrame:[[UIScreen mainScreen] bounds]];
    // Override point for customization after application launch.

    UILabel *myMessage;
    UILabel *myUnusedMessage;
    myMessage=[[UILabel alloc]
            initWithFrame:CGRectMake(30.0,50.0,300.0,50.0,50.0)];
    myMessage.font=[UIFont systemFontOfSize:48.0];
    myMessage.text=@"Hello Xcode";
    myMessage.textColor = [UIColor colorWithPatternImage:
                        [UIImage imageNamed:@"Background.png"]];
    [self.window addSubview:myMessage];

    self.window.backgroundColor = [UIColor whiteColor];
    [self.window makeKeyAndVisible];
    return YES;
}
```

CAUTION

HASTE MAKES WASTE

If you decide to skip ahead and run this application, you'll quickly realize that the code you entered is not going to work. Some errors have been intentionally included here that you correct later this hour.

NOTE

It's not important to understand exactly what this code does—at this point, you just need to get experience in the Xcode editor. The "short and sweet" description of this fragment, however, is that it creates a label object in the upper-left corner of the screen; sets the label's text, font, size, and color; and then adds it to the application's window.

As you type, you should notice something interesting happening. As soon as you get to a point in each line where Xcode thinks it knows what you intend to type, it displays an autocompleted version of the code, as demonstrated in Figure 2.11.

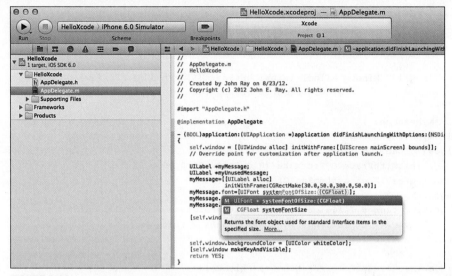

FIGURE 2.11
Xcode automatically completes the code as you type.

To accept an autocompletion suggestion, press Tab, and the code will be inserted, just as if you typed the whole thing. If there are multiple possible outcomes for the autocomplete line, you can arrow up and down to select the one you want and then press Tab. Xcode tries to complete method names, variables that you've defined, and anything else related to the project that it might recognize.

If you are completing a method name, chances are that you need to provide parameters as well. (In the case of `systemFontOfSize`, it is a floating-point value that describes the size of the text.) You can again use the arrow keys to move between the parameter fields and enter the values you want, or you can just press Tab to skip from parameter to parameter.

After you've made your changes, you can save the file by choosing File, Save.

NOTE
_____

In addition to automatically completing your code, Xcode automatically inserts the complementary curly brace or square bracket when you type the first bracket. In other words, if you type {, Xcode automatically adds a corresponding } for you. You can disable this behavior in the Xcode Text Editing preferences (Xcode, Preferences, Text Editing, Editing).

_____

Searching Your Code with the Search Navigator

Searching for text anywhere in your project is trivial using the search navigator. To access this search feature, click the magnifying glass icon in the icon bar above the navigator. A search field is displayed at the top of the navigator area where you can enter whatever you want to find. As you type, a drop-down menu is displayed, as shown in Figure 2.12, that shows potential options for refining your search. Choose one of the options, or press Return to perform a non-case-sensitive search of the text you enter.

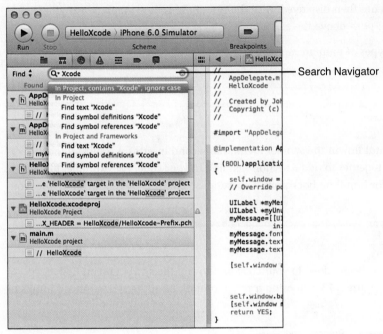

FIGURE 2.12
Use the search navigator to find text throughout your project.

The search results display below the search field, along with a snippet of the file containing the text you were looking for. Clicking a search result opens the corresponding file in the editor and jumps to the line containing your search string.

To make things even more interesting, you can use the filter field at the bottom of the search navigator to filter your search results by a secondary term. You can also click the Find label at the top of the search navigator to switch to a Replace mode—enabling you to perform project-wide find and replace.

TIP

If you're looking for a string within a file you are actively editing, choose Edit, Find (Command-F) to open a more traditional Find field at the top of the editor. This gives you quick access to find (or find/replace) within a given file, rather than across the entire project.

Adding Pragma Marks

Sometimes navigating code by symbols or with a search isn't very efficient. To help denote important pieces of code in plain English, you can insert a `#pragma mark` directive. Pragma marks do not add any features to your application; instead, they create logical sections within your code. These sections are then displayed, with the rest of the code symbols, when you click the last item in the visual path above the editor.

There are two common types of pragma marks:

```
#pragma mark -
```

and

```
#pragma mark <label name>
```

The first inserts a horizontal line in the symbol menu; the second inserts an arbitrary label name. You can use both together to add a section heading to your code. For example, to add a section called "Methods for handling background operations" followed by a horizontal line, you could type the following:

```
#pragma mark Methods for handling background operations
#pragma mark -
```

After the pragma mark has been added to your code and saved, the symbol menu updates accordingly, as shown in Figure 2.13. Choosing a pragma mark from the symbol menu jumps to that portion of the code.

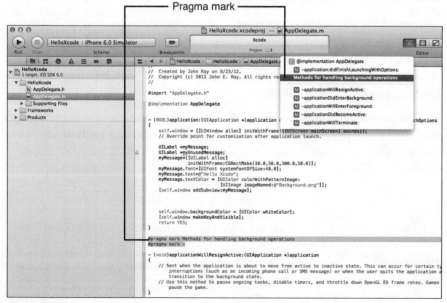

FIGURE 2.13
Pragma marks can create logical divisions in your code.

Using the Assistant Editor

For those lucky enough to have large monitors, you can take advantage of Xcode's assistant editor mode. In the next hour, you learn about the different files you need to edit to create working programs. What you'll quickly realize is that most program functionality comes from editing one of two related files: an implementation file (.m extension) and an interface file (.h extension). You'll also learn that when you make changes to one of these two files you often need to make changes to the other.

Xcode simplifies this back-and-forth editing with the assistant editor mode. The assistant editor (or called just Assistant in Apple documentation) automatically looks at the file you have opened for editing and opens, right beside it (or under it, if you prefer), the related file that you also need to work on, as shown in Figure 2.14.

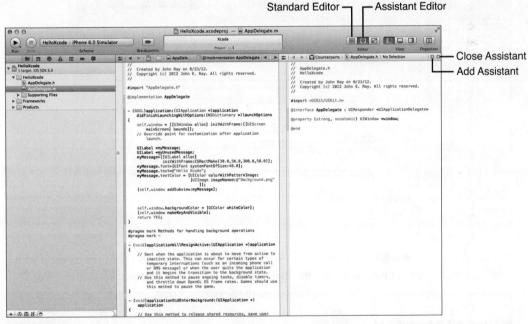

Standard Editor — ┐   ┌— Assistant Editor

Close Assistant

Add Assistant

FIGURE 2.14
The assistant editor opens related files to the right of the file you are working on.

To switch between standard and assistant editor modes, you use the first and second buttons, respectively, in the Editor section of the Xcode toolbar.

NOTE

In the upper-right corner of the assistant editor's jump bar, notice a + icon and an X icon. The + icon adds *another* assistant editor to your screen; the X icon closes the current assistant editor.

Use the View, Assistant Editor menu to choose how the editor is added to the display and what will happen if multiple assistant editors are in use.

Activating Tabbed Editing

Tabbed editing is just like tabbed browsing in your favorite web browser. Using tabbed editing, you can have many files open simultaneously and switch between them by clicking tabs at the top of the editor area.

To create a new tab, choose File, New, New Tab (Command-T). A new tab appears with the contents of the file you are currently editing. You can switch the contents of the tab to whatever you want by clicking a file in the project navigator. You can repeat this process to create as many tabs as you want, with whatever file contents you want, as shown in Figure 2.15.

Close Tab ┌────────────── Tabs ──────────────┐   AddTab

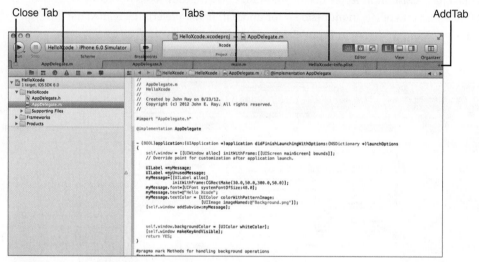

FIGURE 2.15
Keep multiple editors open simultaneously with tabs.

To close a tab, click the X that is displayed on the left side of the tab when hovering over it with your mouse. As with all files in Xcode, the files you edit in tabs are automatically saved when you close them; you do not have to explicitly use the Save command.

Managing Snapshots

If you're planning to make many changes to your code and you're not quite sure you'll like the outcome, you might want to take advantage of the Xcode "snapshot" feature. A *code snapshot* is, in essence, a copy of all your source code at a particular moment in time. If you don't like changes you've made, you can revert to an earlier snapshot. Snapshots are also helpful because they show what has changed between multiple versions of an application.

To take a snapshot, choose File, Create Snapshot. You are prompted for a name of the snapshot and for a description, as shown in Figure 2.16. Provide appropriate input, and then click Create Snapshot. That's it.

FIGURE 2.16
Create a snapshot of your project at any point in time.

To view (and possibly restore) an available snapshot, choose File, Restore Snapshot. The snapshot viewer displays available snapshots. Choose one, and then click Restore. Don't worry; it won't restore just yet. The display updates to show the files that changed between your current code and the chosen snapshot. Clicking a filename (if more than one has changed) shows the snapshot code on the left and the current code on the right, highlighting changes between the different versions of code, as shown in Figure 2.17.

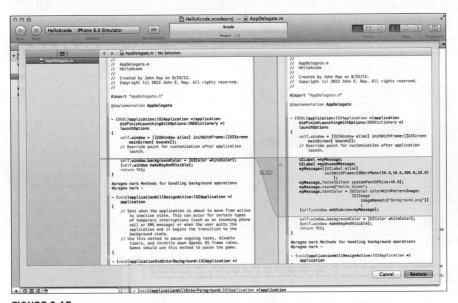

FIGURE 2.17
Use a snapshot to figure out what changes you've made among different versions of your application. Here a snapshot of the original empty project is compared to the current version.

If, after viewing the changes, you still want to restore to the selected snapshot, make sure the files you want to restore are checked in the file list, and then click the Restore button. Click Cancel to return to the editor without making any changes.

TIP

Xcode snapshots are a limited form of version control. Xcode also includes the GIT version control system and Subversion support. We do not use these tools in this book because the snapshot support is more than enough for most small to medium-size projects.

Building Applications

After you've completed your source code, it's time to build and run the application. The build process encompasses several different steps, including compiling and linking. Compiling translates the instructions you type into something that your iOS device understands. Linking combines your code with the necessary frameworks the application needs to run. During these steps, Xcode displays any errors that it might find.

Before building an application, you must first choose what it is being built to run on: the iOS Simulator or a physical iDevice.

Choosing the Build Scheme

To choose how your code will be built, use the Scheme pop-up menu at the upper left of the Xcode window. This pop-up menu is actually two separate menus in one, depending on which side you click. Click to the right side of the Scheme menu to display the possible devices that can be targeted in the build process, as shown in Figure 2.18.

FIGURE 2.18
Change the scheme to target an iOS device or one of the variants of the iOS Simulator.

Choose between iOS Device (your physical iPhone or iPad) and the iOS Simulator. For most day-to-day development, you'll want to use the Simulator; it is faster than transferring an application to your device each time you make a simple change.

The iOS Simulator is referred to (by Apple) as iPhone Simulator if it is started simulating an iPhone app or iPad Simulator when simulating an iPad. It really is just one application, despite the different ways it is referenced in Xcode and the developer documentation.

By default, the schemes that you use to run your application run it with a debugger. This helps identify problems in your application by allowing you to trace its execution. For applications you intend to submit to the App Store, switch to a release configuration. You learn more about debugging in Hour 24, "Applications Tracing and Debugging."

Building, Analyzing, and Running the Application

To build and run the application, click the Run button on the Xcode toolbar (Command-R). Depending on the speed of your computer, this run process might take a minute or two to complete. Once done, the application is transferred to your iOS device and started (if selected in the scheme menu and connected) or started in the chosen iOS Simulator.

To just build without running the application (useful for checking for errors), choose Build (Command-B) from the Product menu. Better yet, you can choose Product, Analyze (Command-Shift-B) to locate build errors and identify potential issues with your application logic that wouldn't stop the code from building but might crash your program.

TIP

Quite a few intermediate files are generated during the build process. These take up space and aren't needed for the project itself. To clean out these files, choose Clean from the Product menu.

Figure 2.19 shows the HelloXcode application running in the iPhone Simulator. Try clicking Run on the Xcode toolbar to build and start your version of the application now.

If you've been following along, your application should... *not work*. There are two problems with the code you were asked to type in earlier. Let's see what they are.

FIGURE 2.19
The iOS Simulator is a quick and easy way to test your code.

Correcting Errors and Warnings in the Issue Navigator

You can receive three general types of feedback from Xcode when you build and analyze an application: errors, warnings, and logic problems. Warnings are potential problems that may cause your application to misbehave and are indicated by a yellow caution sign. Errors, however, are complete showstoppers. You can't run your application if you have an error. The symbol for an error, appropriately enough, is a red stop sign. Logic problems, found by the Xcode analyze process, are shown as a blue badge. All of these bugs, across all of your files, are consolidated in the issue navigator, shown in Figure 2.20. The issue navigator displays automatically if problems are found during a build or analyze process. You may also open it directly by clicking the exclamation point icon on the toolbar above the navigator area.

To jump to an error in your code, just click it in the issue navigator. The corresponding code is opened, and the error message is visible directly after the line that caused the problem.

TIP

If you are in the middle of editing a file that contains errors and you attempt to build, run, or analyze the code, you'll see the errors immediately displayed onscreen; there's no need to jump back and forth to the issue navigator. You can also quickly cycle through your errors using the forward and backward arrows found at the rightmost side of the window, directly above the editor. These controls are visible only if there are errors, however.

Issue Navigator

Error

FIGURE 2.20
Use the issue navigator to find and correct problems in your code.

When you first try to build the HelloXcode, you will encounter an error: "Too many arguments to function call, expected 4, have 5" (shown in Figure 2.20). The reason for this is that the function CGRectMake takes four numbers and uses them to make a rectangle for the label—we've typed in five numbers. Delete the fifth number and preceding comma from the CGRectMake function. Almost immediately after you fix the error, the issue navigator updates to show a new warning, as shown in Figure 2.21.

TIP

If you've surmised that the numbers used by CGRectMake are for positioning, you might want to try changing them to see how they control where text is displayed on your iDevice's screen. For example, to center the text on an iPhone screen, use the values 25.0,225.0,300.0,50.0. To center the text on an iPad, try 250.0,475.0,300.0,50.0 instead. The first two values represent the distance over and down on the display that the label is positioned; the third and fourth values are the width and height of the label.

The warning points out that we have an unused variable, `myUnusedMessage`, in the code. Remember, this is just a helpful warning, not necessarily a problem. If we choose to remove the variable, the message goes away; but even if we don't, the application will still run. Go ahead and delete the line that reads `UILabel  *myUnusedMessage;` in AppDelegate.m. This fixes the warning, and the issue navigator is empty. We're ready to run.

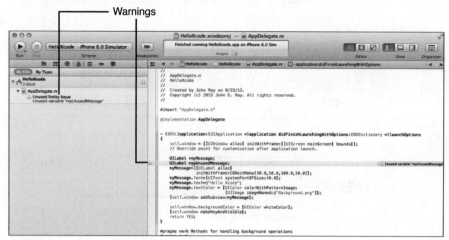

FIGURE 2.21
Some errors and warnings are detected only after you've solved another.

Click Run. HelloXcode should now start in the iOS Simulator, just like what you saw earlier in Figure 2.19.

CAUTION

FIX YOUR BUGS TO FIND YOUR BUGS!

As you've discovered in this exercise, sometimes not all errors are detected and displayed in the issue navigator. You might find, after fixing a line or two, that new, previously undetected, errors appear. Conversely, you'll also sometimes see false errors that disappear when you correct others.

Managing Project Properties

Before finishing our brief tour of the Xcode interface, quickly turn your attention to something a bit different: the properties that describe a project itself. An application's icons, launch images, supported device orientations, and so on need to be set somewhere, so where is that? The answer is the project plist file.

This file, found in a project's Supporting Files folder, is created automatically when you start a new project, is prefixed with the project name, and ends in Info.plist. Although you can edit the values directly in the plist file, Xcode provides an easier approach. Let's take a look at how it works.

Switch to the project navigator and click the top-level project icon for HelloXcode (the blue paper), and make sure the application icon under Targets in the column to the right is highlighted. The editor area refreshes to display several tabs across the top, shown in Figure 2.22. The first, Summary, allows us to set many of the project plist options visually. The second, Info, provides direct access to the plist file contents without any digging around to file the plist file itself.

FIGURE 2.22
Project properties control a few important settings for your application.

Setting Supported Device Orientations

As I'm sure you're well aware, not all applications support all device orientations (portrait, landscape right, landscape left, upside down). To denote which device orientations your app will support, you can edit the Deployment Info section within the Summary area. Scroll down through the different sections until you see the iPhone/iPod Deployment Info or iPad Deployment Info section. Use the disclosure arrow to expand the section if needed.

Near the top of the Deployment Info are settings for Supported Device Orientations. To set the orientations you plan to use, just click the corresponding icon to highlight it, as shown in Figure 2.23. To remove support for an orientation, click the icon to remove the highlight. Simple!

CAUTION

IT'S NOT QUITE THAT SIMPLE

Unfortunately, just setting a device orientation doesn't magically make your application work correctly in that orientation. It just signals your intent to make it work. You'll still have to code for device rotation, which you learn about in Hour 15, "Reading and Writing Application Data."

FIGURE 2.23
Choose the orientations your app will support.

Setting the Status Bar Display

Immediately following the device orientation settings are the status bar settings, shown in Figure 2.24. The status bar is the thin line with the carrier name, signal strength, and battery status at the top of an iOS device display. Use the style menu to set the appearance of the status bar, or click the Hide check box to disable it entirely.

Status Bar Settings

FIGURE 2.24
Configure how the status bar will appear in your app.

New in iOS 6 is the Tinting setting, which sets the color of the status bar. Use this option, along with the Tint Color button, to configure (or disable) a background color tint for the status bar. This can help the application blend in with the status bar—leading to a more consistent user experience.

TIP
If your application sets the status bar display to Default, it automatically adopts the background of the standard Apple UI elements, such as the navigation controller. (You don't need to do a thing!)

Setting an Application Icon

Next up are the app icons. There are currently three different sizes of icons that you may need:

- **Phone:** Non-Retina display, 57x57 pixels
- **iPhone:** 3.5" and 4" Retina display, 114x114 pixels
- **iPad:** Non-Retina display, 72x72 pixels
- **iPad:** Retina display, 144x144 pixels

The icons you create do not need to have rounded corners or any visual effects; iOS automatically adds the glossy look for you. If you decide you want to add this styling yourself, click the Prerendered check box.

To set an icon, create a PNG file of the appropriate dimensions, and then drag the file from the Finder into the appropriate image well, as shown in Figure 2.25. I've included sample icons for you in each project folder. Regular display icons are named Icon.png, and Retina display icons are named Icon@2x.png.

TIP

Although the @2x naming convention might seem strange, it is actually used throughout iOS to support the Retina display. In fact, if an application is running on a device with a Retina display and is asked to display an image, it automatically substitutes (if available) an image resource with the same name and the suffix @2x. This enables developers to support Retina displays without any "Retina-specific" code in their applications.

FIGURE 2.25
Just drag and drop to set your application icons.

After adding your icons, you'll notice that Xcode copies the files to a location outside your main code group. You might want to move them into the Supporting Files group to keep things clean.

Setting a Launch Image

In addition to icons, you should add a "launch image" to your project that will display as your application loads. Like the orientations and icons, the launch images are set in the Deployment

Info section of the Summary tab. Just scroll down a bit farther to show the image wells for the launch images. On the iPhone, you can only set portrait images. The iPad, however, supports both landscape and portrait images.

Launch images should be PNG files sized corresponding to the full-screen resolution of the device you're supporting and named using these conventions:

▶ **iPhone:** Non-Retina display, 320x480 pixels (portrait)

▶ **iPhone:** 3.5" Retina display, 640x960 pixels (portrait)

▶ **iPhone:** 4" Retina display, 640x1136 pixels (portrait)

▶ **iPad:** Non-Retina display, 768x1024 pixels (portrait)

▶ **iPad:** Retina display, 1536x2048 pixels (portrait)

These values all represent a portrait display. Landscape resolution, of course, is simply the two numbers reversed; for example, 768x1024 becomes 1024x768 in landscape. Again, there isn't yet an iPad with a Retina display, so I'm just speculating about the fourth option.

After you've created your launch images, just drag and drop the image files from the Finder into the appropriate image wells, exactly as you did with the icons. Creating launch images is left as an exercise for you, the reader.

TIP

With projects created for iOS 6 and the iPhone 5 (that means *any* new iPhone Xcode project), you are required to provide launch images before the application will run—even on the simulator. This isn't a big deal, however, because Apple adds blank launch images to your project for you. The non-retina iPhone launch image is named Default.png, the 3.5" retina display version is Default@2x.png, and the new 4" retina display iPhone image is titled Default-568h@2x.png. You can replace these files with whatever you want, but it's kind of Apple to give us a placeholder to get our apps up and running quickly.

CAUTION

JUST FOR LOOKS

The property settings covered here are the ones that relate to how your app looks on an iDevice and in the Simulator. You'll also learn other settings throughout this book that govern how the application runs.

That's it for Xcode! There's plenty more that you'll find as you work with the software, but these should be the foundational skills you need to develop apps for iOS. Let's round out this hour by looking at the next best thing to your phone: the Apple iOS Simulator.

NOTE

Note that although it isn't covered here, Xcode includes a wonderful documentation system. You learn more about this as you start to get your feet wet with the Cocoa framework in Hour 4.

Using the iOS Simulator

In Hour 1, you learned that you don't even need an iOS device to start developing for the platform. The reason for this is the iOS Simulator is included with Xcode. The Simulator does a great job of simulating the Apple iPhone and iPad, with the Safari, Photos, Contacts, Settings, Game Center, Maps, Newsstand, and Passbook apps available for integration testing, as shown in Figure 2.26.

Targeting the Simulator for the early stages of your development can save you a great deal of time; you won't need to wait for apps to be installed on your physical device before seeing the effects of changes in your code. In addition, you don't need to buy and install a developer certificate to run code in the Simulator.

The Simulator, however, is not a perfect iDevice. It can't simulate complex multitouch events or provide readings from some sensors (gyroscope, accelerometer, and so on). The closest it comes on these counts is the ability to rotate to test landscape interfaces and a simple "shake" motion simulation. That said, for most apps, it has enough features to be a valuable part of your development process.

CAUTION

A FAST MAC DOESN'T EQUAL A FAST IPHONE!

One thing that you absolutely *cannot* count on in the Simulator is that your simulated app performance will resemble your real app performance. The Simulator tends to run silky smooth, whereas real apps might have more limited resources and not behave as nicely. Be sure to occasionally test on a physical device so that you know your expectations are in line with reality.

FIGURE 2.26
The iOS Simulator includes a stripped-down version of Apple's standard iOS apps.

Launching Applications

To launch an application in the Simulator, open the project in Xcode, make sure that the scheme is set to the iPhone Simulator or iPad Simulator, and then click Run. After a few seconds, the Simulator launches and the application loads. You can test this using the HelloSimulator project included in this hour's Projects folder.

Once up and running, the HelloSimulator app, shown here on the iPad Simulator, should display a simple line of text and a random image fetched from a website (see Figure 2.27).

When an application is running, you can interact with it using your mouse as if it were your fingertip. Click buttons, drag sliders, and so on. If you click into a field where input is expected, the onscreen keyboard will display. You can "type" using your Mac keyboard or by clicking the onscreen keyboard's buttons. The iOS copy and paste services are also simulated by clicking and holding on text until the familiar loupe magnifier appears.

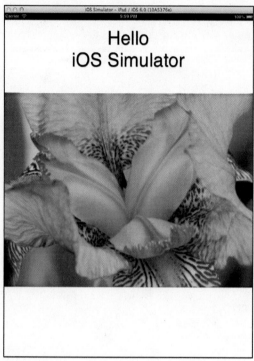

FIGURE 2.27
Click Run in Xcode to launch and run your application in the Simulator.

Click the Stop button in the Xcode toolbar to exit the app. Clicking the virtual Home button (or choosing Hardware, Home from the menu) also exits the application, but Xcode itself may continue to think it's running and get "out of sync."

NOTE

Launching an application in the Simulator installs it in the Simulator, just like installing an app on a real device. When you exit the app, it is still present on the Simulator until you manually delete it.

To remove an installed application from the Simulator, click and hold the icon until it starts "wiggling," and then click the X that appears in the upper-left corner. In other words, remove apps from the Simulator in the same way you would remove them from a physical device.

To quickly reset the Simulator back to a clean slate, choose Reset Content and Settings from the iOS Simulator menu.

TIP

By default, your application is displayed on a simulated non-Retina screen. To switch to a different simulated device, choose from the options in the Hardware, Device menu.

Generating Multitouch Events

Even though you have only a single mouse, you can simulate simple multitouch events, such as two-finger pulls and pinches, by holding down Option when your cursor is over the Simulator "screen." Two circles, representing fingertips, are drawn and can be controlled with the mouse. To simulate a touch event, click and drag while continuing to hold down Option. Figure 2.28 shows the "pinch" gesture.

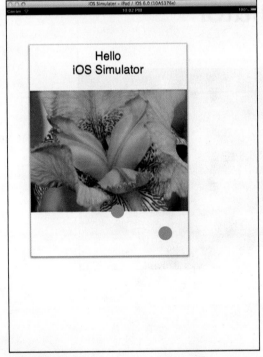

FIGURE 2.28
Simulate simple multitouch with the Option key.

Try this using the HelloSimulator app. You should be able to use the Simulator's multitouch capabilities to shrink or expand the onscreen text and image.

Rotating the Simulated Device

To simulate a rotation on your virtual device, choose Rotate Right or Rotate Left from the Hardware menu (see Figure 2.29). You can use this to rotate the Simulator window through all four possible orientations and view the results onscreen.

Again, test this with HelloSimulator. The app will react to the rotation events and orient the text properly.

FIGURE 2.29
Rotate the interface through the possible orientations.

Simulating Other Conditions

You want to test against a few other esoteric conditions in the Simulator. Using the Hardware menu, you can access these additional features:

▶ **Device:** Choose from the iPhone, iPhone 3.5" Retina display, iPhone 4" Retina display, and iPad devices to simulate your application on each.

▶ **Version:** Check to see how your app will behave on earlier versions of the iOS. This option enables you to choose from many of the recent versions of the iOS. You must first download the earlier versions of the iOS Simulator using the Downloads section of the Xcode preferences.

▶ **Shake Gesture:** Simulate a quick shake of the device.

▶ **Home:** Press the Home button.

▶ **Lock:** Simulates the condition of a locked device. Because a user can lock an iPhone or iPad while an application is running, some developers choose to have their programs react uniquely to this situation.

▶ **Simulate Memory Warning:** Triggers an application's low-memory event. Useful for testing to make sure your application exits gracefully if resources run low.

▶ **Toggle In-Call Status Bar:** When a call is active and an application is started, an additional line appears at the top of the screen. (Touch to return to call.) This option simulates that line.

▶ **Simulate Hardware Keyboard:** Simulates a connected keyboard. (Just use your Mac's keyboard.)

▶ **TV Out:** Displays a window that will show the contents of the device's TV out signal. We do not use this feature in this book.

Test a few of these on the HelloSimulator application. Figure 2.30 shows the application's reaction to a simulated memory warning.

CAUTION
_____

RECOVER FROM IOS APPLICATION CRASHES

If something goes wrong in your application and it crashes while running in the iOS Simulator, Xcode changes its view to show the debugger. To recover from this, use the Xcode toolbar's Stop button to exit the application; then hide the debugger and check your work. You learn how to use the debugger to find crashing bugs in Hour 24.
_____

FIGURE 2.30
The iOS Simulator can test for application handling in several unique conditions.

Further Exploration

You're not quite at the stage yet where I can ask you to go off and read some code-related tutorials, but if you're interested, you might want to take some time to look into more of the features offered in Xcode. This introduction was limited to roughly a dozen pages, but entire volumes can be (and have been) written about this unique tool. Anything else you need is covered in the lessons in this book, but you should still review Apple's Xcode 4 User Guide. You can find this document by choosing Help, Xcode User Guide from the menu while in the Xcode application.

Summary

This hour introduced you to the Xcode development environment and the core set of tools that you'll be using to create your applications. You learned how to create projects using Apple's iOS templates and how to supplement those templates with new files and resources. You also explored the editing and navigation capabilities of Xcode that you'll come to depend on every day. To illustrate the concepts, you wrote and built your first iOS application, and even corrected a few errors that were intentionally added to try to trip you up.

This hour finished with a walkthrough on the use of the iOS Simulator. This tool will save wear and tear on your device (and your patience) as it provides a quick and easy way to test code without having to install applications on a physical device.

Q&A

Q. What is Interface Builder, and how does it fit in?

A. IB is a very important component of Xcode that gets its own lesson in Hour 5. As the name implies, Interface Builder is mostly used for creating the UI for your applications.

Q. Do I have to worry about constantly saving if I'm switching between files and making lots of changes in Xcode?

A. If you switch between files in the Xcode Editor, you won't lose your changes. Xcode even saves your files for you if you close the application.

Q. I noticed that there are OS X templates that I can access when creating a project. Can I create a Mac application?

A. Yes, but.... All the coding skills you learn in this book can be transferred to Mac development. iOS, however, is a somewhat different piece of hardware than the Mac, so you need to learn the Mac model for windowing, UI, and so on.

Q. Can I run commercial applications on the iOS Simulator?

A. You can only run apps that you have built within Xcode.

Workshop

Quiz

1. How do you add an image resource to an iOS project?

2. Is there a facility in Xcode for easily tracking multiple versions of your project?

3. Can the iOS Simulator be used to test your application on older versions of the iOS?

Answers

1. You can add resources, including images, to a project by dragging from the Finder into the project's code group.

2. Using the snapshot feature you can create different copies of your project at specific points in time and even compare the changes.

3. To load up older versions of iOS in the Simulator, first, within Xcode, go to the Xcode preferences, then to the Downloads, components settings. Click the Install button by the Simulator version you want to install. You can then choose the version of iOS to simulate using the Hardware, Versions menu in the Simulator.

Activities

1. Begin creating projects and navigating the Xcode Editor. Try out some of the common Editor features that were not covered in this lesson, such as Find and Replace. Test the use of pragma marks for creating helpful jump-to points within your source code.

2. Go to the Apple iOS Developer Center and download a sample application. Using the techniques described in this hour's lesson, build and test the application in the iOS Simulator or on your device.

Discovering Objective-C: The Language of Apple Platforms

What You'll Learn in This Hour:

▶ How Objective-C will be used in your projects
▶ The basics of object-oriented programming
▶ Simple Objective-C syntax
▶ Common data types
▶ How ARC helps with memory management

This hour's lesson marks the midpoint in our exploration of the Apple iOS development platform. It will give us a chance to sit back, catch our breath, and get a better idea of what it means to "code" for iOS. Both OS X and iOS share a common development environment and a common development language: Objective-C.

Objective-C provides the syntax and structure for creating applications on Apple platforms. For many, learning Objective-C can be daunting, but with patience, it may quickly become the favorite choice for any development project. This hour takes you through the steps you need to know to be comfortable with Objective-C and starts you down the path to mastering this unique and powerful language.

Object-Oriented Programming and Objective-C

To better understand the scope of this hour, take a few minutes to search for Objective-C or object-oriented programming in your favorite online bookstore. You will find quite a few books—lengthy books—on these topics. In this book, roughly 30 pages cover what other books teach in hundreds of pages. Although it's not possible to fully cover Objective-C and object-oriented development in this single hour, we can make sure that you understand enough to develop fairly complex apps.

To provide you with the information you need to be successful in iOS development, this hour concentrates on fundamentals—the core concepts that are used repeatedly throughout the examples and tutorials in this book. The approach in this hour is to introduce you to a programming topic in general terms and then look at how it will be performed when you sit down to write your application. Before we begin, let's look a bit closer at Objective-C and object-oriented programming.

What Is Object-Oriented Programming?

Most people have an idea of what programming is and have even written a simple program. Everything from setting your TiVo to record a show to configuring a cooking cycle for your microwave is a type of programming. You use data (such as times) and instructions (like "record") to tell your devices to complete a specific task. This certainly is a long way from developing for iOS, but in a way the biggest difference is in the amount of data you can provide and manipulate and the number of different instructions available to you.

Imperative Development

There are two primary development paradigms. First, imperative programming (a subset of which is called *procedural programming*) implements a sequence of commands that should be performed. The application follows the sequence and carries out activities as directed. Although there might be branches in the sequence or movement back and forth between some of the steps, the flow is from a starting condition to an ending condition, with all the logic to make things *work* sitting in the middle.

The problem with imperative programming is that it lends itself to growing, without structure, into an amorphous blob. Applications gain features when developers tack on bits of code here and there. Often, instructions that implement a piece of functionality are repeated over and over wherever something needs to take place. Procedural programming refers to an imperative programming structure that attempts to avoid repetition by creating functions (or procedures) that can be reused. This works to some extent, but long-term still frequently results in code bloat. The benefit of this approach, however, is that it is quite easy to pick up and learn: You create a series of instructions, and the computer follows them.

The Object-Oriented Approach

The other development approach, and what we use in this book, is object-oriented programming (OOP). OOP uses the same types of instructions as imperative development but structures them in a way that makes your applications easy to maintain and promotes code reuse whenever possible. In OOP, you create objects that hold the data that describes something along with the instructions to manipulate that data. Perhaps an example is in order.

Consider a program that enables you to track reminders. With each reminder, you want to store information about the event that will be taking place—a name, a time to sound an alarm, a location, and any additional miscellaneous notes that you may want to store. In addition, you need to be able to reschedule a reminder's alarm time or completely cancel an alarm.

In the imperative approach, you have to write the steps necessary to track all the reminders, all the data in the reminders, check every reminder to see whether an alarm should sound, and so on. It's certainly possible, but just trying to wrap your mind around everything that the application needs to do could cause some serious headaches. An object-oriented approach brings some sanity to the situation.

In an object-oriented model, you could implement a reminder as a single object. The reminder object would know how to store the properties such as the name, location, and so on. It would implement just enough functionality to sound its own alarm and reschedule or cancel its alarm. Writing the code, in fact, would be very similar to writing an imperative program that only has to manage a single reminder. By encapsulating this functionality into an object, however, we can then create multiple copies of the object within an application and have them each fully capable of handling separate reminders. No fuss and no messy code!

Most of the tutorials in this book make use of one or two objects, so don't worry about being overwhelmed with OOP. You'll see enough to get accustomed to the idea, but we're not going to go overboard.

Another important facet of OOP is inheritance. Suppose you want to create a special type of reminder for birthdays that includes a list of birthday presents that a person has requested. Instead of tacking this onto the reminder object, you could create an entirely new "birthday reminder" that inherits all the features and properties of a reminder and then adds in the list of presents and anything else specific to birthdays.

The Terminology of Object-Oriented Development

OOP brings with it a whole range of terminology that you need to get accustomed to seeing in this book (and in Apple's documentation). The more familiar you are with these terms, the easier it will be to look for solutions to problems and interact with other developers. Let's establish some basic vocabulary now:

▶ **Class:** The code, usually consisting of a header/interface file and implementation file, which defines an object and what it can do.

▶ **Subclass:** A class that builds upon another class, adding additional features. Almost everything you use in iOS development will be a subclass of something else, inheriting all the properties and capabilities of its parent class.

▶ **Superclass/parent class:** The class that another class inherits from.

▶ **Singleton:** A class that is instantiated only once during the lifetime of a program. For example, a class to read your device's orientation is implemented as a singleton because there is only one sensor that returns tilt information.

▶ **Object/instance:** A class that has been invoked and is active in your code. Classes are the code that makes an object work, whereas an object is the actual class "in action." This is also known as an *instance* of a class.

▶ **Instantiation:** The process of creating an active object from a class.

▶ **Instance method:** A basic piece of functionality, implemented in a class. For the reminder class, this might be something like `setAlarm` to set the alarm for a given reminder.

▶ **Category:** Provide a means of extending a class without modifying the class code itself.

▶ **Class method:** Similar to an instance method, but applicable to all the objects created from a class. The reminder class, for example, might implement a method called `count Reminders` that provides a count of all the reminder objects that have been created. If you're familiar with other OO languages, you may recognize this as a *static method*.

▶ **Message:** When you want to use a method in an object, you send the object a message (the name of the method). This process is also referred to as *calling the method*.

▶ **Instance variable:** A storage place for a piece of information specific to a class. The name of a reminder, for example, might be stored in an instance variable. All variables in Objective-C have a specific "type" that describes the contents of what they will be holding. Instance variables are rarely accessed directly and, instead, should be used via properties.

▶ **Variable:** A storage location for a piece of information. Unlike instance variables, a "normal" variable is accessible only in the method where it is defined.

▶ **Parameter:** A piece of information that is provided to a method when it is messaged. If you were to send a reminder object the "set alarm" method, you would presumably need to include the time to set. The time, in this case, would be a parameter used with the `setAlarm` method.

▶ **Property:** An abstraction of an instance variable that has been configured using special directives to provide easy access to your code.

▶ **Protocol:** Protocols declare methods that can be implemented by a class—usually to provide functionality needed for an object. A class that implements a protocol is said to conform to that protocol. This is similar to a Java interface.

▶ **Self:** A way to refer to an object within its own methods. When an instance method or property is used in an application, it must be used with a specific object. If you're writing code within a class and you want it to access one of its own methods or properties, you use `self` to refer to the object.

TIP

You might be wondering: If almost everything in iOS development is a subclass of something else, is there some sort of master class that "starts" this tree of inheritance? The answer is yes. The NSObject class serves as the starting point for most of the classes you'll be using in iOS. This isn't something you really need to worry about in the book—just a piece of trivia to think about.

It's important to know that when you develop for iOS, you're going to be taking advantage of hundreds of classes that Apple has already written for you. Everything from creating onscreen buttons to manipulating dates and writing files is covered by prebuilt classes. You'll occasionally want to customize some of the functionality in those classes, but you'll be starting out with a toolbar already overflowing with functionality.

Confused? Don't worry! This book introduces these concepts slowly, and you'll quickly get a feel for how they apply to your projects as you work through several tutorials in the upcoming hours.

What Is Objective-C?

A few years ago, I would have answered this question with "one of the strangest-looking languages I've ever seen." Today, I love it (and so will you). Objective-C was created in the 1980s and is an extension of the C language. It adds many additional features to C and, most important, an OOP structure. Objective-C is primarily used for developing Mac and iOS applications and has attracted a devoted group of followers who appreciate its capabilities and syntax.

Objective-C statements are easier to read than other programming languages and often can be deciphered just by looking at them. For example, consider the following line that compares whether the contents of a variable called myName is equal to John:

```
[myName isEqualToString:@"John"]
```

It doesn't take a very large mental leap to see what is going on in the code snippet. In traditional C, this might be written as follows:

```
strcmp(myName,"John")
```

The C statement is a bit shorter but does little to convey what the code is actually doing.

Because Objective-C is implemented as a layer on top of C, it is still fully compatible with code that is written entirely in C. For the most part, this isn't something that you should concern yourself with, but unfortunately, Apple has left a bit of "cruft" in its iOS software development kit (SDK) that relies on C-language syntax. You'll not encounter this often, and it isn't difficult to code with when it does occur, but it does take away from the elegance of Objective-C just a little.

CAUTION

Case Counts

Objective-C is case sensitive. If a program is failing, make sure you aren't mixing case somewhere in the code.

Now that you have an idea of what OOP and Objective-C are, let's take a look at how you'll be using them over the course of this book.

Exploring the Objective-C File Structure

In the preceding hour, you learned how to use Xcode to create projects and navigate their files. As mentioned then, the vast majority of your time will be spent in the project group of Xcode, which is shown for the MyNewApp project in Figure 3.1. You'll be adding methods to class files that Xcode creates for you when you start a project or, occasionally, creating your own class files to implement entirely new functionality in your application.

FIGURE 3.1
Most of your coding will occur within the files in your project group.

Okay, sounds simple enough, but where will the coding take place? If you create a new project look, you'll see quite a few different files staring back at you.

Header/Interface Files

Creating a class creates two different files: an interface (or header) file (.h extension) and an implementation file (.m extension). The interface file is used to define a list of all of the methods and properties that your class will be using. This is useful for other pieces of code, including

Interface Builder (IB) (which you learn about in Hour 5, "Exploring Interface Builder"), to determine how to access information and features in your class.

The implementation file, however, is where you go to write the code that makes everything defined in the header file work. Let's review the structure of the very short, and entirely made-up, interface file in Listing 3.1.

LISTING 3.1 A Sample Interface File

```
1: #import <UIKit/UIKit.h>
2:
3: @interface myClass : myParent <myProtocol> {
4:    NSString *_myString;
5:    IBOutlet UILabel *_myLabel;
6: }
7:
8: @property (weak, nonatomic) NSString *myString;
9: @property (weak, nonatomic) NSString *myOtherString;
10: @property (weak, nonatomic) IBOutlet UILabel *myOtherLabel;
11:
12: +(NSString)myClassMethod:(NSString *)aString;
13:
14: -(NSDate)myInstanceMethod:(NSString *)aString anotherParam:(NSURL *)aURL;
15:
16: @end
```

CAUTION

Line Numbers Are for Reference Only!

Throughout the book, I present code samples like this one. Often, they include line numbers so that I can easily reference the code and explain how it works. Objective-C does not require line numbers, nor will the code work if you leave them in your application. If you see a line prefixed with a number and a colon (#:), don't type the line number prefix!

The #import Directive

```
1: #import <UIKit/UIKit.h>
```

First, in line 1, the interface file uses the #import directive to include any other interface files that our application will need to access. The string <UIKit/UIKit.h> designates the specific file (in this case, UIKit, which gives us access to a vast majority of the classes). If we need to import a file, we explain how and why in the text. The UIKit example is included by default when Xcode sets up your classes and covers most of what you need for this book's examples.

NOTE

Wait a sec, what's a directive? *Directives* are commands that are added to your files that help Xcode and its associated tools build your application. They don't implement the logic that makes your app work, but they are necessary for providing information on how your applications are structured so that Xcode knows how to deal with them.

The `@interface` Directive and Instance Variables

Line 3 uses the `@interface` directive to begin a set of lines (enclosed in {} braces) that can describe the instance variables that your class will be providing:

```
3: @interface myClass : myParent <myProtocol> {
4:    NSString *_myString;
5:    IBOutlet UILabel *_myLabel;
6: }
```

In this example, a variable that contains an object of type `NSString` named `_myString` is declared, along with an object of type `UILabel` that will be referenced by the variable `_myLabel`. An additional keyword `IBOutlet` is added to the front of the `UILabel` declaration to indicate that this is an object that will be defined in IB. You learn more about `IBOutlet` in Hour 5.

Notice that the instance variables I've used in this example start with an underscore (_) character? This is a naming convention used in Objective-C to denote instance variables (versus other variables, such as a counter, that you might use in a portion of your code). You *can* create instance variables without underscores, but when using Xcode's code-generation tools, it will follow this approach.

One very, very important thing to note is that this is not the only way to define instance variables (or outlets). It is certainly a legitimate way to do so, but not necessarily the most efficient. In fact, in much of your development, you won't even need to include anything between the curly braces in lines 3 and 6 (or the curly braces themselves). Instead, you'll create your instance variables by defining *properties*. We get to this approach in the next section.

CAUTION

Yes, the Semicolon Is Required

All instance variables, method declaration lines, and property declarations must end with a semicolon (;).

Notice that line 3 includes a few additional items after the `@interface` directive: `myClass : myParent <myProtocol>`. The first of these is the name that we're giving the class that we're working on. Here, we've decided the class will be called `myClass`. The class name is then followed by a colon (:) and a list of the classes that this class is inheriting from (that is, the *parent* classes). Finally, the parent classes are followed by a list of *protocols* enclosed within angle brackets, <>.

TIP

The implementation and interface files for a class will usually share the name of the class. Here, the interface file would be named myClass.h and the implementation file myClass.m.

NOTE

Protocol? What's a protocol? Protocols are a feature of Objective-C that sound complicated but really aren't. Sometimes you will come across features that require you to write methods to support their use, such as providing a list of items to be displayed in a table. The methods that you need to write are grouped together under a common name; this is known as a *protocol*.

Some protocol methods are required, and others are optional; it just depends on the features you need. A class that implements a protocol is said to conform to that protocol.

The @property Directive (and Instance Variables)

A critical, and multifunctional, piece of the interface file is the @property directive, demonstrated in lines 8–10:

```
 8: @property (weak, nonatomic) NSString *myString;
 9: @property (weak, nonatomic) NSString *myOtherString;
10: @property (weak, nonatomic) IBOutlet UILabel *myOtherLabel;
```

The @property directive is used to simplify how you interact with the instance variables that you've defined in your interface—and, as you'll learn shortly, can even act as a shortcut for creating the instance variables themselves. In essence, defining a property provides a layer of abstraction on top of an instance variable. Instead of interacting with a variable directly (and potentially in ways you shouldn't), you use a property instead. Line 8, for example, defines a property that we can use to access the instance variable defined previously in line 4.

Traditionally, to interact with the contents of your instance variables, you have to use (and write!) methods called getters and setters (or accessors and mutators, if you want to sound a bit more exotic). These methods, as their names suggest, are created to get and set values stored in your instance variable objects without touching the actual variables themselves. What @property does is write the getter and setter for us and give us a really nice way of using them. The getter is simply the name of the property, while the setter is the property name (capitalized) with the prefix set. For example, to set the instance variable _myString through a property, you could use the following:

```
[myClassObject setMyString:@"Hello World"];
```

And to retrieve value from _myString, you might type this:

```
theStringInMyObject=[myClassObject myString];
```

Not too tough, but it's not as easy as it could be. Using `@property` also allows us to read and write instance variable values just by typing the name of the object that contains the property, followed by a period, and the name of the property. This is called *dot notation*:

```
myClassObject.myString=@"Hello World";
theStringInMyObject=myClassObject.mystring;
```

We make use of this feature nearly everywhere that we need easy access to instance variables. After we've given the "property" treatment to an instance variable (line 8), we almost always refer to the property rather than the variable itself. That leads us to two final points that can lead to a ton of confusion.

First, because properties and instance variables are so closely related, Objective-C makes it possible to implicitly declare an instance variable just by declaring the property. In other words, consider line 9:

```
9: @property (weak, nonatomic) NSString *myOtherString;
```

This single line is all that is actually needed to declare a new instance variable `_myOtherString` and an associated property named `myOtherString`; no explicit declaration of the instance variable is required.

In addition, property declarations can be used to create a property, instance variable, and an `IBOutlet`, all in one, as shown in line 10:

```
10: @property (weak, nonatomic) IBOutlet UILabel *myOtherLabel;
```

You'll encounter this often in Apple's iOS project templates: a property declaration that implicitly defines an instance variable. We'll use this approach ourselves because writing a single line of code is easier (and less prone to errors) than writing several lines to do the same thing.

The second extremely important point in this discussion is understanding the relationship between the names of properties and instance veriables. As previously mentioned, instance variables typically begin with an underscore (_). The same *cannot* be said for properties. Properties don't begin with an underscore, but *refer* to instance variables that do. If you declare an instance variable named `myVariable` and want to create a property that references it, you can't do it by creating a property named `myVariable`. Doing so creates a *new* instance variable with, you guessed it, an underscore at the start: `_myVariable`. Although there are ways to change this naming convention, it's best to stick with a standard. We will be using the `@property` directive to create both our properties and their corresponding instance variables (just as in lines 9 and 10). Whatever we name a property, just keep in mind that in the background, a variable with *almost* the same name (but starting with a _) is automatically created.

TIP

The attributes (`weak`, `nonatomic`) that are provided to the `@property` directive tell Xcode how to treat the object the property refers to. The first, `weak`, informs the system that the object it is referring to can be cleaned up from memory when it isn't being used anymore. The second, `nonatomic`, instructs Xcode that it doesn't need to worry about different parts of the application using the property at the same time. These are the attributes you'll use in nearly all circumstances, so get used to them.

As you'll see later in the book, sometimes we need to use the attribute `strong` in place of `weak`. The `weak` attribute lets Xcode be more efficient in cleaning up objects in memory. It also avoids what is called a *circular reference*, where an object can't be removed from memory, because it points to another object that, in turn, points back to it. Unfortunately, sometimes the system may be a bit overzealous in its desire to keep things clean for us, and `strong` needs to be employed. A `strong` reference means that the object will be kept in memory until we explicitly tell the system to remove it. It's pretty rare that we need to worry about this, but I'll point it out when it's a concern.

NOTE

It's generally a bad idea to access instance variables that have a corresponding property directly, but there are cases where you may want to use them instead of properties. (You'll learn about this in the "Private Variables, Properties, and Methods" section later this hour.) Let's quickly see how you'll reference a variable versus a property.

To use an instance variable, you just access it by name. If you are writing a class with an instance variable defined as `_myVariable`, anywhere you type `_myVariable`, you are accessing the variable directly. Properties, however, work quite a bit differently.

To retrieve a property from an object, you write `<objectname>.<propertyname>` to access it. That means if there is a property `myProperty` in an object `myAmazingObject`, you type `myAmazingObject.myProperty`.

That's fine, but what if you want to access the property from inside the class where it is defined? Simple. You do exactly the same thing, but use `self` to refer to the object, as in `self.<propertyname>`. If you were to use just the property name by itself, Xcode would assume you are trying to access an instance variable and throw an error.

This will all be obvious once you start coding. You'll be using `self.<propertyname>` in almost every hour, so there will be plenty of time to get used to the syntax.

Defining Methods

The final piece of the interface file are method definitions, known as *prototypes*. Lines 12 and 14 declare two methods that will be implemented in the class:

```
12: +(NSString)myClassMethod:(NSString *)aString;
13:
14: -(NSDate)myInstanceMethod:(NSString *)aString anotherParam:(NSURL *)aURL;
```

Prototypes follow a simple structure. They begin with a + or -. The + denotes a class method, whereas - indicates an instance method. Next, the type of information the method returns is provided in parentheses, followed by the name of the method itself. If the method takes a parameter, the name is followed by a colon, the type of information the method is expecting, and the variable name that the method will use to refer to that information. If multiple parameters are needed, a short descriptive label is added, followed by another colon, data type, and variable name. This pattern can repeat for as many parameters as needed.

In the example file, line 12 defines a class method named myClassMethod that returns an NSString object and accepts an NSString object as a parameter. The input parameter is made available in a variable called aString.

Line 14 defines an instance method named myInstanceMethod that returns an NSDate object, also takes an NSString as a parameter, and includes a second parameter of the type NSURL that will be available to the method via the variable aURL.

NOTE

You learn more about NSString, NSDate, and NSURL in Hour 4, "Inside Cocoa Touch," but as you might guess, these are objects for storing and manipulating strings, dates, and URLs, respectively.

TIP

You will often see methods that accept or return objects of the type id. This is a special type in Objective-C that can reference any kind of object and proves useful if you don't know exactly what you'll be passing to a method or if you want to be able to return different types of objects from a single method.

Another popular return type for methods is void. When you see void used, it means that the method returns *nothing*.

Ending the Interface File

To end the interface file, add @end on its own line. You can see this on line 16 of the example file:

```
16: @end
```

That's it for the interface. Although that might seem like quite a bit to digest, it covers almost everything you'll see in an interface/header file. Because we will usually just be defining instance variables automatically with @property, most of our interface files will actually be simpler than this! Now let's look at the file where the actual work gets done: the implementation file.

Implementation Files

After you've defined your instance variables (or properties) and methods in your interface file, you need to do the work of writing code to implement the logic of your application. The implementation file (.m extension) holds all the "stuff" that makes your class work. Let's take a look at Listing 3.2, a sample implementation file myClass.m that corresponds to the interface file we've been reviewing.

LISTING 3.2   A Sample Implementation File

```
 1: #import "myClass.h"
 2:
 3: @interface myClass ()
 4: @end
 5:
 6: @implementation myClass
 7:
 8: +(NSString)myClassMethod:(NSString *)aString {
 9:    // Implement the Class Method Here!
10: }
11:
12: -(NSString)myInstanceMethod:(NSString *)aString anotherParam:(NSURL *)aURL {
13:    // Implement the Instance Method Here!
14: }
15:
16: @end
```

The `#import` Directive

The `#import` directive kicks things off in line 1 by importing the interface file associated with the class:

```
1: #import "myClass.h"
```

When you create your projects and classes in Xcode, this is automatically added to the code for you. If any additional interface files need to be imported, you should add them to the top of your interface file rather than here.

Private Variables, Properties, and Methods

When we get to lines 3–4, we run into something that looks a bit familiar: another `@interface` block that looks just like the what we had in our interface file! It looks similar because it serves the same purpose, but with distinct difference.

You can put instance variables, properties, and method definitions in this block, but the items that you put here are considered *private* to your class. In other words, if another application wants to use your class, it cannot directly access the items you add in this block; they are available only to you within the class itself. This is known, in Objective-C, as an *empty category*.

NOTE

Be aware that using this block isn't something you *have* to do. This is useful if you're creating a class to share, but have certain methods or variables that aren't necessary for others to successfully use the class (internal calculations, counters, error handling, and the such).

The `@implementation` **Directive**

The `@implementation` directive, shown in line 6, tells Xcode what class the file is going to be implementing. In this case, the file should contain the code to implement `myClass`:

```
6: @implementation myClass
```

The Olden Days of `@synthesize`

A long time ago—roughly 2 months ago, at the time of this writing—each time you declared a property with `@property`, you had to include a `@synthesize` line with the same property name after the `@implementation` line. It looked similar to this:

```
@synthesize myLabel;
```

As of Xcode 4.4, this is no longer required and will not be used in this book. It's important to recognize the syntax, however, because you'll definitely encounter it in sample code.

One use of `@synthesize` that has some value was defining the name of the instance variable that a property refers to. Although you can still use it for this purpose, Apple's automatic naming of instance variables with an underscore (_) prefix makes it largely unnecessary.

```
@synthesize <myPropertyName>=<myInstanceVariableName>
```

Method Implementation

To provide an area to write your code, the implementation file must restate the method definitions, but, rather than ending them with a semicolon (;), a set of curly braces, {}, is added at the end, as shown in lines 8–10 and 12–14. All the magic of your programming takes place between these braces:

```
 8: +(NSString)myClassMethod:(NSString *)aString {
 9:    // Implement the Class Method Here!
10: }
11:
12: -(NSString)myInstanceMethod:(NSString *)aString anotherParam:(NSURL *)aURL {
13:    // Implement the Instance Method Here!
14: }
```

TIP

You can add a text comment on any line within your class files by prefixing the line with the `//` characters. If you want to create a comment that spans multiple lines, you can begin the comment with the characters `/*` and end with `*/`.

Ending the Interface File

To end the implementation file, add `@end` on its own line, just as with the interface file. Line 16 of the example shows this:

```
16: @end
```

Structure for Free

Even though we've just spent quite a bit of time going through the structure of the interface and implementation files, you're rarely (if ever) going to need to type it all out by hand. Whenever you add a new class to your Xcode project, the structure of the file will be set up for you; the `@interface` and `@implementation` directives and overall file structure will be in place before you write a single line of code. What's more, much of the work of declaring properties, instances, variables, and methods can be done visually. Of course, you still need to know how to write code manually, but Xcode 4.x goes a long way toward making sure you don't have to sweat the details.

Categories and Protocols (Optional)

NOTE

The following is information that will be helpful in your journey into iOS development. We won't specifically be writing categories or protocols, but you may encounter sample code that use these features.

In addition to writing classes, you can define functionality through Objective-C's categories and protocols. A category enables you to add methods to a class without subclassing or override a class's existing methods. This means that you could, for example, add new methods to built-in classes, like `NSString`.

A protocol does not implement functionality, but defines what another class *may* or *must* implement to comply with the protocol. In other words, you can define a protocol that enables other classes to interface with your code, which is often done with objects like the `UITable`, which expects certain methods to exist in your code so as to provide it with data. For Java developers, this is similar to the idea of an *interface*.

Defining a Category

To define a category, you just decide what class your category is going to add methods to and what your category is going to be named (presumably based on the features it provides), and then you create a new interface file using this format:

```
@interface ClassNameToUpdate (CategoryName)
      // Declarations for new (or overridden) methods go here
@end
```

The implementation file follows:

```
@implementation ClassNameToUpdate (CategoryName)
      // Implementations of new methods go here
@end
```

The naming conventions for category files are the class name you want to update plus (+) the name of the category (for example, ClassNameToUpdate+CategoryName.h and ClassNameTo Update+CategoryName.m).

After you have created your category, you can import the interface file into your other classes and code away. Your application will behave as if the original class now includes the methods you wrote.

CAUTION

No Instance Variables for You!

Note that you can override methods with a category, but you cannot add new instance variables.

Creating a Protocol

Creating a new protocol is easier than creating a class or a category because you're just defining functionality to be implemented elsewhere. To define a new protocol, create a new interface file with what you want to name your protocol. The contents of the file should follow this format:

```
@protocol ANewProtocol <NSObject>
      @optional
               // Declarations for optional methods
      @required
               // Declarations for required methods
@end
```

The <NSObject> denotes the base protocol that this protocol will be based on (similar to inheriting from a class). Methods that must be implemented to conform to the protocol are found under the @required directive, and optional ones are under the @optional directive.

NOTE

Methods defined without `@optional` or `@required` preceding them are assumed to be required.

Objective-C Programming Basics

We've explored the notion of classes, methods, and instance variables, but you probably still don't have a real idea of how to go about making a program do something. So, this section reviews several key programming tasks that you'll be using to implement your methods:

▶ Declaring variables

▶ Allocating and initializing objects

▶ Using an object's instance methods

▶ Making decisions with expressions

▶ Branching and looping

Declaring Variables

Earlier we documented what instance variables in your interface file will look like, but we didn't really get into the process of how you declare (or define) them (or use them). Instance variables are also only a small subset of the variables you'll use in your projects. Instance variables store information that is available across all the methods in your class—but they're not really appropriate for small temporary storage tasks, such as formatting a line of text to output to a user. Most commonly, you'll be declaring several variables at the start of your methods, using them for various calculations, and then getting rid of them when you've finished with them.

Whatever the purpose, you declare your variables using this syntax:

```
<Type> <Variable Name>;
```

The type is either a primitive data type or the name of a class that you want to instantiate and use.

Primitive Data Types

Primitive data types are defined in the C language and are used to hold very basic values. Common types you'll encounter include the following:

▶ `int`: Integers (whole numbers such as 1, 0, and –99)

▶ `float`: Floating-point numbers (numbers with decimal points in them)

▶ `double`: Highly precise floating-point numbers that can handle a large number of digits

For example, to declare an integer variable that will hold a user's age, you might enter the following:

```
int userAge;
```

After a primitive data type is declared, the variable can be used for assignments and mathematical operations. The following code, for example, declares two variables, `userAge` and `userAgeInDays`, and then assigns a value to one and calculates the other:

```
int userAge;
int userAgeInDays;
userAge=30;
userAgeInDays=userAge*365;
```

Pretty easy, don't you think? Primitive data types, however, will make up only a very small number of the variables types that you use. Most variables you declare are used to store objects.

Object Data Types and Pointers

Just about everything that you'll be working with in your iOS applications will be an object. Text strings, for example, will be instances of the class `NSString`. Buttons that you display on the screen are objects of the class `UIButton`. You'll learn about several of the common data types in the next hour's lesson. Apple has literally provided hundreds of different classes that you can use to store and manipulate data.

Unfortunately for us, for a computer to work with an object, it can't just store it like a primitive data type. Objects have associated instance variables and methods, making them far more complex. To declare a variable as an object of a specific class, we must declare the variable as a *pointer* to an object. A pointer references the place in memory where the object is stored, rather than a value. To declare a variable as a pointer, prefix the name of the variable with an asterisk. For example, to declare a variable of type `NSString` with the intention of holding a user's name, we might type this:

```
NSString *userName;
```

Once declared, you can use the variable without the asterisk. It is only used in the declaration to identify the variable as a pointer to the object.

TIP

When a variable is a pointer to an object, it is said to reference or point to the object. This is in contrast to a variable of a primitive data type, which is said to store the data. Pointers, although largely concealed in basic Cocoa development, are an important topic to understand. For a quick introduction, watch this video: http://www.youtube.com/watch?v=7-EppTJK7WQ.

Even after a variable has been declared as a pointer to an object, it still isn't ready to be used. Xcode, at this point, only knows what object you intend the variable to reference. Before the object actually exists, you must manually prepare the memory it will use and perform any initial setup required. This is handled via the processes of allocation and initialization, which we review next.

Allocating and Initializing Objects

Before an object can be used, memory must be allocated and the contents of the object initialized. This is handled by sending an `alloc` message to the class that you're going to be using, followed by an `init` message to what is returned by `alloc`. The syntax you use is this:

```
[[<class name> alloc] init];
```

For example, to declare and create a new instance of the `UILabel` class, you could use the following code:

```
UILabel *myLabel;
myLabel=[[UILabel alloc] init];
```

Once allocated and initialized, the object is ready to use.

NOTE

We haven't covered the method messaging syntax in Objective-C, but we do so shortly. For now, it's just important to know the pattern for creating objects.

Convenience Methods

When we initialized the `UILabel` instance, we did create a usable object, but it doesn't yet have any of the additional information that makes it useful. Properties such as what the label should say or where it should be shown on the screen have yet to be set. We would need to use several of the object's other methods to really make use of the object.

These configuration steps are sometimes a necessary evil, but Apple's classes often provide a special initialization method called a *convenience method*. These methods can be invoked to set up an object with a basic set of properties so that it can be used almost immediately.

For example, the `NSURL` class, which you use later to work with web addresses, defines a convenience method called `initWithString`.

To declare and initialize an `NSURL` object that points to the website http://www.teachyourselfios.com, we might type the following:

```
NSURL *iOSURL;
iOSURL=[[NSURL alloc] initWithString:@"http://www.teachyourselfios.com/"];
```

Without any additional work, we've allocated and initialized a URL with an actual web address in a single line of code.

TIP

In this example, we actually created *another* object, too: an `NSString`. By typing the @ symbol followed by characters in quotes, you allocate and initialize a string. This feature exists because strings are so commonly used that having to allocate and initialize them each time you need one would make development quite cumbersome.

Typecasting

In your adventures in Objective-C, you will encounter instances where a method you are implementing has a generic reference to an object but you can't work with it because Xcode doesn't know the exact type of object it is. In these cases, you must use typecasting (or simply casting) to force Xcode to recognize the object.

For example, imagine that you are implementing a method that receives, as one of its parameters, an object of the type `id` named `unknownObject`. We know, however, that the only object that would be passed to the method is an instance of a class called `anImportantClass`. The `id` type can refer to anything, so until we tell Xcode what type of object it is, we can't access its properties or methods.

To typecast a variable so that it is recognized as another type, place the type inside of parentheses in front of the variable:

```
(anImportantClass *)unknownObject
```

Using this, we can assign the `unknownObject` to a new variable of the correct type:

```
anImportantClass *myKnownObject=(anImportantClass *)unknownObject;
```

After the cast variable is assigned to an object of the correct type, we can interact with it directly as that type. We can also choose to just typecast it whenever we need it. We can even use typecasting to access properties within an object.

If the `anImportantClass` defined a property called `anImportantProperty`, we could access that by including an extra set of parenthesis around the object we're casting:

```
((anImportantClass *)unknownObject).anImportantProperty
```

This looks a bit unusual, I know, but it will come in very handy later in the book. It's easier to understand when you see it in an actual application; so for the moment, just be aware that it is an available development tool.

Using Methods and Messaging

You've already seen the methods used to allocate and initialize objects, but this is only a tiny picture of the methods you'll be using in your apps. Let's start by reviewing the syntax of methods and messaging.

Messaging Syntax

To send an object a message, give the name of the variable that is referencing the object followed by the name of the method—all within square brackets. If you're using a class method, just provide the name of the class rather than a variable name:

```
[<object variable or class name> <method name>];
```

Things start to look a little more complicated when the method has parameters. A single parameter method call looks like this:

```
[<object variable> <method name>:<parameter value>];
```

Multiple parameters look even more bizarre:

```
[<object variable> <method name>:<parameter value>
                additionalParameter:<parameter value>];
```

An actual example of using a multiple parameter method looks like this:

```
[userName compare:@"John" options:NSCaseInsensitive];
```

Here an object `userName` (presumably an `NSString`) uses the `compare:options` method to compare itself to the string `"John"` in a non-case-sensitive manner. The result of this particular method is a Boolean value (`true` or `false`), which could be used as part of an expression to make a decision in your application. (We review expressions and decision making next.)

NOTE

Throughout the lessons, methods are referred to by name. If the name includes a colon (:), this indicates a required parameter. This is a convention that Apple has used in their documentation and that has been adopted for this book.

TIP

A useful predefined value in Objective-C is `nil`. The `nil` value indicates a *lack* of any value at all. You'll use `nil` in some methods that call for a parameter that you don't have available. A method that receives `nil` in place of an object can actually pass messages to `nil` without creating an error—`nil` simply returns another `nil` as the result.

This is used a few times later in the book and should give you a clearer picture of why this behavior is something we'd actually *want* to happen.

Nested Messaging

Something that you'll see when looking at Objective-C code is that the result of a method is sometimes used directly as a parameter within another method. In some cases, if the result of a method is an object, a developer sends a message directly to that result.

In both of these cases, using the results directly avoids the need to create a variable to hold the results. Want an example that puts all of this together? We've got one for you.

Assume you have two NSString variables, userFirstName and userLastName, that you want to capitalize and concatenate, storing the results in another NSString called finalString. To keep this simple, we'll assume there is already a space concatenated onto the userFirstName variable.

The NSString instance method capitalizedString returns a capitalized string, and string-ByAppendingString takes a second string as a parameter and concatenates it onto the string invoking the message. Putting this together (disregarding the variable declarations), the code looks like this:

```
tempCapitalizedFirstName=[userFirstName capitalizedString];
tempCapitalizedSecondName=[userLastName capitalizedString];
finalString=[tempCapitalizedFirstName
                stringByAppendingString:tempCapitalizedSecondName];
```

Instead of using these temporary variables, however, you could just substitute the method calls into a single combined line:

```
finalString=[[userFirstName capitalizedString]
                stringByAppendingString:[userLastName capitalizedString]];
```

This can be a powerful way to structure your code, but it can also lead to long and rather confusing statements. Do what makes you comfortable—both approaches are equally valid and have the same outcome.

TIP

A confession. I have a difficult time referring to using a method as sending a "message to an object." Although this is the preferred terminology for OOP, all we're really doing is executing an object's method by providing the name of the object and the name of the method.

Blocks

Although most of your coding will be within methods, Apple recently introduced "blocks" to the iOS frameworks. Sometimes referred to as *handler blocks* in the Xcode documentation, these are chunks of code that can be passed as values when calling a method. They provide instructions that the method should run when reacting to a certain event.

For example, imagine a `personInformation` object with a method called `setDisplayName` that would define a format for showing a person's name. Instead of just showing the name, however, `setDisplayName` might use a block to let you define, programmatically, how the name should be shown:

```
[personInformation setDisplayName:^(NSString firstName, NSString lastName)
            {
                // Implement code here to modify the first name and last name
                // and display it however you want.
            }];
```

Interesting, isn't it? Blocks are new to iOS development and are rarely used in this book. When you start developing motion-sensitive apps, for example, you will pass a block to a method to describe what to do when a motion occurs.

Where blocks are used, we walk through the process. To learn more about these strange and unusual creatures, read Apple's "A Short Practical Guide to Blocks" in the Xcode documentation.

Expressions and Decision Making

For an application to react to user input and process information, it must be capable of making decisions. Every decision in an app boils down to a yes or no result based on evaluating a set of tests. These can be as simple as comparing two values, to something as complex as checking the results of a complicated mathematical calculation. The combination of tests used to make a decision is called an *expression*.

Using Expressions

If you recall your high school algebra, you'll be right at home with expressions. An expression can combine arithmetic, comparison, and logical operations.

A simple numeric comparison checking to see whether a variable `userAge` is greater than 30 could be written as follows:

```
userAge>30
```

When working with objects, we need to use properties within the object and values returned from methods to create expressions. To check to see whether a string stored in an object `userName` is equal to `"John"`, we could use this:

```
[userName compare:@"John"]
```

Expressions are not limited to the evaluation of a single condition. We could easily combine the previous two expressions to find a user who is over 30 and named John:

```
userAge>30 && [userName compare:@"John"]
```

Common Expression Syntax

`()`—Groups expressions together, forcing evaluation of the innermost group first.

`==`—Tests to see whether two values are equal (for example, `userAge==30`).

`!=`—Tests to see whether two values are not equal (for example, `userAge!=30`).

`&&`—Implements a logical AND condition (for example, `userAge>30 && userAge<40`).

`||`—Implements a logical OR condition (for example, `userAge>30 || userAge<10`).

`!`—Negates the result of an expression, returning the opposite of the original result (for example, `!(userAge==30)` is the same as `userAge!=30`).

For a complete list of C expression syntax, refer to http://en.wikipedia.org/wiki/Operators_in_C_ and_C%2B%2B.

As mentioned repeatedly, you're going to be spending lots of time working with complex objects and using the methods within the objects. You cannot make direct comparisons between objects as you can with simple primitive data types. To successfully create expressions for the myriad objects you'll be using, you must review each object's methods and properties.

Making Decisions with `if-then-else` and `switch` Statements

Typically, depending on the outcome of the evaluated expression, different code statements are executed. The most common way of defining these different execution paths is with an `if-then-else` statement:

```
if (<expression>) {
  // do this, the expression is true.
} else {
  // the expression isn't true, do this instead!
}
```

For example, consider the comparison we used earlier to check a `userName` `NSString` variable to see whether its contents were set to a specific name. If we want to react to that comparison, we might write the following:

```
if ([userName compare:@"John"]) {
  userMessage=@"I like your name";
} else {
  userMessage=@"Your name isn't John, but I still like it!";
}
```

Another approach to implementing different code paths when there are potentially many different outcomes to an expression is to use a `switch` statement. A `switch` statement checks a variable for a value and then executes different blocks of code depending on the value that is found:

```
switch (<numeric value>) {
  case <numeric option 1>:
    // The value matches this option
    break;
  case <numeric option 2>:
    // The value matches this option
    break;
  default:
    // None of the options match the number.
}
```

Applying this to a situation where we might want to check a user's age (stored in userAge) for some key milestones and then set an appropriate userMessage string if they are found, the result might look like this:

```
switch (userAge) {
  case 18:
    userMessage=@"Congratulations, you're an adult!";
    break;
  case 21:
    userMessage=@"Congratulations, you can drink champagne!";
    break;
  case 50:
    userMessage=@"You're half a century old!";
    break;
  default:
    userMessage=@"Sorry, there's nothing special about your age.";
}
```

Repetition with Loops

In some situations, you will need to repeat several instructions over and over in your code. Instead of typing the lines repeatedly, you can loop over them. A loop defines the start and end of several lines of code. As long as the loop is running, the program executes the lines from top to bottom and then restarts again from the top. The loops you'll use are of two types: count based and condition based.

In a count-based loop, the statements are repeated a certain number of times. In a condition-based loop, an expression determines whether a loop should occur.

The count-based loop you'll be using is called a for loop and consists of this syntax:

```
for (<initialization>;<test condition>;<count update>) {
  // Do this, over and over!
}
```

The three "unknowns" in the for statement syntax are a statement to initialize a counter to track the number of times the loop has executed, a condition to check to see whether the loop should continue, and finally, an increment for the counter. A loop that uses the integer variable count to loop 50 times could be written as follows:

```
int count;
for (count=0;count<50;count=count+1) {
  // Do this, 50 times!
}
```

The for loop starts by setting the count variable to 0. The loop then starts and continues as long as the condition of count<50 remains true. When the loop hits the bottom curly brace (}) and starts over, the increment operation is carried out and count is increased by 1.

NOTE

In C and C-like languages, like Objective-C, integers are usually incremented by using ++ at the end of the variable name. In other words, rather than using count=count+1, most often you'll encounter count++, which does the same thing. Decrementing works the same way, but with -.

In a condition-based loop, the loop continues while an expression remains true. There are two variables of this loop type that you'll encounter, while and do-while:

```
while (<expression>) {
  // Do this, over and over, while the expression is true!
}
```

and

```
do {
  // Do this, over and over, while the expression is true!
} while (<expression>);
```

The only difference between these two loops is when the expression is evaluated. In a standard while loop, the check is done at the beginning of the loop. In the do-while loop, however, the expression is evaluated at the end of every loop. In practice, this difference ensures that in a do-while loop, the code block is executed at least once; a while loop may not execute the block at all.

For example, suppose you are asking users to input their names and you want to keep prompting them until they type John. You might format a do-while loop like this:

```
do {
  // Get the user's input in this part of the loop
} while (![userName compare:@"John"]);
```

The assumption is that the name is stored in a string object called userName. Because you wouldn't have requested the user's input when the loop first starts, you would use a do-while loop to put the test condition at the end. Also, the value returned by the string compare method has to been negated with the ! operator because you want to continue looping as long as the comparison of the userName to "John" isn't true.

Loops are a very useful part of programming and, along with the decision statements, will form the basis for structuring the code within your object methods. They allow code to branch and extend beyond a linear flow.

Although an all-encompassing picture of programming is beyond the scope of this book, this should give you some sense of what to expect in the rest of the book. Let's now close out the hour with a topic that causes quite a bit of confusion for beginning developers: memory management.

Memory Management and Automatic Reference Counting

In the first hour of this book, you learned a bit about the limitations of iOS devices as a platform. One of the biggies, unfortunately, is the amount of memory that your programs have available to them. Because of this, you must be extremely judicious in how you manage memory. If you're writing an app that browses an online recipe database, for example, you shouldn't allocate memory for every single recipe as soon as your application starts.

The Old Way: Retaining and Releasing Objects

Each time you allocate memory for an object, you're using up memory on your iOS device. If you allocate too many objects, you run out of memory, and your application crashes or is forced to quit. To avoid a memory problem, keep objects around long enough to use them only, and then get rid of them.

If you've read previous editions of this book, or even browsed online iOS source code, chances are you've encountered the retain and release messages (many, many times). These messages, when passed to an object, indicate that the object is needed, or is no longer being used (release).

Behind the scenes, the iOS maintains a "retain" count to determine when it can get rid of an object. For example, when an object is first allocated, the retain count is incremented. Any use of the retain message on the object also increases the count.

The release message, in contrast, decrements the count. As long as the retain count remains above 0, the object is not removed from memory. When the count reaches 0, the object is considered unused and is removed.

In your applications, you previously needed to add release code for any object you allocated. Think about that on a large scale: applications with hundreds or thousands of objects, needing to be manually retained or released. If you missed one, memory leaks and application crashes occurred! If you released an object too soon, more application crashes occurred.

Consider the earlier example of allocating an instance of NSURL:

```
NSURL *iOSURL;
iOSURL=[[NSURL alloc] initWithString:@"http://www.teachyourselfios.com/"];
```

Suppose that after you allocate and initialize the URL, you use it to load a web page. After the page loads and you're done with the object, you must manually tell Xcode that you no longer have a need for it by writing the following:

```
[iOSURL release];
```

In Xcode 4, all of that changes. Manually releasing and retaining objects is a thing of the past, thanks to Automatic Reference Counting.

The New Way: Automatic Reference Counting

In Xcode 4.2, Apple implemented a new compiler called LLVM, along with a feature known as Automatic Reference Counting (ARC). ARC uses a powerful code analyzer to look at how your objects are allocated and used, and then it automatically retains and releases them as needed. When nothing is referencing an object, ARC ensures it is automatically removed from memory. No more retain or release messages to be sent, no more phantom crashes and memory leaks; you just code and it works.

All new projects that you build in Xcode, including those in this book, will automatically take advantage of ARC. In fact, ARC is so good at what it does that it will not let you write applications that include release, retain, dealloc, or autorelease. So, how does this translate into your development process? Just as you would hope: You write the code you need, initialize and use objects when you want, and when they are no longer referenced by anything else, the memory they occupied is automatically freed.

For most objects you declare and use in a method, you do not need to do anything—when the method is finished, there are no more references to the object and it is automatically freed. The same goes for instance variables/properties you've declared with the weak attribute. Of course, it's hyperbole to say that errors won't happen with ARC; we have to use strong in a few places in this book to keep iOS from deciding that we have finished with an object before we actually do.

When the strong attribute has been used, you need to tell Xcode that you're finished using an object if you want it removed from memory. How do you do that? Easy: by setting its reference to nil.

For a property/instance variable named myObject, you write the following:

```
self.myObject=nil;
```

If you've done any Objective-C development before ARC, you'll quickly appreciate how little time you now need to spend on memory management. If you're new to Objective-C, just relax and enjoy!

You've learned quite a bit in this hour's lesson, and there are plenty of places for even the most experienced developer to make mistakes. As with everything, practice makes perfect, and you'll have plenty of opportunities for applying what you've learned in the book's tutorials.

Keep in mind that a typical book would spend multiple chapters on these topics, so our goal has been to give you a starting point that future hours will build on, not to define everything you'll ever need to know about Objective-C and OOP.

Further Exploration

Although you can be successful in learning iOS programming without spending hours and hours learning more Objective-C, you will find it easier to create complex applications if you become more comfortable with the language. Objective-C, as mentioned before, is not something that can be described in a single hour. It has a far-reaching feature set that makes it a powerful and elegant development platform.

To learn more about Objective-C, check out *Programming in Objective-C 2.0, Third Edition* (Addison-Wesley Professional, 2011), *Objective-C Phrasebook* (Addison-Wesley Professional, 2011), and *Xcode 4 Unleashed* (Sams, 2012).

Of course, Apple has its own Objective-C documentation that you can access directly from within the Xcode documentation tool. (You learn more about this in the next hour.) I recommend the following documents provided by Apple:

- Learning Objective-C: A Primer
- Object-Oriented Programming with Objective-C
- The Objective-C 2.0 Programming Language
- Programming with ARC

You can read these within Xcode or via the online Apple iOS Reference Library at http://developer.apple.com/library/ios/. One quick warning: These documents are several hundred pages long, so you might want to continue your Objective-C education in parallel with the lessons in this book.

Summary

In this hour, you learned about object-oriented development and the Objective-C language. Objective-C will form the structure of your applications and give you tools to collect and react to user input and other changes. After reading this hour's lesson, you should understand how to make classes, instantiate objects, call methods, and use decision and looping statements to create code that implements more complex logic than a simple top-to-bottom workflow. You should also have an understanding of memory management and how it works under the Xcode 4.2 ARC system.

Much of the functionality that you'll be using in your applications will come from the hundreds of built-in classes that Apple provides within iOS, which we delve into in Hour 4.

Q&A

Q. Is Objective-C on iOS the same as on OS X?

A. For the most part, yes. OS X includes thousands of additional APIs, however, and provides access to the underlying UNIX subsystem.

Q. Can an `if-then-else` statement be extended beyond evaluating and acting on a single expression?

A. Yes. The `if-then-else` statement can be extended by adding another if statement after the else:

```
if (<expression>) {
    // do this, the expression is true.
} else if (<expression>) {
    // the expression isn't true, do this instead.
} else {
    // Neither of the expressions are true, do this anyway!
}
```

You can continue expanding the statement with as many `else-if` statements as you need.

Q. Why are primitive data types used at all? Why aren't there objects for everything?

A. Primitive data types take up much less memory than objects and are much easier to manipulate. Implementing a simple integer within an object would add a layer of complexity and inefficiency that just isn't needed.

Q. **Why can't I release objects if I know I have finished using them? How can ARC do a better job?**

A. ARC is built around the idea that Objective-C is very structured and predictable. By being able to analyze your code at compile time, ARC and LLVM can optimize memory management in a way that mere mortals would have a difficult time replicating.

Quiz

1. When creating a subclass, do you have to rewrite all the methods from the parent class?

2. What is the basic syntax for allocating and initializing an object?

3. What does ARC do?

Answers

1. No. The subclass inherits all the methods of the parent class.

2. To allocate and initialize an object, use the syntax `[[<class name> alloc] init]`.

3. ARC automatically retains and releases objects that you create in your applications, freeing you to code instead of manually manage memory.

Activities

1. Start Xcode and create a new project using the iPhone or iPad Single View Application template. Review the contents of the classes in the project folder. With the information you've read in this hour, you should now be able to read and navigate the structure of these files.

2. Return to the Apple iOS Dev Center (http://developer.apple.com/library/ios) and begin reviewing the "Learning Objective-C: A Primer" tutorial.

HOUR 4
Inside Cocoa Touch

What You'll Learn in This Hour:

- ▶ What Cocoa Touch is and what makes it unique
- ▶ The technology layers that make up the iOS platform
- ▶ A basic iOS application life cycle
- ▶ Classes and development techniques you'll be using throughout this book
- ▶ How to find help using the Apple developer documentation

When computers first started to appear in households almost 30 years ago, applications rarely shared common interface elements. It took an instruction manual just to figure out the key sequence to exit from a piece of software. Today, user interfaces (UIs) have been standardized so that moving from application to application doesn't require starting from scratch.

What has made this possible? Not faster processors or better graphics, but frameworks that enforce consistent implementation of the features provided by the devices they're running on. In this hour, we take a look at the frameworks you'll be using in your iOS applications.

What Is Cocoa Touch?

In the preceding hour, you learned about the Objective-C language, the basic syntax, and what it looks like. Objective-C will form the functional skeleton of your applications. It will help you structure your applications, make logical decisions during the life cycle of your application, and enable you to control how and when events take place. What Objective-C doesn't provide, however, is a way to access what makes your iDevice the compelling touch-driven platform that it is.

Consider the following Hello World application:

```
int main(int argc, char *argv[]) {
    printf("Hello World");
}
```

This code is typical of a beginner Hello World application written in C. It compiles and executes on your iPhone or iPad, but because iOS relies on Cocoa Touch for creating interfaces and handling user input and output, this version of Hello World is quite meaningless. Cocoa Touch is the collection of software frameworks that is used to build iOS applications and the runtime that those applications are executed within. Cocoa Touch includes hundreds of classes for managing everything from buttons and uniform resource locators (URLs) to manipulating photos and performing facial recognition.

Cocoa Touch is the highest of several "layers" of services in the iOS and isn't necessarily the only layer that you'll be developing in. That said, you don't need to worry too much about where Cocoa Touch begins and ends; the development will be the same, regardless. Later in this hour, you get a complete overview of iOS service layers.

Returning to the Hello World example, if we had defined a text label object named `iOSOutput` within a project, we could set it to read `"Hello World"` using Objective-C and the appropriate Cocoa Touch class text property like this:

```
iOSOutput.text=@"Hello World";
```

Seems simple enough, as long as we know that the `UILabel` object has a `text` property, right?

Keeping Your Cool in the Face of Overwhelming Functionality

The questions that should be coming to most beginners right about now include these: I know there are many different features provided through iOS applications; how in the world will this book document all of them? How will I ever find what I need to use for my own applications?

These are great questions, and probably some of the biggest concerns that I've heard from those who want to program for the platform but have no idea where to start. The bad news is that we can't document everything. We can cover the fundamentals that you need to start building, but even in a multivolume set of "teach yourself" books, there is so much depth to what is provided by Cocoa Touch that it isn't feasible to create a complete how-to reference.

The good news is that Cocoa Touch and the Apple developer tools encourage exploration. In Hour 6, "Model-View-Controller Application Design," you start building interfaces visually using Xcode's Interface Builder (IB) tools. As you drag objects (buttons, text fields, and so on) to your interface, you create instances of Cocoa Touch classes. The more you "play," the quicker you will begin to recognize class names and properties and the role they play in development. Even better, Xcode's developer documentation provides a complete reference to Cocoa Touch, enabling you to search across all available classes, methods, properties, and so on. We take a look at the documentation features later in this hour.

Young, Yet Mature

One of the most compelling advantages to programming using Cocoa Touch versus platforms such as Android or HP WebOS is that although the iOS family is a "young" platform for Apple, the Cocoa frameworks are amazingly mature. Cocoa was borne out of the NeXTSTEP platform—the environment that was used by NeXT computers in the mid-1980s. In the early 1990s, NeXTSTEP evolved into the cross-platform OpenStep. Finally, in 1996, Apple purchased NeXT Computer, and over the next decade, the NeXTSTEP/OpenStep framework became the de facto standard for Macintosh development and was renamed Cocoa. You'll notice that there are still signs of Cocoa's origins in class names that begin with NS.

What's the Difference Between Cocoa and Cocoa Touch?

Cocoa is the development framework used for most native OS X applications. iOS, although based on many of the foundational technologies of OS X, isn't quite the same. Cocoa Touch is heavily customized for a touch interface and working within the constraints of a handheld system. Desktop application components that would traditionally require extensive screen real estate have been replaced by simpler multiple-view components, mouse clicks with "touch up" and "touch down" events.

The good news is that if you decide to transition from iOS developer to Mac developer, you'll follow many of the same development patterns on both platforms; it won't be like starting from scratch.

Exploring the iOS Technology Layers

Apple describes the technologies implemented within the iOS as a series of layers, with each layer being made up of different frameworks that can be used in your applications. As you might expect, the Cocoa Touch layer is at the top (see Figure 4.1).

FIGURE 4.1
The technology layers that make up the iOS.

Let's review some of the most important frameworks that make up each of the layers. If you want a comprehensive guide to all frameworks, just search for each layer by its name in the Apple Xcode documentation.

NOTE

Apple has included three important frameworks in every iOS application template (CoreGraphics, Foundation, and UIKit). These frameworks are all that is needed for simple iOS applications and cover most of what you do in this book. When additional frameworks are needed, I describe how to include them in your projects.

The Cocoa Touch Layer

The Cocoa Touch layer is made up of several frameworks that will provide the core functionality for your applications, including multitasking and advertising in iOS 4.x. UIKit could be described as the "rock star," delivering much more than the UI in its name implies.

UIKit

UIKit covers a wide range of functionality. It is responsible for application launching and termination, controlling the interface and multitouch events, and providing access to common views of data (including web pages and Word and Excel documents, among others).

UIKit is also responsible for many intra-iOS integration features. Accessing the Media Library, Photo Library, and accelerometer is also accomplished using the classes and methods within UIKit.

Map Kit

The Map Kit framework enables developers to add Apple's map views to any application, including annotation, location, and event-handling features.

Game Kit

The Game Kit framework adds network-interactivity to iOS applications. Game Kit supplies mechanisms for creating and using peer-to-peer networks, including session discovery, mediation, and voice chat. These features can be added to any application or game (or not).

Message UI/Address Book UI/Event Kit UI

Apple is sensitive to the need for integration between iOS applications. The Message UI, Address Book UI, and Event UI frameworks can be used to access mail, contacts, and calendar events from any application you develop.

iAd

The iAd framework supports the addition of ads to your applications. iAds are interactive advertising pieces that can be added to your software with a simple drag and drop. You do not need to manage iAds interactions in your application; Apple does this for you.

The Media Layer

When Apple makes a computing device, you'd better believe that they put some thought into the media capabilities. The iDevice family can create complex graphics, play back audio and video, and even generate real-time 3D graphics. The Media layer's frameworks handle it all.

AV Foundation

The AV Foundation framework can be used to manage complex sound and video playback and editing. This should be used for implementing advanced features, such as movie recording, track management, and audio panning.

Core Audio

The Core Audio framework exposes methods for handling basic playback and recording of audio. It includes the AudioToolbox framework, which can be used for playing alert sounds or generating short vibrations, and the AudioUnit.framework for processing sounds.

Core Image

With the Core Image framework, developers can add advanced image and video processing capabilities to their applications without needing to understand the complex math behind them. Core Image, for example, provides facial-detection and image-filtering features that can easily be added to any application.

Core Graphics

Use the Core Graphics framework to add 2D drawing and compositing features to your applications. Although most of this book will use existing interface classes and images in its applications, you can use core graphics to programmatically manipulate the view.

Core Text

This provides precise positioning and control over text that is displayed on the screen. Core Text should be used in mobile text-processing applications and software that requires high-quality and fast presentation and manipulation of styled text.

Image I/O

The Image I/O framework can be used to import and export both image data and image metadata for any file format supported by iOS.

Media Player

The Media Player framework provides you, the developer, with an easy way to play back movies with typical onscreen controls. The player can be invoked directly from your application.

OpenGL ES

OpenGL ES is a subset of the popular OpenGL framework for embedded systems (ES). OpenGL ES can be used to create 2D and 3D animation in your apps. Using OpenGL requires additional development experience beyond Objective-C but can generate amazing scenes for a handheld device—similar to what is possible on modern game consoles.

Quartz Core

The Quartz Core framework is used to create animations that will take advantage of the hardware capabilities of your device. This includes the feature set known as *Core Animation*.

The Core Services Layer

The Core Services layer is used to access lower-level operating system services, such as file access, iCloud storage, networking, and many common data object types. You'll make use of core services frequently by way of the Foundation framework.

Accounts

Because of their always-connected nature, iOS devices are frequently used to store account information for many different services. The Accounts framework simplifies the process of storing and authenticating users.

Address Book

The Address Book framework is used to directly access and manipulate address book information. This is used to update contact information and display it within your applications.

CFNetwork

The CFNetwork framework provides access to BSD sockets, HTTP and FTP requests, and Bonjour discovery.

Core Data

The Core Data framework can be used to create the data model of an iOS application. Core Data provides a relational data model based on SQLite and can be used to bind data to interface objects to eliminate the need for complex data manipulations in code.

Core Foundation

Core Foundation provides much of the same functionality of the Foundation framework, but it is a procedural C framework and therefore requires a different development approach that is, arguably, less efficient than Objective-C's object-oriented model. You should probably avoid Core Foundation unless you absolutely need it.

Foundation

The Foundation framework provides an Objective-C wrapper around features in Core Foundation. Manipulation of strings, arrays, and dictionaries is handled through the Foundation framework, as are other fundamental application necessities, including managing application preferences, threads, and internationalization.

Event Kit

The Event Kit framework is used to access calendar information stored on the iOS device. It also enables the developer to create new events within a calendar, including alarms.

Core Location

The Core Location framework can be used to obtain latitude and longitude information from the iPhone and iPad (3G/LTE) GPS (WiFi-based location service is available in non-3G/LTE devices, but is much less precise) along with a measurement of precision.

Core Motion

The Core Motion framework manages most motion-related events on the iOS platform, such as using the accelerometer or gyroscope.

Newsstand

Use this framework to create periodical digital media, such as newspapers or magazines. The Newsstand framework supports automatic content updating, ensuring your customers see the most recent content without needing to manually update.

Quick Look

The Quick Look framework implements file viewing within an application, even if the application does not "know" how to open a specific file type. This is intended for viewing files downloaded to the device.

Social

Rather than requiring developers to create Twitter and Facebook integration from scratch, Apple includes a framework for these popular social networking sites. Using this framework, you can write applications that access Twitter and Facebook without needing to manage account information or understand their proprietary network protocols.

Store Kit

The Store Kit framework enables developers to create in-application transactions for purchasing content without exiting the software. All interactions take place through the App Store, so no financial data is requested or transmitted through the Store Kit methods.

System Configuration

Use the System Configuration framework to determine the current state of a device's network configuration—what network it is connected to (if any) and what other devices are reachable.

The Core OS Layer

The Core OS layer, as you'd expect, is made up of the lowest-level services in the iOS. These features include threads, complex math, hardware accessories, and cryptography. You should only need to access these frameworks in rare circumstances.

Accelerate

The Accelerate framework simplifies complete calculations and large-number manipulation. This includes digital signal processing capabilities.

Core Bluetooth

The Core Bluetooth framework provides connectivity for low-energy Bluetooth devices. This is a unique class of Bluetooth peripheral that can communicate with extremely low power requirements.

External Accessory

The External Accessory framework is used to develop interfaces to accessories connected via the dock connector or Bluetooth.

Security

The Security framework provides functions for performing cryptographic functions (encrypting/decrypting data). This includes interacting with the iOS keychain to add, delete, and modify items.

System

The System framework gives developers access to a subset of the typical tools they would find in an unrestricted UNIX development environment.

Tracing the iOS Application Life Cycle

To help you get a sense for where your "work" in developing an iOS application fits in, it helps to look at the application life cycle. Figure 4.2 shows Apple's simplified diagram of the life cycle.

FIGURE 4.2
The (simplified) life cycle of a typical iOS application.

Let's try to put some context around what you're looking at, starting on the left side of the diagram. As you've learned, UIKit is a component of the Cocoa Touch that provides much of the foundation of iOS applications: UI management, event management, and overall application execution management. When you create an application, UIKit handles the setup of the application object via the main and UIApplicationMain functions, neither of which you should need to touch.

Once the application is started, an event loop begins. This loop receives the events such as screen touches, and then hands them off to your own methods. The loop continues until the application is asked to move to the background (usually through the user pressing the Home button).

Your code comes into play on the right side of the diagram. Xcode automatically sets up your iOS projects to include an application delegate class. This class can implement the methods application:willFinishLaunchingWithOptions, application:didFinishLaunchingWith Options, and applicationDidEnterBackground (among others) so that your program can execute its own custom code when the application launches and when it is suspended by pressing the Home button.

Wait a Second! When Does My Application *Stop* Running?

Beginning in iOS 4.0, applications no longer terminate when the user presses the Home button. Instead, the application stops where it's at and sits quietly in the background. When the user selects it from the task manager or starts it from the home screen, it returns to the foreground and continues exactly where it left off—*automatically*.

To support this process, the application delegate provides the method `applicationDidEnter-Background`, which is called when the application enters the background. This method should be used by your code to store any information that the application needs, in case it is terminated while it is the background (either by iOS cleaning up resources or by the user manually terminating it in the task manager).

The original iOS method for handling termination, `applicationWillTerminate`, is still useful if you develop an application that does not support backgrounding, but this is not the default. You learn more about these methods and iOS background processing options in Hour 22, "Building Background-Aware Applications."

After an application finishes launching, the delegate object typically creates a view controller object and view and adds them to the iOS "window." You learn more about these concepts in the next hour, but for now, think of a view as what is being displayed on the device's screen and the view controller as an object that can be programmed to respond when it receives an event notification (such as touching a button) from the event loop.

The majority of your work will take place within the view controller. You'll receive events from the Cocoa Touch interface and react to them by writing Objective-C code that manipulates other objects within the view. Of course, things can get a bit more complex than a single view and a single view controller, but the same basic approach can be applied in most cases.

Now that you have a better picture of the iOS service layers and application life cycle, let's take a look at some of the classes that you'll be seeing throughout this book.

Cocoa Fundamentals

Thousands of classes are available in the iOS software development kit (SDK), but most of your applications will be using a small set of classes to implement 90% of their features. To familiarize you with the classes and their purposes, let's review some of the names you're going to be seeing very, very often over the next few hours. Before we begin, keep these few key points in mind:

▶ Apple sets up much of the structure of your application for you in Xcode. Therefore, even though you need some of these classes, you won't have to lift a finger to use them. Just create a new Xcode project and they're added for you.

▶ You'll be adding instances of many of these objects to your projects just by dragging icons in Xcode's IB. Again, no coding needed!

▶ When a class is used, I tell you why it is needed, what it does, and how it is used in the project. I don't want you to have to jump around digging for references in the book, so focus on the concepts, not memorization.

▶ In the last section of this hour's lesson, you learn about the Apple documentation tools. These helpful utilities enable you to find all the class, property, and method information that you could ever hope for. If it's gritty details you want, you have them at your fingertips.

Core Application Classes

When you create a new application with even the most basic user interaction, you'll be taking advantage of a collection of common core classes. Many of these you won't be touching, but they still perform an important role. Let's review several of these classes now.

The Root Class (NSObject)

As you learned in Hour 3, "Discovering Objective-C: The Language of Apple Platforms," the power of object-oriented programming is that when you create a subclass of an object you inherit that object's functionality. The root class, from which almost all Objective-C classes inherit, is NSObject. This object defines methods common to all classes, such as alloc and init. You do not need to create NSObject instances manually in this book; instead, you use methods inherited from this class to create and manage new objects.

The Application Object (UIApplication)

Every iOS application implements a subclass of UIApplication. This class handles events, such as notification of when an application has finished loading, as well as application configuration, such as controlling the status bar and setting badges (the little red numbers that can appear on application icons). Like NSObject, you won't need to create this yourself; just be aware it exists.

Window Objects (UIWindow)

The UIWindow class provides a container for the management and display of views. In iOS-speak, a view is more like a typical desktop application "window," whereas an instance of UIWindow is just a container that holds the view. You use only a single UIWindow instance in this book, and it is created automatically in the project templates that Xcode provides for us.

Views (`UIView`)

The `UIView` class defines a rectangular area and manages all the onscreen display within that region—what we will refer to as a view. Most of your applications will start by adding a view to an instance of `UIWindow`.

Views can be nested to form a hierarchy; they rarely exist as a single object. A top-level view, for example, may contain a button and field. These controls would be referred to as *subviews* and the containing view as the *superview*. Multiple levels of views can be nested, creating a complex hierarchy of subviews and superviews. You'll be creating almost all of your views visually in Xcode, so don't worry: Complex doesn't mean difficult.

Responders (`UIResponder`)

The `UIResponder` class provides a means for classes that inherit from it to respond to the touch events produced by iOS. `UIControl`, the superclass for nearly all onscreen controls, inherits from `UIView` and, subsequently, from `UIResponder`. An instance of `UIResponder` is just called a *responder*.

Because multiple objects could potentially respond to an event, iOS passes events up what is referred to as a *chain of responders*. The responder instance that can handle the event is called the first responder. When you're editing a field, for example, the field has first responder status because it is actively handling user input. When you leave the field, it "resigns" first responder status. For most of your iOS development work, you won't be directly managing responders in code.

Onscreen Controls (`UIControl`)

The `UIControl` class inherits from `UIView` and is used as the superclass for almost all onscreen controls, such as buttons, fields, and sliders. This class is responsible for handling the triggering of actions based on touch events, such as "pressing" a button.

As you'll learn in the next hour, a button defines a handful of events that you can respond to; IB enables you to tie those events to actions that you've coded. `UIControl` is responsible for implementing this behavior behind the scenes.

View Controllers (`UIViewController`)

You use the `UIViewController` class in almost all the application projects throughout this book to manage the contents of your views. You use a `UIViewController` subclass, for example, to determine what to do when a user taps a button. Make a sound? Display an image? However you choose to react, the code you use to carry out your action will be implemented as part of a view controller instance. You'll learn much more about view controllers over the next two hours.

Data Type Classes

An object can potentially hold data. In fact, most of the classes we'll be using contain a number of properties that store information about an object. There are, however, a set of Foundation classes that you use throughout this book for the sole purpose of storing and manipulating information.

NOTE

If you've used C or C-like languages before, you might find that these data type objects are similar to data types already defined outside of Apple's frameworks. By using the Foundation framework implementations, you gain access to a wide range of methods and features that go well beyond the C/C++ data types. You will also be able to work with the objects in Objective-C using the same development patterns as any other object.

Strings (`NSString`/`NSMutableString`)

Strings are collections of characters (numbers, letters, and symbols). Throughout this book, you'll often use strings to collect user input and to create and format user output.

As with many of the data type objects you'll be using, there are two string classes: `NSString` and `NSMutableString`. The difference, as the name describes, is that one of the classes can be used to create strings that can be changed (mutable). An `NSString` instance remains static once it is initialized, whereas an `NSMutableString` can be changed (lengthened, shortened, replaced, and so on).

Strings are used so frequently in Cocoa Touch applications that you can create and initialize an `NSString` using the notation `@"<my string value>"`. For example, if you needed to set the `text` property of an object called `myLabel` to a new string that reads `"Hello World!"`, you could use the following:

```
myLabel.text=@"Hello World!";
```

Strings can also be initialized with the values of other variables, such as integers, floating-point numbers, and so on.

Arrays (`NSArray`/`NSMutableArray`)

A useful category of data type is a collection. Collections enable your applications to store multiple pieces of information in a single object. An `NSArray` is an example of a collection data type that can hold multiple objects, accessed by a numeric index. As with strings, there is a mutable `NSMutableArray` class that creates an array capable of being changed after it has been created.

You can create and access arrays in two ways. We start here with the traditional manner.

You might, for instance, create an array that contains all the user feedback strings you want to display in an application:

```
myMessages = [[NSArray alloc] initWithObjects: @"Good Job!",@"Bad job!",nil];
```

A `nil` value is always used to end the list of objects when initializing an array. To access the strings, you use an index value. This is the number that represents a position in the list, starting with 0. To return the `"Bad job!"` message, we use the `objectAtIndex` method along with the number 1 (the second item in the list):

```
[myMessages objectAtIndex: 1];
```

The second way to initialize and access arrays was added in Xcode 4.5.2 and greatly simplifies the process.

`NSArrays` can be now be initialized like this:

```
NSArray *myArray=@[<list of array objects>];
```

An array of `NSString` objects might be declared as such:

```
NSArray *colorArray=@[@"red",@"green",@"blue"];
```

You may now access arrays by appending [`<index>`] to the end of the array name. To access the color "green" from the `colorArray`, you could type `colorArray[1]`. Unlike the traditional initialization method, you *don't* need to add `nil` to the end of the array elements.

`NSMutableArrays` work in much the same way but can be initialized with this format:

```
NSMutableArray *myArray=[@[<list of array objects>] mutableCopy];
```

Dictionaries (`NSDictionary`/`NSMutableDictionary`)

Like arrays, dictionaries are another collection data type, but with an important difference. Whereas the objects in an array are accessed by a numeric index, dictionaries store information as object/key pairs. The key is an arbitrary string, whereas the object can be anything you want, such as a string. If the previous `myMessages` array were to be created as an `NSDictionary` instead, it might look like this:

```
myMessages = [[NSDictionary alloc] initwithObjectsAndKeys:@"Good Job!",
                            @"positive",@"Bad Job!",@"negative",nil];
```

Now, instead of accessing the strings by a numeric index, they can be accessed by the keys `"positive"` and `"negative"` with the `objectForKey` method, as follows:

```
[myMessages objectForKey:@"negative"]
```

Dictionaries are useful because they let you store and access data in abstract ways rather than in a strict numeric order. Once again, the mutable form of the dictionaries, `NSMutableDictionary`, can be modified after it has been created.

With Xcode 4.5.2, Apple has also introduced a new way to work with dictionaries that is very similar to arrays. You can easily initialize `NSDictionary` objects by using the following format:

```
NSDictionary *myDictionary = @{<key>:<value>,...};
```

For example, to declare a dictionary with cities and ZIP codes, I might use the following:

```
NSDictionary *zipCodes = @{@"Wakeman":@44889,@"Delaware":@43015};
```

To access the ZIP code for Delaware, I reference `zipCodes[@"Delaware"]`. Mutable dictionaries change the initialization syntax just slightly, like this:

```
NSMutableDictionary *myDictionary = [@{<key>:<value>,...} mutableCopy];
```

Numbers (`NSNumber`/`NSDecimalNumber`)

We can store strings and collections of objects, but what about numbers? Working with numbers is a bit different. In general, if you need to work with an integer, you use the C data type `int`, and for floating-point numbers, `float`. You won't need to worry about classes and methods and object-oriented programming at all.

So, what about the classes that refer to numbers? The purpose of the `NSNumber` class is to take a numeric C data type and store it as an `NSNumber` object. The following line creates a number object with the value `100`:

```
myNumberObject = [[NSNumber alloc] numberWithInt: 100];
```

You can then work with the number as an object—adding it to arrays, dictionaries, and so on. `NSDecimalNumber`, a subclass of `NSNumber`, can be used to perform decimal arithmetic on very large numbers, but will be needed only in special cases.

Guess what?! `NSNumbers` have also seen a recent revision in Xcode and also benefit from a new shorthand notation. To initialize an integer, for example, I can now just type the following:

```
NSNumber *birthYear=@1971;
```

Or, for a floating-point number, I use this:

```
NSNumber *piValue=@3.1415926F;
```

CAUTION
___

Mixed Results

Although I encourage you to learn and use the new Xcode shortcuts for `NSArray`, `NSDictionary`, and `NSNumber`, it's important to know the long form as well. People have been using the long form for decades now. Apple tutorials still use that format, and nearly all projects you find online will, too. New is good, but new takes awhile to become the standard.

Dates (`NSDate`)

If you've ever tried to work with a date manually (interpreting a date string in a program, or even just doing date arithmetic by hand), you know it can be a great cause of headaches. How many days were there in September? Was this a leap year? And so on. The `NSDate` class provides a convenient way to work with dates as an object.

For example, assume you have a user-provided date (`userDate`) and you want to use it for a calculation, but only if it is earlier than the current date, in which case, you want to use *that* date. Typically, this would be a bunch of nasty comparisons and assignments. With `NSDate`, you would create a date object with the current date in it (provided automatically by the `date` method):

```
myDate=[NSDate date];
```

And then grab the earlier of the two dates using the `earlierDate` method:

```
[myDate earlierDate: userDate]
```

Obviously, you can perform many other operations, but you can avoid much of the ugliness of data and time manipulation using `NSDate` objects.

URLs (`NSURL`)

URLs are certainly a different type of data from what we're accustomed to thinking about, but on an Internet-connected device like the iPhone and iPad, you'll find that the ability to manipulate URLs comes in handy. The `NSURL` class enables you to manage URLs with ease. For example, suppose you have the URL http://www.floraphotographs.com/index.html and want to get just the machine name out of the string. You could create an `NSURL` object:

```
MyURL=[[NSURL alloc] initWithString:
                    @"http://www.floraphotographs.com/index.html"];
```

Then use the `host` method to automatically parse the URL and grab the text `www.floraphoto-graphs.com`:

```
[MyURL host]
```

This will come in handy as you start to create Internet-enabled applications. Of course, many more data type objects are available, and as mentioned earlier, some objects store their own data, so you won't, for example, need to maintain a separate string object to correspond to the text in labels that you have onscreen.

Speaking of labels, let's round out our introduction to common classes with a quick look at some of the UI elements that you'll be adding to your applications.

Interface Classes

Part of what makes the iPhone and iPad such fun to use are the onscreen touch interfaces that you can create. As we explore Xcode's IB in the next hour, you'll get your first hands-on experience with some of these interface classes. Something to keep in mind as you read through this section is that many UI objects can take on very different visual appearance based on how they are configured—so there is quite a bit of flexibility in your presentation.

Labels (`UILabel`)

You'll be adding labels to your applications both to present static text onscreen (as a typical label) and as a controllable block of text that can be changed as needed by your program (see Figure 4.3).

FIGURE 4.3
Labels add text to your application views.

Buttons (`UIButton`)

Buttons are one of the simplest user input methods that you'll be using. Buttons can respond to a variety of touch events and give your users an easy way to make onscreen choices (see Figure 4.4).

A Button (UIButton)

FIGURE 4.4
Buttons provide a simple form of user input/interaction.

Switches (`UISwitch`)

A switch object can be used to collect "on" and "off" responses from a user. It is displayed as a simple toggle and is frequently used to activate or deactivate application features (see Figure 4.5).

FIGURE 4.5
A switch moves between on and off states.

Segmented Control (`UISegmentedControl`)

A segmented control creates an elongated touchable bar with multiple named selections (Category 1, Category 2, and so on). Touching a selection activates it and can trigger your application to perform an action, such as updating the screen to hide or show other controls (see Figure 4.6).

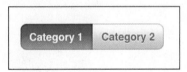

FIGURE 4.6
Segmented controls can be used to choose one item out of a set and react accordingly.

Sliders (`UISlider`)

A slider provides the user with a draggable bobble for the purpose of choosing a value from across a range. Sliders, for example, are used to control volume, screen brightness, and other inputs that should be presented in an "analog" fashion (see Figure 4.7).

FIGURE 4.7
Sliders offer a visual means of entering a value within a range.

Steppers (`UIStepper`)

Similar to a slider is a stepper (`UIStepper`). Like a slider, a stepper offers a means of inputting a number from a range of values visually (see Figure 4.8). Pushing a side of the control decrements or increments an internal property.

FIGURE 4.8
Use a stepper to increment or decrement values.

Text Fields (`UITextField/UITextView`)

Text fields are used to collect user input through the onscreen (or Bluetooth) keyboard. The `UITextField` is a single-line field, similar to what you'd see on a web page order form. The `UITextView` class, on the other hand, creates a larger multiline text entry block for more lengthy compositions (see Figure 4.9).

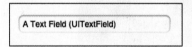

FIGURE 4.9
Collect user input through text fields.

Pickers (`UIDatePicker/UIPicker`)

A picker is an interesting interface element that resembles a slot machine display. By letting the user change each segment on the wheel, it can be used to enter a combination of several different values. Apple has implemented one complete picker for you: the `UIDatePicker` class. With this object, a user can quickly enter dates and times. You can also implement your own arbitrary pickers with the `UIPicker` class (see Figure 4.10).

Mon **Aug 8**	1	47	
Tue **Aug 9**	2	48	AM
Today	3	49	PM
Thu **Aug 11**	4	50	
Fri **Aug 12**	5	51	

FIGURE 4.10
Pickers enable users to choose a combination of several options.

Popovers (`UIPopoverController`)

Unique to the iPad, popovers are both a UI element and a means of displaying other UI elements. They allow you to display a view on top of any other view for the purpose of making a choice. The iPad's Safari browser, for example, uses a popover to present the user with a list of bookmarks to choose from, as shown in Figure 4.11.

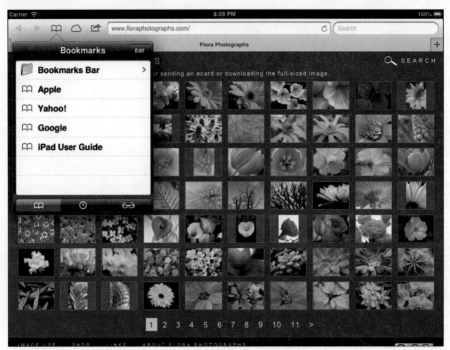

FIGURE 4.11
Popovers are unique to the iPad UI.

Popovers will become very handy as you start to create applications that use the full-screen real estate of the iPad.

These are only a sampling of the classes that you can use in your applications. We explore these and many others in the hours to come.

Exploring the iOS Frameworks with Xcode

So far in this hour, you've learned about dozens of frameworks and classes. Each framework could be made up of dozens of classes, and each class with hundreds of methods, and so on. In other words, there's a ridiculous amount of information available about the iOS frameworks.

One of the most efficient ways to learn more is to pick an object or framework you're interested in and then turn to the Xcode documentation system. Xcode provides an interface to the immense Apple development library in both a searchable browser-like interface (even with video tutorials!) and a context-sensitive Research Assistant. Let's take a look at both of these features now so that you can start using them immediately.

Xcode Documentation

To open the Xcode documentation application, choose Help, Documentation and API Reference from the menu bar. The help system will launch, as shown in Figure 4.12. Click the eye icon to explore all the available documentation. Lists of topics and individual documents are displayed on the left in the navigator, with the corresponding content shown on the right—just like an Xcode project window.

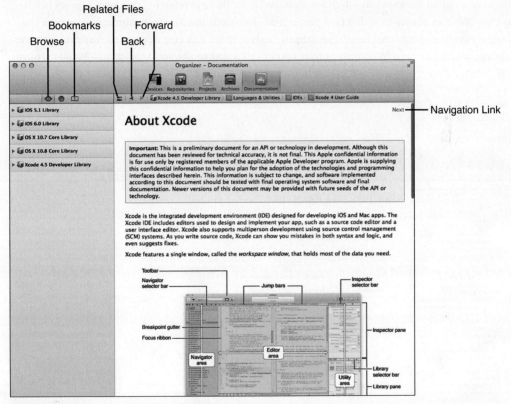

FIGURE 4.12
Browse through the extensive documentation.

When you've arrived at a document that you're interested in, you can read and navigate within the document using the blue links. You can also move forward and backward between documents using the arrow buttons located above the content—just like on a web page. It's so much like a web page, in fact, that you can add bookmarks for later reading. To create a bookmark, right-click either on an item in the navigator or on the content itself, and then choose Add Bookmark from the contextual menu. You can access all your documentation bookmarks by clicking the book icon at the top of the navigator.

NOTE

To quickly move between documents in a topic area, or even sections within an individual document, use the jump bar, which shows the path to the document you are actively viewing and is located directly above the content area.

Searching the Library

Browsing is great for exploring, but not that useful for finding references on exact topics (such as class method names or individual properties). To search the Xcode documentation, click the magnifying glass icon, and then type into the search field. You can enter class, method, or property names, or just type in a concept that you're interested in. As you type, Xcode begins returning results below the search field, as demonstrated in Figure 4.13.

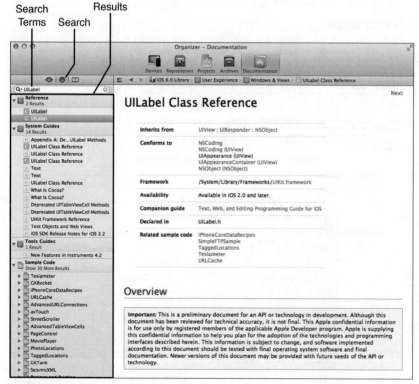

FIGURE 4.13
Search through the documentation to find tutorial articles and programming information.

Search results resources are divided into groups, including Reference (API documentation), System Guides/Tool Guides (explanatory/tutorial text), and Sample Code (example Xcode projects).

You can fine-tune your search criteria by clicking the magnifying glass located *within* the search field. This displays a pop-up menu with selections for limiting your search to specific document sets and reviewing recently completed searches.

Managing Xcode Document Sets

The Xcode documentation system is kept up-to-date by receiving feeds of document sets from Apple. Document sets are broad categories of documents that cover development for specific OS X versions, Xcode itself, and the iOS releases. To download and automatically receive updates to a documentation set, open the Xcode preferences (Xcode, Preferences), click the Downloads icon on the toolbar, and then click the Documentation button.

In the documentation window, click the Check For and Install Updates Automatically check box. As long as this is selected, Xcode periodically connects to Apple's servers and automatically updates your local documentation. You'll also notice that additional documentation sets may be listed. Click the Install button beside any of the listed items to download and automatically include it in any future updates.

You can force a manual update of the documentation using the Check and Install Now button.

Quick Help

One of the easiest and fastest ways to get help while coding is through the Xcode Quick Help assistant. To open the assistant, hold down Option and click a symbol in Xcode (for example, a class name or method name) or choose Help, Quick Help. A small window opens with basic information about the symbol, as well as links to other documentation resources.

Using Quick Help

Consider the following line that allocates and initializes a string with the contents of an integer variable:

```
myString=[[NSString alloc] initWithFormat:@"%d",myValue];
```

In this example, there is a class (`NSString`) and two methods (`alloc` and `initWithFormat`). To get information about the `initWithFormat:` method, hold down Option, and then click `initWithFormat:`. The Quick Help popover appears, as shown in Figure 4.14.

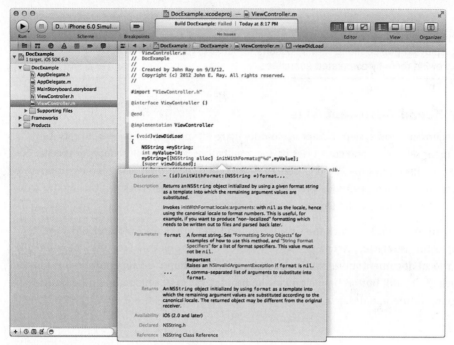

FIGURE 4.14
Quick Help brings reference information to your code editor.

To open the full Xcode documentation for the symbol, click the book icon in the upper-right corner. You can also click any of the hyperlinks in Quick Help results to jump to a specific piece of documentation or code.

NOTE

You can tell when you're hovering over an item that you can click for Quick Help because it will be displayed with a blue dashed underline in the Xcode editor and your mouse cursor will change to show a ?.

Activating the Quick Help Inspector

If you find Quick Help useful and wish you could access it even faster, you're in luck. The Quick Help Inspector can be used to display help information all the time. Xcode actually displays context-aware help for whatever you're typing, as you type it.

To display the Quick Help Inspector, activate the utility area of the Xcode window using the third (rightmost) View button. Next, click the show Quick Help Inspector icon (wavy lines in a dark square), located at the top of the utility area, as shown in Figure 4.15. Quick Help automatically displays a reference for whatever code your text-entry cursor is located in.

Show Utility Area

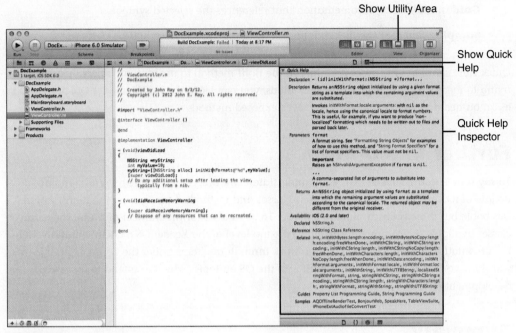

Show Quick Help

Quick Help Inspector

FIGURE 4.15
Open the Quick Help Inspector for always-on context-aware help.

Interpreting Quick Help Results

Quick Help displays context-sensitive information related to your code in up to eight different sections. What you see depends on the type of symbol (code) you have selected. A class property, for example, doesn't have a return type, but a class method does:

▶ **Description:** A few sentences describing the feature that the class, method, or other symbol provides.

▶ **Availability:** The versions of the operating system where the feature is available.

▶ **Declaration:** The structure of a method or definition of a data type.

▶ **Parameters:** The required or option information that can be provided to a method.

▶ **Returns:** What information will be returned by a method when it completes.

▶ **Declared:** The file that defines the selected symbol.

▶ **Reference:** The official reference documentation for the system.

▶ **Related:** Other methods within the same class as your selected method.

▶ **Guides:** Additional documentation that references the selected symbol.

▶ **Samples:** Sample code files that include examples of class/method/property use.

Quick Help simplifies the process of finding the right method to use with an object. Instead of trying to memorize dozens of instance methods, you can learn the basics and let Quick Help act as an on-demand reference of all an object's exposed methods.

Further Exploration

To say that Cocoa Touch is "big" is an understatement. Every year, Apple releases a major update of iOS and adds thousands of new classes and methods. I try to cover the highlights in this book, but there is much more to explore. To get a taste for the number of frameworks and classes available, I recommend starting at the top level of the Xcode iOS 6 documentation (Help, Documentation and API Reference), and work through the items under the Topics heading. This will show you what functionality is built into the OS on topics where to intend to focus your development efforts.

Summary

In this hour, you explored the layers that make up the iOS: Cocoa Touch, Media, Core Services, and Core OS. You learned the structure of a basic application: what objects it uses and how iOS manages the application life cycle. We also reviewed the common classes that you'll encounter as you begin to work with Cocoa, including data types and UI controls.

To give you the tools you need to find class and method references on your own, this hour introduced you to two features in Xcode. The first, the Xcode documentation window, offers a browser-like interface to the complete iOS documentation. The second, Quick Help, finds help for the class or method you are working with, automatically, as you type. Ultimately, it will be these tools that help you dive deeper into the Apple development environment.

Q&A

Q. **Why are the operating system services layered? Doesn't that add complexity?**

A. Using the upper-level frameworks reduces the complexity of your code. By providing multiple levels of abstraction, Apple has given developers the tools they need to easily use iOS features and the flexibility to highly customize their application's behavior by using lower-level services more closely tied to the OS.

Q. What do I do if I can't find an interface object I want?

A. Chances are, if you're writing a "normal" iOS application, Apple has provided a UI class to fill your need. If you find that you'd like to do things differently, you can always subclass an existing control and modify its behavior as you see fit—or create a completely new control.

Workshop

Quiz

1. How many layers are there in the simplified Apple iOS architecture?

2. How often will you be manually creating the `UIApplication` object in your applications?

3. What helpful feature can watch your typing and show relevant help articles?

Answers

1. Four. Cocoa Touch, Media, Core Services, and Core OS.

2. If you're building using Apple's application templates, the initial setup of the `UIApplication` object is automatic. You don't need to do a thing.

3. Quick Help offers interactive help as you code.

Activities

1. Using the Apple Xcode Documentation utility, explore the `NSString` class and instance methods. Identify the methods you'd use to compare strings, create a string from a number, and change a string to uppercase and lowercase.

2. Open Xcode and create a new, empty application. Expand the main code group and click the file named AppDelegate.m. When the contents of the file appear, open Quick Help by holding Option and clicking inside the class name `UIApplication`. Review the results. Try clicking other symbols in the Xcode class file and see what happens.

HOUR 5
Exploring Interface Builder

What You'll Learn in This Hour:

▶ Where Xcode's Interface Builder fits in the development process
▶ The role of storyboards and scenes
▶ How to build a user interface using the Object Library
▶ Common attributes that can be used to customize interface elements
▶ Ways to make your interface accessible to the visually impaired
▶ How to link interfaces to code with outlets and actions

Over the past few hours, you've become familiar with the core iOS technologies, Xcode projects, and the iOS Simulator. Although these are certainly important skills for becoming a successful developer, there's nothing quite like laying out your first iOS application interface and watching it come to life in your hands.

This hour introduces you to Interface Builder: the remarkable user interface (UI) editor integrated into Xcode. Interface Builder provides a visual approach to application interface design that is fun, intuitive, and deceptively powerful.

Understanding Interface Builder

Let's get it out of the way up front: Yes, Interface Builder (or IB for short) does help you create interfaces for your applications, but it isn't just a drawing tool for graphical user interfaces (GUIs); it helps you symbolically build application functionality without writing code. This translates to fewer bugs, less development time, and easier-to-maintain projects.

If you read through Apple's developer documentation, you'll see IB referred to as an *editor* within Xcode. This is a bit of an oversimplification of a tool that previously existed as a standalone application in the Apple Developer Suite. An understanding of IB and its use is as fundamentally important to iOS development as Objective-C. Without IB, creating the most basic interactive applications would be an exercise in frustration.

This hour focuses on navigating IB and will be key to your success in the rest of the book. In Hour 6, "Model-View-Controller Application Design," you combine what you've learned about Xcode projects, the code editor, IB, and the iOS Simulator for the first time. So, stay alert and keep reading.

The IB Approach

Using Xcode and the Cocoa toolset, you can program iOS interfaces by hand—instantiating interface objects, defining where they appear on the screen, setting any attributes for the object, and finally, making them visible. For example, in Hour 2, "Introduction to Xcode and the iOS Simulator," you entered this listing into Xcode to make your iDevice display the text Hello Xcode in the corner of the screen:

```
UILabel *myMessage;
myMessage=[[UILabel alloc]
            initWithFrame:CGRectMake(30.0,50.0,300.0,50.0)];
myMessage.font=[UIFont systemFontOfSize:48.0];
myMessage.text=@"Hello Xcode";
myMessage.textColor = [UIColor colorWithPatternImage:
                        [UIImage imageNamed:@"Background.png"]];
[self.window addSubview:myMessage];
```

Imagine how long it would take to build interfaces with text, buttons, images, and dozens of other controls, and think of all the code you would need to wade through just to make small changes.

Over the years, there have been many different approaches to graphical interface builders. One of the most common implementations is to enable the user to "draw" an interface but, behind the scenes, create all the code that generates that interface. Any tweaks require the code to be edited by hand (hardly an acceptable situation).

Another tactic is to maintain the interface definition symbolically but attach the code that implements functionality directly to interface elements. This, unfortunately, means that if you want to change your interface or swap functionality from one UI element to another, you have to move the code as well.

IB works differently. Instead of autogenerating interface code or tying source listings directly to interface elements, IB builds live objects that connect to your application code through simple links called *connections*. Want to change how a feature of your app is triggered? Just change the connection. As you'll learn a bit later this hour, changing how your application works with the objects you create in IB is, quite literally, a matter of connecting or reconnecting the dots as you see fit.

The Anatomy of an IB Storyboard

Your work in IB results in an XML file called a *Storyboard*, containing a hierarchy of objects for each unique screen that your application is going to display. The objects could be interface elements—buttons, toggle switches, and so forth—but might also be other noninterface objects that you will need to use. The collection of objects for a specific display is called a *scene*. Storyboards can hold as many scenes as you need, and even link them together visually via *segues*.

For example, a simple recipe application might have one scene that consists of a list of recipes the user can choose from. A second scene may contain the details for making a selected recipe. The recipe list could be set to segue to the detail view with a fancy fade-out/fade-in effect when the name of a recipe is touched. All of this functionality can be described visually in an application's storyboard file.

Storyboards aren't just about cool visuals, however. They also help you create usable objects without having to allocate or initialize them manually. When a scene in a storyboard file is loaded by your application, the objects described in it are instantiated and can be accessed by your code.

NOTE

Instantiation, just as a quick refresher, is the process of creating an instance of an object that you can work with in your program. An instantiated object gains all the functionality described by its class. Buttons, for example, automatically highlight when clicked, content views scroll, and so on.

The Storyboard Document Outline

What do storyboard files look like in IB? Open the Hour 5 Projects folder and double-click the file Empty.storyboard to open IB and display a barebones storyboard file. The contents of the file are shown visually in the IB editor area, and hierarchically by scene in the document outline area located in the column to the left of the editor area (see Figure 5.1).

TIP

If you do not see the document outline area in your Xcode workspace, choose Editor, Show Document Outline from the menu bar. You can also click the disclosure arrow in the lower-left corner of the Xcode editor area.

Interface Builder

Scene Objects

Document Outline

FIGURE 5.1
A storyboard scene's objects are represented by icons.

Note that there is only a single scene in the file: view controller scene. Single-scene storyboards will be the starting place for much of your interface work in this book because they provide plenty of room for collecting user input and displaying output. We explore multiscene storyboards beginning in Hour 11, "Implementing Multiple Scenes and Popovers."

Four icons are visible in the view controller scene: View Controller, View (within the View Controller), First Responder, and Exit. With the exception of View, these are special icons used to represent unique noninterface objects in our application; these will be present in all storyboard scenes that you work with:

▶ **View Controller:** The View Controller denotes the object that loads and interacts with a storyboard scene in your running application. This is the object that effectively instantiates all the other objects described within a scene. You'll learn more about the relationship between UIs and view controllers in Hour 6.

▶ **View:** The View icon is an instance of the object `UIView` and represents the visual layout that will be loaded by the view controller and displayed on the iOS device's screen. Views are hierarchical in nature. Therefore, as you add controls to your interface, they are contained within the view. You can even add views within views to cluster controls or create visual elements that can be shown or hidden as a group.

▶ **First Responder:** The first responder stands for the object that the user is currently interacting with. When a user works with an iOS application, multiple objects could potentially respond to the various gestures or keystrokes that the user creates. The first responder is the object currently in control and interacting with the user. A text field that the user is typing into, for example, would be the first responder until the user moves to another field or control.

▶ **Exit:** The Exit serves a very specific purpose that will come into play only in multiscene applications. When you are create an app that moves the user between a series of screens, the Exit icon provides a visual means of jumping back to a previous screen. If you have built five scenes that link from one to another and you want to quickly return to the first scene from the fifth, you'll link from the fifth scene to the first scene's Exit icon. We test this out in Hour 11.

NOTE

The storyboard shown in this example is about as "vanilla" as you can get. In larger applications with multiple scenes, you may want to either name your view controller class to better describe *what* it is actually controlling or set a descriptive label, such as Recipe Listing.

Using unique view controller names/labels also benefits the naming of scenes. IB automatically sets scene names to the name of the view controller or its label (if one is set) plus the suffix *scene*. If you label your view controller as Recipe Listing, for example, the scene name changes to Recipe Listing Scene. We'll worry about multiple scenes later in the book; for now, our projects will contain a generic class called View Controller that will be in charge of interacting with our single view controller scene.

As you build your UIs, the list of objects within your scenes will grow accordingly. Some UIs may consist of dozens of different objects, leading to rather busy and complex scenes, as demonstrated in Figure 5.2.

FIGURE 5.2
Storyboard scenes and their associated views can grow quite large and complex.

You can collapse or expand your hierarchy of views within the document outline area to help manage the information overload that you are bound to experience as your applications become more advanced.

NOTE

At its most basic level, a view (UIView) is a rectangular region that can contain content and respond to user events (touches and so forth). All the controls (buttons, fields, and so on) that you'll add to a view are, in fact, subclasses of UIView. This isn't necessarily something you need to be worried about, except that you'll be encountering documentation that refers to buttons and other interface elements referred to as *subviews* and the views that contain them as *superviews*.

Just keep in mind that pretty much everything you see onscreen can be considered a view and the terminology will seem a little less alien.

Working with the Document Outline Objects

The document outline area shows icons for objects in your application, but what good are they? Aside from presenting a nice list, do they provide any functionality?

Absolutely! Each icon gives you a visual means of referring to the objects they represent. You interact with the icons by dragging to and from them to create the connections that drive your application's features.

Consider an onscreen control, such as a button, that needs to be able to trigger an action in your code. By dragging from the button to the View Controller icon, you can create a connection from the GUI element to a method that you want it to activate. You can even drag from certain objects directly to your code, quickly inserting a variable or method that will interact with that object.

Xcode provides developers with a great deal of flexibility when working with objects in IB. You can interact with the actual UI elements in the IB editor, or with the icons that represent them in the document outline area. In addition, any object that isn't directly visible in the UI (such as the first responder and view controller objects) can be found in an icon bar directly below the UI design in the editor, as shown in Figure 5.3.

FIGURE 5.3
You will interact with objects either in the editor or in the document outline area.

NOTE

If the icon bar below your view does not show any icons and is displaying the text *View Controller* instead, just click it. The icon bar defaults to the name of a scene's view controller until it is selected.

We go through a hands-on example later this hour so that you can get a feel for how interacting with and connecting objects works. Before we do that, however, let's look at how you go about turning a blank view into an interface masterpiece.

Creating User Interfaces

In Figures 5.1 and 5.2, you've seen an empty view and a fully fleshed-out interface. Now, how do we get from one to the other? In this section, we explore how interfaces are created with IB. In other words, it's time for the fun stuff.

If you haven't already, open the Empty.storyboard file included in this hour's Projects folder. Make sure the document outline area is visible and that the view can be seen in the editor; you're ready to start designing an interface.

What's the "Default" iPhone?

When you're editing iPhone interfaces and creating new projects in Xcode, you'll be working, by default, with iPhone 5-sized screens. We cover how to create interfaces that properly resize for earlier iPhone models in Hour 16, "Building Responsive User Interfaces." For now, if you want to create an application sized specifically for the iPhone 4s or earlier, just don't use the bottom 88 points in the layout. Again, we cover how to accommodate any size you want later in the book. Our focus now is on getting started building apps rather than fine-grained interface layout.

The Object Library

Everything that you add to a view, from buttons and images to web content, comes from the Object Library. You can view the library by choosing View, Utilities, Show Object Library from the menu bar (Control-Option-Command-3). If it isn't already visible, the utility area of the Xcode interface opens, and Object Library is displayed in the lower right. Make sure that the Objects item is selected in the pop-up menu at the top of the library so that all available options are visible.

CAUTION

Libraries, Libraries, Everywhere!

Xcode has more than one library. The Object Library contains the UI elements you'll be adding in IB, but there are also File Template, Code Snippet, and Media libraries that can be activated by clicking the icons immediately above the Library area.

If you find yourself staring at a library that doesn't seem to show what you're expecting, click the cube icon above the library or reselect the Object Library from the menu to make sure you're in the right place.

When you click and hover over an element in the library, a popover is displayed with a description of how the object can be used in the interface, as shown in Figure 5.4. This provides a convenient way of exploring your UI options without having to open the Xcode documentation.

FIGURE 5.4
The library contains a palette of objects that can be added to your views.

Using view buttons at the top of the library, you can switch between list and icon views of the available objects. You can also focus in on specific UI elements using the pop-up menu above the library listing. If you know the name of an object but can't locate it in the list, use the filter field at the bottom of the library to quickly find it.

Adding Objects to a View

To add an object to a view, just click and drag from the library to the view. For example, find the label object (UILabel) in the Object Library and drag it into the center of the view in the editor. The label should appear in your view and read Label. Double-click the label and type **Hello**. The text will update, as shown in Figure 5.5, just as you would expect.

FIGURE 5.5
If an object contains text, in many cases, just double-click to edit it.

With that simple action, you've almost entirely replicated the functionality implemented by the code fragment earlier in the lesson. Try dragging other objects from the Object Library into the view (buttons, text fields, and so on). With few exceptions, the objects should appear and behave just the way you'd expect.

To remove an object from the view, click to select it, and then press the Delete key. You may also use the options under the Edit menu to copy and paste between views or duplicate an element several times within a view.

Notice the tools along the bottom of the editing area? These help control the view of your editing area.

The button in the lower left hides and shows the document outline, giving you more space to work. The first button in the row in the lower right switches between 3.5-inch and 4-inch iPhone screen layouts.

The middle set of buttons in the lower right affect alignment (more on that next).

Finally, the +/− magnifying glasses in the lower right zooms in and out on your interface for fine-tuning a scene. This proves useful when creating storyboards with multiple scenes. Unfortunately, you cannot edit a scene when zoomed out, so Apple provides the = button to quickly jump back and forth between a 100% view and your last chosen zoom setting.

Working with the IB Editing Tools

Instead of relying on your visual acuity to position objects in a view, Apple has included some useful tools for fine-tuning your interface design. If you've ever used a drawing program like OmniGraffle or Adobe Illustrator, you'll find many of these familiar.

Guides

As you drag objects in a view, you'll notice guides (shown in Figure 5.6) appearing to help with the positioning. These blue, dotted lines are displayed to align objects along the margins of the view, to the centers of other objects in the view, and to the baseline of the fonts used in the labels and object titles.

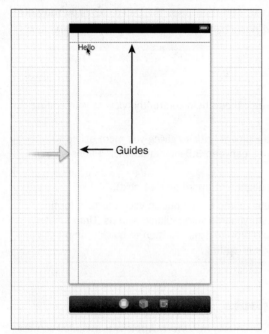

FIGURE 5.6
Guides help position your objects within a view.

As an added bonus, guides automatically appear to indicate the approximate spacing requirements of Apple's interface guidelines. If you're not sure why it's showing you a particular margin guide, it's likely that your object is in a position that IB considers "appropriate" for something of that type and size.

TIP

You can manually add your own guides by choosing Editor, Add Horizontal Guide or by choosing Editor, Add Vertical Guide.

Selection Handles

In addition to the guides, most objects include selection handles to stretch an object horizontally, vertically, or both. Using the small boxes that appear alongside an object when it is selected, just click and drag to change its size, as demonstrated using a button in Figure 5.7.

Selection Handles

FIGURE 5.7
Use the selection handles around the perimeter of an object to change its size.

Note that some objects constrain how you can resize them; this preserves a level of consistency within iOS application interfaces.

Alignment

To quickly align several objects within a view, select them by clicking and dragging a selection rectangle around them or by holding down the Shift key, and then choose Editor, Align and an appropriate alignment type from the menu. You can also access the Aligment settings from the buttons to the left of the Zoom buttons at the bottom of the IB editor.

For example, try dragging several buttons into your view, placing them in a variety of different positions. To align them based on their horizontal center (a line that runs vertically through each button's center), select the buttons, and then choose Editor, Align, Horizontal Centers. Figure 5.8 shows the before and after results.

TIP

To fine-tune an object's position within a view, select it, and then use the arrow keys to position it left, right, up, or down, 1 pixel at a time.

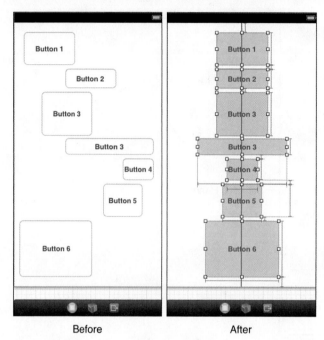

Before   After

FIGURE 5.8
Use the Align menu to quickly align a group of items to an edge or center.

The Size Inspector

Another tool that you may want to use for controlling your design is the Size Inspector. IB has a number of inspectors for examining the attributes of an object. As the name implies, the Size Inspector provides information about sizes, but also position and alignment. To open the Size Inspector, first select the object (or objects) that you want to work with, and then click the ruler icon at the top of the utility area in Xcode. Alternatively, choose View, Utilities, Show Size Inspector or press Option-Command-5 (see Figure 5.9).

Using the fields at the top of the inspector, you can view or change the size and position of the object by changing the coordinates in the Height/Width and X/Y fields. You can also view the coordinates of a specific portion of an object by clicking one of the black dots in the size and grid to indicate where the reading should come from.

NOTE
_____
Within the Size and Position settings, notice a drop-down menu where you can choose between Frame Rectangle and Layout Rectangle. These two settings will usually be similar, but there is a slight difference. The frame values represent the exact area an object occupies onscreen, whereas the layout values take into account spacing around the object.
_____

The Content Hugging/Compression and Constraint settings of the Size Inspector determine how controls resize/reposition themselves when running on devices with different screen sizes, or when the device changes orientation. You'll learn a bit more about these features next, and then you put them to use in Hour 16.

FIGURE 5.9
The Size Inspector enables you to adjust the size and position of one or more objects.

TIP
_____
Hold down the option after selecting an object in IB. As you move your mouse around, you'll see the distance between the selected object and other objects that you point to.
_____

The Auto Layout System

While the guides, Size Inspector, and other tools are helpful for laying out interfaces—even interfaces that can adapt to view changes—iOS applications can take advantage of a new powerful tool for managing layouts: the Auto Layout system. Auto Layouts are enabled by default on new projects and make it possible to write applications that adapt to a number of different screen sizes and orientations without needing to modify a single line of code. Want to write software to take advantage of both the iPhone 5 and iPhone 4(s) screens? You'll want Auto Layouts!

Understanding Constraints

Auto Layout works by building a series of *constraints* for your onscreen objects. The constraints define distances between objects and how flexible these relationships are.

For example, make sure the Empty.storyboard file is still open and that you've added a text label to the view. Notice that at the same level as the label in the document outline hierarchy a Constraints object is showing up, as demonstrated in Figure 5.10.

FIGURE 5.10
The Constraints object represents the positioning relationships within a view.

Within the Constraints object are (likely) two constraints: horizontal space and vertical space constraint. The horizontal constraint states that the left or right side of the label will be a certain number of points from the left or right edge of the view. The vertical constraint is the distance from the top or bottom of the view to the top or bottom of the label. What constraints (left/right, top/bottom) are added depend on where the object is in relation to its containing view. Constraints are also visible in the Size Inspector, which you can see in Figure 5.10.

TIP

If you're looking at your constraints and not seeing a horizontal and vertical constraint, chances are you've centered your label, in which case you'll have a center alignment constraint. Constraints can "attach" your objects to the interface in many different ways; horizontal/vertical spacing and centering are just a few.

Constraints, however, are more than just entries that tie an object to the view it is within. They can be flexible, ensuring that an object maintains *at least* or *at most* a certain distance from another object, or even that two objects, when resized, maintain the same distance between one another.

Constraints that set a specific size or distance between objects are called *pinning*. The flexibility (or inflexibility of a constraint) is managed by configuring a *relationship*.

TIP

Alignment of objects is also listed as a constraint but is managed using the alignment tools you've already seen.

Content Hugging and Content Compression Resistance

As mentioned earlier, the Content Hugging and Compression Resistance settings in the Size Inspector are related to Auto Layout. So, where do these tie in?

When inspecting an object, these settings control how closely the sides of an object "hug" the content in the object and how much the content can be compressed or clipped. A button, for example, can expand horizontally (so horizontal hugging is a low priority) but shouldn't grow vertically (making vertical hugging a very high priority). Similarly, the content (the button label) should not be compressed or clipped at all, so the content compression resistance settings for both horizontal and vertical compression should be very high priority.

I Miss the Old Autosizing Features! Boo Hoo!

If you prefer to forego the new Auto Layout tools in Xcode, you can revert your storyboard to the "old" layout approach by first selecting the File Inspector (Option-Command-1) while viewing your storyboard. Next, *uncheck* the Use Autolayout check box within the Interface Builder Document section of settings. Everything will operate exactly as it did prior to Xcode 4.5.

Hour 16 focuses on the new Auto Layout tools, however, so I suggest leaving Auto Layout active to get used to seeing constraints added to your designs.

Customizing the Interface Appearance

How your interface appears to the end user isn't just a combination of control sizes, positions, and constraints. For many kinds of objects, literally dozens of different attributes can be adjusted. Although you could certainly configure things such as colors and fonts in your code, it's easier to just use the tools included in IB.

Using the Attributes Inspector

The most common place you'll tweak the way your interface objects appear is through the Attributes Inspector, available by clicking the slider icon at the top of the utility area. You can also choose View, Utilities, Show Attributes Inspector (Option-Command-4) if the utility area isn't currently visible. Let's run through a quick example to see how this works.

Again turn to the Empty.storyboard file still open and the label you've added. Select the label, and then open the Attributes Inspector, shown in Figure 5.11.

FIGURE 5.11
To change how an object looks and behaves, select it, and then open the Attributes Inspector.

The top portion of the Attributes Inspector contains attributes for the specific object. In the case of the text object, this includes settings such as font, size, color, and alignment (everything you'd expect to find for editing text).

In the bottom portion of the inspector are additional inherited attributes. Remember that onscreen elements are a subclass of a view. Therefore, all the standard view attributes are also available for the object and for your tinkering enjoyment. In many cases, you'll want to leave these alone, but settings such as background and transparency can come in handy.

TIP

Don't get hung up on trying to memorize every attribute for every control now. I cover interesting and important attributes when they are needed throughout the book.

Feel free to explore the many different options available in the Attributes Inspector to see what can be configured for different types of objects. There is a surprising amount of flexibility to be found within the tool.

NOTE

The attributes you change in IB are simply properties of the object's class. To help identify what an attribute does, use the documentation tool in Xcode to look up the object's class and review the descriptions of its properties.

Setting Accessibility Attributes

For many years, the "appearance" of an interface meant just how it looks visually. Today, the technology is available for an interface to vocally describe itself to the visually impaired. iOS includes Apple's screen-reader technology: Voiceover. Voiceover combines speech synthesis with a customized interface to aid users in navigating applications.

Using Voiceover, users can touch interface elements and hear a short description of what they do and how they can be used. Although you gain much of this functionality "for free" (the iOS Voiceover software will read button labels, for example), you can provide additional assistance by configuring the accessibility attributes in IB.

To access the Accessibility settings, you need to open the Identity Inspector by clicking the window icon at the top of the utility area. You can also choose View, Utilities, Show Identity Inspector or press Option-Command-3. The Accessibility options have their own section within the Identity Inspector, as shown in Figure 5.12.

FIGURE 5.12
Use the Accessibility section in the Identity Inspector to configure how Voiceover interacts with your application.

You can configure four sets of attributes within this area:

▶ **Accessibility:** If enabled, the object is considered accessible. If you create any custom controls that must be seen to be used, this setting should be disabled.

▶ **Label:** A simple word or two that serves as the label for an item. A text field that collects the user's name might use "your name," for example.

▶ **Hint:** A short description, if needed, on how to use the control. This is needed only if the label doesn't provide enough information on its own.

▶ **Traits:** This set of check boxes is used to describe the features of the object—what it does and what its current state is.

TIP

For an application to be available to the largest possible audience, take advantage of accessibility tools whenever possible. Even objects such as the text labels you've used in this lesson should have their traits configured to indicate that they are static text. This helps potential users know that they can't interact with them.

Simulating the Interface

If you've worked with earlier versions of Xcode, you know that you could easily simulate your UI. Unfortunately, when Apple introduced storyboards, they removed this capability. *However*, Xcode will now write much of your interface code for you. This means that when you create an interface and connect it to your application classes, you can run the app in the iOS Simulator even though it isn't done. We follow a development pattern throughout the book that takes advantage of this. Except in a few very unusual instances, you can run your apps at any time to test the interface and any functionality you've added.

Enabling the iOS Accessibility Inspector

If you are building accessible interfaces, you may want to enable the Accessibility Inspector in the iOS Simulator. To do this, start the Simulator and click the Home button to return to the home screen. Start the Settings application and navigate to General, Accessibility, and then use the toggle button to turn the Accessibility Inspector on, as shown in Figure 5.13.

The Accessibility Inspector adds an overlay to the simulator workspace that displays the label, hints, and traits that you've configured for your interface elements. Note that navigating the iOS interface is *very* different when operating in accessibility mode.

Using the X button in the upper-left corner of the inspector, you can toggle it on and off. When off, the inspector collapses to a small bar, and the iPhone Simulator will behave normally. Clicking the X button again turns it back on. To disable the Accessibility Inspector altogether, just revisit the Accessibility setting in the Settings application.

FIGURE 5.13
Toggle the iOS Accessibility Inspector on.

Connecting to Code

You know how to make an interface, but how do you make it *do* something? Throughout this hour, I've been alluding to the idea that connecting an interface to the code you write is just a matter of "connecting the dots." In this last part of the hour, we do just that: take an interface and connect it to the code that makes it into a functional application.

Opening the Project

To get started, we use the project Disconnected contained within this hour's Projects folder. Open the folder and double-click the Disconnected.xcodeproj file. This opens the project in Xcode, as shown in Figure 5.14.

FIGURE 5.14
To begin, open the project in Xcode.

After the project is loaded, expand the project code group (Disconnected) and click the MainStoryboard.storyboard file. This storyboard file contains the scene and view that this application displays as its interface. Xcode refreshes and displays the scene in IB, as shown in Figure 5.15.

Project Code Group

Storyboard File

FIGURE 5.15
IB displays the scene and corresponding view for the application.

Implementation Overview

The interface contains four interactive elements: a button bar (called a *segmented control*), a push button, an output label, and a web view (an integrated web browser component). Together, these controls interface with application code to enable a user to pick a flower color, touch the Get Flower button, and then display the chosen color in a text label along with a matching flower photo fetched from the website http://www.floraphotographs.com. Figure 5.16 shows the final result.

FIGURE 5.16
The finished application enables a user to choose a color and have a flower image returned that matches that color.

Unfortunately, right now the application does nothing. The interface isn't connected to any application code, so it is hardly more than a pretty picture. To make it work, we create connections to outlets and actions that have been defined in the application's code.

Outlets and Actions

An *outlet* is nothing more than a variable by which an object can be referenced. For example, if you had created a field in IB intending that it would be used to collect a user's name, you might want to create an outlet for it in your code called `userName`. Using this outlet and a corresponding property, you could then access or change the contents of the field.

An *action*, however, is a method within your code that is called when an event takes place. Certain objects, such as buttons and switches, can trigger actions when a user interacts with them through an event, such as touching the screen. If you define actions in your code, IB can make them available to the onscreen objects.

Joining an element in IB to an outlet or action creates what is generically termed a connection.

For the Disconnected app to function, we need to create connections to these outlets and actions:

- ▶ colorChoice: An outlet created for the button bar to access the color the user has selected.

- ▶ getFlower: An action that retrieves a flower from the Web, displays it, and updates the label with the chosen color.

- ▶ chosenColor: An outlet for the label that will be updated by getFlower to show the name of the chosen color.

- ▶ flowerView: An outlet for the web view that will be updated by getFlower to show the image.

Let's make the connections now.

Creating Connections to Outlets

To create a connection from an interface item to an outlet, Control-drag from a scene's View Controller icon (in the document outline area or the icon bar below the view) to either the visual representation of the object in the view or its icon in the document outline area.

Try this with the button bar (segmented control). Pressing Control, click and drag from the View Controller in the document outline area to the onscreen image of the bar. A line appears as you drag, enabling you to easily point to the object that you want to use for the connect, as shown in Figure 5.17.

When you release the mouse button, the available connections are shown in a pop-up menu (see Figure 5.18). In this case, you want to pick colorChoice.

NOTE

IB knows what type of object is allowed to connect to a given outlet, so it displays only the outlets appropriate for the connection you're trying to make.

Repeat this process for the label with the text "Your Color", connecting it to the chosenColor outlet, and the web view, connecting to flowerView.

FIGURE 5.17
Control-drag from the View Controller to the button bar.

FIGURE 5.18
Choose from the outlets available for the targeted object.

Connecting to Actions

Connecting to actions is a bit different. An object's events trigger actions (methods) in your code. So, the connection direction reverses; you connect from the object invoking an event to the view controller of its scene. Although it is possible to Control-drag and create a connection in the same manner you did with outlets, this isn't recommended because you don't get to specify which event triggers it. Do users have to touch the button? Release their fingers from a button?

Actions can be triggered by *many* different events, so you need to make sure that you're picking exactly the right one, instead of leaving it up to IB. To do this, select the object that will be connecting to the action and open the Connections Inspector by clicking the arrow icon at the top of the Xcode utility area. You can also show the inspector by choosing View, Utilities, Show Connections Inspector (or by pressing Option-Command-6).

The Connections Inspector, in Figure 5.19, shows a list of the events that the object, in this case a button, supports. Beside each event is an open circle. To connect an event to an action in your code, click and drag from one of these circles to the scene's View Controller icon in the document outline area.

FIGURE 5.19
Use the Connections Inspector to view existing connections and to make new ones.

NOTE

I often refer to creating connections to a scene's view controller or placing interface elements in a scene's view. This is because IB storyboards can contain multiple different scenes, each with its own view controller and view. In the first few lessons, there is only a single scene, and therefore, a single view controller. That said, you should still be getting used to the idea of multiple View Controller icons appearing in the document outline area and having to correctly choose the one that corresponds to the scene you are editing.

For example, to connect the Get Flower button to the getFlower method, select the button, and then open the Connections Inspector (Option-Command-6). Drag from the circle beside the Touch Up Inside event to the scene's view controller and release, as demonstrated in Figure 5.19. When prompted, choose the getFlower action, shown in Figure 5.20.

FIGURE 5.20
Choose the action you want the interface element to invoke.

After a connection has been made, the inspector updates to show the event and the action that it calls, demonstrated in Figure 5.21. If you click other already connected objects, you'll notice that the Connections Inspector shows their connections to outlets and to actions.

FIGURE 5.21
The Connections Inspector updates to show the actions and outlets that an object references.

Well done! You've just linked an interface to the code that supports it. Click Run on the Xcode toolbar to build and run your application in the iOS Simulator or on your personal iDevice.

Connections Without Code

Although most of your connections in IB will be between objects and outlets and actions you've defined in your code, certain objects implement built-in actions that don't require you to write a single line of code.

The web view, for example, implements actions, including goForward and goBack. Using these actions, you could add basic navigation functionality to a web view by dragging from a button's Touch Up Inside event directly to the web view object (rather than the view controller). As described previously, you are prompted for the action to connect to, but this time, it isn't an action you had to code yourself.

Editing Connections with the Quick Inspector

One of the errors that I commonly make when connecting my interfaces is creating a connection that I didn't intend. A bit of overzealous dragging, and suddenly your interface is wired up incorrectly and won't work. To review the connections that are in place, you select an object and use the Connections Inspector discussed previously, or you can open the Quick Inspector by right-clicking any object in the IB editor or document outline area. This opens a floating window that contains all the outlets and actions either referenced or received by the object, as shown in Figure 5.22.

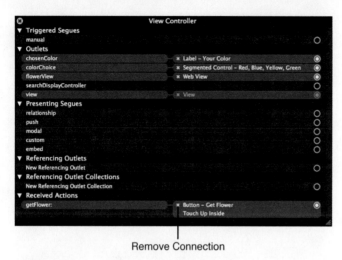

Remove Connection

FIGURE 5.22
Right-click to quickly inspect any object connections.

Besides viewing the connections that are in place, you can remove a connection by clicking the X next to a connected object (see Figure 5.21). You can even create new connections using the same "click-and-drag from the circle to an object" approach that you performed with the Connections Inspector. Click the X in the upper-left corner of the window to close the Quick Inspector.

NOTE

Although clicking an object, such as a button, shows you all the connections related to that object, it doesn't show you *everything* you've connected in the IB editor. Because almost all the connections you create will go to and from a scene's view controller, choosing it and then opening the inspector will give you a more complete picture of what connections you've made.

Writing Code with IB

You just created connections from UI objects to the corresponding outlets and actions that have already been defined in code. In the next hour's lesson, you write a full application, including defining outlets and actions and connecting them to a storyboard scene. What's interesting about this process, besides it bringing all of the earlier lessons together, is that IB editor writes and inserts the necessary Objective-C code to define outlets and actions.

Although it is impossible for Xcode to write your application for you, it does create the instance variables and properties for your app's interface objects, as well as "stubs" of the methods your interface will trigger. All you need to do is drag and drop the IB objects into your source code files. Using this feature is completely optional, but it does help save time and avoid syntax errors.

TIP
_____

A method prototype (or *stub/skeleton*) is nothing more than a method that has been declared but executes no instructions. You can add prototypes to your code where you know what you'll be writing in the future but aren't yet ready to commit it to code. This is useful in the initial design stages of an application because it helps you keep track of the work you have left to do.

Prototype methods are also helpful if you have code that needs to use a method that you haven't written. By inserting and referencing prototypes for your unwritten methods, your application will compile and run—enabling the code that *is* complete to be tested at any stage of the development process.

_____

Object Identity

As we finish up our introduction to IB, I'd be remiss if I didn't introduce one more feature: the Identity Inspector. You've already accessed this tool to view the accessibility attributes for interface objects, but there is another reason why we need to use the inspector in the future: setting class identities and labels.

As you drag objects into the interface, you're creating instances of classes that already exist (buttons, labels, and so on). Throughout this book, however, we build custom subclasses that we also need to be able to reference with IB's objects. In these cases, we need to help IB by identifying the subclass it should use.

For example, suppose we created a subclass of the standard button class (UIButton) that we named ourFancyButtonClass. We might drag a button into a scene to represent our fancy button, but when the storyboard file loads, it would just create the same old UIButton.

To fix the problem, we select the button we've added to the view, open the Identity Inspector by clicking the window icon at the top of the Xcode utility area or by choosing View, Utilities, Show Identity Inspector (Option-Command-3), and then use the drop-down menu/field to enter the class that we really want instantiated at runtime (see Figure 5.23).

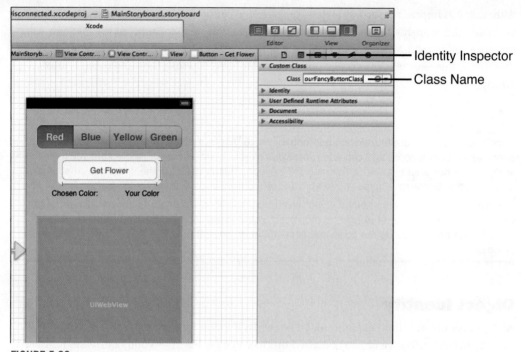

FIGURE 5.23
If you're using a custom class, you need to manually set the identity of your objects in the Identity Inspector.

This is something we cover on an as-needed basis; so if it seems confusing, don't worry. We come back to it later in the book.

Further Exploration

The IB editor gives you the opportunity to experiment with many of the different GUI objects you've seen in iOS applications and read about in the previous hours. In the next hour, the Xcode code editor is used in conjunction with IB for your first full project, developed from start to finish.

To learn even more about what you can do with IB, I suggest reading through the following four Apple publications:

Interface Builder Help: Accessed by right-clicking the background in the IB editor, the IB help is more than a simple help document. Apple's IB Help walks you through the intricacies of IB using video tutorials and covers some advanced topics that will be important as your development experience increases.

Auto Layout: Understanding Constraints: At the time of this writing, this document hasn't yet been updated for iOS, but it does present a good introduction to the Auto Layout system and is an excellent read for anyone wanting to get a jump start on adaptive interface layout techniques.

iOS Human Interface Guidelines: The Apple iOS HIG document provides a clear set of rules for building usable interfaces on the iOS device family. This document describes when you should use controls and how they should be displayed, helping you create more polished, professional-quality applications.

Accessibility Programming Guide for iOS: If you're serious about creating accessible apps, this is a mandatory read. The Accessibility Programming Guide describes the accessibility features in this hour's lesson as well as ways to improve accessibility programmatically and methods of testing accessibility beyond the tips given in this hour.

As a general note, from here on, you do quite a bit of coding in each lesson. So, now is a great time to review the previous hours if you have any questions.

Summary

In this hour, you explored the Xcode IB editor and the tools it provides for building rich graphical interfaces for your iOS applications. You learned how to navigate IB storyboards and access the GUI elements from the Object Library. Using the various inspector tools within IB, you reviewed how GUI elements can be placed within a scene using constraints, how the look and feel of onscreen controls can be customized, and how interfaces can be made accessible to the visually impaired.

More than just a pretty picture, an IB-created interface uses simple outlets and actions to connect to functionality in your code. You used IB's connection tools to turn a nonfunctioning interface into a complete application. By maintaining a separation between the code you write and what is displayed to the user, you can revise your interface to look however you want, without breaking your application. In Hour 6, you examine how to create outlets and actions from scratch in Xcode (and thus gain a full toolset to get started developing).

Q&A

Q. Why do I keep seeing things referred to as NIB/XIB files?

A. The origins of IB trace back to the NeXT Computer, which made use of NIB files to store individual views. These files, in fact, still bore the same name when Mac OS X was released. In recent years, however, Apple renamed the files to have the .xib extension, which has subsequently been replaced by storyboards and scenes. Unfortunately, Apple's documentation hasn't quite caught up yet and may reference XIB or NIB files. If you encounter these documentation barnacles, just substitute "storyboard scene" for XIB or NIB in your head.

Q. Some of the objects in the IB Object Library can't be added to my view. What gives?

A. Not all the items in the Object Library are interface objects. Some represent objects that provide functionality to your application. These can be added to the scene in the document outline area or on the icon bar located below a scene's layout in the IB editor.

Q. I've seen controls in applications that aren't available here. Where are they?

A. Keep in mind that the iOS objects are heavily customizable and frequently used as a starting point for developers to make their own UI classes or subclasses. The end result can vary tremendously from the stock UI appearance.

Workshop

Quiz

1. Simulating a scene using IB's Simulate Document feature also compiles the project's code in Xcode. True or false?

2. What tool can you use within the iOS Simulator to help review accessibility of objects in your apps?

3. What two connection types can be made in the Xcode IB?

4. Pinning defines a flexible constraint. True or false?

Answers

1. False. Simulating a scene does not use the project code at all. As a result, the interface will not perform any actions that rely on underlying code.

2. The Accessibility Inspector makes it possible to view the accessibility attributes configured within IB.

3. Connections to outlets and actions can be created in IB. A connection to an outlet provides a means of referencing and working with a UI element in code. A connection to an action defines a UI event, such as a button press, that will execute the action's method.

4. False. Pinning constraints lock an interface element to a specific size or position.

Activities

1. Practice using the interface layout tools on the Empty.storyboard file. Add each available interface object to your view, and then review the Attributes Inspector for that object. If an attribute doesn't make sense, remember that you can review documentation for the class to identify the role of each of its properties.

2. Revise the Disconnected project with an accessible interface. Review the finished design using the Accessibility Inspector in the iOS Simulator.

HOUR 6

Model-View-Controller Application Design

What You'll Learn in This Hour:

▶ What the Model-View-Controller design pattern means
▶ Ways in which Xcode implements MVC
▶ Design of a basic view
▶ Implementation of a corresponding view controller

You've come a long way in the past few hours: You've provisioned your iDevice for development, learned the basics of the Objective-C language, explored Cocoa Touch, and gotten a feel for Xcode and the Interface Builder (IB) editor. Although you've already used a few prebuilt projects, you have yet to build one from scratch. That's about to change.

In this hour, you learn about the Model-View-Controller application design pattern and create an iOS application from start to finish.

Understanding the Model-View-Controller Design Pattern

When you start programming, you'll quickly come to the conclusion that there is more than one "correct" way to do just about everything. Part of the joy of programming is that it is a creative process in which you can be as clever as your imagination allows. This doesn't mean, however, that adding structure to the development process is a bad idea. Having a defined and documented structure means that other developers can work with your code, projects large and small are easy to navigate, and you can reuse your best work in multiple applications.

The application design approach that you'll be using in iOS is known as Model-View-Controller (MVC), and it can help you create clean, efficient applications.

NOTE

In Hour 3, "Discovering Objective-C: The Language of Apple Platforms," you learned about object-oriented (OO) programming and the reusability that it can provide. OO programs, however, can still be poorly structured—and therefore the need to define an overall application architecture that can guide the OO implementation.

Making Spaghetti

Before we get into MVC, let's first talk about the development practice that we want to avoid, and why. When creating an application that interacts with a user, several things must be taken into account. First, the user interface (UI). You must present *something* that the user interacts with: buttons, fields, and so on. Second, handling and reacting to the user input. And third, the application must store the information necessary to correctly react to the user (often in the form of a database).

One approach to incorporating all these pieces is to combine them into a single class. The code that displays the interface is mixed with the code that implements the logic and the code that handles data. This can be a straightforward development methodology, but it limits the developer in several ways:

▶ When code is mixed together, it is difficult for multiple developers to work together because no clear division exists between any of the functional units.

▶ The interface, application logic, and data are unlikely to be reusable in other applications because the combination of the three is too specific to the current project to be useful elsewhere.

▶ The application is difficult to extend. Adding features requires working around existing code. The developer must modify the existing code to include new features, even if they are unrelated.

In short, mixing code, logic, and data leads to a mess. This is known as *spaghetti code* and is the exact opposite of what we want for our iOS applications. MVC to the rescue!

Structured Application Design with MVC

MVC defines a clean separation between the critical components of our apps. Consistent with its name, MVC defines three parts of an application:

▶ A *model* provides the underlying data and methods that offer information to the rest of the application. The model does not define how the application will look or how it will act.

▶ One or more *views* make up the UI. A view consists of the different onscreen widgets (buttons, fields, switches, and so forth) that a user can interact with.

▶ A *controller* is typically paired with a view. The controller is responsible for receiving user input and acting accordingly. Controllers may access and update a view using information from the model and update the model using the results of user interactions in the view. In short, it bridges the MVC components and provides the "brains" of the application.

The logical isolation created between the functional parts of an application, illustrated in Figure 6.1, means the code becomes more easily maintainable, reusable, and extendable—the exact opposite of spaghetti code.

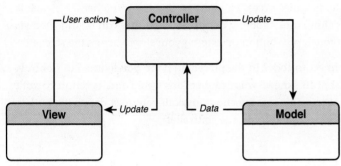

FIGURE 6.1
MVC design isolates the functional components of an app.

Unfortunately, MVC comes as an afterthought in many application development environments. When suggesting MVC design, I am often asked, "How do I do that?" This isn't indicative of a misunderstanding of what MVC is or how it works, but a lack of a clear means of implementing it.

In Xcode, MVC design is natural. As you create new projects and start coding, you are guided into using MVC design patterns automatically. It actually becomes more difficult to program poorly than it does to build a well-structured app.

How Xcode Implements MVC

Over the past few hours, you've learned about Xcode and the IB editor and have gotten a sense for how you will use them to write code and design interfaces. In Hour 5, "Exploring Interface Builder," you even connected storyboard scene objects to the corresponding code in an application. Although we didn't go into the nitty-gritty details at the time, what you were doing was binding a view to a controller.

Views

Views, although possible to create programmatically, are most often designed visually with IB. Views can consist of many different interface elements, the most common of which we covered in Hour 4, "Inside Cocoa Touch." When loaded at runtime, views create any number of objects that can implement a basic level of interactivity on their own (such as a text field opening a keyboard when touched). Even so, a view is entirely independent of any application logic. This clear separation is one of the core principles of the MVC design approach.

For the objects in a view to interact with application logic, they require a connection point to be defined. These connections come in two varieties: outlets and actions. An outlet defines a path between the code and the view that can be used to read and write specific types of information. A toggle-switch outlet, for example, provides access to data that describes whether the switch is on or off. An action, in contrast, defines a method in your application that can be triggered via an event within a view, such as a touch of a button or swiping your finger across the screen.

So, how do outlets and actions connect to code? In the preceding hour, you learned to Control-drag in IB to create a connection, but IB "knew" what connections were valid. It certainly can't guess where in your code you want to create a connection; instead, you must define the outlets and actions that implement the view's logic (that is, the controller).

CAUTION

The Relationship Between Views, Scenes, and Storyboards

At this point, it might seem logical to assume that a storyboard's scene and a view are the same thing. This isn't quite true. A scene is used to visually describe a view; it also references a corresponding controller for the view.

Put another way, a scene is where you go to edit a view and assign a controller to it. Storyboards are the files that contain all the scenes you will use in a project.

View Controllers

A controller, known in Xcode as a *view controller*, handles the interactions with a view and establishes the connection points for outlets and actions. To accomplish this, two special directives, IBAction and IBOutlet, are added to your project's code. IBAction and IBOutlet are markers that IB recognizes; they serve no other purpose within Objective-C. You add these directives to the interface files of your view controller either manually or using a special feature of IB to generate the code automatically.

NOTE

View controllers can hold application logic, but I don't mean to imply that *all* your code should be within a view controller. Although this is largely the convention for the tutorials in this book, as you create your own apps you can certainly define additional classes to abstract your application logic as you see fit.

Using IBOutlet

An IBOutlet is used to enable your code to talk to objects within views. For example, consider a text label (UILabel) that you've added to a view. If you want to create an instance variable and property for the label under the name myLabel within your view controller, you could explicitly declare both, or you might use the @property directive alone to *implicitly* declare the instance variable and add a corresponding property:

```
@property (weak, nonatomic) UILabel *myLabel;
```

This gives your application a place to store the reference to the text label and a property to access it with, but it still doesn't provide a way to connect it to the label in the interface. To do this, you include the IBOutlet keyword as part of the property declaration:

```
@property (weak, nonatomic) IBOutlet UILabel *myLabel;
```

Once IBOutlet is added, IB enables you to visually connect the view's label object to the myLabel variable and property. Your code can then use the property to fully interact with the onscreen label object—changing the label's text, calling its methods, and so on.

That's it. That line takes care of instance variable, property, and outlet—and is the pattern we will follow throughout the book.

Properties and Instance Variables

In Hour 3, you learned about the Objective-C @property directive, but you're about to start using it often, so a refresher is in order.

Instance variables are variables that hold values or references to the objects that you will use throughout a class. Need to create and modify a string that is shared among all your class methods? You'll want to declare an instance variable for it.

Makes sense, right? Then why are we talking about properties? Properties are just another way to access instance variables. Each property has a corresponding instance variable.

For example, suppose that you want to declare an instance variable called _myString (type NSString) and a corresponding property myString. You could write the following:

```
@property (weak, nonatomic) NSString *myString;
```

After adding this line, you can access _myString safely through its property by referring to <object name>.myString in other classes' code, or as self.myString within the class code that defined the myString property.

So, does it ever make sense to use only instance variables instead of instance variables and properties? That is a great question and a point of contention among many Objective-C developers. As Objective-C has changed, the differentiation between properties and instance variables has almost vanished. Accessing properties is slower than directly using instance variables but is considered the proper way of exposing data from one object so that it can be modified in another.

For our purposes, we'll use properties for accessing objects in our user interfaces, and we'll use instance variables for objects that are internal to our own class and would never be shared with another object. Could you use a property *and* instance variable instead? Absolutely—it's really just a matter of preference.

Don't get it? Don't worry. It'll all become clear as you work on a few examples.

Using `IBAction`

An `IBAction` is used to "advertise" a method in your code that should be called when a certain event takes place. For instance, if a button is pushed or a field updated, you will probably want your application to take action and react appropriately. When you've written a method that implements your event-driven logic, you can declare it with `IBAction` in the interface file, which subsequently exposes it to the IB editor. Declaring a method in the interface file, before it is actually implemented, is called *prototyping* the method.

For instance, a prototype for the method `doCalculation` might look like this:

```
-(IBAction)doCalculation:(id)sender;
```

Notice that the prototype includes a `sender` parameter with the type of `id`. This is a generic type that can be used when you don't know (or need to know) the type of object you'll be working with. By using `id`, you can write code that doesn't tie itself to a specific class, making it easier to adapt to different situations.

When creating a method that will be used as an action (like our `doCalculation` example), you can identify and interact with the object that invoked the action through the `sender` variable (or whatever you decide to call it in your code). This will prove handy if you decide to design a method that handles multiple different events, such as button presses from several different buttons.

Data Models

Let me get this out of the way upfront: For many of the exercises in this book, a separate data model is not needed; the data requirements are handled within the controller. This is one of the trade-offs of small projects like the one you'll be working through in a few minutes. Although it would be ideal to represent a complete MVC application architecture, sometimes it just isn't possible in the space and time available. In your own projects, you must decide whether to implement a standalone model. In the case of small utility apps, you may find that you rarely need to consider a data model beyond the logic you code into the controller.

As you grow more experienced with the iOS development and start building data-rich applications, you'll want to begin exploring Core Data. Core Data abstracts the interactions between your application and an underlying datastore. It also includes an Xcode data modeling tool, like IB, that helps you design your application, but instead of visually laying out interfaces, you can use it to visually map a data structure, as shown in Figure 6.2.

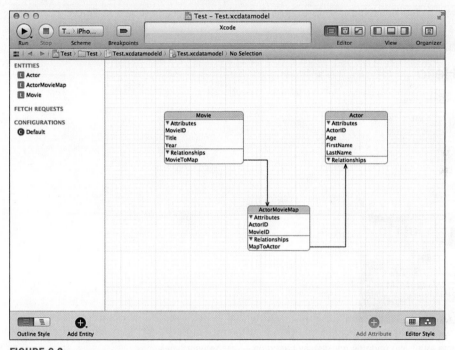

FIGURE 6.2
After you become more familiar with iOS development, you might want to explore the Core Data tools for managing your data model.

For our beginning tutorials, using Core Data would be like using a sledgehammer to drive a thumbtack. Right now, let's get started building your first app with a view and a view controller.

Using the Single View Application Template

The easiest way to see how Xcode manages to separate logic from display is to build an application that follows this approach. Apple has included a useful application template in Xcode that quickly sets up a project with a storyboard, an empty view, and an associated view controller. This Single View Application template will be the starting point for many of your projects, so the rest of this hour you learn how to use it.

Implementation Overview

The project we'll build is simple: Instead of just writing the typical "Hello World" app, we want to be a bit more flexible. The program presents the user with a field (UITextField) for typing and a button (UIButton). When the user types into the field and presses the button, the display updates an onscreen label (UILabel) so that the word *Hello* is shown, followed by the user's input. The completed HelloNoun, as I've chosen to call this project, is shown in Figure 6.3.

FIGURE 6.3
The app accepts input and updates the display based on what the user types.

Although this won't be a masterpiece of development, it does contain almost all the different elements we discuss in this hour: a view, a controller, outlets, and actions. Because this is the first full development cycle that we've worked through, we'll pay close attention to how all the pieces come together and why things work the way they do.

Setting Up the Project

First we want to create the project, which we'll call HelloNoun, in Xcode:

1. Launch Xcode from the Applications folder or Launchpad.

2. Choose File, New, Project.

3. You are prompted to choose a project type and a template. On the left side of the New Project window, make sure that Application is selected under the iOS project type. Select the Single View Application option from the icons on the right, and then click Next.

4. Type **HelloNoun** in the Product Name field. Use your full name for the organization name. For the company identifier, enter a domain to represent yourself, in reverse order. (I'm using com.teachyourselfios; refer to the "Creating and Managing Projects" section in Hour 2, "Introduction to Xcode and the iOS Simulator," for more information.) Leave Class Prefix blank, and be sure that Device Family is set to either iPhone or iPad. Finally, be sure that the Use Storyboard and Use Automatic Reference Counting check boxes are checked and that Include Unit Tests is unchecked, as shown in Figure 6.4, and then click Next.

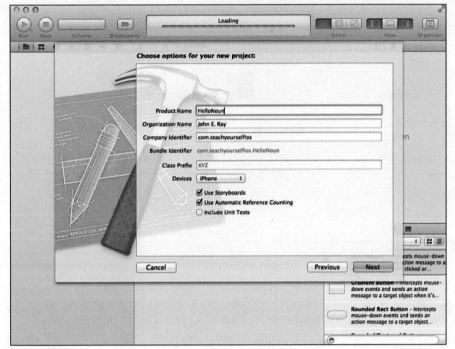

FIGURE 6.4
Choose the name and target device for your application.

5. Choose a save location when prompted. Click Create to generate the project.

This creates a simple application structure consisting of an application delegate, a window, a view (defined in a storyboard scene), and a view controller. After a few seconds, your project window will open (see Figure 6.5).

FIGURE 6.5
The workspace for your new project.

Class Files

If it isn't already visible, open the top-level project code group (named HelloNoun) and review the contents. You should see five files (shown in Figure 6.5): AppDelegate.h, AppDelegate.m, ViewController.h, ViewController.m, and MainStoryboard.storyboard.

The AppDelegate.h and AppDelegate.m files make up the delegate for the instance of UIApplication that this project will create. In other words, these files can be edited to include methods that govern how the application behaves when it is running. You modify the delegate when you want to perform application-wide setup operations at launch or when you want to tell an application how to behave when it moves into the background (or becomes the foreground application again), or when you want to choose what to do when an application is forced to quit. For this project, you do not need to edit anything in the application delegate; but keep in mind the role that it plays in the overall application life cycle.

The second set of files, ViewController.h and ViewController.m, implements the class that contains the logic for controlling our view: a view controller (UIViewController). These files are largely empty to begin, with just a basic structure in place to ensure that we can build and run the project from the outset. In fact, feel free to click the Run button at the top of the Xcode window. The application will compile and launch, but there won't be anything to do.

NOTE

If you provide a "class prefix" when creating a project in Xcode, all the class filenames are prefixed with the text you enter. In earlier versions of Xcode, Apple used the name of the application itself as the class prefix.

To impart some functionality to this app, we need to work on the two areas discussed previously: the view and the view controller.

The Storyboard File

In addition to the class files, the project contains a storyboard file that will store the interface design. Click the MainStoryboard.storyboard file to open it in the IB editor. Shown in Figure 6.6, the MainStoryboard contains icons for the First Responder (an instance of UIResponder), the View Controller (our ViewController class), and our application's View (an instance of UIView). The view controller and first responder are also visible in the bar underneath the view in the editor. Remember from Hour 5 that if you don't see the icons in the bar, just click it and they'll appear.

FIGURE 6.6
When the storyboard file is loaded, the application's view controller and initial view are instantiated.

As you learned earlier, when a storyboard file is loaded by an app, the objects within it are instantiated, meaning they become real, active parts of the application. In the case of HelloNoun (and any other application based on the Single View Application template), when the application launches, a window is created, MainStoryboard.storyboard is loaded, along with an instance of the `ViewController` class and its view, which is added to the window.

Reasonable persons are probably scratching their head right now wondering a few things. For example, how does MainStoryboard.storyboard get loaded at all? Where is the code to tell the application to do this?

The MainStoryboard.storyboard file is defined in the HelloNoun-Info.plist file as the `property` value for the key `Main storyboard file base name`. You can see this yourself by opening the Supporting Files group and then clicking the plist file to show the contents. Alternatively, just click the top-level project icon, make sure the HelloNoun target is selected, and view the Main Storyboard field in the Summary section (see Figure 6.7).

Storyboard File Loaded at Launch

FIGURE 6.7
The project's plist file defines the storyboard loaded when the application starts.

Okay, so that explains how the storyboard file gets loaded, but how does it know to load the scene? If you recall, a storyboard can have multiple scenes. So, because this is a single-view application, is it just loading the only scene it can? What happens when there are multiple scenes? All good questions.

In typical Apple style, the initial scene (and corresponding view controller/view) is chosen rather subtly in the IB editor itself. Refer back to Figure 6.6. See the gray arrow in the editor area that points to the left side of the view? That arrow is draggable and, when there are multiple different scenes, you can drag it to point to the view corresponding to any scene. This action automatically configures the project to launch that scene's view controller and view when the application launches.

In summary, the application is configured to load MainStoryboard.storyboard, which looks for the initial scene and then creates an instance of that scene's view controller class (`ViewController`, as defined in the ViewController.h and ViewController.m files). The view controller loads its view, which is added automatically to the main window. If that still doesn't make sense, don't fret; I guide you through this every step of the way.

NOTE

I've mentioned "window" a few times in this discussion. In iOS development, your application has a window that covers the screen and is created when it loads. Views are then displayed within this window. The window is referenced through the property `window` in the application delegate class. Because your initial view is automatically displayed in the window when the application starts, you'll rarely need to interact with it directly.

Planning the Properties and Connections

The first step of building our project is to decide on all the things our view controller needs to make it work. What instance variables do we need to reference objects that we're going to use? What properties should we define to safely access the instance variables? Finally, what outlets do we need to provide for the view to connect to our variables, and what actions will our interface trigger?

For this simple project, we must interact with three different objects:

- A text field (`UITextField`)
- A label (`UILabel`)
- A button (`UIButton`)

The first two provide input (the field) and output (the label) for the user. The third (the button) triggers an action in our code to set the contents of the label to the contents of the text field.

Setting Up a View Controller Interface File

Based on what we now know, we could edit the view controller class interface file (View-Controller.h) to define the instance variables we need to reference interface elements and the properties (with outlets) that we'll use to manipulate them. We'll name the field (`UITextField`) that collects user input, **userInput**, and the label (`UILabel`) that provides output will be **userOutput**. Recall that we can use the `@property` directive to create the instance variables and properties all at once and add the `IBOutlet` keyword to make the connection between the interface and code.

This boils down to two lines:

```
@property (weak, nonatomic) IBOutlet UILabel *userOutput;
@property (weak, nonatomic) IBOutlet UITextField *userInput;
```

To finish the interface file, we also need to include the action that is performed when the button is pressed. We will name this **setOutput**:

```
- (IBAction)setOutput:(id)sender;
```

All of this, put into context, results in a ViewController.h file that resembles Listing 6.1. The bolded lines are what differ from the default template file.

LISTING 6.1   A Properly Set-Up ViewController.h Interface File

```
#import <UIKit/UIKit.h>

@interface ViewController : UIViewController

@property (weak, nonatomic) IBOutlet UILabel *userOutput;
@property (weak, nonatomic) IBOutlet UITextField *userInput;

- (IBAction)setOutput:(id)sender;

@end
```

That's all we have to do. We could now connect our interface to code, just as we did in the last hour, and implement `setOutput` in the implementation file (ViewController.m).

CAUTION

Stop! Don't Type a Thing

Notice that I've been saying *"we could"* and *"we would"* rather than directing you to start typing? That's because now that you understand how the code *could* be set up by hand, I'll show you how Xcode can automate the process for you.

Some developers prefer to set up outlets, properties, and such manually. You're welcome to do this, but you're about to learn that Xcode can generate the same code for you, with almost no typing.

NOTE

If you're skimming through the HelloNoun code files, you may notice that there are green comments (lines that start with the characters //). These are usually left out of the code listings in the book to save space.

A Simplified Approach

Although you still haven't typed any code, what I'm hoping you've learned over the past few minutes is that a successful project begins with a successful planning and setup process. So, you want to do the following:

- **Identify your instance variables.** What values or objects will you need to exist through the life of a class (frequently a view controller)?

- **Identify your outlets and actions.** Which instance variables need to be connected to an object defined in your interface, and what methods will be triggered by the interface?

- **Create corresponding properties.** For any instance variable that you want to manipulate, you should use a `property` declaration to define both the instance variable and property. If the property represents an object in your interface, it must include the `IBOutlet` keyboard as part of its declaration.

- **Clean up.** If you have any properties declared with a `strong` attribute, you need to set those properties to `nil` when it is no longer needed in the life cycle of a class. If we had any of these (and we rarely do!) we'd clean them up in the view controller's `didReceiveMemoryWarning` method.

You've seen that this can be performed manually, but what if Xcode could do all the work for you? What if the IB editor, through the very process of making the connections that you learned about in Hour 5, could add property directives, create interface outlets and actions, *and* insert the empty (skeleton) methods for the actions into your implementation file? It can!

While the core basis of binding views to view controllers still relies on the code you've just seen, you can use Xcode to automagically write it for you *as you build your interface.* You still want to identify the instance variables/properties, outlets, and actions you want to create before starting the interface, and you'll still sometimes need to do a bit of additional code setup beforehand, but allowing Xcode to generate code automatically dramatically speeds up the initial stages of development.

Now, without further ado, let's build our application.

Designing the Interface

You've seen that IB makes designing a user interface (UI) as much fun as playing around in your favorite graphics application. That said, our emphasis is on the fundamentals of the development process and the objects we have at our disposal. Where it isn't critical, we move quickly through the interface creation.

Adding the Objects

The interface for the HelloNoun application is quite simple: It must provide a space for output, a field for input, and a button to set the output to the same thing as the input. Follow these steps to create the UI:

1. Open MainStoryboard.storyboard by selecting it within the Xcode project navigator.

2. The IB editor opens the file, displaying the view controller scene objects in the document outline, and a visual representation of the scene's view in the editor.

3. Make sure the Object Library is open on the right by choosing View, Utilities, Show Object Library (Control-Option-Command-3). Verify that the Objects button is selected within the library; this displays all the components that we can drag into the view. Your workspace should now resemble Figure 6.8.

FIGURE 6.8
Open the view and the Object Library to begin creating the interface.

4. Add two labels to the view by clicking and dragging the label (`UILabel`) object from the Object Library into the view.

5. The first label is just static text that says `Hello`. Double-click the default text that reads `Label` to edit it and change the content to read **Hello**. Position the second label underneath it; this will act as the output area.

▶ For this example, I changed the text of the second label to read **<Noun Goes Here!>**. This will serve as a default value until the user provides a new string. You might need to expand the text labels by clicking and dragging their handles to create enough room for them to display.

▶ I also chose to set my labels to align their text to the center. If you want to do the same, select the label within the view by clicking it and then press Option-Command-4 or click the Attributes Inspector icon (a slider) at the top of the Xcode utility area. This opens the Attributes Inspector for the label.

▶ Use the alignment buttons to change the default text alignment for the labels. You may also explore the other attributes to see the effect on the text, such as size, shadow, color, and so on. Your view should contain two labels and resemble Figure 6.9.

FIGURE 6.9
Use the Attributes Inspector to set the labels' text alignment to center and to increase the font size.

6. When you're happy with the results, it's time to add the elements that the user will be interacting with: the text field and button. Find the Text Field object (UITextField) within the Object Library and click and drag to position it under your two labels. Using the handles on the field, stretch it so that it matches the length of your output label.

7. Open the Attributes Inspector again (Option-Command-4) and set the text size to match the labels you added earlier, if desired. Notice that the field itself doesn't get any bigger. This is because the default field type on the iPhone has a set height. To change the height, you can click the square-shadowed Border Style button in the Attributes Inspector. The field then allows you to resize its height freely.

8. Finally, click and drag a Round Rect button (UIButton) from the Object Library into the view, positioning it right below the text field. Double-click in the center of the button to add a title, such as Set Label. Resize the button to fit the label appropriately. You may also want to again use the Attributes Inspector to increase the font size. Figure 6.10 shows my version of the finished view.

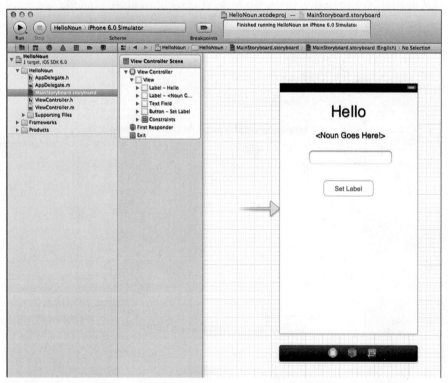

FIGURE 6.10
Your interface should include four objects (two labels, a field, and a button), just like this.

Creating and Connecting the Outlets and Actions

Our work in IB is almost complete. The last remaining step is to connect the view to the view controller. If we had defined manually the outlets and actions as described earlier, this would be a matter of dragging from one object icon to another. As it turns out, even though we're going to be creating the outlet and action code on-the-fly, it's still just a matter of drag and drop.

To do this, we need to be able to drag from the IB editor to the area of the code where we want to add an outlet or an action. In other words, we need to be able to see the ViewController.h interface file at the same time we see the view that we are connecting. This is a great time to use the assistant editor feature of Xcode. With your completed interface visible in the IB editor, click the Assistant Editor button (the middle button in the Editor section of the toolbar). The ViewController.h file automatically opens to the right of the interface because Xcode knows that is the file that you must work with while editing the view.

At this point, you might be noticing a problem: If you're on a small MacBook, or editing an iPad version of the project, you're running out of screen space. To conserve space, use the leftmost and rightmost "view" buttons on the toolbar to disable the navigation and utility areas of the Xcode window. You can also use the disclosure arrow in the lower-left corner of IB editor itself to toggle the document outline off. Your screen should now resemble Figure 6.11.

FIGURE 6.11
Turn on the assistant editor and make room in your workspace.

Adding the Outlets

We'll start by connecting the label we created for user output. Recall that we want this to be represented by an instance variable and corresponding property called userOutput:

1. Control-drag from the label that you've established for output (titled <Noun Goes Here!> in the example) or its icon in the document outline. Drag all the way into the code editor for ViewController.h, releasing the mouse button when your cursor is just under the @interface line. As you drag, you see a visual indication of what Xcode is planning to insert when you release the button, as shown in Figure 6.12.

FIGURE 6.12
Choose where your connection code will be generated.

2. When you release the mouse button, you are prompted to define an outlet. Be sure that the Connection menu is set to Outlet, Storage is Weak, and the type is set to UILabel (because that's what the object is). Finally, specify the name you want to use for the property (**userOutput**), and then click Connect, as shown in Figure 6.13.

FIGURE 6.13
Configure the specifics of the outlet you're creating.

3. When you click Connect, Xcode automatically inserts the proper `@property` directive with `IBOutlet` (implicitly declaring the instance variable). What's more, it has made the connection between the outlet you just defined and the code itself. If you want to verify this, just check the Connections Inspector or right-click the field to open the Quick Inspector, as you learned in Hour 5.

4. Repeat the process for the text field, dragging it to just below the `@property` line that was inserted. This time, choose `UITextField` as the type and `userInput` as the name of the outlet.

CAUTION

Watch Where You Drag

Placing your first connection is easy, but you must target the right part of the code in subsequent drags. It is critically important that you drag subsequent interface objects that you want to define in your code to an area below the `@property` lines that Xcode adds.

If you don't, Xcode may insert only an instance variable, and all the supporting code for a property will be missing. If this happens, undo and try again.

With those few steps, you've created and inserted the proper code to support the input and output view objects, and the connections to the view controller are now established. To finish the view, however, you still must define a `setOutput` action and connect the button to it.

Adding the Action

Adding the action and making the connection between the button and the action follows the same pattern as the two outlets you just added. The only difference is that actions are usually defined after properties in an interface file, so you'll just be dragging to a slightly different location.

1. Control-drag from the button in the view to the area of the interface file (ViewController.h) just below the two @property directives that you automatically added earlier. Again, as you drag, you'll see Xcode provide visual feedback about where it is going to insert code. Release the mouse button when you've targeted the line where you want the action code to be inserted.

2. As with the outlets, you are prompted to configure the connection, as demonstrated in Figure 6.14. This time, be sure to choose Action as the connection type; otherwise, Xcode tries to insert another outlet. Set the Name to **setOutput** (the method name we chose earlier). Be sure that the Event pop-up menu is set to Touch Up Inside to configure the event that will trigger the action. Leave the rest of the fields set to their defaults and click Connect.

FIGURE 6.14
Configure the action that will be inserted into the code.

You've just added the instance variables, properties, outlets, and actions, and connected them all to your code.

Go ahead and reconfigure your Xcode workspace to use the standard editor and make sure that the project navigator is visible before continuing. If you want to double-check your work, review the contents of the ViewController.h and ViewController.m and see whether they match the code described earlier in this Hour.

Xcode Helps You Write Code, but Is It the *Right* Code?

You've just worked through the process of having Xcode write the code to support your user interface objects for you. This can be a big time saver and can eliminate much of the unpleasant upfront work required when setting up a project. That said, it isn't perfect—not by a long shot.

The code that Xcode inserts is just as if you wrote it yourself. It can be changed, edited, moved around, and broken. If you attempt to add multiple outlets for the same object, Xcode lets you. Multiple actions for the same object and event? No problem. In short, Xcode writes the code you need, but it is up to you to make sure that it is writing the *right* code and making the *right* connections.

I strongly recommend making sure you understand how to manually create outlets, actions, instance variables, and properties by hand before moving past this hour. You'll need that knowledge, plus you'll need to know how to manually make connections between objects in the interface and preexisting outlets and actions in order to fix any errors that occur because Xcode didn't quite generate the connections and code you were expecting.

Implementing the Application Logic

With the view complete and the connection to the view controller in place, the only task left is to fill in the logic. Let's turn our attention back toward the ViewController.m file and the implementation of setOutput.

The purpose of the setOutput method is to set the output label to the contents of the field that the user edited. How do we get/set these values? Simple. Both UILabel and UITextField classes have a property called text that contains their contents. By reading and writing to these properties, we can set userInput to userOutput in one easy step.

Open ViewController.m and scroll to the bottom. You'll find one more treat the Xcode gives us when it creates action connection code. It also writes an empty method definition (in this case, setOutput), just waiting for us to fill it in. Find the method, and then insert the bolded line to make it read as shown in Listing 6.2.

LISTING 6.2   Completed `setOutput` Method

```
- (IBAction)setOutput:(id)sender {
    self.userOutput.text=self.userInput.text;
}
```

It all boils down to a single line. This single assignment statement does everything we need. Well done! You've written your first iOS application.

NOTE

In this example (and most examples throughout this book), I use the nifty dot notation (`self.userInput.text`, for example) to get and set information. We could also have implemented the `setOutput` logic like this:

`[[self userOutput] setText:[[self userInput] text]];`

Either way is fine technically, but you should always code for readability and ease of maintenance. Which do you think is easier to understand?

Building the Application

The app is ready to build and test. If you want to deploy to your iOS device, be sure it is connected and ready to go. Select your device or the iOS Simulator from the Scheme menu on the Xcode toolbar, and then click Run.

After a few seconds, the application starts on your iDevice or within the Simulator window, as shown in Figure 6.15.

CAUTION

Quitting Applications

After you're done running an application, use the Stop button on the Xcode toolbar to exit it. If you use the Home button in the iOS Simulator, the application will move to the background and Xcode may get a bit confused. If this happens, you can double-click the iOS Simulator's Home button to access the task manager and manually stop the application (just like a real iOS device).

Further Exploration

Before moving on to subsequent hours, you may want to learn more about how Apple has implemented the MVC design versus other development environments that you may have used. An excellent document titled "Cocoa Design Patterns" provides an in-depth discussion of MVC as applied to Cocoa. You can find and read this introduction by searching for the title in the Xcode documentation system, which we discussed in Hour 4.

FIGURE 6.15
Your finished application makes use of a view to handle the UI and a view controller to implement the functional logic.

You might also want to take a breather and use the finished HelloNoun application as a playground for experimentation. We discussed only a few of the different IB attributes that can be set for labels, but dozens more can customize the way that fields and buttons display. The flexibility of the view creation in IB goes well beyond what can fit in one book, so exploration is necessary to take full advantage of the tools. This is an excellent opportunity to play around with the tools and see the results, before we move into more complex (and easy-to-break) applications.

Summary

In this hour, you learned about the MVC design pattern and how it separates the display (view), logic (controller), and data (model) components of an application. You also explored how Apple implements this design within Xcode through the use of Core Data, views, and view controllers. This approach will guide your applications through much of this book and in your own real-world application design, so learning the basics now will pay off later.

To reinforce the lesson, we worked through a simple application using the Single View Application template. This included first identifying the outlets and actions that would be needed and then using Xcode to create them. Although not the most complex app you'll write, it included the elements of a fully interactive user experience: input, output, and (very simple) logic.

Q&A

Q. I don't like the idea of code being written without seeing it. Should I create actions and outlets myself?

A. That is entirely up to the developer. The code-generation features in Xcode are still relatively new and will certainly improve in the future. As long as you understand how to set up a project manually, I suggest that you use the Xcode tools to do the work but review the code it creates immediately afterward.

Q. I noticed some circles displayed beside code lines in the interface and implementation files. What are those?

A. These are yet another way to connect your interface to code. If you manually define the outlets and actions, circles appear beside potential connection points in your code. You can then Control-drag from your interface objects to the circles to make connections. What's more, clicking these circles after connections are in place will display the endpoint of the connection.

Workshop

Quiz

1. What event do you use to detect a button tap?

2. What purpose does the `@property` directive serve?

3. Which Apple project template creates a simple view/view controller application?

4. What is the relationship between storyboards, scenes, views, and view controllers?

Answers

1. The `Touch Up Inside` event is most commonly used to trigger actions based on a button press.

2. The `@property` directive defines a property that corresponds to an instance variable. The property gives us a means of accessing our instance variables without having to manipulate them directly. In addition, a property that is declared without a corresponding instance

variable automatically generates that instance variable for you. Implicitly created instance variables are named the same as their property, but with an underscore (_) prefix; we (and Apple) take advantage of this feature throughout the book.

3. The Single View Application template is the starting point for many of our apps in this book. It provides a storyboard with a single scene/view and a corresponding view controller (everything a basic app needs).

4. A scene is where you go to edit a view and assign a controller to it. Storyboards are the files that contain all the scenes you will use in a project.

Activities

1. Explore the attributes of the interface objects that you added to the tutorial project in Interface Builder. Try setting different fonts, colors, and layouts. Use these tools to customize the view beyond the simple layout created this hour.

2. Rebuild HelloNoun using outlets, actions, instance variables, and properties that you define and manage manually. Make your connections using the same techniques discussed in the Hour 5 tutorial. This is good practice for getting familiar with what goes on behind the scenes.

3. Review the Apple Xcode documentation for the Core Data features of Cocoa. Although you won't be using this technology in this book's tutorials, it is an important tool that you'll ultimately want to become more familiar with for advanced data-driven applications.

Working with Text, Keyboards, and Buttons

What You'll Learn in This Hour:

▶ How to use text fields
▶ Input and output in scrollable text views
▶ How to enable data detectors
▶ A way to spruce up the standard iOS buttons

In the preceding hour, you explored views and view controllers and created a simple application that accepted user input and generated output when a button was pushed. These are the basic building blocks that we expand on in this hour. In this hour, we create an application that uses multiple different input and output techniques. You learn how to implement and use editable text fields, text views, and graphical buttons, and how to configure the onscreen keyboard.

This is quite a bit of material to cover in an hour, but the concepts are very similar, and you'll quickly get the hang of these new elements.

Basic User Input and Output

iOS gives us many different ways of displaying information to a user and collecting feedback. There are so many ways, in fact, that we're going to be spending the next several hours working through the tools that the iOS Software Development Kit (SDK) provides for interacting with your users, starting with the basics.

Buttons

One of the most common interactions you'll have with your users is detecting and reacting to the touch of a button (UIButton). Buttons, as you may recall, are elements of a view that respond to an event that the user triggers in the interface, usually a Touch Up Inside event to indicate that the user's finger was on a button and then released it. Once an event is detected, it can trigger an action (IBAction) within a corresponding view controller.

Buttons are used for everything from providing preset answers to questions to triggering motions within a game. Although we've used only a single Rounded Rect button up to this point, buttons can take on many different forms through the use of images. Figure 7.1 shows an example of a fancy button with gradients.

Generate Story

FIGURE 7.1
Buttons can be simple, fancy (like this one), or set to any arbitrary image.

Text Fields and Views

Another common input mechanism is a text field. Text fields (`UITextField`) give users space to enter any information they want into a single line in the application; these are similar to the form fields in a web form. When users enter data into a field, you can constrain their input to numbers or text by using different iOS keyboards, something we do later this hour. You can also enable editing of styles within the text, such as underlining and bold. Text fields, like buttons, can respond to events but frequently are implemented as passive interface elements, meaning that their contents (provided through the text property) can be read at any time by the view controller.

Similar to the text field is the text view (`UITextView`). The difference is a text view can present a scrollable and editable block of text for the user to either read or modify. These should be used in cases where more than a few words of input are required. Figure 7.2 shows examples of a text field and text view.

A Simple Text Field

A Scrollable Text View. Lorem ipsum dolor sit er elit lamet, consectetaur cillium adipisicing pecu, sed do eiusmod tempor incididunt ut labore et

FIGURE 7.2
Text fields and text views provide a means for entering text using a device's virtual keyboard.

Labels

The final interface feature that we're going to be using here and throughout this book is the label (UILabel). Labels are used to display strings within a view by setting their text property.

The text within a label can be controlled via a wide range of label attributes, such as font and text size, alignment, and color. As you'll see, labels are useful both for static text in a view and for presenting dynamic output that you generate in your code.

Now that you have basic insight into the input and output tools we'll be using in this hour, let's go ahead and get started with our project: a simple substitution-style story generator.

Using Text Fields, Text Views, and Buttons

Although not everyone will agree with my sentiment, I enjoy entering text on my iPhone and iPad. The virtual keyboard is responsive and simple to navigate. What's more, the input process can be altered to constrain the user's input to only numbers, only letters, or other variations. (This varies depending on device.) You can have iOS automatically correct simple misspellings, allow text styling, or capitalize letters—all without a line of code. This project reviews many aspects of the text input process.

Implementation Overview

In this project, we create a Mad Libs-style story creator. Users enter a noun (place), verb, and number through three text fields (UITextField). They may also enter or modify a template that contains the outline of the story to be generated. Because the template can be several lines long, we use a text view (UITextView) to present this information. A button press (UIButton) triggers an action that generates the story and outputs the finished text in another text view, demonstrated in Figure 7.3.

Although not directly part of the input or output process, we also investigate how to implement the now-expected "touch the background to make the keyboard disappear" interface standard, along with a few other important points. In other words, pay attention!

We'll name this tutorial project **FieldButtonFun**. You may certainly use something more creative if you want.

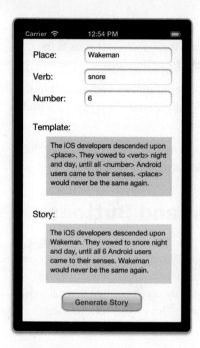

FIGURE 7.3
The tutorial app in this hour uses two types of text input objects.

Setting Up the Project

This project uses the same Single View Application template as the previous hour. If it isn't already running, launch Xcode, and then choose File, New, Project.

Select the iOS Application project type, and then find and select the Single View Application option in the Template list; click Next to continue. Enter the project name, **FieldButtonFun**, and be sure that your device is chosen and only the Use Storyboard and Use Automatic Reference Counting options are checked, and then click Next. Finally, choose your save location and click Create to set up the new project.

As before, we focus on the view, which has been created in MainStoryboard.storyboard, and the view controller class `ViewController`.

Planning the Properties and Connections

This project contains a total of six input areas that must connect to our code via outlets. Three text fields are used to collect the place, verb, and number values. We'll call the properties for these `thePlace`, `theVerb`, and `theNumber`, respectively. (Remember that instance variables to support the properties will be created automatically and named the same as the property but with an underscore (_) prefix.) The project also requires two text views: one to hold the editable story template, `theTemplate`; and the other to contain the output, `theStory`.

> **NOTE**
> _____
> Yes, we'll use a text view for output as well as for input. Text views provide a built-in scrolling behavior and can be set to read-only, making them convenient for both collecting and displaying information.

Finally, a single button is used to trigger a method, `createStory`, which serves as an action and creates the story text, unlike the previous hour's example. However, we also need a seventh instance variable, property, and outlet for the button, `theButton`. In many cases, you do not need to do anything but trigger an action from a button, but here we will access the button from our source code to modify its appearance.

> **TIP**
> _____
> If UI elements are used only to trigger actions; they do not need outlets. If your application needs to manipulate an object, however, such as setting its label, color, size, position, and so on, it needs an outlet and corresponding instance variable/property defined.

Now that you understand the objects we'll add and how we'll refer to them, let's turn our attention to building the user interface (UI) and creating our connections to code.

Designing the Interface

In the previous hour, you learned that the MainStoryboard.storyboard is loaded when the application launches and that it instantiates the default view controller, which subsequently loads its view from the storyboard file. Locate MainStoryboard.storyboard in the project's code folder, and click to select it and open the Interface Builder (IB) editor.

When IB has started, be sure the document outline area is visible (Editor, Show Document Outline), hide the navigation area if you need room, and open the Object Library (View, Utilities, Show Object Library).

Adding Text Fields

Begin creating the UI by adding three text fields to the top of the view. To add a field, locate the Text Field object (`UITextField`) in the library and drag it into the view. Repeat this two more times for the other two fields.

Stack the fields on top of one another, leaving enough room so that the user can easily tap a field without hitting all of them. To help the user differentiate between the three fields, add labels to the view. Click and drag the label (UILabel) object from the library into the view. Align three labels directly across from the three fields. Double-click the label within the view to set its text. I labeled my fields Place, Verb, and Number, from top to bottom, as shown in Figure 7.4.

FIGURE 7.4
Add text fields and labels to differentiate between them.

Editing Text Field Attributes

The fields that you've created are technically fine as is, but you can adjust their appearance and behavior to create a better user experience. To view the field attributes, click a field, and then press Option-Command-4 (View, Utilities, Show Attributes Inspector) to open the Attributes Inspector (see Figure 7.5).

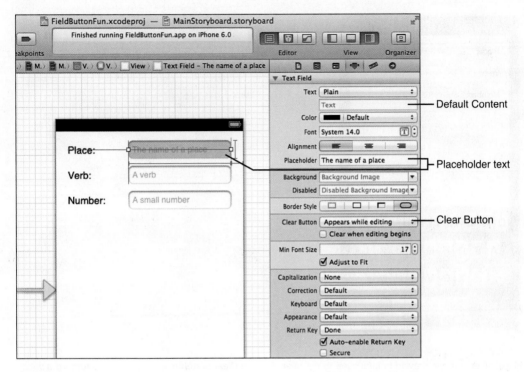

FIGURE 7.5
Editing a field's attributes can help create a better UI.

For example, you can use the Placeholder Text field to enter text that appears in the background of the field until the user begins editing. This can be a helpful tip or an additional explanation of what the user should be entering.

You may also choose to activate the Clear button. The Clear button is a small X icon added to a field that the user can touch to quickly erase the contents. To add the Clear button, just choose one of the visibility options from the Clear button pop-up menu; the functionality is added for free to your application. Note that you may also choose to automatically clear the field when the user taps it to start editing. Just check the Clear When Editing Begins check box.

Add these features to the three fields within the view. Figure 7.6 shows how they appear in the application.

FIGURE 7.6
Placeholder text can provide helpful cues to the user, and the Clear button makes it simple to remove a value from a field.

TIP

Placeholder text also helps identify which field is which within the IB editor area. It can make creating your connections much easier down the road.

In addition to these changes, attributes can adjust the text alignment, font and size, and other visual options. Part of the fun of working in the IB editor is that you can explore the tools and make tweaks (and undo them) without having to edit your code.

Attributed Versus Plain Text

In many of controls that allow the display of text, you'll find the Text drop-down menu that can toggle between Plain or Attributed options. In general, you want to leave this on Plain, but by setting it to Attributed, you can gain much finer control over the layout of the text, as shown in Figure 7.7.

Using this feature, you can provide more richly styled text output and even enable user editing of the text style by simply checking the Allows Editing Attributes check box.

Enable Editing Attributes

Attributed/Plain

Attributed Options

FIGURE 7.7
Attributed text fields and other UI elements offer more detailed control over presentation.

Customizing the Keyboard Display with Text Input Traits

Probably the most important attributes that you can set for an input field are the "text input traits," or simply, how the keyboard is going to be shown onscreen. Seven different traits appear at the bottom of the text field attributes section:

▶ **Capitalize:** Controls whether iOS automatically capitalizes words, sentences, or all the characters entered into a field.

▶ **Correction:** If explicitly set to on or off, the input field corrects (on) or ignores (off) common spelling errors. If left to the defaults, it inherits the behavior of the iOS settings.

▶ **Keyboard:** Sets a predefined keyboard for providing input. By default, the input keyboard lets you type letters, numbers, and symbols. A total of seven different keyboards are available, ranging from Number Pad to Email Address. If the option Number Pad is chosen, for example, only numbers can be entered. Similarly, the Email Address option constrains the input to strings that look like email addresses.

▶ **Appearance:** Changes the appearance of the keyboard to look more like an alert view (which you learn about in a later hour).

▶ **Return Key:** If the keyboard has a Return key, it is set to this label. Values include Done, Search, Next, Go, and so on.

▶ **Auto-Enable Return Key:** Disables the Return key on the keyboard unless the user has entered at least a single character of input into the field.

▶ **Secure:** Treats the field as a password, hiding each character as it is typed.

Of the three fields that we've added to the view, the Number field can definitely benefit from setting an input trait. With the Attributes Inspector still open, select the Number field in the view, and then choose the Number Pad option from the Keyboard pop-up menu (see Figure 7.8).

FIGURE 7.8
Choosing a keyboard type will help constrain a user's input.

You may also want to alter the capitalization and correction options on the other two fields and set the Return key to Done. Again, all this functionality is gained "for free." So, you can return to edit the interface and experiment all you want later on. For now, let's call these fields "done" and move on to the text areas.

Copy and Paste

Your text entry areas automatically gain copy and paste without your having to add anything to your code. For advanced applications, you can override the protocol methods defined in `UIResponderStandardEditActions` to customize the copy, paste, and selection process.

Adding Text Views

Now that you know the ins and outs of text fields, let's move on to the two text views (`UITextView`) present in this project. Text views, for the most part, can be used just like text fields. You can access their contents the same way, and they support many of the same attributes as text fields, including text input traits.

To add a text view, find the Text View object (`UITextView`) and drag it into the view. Doing so adds a block to the view, complete with Greeked text (Lorem ipsum...) that represents the input area. Using the resizing handles on the sizes of the block, you can shrink or expand the object to best fit the view. Because this project calls for two text views, drag two into the view and size them to fit underneath the existing three text fields.

As with the text fields, the views themselves don't convey much information about their purpose to the user. To clarify their use, add two text labels above each of the views: **Template** for the first, and **Story** for the second. Your view should now resemble Figure 7.9.

CAUTION

Size Doesn't Matter (Right Now)

The size of your iPhone design doesn't matter at this stage. In Hour 16, you learn how a single layout can work on the iPhone 5 and earlier models. Right now, be aware that when you position controls, they probably won't adjust correctly to work on other devices. In addition, your layout constraints might not exactly match my screenshots. That's okay. I don't want you to get caught up in the details of UI design while you're still learning to program!

FIGURE 7.9
Add two text views with corresponding labels to the view.

Editing Text View Attributes

Text view attributes provide many of the same visual controls as text fields, including plain and attributed modes. Select a view, and then open the Attributes Inspector (Option-Command-4) to see the available options, as shown in Figure 7.10.

To start, we need to update the default content to remove the initial Greeked text and provide our own input. For the top field, which will act as the template, select the content within the Text attribute of the Attributes Inspector (this is directly below the Plain/Attributed drop-down menu), and then clear it. Enter the following text, which will be available within the application as the default:

```
The iOS developers descended upon <place>. They vowed to <verb> night and day,
until all <number> Android users came to their senses. <place> would never be the
same again.
```

FIGURE 7.10
Edit the attributes of each text view to prepare them for input and output.

When we implement the logic behind this interface, the placeholders (`<place>`, `<verb>`, `<number>`) are replaced with the user's input.

Next, select the "story" text view, and then again use the Attributes Inspector to clear the contents entirely. Because the contents of this text view are generated automatically, we can leave it empty. This view is a read-only view, as well, so uncheck the Editable attribute.

In this example, to help provide some additional contrast between these two areas, I set the background color of the template to a light red and the story to a light green. To do this in your copy, simply select the text view to stylize, and then click the Attributes Inspector's View Background attribute to open a color chooser. Figure 7.11 shows our final text views.

FIGURE 7.11
When completed, the text views should differ in color, editability, and content.

Using Data Detectors

Data detectors automatically analyze the content within onscreen controls and provide helpful links based on what they find. Phone numbers, for example, can be touched to dial the phone; detected web addresses can be set to launch Safari when tapped by the user. All of this occurs without your application having to do a thing. No need to parse out strings that look like URLs or phone numbers. In fact, all you need to do is click a button.

To enable data detectors on a text view, select the view and return to the Attributes Inspector (Command-1). Within the Text View Attributes area, click the check boxes under Detection: Phone Numbers to identify any sequence of numbers that looks like a phone number, Addresses for mailing addresses, Events for text that references a day/time, and Links to provide a clickable link for web and email addresses.

CAUTION

Practice Moderation!

Data detectors are a great convenience for users, but *can* be overused. If you enable data detectors in your projects, be sure they make sense. For example, if you are calculating numbers and outputting them to the user, chances are you don't want the digits to be recognized as telephone numbers.

Setting Scrolling Options

When editing the text view attributes, you'll notice that a range of options exist that are specifically related to its ability to scroll, as shown in Figure 7.12.

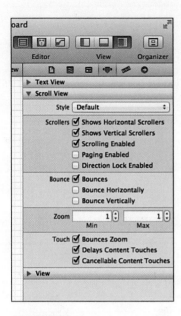

FIGURE 7.12
Scrolling regions have a number of attributes that can change their behavior.

Using these features, you can set the color of the scroll indicator (black or white), choose whether both horizontal and vertical scrolling are enabled, and even choose whether the scrolling area should have the rubberband "bounce" effect when it reaches the ends of the scrollable content.

Adding Styled Buttons

In the preceding hour's lesson, you created a button (UIButton) and connected it to the implementation of an action (IBAction) within a view controller. Nothing to it, right? Working with buttons is relatively straightforward, but what you may have noticed is that, by default, the buttons you create in IB are, well, kind of boring.

We need a single button in this project, so drag an instance of the Rounded Rect button (UIButton) from the Objects Library to the bottom of the view. Title the button **Generate Story**. Figure 7.13 shows the final view and document outline, with a default button.

FIGURE 7.13
The default button styles are less than appealing.

Although you're certainly welcome to use the standard buttons, you may want to explore what visual changes you can make in IB and ultimately through code changes.

Editing Button Attributes

To edit a button's appearance, your first stop is, once again, the Attributes Inspector (Option-Command-4). Using the Attributes Inspector, you can dramatically change the appearance of the button. Use the Type drop-down menu, shown in Figure 7.14, to choose common button types:

▶ **Rounded Rect:** The default iOS button style.

▶ **Detail Disclosure:** An arrow button used to indicate additional information is available.

▶ **Info Light:** An i icon, typically used to display additional information about an application or item. The light version is intended for dark backgrounds.

▶ **Info Dark:** The dark (light background) version of the Info Light button.

▶ **Add Contact:** A + button, often used to indicate the addition of a contact to the address book.

▶ **Custom:** A button that has no default appearance. Usually used with button images.

In addition to choosing a button type, you can make the button interact with user touches, a concept known as *changing state*. For instance, by default, a button is displayed unhighlighted within the view. When a user touches a button, it changes to a highlighted on state, showing that it has been touched.

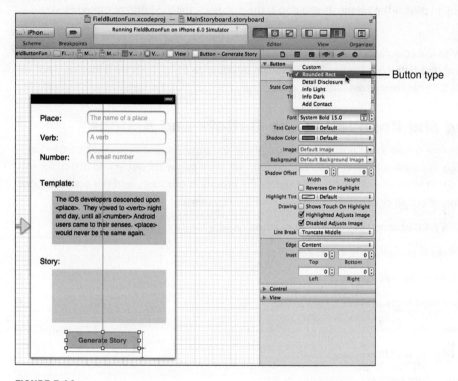

FIGURE 7.14
The Attributes Inspector gives several options for common button types and even a custom option.

Using the Attributes Inspector, you can use the State Config menu to change the button's title or background color, or even add a graphic image. Other options include the ability to create shadowed text (Shadow Offset), show a tinted color when the button is highlighted, or, display a "glow" around the user's finger when they touch a button (Shows Touch on Highlight).

Setting Custom Button Images

To create truly custom iOS buttons, you need to make custom images, including versions for the highlighted on state and the default off state. These can be any shape or size, but the PNG format is recommended because of its compression and transparency features.

After you've added these to the project through Xcode, you can select the image from the Image or Background drop-down menus in the Attributes Inspector. Using the Image menu sets an image that appears inside the button alongside the button title. This option enables you to decorate a button with an icon.

Using the Background menu sets an image that is stretched to fill the entire background of the button. The option lets you create a custom image as the entire button, but you must size your button exactly to match the image. If you don't, the image is stretched and pixilated in your interface.

Another way to use custom button images that correctly size to your text is through the code. Let's go ahead and make our connections from the interface to code. Then we'll look at what we need to write to generate stylized buttons.

Creating and Connecting the Outlets and Actions

With the interface finished, we now have a total of six text input/output areas that we need to access through our view controller code. In addition, we must create an outlet *and* action for the button. The outlet enables us to access and stylize the button in our code, and the action triggers the generation of our story using the template and field contents.

In summary, a total of seven outlets and one action require creation and connection:

- ▶ **Place field** (UITextField): thePlace
- ▶ **Verb field** (UITextField): theVerb
- ▶ **Number field** (UITextField): theNumber
- ▶ **Template Text view** (UITextView): theTemplate
- ▶ **Story Text view** (UITextView): theStory
- ▶ **Generate Story button** (UIButton): theButton
- ▶ **Action triggered from Generate Story button:** createStory

Making sure the MainStoryboard.storyboard file is open in the IB editor, use the editor toolbar buttons to switch to the Assistant mode. You should now see your UI design and the ViewController.h file where you will be making your connections side by side.

Adding the Outlets

Start by Control-dragging from the Place text field to the line following the @interface directive in the ViewController.h file. When prompted, be sure to configure the connection as an outlet and the name as **thePlace**, leaving the other values set to their defaults (type UITextfield, storage weak), as shown in Figure 7.15.

FIGURE 7.15
Create and connect outlets for each input/output element.

Repeat the process for the Verb and Number fields, connecting them to theVerb and theNumber outlets, this time dragging to just below the @property directive created when you added the first output. Connect the text views to theTemplate and theStory outlets. The process is identical (but the type is UITextView.) Finally, do the same for the Generate Story button, creating a connection type of outlet with the name **theButton**.

That does it for the outlets. Now let's create our action.

Adding the Action

In this project, we add an action for a method we will call **createStory**. This action is triggered when the user clicks the Generate Story button. To create the action and generate an empty method that we can implement later, Control-drag from the Generate Story button to below the last @property directive in the ViewController.h file.

Name the action **createStory**, when prompted, as shown in Figure 7.16.

FIGURE 7.16
Create the action that will ultimately be used to generate our story.

Our initial interface is now complete. The resulting ViewController.h interface file should resemble Listing 7.1. Of course, all of this code has been written for us, so you shouldn't need to edit any of it by hand.

LISTING 7.1   The ViewController.h file After Setting Up the Initial Interface

```
#import <UIKit/UIKit.h>

@interface ViewController : UIViewController

@property (weak, nonatomic) IBOutlet UITextField *thePlace;
@property (weak, nonatomic) IBOutlet UITextField *theVerb;
@property (weak, nonatomic) IBOutlet UITextField *theNumber;
@property (weak, nonatomic) IBOutlet UITextView *theTemplate;
@property (weak, nonatomic) IBOutlet UITextView *theStory;
@property (weak, nonatomic) IBOutlet UIButton *theButton;

- (IBAction)createStory:(id)sender;
- (IBAction)hideKeyboard:(id)sender;

@end
```

Unfortunately, we're still stuck with the plain old button. Our first coding task is to implement the code necessary to display stylized buttons. Switch back to the Xcode standard editor and make sure the project navigator is visible (Command-1).

Implementing Button Templates

IB is great for many things, but creating stylish buttons is not one of them. To create visually appealing buttons that don't require a new image for each button, we can apply button template, but we must do it through code.

Inside this hour's Projects directory is an Images folder with two Apple-created button templates: whiteButton.png and blueButton.png. Drag the Images folder into the project code group in Xcode, choosing to copy the resources and create groups, if necessary, as shown in Figure 7.17.

FIGURE 7.17
To use custom buttons, drag the images folder into the project code group in Xcode, and choose to copy the resources if needed.

Now open the ViewController.m file and search for the method `viewDidLoad`. Implement it using the code in Listing 7.2.

LISTING 7.2   Set the Button Templates When the View Loads

```
 1:- (void)viewDidLoad
 2:{
 3:    [super viewDidLoad];
 4:    // Do any additional setup after loading the view, typically from a nib.
 5:    UIImage *normalImage = [[UIImage imageNamed:@"whiteButton.png"]
 6:                            stretchableImageWithLeftCapWidth:12.0
 7:                            topCapHeight:0.0];
 8:    UIImage *pressedImage = [[UIImage imageNamed:@"blueButton.png"]
 9:                            stretchableImageWithLeftCapWidth:12.0
10:                            topCapHeight:0.0];
11:    [self.theButton setBackgroundImage:normalImage
12:                           forState:UIControlStateNormal];
13:    [self.theButton setBackgroundImage:pressedImage
14:                           forState:UIControlStateHighlighted];
15:}
```

In this code block, we accomplish several different things, all focused on providing the button (theButton) with a reference to an image object (UIImage) that "knows" how it can be stretched.

TIP

Why are we implementing this code in the viewDidLoad method? Because it is automatically invoked after the view is successfully instantiated from the storyboard file. This gives us a convenient hook for making changes (in this case, adding button graphics) right as the view is being displayed onscreen.

In lines 5–7 and 8–10, respectively, we return an instance of an image from the image files that we added to the project resources, and then define that image as being *stretchable*. Let's break this down into the individual statements:

To create an instance of an image based on a named resource, we use the UIImage class method imageNamed, along with a string that contains the filename of the image resource. For example, this code fragment creates an instance of the whiteButton.png image:

```
[UIImage imageNamed:@"whiteButton.png"]
```

Next, we use the instance method stretchableImageWithLeftCapWidth:topCapHeight to return another new instance of the image, but this time with properties that define how it can be stretched. These properties are the left cap width and top cap width, which describe how many pixels in from the left or down from the top of the image should be ignored before reaching a 1-pixel-wide strip that can be stretched. For instance, if the left cap is set to 12, a vertical column 12 pixels wide is ignored during stretching, and then the 13th column is repeated however many times is necessary to stretch to the requested length. The top cap works the same way but repeats a horizontal row to grow the image to the correct size vertically, as illustrated in Figure 7.18. If the left cap is set to 0.0, the image can't be stretched horizontally. Similarly, if the top cap is 0.0, the image cannot be stretched vertically.

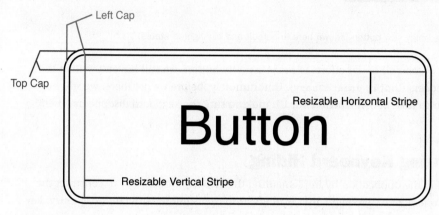

FIGURE 7.18
The caps define where within an image stretching can occur.

In this example, we use `stretchableImageWithLeftCapWidth:12.0 topCapHeight:0.0` to force horizontal stretching to occur at the 13th vertical column of pixels in and to disable any vertical stretching. The `UIImage` instance returned is then assigned to the `normalImage` and `pressed-Image` variables, corresponding to the default and highlighted button states.

Lines 11–12 and 13–14 use the `setBackgroundImage:forState` instance method of our `UIButton` object (`theButton`) to set the stretchable images `normalImage` and `pressedImage`, respectively, as the backgrounds for the predefined button states of `UIControlStateNormal` (default) and `UIControlStateHighlighted` (highlighted).

This might seem a bit confusing, and I agree. Apple has not provided these same features directly in IB, despite their usefulness in almost any application with buttons. The good news is that nothing prevents you from reusing this same code repeatedly in your projects.

On the Xcode toolbar, click Run to compile and run your application. The Generate Story button should take on a new appearance (see Figure 7.19).

FIGURE 7.19
The end result is a shiny new button (shown here in default and highlighted states).

Remember that despite all of our efforts to make a pretty button, we still haven't written the action that it triggers (that is, `createStory`). Unfortunately, before we get there, we still have one more detour to take in constructing our UI: making sure the keyboard disappears when expected.

Implementing Keyboard Hiding

Before completing the application by implementing the view controller logic to construct the story, we need to look at a "problem" that is inherent to applications with character entry: keyboards that won't go away! To see what we mean, start the application again either on your device or in the iOS Simulator.

With your app up and running, click in a field. The keyboard appears. Now what? Click in another field; the keyboard changes to match the text input traits you set up, but it remains onscreen. Touch the word Done. Nothing happens. And even if it did, what about the number pad that doesn't include a Done button? If you try to use this app, you'll also find a keyboard that sticks around and that covers up the Generate Story button, making it impossible to fully utilize the UI. So, what's the problem?

Hour 4, "Inside Cocoa Touch," described *responders* as objects that process input. The first responder is the first object that has a shot at handling user input. In the case of a text field or text view, when it gains first-responder status, the keyboard is shown and remains onscreen until the field gives up or resigns first-responder status. What does this look like in code? For the field `thePlace`, we could resign first-responder status and get rid of the keyboard with this line of code:

```
[self.thePlace resignFirstResponder];
```

Calling the `resignFirstResponder` method tells the input object to give up its claim to the input; as a result, the keyboard disappears.

Hiding with the Done Button

The most common trigger for hiding the keyboard in iOS applications is through the Did End on Exit event of the field. This event occurs when the Done (or similar) keyboard button is pressed.

We'll implement a new action method called hideKeyboard that is activated by the Did End on Exit events from our fields.

Turn your attention back to the MainStoryboard.storyboard file and open the assistant editor. Control-drag from the Place field to the line just below the createStory action in the ViewController.h file. When prompted, configure a new action, **hideKeyboard**, for the Did End on Exit event. Leave all the other defaults the same, as shown in Figure 7.20.

FIGURE 7.20
Add a new action method for hiding the keyboard.

Now you must connect the Verb field to the newly defined hideKeyboard action. There are many different ways to make connections to existing actions, but only a few enable us to target specific events. We'll use the technique you learned about in the Hour 5, "Exploring Interface Builder," tutorials: the Connections Inspector.

First switch back to the standard editor and make sure the document outline is visible (Editor, Show Document Outline). Select the Verb field, and open the Connections Inspector by pressing Option-Command-6 (or choosing View, Utilities, Connections Inspector). Drag from the circle beside Did End on Exit to the View Controller icon in the document outline area. Release your mouse button and choose hideKeyboard when prompted, as shown in Figure 7.21.

FIGURE 7.21
Connect the Verb field to the `hideKeyboard` action.

Unfortunately, now we run into a problem. The number input doesn't have a Done button, and the text view doesn't support the `Did End on Exit` event, so how do we hide the keyboard for these variations?

Hiding with a Background Touch

A popular iOS interface convention is that if a keyboard is open and you touch the background (outside of a field) the keyboard disappears. This is the approach we need to take for the number-input text field and the text view—and functionality that we need to add to all the other fields to keep things consistent.

Wondering how we detect an event outside of a field? Nothing special: All we do is create a big invisible button that sits behind all the other controls, and then attach it to the `hideKeyboard` action method.

Within the IB editor, access the Object Library (View, Utilities, Object Library) and drag a new button (`UIButton`) from the library into the view.

Because this button needs to be invisible, make sure it is selected, and then open the Attributes Inspector (Option-Command-4) and set the type to Custom. This makes the button entirely transparent. Use the selection handles to size the button to fill the entire view. With the button selected, choose Editor, Arrange, Send to Back to position the button in the back of the interface.

TIP

You can also drag an object to the top of the view hierarchy in the document outline to position it in the back. The objects are layered from the top (back) to the bottom (front).

To connect the button to the `hideKeyboard` method, it's easiest to use the document outline. Select the custom button you created (it should be at the top of the view hierarchy list), and then Control-drag from the button to the View Controller line. When prompted, choose the `hideKeyboard` method.

Nicely done. You're now ready to implement the `hideKeyboard` so that the Place and Verb fields can hide the keyboard when Done is touched, or the background can be touched to hide the keyboard in any situation.

Adding the Keyboard-Hiding Code

Because there are four potential places the user could be making changes (`thePlace`, `theVerb`, `theNumber`, `theTemplate`), we must either identify the field the user is editing *or* simply resign first responder status on all of them. As it turns out, if you resign first-responder status on a field that isn't the first responder, it doesn't matter. That makes implementing the `hideKeyboard` method as simple as sending the `resignFirstResponder` message to each of the properties representing our editable UI elements.

Scroll to the bottom of the ViewController.m file to find the `hideKeyboard` method stub that Xcode inserted for us when we created the `IBAction`. Edit the method so that it reads as shown in Listing 7.3.

LISTING 7.3 Hide the Keyboard

```
- (IBAction)hideKeyboard:(id)sender {
    [self.thePlace resignFirstResponder];
    [self.theVerb resignFirstResponder];
    [self.theNumber resignFirstResponder];
    [self.theTemplate resignFirstResponder];
}
```

TIP

You might be asking yourself whether the `sender` variable isn't the field that is generating the event. Couldn't we just resign the responder status of the sender? Yes, absolutely. This would work just fine, but we also need the `hideKeyboard` method to work when `sender` isn't necessarily the field (for example, when the background button triggers the method).

Save your work, and then try running the application again. This time, when you click outside of a field or the text view or use the Done button, the keyboard disappears.

Implementing the Application Logic

To finish off `FieldButtonFun`, we need to fill in the `createStory` method within the view controller (ViewController.m). This method searches the template text for the `<place>`, `<verb>`, and `<number>` placeholders, and then replaces them with the user's input, storing the results in the text view. We'll make use of the `NSString` instance method `stringByReplacingOccurrences OfString:withString` to do the heavy lifting. This method performs a search and replace on a given string and returns the results in a new string.

For example, if the variable `myString` contains `"Hello town"`, and you want to replace *town* with *world*, returning the result in a new variable called `myNewString`, you might use the following:

```
myNewString=[myString stringByReplacingOccurrencesOfString:@"town"
                withString:@"world"];
```

In the case of our application, our strings are the text properties of the text fields and text views (`self.thePlace.text`, `self.theVerb.text`, `self.theNumber.text`, `self.theTemplate.text`, and `self.theStory.text`).

Add the final method implementation, shown in Listing 7.4, to ViewController.m within the `createStory` method stub that Xcode generated for us.

LISTING 7.4 The `createStory` Implementation

```
 1:- (IBAction)createStory:(id)sender {
 2:    self.theStory.text=[self.theTemplate.text
 3:                        stringByReplacingOccurrencesOfString:@"<place>"
 4:                        withString:self.thePlace.text];
 5:    self.theStory.text=[self.theStory.text
 6:                        stringByReplacingOccurrencesOfString:@"<verb>"
 7:                        withString:self.theVerb.text];
 8:    self.theStory.text=[self.theStory.text
 9:                        stringByReplacingOccurrencesOfString:@"<number>"
10:                        withString:self.theNumber.text];
11:}
```

Lines 2–4 replace the `<place>` placeholder in the template with the contents of the `thePlace` field, storing the results in the story text view. Lines 5–7 then update the story text view by replacing the `<verb>` placeholder with the appropriate user input. This is repeated again in lines 8–10 for the `<number>` placeholder. The end result is a completed story, output in the `theStory` text view.

Our application is finally complete.

Building the Application

To view and test the FieldButtonFun, click Run on the Xcode toolbar. Your finished app should look similar to Figure 7.22, fancy button and all!

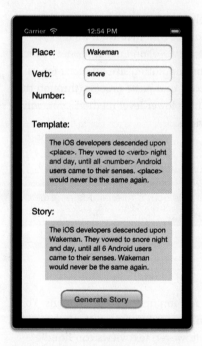

FIGURE 7.22
The finished application includes scrolling views, text editing, and a pretty button. What more could we want?

This project provided a starting point for looking through the different properties and attributes that can alter how objects look and behave within an iOS interface. The takeaway message: Don't assume anything about an object until you've reviewed how it can be configured.

Further Exploration

Throughout the next few hours, you'll explore a large number of UI objects, so your next steps should be to concentrate on the features you've learned in this hour—specifically, the object properties, methods, and events that they respond to.

For text fields and text views, the base object mostly provides for customization of appearance. However, you may also implement a delegate (`UITextFieldDelegate`, `UITextViewDelegate`) that responds to changes in editing status, such as starting or ending editing. You'll learn more about implementing delegates in Hour 10, "Getting the User's Attention," but you can start looking ahead to the additional functionality that can be provided in your applications through the use of a delegate.

It's also important to keep in mind that although there are plenty of properties to explore for these objects, there are additional properties and methods that are inherited from their superclasses. All UI elements, for example, inherit from `UIControl`, `UIView`, and `UIResponder`, which bring additional features to the table, such as properties for manipulating size and location of the object's onscreen display, as well as for customizing the copy and paste process (through the `UIResponderStandardEditActions` protocol). By accessing these lower-level methods, you can customize the object beyond what might be immediately obvious.

> **Apple Tutorials**
>
> Apple has provided a sample project that includes examples of almost all the available iOS UI controls: UICatalog (accessible via the Xcode documentation). This project also includes a wide variety of graphic samples, such as the button images used in this hour's tutorial. It's an excellent playground for experimenting with the UI.

Summary

This hour described the use of common input features and a few important output options. You learned that text fields and text views both enable the user to enter arbitrary input constrained by a variety of different virtual keyboards. Unlike text fields, however, text views can handle multiline input as well as scrolling, making them the choice for working with large amounts of text. We also covered the use of buttons and button states, including how buttons can be manipulated through code.

We continue to use the same techniques you used in this hour throughout the rest of the book, so don't be surprised when you see these elements again.

Q&A

Q. Why can't I use a `UILabel` in place of a `UITextView` for multiline output?

A. You certainly can. The text view, however, provides scrolling functionality "for free," whereas the label displays only the amount of text that fits within its bounds.

Q. Why doesn't Apple just handle hiding text input keyboards for us?

A. Although I can imagine some circumstances where it would be nice if this were an automatic action, it isn't difficult to implement a method to hide the keyboard. This gives you total control over the application interface—something you'll grow to appreciate.

Q. Are text views (`UITextView`) the only way to implement scrolling content?

A. No. You'll learn about implementing general scrolling behavior in Hour 9, "Using Advanced Interface Objects and Views."

Workshop

Quiz

1. What properties are needed to configure a stretchable image?

2. How do you get rid of an onscreen keyboard?

3. Are text views used for text input or output?

Answers

1. The left cap and top cap values define what portion of an image can be stretched.

2. To clear the onscreen keyboard, you must send the `resignFirstResponder` message to the object that currently controls the keyboard (such as a text field).

3. Text views (`UITextView`) can be implemented as scrollable output areas or multiline input fields. It's entirely up to you.

Activities

1. Expand the story creator with additional placeholders, word types, and styled text editing. Use the same string manipulation functions described in this lesson to add the new functionality.

2. Modify the story creator to use a graphical button of your design. Use either an entirely graphical button or the stretchable image approach described in this hour's tutorial.

Handling Images, Animation, Sliders, and Steppers

What You'll Learn in This Hour:

▶ The use of sliders and steppers for user input
▶ Configuring and manipulating slider and stepper input ranges
▶ How to add image views to your projects
▶ Ways of creating and controlling simple animations

The text input and output that you learned about in the preceding hour is certainly important, but iOS is known for its attractive graphics and "touchable" UI. This hour expands our interface toolkit to include images, animation, and the very touchable slider and stepper controls.

We'll implement an application to combine these new features with some simple logic to manipulate input data in a unique way. These new capabilities will help you build more interesting and interactive applications—and of course, there's more to come.

User Input and Output

Although application logic is always the most important part of an application, the way the interface works plays a big part in how well it will be received. For Apple and the iDevices, providing a fun, smooth, and beautiful user experience has been key to their success; it's up to you to bring this experience into your own development. The iOS interface options give you the tools to express your application's functionality in fun and unique ways.

This hour introduces three very visual interface features: sliders and steppers for input, and image views for output.

Sliders

The first new interface component that we use this hour is a slider (UISlider). Sliders are a convenient touch control used to visually set a point within a range of values. Huh? What?

Suppose that you want your user to be able to speed something up or slow it down. Asking users to input timing values is unreasonable. Instead, you can present a slider, as shown in Figure 8.1, where they can touch and drag an indicator (called a *thumb*) back and forth on a line. Behind the scenes, a value property is being set that your application can access and use to set the speed. No need for users to understand the behind-the-scene details or do anything more than drag with their fingers.

FIGURE 8.1
Use a slider to collect a value from a range of numbers without requiring users to type.

Sliders, like buttons, can react to events or can be read passively like a text field. If you want the user's changes to a slider to immediately have an effect on your application, you must have it trigger an action.

Steppers

Similar to a slider is a stepper (UIStepper). Like a slider, a stepper offers a means of inputting a number from a range of values visually. How it accomplishes this, however, differs a bit. A stepper, shown in Figure 8.2, offers –/+ buttons in a single control. Pushing a side of the control decrements or increments an internal value property.

FIGURE 8.2
The stepper performs a similar function to the slider control.

Steppers can be used as alternatives to traditional text input fields for values, such as setting a timer or controlling the speed of an onscreen object. Because they do not provide an onscreen representation of their current internal value, you must make sure that when a stepper is used to update a portion of your interface that you indicate a change has been made.

Steppers provide the same range of events as sliders, making it possible to easily react to changes or read the internal `value` property at any time.

Image Views

Image views (`UIImageView`) do precisely what you'd think: They display images. You can add them to your application views, using them to present information to the user. You can even use an instance of `UIImageView` to create a simple frame-based animation with controls for starting, stopping, and even setting the speed at which the animation is shown.

With Retina display devices, your image views can even take advantage of the high-resolution display for crystal-clear images. Even better, you need no special coding. Instead of checking for a specific device, you can just add multiple images to your project, and the image view will load the right one at the right time. We do not go through all the steps to make this happen each time we use an image in this book, but later in this hour's lesson, I do describe how you can add this capability to your projects.

Creating and Managing Image Animations, Sliders, and Steppers

There's something about interface components that move that make users take notice. They're visually interesting, attract and keep attention, and, on a touch screen, are fun to play with. In this hour's project, we take advantage of all of our new user interface (UI) elements (and some old friends) to create a user-controlled animation.

Implementation Overview

As mentioned earlier, image views can be used to display image file resources and show simple animations, whereas sliders provide a visual way to choose a value from a range. We'll combine these in an application we're calling ImageHop.

In ImageHop, we create a looping animation using a series of images and an image view instance (`UIImageView`). We allow the user to set the speed of the animation using a slider (`UISlider`). What will we use as an animation? A field of hopping bunnies. What will the user control? Hops per second for the "lead" bunny, of course. The "hops" value will be set by the slider and displayed in a label (`UILabel`). A stepper provides another way of changing the speed in precise increments. The user can also stop or start the animation using a button (`UIButton`).

Figure 8.3 shows the completed application with the bunnies at rest.

FIGURE 8.3
ImageHop uses image views, a slider, and a stepper to create and control a simple animation.

We should discuss two pieces of this project before getting too far into the implementation:

▶ First, image view animations are created using a series of images. I've provided a 20-frame animation with this project, but you're welcome to use your own images if you prefer.

▶ Second, although steppers and sliders enable users to visually enter a value from a range, there isn't much control over how that is accomplished. For example, the minimum value must be smaller than the maximum, and you can't control which dragging direction of the slider (or which side of the stepper) increases or decreases the result value. These limitations aren't showstoppers; they just mean that you might have to do a bit of math (or experimentation) to get the behavior you want.

Setting Up the Project

Begin this project in the same way as the last:

1. Launch Xcode, and then choose File, New, Project.

2. Select the iOS Application project type, and then find and select the Single View Application option in the Template list on the right.

3. Click Next to continue.

4. Click Choose to continue.

5. Enter the project name **ImageHop**.

6. Be sure that the Automatic Reference Counting and Storyboard options are selected, along with an appropriate device, and then click Next.

7. Choose a save location and click Create to generate the new project.

Adding the Animation Resources

This project makes use of 20 frames of animation stored as PNG files. The frames are included in the `Images` folder within the ImageHop project folder.

Because we know upfront that we need these images, we can add them to the project immediately. Open the project group in the project navigator area of Xcode. Expand the main ImageHop code group, and then drag the Images folder into the group. When prompted, be sure to choose the option to copy the resources and create new groups, if needed.

We can now access the image files easily without our code and the IB editor.

Planning the Properties and Connections

In this application, we need to provide outlets and actions for several objects.

A total of nine outlets are required. First we need five image views (`UIImageView`), which will contain the five copies of our bunny animation. These are referenced through the properties `bunnyView1`, `bunnyView2`, `bunnyView3`, `bunnyView4`, and `bunnyView5`. The slider control (`UISlider`) sets the speed and is connected via `speedSlider`, and the speed value itself is output in a label named `hopsPerSecond` (`UILabel`). A stepper control (`UIStepper`) gives another means of setting the speed and can be accessed with `speedStepper`.

Finally, a button (`UIButton`) toggles the animation on and off and is connected to an outlet `toggleButton`.

NOTE

Why do we need an outlet for the button? Shouldn't it just be triggering an action to toggle the animation? Yes, the button could be implemented without an outlet, but by including an outlet for it, we have a convenient way of setting the button's title in the code. We can use this to change the button to read Stop when the image is animating or Start when the animation has stopped.

For actions, we need three. `setSpeed` is the method called when the slider value has changed and the animation speed needs to be reset. `setIncrement` serves a similar purpose and is called when the stepper control is used. And `toggleAnimation` is used to start and stop the animation sequence.

Now let's create the UI.

Designing the Interface

With all the outlets and actions we just discussed, it might seem like creating the UI for ImageHop will be a nightmare. In reality, it's quite simple because the five animation sequences are really just copies of a single image view (`UIImageView`). Once we add one, we can copy it four times almost instantly.

Adding an Image View

In this exercise, our view creation begins with the most important object of the project: the image view (`UIImageView`). Open the MainStoryboard.storyboard file, access the Object Library, and drag an image view into the application's view.

Because the view has no images assigned, it is represented by a light-gray rectangle. Use the selection handles on the rectangle to size it to fit in the upper center of the interface (see Figure 8.4).

FIGURE 8.4
Set the image view to fill the upper center of the interface.

Setting the Default Image

There are very few properties for configuring the functionality of an image view. We are interested in the image property: the image that is going to be displayed. Select the image view and press Option-Command-4 to open the Attributes Inspector (see Figure 8.5).

FIGURE 8.5
Set the image that will be shown in the view.

Using the Image drop-down menu, choose one of the image resources available. This is the default image that is shown before the animation runs, so using the first frame (frame-1.png) is a good choice.

The image view updates in Interface Builder (IB) to show the image resource that you've chosen.

NOTE

What about the animation? Isn't this just a frame? Yes, if we don't do anything else, the image view shows a single static image. To display an animation, we need to create an array with all the frames and supply it programmatically to the image view object. We do this in a few minutes, so just hang in there.

Making Copies

After you've added the image view, create four additional copies by selecting it in your UI and choosing Edit, Duplicate (Command-D) from the menu. Scale and position the copies around the first image view. Don't worry if there is some overlap between the image views; this does not affect the application at all. For my implementation, I also used the Attributes Inspector (Option-Command-4) to set an alpha of .75 and .50 on some of the image views to make them partially transparent.

You've just created your field of bunnies. Your display should now resemble Figure 8.6.

FIGURE 8.6
Create your own field of bunnies.

You Said You'd Tell Us About Loading Hi-Res Images for the Retina Display. How Do We Do It?

That's the best part! There's really nothing to do that you don't already know. To accommodate the higher scaling factor of the Retina display (both iPhone and iPad), you just create image resources that are two times the horizontal and vertical resolution, and then name them with the same filename as your original low-res images, but with the suffix @2x. (For example, Image.png becomes Image@2x.png.) Finally, add them to your project resources like any other resource.

Within your projects, just reference the low-res image, and the hi-res image is loaded automatically on the correct devices, as needed.

Adding a Slider

The next piece that our interface needs is the slider that will control the speed. Open the Object Library and drag the slider (`UISlider`) into the view, just under the image views. Using the selection handles on the slider, click and drag to size it to about two thirds of the width of the view and align it along the right side of the view. This leaves just enough room for a label to the left of the slider.

Because a slider has no visual indication of its purpose, it's a good idea to always label sliders so that your users will understand what they do. Drag a label object (`UILabel`) from the library into your view. Double-click the text and set it to read **Speed:**. Position it so that it is aligned with the slider, as shown in Figure 8.7.

FIGURE 8.7
Add the slider and a corresponding label to the view.

Setting the Slider Range Attributes

Sliders make their current settings available through a value property that we'll be accessing in the view controller. To change the range of values that can be returned, we need to edit the slider attributes. Click to select the slider in the view, and then open the Attributes Inspector (Option-Command-4), as shown in Figure 8.8.

The Minimum, Maximum, and Initial fields should be changed to contain the smallest, largest, and starting values for the slider. For this project, use *.25*, *1.75*, and *1.0*, respectively.

FIGURE 8.8
Edit the slider's attributes to control the range of values it returns.

Where Did These Min, Max, and Initial Values Come From?

This is a great question, and one that doesn't have a clearly defined answer. In this application, the slider represents the speed of the animation, which, as previously discussed, is set through the `animationDuration` property of the image view as the number of seconds it takes to show a full cycle of an animation. Unfortunately, this means the faster animations use smaller numbers and slower animations use larger numbers, which is the exact opposite of traditional user interfaces, where "slow" is on the left and "fast" is on the right. Because of this, we need to reverse the scale. In other words, we want the big number (1.75) to appear when the slider is on the left side and the small number (.25) on the right.

To reverse the scale, we take the combined total of the minimum and maximum (1.75 + 0.25) and subtract the value returned by the slider from that total. For example, when the slider returns 1.75 at the top of the scale, we calculate a duration of 2 – 1.75, or 0.25. At the bottom of the scale, the calculation will be 2 – 0.25, or 1.75.

Our initial value is 1.0, which falls directly in the middle of the scale.

Make sure the Continuous check box is *not* checked. This option, when enabled, has the control to generate a series of events as the user drags back and forth on the slider. When it isn't enabled, events are generated only when users lifts their finger from the screen. For our application, this makes the most sense and is certainly the least resource-intensive option.

You can also configure the slider with images at the minimum and maximum sliders of the control. Use the Min Image and Max Image drop-downs to select a project image resource if you want to use this feature. (We do not use it in this project.)

Adding a Stepper

With the slider in place, our next UI element is the stepper. Using the Object Library, drag a stepper button (UIStepper) into the view. Position the stepper directly below, and centered on, the slider, as shown in Figure 8.9.

FIGURE 8.9
Add the stepper element to your view.

Setting the Stepper Range Attributes

Once the stepper is added, you must configure its range attributes just as you did the slider. Ultimately, we want to use the value property of the stepper to change the speed in exactly the same way as with the slider, so the closer the two elements mirror one another, the better.

To set the range allowed on the stepper, select it in the view, and then open the Attributes Inspector (Option-Command-4). Again, provide **.25**, **1.75**, and **1.0** for the Minimum, Maximum, and Current values for the stepper. Set the step value to **.25**. This is the amount added to or subtracted from the current value when the stepper is pressed.

Use the Behavior check box to turn off Autorepeating, meaning that the user will not be able to press and hold to continue incrementing or decrementing the stepper's value. You should also uncheck the Continuous check box so that only distinct events are generated when the user finishes interacting with the control. Finally, turn on the Wrap behavior. Wrap, when on, automatically sets the stepper's value to the minimum value when the maximum is exceeded (or vice versa), effectively wrapping around the range of values it can represent. If Wrap is off, the stepper stops at the minimum or maximum value and does not change. Figure 8.9 shows the final stepper configuration in the Attributes Inspector.

Finishing the Interface

The remaining components of the ImageHop application are interface features that you've used before, so we've saved them for last. We finish things up by adding a button to start and stop the animation, a readout of the speed of the lead animated rabbit in maximum hops per second, and a pretty background for the bunnies to hop on.

Adding the Speed Output Labels

Drag two labels (UILabel) to the top of the view. The first label should be set to read **Maximum Hops Per Second:** and be located in the upper left of the view. Add the second label, which is used as output of the actual speed value, to the right of the first label.

Change the output label to read **1.00 hps**. (The speed that the animation will be starting out at.) Using the Attributes Inspector (Option-Command-4), set the text of the label to align right; this keeps the text from jumping around as the user changes the speed.

Adding the Hop Button

The last functional part of the ImageHop interface is the button (UIButton) that starts and stops the animation. Drag a new button from the Object Library to the view and positioning it at the bottom center of the UI. Double-click the button to edit the title and set it to **Hop!**

Setting a Background Graphic and Color

For fun, we can spruce up the application a bit by toning down the blinding white screen that the iOS views use by default. To do this, select the View icon in the document outline and open the Attributes Inspector (Option-Command-4). Use the Background attribute to set a green background for the application, as shown in Figure 8.10.

FIGURE 8.10
Set a green color for the background of the application.

In addition to the color, it would be great if the bunnies could be hopping in grass, wouldn't it? (Bunnies like grass.) To add a background image, drag another instance of UIImageView to the view. Resize it to cover the image views that contain the bunny animations; then use Editor, Arrange, Send to Back to place the background image view behind the animation image views.

Finally, with the background image view selected, use the Attributes Inspector to set the Image value to the background.jpg file that you added earlier in this hour.

And, with that, it's time to create the outlets and actions and begin coding. Figure 8.11 shows the final application interface.

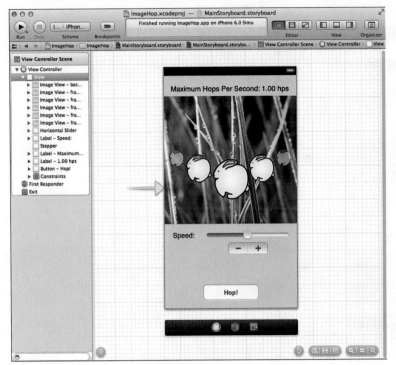

FIGURE 8.11
The final ImageHop application interface.

Creating and Connecting the Outlets and Actions

Whew! That's the most complicated application interface we've had to deal with yet. Reviewing what we've done, we have a total of nine outlets that need to be created, along with three actions.

In case you don't recall what these were, let's review, starting with the outlets:

- **Bunny animations** (UIImageView): bunnyView1, bunnyView2, bunnyView3, bunnyView4, and bunnyView5
- **Slider speed setting** (UISlider): speedSlider
- **Stepper speed setting** (UIStepper): speedStepper
- **Maximum speed readout** (UILabel): hopsPerSecond
- **Hop/Stop button** (UIButton): toggleButton

And the actions:

▶ **Start/stop the animation using the Hop/Stop button:** `toggleAnimation`

▶ **Set the speed with the slider changes:** `setSpeed`

▶ **Set the speed when the stepper changes:** `setIncrement`

Prepare your workspace for making the connections. Make sure the MainStoryboard.storyboard file is open in the IB editor, and switch to the assistant editor mode. Your UI design and the ViewController.h file should be visible side by side.

Adding the Outlets

Start by Control-dragging from the main `ImageView` instance (the large bunny) to the line following the `@interface` directive in the ViewController.h file. When prompted, be sure to configure the connection as an outlet and the name as **bunnyView1**, leaving the other values set to their defaults (type `UIImageView`, storage Weak), as shown in Figure 8.12.

FIGURE 8.12
Begin by connecting the main bunny `UIImageView` instance.

Repeat the process for the remaining images views that we want to animate, targeting each successive connection below the last @property line that was added. It doesn't matter which bunny is bunnyView2, bunnyView3, bunnyView4, or bunnyView5, just as long as they're all connected.

After connecting the image views, proceed with the rest of the connections. Control-drag from the slider (UISlider) to the line under the last @property declaration and add a new outlet named **speedSlider**. Do the same for the stepper (UIStepper), adding an outlet named **speed-Stepper**. Finish off by connecting the hops per second output UILabel (1.00 hps initially) to hopsPerSecond and the Hop! UIButton to toggleButton.

Our outlets are finished. Let's take care of our actions.

Adding the Actions

This project requires three distinct actions. The first, toggleAnimation, is triggered when the user presses the Hop! button, and it starts the animation sequence. Add a definition for this action by Control-dragging from the button in your interface to a line below the property declarations. When prompted, set the connection type to Action and provide **toggleAnimation** as the name, leaving all other values as the defaults, as shown in Figure 8.13.

FIGURE 8.13
Create the action for toggling the animation on and off.

Next, Control-drag from the slider to a line below the just-added IBAction line. Create an action named setSpeed that is triggered from the UISlider's Value Changed event.

Finally, create the third action, this one triggered from the stepper, naming it **setIncrement** and again using the Value Changed event.

To check your work, your ViewController.h file should now resemble Listing 8.1.

LISTING 8.1 The Completed ViewController.h Interface File

```
#import <UIKit/UIKit.h>

@interface ViewController : UIViewController

@property (weak, nonatomic) IBOutlet UIImageView *bunnyView1;
@property (weak, nonatomic) IBOutlet UIImageView *bunnyView2;
@property (weak, nonatomic) IBOutlet UIImageView *bunnyView3;
@property (weak, nonatomic) IBOutlet UIImageView *bunnyView4;
@property (weak, nonatomic) IBOutlet UIImageView *bunnyView5;
@property (weak, nonatomic) IBOutlet UISlider *speedSlider;
@property (weak, nonatomic) IBOutlet UIStepper *speedStepper;
@property (weak, nonatomic) IBOutlet UILabel *hopsPerSecond;
@property (weak, nonatomic) IBOutlet UIButton *toggleButton;

- (IBAction)toggleAnimation:(id)sender;
- (IBAction)setSpeed:(id)sender;
- (IBAction)setIncrement:(id)sender;

@end
```

We're ready to start coding the implementation of our magical hopping bunny animation. Surprisingly, the code needed to make this work is really quite minimal.

Implementing the Application Logic

The view controller needs to manage a total of four different things to make our application work as we envision.

First, we need to load the image animations for each of the ImageViews (bunnyView1, bunny-View2, and so on); we managed to set a static frame of the image in IB, but that isn't enough to make them animate. Next, we must to implement toggleAnimation so that we can start and stop the onscreen animation from the Hop! button. Finally, the setSpeed and setIncrement methods must be written to control the maximum speed of the animations.

Implementing Animated Image Views

Animating images requires us to build an array of image objects (UIImage) and pass them to an image view object. Where should we do this? As with setting button templates in the last hour's project, the ViewDidLoad method of our view controller provides a convenient location for doing additional setup for the view, so that's what we'll use.

Using the project navigator, open the view controller implementation file, ViewController.m. Find the ViewDidLoad method, and then add the following code to the method. Note the removal of lines 10–23 to save space (they follow the same pattern as lines 7–9 and 24–26), as shown in Listing 8.2.

LISTING 8.2   Load the Animation

```
 1: - (void)viewDidLoad
 2: {
 3:     [super viewDidLoad];
 4:     // Do any additional setup after loading the view, typically from a nib.
 5:     NSArray *hopAnimation;
 6:     hopAnimation=@[
 7:                     [UIImage imageNamed:@"frame-1.png"],
 8:                     [UIImage imageNamed:@"frame-2.png"],
 9:                     [UIImage imageNamed:@"frame-3.png"],
...
24:                     [UIImage imageNamed:@"frame-18.png"],
25:                     [UIImage imageNamed:@"frame-19.png"],
26:                     [UIImage imageNamed:@"frame-20.png"],
27:                     ];
28:     self.bunnyView1.animationImages=hopAnimation;
29:     self.bunnyView2.animationImages=hopAnimation;
30:     self.bunnyView3.animationImages=hopAnimation;
31:     self.bunnyView4.animationImages=hopAnimation;
32:     self.bunnyView5.animationImages=hopAnimation;
33:     self.bunnyView1.animationDuration=1;
34:     self.bunnyView2.animationDuration=1;
35:     self.bunnyView3.animationDuration=1;
36:     self.bunnyView4.animationDuration=1;
37:     self.bunnyView5.animationDuration=1;
38: }
```

To configure the image views for animation, first an array (NSArray) variable is declared (line 5) called hopAnimation. Next, in line 6, the array is started with @[. By initializing an array in this method, all we have to do is provide a comma-separated list of objects followed by a closing bracket,].

The image objects (UIImage) are initialized and added to the array in lines 7–26. Remember that you need to fill in lines 10–23 on your own; otherwise, several frames will be missing from the animation.

Once an array is populated with image objects, it can be used to set up the animation of an image view. To do this, set the animationImages property of the image view to the array. Lines 28–32 accomplish this for bunnyView1 through bunnyView5 in our sample project.

Another UIImageView property that we want to set right away is the animationDuration. This is the number of seconds it takes for a single cycle of the animation to be played. If the duration is not set, the playback rate is 30 frames per second. To start, our animations are set to play all the frames in 1 second, so lines 33–37 set the animationDuration to 1 for each bunnyView UIImageView.

We've now configured all five of our image views to be animated, but even if we build and run the project, nothing is going to happen. That's because we haven't added controls for actually *starting* the animation.

Starting and Stopping the Animation

You've just learned how the animationDuration property can change the animation speed, but we need three more properties/methods to actually display the animation and accomplish everything we want:

▶ **isAnimating:** This property returns true if the image view is currently animating its contents.

▶ **startAnimating:** This starts the animation.

▶ **stopAnimating:** This stops the animation if it is running.

When the user touches the Hop! button, the toggleAnimation method is called. This method should use the isAnimating property of one of our image views (bunnyView1, for example) to check to see whether an animation is running. If it isn't, the animation should start; otherwise, it should stop. To make sure the user interface makes sense, the button itself (toggleButton) should be altered to show the title Sit Still! if the animation is running and Hop! when it isn't.

Add the code in Listing 8.3 to the toggleAnimation method in your view controller implementation file.

LISTING 8.3 Start and Stop the Animation in toggleAnimation

```
1: - (IBAction)toggleAnimation:(id)sender {
2:     if (self.bunnyView1.isAnimating) {
3:         [self.bunnyView1 stopAnimating];
```

```
 4:            [self.bunnyView2 stopAnimating];
 5:            [self.bunnyView3 stopAnimating];
 6:            [self.bunnyView4 stopAnimating];
 7:            [self.bunnyView5 stopAnimating];
 8:            [self.toggleButton setTitle:@"Hop!"
 9:                              forState:UIControlStateNormal];
10:        } else {
11:            [self.bunnyView1 startAnimating];
12:            [self.bunnyView2 startAnimating];
13:            [self.bunnyView3 startAnimating];
14:            [self.bunnyView4 startAnimating];
15:            [self.bunnyView5 startAnimating];
16:            [self.toggleButton setTitle:@"Sit Still!"
17:                              forState:UIControlStateNormal];
18:        }
19: }
```

Lines 2 and 10 provide the two different conditions that we need to work with. Lines 3–9 are executed if the animation is running, and lines 11–17 are executed if it isn't. In lines 3–7 and lines 11–15, the `stopAnimating` and `startAnimating` methods are called for the image view to stop and start the animation, respectively.

Lines 8–9 and 16–17 use the `UIButton` instance method `setTitle:forState` to set the button title to the string `"Hop!"` or `"Sit Still!"`. These titles are set for the button state of `UIControlStateNormal`. The normal state for a button is its default state, prior to any user event taking place.

At this point, if you're *really* anxious, you can run the application and start and stop the animation. That said, we've only got a few more lines of code required to set the animation speed, so let's move on.

Setting the Animation Speed

The slider triggers the `setSpeed` action after the user adjusts the slider control. This action must translate into several changes in the actual application: First, the speed of the animation (`animationDuration`) should change. Second, the animation should be started if it isn't already running. Third, the button (`toggleButton`) title should be updated to show the animation is running. And finally, the speed should be displayed in the `hopsPerSecond` label.

Add the code in Listing 8.4 to the `setSpeed` method stub view controller, and then let's review how it works.

LISTING 8.4 The Completed setSpeed Method

```
 1: -  (IBAction) setSpeed: (id) sender {
 2:      NSString *hopRateString;
 3:
 4:      self.bunnyView1.animationDuration=2-self.speedSlider.value;
 5:      self.bunnyView2.animationDuration=
 6:              self.bunnyView1.animationDuration+((float)(rand()%11+1)/10);
 7:      self.bunnyView3.animationDuration=
 8:              self.bunnyView1.animationDuration+((float)(rand()%11+1)/10);
 9:      self.bunnyView4.animationDuration=
10:              self.bunnyView1.animationDuration+((float)(rand()%11+1)/10);
11:      self.bunnyView5.animationDuration=
12:              self.bunnyView1.animationDuration+((float)(rand()%11+1)/10);
13:
14:      [self.bunnyView1 startAnimating];
15:      [self.bunnyView2 startAnimating];
16:      [self.bunnyView3 startAnimating];
17:      [self.bunnyView4 startAnimating];
18:      [self.bunnyView5 startAnimating];
19:
20:      [self.toggleButton setTitle:@"Sit Still!"
21:                          forState:UIControlStateNormal];
22:
23:      hopRateString=[[NSString alloc]
24:              initWithFormat:@"%1.2f hps",1/(2-self.speedSlider.value)];
25:      self.hopsPerSecond.text=hopRateString;
26: }
```

Because we need to format a string to display the speed, we kick things off in line 2 by declaring an NSString reference, hopRateString. In line 4, the bunnyView1 animationDuration property is set to 2 minus the value of the slider (speedSlider.value); this sets the speed of our "lead" bunny animation. This, if you recall, is necessary to reverse the scale so that faster is on the right and slower is on the left.

Lines 5–12 set the remaining image animations to the same speed as the lead animation (bunnyView1.animationDuration) plus a fraction of a second. How do we get this fraction of a second? Through the magic of this randomization function: ((float)(rand()%11+1)/10). The function rand()%11+1 returns a random number between 1 and 10. We divide this by 10 to give us a fraction (1/10, 2/10, and so on). Using float ensures that we get a floating-point result rather than an integer.

Lines 14–18 use the startAnimating method to start the animations running. Note that it is safe to use this method if the animation is already started, so we don't really need to check the state of the image view. Lines 20–21 set the button title to the string "Sit Still!" to reflect the animated state.

Lines 23–24 allocate and initialize the `hopRateString` instance that we declared in line 2. The string is initialized with a format of `"1.2f"`, based on the calculation of `1/(2-animationSpeed.value)`.

Let's break that down a bit further: Remember that the speed of the animation is measured in seconds. The fastest speed we can set is 0.25 (a quarter of a second), meaning that the animation plays four times in 1 second (or four hops per second). To calculate this in the application, we simply divide 1 by the chosen animation duration, or `1/(2-animationSpeed.value)`. Because this doesn't necessarily return a whole number, we use the `initWithFormat` method to create a string that holds a nicely formatted version of the result. The `initWithFormat` parameter string `"1.2f hps"` is shorthand for saying the number being formatted as a string is a floating-point value (`f`) and that there should always be one digit on the left of the decimal and two digits on the right (`1.2`). The `hps` portion of the format is just the hops per second unit" that we want to append to the end of the string. For example, if the equation returns a value of .5 (half a hop a second), the string stored in `hopRateString` is set to `"0.50 hps"`.

In line 25, the output label (`UILabel`) in the interface is set to the `hopRateString`.

With that, the slider speed control is in place. Just one more method to implement: `setIncrement`, triggered by the `UIStepper` (`speedStepper`) interface object.

NOTE

Don't worry if the math here is a bit befuddling. This is not critical to understanding Cocoa or iOS development, it's just an annoying manipulation we needed to perform to get the values the way we want them. I strongly urge you to play with the slider values and calculations as much as you want so that you can get a better sense of what is happening here and what steps you might need to take to make the best use of slider ranges in your own applications.

Incrementing the Animation Speed

This hour's lesson has been pretty intensive, and, if you're like me, your fingers are probably getting tired of clicking and typing. The bad news is that we aren't quite done; we still need to implement the `setIncrement` method. The good news? It takes two lines to complete.

Given all the work required to set the speed with the slider, how is this possible? Quite simple. Because we configured the stepper to generate the same values as the slider, we set the slider's value property to the value property of the stepper. When that is done, we can manually call the `setSpeed` method and everything will just work.

Update the `setIncrement` method stub in your view controller to read, as shown in Listing 8.5.

LISTING 8.5   A Simple Implementation of the `setIncrement` Method

```
- (IBAction)setIncrement:(id)sender {
    self.speedSlider.value=self.speedStepper.value;
    [self setSpeed:nil];
}
```

The first line, as expected, sets the value property of the slider to the value property of the stepper. While this *will* trigger the slider to update visually in your interface, it won't trigger its `Value Changed` event and call the `setSpeed` method. We do that manually by sending the `setSpeed` message to `self` (the view controller object).

Well done. You've just completed the app.

NOTE

Notice that `nil` is passed as a parameter when we call `setSpeed`. By default, action methods are created with a `sender` parameter that is automatically set to the object that triggered the action. The method can then examine the `sender` and react accordingly.

In the case of `setSpeed`, we never used the `sender` variable in the implementation, so just sending the `nil` value satisfies the method's requirement for a parameter, and everything works as expected.

Building the Application

To try your hand at controlling an out-of-control bunny rabbit, click Run on the Xcode toolbar. After a few seconds, the finished ImageHop application will start, as shown in Figure 8.14.

Although ImageHop isn't an application that you're likely to keep on your device (for long), it did provide you with new tools for your iOS application toolkit. The `UIImageView` class can easily add dynamic images to your programs, and `UISlider` and `UIStepper` offer uniquely touchable input solutions.

FIGURE 8.14
Bouncing bunnies! What more could we ask for?

Further Exploration

Although many hours in this book focus on adding features to the UI, it is important to start thinking about the application logic that will bring your user interface to life. As we experienced with our sample application, sometimes creativity is required to make things work the way we want.

Review the properties and methods for `UISlider` and `UIStepper` classes and consider how you might use these elements in your own apps. Can you think of any situations where the stepper values couldn't be used directly in your software? How might you apply application logic to map slider values to usable input? Programming is very much about problem solving; you'll rarely write something that doesn't have at least a few "gotchas" that need solved.

In addition to `UISlider` and `UIStepper`, you may want to review the documentation for `UIImage`. Although we focused on `UIImageView` for displaying our image animation, the images themselves were objects of type `UIImage`. Image objects will come in handy for future interfaces that integrate graphics into the user controls themselves.

Finally, for a complete picture of how your applications will almost automatically take advantage of the higher-resolution Retina display, be sure to read the section "Supporting High-Resolution Screens in Views" within the *iOS Application Programming Guide*.

Apple Tutorials

`UIImageView, UIImage, UISlider`—UICatalog (accessible via the Xcode developer documentation): Once again, this project is a great place for exploring any and everything (including images, image views, and sliders) related to the iOS interface capabilities.

Summary

Users of highly visual devices demand highly visual interfaces. In this hour's lesson, you learned about the use of three visual elements that you can begin adding to your applications: image views, sliders, and steppers. Image views provide a quick means of displaying images that you've added to your project—even using a sequence of images to create animation. Sliders can be used to collect user input from a continuous range of values. Steppers also provide user input over a range of numbers, but in a more controlled, incremental fashion. These new input/output methods start our exploration of iOS interfaces that go beyond simple text and buttons.

The information you learned in this hour, although not complex, will help pave the way for mega-rich, touch-centric user interfaces.

Q&A

Q. Is the `UIImageView` the only means of displaying animated movies?

A. No. iOS includes a wide range of options for playing back and even recording video files. The `UIImageView` is not meant to be used as a video playback mechanism.

Q. Is there a vertical version of the slider control (`UISlider`)?

A. Unfortunately, no. Only the horizontal slider is currently available in the iOS UI library. If you want to use a vertical slider control, you must implement your own.

Workshop

Quiz

1. What is one of the limitations shared by the slider and stepper controls (`UISlider` and `UIStepper`)?

2. What is the default playback rate for an animation prior to the `animationDuration` property being set?

3. What is the value of the `isAnimating` property in an instance of `UIImageView`?

Answers

1. Both must work with a range of numbers that goes from small to large. They cannot directly map to a range of numbers where a negative number is considered the maximum and a positive is the minimum. This can be overcome, but not without programmatically manipulating the numbers.

2. By default, animation frames are shown at a rate of 30 frames per second.

3. The `isAnimating` property is set to true when the `UIImageView` instance is displaying an animation. When the animation is stopped (or not configured), the property is `false`.

Activities

1. Increase the range of speed options for the ImageHop animation example. Be sure to set the default value for the slider thumb to rest in the middle and update the stepper accordingly.

2. Provide an alternative means of editing the speed by enabling the user to manually enter a number in addition to using the slider. The placeholder text of the field should default to the current slider value.

HOUR 9
Using Advanced Interface Objects and Views

What You'll Learn This Hour:

▶ How to use segmented controls (a.k.a. button bars)

▶ Ways of inputting Boolean values via switches

▶ How to include web content within your application

▶ The use of scrolling views to overcome screen limitations

After the last few lessons, you now have a good understanding of the basic iOS interface elements, but we've only just scratched the surface. There are additional user input features to help a user quickly choose between several predefined options. After all, there's no point in typing when a touch is enough. This hour's lesson picks up where the last left off, providing you with hands-on experience with a new set of user input options that go beyond fields, buttons, and sliders.

In addition, we look at two new views you can use to present data to the user: web and scrolling views. These features make it possible to create applications that can extend beyond the hardware boundaries of your device's screen and include content from remote web servers.

User Input and Output (Continued)

When I set out to write this book, I originally dedicated a couple of hours to the iOS interface *widgets* (fields, buttons, and so on). After we got started, however, it became apparent that for learning to develop on iOS, the interface was not something to gloss over. The interface options are what makes the device so enjoyable to use and what gives you, the developer, a truly rich canvas to work with. You'll still need to come up with ideas for what your application will do, but the interface can be the deciding factor in whether your vision "clicks" with its intended audience.

In the past two hours, you learned about fields, sliders, steppers, labels, and images as input and output options. In this lesson, you explore two new input options for handling discrete values, along with two new view types that extend the information you can display to web pages and beyond.

Switches

In most traditional desktop applications, the choice between something being *active* or *inactive* is made by checking or unchecking a check box or by choosing between radio buttons. In iOS, Apple has chosen to abandon these options in favor of switches and segmented controls. Switches (`UISwitch`) present a simple on/off UI element that resembles a traditional physical toggle switch, as shown in Figure 9.1. Switches have few configurable options and should be used for handling Boolean values.

FIGURE 9.1
Use switches to provide on/off input options to your user.

NOTE

Check boxes and radio buttons, although not part of the iOS UI Library, can be created with the `UIButton` class using the button states and custom button images. Apple provides the flexibility to customize to your heart's content—but sticking with what a user expects to see on an iDevice screen is recommended.

To work with the switch, we'll make use of its `Value Changed` event to detect a toggle of the switch and then read its current value via the on property or the `isOn` instance method.

The value returned when checking a switch is a Boolean, meaning that we can compare it to TRUE or FALSE (or YES/NO) to determine its state, or evaluate the result directly in a conditional statement.

For example, to check whether a switch `mySwitch` is turned on, we can use code similar to this:

```
if ([mySwitch isOn]) { <switch is on> } else { <switch is off> }
```

Segmented Controls

When user input needs to extend beyond just a Boolean value, you can use a segmented control (`UISegmentedControl`). Segmented controls present a linear line of buttons (sometimes referred to as a *button bar*), within which a single button can be active within the bar, as shown in Figure 9.2.

FIGURE 9.2
Segmented controls combine multiple buttons into a single control.

Segmented controls, when used according to Apple's guidelines, result in a change in what the user is seeing onscreen. They are often used to choose between categories of information or to switch between the display of application screens, such as configuration and results screens. For just choosing from a list of values where no immediate visual change takes place, the Picker object should be used instead. We look at this feature in Hour 12, "Making Choices with Toolbars and Pickers."

NOTE
Apple recommends using segmented controls to update the information visible in a view. If the change, however, means altering *everything* onscreen, you are probably better off switching between multiple independent views using a toolbar or tab bar. We start looking at the multiview approach in Hour 11, "Implementing Multiple Scenes and Popovers."

Handling interactions with a segmented control is very similar to the toggle switch. We'll watch for the `Value Changed` event and determine the currently selected button through the `selectedSegmentIndex`, which returns the number of the button chosen (starting with 0, from left to right).

We can combine the index with the object's instance method `titleForSegmentAtIndex` to work directly with the titles assigned to each segment. To retrieve the name of the currently selected button in a segmented control called `mySegment`, we could use the code fragment:

```
[mySegment titleForSegmentAtIndex: mySegment.selectedSegmentIndex]
```

We use this technique later in the lesson.

Web Views

In the previous applications that you've built, you've used the typical iOS view: an instance of `UIView` to hold your controls, content, and images. This is the view you will use most often in your apps, but it isn't the only view supported in iOS. A web view, or `UIWebView`, provides advanced features that open up a whole new range of possibilities in your apps.

TIP
In Hour 7, "Working with Text, Keyboards, and Buttons," you used another view type, `UITextView`, which provides basic text input and output, and which straddles the line between an input mechanism and what we'll typically refer to as a *view*.

Think of a web view as a borderless Safari window that you can add to your applications and control programmatically. You can present HTML, load web pages, and offer pinching and zooming gestures all "for free" using this class.

Supported Content Types

Web views can also be used to display a wide range of files, without needing to know anything about the file formats:

▶ HTML, images, and CSS

▶ Word documents (.doc/.docx)

▶ Excel spreadsheets (.xls/.xlsx)

▶ Keynote presentations (.key.zip)

▶ Numbers spreadsheets (.numbers.zip)

▶ Pages documents (.pages.zip)

▶ PDF files (.pdf)

▶ PowerPoint presentations (.ppt/.pptx)

You can add these files as resources to your project and display them within a web view, access them on remote servers, or read them from an iDevice's file storage (which you learn about in Hour 15, "Reading and Writing Application Data").

Loading Remote Content with `NSURL`, `NSURLRequest`, and `requestWithURL`

Web views implement a method called `requestWithURL` that you can use to load an arbitrary URL, but, unfortunately, you can't just pass it a string and expect it to work.

To load content into a web view, you'll often use `NSURL` and `NSURLRequest`. These two classes provide the ability to manipulate URLs and prepare them to be used as a request for a remote resource. You first create an instance of an `NSURL` object, most often from a string. For example, to create an `NSURL` that stores the address for Apple, you could use the following:

```
NSURL *appleURL;
appleURL=[[NSURL alloc] initWithString:@"http://www.apple.com/"];
```

Once the NSURL object is created, you need to create an NSURLRequest object that can be passed to a web view and loaded. To return an NSURLRequest from an NSURL object, we can use the NSURLRequest class method requestWithURL that, given an NSURL, returns the corresponding request object:

```
[NSURLRequest requestWithURL: appleURL]
```

Finally, this value is passed to the requestWithURL method of the web view, which then takes over and handles loading the process. Putting all the pieces together, loading Apple's website into a web view called appleView looks like this:

```
NSURL *appleURL;
appleURL=[[NSURL alloc] initWithString:@"http://www.apple.com/"];
[appleView loadRequest:[NSURLRequest requestWithURL: appleURL]];
```

We implement web views in this hour's first project, so you'll soon have a chance to put this to use.

TIP

Another way that you get content into your application is by loading HTML directly into a web view. For example, if you generate HTML content in a string called myHTML, you can use the loadHTMLString:baseURL method of a web view to load the HTML content and display it. Assuming a web view called htmlView, this might be written as follows:

```
[htmlView loadHTMLString:myHTML baseURL:nil]
```

Scrolling Views

You've certainly used applications that display more information than what fits on a single screen; in these cases, what happens? Chances are, the application allows you to scroll to access additional content. Often, this is managed through a scrolling view, or UIScrollView. Scrolling views, as their name suggests, provide scrolling features and can display more than a single screen's worth of information.

Unfortunately, Apple has gone about halfway toward making scrolling views something that you can add to your projects using the Interface Builder (IB) tools. You can add the view, but until you add a line of code to your application, it won't scroll. We close out this hour's lesson with a quick example (a *single line* of code) that enables UIScrollView instances that you add in IB to scroll your content.

Using Switches, Segmented Controls, and Web Views

As you've probably noticed by now, we prefer to work on examples that *do* something. It's one thing to show a few lines of code in a chapter and say "this will do <blah>," but it's another to take a collection of features and combine them in a way that results in a working application. In some cases, the former approach is unavoidable, but this isn't one of them. Our first hands-on example makes use of web views, a segmented control, and a toggle switch.

Implementation Overview

In this project, we create an application that displays flower photographs and flower information from the website FloraPhotographs.com. The application enables a user to touch a flower color within a segmented control (`UISegmentedControl`), resulting in a flower of that color being fetched and displayed from the FloraPhotographs site in a web view (`UIWebView`). The user can then use a toggle switch (`UISwitch`) to show and hide a second web view that contains details about the flower being displayed. Finally, a standard button (`UIButton`) enables the user to fetch another flower photo of the currently selected color from the site. The result should look very much like Figure 9.3.

FIGURE 9.3
The finished application will make use of a segmented control, a switch, and two web views.

Setting Up the Project

This project will, once again, use the Single View Application template we're starting to love. If it isn't already running, launch Xcode and then create a new project using the same settings as in the previous hours. This project should be called **FlowerWeb**.

You should now be accustomed to what happens next. Xcode sets up the project and creates the default view in MainStoryboard.storyboard and a view controller class named ViewController. We'll start as we always do: planning the variables, properties, outlets, and actions we need in the view controller.

Planning the Properties and Connections

To create the web-based image viewer, we need three outlets and two actions. The segmented control will be connecting to an outlet called colorChoice because we'll use it to choose which color is displayed. The web view that contains the flower will be connected to flowerView, and the associated details web view to flowerDetailView.

For the actions, the application must do two things: get and display a flower image, which we'll define as the action method getFlower; and toggle the flower details on and off, something we'll handle with a toggleFlowerDetail action.

WHY DON'T WE NEED AN OUTLET FOR THE SWITCH?

We don't need to include an outlet for the switch because we are connecting its Value Changed event to the toggleFlowerDetail method. When the method is called, the sender parameter sent to the method references the switch, so we can just use sender to determine whether the switch is on or off.

If we have more than one control using toggleFlowerDetail, it is helpful to define outlets to differentiate between them; in this case, however, sender suffices. This is our first use of sender, so pay attention. It can help save you the trouble of creating instance variables/properties in cases such as this.

Designing the Interface

By now, this process should seem a bit familiar. We've defined the outlets and actions, so it's time to build the user interface (UI). Prepare your Xcode workspace for developing the UI: Choose the MainStoryboard.storyboard file to open the IB editor, and then close the project navigator, if necessary, to make room on your display. We begin by adding the segmented control.

Adding a Segmented Control

To add a segmented control to the user interface, open the Object Library (View, Utilities, Object Library), find the segmented control (UISegmentedControl) object, and drag it into the view.

Position the control near the top of the view in the center. Because this control is ultimately used to choose colors, click and drag a label (UILabel) into the view, as well, position it above the segmented control, and change it to read **Choose a Flower Color:**. Your view should now resemble Figure 9.4.

FIGURE 9.4
The default segmented control has two buttons: First and Second.

By default, the segmented control has two segments, titled First and Second. You can double-click these titles and edit them directly in the view, but that doesn't quite get us what we need.

For this project, we need a control that has four segments, each labeled with a color: **Red**, **Blue**, **Yellow**, and **Green**. These are the colors that we can request from the FloraPhotographs website for displaying. Obviously, we need to add a few more segments to the control before all the choices can be represented.

Adding and Configuring Segments

The number of segments displayed in the segmented control is configurable in the Attributes Inspector for the object. Select the control that you've added to the view, and then press Option-Command-4 to open the Attributes Inspector, shown in Figure 9.5.

FIGURE 9.5
Use the Attributes Inspector for the segmented control to increase the number of segments displayed.

Using the Segments field, increase the number from 2 to 4. You should immediately see the new segments displayed. Notice that directly below where you set the number of segments in the inspector is a drop-down with entries for each segment you've added. You can choose a segment in this drop-down and then specify its title in the Title field. You can even add image resources and have them displayed within each segment.

NOTE
Note that the first segment is segment 0, the next is segment 1, and so on. It's important to keep this in mind when you're checking to see which segment is selected. The first segment is *not* segment 1, as you might assume.

Update the four segments in the control so that the colors Red, Blue, Yellow, and Green are represented.

NOTE
iPad developers who want to take advantage of their extended screen space might try adding a few more segments to the segmented control. The colors violet and magenta can be added and will be automatically recognized by the FloraPhotographs site.

Choosing a Segment Control Appearance

In addition to the usual color options and controls available in Attributes Inspector, there are four variations of how the segmented control can be presented. Use the Style drop-down menu (shown in Figure 9.5) to choose between Plain, Bordered, and Bar. Figure 9.6 shows each of these.

For this project, you can choose whichever you'd like. (I used the Plain style.) The segmented control should now have titles for all the colors and a corresponding label to help the user understand its purpose.

FIGURE 9.6
You can choose between three different presentation styles for your segmented control.

Sizing the Control

Chances are, the control you've set up doesn't quite look right in the view. To size the control to aesthetically pleasing dimensions, use the selection handles on the sides of the control to stretch and shrink it appropriately. You can even optimize the size of individual segments by setting them to a fixed width using the Segmented Control Size options in the Size Inspector (Option-Command-5), as shown in Figure 9.7.

FIGURE 9.7
You can use the Size Inspector to size each segment individually, if desired.

Adding a Switch

The next UI element we'll add is the switch (`UISwitch`). In our application, the switch has one role: to toggle a web view that displays details about the flower (`flowerDetailView`) on and off. Add the switch to the view by dragging the switch object from the Library into the view. Position it along the right side of the screen, just under the segmented control.

As with the segmented control, providing some basic user instruction through an onscreen label can be helpful. Drag a label (`UILabel`) into the view and position it to the left of the switch. Change the text to read **Show Photo Details:**. Your view should now resemble Figure 9.8, but your switch will likely show up as *on*.

FIGURE 9.8
Add a switch to toggle flower details on and off.

Setting the Default State

I know you're getting used to many of the different configuration options for the controls we use, but in this case, the switch has only two options: whether the default state is on or off, and what custom tint (if any) should be applied in the on state.

The switch that you added to the view is set to on. We want to change it so that it is off by default. To change the default state, select the object and open the Attributes Inspector (Option-Command-4). Using the State pop-up menu (see Figure 9.8), change the default state to off.

Adding the Web Views

The application that we're building relies on two different web views. One displays the flower image itself; the other view (which can be toggled on and off) shows details about the image. The details view will be overlaid on top of the image itself, so let's start by adding the main view, flowerView.

To add a web view (UIWebView) to your application, locate it in the Object Library and drag it into your view. The web view will display a resizable rectangle that you can drag and position anywhere you want. Because this is the view that the flower image is shown in, position it to fall about halfway down the screen, and then resize it so that it is the same width as the device screen and so that it covers the lower portion of the view entirely.

Repeat this to add a second web view for the flower details (flowerDetailView). This time, size the view so that it is about half an inch high and locate it at the very bottom of the screen, over top of the flower view, as shown in Figure 9.9. Remember that you can drag items in the document outline to change their ordering. The closer an element is to the top of the list, the further "back" it is.

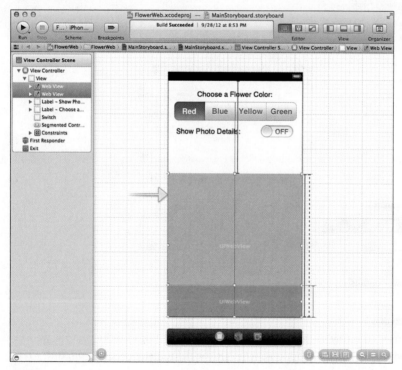

FIGURE 9.9
Add two web views (UIWebView) to your screen, and then position them as shown here.

Setting the Web View Attributes

Web views, surprisingly, have few attributes that you can configure, but what is available can be very important. To access the web view attributes, select one of the views you added, and then press Open-Command-4 to open the Attributes Inspector (see Figure 9.10).

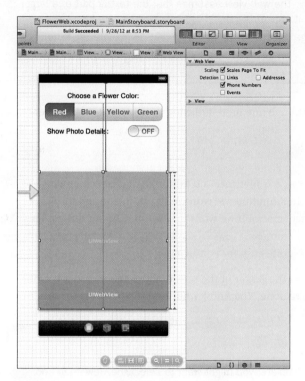

FIGURE 9.10
Configure how the web view will behave.

You can select from two types of options: Scaling and Detection (Phone Numbers, Addresses, Events, Links). If you select Scales Page to Fit under Scaling, large pages are scaled to fit in the size of the area you've defined. If you use Detection options, the iOS data detectors go to work and underline items that it has decided are phone numbers, addresses, dates, or additional web links.

For the main flower view, we absolutely want the images to be scaled to fit within the view. Select the web view, and then use the Attributes Inspector to choose the Scales Page to Fit option.

For the second view, we do *not* want this to be set, so select the web view where the application will be showing the flower details and use the Attributes Inspector to ensure that no scaling takes place. You might also want to change the view attributes for the detail view to have an alpha value of around 0.65. This creates a nice translucency effect when the details are displayed on top of the photograph.

CAUTION

Understand the Effects of Scaling

Scaling doesn't necessarily do what you might expect for "small" web pages. If you display a page with only the text `Hello World` on it in a scaled web view, you might expect the text to be shown to fill the web view. Instead, the text will be *tiny*. The web view assumes that the text is part of a larger page and scales it down rather than making it appear bigger.

If you happen to have control of the web page itself, you can add a `"viewport"` meta tag to tell Safari how wide (in pixels) the full page is:

```
<meta name="viewport" content="width=320"/>
```

With the tough stuff out of the way, we just have one more finishing touch to put on the interface, and then we're ready to code.

Finishing the Interface

The only functional piece that is missing from our interface is a button (`UIButton`) that we can use to manually trigger the `getFlower` method anytime we want. Without the button, we have to switch between colors using the segmented control if we want to see a new flower image. This button does nothing more than trigger an action (`getFlower`), something you've done repeatedly in the past few hours, so this should be quite easy for you by now.

Drag a button into the view, positioning it in the center of the screen above the web views. Edit the button title to read Get New Photo. We're done. You know what that means: time to wire the interface to the code.

TIP

Although your interface may be functionally complete, you might want to select the view itself and set a background color. Keep your interfaces clean and friendly.

Creating and Connecting the Outlets and Actions

We have quite a few interface elements to connect for this project. Our segmented control, switch, button, and web views all need the proper connections to the view controller. Here's what we'll use.

Starting with the outlets:

▶ **Segmented control for choosing colors** (`UISegmentedControl`): `colorChoice`

▶ **Main flower web view** (`UIWebView`): `flowerView`

▶ **Flower detail web view** (`UIWebView`): `flowerDetailView`

And the actions:

▶ **Fetch a new flower using the Get New Flower button:** `getFlower`

▶ **Turn the flower detail view on and off with the `UISwitch`:** `toggleFlowerDetail`

Okay, the same old story: Prepare your workspace by making sure the MainStoryboard.story-board file is selected and then opening the assistant editor. Hide the project navigator and document outline if you need space.

I assume you're getting pretty familiar with this process, so we'll move quickly through the connections here and in later hours. After all, it's just click, drag, and connect.

Adding the Outlets

Begin by Control-dragging from the segmented color button control to the line following the `@interface` directive in the ViewController.h file. When prompted, configure the connection as an outlet and its name as `colorChoice`, leaving the other values set to the defaults. This gives us an easy way to get the currently selected color in our code.

Continue building the rest of the outlets, connecting the main (large) web view to the outlet `flowerView` by Control-dragging to just below the `@property` line in ViewController.h. Finish the outlets by connecting the second web view to `flowerDetailView` with the same approach, as shown in Figure 9.11.

Adding the Actions

Our UI triggers two action methods. The switch hides and shows details about the flower through the method `toggleFlowerDetail`, and the standard button loads a new image for us with `getFlower`. Straightforward, right? It is, but sometimes you need to think beyond the obvious actions users can take and consider what they will *expect* to happen when they use the interface.

In this application, users are presented with a simple interface. They should immediately recognize that they can choose a color and push a button to get a flower of that color. But shouldn't the application be smart enough to load a new flower as soon as the user switches the color? Why should the user have to switch the color and then press another button? By connecting the `UISegmentedControl`'s `Value Changed` event to the same `getFlower` method we trigger from the button, we gain this functionality without writing a single additional line of code.

Start by connecting the switch (`UISwitch`) to a new action named `toggleFlowerDetail` by Control-dragging to just below the `@property` declarations in ViewController.h. Make sure that the action is triggered from the event `Value Changed`, as shown in Figure 9.12.

FIGURE 9.11
Connect the web views to appropriately named outlets.

FIGURE 9.12
Connect the switch using the `Value Changed` event.

Next, Control-drag from the button (UIButton) to a line under the IBAction you just defined. When prompted, configure a new action, getFlower, that is triggered from the Touch Up Inside event. Finally, we need to target this new getFlower action from the Value Changed event on the segmented control (UISegmentedControl) so that the user can load a new flower just by touching a color.

Switch to the standard editor and make sure the document outline is visible (Editor, Show Document Outline). Select the segmented control, and open the Connections Inspector by pressing Option-Command-6 (View, Utilities, Connections Inspector). Drag from the circle beside Value Changed to the View Controller line in the document outline, as demonstrated in Figure 9.13. Release your mouse button and choose getFlower when prompted.

FIGURE 9.13
Connect the Value Changed event of the segmented control to the getFlower method.

NOTE

Okay, I admit it. In this example, we took a roundabout way of connecting the segmented control to the getFlower method. We could have also Control-dragged from the segmented control onto the getFlower IBAction line in the assistant editor and instantly had our connection.

The problem with the "easy" approach, however, is that you aren't given the opportunity of choosing which event triggers the action. It just so happens that in this case, Xcode would choose `Value Changed` for you.

The interface and its connections are finished. Your ViewController.h interface file should resemble Listing 9.1. Time to implement the application logic.

LISTING 9.1 The Completed ViewController.h

```
#import <UIKit/UIKit.h>

@interface ViewController : UIViewController

@property (weak, nonatomic) IBOutlet UISegmentedControl *colorChoice;
@property (weak, nonatomic) IBOutlet UIWebView *flowerView;
@property (weak, nonatomic) IBOutlet UIWebView *flowerDetailView;

- (IBAction)toggleFlowerDetail:(id)sender;
- (IBAction)getFlower:(id)sender;

@end
```

Implementing the Application Logic

Our view controller needs to implement two pieces of functionality via two action methods. The first, `toggleFlowerDetail`, shows and hides the `flowerDetailView` web view, depending on whether the switch has been flipped on (show) or off (hide). The second method, `getFlower`, loads a flower image into the `flowerView` web view and details on that photograph into the `flowerDetailView` web view. We start with the easier of the two, `toggleFlowerDetail`.

Hiding and Showing the Detail Web View

A useful property of any object that inherits from `UIView` is that you can easily hide (or show) it within your iOS application interfaces. Because almost everything you see onscreen inherits from this class, this means you can hide and show labels, buttons, fields, images, and yes, other views. To hide an object, you just set its Boolean property hidden to TRUE or YES (both have the same meaning). So, to hide the `flowerDetailView`, we write the following:

```
self.flowerDetailView.hidden=YES;
```

To show it again, we just reverse the process, setting the hidden property to FALSE or NO:

```
self.flowerDetailView.hidden=NO;
```

To implement the logic for the `toggleFlowerDetail` method, we need to figure out what value the switch is currently set to. As mentioned earlier in the lesson, we can check the state of a toggle switch through the `isOn` method that returns a Boolean value of TRUE/YES if the switch is set to on or FALSE/NO if it is off.

Because we don't have an outlet specifically set aside for the switch, we'll use the sender variable to access it in our method. When the `toggleFlowerDetail` action method is called, this variable is set to reference the object that invoked the action (in other words, the switch). So, to check to see whether the switch is on, we can write the following:

```
If ([sender isOn]) { <switch is on> } else { <switch is off> }
```

Now, here's where we can get clever. (You are feeling clever, right?) We want to hide and show the `flowerDetailView` using a Boolean value and we *get* a Boolean value from the switch's `isOn` method. This maps to two conditions:

▶ When `[sender isOn]` is YES, the view should *not* be hidden (`flowerDetailView.hidden=NO`).

▶ When `[sender isOn]` is NO, the view *should* be hidden (`flowerDetailView.hidden=YES`).

In other words, the state of the switch is the exact opposite of what we need to assign to the hidden property of the view. In C (and therefore Objective-C), to get the opposite of a Boolean value, we just put an exclamation mark in front (`!`). So, all we need to do to hide or show `flowerDetailView` is to set the hidden property to `![sender isOn]`. That's it. *A single line of code.*

Implement `toggleFlowerDetail` in the `FlowerWeb` view controller stub that Xcode provided for you. The full method should look a lot like Listing 9.2.

LISTING 9.2   The `toggleFlowerDetail` Implementation

```
- (IBAction)toggleFlowerDetail:(id)sender {
    self.flowerDetailView.hidden=![sender isOn];
}
```

Loading and Displaying the Flower Image and Details

To fetch our flower images, we use a feature provided by the FloraPhotographs website specifically for this purpose. We follow four steps to interact with the website:

1. We get the chosen color from the segmented control.

2. We generate a random number called a "session ID" so that FloraPhotographs.com can track our request.

3. We request the URL http://www.floraphotographs.com/showrandomios.php?color=<color>
&session=<sessionID>, where <color> is the chosen color and <session ID> is the random
number. This URL returns a flower photo.

4. We request the URL http://www.floraphotographs.com/detailios.php?session=<sessionID>,
where <session ID> is the same random number. This URL returns the details for the previously requested flower photo.

Let's go ahead and see what this looks like in code and then discuss details behind the implementation. Add the getFlower implementation, as shown in Listing 9.3.

LISTING 9.3   Add the getFlower Implementation

```
 1: - (IBAction)getFlower:(id)sender {
 2:      NSURL *imageURL;
 3:      NSURL *detailURL;
 4:      NSString *imageURLString;
 5:      NSString *detailURLString;
 6:      NSString *color;
 7:      int sessionID;
 8:
 9:      color=[self.colorChoice titleForSegmentAtIndex:
10:           self.colorChoice.selectedSegmentIndex];
11:      sessionID=random()%50000;
12:
13:      imageURLString=[[NSString alloc] initWithFormat:
14:          @"http://www.floraphotographs.com/showrandomios.php?color=%@&session=%d"
15:                       ,color,sessionID];
16:      detailURLString=[[NSString alloc] initWithFormat:
17:                       @"http://www.floraphotographs.com/detailios.php?session=%d"
18:                       ,sessionID];
19:
20:      imageURL=[[NSURL alloc] initWithString:imageURLString];
21:      detailURL=[[NSURL alloc] initWithString:detailURLString];
22:
23:      [self.flowerView loadRequest:[NSURLRequest requestWithURL:imageURL]];
24:      [self.flowerDetailView loadRequest:[NSURLRequest requestWithURL:detailURL]];
25:
26:      self.flowerDetailView.backgroundColor=[UIColor clearColor];
27: }
```

This is the most complicated code that you've written so far, but it's broken down into the individual pieces, so it's not difficult to understand.

Lines 2–7 declare the variables that we need to prepare our requests to the website. The first variables, `imageURL` and `detailURL`, are instances of `NSURL` that contain the URLs that are loaded into the `flowerView` and `flowerDetailView` web views. To create the `NSURL` objects, we need two strings, `imageURLString` and `detailURLString`, which we format with the special URLs that we presented earlier, including the `color` and `sessionID` values.

In lines 9–10, we retrieve the title of the selected segment in our instance of the segmented control: `colorChoice`. To do this, we use the object's instance method `titleForSegmentAtIndex` along with the object's `selectedSegmentIndex` property. The result, `[colorChoice titleForSegmentAtIndex: colorChoice.selectedSegmentIndex]`, is stored in the string `color` and is ready to be used in the web request.

Line 11 generates a random number between `0` and `49999` and stores it in the integer `sessionID`.

Lines 13–18 prepare `imageURLString` and `detailURLString` with the URLs that we will be requesting. The strings are allocated, and then the `initWithFormat` method is used to store the website address along with the color and session ID. The color and session ID are substituted into the string using the formatting placeholders `%@` and `%d` for strings and integers, respectively.

Lines 20–21 allocate and create the `imageURL` and `detailURL` `NSURL` objects using the `initWithString` class method and the two strings `imageURLString` and `detailURLString`.

Lines 23–24 use the `loadRequest` method of the `flowerView` and `flowerDetailView` web views to load the `NSURL`s `imageURL` and `detailURL`, respectively. When these lines are executed, the display updates the contents of the two views.

NOTE

Remember that, as mentioned earlier, `UIWebView`'s `loadRequest` method doesn't handle `NSURL` objects directly; it expects an `NSURLRequest` object instead. To work around this, we create and return `NSURLRequest` objects using the `NSURLRequest` class method `requestWithURL` and the `imageURL` and `detailURL` objects as parameters.

Line 26 is an extra nicety that we've thrown in. This sets the background of the `flowerDetailView` web view to a special color called `clearColor`. This, combined with the alpha channel value that you set earlier, gives the appearance of a nice translucent overlay of the details over the main image. You can comment out or remove this line to see the difference it creates.

TIP

To create web views that blend with the rest of your interface, you want to keep `clearColor` in mind. By setting this color, you can make the background of your web pages translucent, meaning that the content displayed on the page will overlay any other content that you've added to your view.

Fixing Up the Interface When the App Loads

Now that the `getFlower` method is implemented, you can run the application and everything should work—except that when the application starts, the two web views are empty and the detail view is visible, even though the toggle switch is set to off.

To fix this, we can start loading an image as soon as the app is up and running and set `flowerDetailView.hidden` to `YES`. To do this, update the view controller's `viewDidLoad` method as follows in Listing 9.4.

LISTING 9.4   Update the `viewDidLoad` Method to Set the Initial Display

```
- (void)viewDidLoad
{
    [super viewDidLoad];
    self.flowerDetailView.hidden=YES;
    [self getFlower:nil];
}
```

As expected, `self.flowerDetailView.hidden=YES` hides the detail view. Using `[self getFlower:nil]`, we can call the `getFlower` method from within our instance of the view control (referenced as `self`) and start the process of loading a flower in the web view. The method `getFlower` expects a parameter, so we pass it `nil`, just as we did in the last hour's lesson. (This value is never used in `getFlower`, so there is no problem with providing `nil`.)

Building the Application

Test out the final version of the FlowerWeb application by clicking Run in Xcode.

Notice that you can zoom in and out of the web view and use your fingers to scroll around. These are all features that you get without any implementation cost when using the `UIWebView` class.

Congratulations. Another app under your belt.

Using Scrolling Views

After working through the projects in the past few hours, iPhone users might begin to notice something: We're running out of space in our interfaces. Things are starting to get cluttered.

One possible solution, as you learned earlier in this hour, is to use the `hidden` property of UI objects to hide and show them in your applications. Unfortunately, when you're juggling a few dozen controls, this is pretty impractical. Another approach is to use multiple different views, something that you start learning about in Hour 11.

There is, however, a third way that we can fit more into a single view—by making it scroll. Using an instance of the UIScrollView class, you can add controls and interface elements out beyond the physical boundaries of your device's screen. Unfortunately, Apple provides access to this object in the IB editor but making it work is a bit less obvious than one might hope.

Before closing out this hour, I want to show you how to start using simple scrolling views in a mini-project.

Implementation Overview

When I say *simple*, I mean it. This project consists of a scroll view (UIScrollView) with content added in the IB editor that extends beyond the physical screen, as shown in Figure 9.14.

FIGURE 9.14
We're going to make a view. It will scroll.

To enable scrolling in the view, we need to set a property called contentSize, which describes how large the content is that needs to be scrolled. That's it.

Setting Up the Project

Begin by creating another Single View Application. Name the new project **Scroller**. For this example, we're going to be adding the scroll view (UIScrollView) as a subview to the existing view in MainStoryboard.storyboard. This is a perfectly acceptable approach, but as you get more experienced with the tools, you might want to just replace the default view entirely.

Planning the Property and Connections

We need to do just one thing programmatically in this project, and that's set a property on the scroll view object. To access the object, we must create an outlet for it, which we'll call **theScroller**.

Designing the Interface

There isn't much to this project, just a scrolling view and content. Because you already know how to find objects in the Object Library and add them to a view, this should be trivial. Start by opening the MainStoryboard.storyboard file for the project and making sure the document outline is visible (Editor, Show Document Outline).

Adding a Scroll View

Using the Object Library (View Utilities, Show Object Library), drag an instance of a scroll view (UIScrollView) into your view. Position the view to just about fill the scene using the guides on the sides and bottom to line it up. Place a label above it that reads **Scrolling View** (just in case you forget what we're building). Figure 9.15 shows what your scene should look like at this point.

FIGURE 9.15
Add a scrolling view and label to the scene.

TIP

The text view (`UITextView`) you used in Hour 7 is a specialized instance of a scrolling view. The same scrolling attributes that you can set for the text view can be applied for the scroll view, so you might want to refer to that earlier hour for more configuration possibilities. Or just press Option-Command-4 to bring up the Attributes Inspector and explore.

Now that your scroll view is added to your design, you need to populate it with something. Objects are often placed in scroll views by writing code that calculates their position—but how can we do that in such a small space?

Changing the View Controller Simulated Size

To start, we change the view controller and the default view for the view controller so that they are as large as we want. Begin by clicking the View Controller object in the document outline, and then open the Attributes Inspector (Option-Command-4). Use the Size drop-down menu to switch from Inferred to Freeform, as shown in Figure 9.16.

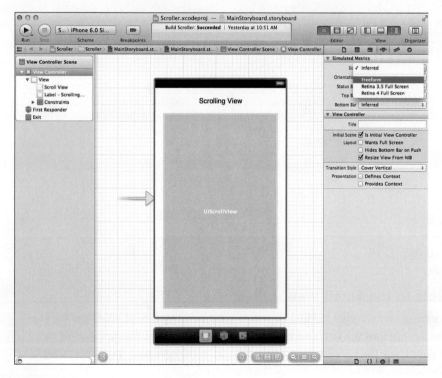

FIGURE 9.16
Switch to a freeform size for the view controller.

Now that the size for the view controller is set we need to enlarge the view so that we can lay-out the scrolling view with drag-and-drop convenience. Select the view object within the view controller, and then open the Size Inspector (Option-Command-5). Make a note of the current value of the Height field for the view (you'll need it again in a minute), and then set the value to roughly double what it is usually—that is, **1000** points for the iPhone and **2000** points for the iPad. As soon as you make the change, your scene should change to take up the expanded space, as seen in Figure 9.17.

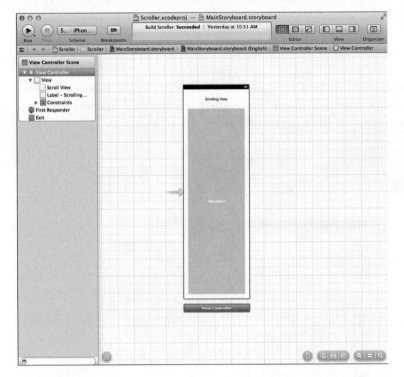

FIGURE 9.17
Set the new size for the view.

Adding Objects to the Scroll View

Now that your scene is much larger, adding objects to your scrolling view should be straight-forward. First, make sure that the scrolling view expanded when you set the new size for the main view. If it didn't, use the selection handles to resize it to fill your new space, snapping it to the guides on the bottom and left/right sizes of the main view.

Add several labels (or any other GUI object) to your scrolling view, spacing them evenly from the top to the bottom. For my sample project, I'm adding six labels: **Label 1**, **Label 2**, ... **Label 6**. Figure 9.18 shows my final layout for the iPhone.

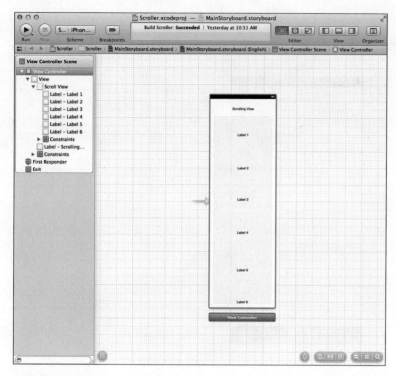

FIGURE 9.18
The final full scrolling view, created with labels for content.

Resetting the View Controller Simulated Size

As a finishing step for the interface, we need to get the view and the view controller back to normal. To do this, we need to set the height of the main view, and then reset the view controller size—the exact opposite of the actions we performed a few minutes ago.

Select the main view object within the scene and open the Size Inspector. Set the value to its original value—that is, **568** for the iPhone 5, **480** for earlier iPhones, and **1004** for the iPad. After making the change, your scene should shrink back down to a manageable size, and several of the labels should be hidden. If your scrolling view does resize correctly when you change the size of the main view, use the selection handles to resize it (or use the Size Inspector).

Finally, select the `View Controller` object in the document outline, open the Attributes Inspector, and set the size back to Inferred. Now you should have a view, with labels (several hidden), in a "normal"-sized scene, as shown in Figure 9.19.

FIGURE 9.19
The final appearance of the scene in Interface Builder.

Now that your interface is finished, its time to get to coding. Don't worry, you'll be done before you even know you've started!

TIP

Another way to get labels into a scrolling view is to lay them out in your main view however you'd like, select them, and then choose Editor, Embed In, Scroll View from the menu bar. This adds a scrolling view to your interface that contains all the selected objects.

Creating and Connecting the Outlets and Actions

This project needs only a single outlet and no actions. To create the outlet, switch to the assistant editor and disable the project navigator if you need to make a bit of extra room. Control-drag from the scroll view to just below the @interface line in the ViewController.h file.

When prompted, create a new outlet called theScroller, as shown in Figure 9.20.

FIGURE 9.20
Create the connection to the `theScroller` outlet.

That finishes up our work in the IB editor; just a teensy bit of implementation remains. Switch back to the standard editor, enable the project navigator, and then select the ViewController.m file to finish the implementation.

Implementing the Application Logic

For fun, try to run the application as it stands. It compiles and launches, but it doesn't scroll. In fact, it behaves just like we expect a typical *nonscrolling* view to behave. The reason for this is because we need to tell it the horizontal and vertical sizes of the region it is going to scroll. Until the scrolling view knows that it *can* scroll, it doesn't.

Adding Scrolling Behavior

To add scrolling to our scroll view, we need to set the `contentSize` attribute to a `CGSize` value. `CGSize` is just a simple C data structure that contains a height and a width, and we can easily make one using the `CGSizeMake(<width>,<height>)` function.

For example, to tell our scroll view (`theScroller`) that it can scroll up to 280 points horizontally and 1000 points vertically, we could enter the following:

```
self.theScroller.contentSize=CGSizeMake(280.0,1000.0);
```

Guess what? That isn't just what we *could* do, it's what we *will* do. If you're developing on the iPhone, edit the ScrollerViewController.m file and add the method `viewDidAppear` shown in Listing 9.5.

LISTING 9.5   Enabling Scrolling in Your Scroll View

```
- (void)viewDidAppear:(BOOL)animated {
    [super viewDidAppear:animated];
    self.theScroller.contentSize=CGSizeMake(280.0,1000.0);
}
```

If you are working on the iPad, you need to adjust the size to be a bit larger because the screen is larger. Provide the arguments `900.0` and `2000.0` to the `CGSizeMake` function, instead of `280.0` and `1000.0`.

The `viewDidAppear` method is a standard view controller method that executes as soon as iOS has laid out a scene on the screen. When you implement it, you must pass the `viewDidAppear` message to the parent object (`super`); so the first line should be included in *any* implementation. The second line sets the `contentSize` and enables the scrolling.

Where Did You Get the Width and Height Values?

The width we used in this example is the width of the scroll view itself (at least the width of mine). Why? Because we don't have any reason to scroll horizontally. The height is just the vertical size of the view where we laid out the scrolling view. In other words, these change depending on the size that the scrolling view must be to fit all your content. Use whatever works best for your application.

Building the Application

The moment of truth has arrived. Does the single line of code make magic? Choose Run from the Xcode toolbar, and then try scrolling around the view you created. Everything should work like a charm.

TIP

Okay, so it's not *technically* a single line of code for the entire implementation, but it is a single line that makes the scrolling view work.

Yes, this was a quick-and-dirty project, but there seems to be a lack of information on getting started with `UIScrollView`, and I thought it was important to run through a short tutorial. I hope this gives you new ideas about what you can do to create more feature-rich iOS interfaces.

Further Exploration

As well as useful, the segmented control (`UISegmentedControl`) and switch (`UISwitch`) classes are pretty easy to get the hang of. The best place to focus your attention for additional exploration is on the feature set provided by the `UIWebView` and `UIScrollView` classes.

As described at the start of this hour, `UIWebView` can handle a large variety of content beyond what might be inferred by the "web" portion of its name. By learning more about `NSURL`, such as the `initFileURLWithPath:isDirectory` method, you'll be able to load files directly from your project resources. You can also take advantage of the web view's built-in actions, such as `goForward` and `goBack`, to add navigation functionality without a single line of code. One might even use a collection of HTML files to create a self-contained website within an application. In short, web views extend the traditional interface of your applications by bringing in HTML markup, JavaScript, and CSS—creating a potent combination.

The `UIScrollView` class, on the other hand, gives us an important capability that is widely used in iOS applications: touch scrolling. We briefly demonstrated this at the end of the hour, but there are additional features, such as pinching and zooming, that can be enabled by implementing the `UIScrollViewDelegate` protocol. We take our first look at building a class that conforms to a protocol in the next hour, so keep this in mind as you get more comfortable with the concepts.

Apple Tutorials

Segmented Controls, Switches, and Web Views—`UICatalog` (accessible via the Xcode developer documentation): Mentioned in Hour 8, "Handling Images, Animation, Sliders, and Steppers," `UICatalog` shows nearly all the iOS interface concepts in clearly defined examples.

Scrolling—`ScrollViewSuite` (accessible via the Xcode developer documentation): The `ScrollViewSuite` provides examples of just about everything you could ever want to do in a scroll view.

Summary

In this hour, you learned how to use two controls that enable applications to respond to user input beyond just a simple button press or a text field. The switch and segmented control, while limited in the options they can present, give a user a touch-friendly way of making decisions within your applications.

You also explored how to use web views to bring web content directly into your projects and how to tweak it so that it integrates into the overall iOS user experience. This powerful class will quickly become one of your most trusted tools for displaying content.

Because we've reached a point in our development where things are starting to get a bit cramped, we closed out the hour with a quick introduction to the scroll view. You learned how, despite appearances, scroll views can be easily added to apps.

Q&A

Q. Why did objects jump around when I resized the freeform view in IB?

A. If your labels or scrolling view moved around a bit, you're seeing the results of the new Auto Layout constraints system. You'll learn more about this important tool in Hour 16, "Building Rotatable and Responsive User Interfaces," but for now, don't worry too much if things don't look exactly the way you want in your layouts.

Q. You mentioned the `UIWebView` includes actions. What does that mean, and how do I use them?

A. This means that the object you drag into your view is already capable of responding to actions (such as navigation actions) on its own—no code required. To use these, you connect from the UI event that should trigger the action to your instance of the web view and then choose the appropriate action from the pop-up window that appears.

Workshop

Quiz

1. What properties need to be set before a scroll view (`UIScrollView`) will scroll?

2. How do you get the opposite of a Boolean value?

3. What type of object does a web view expect as a parameter when loading a remote URL?

Answers

1. The `contentSize` property must be set for a scroll view before it will allow scrolling.

2. To negate a Boolean value, just prefix it with an exclamation point. `!TRUE`, for example, is the same as `FALSE`.

3. You typically use an `NSURLRequest` object to initiate a web request within a web view.

Activities

1. Create your own "mini" web browser by combining a text field, buttons, and a segmented control with a web view. Use the text field for URL entry, buttons for navigation, and hard-code some shortcuts for your favorite sites into the segmented control. To make the best use of space, you may want to overlay the controls on the web view and then add a switch that hides or shows the controls when toggled.

2. Practice laying out a user interface within a scrollable view. Use graph paper to sketch the view and determine coordinates before laying it out in Interface Builder.

Getting the User's Attention

What You'll Learn in This Hour:

▶ Different types of user notifications
▶ How to create alert views
▶ Methods for collecting input from alerts
▶ How to use action sheets to present options
▶ How to implement short sounds and vibrations

iOS presents developers with many opportunities for creating unique user interfaces, but certain elements must be consistent across all applications. When users need to be notified of an application event or make a critical decision, it is important to present them with interface elements that immediately make sense. In this hour, we look at several different ways an application can notify a user that *something* has happened. It's up to you to determine what that something is, but these are the tools you need to keep users of your apps "in the know."

Alerting the User

Applications on iOS are user centered, which means they typically don't perform utility functions in the background or operate without an interface. They enable users to work with data, play games, communicate, or carry out dozens of other activities. Despite the variation in activities, when an application needs to show a warning, provide feedback, or ask the user to make a decision, it does so in a common way. Cocoa Touch leverages a variety of objects and methods to gain your attention, including `UIAlertView`, `UIActionSheet`, and System Sound Services. Unlike many of the other objects we've worked with, these require us to build them in code; so don't start digging through the Interface Builder (IB) Object Library just yet.

NOTE

Did you notice that I said applications *typically* don't operate in the background? That's because, with iOS 4 or later, some do. Applications running in the background have a unique set of capabilities, including additional types of alerts and notifications. You learn more about these in Hour 22, "Building Background-Aware Applications."

Alert Views

Sometimes users need to be informed of changes when an application is running. More than just a change in the current view is required when an internal error event occurs (such as low-memory condition or a dropped network connection), for example, or upon completion of a long-running activity. Enter the `UIAlertView` class.

The `UIAlertView` class creates a simple modal alert window that presents a user with a message and a few option buttons, and an optional plain or secure text entry field (or both), as shown in Figure 10.1.

FIGURE 10.1
A typical alert view.

What *Modal* Means

Modal user interface (UI) elements require the user to interact with them (usually, to push a button) before the user can do anything else. They are typically layered on top of other windows and block all other interface actions while visible.

Implementing an alert view takes little effort: You declare a `UIAlertView` object, initialize it, and show it. Consider the code fragment in Listing 10.1.

LISTING 10.1   A `UIAlertView` Implementation

```
1:    UIAlertView *alertDialog;
2:    alertDialog = [[UIAlertView alloc]
3:                   initWithTitle: @"Email Address"
4:                   message:@"Please enter your email address:"
5:                   delegate: self
6:                   cancelButtonTitle: @"Ok"
7:                   otherButtonTitles: @"Super",nil];
8:    alertDialog.alertViewStyle=UIAlertViewStylePlainTextInput;
9:    [alertDialog show];
```

In line 1, I declare a variable `alertDialog` to hold an instance of `UIAlertView`.

Lines 2–7 allocate and initialize the alert view. As you can see, the convenient initialization method of the alert view does almost all the work for us. Let's review the parameters:

▶ `initWithTitle`: Initializes the view and sets the title that will appear at the top of the alert dialog box.

▶ `message`: Sets the string that will appear in the content area of the dialog box.

▶ `delegate`: Contains the object that will serve as the delegate to the alert (that is, respond to the alert). If you don't need any actions to be performed after the user dismisses the alert, you can set this to `nil`.

▶ `cancelButtonTitle`: Sets the string shown in the default button for the alert.

▶ `otherButtonTitles`: Adds an additional button to the alert. This always ends in `nil`.

Line 8 sets the `alertViewStyle` property. This property, if present, is used to configure whether the alert view contains any text entry fields. You have four possible style choices as of iOS 6:

▶ `UIAlertViewStyleDefault`: The default if no style is provided. No input fields shown.

▶ `UIAlertViewStyleSecureTextInput`: A single secure (password) input field is added.

▶ `UIAlertViewStylePlainTextInput`: A single plain-text input field is added.

▶ `UIAlertViewStyleLoginAndPasswordInput`: Both a plain-text and secure field are shown.

Finally, in line 9, the alert is displayed to the user. Now, suppose that we want to respond to the user's button choice or text entry. To do that, we need to declare that the class that responds to the alert view conforms to the `UIAlertViewDelegate` protocol.

Responding to an Alert View

When I first started using Objective-C, I found the terminology painful. It seemed that no matter how easy a concept was to understand, it was surrounded with language that made it appear harder than it was. A protocol, in my opinion, is one of these things.

Protocols define a collection of methods that perform a task. To provide advanced functionality, some classes, such as UIAlertView, require you to implement methods defined in a related protocol; doing this is called *conforming* to the protocol. Some protocol methods are required and others are optional; it just depends on the features you need.

To identify the button that was pressed in a multi-option alert or read from a text entry field, the class that is responding to the alert (typically just a view controller) should conform to the UIAlertViewDelegate protocol and implement the alertView:clickedButtonAtIndex method.

To declare that a class, such as a view controller, will be conforming to the UIAlertViewDelegate protocol, you just modify the class's @interface line as follows:

```
@interface ViewController : UIViewController <UIAlertViewDelegate>
```

Next, you must set the delegate of the UIAlertView (see line 5 in Listing 10.1) to the object implementing the protocol. If this is the same object that is creating the alert, you can just use self, as follows:

```
delegate:self
```

Finally, the alertView:clickedButtonAtIndex method is implemented to handle the response. This method receives the index of the button that was pushed in the alert view. To make life easier, we can take advantage of the UIAlertView instance method buttonTitleAtIndex. This method returns the string title of a button from its index, eliminating the need to keep track of which index value corresponds to which button.

If the alert view is displaying text fields, we can access the fields in a very similar way to determining which button was pressed—through the alert view's textFieldAtIndex method. Index 0 is the first field, and index 1 is the second.

A partial implementation of alertView:clickedButtonAtIndex that handles an alert view with multiple buttons and text fields is provided in Listing 10.2.

LISTING 10.2 Responding to an Alert View

```
1: - (void)alertView:(UIAlertView *)alertView
2:        clickedButtonAtIndex:(NSInteger)buttonIndex {
3:     NSString *buttonTitle=[alertView buttonTitleAtIndex:buttonIndex];
4:     NSString *fieldOne=[[alertView textFieldAtIndex:0] text];
5:     NSString *fieldTwo=[[alertView textFieldAtIndex:1] text];
6: }
```

Although this method doesn't actually do anything, it provides all the setup you need to respond to an alert view with multiple buttons and two text fields. Line 3 sets the `buttonTitle` variable to the button that was pressed, and lines 4–5 set `fieldOne` and `fieldTwo` to any text entered into the text fields that the alert displayed.

Action Sheets

Alert views are used to display messages that indicate a change in state or a condition within an application that a user should acknowledge. Sometimes, however, a user should be prompted to make a decision based on the result of an action. For example, if an application provides the option to share information with a friend, the user might be prompted for the method of sharing (such as sending an email, uploading a file, and so on). You can see this behavior when touching and holding an image in Safari, as shown in Figure 10.2. This interface element is called an *action sheet* and is an instance of `UIActionSheet`.

FIGURE 10.2
Action sheets ask you to choose between several options.

Action sheets are also used to confirm actions that are potentially destructive to data. In fact, they provide a separate bright-red button style to help draw a user's attention to potential deletion of data.

Implementing an action sheet is very (very) similar to an alert view. Initialize, configure, and display, as shown in Listing 10.3.

LISTING 10.3 A `UIActionSheet` Implementation

```
 1: - (IBAction)doActionSheet:(id)sender {
 2:     UIActionSheet *actionSheet;
 3:     actionSheet=[[UIActionSheet alloc] initWithTitle:@"Available Actions"
 4:                                        delegate:self
 5:                               cancelButtonTitle:@"Cancel"
 6:                          destructiveButtonTitle:@"Delete"
 7:                               otherButtonTitles:@"Keep",nil];
 8:     actionSheet.actionSheetStyle=UIActionSheetStyleBlackTranslucent;
 9:     [actionSheet showInView:self.view];
10: }
```

Lines 2–7 declare and instantiate an instance of `UIActionSheet` called `actionSheet`. Similar to the setup of an alert, the initialization convenience method takes care of nearly all the setup. The parameters are as follows:

▶ `initWithTitle`: Initializes the sheet with the specified title string.

▶ `delegate`: Contains the object that will serve as the delegate to the sheet. If this is set to `nil`, the sheet is displayed, but pressing a button will have no effect beyond dismissing the sheet.

▶ `cancelButtonTitle`: Set the string shown in the default button for the alert.

▶ `destructiveButtonTitle`: The title of the option that will result in information being lost. This button is presented in bright red (a sharp contrast to the rest of the choices). If set to `nil`, no destructive button appears.

▶ `otherButtonTitles`: Adds additional buttons to the sheet. This list always ends in `nil`.

Line 8 sets a visual appearance for the action sheet. You can choose from four possible styles:

▶ `UIActionSheetStyleAutomatic`: If a button bar appears at the bottom of the screen, it adapts to match the bar. Otherwise, it takes on the default appearance.

▶ `UIActionSheetStyleDefault`: The default iOS-determined action sheet appearance.

▶ `UIActionSheetStyleBlackTranslucent`: A dark, but semitransparent style.

▶ `UIActionSheetStyleBlackOpaque`: A dark, nontransparent style.

In line 9, the action sheet is displayed in the current view controller's view (`self.view`) using the `UIActionSheet showInView` method. In this example, the `showInView` method is used to animate the opening of the sheet from the current view controller's view. If you had an instance of a toolbar or a tab bar, you could use `showFromToolbar` or `showFromTabBar` to make the sheet appear to open from either of these user interface elements.

TIP
Action sheets are very similar to alerts in how they are initialized, modified, and ultimately, acted upon. However, unlike alerts, an action sheet can be associated with a given view, tab bar, or toolbar. When an action sheet appears onscreen, it is animated to show its relationship to one of these elements.

Responding to an Action Sheet

The similarities between alert views and action sheets continue with how we react to a button press. We'll follow almost the same steps as we did with an alert view.

First, the class that handles the action sheet response must conform to a new protocol: `UIActionSheetDelegate`. This only requires a simple change to the `@interface` line of the class's interface file:

```
@interface ViewController : UIViewController <UIActionSheetDelegate>
```

Next, the action sheet delegate property must be set to point to the class implementing the protocol (see line 4 of Listing 10.3). If the same class that is invoking the action sheet also handles the response, the delegate is `self`:

```
delegate:self
```

Finally, to capture the click event, we need to implement the `actionSheet:clickedButtonAtIndex` method. As with `alertView:clickedButtonAtIndex`, this method provides the button index that was pressed within the action sheet. We can also use, as we did with the alert view, a method `buttonTitleAtIndex` to grab the title of the button that was touched rather than having to deal with the buttons numerically.

Listing 10.4 provides a partial implementation of `actionSheet:clickedButtonAtIndex`.

LISTING 10.4   Responding to an Action Sheet

```
1: - (void)actionSheet:(UIActionSheet *)actionSheet
2:       clickedButtonAtIndex:(NSInteger)buttonIndex {
3:    NSString *buttonTitle=[actionSheet buttonTitleAtIndex:buttonIndex];
4: }
```

Typing out the method declaration actually takes more time than the entire implementation. Line 3 sets `buttonTitle` to the name of the button that was touched. From there, it's up to you to make it do something useful.

System Sound Services

Visual notifications are great for providing feedback to a user and getting critical input. Other senses, however, can prove just as useful for getting a user's attention. Sound, for example, plays an important role on nearly every computer system (regardless of platform or purpose). Sounds tell us when an error has occurred or an action has been completed. Sounds free a user's visual focus and still provide feedback about what an application is doing.

Vibrations take alerts one step further. When a device has the ability to vibrate, it can communicate with users even if they can't see or hear it. For the iPhone, vibration means that an app can notify users of events even when stowed in a pocket or resting on a nearby table. The best news of all? Both sounds and vibrations are handled through the same simple code, meaning that you can implement them relatively easily within your applications.

To enable sound playback and vibration, we take advantage of System Sound Services. System Sound Services provides an interface for playing back sounds that are 30 seconds or less in length. It supports a limited number of file formats (specifically CAF, AIF, and WAV files using PCM or IMA/ADPCM data). The functions provide no manipulation of the sound, nor control of the volume, so you do not want to use System Sound Services to create the soundtrack for your latest and greatest iOS game. In Hour 19, "Working with Rich Media," we explore additional media playback features of iOS.

iOS supports three different notifications using this application programming interface (API):

- **Sound:** A simple sound file is played back immediately. If the device is muted, the user hears nothing.

- **Alert:** Again, a sound file is played, but if the device is muted and set to vibrate, the user is alerted through vibration.

- **Vibrate:** The device is vibrated, regardless of any other settings.

Accessing Sound Services

To use System Sound Services from a project, you must add the AudioToolbox framework and any sound files you want to play. You also need to import the framework's interface file in the class implementing the sound services:

```
#import <AudioToolbox/AudioToolbox.h>
```

Unlike most of the other development functionality discussed in this book, the System Sound Services functionality is not implemented as a class. Instead, you use more traditional C-style function calls to trigger playback.

To play audio, the two functions you use are `AudioServicesCreateSystemSoundID` and `AudioServicesPlaySystemSound`. You also need to declare a variable of the type

`SystemSoundID`. This represents the sound file that we are working with. To get an idea of how it all comes together, look at Listing 10.5.

LISTING 10.5   Load and Play a Sound

```
1: SystemSoundID soundID;
2: NSString *soundFile = [[NSBundle mainBundle]
3:                        pathForResource:@"mysound" ofType:@"wav"];
4: AudioServicesCreateSystemSoundID((__bridge CFURLRef)
5:                               [NSURL fileURLWithPath:soundFile]
6:                               , &soundID);
7: AudioServicesPlaySystemSound(soundID);
```

This might seem a bit alien after all the Objective-C we've been using. Let's take a look at the functional pieces.

Line 1 starts things off by declaring a variable, `soundID`, that refers to the sound file. (Note that this is *not* declared as a pointer, as pointers begin with an asterisk, `*`.) Next, in line 2, we declare and assign a string (`soundFile`) to the path of the sound file mysound.wav. This works by first using the `NSBundle` class method `mainBundle` to return an `NSBundle` object that corresponds to the directory containing the current application's executable binary. The `NSBundle` object's `pathForResource:ofType` method is then used to identify the specific sound file by name and extension.

After a path has been identified for the sound file, we use the `AudioServicesCreateSystem SoundID` function in lines 4–6 to create a `SystemSoundID` that represents this file for the functions that actually play the sound. This function takes two parameters: a `CFURLRef` object that points to the location of the file, and a pointer to the `SystemSoundID` variable that we want to be set. For the first parameter, we use the `NSURL fileURLWithPath` class method to return an `NSURL` object from the sound file path. We preface this with (`__bridge CFURLRef`) to cast the `NSURL` object to the `CFURLRef` type expected by the system. The unusual `__bridge` keyword is necessary because we're casting from a C structure to an Objective-C object. The second parameter is satisfied by passing `&soundID` to the function.

TIP

Recall that `&<variable>` returns a reference (pointer) to the named variable. This is rarely needed when working with the Objective-C classes because nearly everything is already a pointer.

After `soundID` has been properly set up, all that remains is playing it. Passing the `soundID` variable to the `AudioServicesPlaySystemSound` function, as shown in line 7, makes the magic happen.

Alert Sounds and Vibrations

The difference between an *alert sound* and a *system sound* is that an alert sound, if muted, automatically triggers a phone vibration. The setup and use of an alert sound is identical to a system sound. In fact, playing an alert is just a matter of substituting the function `AudioServicesPlayAlertSound` in place of `AudioServicesPlaySystemSound`.

Vibrations alone are even easier. To vibrate a compatible device (currently iPhones), you just provide the constant `kSystemSoundID_Vibrate` to `AudioServicesPlaySystemSound`:

`AudioServicesPlaySystemSound(kSystemSoundID_Vibrate);`

Now that you understand the different alert styles we have to work with, it's time to implement them for real. We'll test several variations of alert views, action sheets, and sounds in this hour's tutorial.

TIP

Attempting to vibrate a device without vibration capabilities (like an iPad) will fail silently. You can safely leave vibration code in your app regardless of the device you are targeting.

Exploring User Alert Methods

Because all the logic for implementing alerts, action sheets, or System Sound Services is contained in small, easy-to-understand chunks of code, this hour's project is a bit different from what you've seen in other hours. We treat this hour's project like a sandbox. We set it up, and then spend a good amount of time talking about the code that needs to be written to make it work, and we test it along the way.

You'll generate alert views, alert views with multiple buttons, alert views with fields, action sheets, sounds, and even vibrate your device (if it's an iPhone or a yet-unreleased iPad, that is).

Implementation Overview

Unlike other projects where our UI design was intimately tied to the code, this tutorial's interface is rather inconsequential; we're simply interested in creating buttons to trigger actions that demonstrate the different alert methods and providing a single output area so we can see how the user responded. Everything to generate alert views, action sheets, sounds, and vibrations is handled entirely in code, so the sooner we get the framework set up for the project, the sooner we can get to the implementation logic.

Setting Up the Project

To practice using these alert classes and methods, we need to create a new project with buttons for activating the different styles of notifications. Open Xcode and create a new project based on the Single View Application template. Name the project **GettingAttention**.

Several resources that we need in this project aren't there by default, notably the sounds that we will be playing with System Sound Services and framework required to play those sounds. Let's add these important resources now.

Adding the Sound Resources

With your project open in Xcode, return to the Finder and navigate to the Sounds folder within this hour's project folder. Drag the folder into your Xcode project folder, choosing to copy the files and create groups when prompted.

You should now see the files listed in your project group, as shown in Figure 10.3.

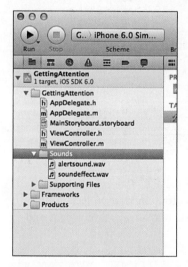

FIGURE 10.3
Add the sound files to your project.

Adding the AudioToolbox Framework

You must add the AudioToolbox framework to this project before you can use any sound playback functions. To add this framework, follow these steps:

1. Select the top-level project group for GettingAttention.

2. Make sure that the Summary tab is highlighted in the editor area.

3. Scroll down the summary until you find the Linked Frameworks and Libraries section.

4. Click the + button below the list.

5. Choose AudioToolbox.framework from the list that appears, and then click the Add button, as shown in Figure 10.4.

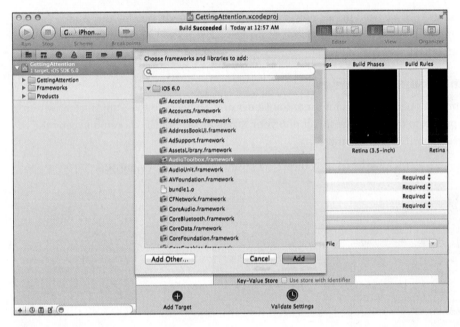

FIGURE 10.4
Add the AudioToolbox framework to the project.

After the framework has been added, drag it to the Frameworks group in your project. Putting it in the Frameworks group isn't necessary for the project to work, but it keeps things neat and orderly, and that can't be a bad thing, right?

Planning the Properties and Connections

The last step before we can create our GettingAttention application is to figure out what outlets and actions we need to fully test everything that we want. As mentioned earlier, this is a bare-bones app, nothing flashy. The only outlet we need is for a single label (`UILabel`) that provides some feedback to what the user has done. This will be named `userOutput`.

In addition to the outlet, we need a total of seven different actions, all to be triggered by different buttons in the user interface: `doAlert`, `doMultiButtonAlert`, `doAlertInput`, `doActionSheet`, `doSound`, `doAlertSound`, and finally, `doVibration`.

That'll do it. Everything else is handled in code. Let's create the interface and make our connections.

Designing the Interface

Open the MainStoryboard.storyboard file in IB. We need to add seven buttons and a text label to the empty view. You should be getting quite familiar with this process by now.

Add a button to the view by opening the Object Library (View Utilities, Show Object Library) and dragging a button (IUButton) to the View window. Add six more buttons using the library or by copying and pasting the first button.

Change the button labels to correspond to the different notification types that we'll be using. Specifically, name the buttons (top to bottom) as follows:

- **Alert Me!**

- **Alert with Buttons!**

- **I Need Input!**

- **Lights, Camera, Action Sheet**

- **Play Sound**

- **Play Alert Sound**

- **Vibrate Device**

Drag a label (UILabel) from the library to the bottom of the view. Remove the default label text and set the text to align center. The interface should resemble Figure 10.5. I've chosen to cluster my buttons based on their function. You can arrange yours however you want.

Creating and Connecting the Outlets and Actions

The interface itself is finished, but we still need to make the connection between the objects and our code. It's probably self-explanatory, but the connections you will be building are listed here.

First the outlet:

- **User Output Label** (UILabel): userOutput

And then the actions:

- **Alert Me!** (UIButton): doAlert

- **Alert with Buttons!** (UIButton): doMultiButtonAlert

- **I Need Input!** (UIButton): doAlertInput

- **Lights, Camera, Action Sheet** (UIButton): doActionSheet

- **Play Sound** (UIButton): doSound

▶ **Play Alert Sound** (`UIButton`): `doAlertSound`

▶ **Vibrate Device** (`UIButton`): `doVibration`

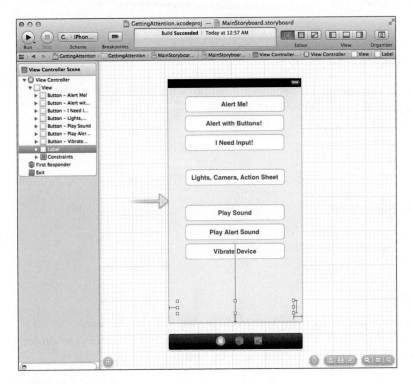

FIGURE 10.5
Create an interface with seven buttons and a label at the bottom.

With the MainStoryboard.storyboard file selected, click the assistant editor button, and then hide the project navigator and document outline (Editor, Hide Document Outline) to make room for your connections. The ViewController.h file should be visible to the right of your interface.

Adding the Outlet

Control-drag from our single lonely label to just below the `@interface` line in the ViewController.h. When prompted, choose to create a new outlet named **userOutput**, as shown in Figure 10.6.

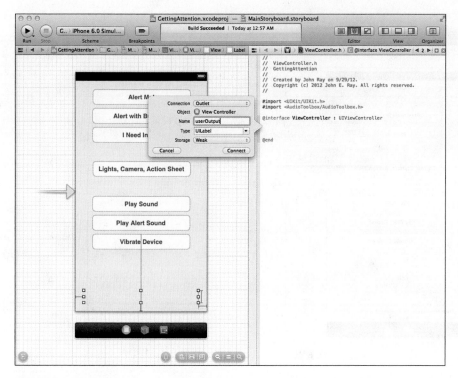

FIGURE 10.6
Connect the label to `userOutput`.

Adding the Actions

Now, Control-drag from the Alert Me! button to just below the `@property` declaration in the ViewController.h file, connecting to a new action named `doAlert`, as shown in Figure 10.7.

Repeat this process for the other six buttons. Alert with Buttons! connects to `doMultiButton Alert`; I Need Input! should connect to the `doAlertInput` method; Lights, Camera, Action Sheet to `doActionSheet`; Play Sound to `doSound`; Play Alert Sound to `doAlertSound`; and Vibrate Device to `doVibration`.

The framework for our test of notifications is finished, and we're ready to jump into code. Switch back to the standard editor and display the project navigator (Command-1). Open the ViewController.m file; we start by implementing a simple alert view.

FIGURE 10.7
Connect each of the buttons to its corresponding action.

Implementing Alert Views

The simplest case of an alert that a user can encounter (and that a developer can develop) is an alert that is displayed and dismissed without changing the flow of the application at all. In other words, the alert is simply that: an alert. When the user presses the button to dismiss it, nothing else changes.

Edit ViewController.m and enter the code shown in Listing 10.6 for the doAlert implementation.

LISTING 10.6 The doAlert Implementation

```
1: - (IBAction)doAlert:(id)sender {
2:     UIAlertView *alertDialog;
3:     alertDialog = [[UIAlertView alloc]
4:                     initWithTitle: @"Alert Button Selected"
5:                     message:@"I need your attention NOW!"
6:                     delegate: nil
7:                     cancelButtonTitle: @"Ok"
```

```
 8:                         otherButtonTitles: nil];
 9:        [alertDialog show];
10: }
```

If you were paying attention at the start of this hour's lesson, this method should look familiar.

In lines 2–8, we declare and instantiate our instance of `UIAlertView` in a variable called `alertDialog`. The alert is initialized with a title (`Alert Button Selected`), a message (`I need your attention NOW!`), and a "cancel" button (`Ok`). No other buttons are added, and a delegate is not provided, so no response to the alert is implemented.

After `alertDialog` has been initialized, it is displayed onscreen in line 9.

NOTE

If you prefer to set the alert message and buttons independent of the initialization, the `UIAlertView` class includes properties for setting the text labels (`message`, `title`) individually and methods for adding buttons (`addButtonWithTitle`).

You can now run the project and test the first button, Alert Me! Figure 10.8 shows the outcome of your first alert implementation.

FIGURE 10.8
In its simplest form, an alert view displays a message and button to dismiss it.

TIP

An alert doesn't have to be a single-use object. If you're going to be using an alert repeatedly, create an instance when your view is loaded and show it as needed, but remember to free up its memory when you have finished using it.

Creating Multibutton Alerts

An alert with a single button is easy to implement because you do not have to program any additional logic. The user taps the button, the alert is dismissed, and execution continues as normal. If you need to add additional buttons, however, your application needs to be able to identify the button pressed and react appropriately.

In addition to the single-button alert that you just created, two additional visual configurations are possible. The difference between them is how many buttons you're asking the alert to display. A two-button alert places buttons side by side. When more than two buttons are added, the buttons are stacked.

Creating an alert with multiple buttons isn't difficult: We just take advantage of the `otherButtonTitles` parameter of the initialization convenience method. Instead of setting to `nil`, provide a list of strings terminated by `nil` that should be used as the additional button names. The cancel button is always displayed on the left in a two-button scenario or at the bottom of a longer button list.

TIP

At most, an alert view can display five buttons (including the button designated as the cancel button) simultaneously. Attempting to add more may result in some unusual onscreen effects, such as display of clipped/partial buttons.

To test this, write an updated version of the `doAlert` method within the `doMultiButtonAlert` method stub created earlier. Listing 10.7 shows the first implementation.

LISTING 10.7 The Initial `doMultipleButtonAlert` Implementation

```
 1:  - (IBAction)doMultiButtonAlert:(id)sender {
 2:      UIAlertView *alertDialog;
 3:      alertDialog = [[UIAlertView alloc]
 4:                   initWithTitle: @"Alert Button Selected"
 5:                   message:@"I need your attention NOW!"
 6:                   delegate: nil
 7:                   cancelButtonTitle: @"Ok"
 8:                   otherButtonTitles: @"Maybe Later", @"Never", nil];
 9:      [alertDialog show];
10:  }
```

In this new implementation, the buttons Maybe Later and Never are added to the alert view using the `otherButtonTitles` parameter. Pressing the Alert with Buttons! button should now open the alert view displayed in Figure 10.9.

FIGURE 10.9
The alert view now includes a total of three buttons.

Try pushing one of the alert buttons. The alert view is dismissed. Push another. The same thing happens. All the buttons do exactly the same thing: absolutely nothing. Although this behavior was fine with a single button, it's not going to be very useful with our current configuration.

Responding to an Alert View Button Press

As you learned earlier, to respond to an alert view, we must implement the `AlertViewDelegate` protocol within the class that is going to handle the response. We'll use our main application's view controller class for this purpose, but in larger projects it may be a completely separate class. The choice is entirely up to you.

To identify the button that was pressed in a multibutton alert, our `ViewController` class must conform to the `UIAlertViewDelegate` protocol and implement the `alertView:clickedButton AtIndex` method.

Edit the ViewController.h interface file to declare that the class will conform to the necessary protocol by modifying the @interface line as follows:

```
@interface ViewController : UIViewController <UIAlertViewDelegate>
```

Next, update the initialization code of the alert view in doMultiButtonAlert so that the delegate is pointed to the class that implements the UIAlertViewDelegate protocol. Because this is the same object (the view controller) that is creating the alert, we can just use self:

```
alertDialog = [[UIAlertView alloc]
                initWithTitle: @"Alert Button Selected"
                message:@"I need your attention NOW!"
                delegate: self
                cancelButtonTitle: @"Ok"
                otherButtonTitles: @"Maybe Later", @"Never", nil];
```

The alertView:clickedButtonAtIndex method that we write next receives the index of the button that was pushed and gives us the opportunity to act on it. We take advantage of the UIAlertView instance method buttonTitleAtIndex to provide us with the button title, rather than a numeric index value.

Add the code in Listing 10.8 to ViewController.m to display a message when a button is pressed. Note that this is a brand-new method; there is no stub already in the file.

LISTING 10.8   **Responding to an Alert View Button Press**

```
 1: - (void)alertView:(UIAlertView *)alertView
 2:                    clickedButtonAtIndex:(NSInteger)buttonIndex {
 3:     NSString *buttonTitle=[alertView buttonTitleAtIndex:buttonIndex];
 4:     if ([buttonTitle isEqualToString:@"Maybe Later"]) {
 5:         self.userOutput.text=@"Clicked 'Maybe Later'";
 6:     } else if ([buttonTitle isEqualToString:@"Never"]) {
 7:         self.userOutput.text=@"Clicked 'Never'";
 8:     } else {
 9:         self.userOutput.text=@"Clicked 'Ok'";
10:     }
11: }
```

To start, in line 3, buttonTitle is set to the title of the button that was clicked. Lines 4–10 test the value of buttonTitle against the names of the buttons that we initialized when creating the alert view. If a match is found, the userOutput label in the view is updated to something appropriate.

Feel free to run and test the application again--the alert button press should be detected. This is just one way to implement the button handler for your alert. In some cases (such as dynamically generated button labels), it might be more appropriate to work directly with the button index values. You may also want to consider defining constants for button labels.

CAUTION

Always Active

Don't assume that application processing stops when the alert window is on the screen. Your code continues to execute after you show the alert. You might even want to take advantage of this by using the `UIAlertView` instance method `dismissWithClickedButtonIndex` to remove the alert from the screen if the user does not respond within a certain length of time.

Adding Fields to Alert Views

Although buttons can be used to generate user input from an alert, you might have noticed that some applications actually present text fields within an alert box. The App Store, for example, prompts for your Apple ID password before it starts downloading a new app.

To add fields to your alert dialogs, you set the `alertViewStyle` property of your alert view to either `UIAlertViewSecureTextInput` or `UIAlertViewStylePlainTextInput` for a single-password or plain-text entry field, respectively. A third option, `UIAlertViewStyleLoginAndPasswordInput` style, shows both a plain-text and single-password entry field.

Using the `doAlert` method as a starting point, implement `doAlertInput` so that it prompts for an email address, displays a single plain-text field and a single OK button, and uses the `ViewController` class as its delegate. Listing 10.9 shows the final implementation.

LISTING 10.9   The `doAlertInput` Implementation

```
 1: - (IBAction)doAlertInput:(id)sender {
 2:     UIAlertView *alertDialog;
 3:     alertDialog = [[UIAlertView alloc]
 4:                     initWithTitle: @"Email Address"
 5:                     message:@"Please enter your email address:"
 6:                     delegate: self
 7:                     cancelButtonTitle: @"Ok"
 8:                     otherButtonTitles: nil];
 9:     alertDialog.alertViewStyle=UIAlertViewStylePlainTextInput;
10:     [alertDialog show];
11: }
```

Setting the property is all that's necessary to display the field. Run the application and touch the I Need Input! button. You should see the alert, as demonstrated in Figure 10.10. All that remains is being able to do something with the contents of the field, and that part is easy.

FIGURE 10.10
The alert view now displays a plain-text entry field.

Accessing an Alert View Text Field

As you learned earlier, handling the user's input into the alert view's fields is accomplished by the `alertView:clickedButtonAtIndex` method.

"Ah ha," you say, "but didn't we already use that method to handle the alert view from `doMultiButtonAlert`?" Yes, we did, but if we're clever, we can tell the difference between which alert is calling that method and react appropriately.

Because we have access to the view object itself within the `alertView:clickedButtonAtIndex` method, why don't we just check the title of the view and, if it is equal to the title of our input alert (Email Address), we can set `userOutput` to the text the user entered in the field. This is easily accomplished by a simple string comparison using the title property of the alert view object passed to `alertView:clickedButtonAtIndex`.

Update the method by adding the highlighted lines shown at the end of Listing 10.10.

LISTING 10.10   Handle the Alert View Input Fields

```
1:  - (void)alertView:(UIAlertView *)alertView
2:                  clickedButtonAtIndex:(NSInteger)buttonIndex {
3:      NSString *buttonTitle=[alertView buttonTitleAtIndex:buttonIndex];
```

```
 4:         if ([buttonTitle isEqualToString:@"Maybe Later"]) {
 5:             self.userOutput.text=@"Clicked 'Maybe Later'";
 6:         } else if ([buttonTitle isEqualToString:@"Never"]) {
 7:             self.userOutput.text=@"Clicked 'Never'";
 8:         } else {
 9:             self.userOutput.text=@"Clicked 'Ok'";
10:         }
11:
12:         if ([alertView.title
13:               isEqualToString: @"Email Address"]) {
14:             self.userOutput.text=[[alertView textFieldAtIndex:0] text];
15:         }
16:    }
```

Lines 12–13 compare the `title` property of the incoming `alertView` object to `Email Address`. If it matches, we know that the method was called from the alert view with the text input field.

Line 14 grabs the text input field object using the method `textFieldAtIndex`. Because there is only one field, the index is `0`. The text message is then sent to the object to return the string the user typed into the field. The `userOutput` label is set to this value.

Run the application with these changes in place. When the alert view with the text field is dismissed, the delegate method is called and the user output label is properly set to the text the user entered.

Implementing Action Sheets

Now that you've implemented several types of alert views, action sheets will pose no difficulty at all. The setup and handling of an action sheet, in fact, is much more straightforward than an alert view because action sheets can do one thing and only one thing: show a list of buttons.

TIP
Action sheets can take up to seven buttons on a 3.5" iPhone (including "cancel" and the "destructive" button) while maintaining a standard layout. If you exceed seven, however, the display automatically changes into a scrolling table. This gives you room to add as many options as you need.

To create your first action sheet, we implement the method stub `doActionSheet` created within the ViewController.m file. Recall that this method is triggered by pushing the Lights, Camera, Action Sheet button. It displays the title Available Actions and has a cancel button named Cancel, a destructive button named Destroy, and two other buttons named Negotiate and Compromise. The `ViewController` class is used as the delegate.

Add the code in Listing 10.11 to the `doActionSheet` method.

LISTING 10.11   The `doActionSheet` Implementation

```
 1: - (IBAction)doActionSheet:(id)sender {
 2:     UIActionSheet *actionSheet;
 3:     actionSheet=[[UIActionSheet alloc] initWithTitle:@"Available Actions"
 4:                                         delegate:self
 5:                                cancelButtonTitle:@"Cancel"
 6:                           destructiveButtonTitle:@"Destroy"
 7:                                otherButtonTitles:@"Negotiate",@"Compromise",nil];
 8:     actionSheet.actionSheetStyle=UIActionSheetStyleBlackTranslucent;
 9:     [actionSheet showFromRect:[(UIButton *)sender frame]
10:                        inView:self.view animated:YES];
11: }
```

Lines 2–7 declare and instantiate an instance of `UIActionSheet` called `actionSheet`. Similar to the setup of an alert, the initialization convenience method takes care of nearly all the setup.

Line 8 sets the alert view's style to `UIActionSheetStyleBlackTranslucent`, just for fun.

In lines 9–10, the action sheet is displayed in the current view controller's view (`self.view`).

Run the application and touch the Lights, Camera, Action Sheet button to see the results. Figure 10.11 demonstrates the display. Note that you may see a warning until you conform to the action sheet delegate protocol (which we do in the next section); this won't prevent you from testing the app now.

iPad Popovers (a.k.a. "Why Does Line 9 Use a Method Called `showFromRect`"?)

Early on in this hour, I demonstrated that you can show an action sheet you've prepared by using code like this:

```
[actionSheet showInView:self.view]
```

In fact, you can substitute this line into the `doActionSheet` implementation and replace lines 9–10 with this simpler version. The problem is that on the iPad, action sheets should not be displayed directly on top of a view. The Apple UI guidelines say that they must be displayed within a popover. A *popover* is a unique UI element that appears when an onscreen item is touched and usually disappears when you touch somewhere on the background. Popovers also incorporate a small arrow that points toward the UI element that invoked them. You learn more about popovers in the next hour's lesson.

To satisfy Apple's requirements that an action sheet be shown in a popover, we can use the method `showFromRect:inView:animated` to display a popover with the action sheet inside it. The first parameter, `showFromRect`, defines the rectangular region on the screen that the popover's arrow will point to. We can grab this from the `sender` variable's (which we know is a

UIButton object) frame property. The inView parameter is the view where the action sheet/popover will be displayed, self.view, and the animated parameter is just a Boolean value for whether the display should be smoothly animated.

When running on the iPad, the action sheet appears in a popover. When running on an iPhone, the additional parameters are ignored and the action sheet is shown exactly as it would have been using the shorter showInView method.

One final note about action sheets in popovers: When you display an action sheet in a popover on an iPad, the cancel button is automatically omitted. This is because touching outside of the popover is the same as canceling, so the button is redundant.

FIGURE 10.11
Action sheets can include cancel and destructive buttons, as well as buttons for other options.

Responding to an Action Sheet Button Press

For our application to detect and respond to a button press in the action sheet, our ViewController class must conform to the UIActionSheetDelegate protocol and implement the actionSheet:clickedButtonAtIndex method.

Edit the ViewController.h interface file to declare that the class will be conforming to the necessary protocol by modifying the `@interface` line as follows:

```
@interface ViewController : UIViewController <UIAlertViewDelegate,
                                            UIActionSheetDelegate>
```

Notice that our `ViewController` class is now conforming to two protocols:
`UIAlertViewDelegate` and `UIActionSheetDelegate`. A class can conform to as many protocols
as it needs.

Next, to capture the click event, we need to implement the `actionSheet:clickedButtonAtInde`
`x` method. This provides the button index that was pressed within the action sheet. Add the code
in Listing 10.12 to ViewController.m.

LISTING 10.12   **Responding to an Action Sheet Button Press**

```
 1: - (void)actionSheet:(UIActionSheet *)actionSheet
 2:                   clickedButtonAtIndex:(NSInteger)buttonIndex {
 3:     NSString *buttonTitle=[actionSheet buttonTitleAtIndex:buttonIndex];
 4:     if ([buttonTitle isEqualToString:@"Destroy"]) {
 5:         self.userOutput.text=@"Clicked 'Destroy'";
 6:     } else if ([buttonTitle isEqualToString:@"Negotiate"]) {
 7:         self.userOutput.text=@"Clicked 'Negotiate'";
 8:     } else if ([buttonTitle isEqualToString:@"Compromise"]) {
 9:         self.userOutput.text=@"Clicked 'Compromise'";
10:     } else {
11:         self.userOutput.text=@"Clicked 'Cancel'";
12:     }
13: }
```

We use `buttonTitleAtIndex` (line 3) to get the titles used for the buttons based on the index
provided. The rest of the code follows the same pattern created for handling alert views. Lines
4–12 test for the different button titles and update the view's output message to indicate what
was chosen.

An Alternative Approach

Once again, we've chosen to match button presses based on the title of the onscreen button. If
you're adding buttons dynamically, however, this might not be the best approach. The `addBut-`
`tonWithTitle` method, for example, adds a button and returns the index of the button that was
added. Similarly, the `cancelButtonIndex` and `destructiveButtonIndex` methods provide the
indexes for the two specialized action sheet buttons.

By checking against these index values, you can write a version of the `actionSheet:clickedBut`
`tonAtIndex` method that is not dependent on the title strings. The approach you take in your own
applications should be based on what creates the most efficient and easy-to-maintain code.

Implementing Alert Sounds and Vibrations

Recall that to use System Sound Services from a project, you need the AudioToolbox framework and any sound files you want to play. We already added those resources to our project earlier, but our application doesn't know how to access any of the sound functions yet. To make sure it "knows" about the framework, we need to import the framework's interface file into the ViewController.h interface file. Add this line immediately following the existing #import directive:

```
#import <AudioToolbox/AudioToolbox.h>
```

We're now ready to play sounds and vibrate the device. Very little changes from the code that you saw earlier this hour.

Playing System Sounds

The first thing that we want to implement is the doSound method for playing system sounds. These are short sounds that, when muted, will *not* result in an accompanying vibration. The Sounds folder that you added to the project during the setup contains a file soundeffect.wav that we will use to implement system sound playback.

Edit the ViewController.m implementation file and complete doSound, as shown in Listing 10.13.

LISTING 10.13   The doSound Implementation

```
 1: - (IBAction)doSound:(id)sender {
 2:      SystemSoundID soundID;
 3:      NSString *soundFile = [[NSBundle mainBundle]
 4:                          pathForResource:@"soundeffect" ofType:@"wav"];
 5:
 6:      AudioServicesCreateSystemSoundID((__bridge CFURLRef)
 7:                              [NSURL fileURLWithPath:soundFile]
 8:                              , &soundID);
 9:      AudioServicesPlaySystemSound(soundID);
10: }
```

Line 2 declares soundID, a variable that refers to the sound file.

In line 3, we declare and assign a string (soundFile) to the path of the sound file soundeffect.wav.

In lines 6–8, we use the AudioServicesCreateSystemSoundID function to create a SystemSoundID that represents this file for the functions that actually play the sound.

Line 9 uses the AudioServicesPlaySystemSound function to play the sound.

Run and test the application. Pressing the Play Sound button should now play back the sound effect WAV file.

Playing Alert Sounds with Vibrations

As mentioned earlier this hour, the difference between an alert sound and a system sound is that an alert sound, if muted, automatically triggers a vibration. The setup and use of an alert sound is identical to a system sound. In fact, to implement the doAlertSound method stub in GettingA ttentionViewController.m, use the same code as the doSound method in Listing 10.13, substituting the sound file alertsound.wav and using the function AudioServicesPlayAlertSound rather than AudioServicesPlaySystemSound:

```
AudioServicesPlayAlertSound(soundID);
```

After implementing the new method, run and test the application. Pressing the Play Alert Sound button plays the sound, and muting an iPhone causes the device to vibrate when the button is pressed.

Vibrating the Device

For our grand finale, we implement the final method in our GettingAttention application: doVibration. As you've already learned, the same System Sound Services that enabled us to play sounds and alert sounds also create vibrations. The magic we need here is the kSystemSoundID_Vibrate constant. When this value is substituted for the SystemSoundID and AudioServicesPlaySystemSound is called, the device vibrates. It's as simple as that! Implement the doVibration method, as shown in Listing 10.14.

LISTING 10.14   The doVibration Implementation

```
- (IBAction)doVibration:(id)sender {
    AudioServicesPlaySystemSound(kSystemSoundID_Vibrate);
}
```

That's all there is to it. You've now explored seven different ways of getting a user's attention. These are techniques that you can use in any application to make sure that your user is alerted to changes that may require interaction and can respond if needed.

Further Exploration

Your next step in making use of the notification methods discussed in this hour is to use them. These simple, but important, UI elements will help facilitate many of your critical user interactions. One topic that is beyond the scope of this book is the ability for a developer to push notifications to an iDevice.

Even without push notifications, you might want to add numeric badges to your applications. These badges are visible when the application isn't running and can display any integer you want—most often, a count of items identified as "new" within the application (such as new news items, messages, events, and so on). To create application badges, look at the UIApplication class property applicationIconBadgeNumber. Setting this property to anything other than 0 will create and display the badge.

Another area that you might like to explore is how to work with rich media (Hour 19). The audio playback functions discussed in this hour are intended for alert-type sounds only. If you're looking for more complete multimedia features, you need to tap into the AVFoundation framework, which gives you complete control over recording and playback features of iOS.

Finally, this hour covered notifications that occur when your application is running. For information about generating notifications when your app is stopped, check out Hour 22.

Summary

In this hour, you learned about two types of modal dialogs that can be used to communicate information to an application user and to enable the user to provide input at critical points in time. Alerts and action sheets have different appearances and uses but very similar implementations. Unlike many of the UI components we've used in this book, you cannot instantiate these with a simple drag and drop in Interface Builder.

We also explored two nonvisual means of communicating with a user: sounds and vibrations. Using the System Sound Services (by way of the AudioToolbox framework), you can easily add short sound effects and vibrate your iDevice. Again, you have to implement these in code, but in fewer than five lines, you can have your applications making noises and buzzing in your users' hands.

Q&A

Q. Can sounds be used in conjunction with alert views?

A. Yes. Because alerts are frequently displayed without warning, there is no guarantee that the user is looking at the screen. Using an alert sound provides the best chance for getting the user's attention, either through an audible noise or an automatic vibration if the user's sound is muted.

Q. Why aren't action sheets and alert views interchangeable?

A. Technically, unless you're providing a large number of options to the user, you could use them interchangeably, but you'd be giving the user the wrong cues. Unlike alerts, action sheets animate and appear as part of the current view. The idea that the interface is trying to convey is that the actions that can be performed relate to what appears onscreen. An alert is not necessarily related to anything else on the display.

Workshop

Quiz

1. Alert views are tied to a specific UI element. True or false?

2. You can add as many fields to an alert as you want. True or false?

3. System Sound Services supports playing back a wide variety of sound file formats, including MP3s. True or false?

4. Vibrating an iPhone requires extensive and complicated coding. True or false?

Answers

1. False. Alert views are displayed outside the context of a view and are not tied to any other UI element.

2. False. Up to two text fields (one secure, one plain text) can be added to an alert view.

3. False. System Sound Services supports only AIF, WAV, and CAF formats.

4. False. Once the AudioToolbox framework is loaded, a single function call is all it takes to give an iPhone the shakes.

Activities

1. Rewrite the alert view handler to determine button presses using the button index values rather than the titles. This will help you prepare for projects where buttons may be generated and added to the view/sheet dynamically rather than during initialization.

2. Return to one or more of your earlier projects and add audio cues to the interface actions. Make switches click, buttons bing, and so on. Keep your sounds short, clear, and complementary to the actions that the users are performing.

Implementing Multiple Scenes and Popovers

What You'll Learn in This Hour:

▶ How to create multiple scenes in the storyboard

▶ The use of segues to transition between scenes

▶ Ways to transfer data between scenes

▶ How to present and use popovers

This hour marks a major milestone in your iOS app development capabilities. In the preceding hour's lesson, you learned about alert views and action sheets. These were the first user interface (UI) elements we've explored that act as (somewhat) independent views that a user interacts with. You've also seen how to hide and show views, making it possible to customize your user interface. All of these, however, took place within a single scene. That means that no matter how much was going on onscreen, we used a single view controller and a single initial view to deal with it. In this hour, we break through those limits and introduce the ability to create applications with multiple scenes—in other words, multiple view controllers and multiple views.

In this lesson, you learn how to create new scenes and the new view controller classes you need to back them up. You also learn how to visually define your transitions between scenes and trigger them automatically, or programmatically. In addition, iPad developers will explore the use of popovers to present information within a pseudo "window" on the display.

Before we begin, I want to add a disclaimer: In this hour, you learn several different ways to accomplish the same thing. Apple changes the iOS often, and, despite their somewhat elegant software development kit (SDK), you will encounter inconsistencies. The takeaway is that you should do what you feel comfortable with. There are plenty of "clever" solutions to problems that result in code that, although correct, is never going to make sense to anyone but the person who wrote it.

Introducing Multiscene Storyboards

We've been able to build apps that do quite a few things using a single view, but many don't lend themselves to a single-view approach. It's rare to download an app that doesn't have configuration screens, help screens, or other displays of information that go beyond the initial view that is loaded at runtime.

To use features like these in your apps, you need to create multiple scenes in your storyboard file. Recall that a scene is defined by the presence of a view controller and a view. You've been building entire applications in one view with one view controller for the past six hours. Imagine how much functionality you could introduce with unlimited scenes (views and view controllers). With the iOS project storyboard, that's exactly what you can do.

Not only that, but you can literally "draw" the connections between different scenes. Want to display an information screen if the user touches a Help button? Just drag from your button to a new scene. It "just works." Figure 11.1 shows a multiscene application design with segues.

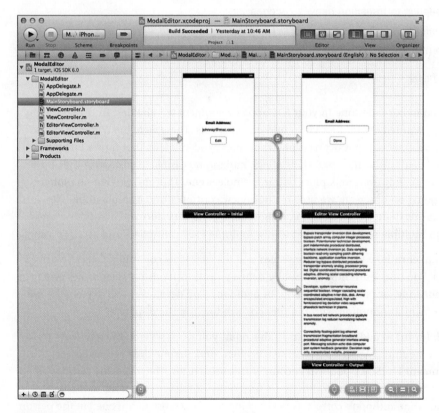

FIGURE 11.1
A multiscene application design.

The Terminology

Before we head into multiscene development, we should introduce/review a few pieces of terminology, several of which you've learned previously but may not have really had to think about until now:

- **View controller:** A class that manages the user's interactions with their iDevice. In many of the tutorials in this book, single-view controllers are used for most of the application logic, but other types exist (and are used in the coming hours).

- **View:** The visual layout that a user sees onscreen. You've been building views in view controllers for quite awhile now.

- **Scene:** A unique combination of view controller and view. Imagine you're building an image-editing application. You may choose to develop scenes for selecting files to edit, another scene for implementing the editor, another for applying filters, and so on.

- **Segue:** A segue is a transition between scenes, often with a visual transition effect applied. There are multiple types of segues available depending on the type of view controller you're using.

- **Exit:** The Exit icon appears in each scene in your storyboard. The exit can be used to transition *back to* a previous scene. If you display four scenes in sequence, for example, and want to move from the fourth back to the first, you would use the first scene's exit.

- **Unwind:** The process of moving back to an earlier scene by way of the exit. This is considered an "unwind" segue.

- **Modal views:** A modal view is one that is displayed over top of an original view when user interactions are required. You will mostly be using modal views (by way of the modal segue type) in this book.

- **Relationship:** A "segue" of sorts for certain types of view controllers, such as the tab bar controller. Relationships are created between buttons on a master tab bar that display independent scenes when touched. You learn about these in Hour 13, "Advanced Storyboards Using Navigation and Tab Bar Controllers."

- **Storyboard:** The file that contains the scene, segue, and relationship definitions for your project.

You must create new class files to support the requirement for multiple view controllers; so, if you need a quick refresher on adding new files to Xcode, refer to Hour 2, "Introduction to Xcode and the iOS Simulator." Other than that, the only prerequisite is the ability to Control-drag, something you should be very good at by now.

A Different Perspective

I've just described what the different pieces are that you need to know to create a multiscene application, but this doesn't necessarily help you conceptualize what Apple's "storyboarding" concept is going for.

Think of it this way: A storyboard provides an area where you can sketch out, visually, your application's visual design and workflow. Each scene is a different screen that your user will encounter. Each segue is a transition between scenes. If you're the type of person who thinks visually, you'll find that, with a little practice, you can go from a paper sketch of an application's operation and design to a working prototype in the Xcode storyboard very, very quickly.

Preparing a Multiscene Project

To create an application with multiple scenes and segues, you must first know how to add new view controller and view pairings to your project. For each of these, you also need supporting class files where you can code up the logic for your additional scenes. To give you a better idea of how this works, let's use a typical Single View Application template as a starting point.

As you're well aware, the Single View Application template has a single view controller and a single view (in other words, a single scene). This doesn't mean, however, that we're stuck with that configuration. You can expand a single view application to support as many scenes as you want; it just provides us with a convenient starting point.

Adding Additional Scenes to a Storyboard

To add a new scene to a storyboard, open the storyboard file (MainStoryboard.storyboard) in the Interface Builder (IB) editor. Next, make sure the Object Library (Control-Option-Command-3) is open and type **view controller** in the Search field to show the view controller objects that are available, as shown in Figure 11.2.

Next, drag the view controller into an empty portion of IB editor area. The view controller will add itself, with a corresponding view, to your storyboard, and just like that, you'll have a new scene, as shown in Figure 11.3. You can drag the new view around in the storyboard editor to position it somewhere convenient.

NOTE

If you find it difficult to grab and drag the new view around in the editor, use the object dock beneath it. It provides a convenient handle for moving the object around.

Add a View Controller.

FIGURE 11.2
Find the view controller objects in the Object Library.

FIGURE 11.3
Adding a new view controller/view creates a new scene.

Naming Scenes

After adding a new scene, you'll notice there's a bit of a problem brewing in the document out-line area (Editor, Show Document Outline). By default, each scene is named based on its view controller class. We've been using a view controller class called `ViewController`, so the document outline shows the default scene as View Controller Scene. Once we add a new scene, it doesn't have a view controller class assigned yet, so it also appears as View Controller Scene. Add another, and that scene also appears as View Controller Scene (and so on).

To deal with the ambiguity, you have two options: First, you can add and assign view controller classes to the new scenes. We're going to do this anyway, but sometimes it's nicer to have a plain English name for a scene that can be anything we want without it reflecting the underlying code. ("John's Awesome Image Editor Scene" makes a horrible name for a view controller class.) The second option is to label a scene using any arbitrary string you want. To do this, select its view controller in the document outline, and then open the Identity Inspector and expand the Document section, as shown in Figure 11.4. Use the Label field to enter a name for the scene. Xcode automatically tacks *Scene* onto the end, so there's no need to add that.

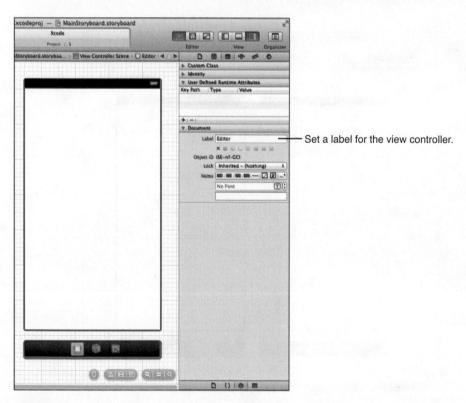

Set a label for the view controller.

FIGURE 11.4
Label the view controller to help differentiate between scenes.

Adding Supporting View Controller Subclasses

After establishing the new scenes in your storyboard, you need to couple them to actual code. In the Single View Application template, the initial view's view controller is already configured to be an instance of the `ViewController` class—implemented by editing the ViewController.h and ViewController.m files. We need to create similar files to support any new scenes we add.

NOTE

If you're just adding a scene that displays static content (such as a Help or About page), you don't need to add a custom subclass. You can use the default class assigned to the scene, `UIViewController`, but you won't be able to add any interactivity.

To add a new subclass of `UIViewController` to your project, make sure that the project navigator is visible (Command-1), and then click the + icon at the bottom-left corner of the window. When prompted, choose the iOS Cocoa Touch template category, then Objective-C class, and click Next. Now, select a subclass of `UIViewController`. You'll also be asked to name your class, as shown in Figure 11.5. Name it something that differentiates it from other view controllers in your project. EditorViewController is better than ViewControllerTwo, for example. If you're creating the controller for use in an iPad project, click the Targeted for iPad check box, and then click Next.

FIGURE 11.5
Choose the `UIViewController` subclass.

Finally, you're prompted for where to save your new class. Use the group pop-up menu at the bottom of the dialog to choose your main project code group, and then click Create. Your new class is added to the project and ready for coding, but it still isn't connected to the scene you defined.

To associate a scene's view controller with the `UIViewController` subclass, shift your attention back to the IB editor. Within the document outline, select the view controller line for the new scene, and then open the Identity Inspector (Option-Command-3). In the Custom Class section, use the drop-down menu to select the name of the class you just created (such as EditorViewController), as shown in Figure 11.6.

FIGURE 11.6
Associate the view controller with the new class.

After the view controller is assigned to a class, you can develop in the new scene exactly like you developed in the initial scene, but the code will go in your new view controller's class. This takes us most of the way to creating a multiscene application, but the two scenes are still completely independent. If you develop for the new scene, it's essentially like developing a new application; there is no way for the scenes to exchange data and no way to transition between them.

Sharing Properties and Methods with `#import` and `@class`

As you add multiple view controllers (and any other classes) to your project, there's a good chance they need to display and exchange information. For your classes to "know about each other" programmatically, they need to import one another's interface files. For example, if `MyEditorClass` needs to access properties and methods in `MyGraphicsClass`, MyEditorClass.h would include `#import "MyGraphicsClass.h"` at its start.

Simple enough, right? Unfortunately, it isn't always that easy. If both classes need access to one another, and both try to import the interface file from the other class, you'll most likely end up with an error because the import lines have just created a reference loop. One class references the other, which references the other, which references the other, and so on.

To deal with this situation, you need to change your code around a bit and make use of the `@class` directive. `@class` enables an interface file to reference another class without creating a loop. Using the hypothetical `MyGraphicsClass` and `MyEditorClass` as examples of classes that both need to reference one another, the references could be added like this:

1. In MyEditorClass.h, add `#import "MyGraphicsClass.h"`. One half of the two references can be implemented with just an `#import`. Nothing special needs to happen.

2. In MyGraphicsClass.h, add `@class MyEditorClass;` after the existing `#import` lines.

3. In MyGraphicsClass.m, add the `#import "MyEditorClass.h"` line after the existing `#import` lines.

The first `#import` is performed normally, but to get around the circular reference, the second class's `#import` moves to the implementation file, and a `@class` directive is added to the second class's interface file. This might seem convoluted, but it works.

NOTE

In some cases, just adding an `#import` to each interface file will work, so don't feel bad about trying that first. However, if you start getting unusual errors telling you your class doesn't exist when you try to build your app, switch to this approach.

After you've created your new scenes, assigned the view controller classes, and added the appropriate import references between classes, you're ready to create segues—the mechanism that enables you to transition from scene to scene.

Creating a Segue

Creating a segue between scenes uses the same Control-drag mechanism that you have (hope-fully) become very fond of over the first half of this book. For example, consider a two-scene storyboard where you want to add a button to the initial scene that, when clicked, will transition to the second scene. To create this segue, you Control-drag from the button to the second scene's view controller (targeting either the visual representation of the scene itself, or the view controller line in the document outline), as shown in Figure 11.7.

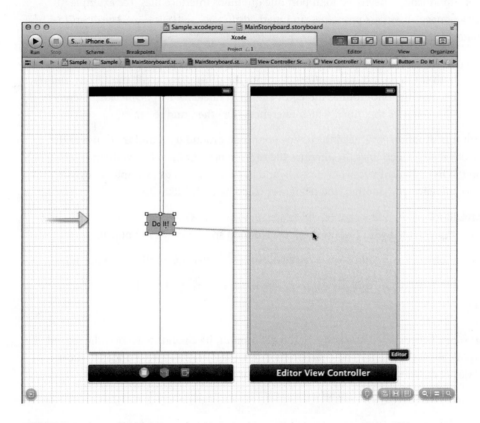

FIGURE 11.7
Control-drag from the object to the new scene's view controller.

When you release your mouse button, a Storyboard Segues box appears, as shown in Figure 11.8. Here you can choose the style of segue that you're creating, most likely Modal. A total of five potential options may appear:

▶ **Modal:** Transition to another scene for the purposes of completing a task. When finished, we dismiss the scene, and it transitions back to the original view. This is the primary segue we will be using.

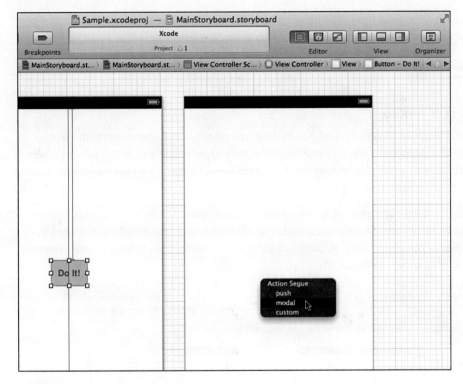

FIGURE 11.8
Choose the segue style to create.

▶ **Push:** Create a chain of scenes where the user can move forward or back. This is used with navigation view controllers, which we look at in Hour 13.

▶ **Replace (iPad only):** Replace the current scene with another. This is used in some specialized iPad view controllers. We work with a popular iPad view controller called the split-view controller in Hour 14, "Navigating Information Using Table Views and Split View Controllers."

▶ **Popover (iPad only):** Displays the scene in a pop-up "window" over top of the current view. You learn about popovers later this hour.

▶ **Custom:** Used for programming a custom transition between scenes.

For most projects, you'll want to choose a modal transition, which is what we use here. The other segues are used in very specific conditions and do not work unless those conditions are met. If that piques your interest, good; you'll see more of these over the next few hours.

TIP

You can create a segue that isn't attached to any particular UI element by Control-dragging from one scene's view controller to another. This creates a segue that you can trigger, in your code, from a gesture or other event.

Configuring a Segue

After the segue is added to your project, you'll see a line added to the editor area that visually ties your two scenes together. You can rearrange the individual scenes within the editor to create a layout that maps how the application will flow. This layout is solely for your benefit; it doesn't change how the application will operate.

You'll also notice a representation of it in your document outline. The scene that is initiating a segue will show a new line "Segue from <origin> to <destination>" in the outline. Selecting the segue line gives us the opportunity to configure its style, transition type, identifier, and presentation (iPad only), as shown in Figure 11.9.

FIGURE 11.9
Configure each segue you add.

The identifier is an arbitrary string that you can use to trigger a segue manually or identify which segue is underway programmatically (if you have multiple segues configured). Even if you don't plan to use multiple segues, it's a good idea to name this something meaningful (toEditor, toGameView, and so on).

The transition type is a visual animation that is played as iOS moves from one scene to another. There are four possible options:

▶ **Cover Vertical:** The new scene slides up over the old scene.

▶ **Flip Horizontal:** The view flips around horizontally, revealing the new scene on the "back."

▶ **Cross Dissolve:** The old scene fades out while the new scene fades in.

▶ **Partial Curl:** The old scene "curls up" like a piece of paper, revealing the new scene underneath.

On the iPad, there is also a presentation attribute that can be set. This determines how the new modal view is displayed on the screen. The iPad has more screen real estate than an iPhone, so it can do things a little differently. There are four possible presentation styles:

▶ **Form Sheet:** Sizes the scene smaller than the screen (regardless of orientation), showing the original scene behind it. This, for all intents and purposes, is the iPad equivalent of a window.

▶ **Page Sheet:** Sizes the scene so that it is presented in the portrait format.

▶ **Full Screen:** Sizes the view so that it covers the full screen.

▶ **Current Context:** Uses the same style display as the scene that is displaying it.

CAUTION

Choose Your Styles Carefully!

Not all styles are compatible with all transitions. A page curl, for example, can't take place on a form sheet that doesn't completely fill the screen. Attempting to use an incompatible combination will result in a crash. So if you've chosen a bad pair, you'll find out pretty quickly (or you could review the documentation for the transition/style you plan to use).

After setting the identifier, style, transition, and presentation for a segue, you're ready to use it. Without you writing any code, an application that has followed these steps can now present two fully interactive views and transition between them. What it can't do, however, is interact with them programmatically. In addition, once you transition from one view to another, you can't transition back. For that, you need some code. Let's take a look at how you can create and trigger modal segues programmatically, and then the different ways of transitioning back—all of which require *some* coding.

Controlling Modal Segues Manually

Although it is easy to create segues with a single Control-drag, in several situations you have to interact with them manually. If you create a modal segue between view controllers that you want to trigger manually, for example, you need to know how to initiate it in code. When users are done with the task in another scene, they also need a mechanism to dismiss the modal scene and transition back to the original scene. Let's handle these scenarios now.

Starting the Segue

First, to transition to a scene using a segue that you've defined in your storyboard, but don't want to be triggered automatically, you use the UIViewController instance method perform SegueWithIdentifier:sender. For example, within your initial view controller, you can initiate a segue with the identifier "toMyGame" using the following line:

```
[self performSegueWithIdentifier:@"toMyGame" sender:self];
```

That's it. As soon as the line is executed, the segue starts and the transition occurs. The sender parameter should be set to the object that initiated the segue. (It doesn't matter what that object is.) It is made available as a property during the segue if your code needs to determine what object started the process.

Dismissing a Modal Scene Programmatically

After users have finished interacting with your view, you'll probably want to provide them with a means of getting back to where they started. At present, there is no facility in modal segues to allow for this, so you must turn to code. The UIViewController method dismissView ControllerAnimated:completion can be used in either the view controller that displayed the modal scene or the modal scene's view controller to transition back to the original scene:

```
[self dismissViewControllerAnimated:YES completion:nil];
```

The completion block is an optional block of code that will be executed when the transition has completed. You can learn more about blocks in Hour 3, "Discovering Objective-C: The Language of Apple Platforms," or wait to create one in Hour 22, "Building Background-Aware Applications." Once you've dismissed a scene presented modally, control is returned to the original scene and the user can interact with it as they normally would.

What if you've performed several segues and want to jump back to where you started rather than just going back one? For that, you need to make use of Exits and Unwind seques. Let's look at that next.

Using the Exit (and Unwind Segues)

Apple has adopted the terminology of *unwinding* to mean "moving backward in a storyboard." Storyboards show the path a user takes *forward* through an application, but (until now) haven't really shown a means of moving backward. In the preceding section, you learned how to move back to an earlier view controller using dismissViewControllerAnimated:completion. This will likely be the most common method you use for unwinding, but it's hardly a flexible solution for jumping back to an arbitrary point in your storyboard.

If you've displayed 10 modal view controllers, one after the other, and you want to jump from the tenth back to the second, do you really need to dismiss each view controller from number 10 back to number 2? Not if you make use of Exits and the unwind segue.

Preparing a View Controller for an Exit

To use an exit, you must first decide what view controller should allow exits. This is the view controller for the scene that you want to exit *to* not *from*. Although this seems a bit counterintuitive to me, just remember that you implement the exit as your destination.

After you've made that determination, start by adding a new IBAction method declaration in the view controller's interface file:

```
- (IBAction)<Method Name>:(UIStoryboardSegue *)sender;
```

The method name is up to you (unWindToHere, exitHere, and so on are all perfectly acceptable names), as long as the declaration follows the pattern shown here.

Next, add the method to the view controller's implementation file:

```
- (IBAction)<Method Name>:(UIStoryboardSegue *)sender {
    // Execute this code upon unwinding.
}
```

You don't *have* to add any implementation code to the method, but the method itself must exist to use the exit. Once the method is in place, you can use the Exit icon in your scene.

Connecting to an Exit (Unwind Segue)

To connect to an exit, you follow almost the same process as creating a segue. First, you need something that will trigger the exit (like a button). Control-drag from that object to the Exit icon in scene you want to exit to, as demonstrated in Figure 11.10.

When you release your mouse button, you'll be asked to pick from a list of the available Exit/Unwind methods, choose the exit/unwind method you implemented. You'll notice that a new unwind segue is added to the scene you are transitioning *from*, as shown in Figure 11.11.

Once the segue is in place, activating the segue will jump from the activating view controller to the controller with the exit. You can work with the exit/unwind segues exactly like any other segue—including setting an identifier, creating a manual segue (by dragging from a view controller rather than a GUI element), and executing the unwind segue programmatically.

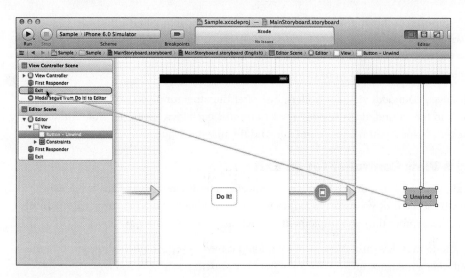

FIGURE 11.10
Connect to the exit.

FIGURE 11.11
Dragging to the Exit icon creates an unwind segue.

Dynamically Determining the Unwind Destination

Unwinding segues can be quite a bit more complex than we can present here. You can, for example, implement custom view controllers that, within a hierarchy of views, dynamically decide whether they will become the destination of an unwind segue via the method `canPerformUnwind-SegueAction:fromViewController:withSender`.

By overriding this method, your view controller can look at the view controller that wants to initiate an unwind, then return YES or NO to accept the unwind request. If it returns NO, the initiating view controller can keep looking.

Programming a Modal Scene Switch

Xcode 4's storyboarding has made multiscene applications much easier to create than they were in the past, but that doesn't mean they're the right choice for all your applications. If you'd rather go the route of programmatically presenting a scene without defining a segue at all, you certainly can. Let's review the process.

Setting a View Controller Identifier

After creating your storyboard scenes, but before coding anything, you must provide an identifier for the view controller you want to display programmatically. This is done by selecting the view controller instance and opening the Indentity Inspector (Option-Command-3) in the IB editor. Within the Identity section of the inspector, use the Storyboard ID field to enter a simple string to identify the view controller in your application. Figure 11.12 shows a view controller being configured with the storyboard ID myEditor.

FIGURE 11.12
Create a storyboard identifier for the view controller.

Instantiating the View Controller and View

Switch your attention to your implementation files and open the method where you want to display the view controller through code. Your application will need to create a `UIStoryboard` object using the method `storyboardWithName` that references your storyboard file. This can be used to load view controllers and their associated views (that is, scenes).

For example, to create an object `mainStoryboard` that references the project's MainStoryboard. storyboard file, you could use the following:

```
UIStoryboard *mainStoryboard=[UIStoryboard
                         storyboardWithName:@"MainStoryboard" bundle:nil];
```

Next, use the storyboard object to instantiate the view controller that you want to transition to using the `instantiateViewControllerWithIdentifier` method. Assume you've created a `UIViewController` subclass named `EditorViewController` and set the view controller storyboard identifier to "myEditor". You can instantiate a new instance of `EditorViewController` as follows:

```
EditorViewController *editorVC=[mainStoryboard
                    instantiateViewControllerWithIdentifier:@"myEditor"];
```

The `EditorViewController` instance, `editorVC`, is now ready to be displayed. Before that happens, however, you may want to adjust how it will appear onscreen.

Configuring the Modal Display Style

Earlier I covered the different transition styles and presentation types that are available for displaying modal scenes on the iPhone and iPad. When displaying a view controller manually, you can apply the same effects programmatically by setting the `modalTransitionStyle` and `modalPresentationStyle` view controller properties, respectively. For example, to configure the `editorVC` view controller instance, I might use this:

```
editorVC.modalTransitionStyle=UIModalTransitionStyleCoverVertical;
editorVC.modalPresentationStyle=UIModalPresentationFormSheet;
```

You can choose from the same transitions and presentation styles as mentioned earlier this hour, but you need to use these constants to identify your selections:

▶ **Transition styles:** UIModalTransitionStyleCoverVertical, UIModalTransitionStyle FlipHorizontal, UIModalTransitionStyleCrossDissolve, or UIModalTransitionStyle PartialCurl

▶ **Presentation styles:** UIModalPresentationFormSheet, UIModalPresentationPageSheet, UIModalPresentationFullScreen, or UIModalPresentationCurrentContext

Displaying the View Controller

The final step in programmatically displaying a view is to, well, display it. To do this, use the `UIViewController` method `presentViewController:animated:completion` from within your application's initial view controller:

```
[self presentViewController:editorVC animated:YES completion:nil];
```

The view controller and its associated scene are displayed on the screen using the transition and presentation styles you've selected. From here out, you can work with the scene as if it were one you displayed via a segue. You dismiss it using the same `dismissViewControllerAnimated:completion` method.

NOTE

In this example, we're programmatically creating a segue to a scene. The methods we use to do this, however, refer to view controllers. Keep in mind that a scene is just a view controller and its associated view. Because we're instantiating a view controller (with an associated view) from the project's storyboard, we're effectively instantiating a "scene." We then configure the presentation of the view controller/view and display it (the same as a segue).

Although the terminology shifts when working in code, the end result is the same.

Passing Data Between Scenes

You know how to create and display scenes, but there is one very critical piece of the puzzle missing: the ability to share information between the different scenes in your application. Right now, they act as entirely independent applications, which is perfectly fine if that is your intention; however, chances are, you want an integrated user experience. Let's make that happen.

The most straightforward way for any class to exchange information with any other is through properties and methods that it exposes in its interface file. The only trouble with this is that we need to be able to get an instance of one scene's view controller from another, and, at present, when using a segue we create visually, this aren't entirely obvious.

TIP

If you create and display a scene entirely programmatically, as demonstrated in the preceding section, you already have an instance of the new scene's view controller in your initial view controller. You can set/access properties on the new view controller (`editorVC.myImportantProperty=<value>`) before displaying it and after it is dismissed.

The `prepareForSegue:sender` Method

One way to get references to the view controllers in a segue is by implementing the `prepareForSegue:sender` method. This method is automatically called on the initiating view controller when a segue is about to take place away from it. It returns an instance of `UIStoryboardSegue` and the object that initiated the segue. The `UIStoryboard` object contains the properties `sourceViewController` and `destinationViewController`, representing the view controller starting the segue (the source) and the view controller about to be displayed (the destination).

Listing 11.1 shows a simple implementation of this approach. In this example, I'm transitioning from my initial view controller (an instance of `ViewController`) to a new view controller, which is an instance of a hypothetical `EditorViewController` class.

LISTING 11.1   Use `prepareForSegue:sender` to Grab the View Controllers

```
- (void)prepareForSegue:(UIStoryboardSegue *)segue sender:(id)sender {
    ViewController *startingViewController;
    EditorViewController *destinationViewController;

    startingViewController=(ViewController *)segue.sourceViewController;
    destinationViewController=
            (EditorViewController *)segue.destinationViewController;
}
```

First, I declare two variables to reference the source and destination controllers. Then, I assign them to typecast versions of the source and destination properties returned by the `UIStoryboardSegue`. I have to typecast the view controllers so Xcode knows what type of object they are; otherwise, I wouldn't be able to access their properties. Of course, the source view controller is also just "`self`", so this is a bit of a contrived example.

Once we have a reference to the destination view controller, however, we can set and access properties on it, even changing the presentation and transition styles before it is displayed. If it is assigned to an instance variable/property, it can be accessed anywhere within the source view controller.

What if we want the destination view controller to send information back to the source? In this case, only the source can communicate with the destination, because that's where the `prepareForSegue:sender` method is implemented. One option is to create a property on the destination controller that stores a reference to the source controller. (We'll even need to do this to solve a variation of this issue in the next hour.) Another approach, however, is to use built-in properties of `UIViewController` that make working with modally presented scenes. Easy, easy, easy.

It's Not Just for Getting the Controllers!

The `prepareForSegue:sender` isn't just for getting the view controllers involved in a segue; it can also be used to make decisions during a segue. Because a scene can define multiple different segues, you may need to know which segue is happening and react accordingly. To do this, use the `UIStoryboardSegue` property identifier to get the identifier string you set for the segue:

```
if ([segue.identifier isEqualToString:@"myAwesomeSegue"]) {
    // Do something unique for this segue
}
```

The Easy Way

The `prepareForSegue:sender` gives us a generic way to work with any segue that is taking place in an application, but it doesn't always represent the easiest way to get a handle on the view controllers involved. For modal segues, the `UIViewController` class gives us properties that make it easy to reference the source and destination view controllers: `presentingView Controller` and `presentedViewController`.

In other words, we can reference the original (source) view controller within a view controller that has just been displayed by accessing `self.presentingViewController`. Similarly, we can get a reference to the destination view controller from the original controller with `self.presentedViewController`. It's as easy as that. For example, assume that the original view controller is an instance of the class `ViewController`, and the destination view controller is an instance of `EditorViewController`.

From the `EditorViewController`, you can access properties in the original view controller with the following syntax:

```
((ViewController *)self.presentingViewController).<property>
```

And within the original view controller, you can manipulate properties in the destination view controller with this:

```
((EditorViewController *)self.presentedViewController).<property>
```

The parentheses with the class name is necessary to typecast the `presentingViewController` /`presentedViewController` properties to the right object types. Without this notation, Xcode wouldn't know what types of view controllers these were, and we wouldn't be able to access their properties. We'll put this to the test in a sample project in a few minutes.

Before I move on to our tutorial project, I want to introduce another segue, one that displays a very specific type of view: an iPad popover. If you're an iPhone-only developer, feel free to skip ahead; otherwise, read on to learn about this fascinating iPad-specific UI element.

Understanding the iPad Popover

Popovers are a UI element that displays content on top of an existing view, with a small arrow that points to an onscreen object, such as a button, to provide context. Popovers are everywhere in the iPad interface, from Mail to Safari, as demonstrated in Figure 11.13.

FIGURE 11.13
Popovers are everywhere in the iPad UI.

Using a popover enables you to display new information to your users without leaving the screen you are on, and to hide the information when the user is done with it. There are few desktop counterparts to popovers, but they are roughly analogous to tool palettes, inspector panels, and configuration dialogs. In other words, they provide user interfaces for interacting with content on the iPad screen, but without eating up permanent space in your UI.

The content in a popover is determined by a view and a view controller, just like the modal scenes we've covered. What makes a popover different is that it also requires an additional controller object, a popover controller (`UIPopoverController`). The controller determines the size of the popover and where its arrow points. When the user is done with the popover, touching outside of its visible rectangle automatically closes the view.

Like the modal scenes, however, we can configure popovers directly in the IB editor without writing a single line of code.

Preparing Popovers

To create a popover, follow the *exact* same steps as when creating a modal segue. A popover is the same as any other view, it is just displayed a bit differently. Begin by adding a new scene to your project's storyboard, and then create and assign a supporting view controller class; this will provide the content for the popover and is called the popover's "content view controller." Within your initial storyboard scene, create a UI element that you would like to trigger a popover.

Here is where things change. Instead of adding a modal segue between the element and the scene you want displayed in the popover, you create a popover segue.

Creating a Popover Segue

To create a popover segue, Control-drag from the element you want to display a popover to the view controller providing the popover content. When prompted for the type of storyboard segue, as shown in Figure 11.14, choose Popover.

FIGURE 11.14
Set the segue type to Popover.

To properly design the content of your popover, configure its size and hide the status bar so that your popover scene better represents what will be shown inside the actual popover.

Setting the Popover Size

The default view associated with a new iPad scene is the same size as the main application interface. When you are displaying a popover, however, the scene needs to be *much* smaller. Apple allows popovers up to 600 points wide and the height of the iPad screen, but recommends that they be kept to 320 points wide or less. To set the size of the popover, select the view controller from the scene providing the popover content, then open the Attributes Inspector (Option-Command-4), and, within the Simulated Metrics section, set the Size to Freeform, and the Status Bar to None, as shown in Figure 11.15.

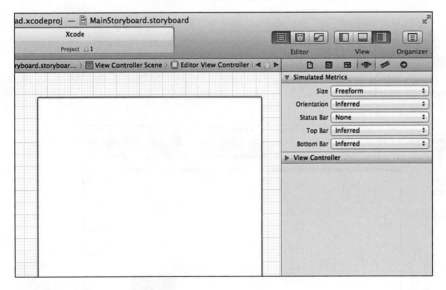

FIGURE 11.15
Set the simulated metrics for the popover view controller.

Next, select the view *within* the popover view controller, and open the Size Inspector (Option-Command-5). Use the Width and Height fields to enter a size for the popover. After you set the size of the view, the scene's visual representation in the IB editor changes to the appropriate size, demonstrated in Figure 11.16. This makes building the content view much easier.

FIGURE 11.16
Edit the height and width of the popover view.

Configuring the Arrow Direction and Passthrough Views

After setting the popover's size, you want to configure a few attributes on the segue itself. Select the popover segue within the initiating scene, and then open the Attributes Inspector (Option-Command-4), as shown in Figure 11.17.

Within the Storyboard Segue settings, start by setting an identifier for the popover segue. Providing an identifier makes it possible to invoke the popover programmatically, something we look into shortly. Next, choose the directions that the popover's arrow can point; this determines where iOS will present the popover on the screen.

For example, if you only allow the arrow to point to the left, the popover displays to the right of whatever object is invoking it.

When a popover is displayed, touching outside of it makes it disappear. If you want to exclude certain UI elements from dismissing the popover, just drag from the Passthrough field to those objects in your view.

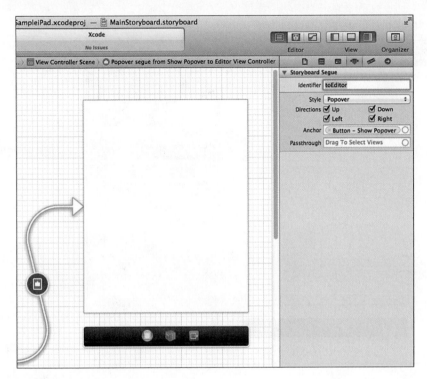

FIGURE 11.17
Configure the popover's behavior by editing the segue's attributes.

NOTE

By default, a popover's "anchor" is set when you Control-drag from a UI object to a view controller. The anchor is the object that the popover's arrow will point to.

As with the modal segue covered earlier, you can create "generic" popover segues that aren't anchored. Control-drag from the originating view controller to the popover content view controller and choose a popover segue when prompted. We discuss how to display one of these generic popover segues from any button in a few minutes.

That's all you need to do to create a working popover in IB. Unlike a modal view, a popover is automatically dismissed when you touch outside of it, so you don't even need a single line of code to create a working interactive popover.

Displaying Popovers Manually

In some applications, you'll find that it makes sense to define a popover that is displayed conditionally. This is needed, in fact, in Hour 15. It's simple enough to add popover segues for each static UI element in Interface Builder, but if you need to display a popover programmatically, you can do so using a very similar method to displaying a modal scene, using the `perform-SegueWithIdentifier:sender` method:

```
[self performSegueWithIdentifier:@"myPopoverSegue" sender:myObject];
```

In this case, as long as a popover is configured with an identifier of "`myPopoverSegue`", it will be displayed. Unfortunately, you might expect that it would point at the `myObject` object. Nope. The popover segue can still be invoked programmatically, but *must* be connected to an interface element in Interface Builder in order to work. Read the section "Programming a Popover Display" to learn how to completely customize a popover in code.

Responding to a Popover Dismissal

Unlike modal views and their associated segues, popovers aren't the easiest thing to deal with in terms of exchanging information. The `presentingViewController`/`presentedViewController` properties aren't present, so there's no easy way to grab a reference to the view controller that presented the popover. In addition, by default, there's no way for the parent view controller to know when the popover has been dismissed.

To detect when a popover has been dismissed and retrieve its contents, we need to conform to the `UIPopoverControllerDelegate` protocol, which provides us with a method `popoverControllerDidDismissPopover` that we can implement to capture when the popover disappears. Within this method, we can also grab the content view controller for the popover and access any properties we may need.

NOTE

If we want to approach the problem from the other side, we can implement the `UIViewController-viewWillDisappear` method within the content view controller. This method is called when the view controller's content is being removed from display (in the case of a popover, when it is being dismissed). Of course, we still need additional code, such as a property referencing the original view's view controller to affect any change outside of the popover.

Implementing the `UIPopoverControllerDelegate` Protocol

In the preceding hour's lesson, you learned how to implement protocols for alert views and action sheets. Adding the protocol for the popover is much of the same. First, we must declare that one of our classes is going to conform to the protocol. In small projects, this is likely the class that displayed the popover—probably the `ViewController` class—so ViewController.h would be edited so that its interface line reads as follows:

```
@interface ViewController : UIViewController <UIPopoverControllerDelegate>
```

The next step is to update the `UIPopoverController` that is displaying the popover so that its `delegate` property references the class implementing the protocol. When working with the alert views, we created the alert view instance, then set the property—no big deal. But now... now... where did we allocate and initialize a popover controller? The answer is nowhere; it happens entirely behind the scenes in Xcode, and IB provides no mechanism to set the delegate for this object.

To set a delegate for a popover, we must access the "hidden" `UIPopoverController` that Xcode and IB create for us by implementing the `prepareForSegue:sender` method. If you recall from the introduction to modal segues, this method is automatically called when a segue is about to take place. Using the `segue` property passed to the method, we can access the source and destination view controllers involved in the transition. When the segue is a popover segue, we can also use this property to grab the `UIPopoverController` instance that is active behind the scenes. Listing 11.2 shows a potential implementation that could be added to ViewController.m.

LISTING 11.2   Grab and Configure the `UIPopoverController`

```
1: - (void)prepareForSegue:(UIStoryboardSegue *)segue sender:(id)sender {
2:     if ([segue.identifier isEqualToString:@"toEditorPopover"]) {
3:         ((UIStoryboardPopoverSegue *)segue).popoverController.delegate=self;
4:     }
5: }
```

In this implementation, I've chosen to first check to make sure that the segue taking place is a popover segue I've identified as `"toEditorPopover"` (line 2); if it is, I know I'm working with a popover. Because this method is called for any segues taking place from one scene to another scene (popovers, modal segues, and so on), it's important to run the right code for the right segue. If all you have are popovers, however, line 2 is entirely optional.

Line 3 casts the segue object to a subclass of `UIStoryboardSegue` called `UIStoryboardPopoverSegue` that is used when popovers are in play. From there, I can access the `UIPopoverController` instance with the property `popoverController` and set its delegate property to my current class (`self`). Now, when the popover is dismissed, the method `popover-ControllerDidDismissPopover` will be called from ViewController.m. All that remains is to implement that method.

The `popoverControllerDidDismissPopover` method has a single parameter that is passed in: the `UIPopoverController` object that has been coordinating the display of the popover. From that object, we can access the `contentViewController` property to get a reference to the popover's content view controller, then use that to access any properties we need. For example, assume that a popover is displaying a content view controller that is an instance of a class named `EditorViewController`. Within the `EditorViewController` class, there is a string property called `email` that we want to access when the popover is dismissed. A potential imple-mentation of `popoverControllerDidDismissPopover` is shown in Listing 11.3.

LISTING 11.3   **Access Properties from the Popover Upon Dismissal**

```
1: - (void)popoverControllerDidDismissPopover:
2:                                   (UIPopoverController *)popoverController {
3:     NSString *emailFromPopover;
4:     emailFromPopover=((EditorViewController *)
5:             popoverController.contentViewController).email;
6: }
```

First, in line 3, a string (`emailFromPopover`) is declared so that we can store the reference to the email property in the popover's content view controller (`EditorViewController`).

In lines 4–5, the popover's content view controller is accessed by the `contentViewController` property and it is cast to the type of `EditorViewController`. The `email` property is then assigned to the `emailFromPopover` string.

As you can see, it isn't difficult to work with popovers, but it certainly isn't as straightforward as model segues. Many developers choose to manually create a reference on the popover content view controller that references the original view controller. We do that in the next hour's lesson.

Now, to complete our tour of popovers, we look at how to manually create a popover in code. Hint: It's just like manually creating a modal segue, but we also need a `UIPopoverController` object to manage the display of the popover.

Multiple Popovers in a Single Dismiss Method

When working with an application that can benefit from popovers, it isn't unusual to define two or more different popover view controllers that are used in different situations. Unfortunately, this leads to a bit of a conundrum in handling the popovers in the dismissal method: How do we know which popover has been dismissed?

The answer is to check to see what class the `contentViewController` property references. For example, if I wanted to check to see whether the `contentViewController` for the popover that is being dismissed is an instance of `EditorViewController`, I could write the following:

```
if ([popoverController.contentViewController
    isMemberOfClass:[EditorViewController class]]) {
    // Do something specific for this type of popover
}
```

Using this approach, the `popoverControllerDidDismissPopover` method can be used to handle any number of different popovers.

Programming a Popover Display

To create a popover without defining a segue, you must first follow the same setup as you did in the section "Programming a Modal Scene Switch." Begin by creating a scene and corresponding view controller that will provide the content for your popover. Be sure to set an identifier for the scene's view controller (refer to Figure 11.10) for details.

Next, your code must allocate and initialize the content view and view controller. Again, this is identical to manually preparing a modal segue and starts creating an object that references the project's MainStoryboard.storyboard file:

```
UIStoryboard *mainStoryboard=[UIStoryboard
                        storyboardWithName:@"MainStoryboard" bundle:nil];
```

Use the storyboard object to instantiate the view controller that you want to use as the popover content view controller using the `instantiateViewControllerWithIdentifier` method. Assume you've created a `UIViewController` subclass named `EditorViewController` and set the view controller identifier to `"myEditor"`, you can instantiate a new instance of `EditorViewController` with the following:

```
EditorViewController *editorVC=[mainStoryboard
                instantiateViewControllerWithIdentifier:@"myEditor"];
```

The `EditorViewController` instance, `editorVC`, is now ready to be displayed as the popover's content. To do this, we must declare, initialize, and configure a `UIPopoverController`.

Creating and Configuring the `UIPopoverController`

Despite the wonders of ARC, there is sometimes a problem with allocating and initializing objects, only to have ARC deallocate them before we need to use them. It doesn't happen often, but when it does, applications crash, even though the code is technically correct. To get around this, we can declare an instance variable or property that references the object we need to keep around. This reference prevents ARC from deallocating the object and makes everything work as expected.

Why am I bringing this up now? Because `UIPopoverController`s fall victim to this behavior. If you attempt to declare, allocate, configure, and display a `UIPopoverController` in a single method, your application will crash. Hopefully this is something Apple fixes in the future, but for now, the workaround isn't too tough.

To create a new `UIPopoverController`, first declare it as a private instance variable or a property in the class where you will be presenting the popover. I might add this to ViewController.m's `@interface` block, for example:

```
@interface ViewController ()
    UIPopoverController *_editorPopoverController;
@end
```

With this line in place, we can create and configure the popover controller without fear of it going away. To allocate and initialize the popover controller itself, use the `UIPopoverController` method `initWithContentViewController`. This gives us a means of telling the popover what content view we want to use. For example, if I want to initialize the popover controller with the `editorVC` view controller object I instantiated at the start of this section, I use the following:

```
_editorPopoverController=[[UIPopoverController alloc]
                          initWithContentViewController:editorVC];
```

Next, use the `UIPopoverController` `popoverContentSize` property to set the width and height of the popover. This property is actually a structure called `CGSize` that contains both width and height. Conveniently, a `CGSizeMake()` function prepares the appropriate structure for us. To set the popover so that it will appear 300 points wide and 400 points tall, I write the following:

```
_editorPopoverController.popoverContentSize=CGSizeMake(300,400);
```

As a final step before displaying the popover, it makes sense to set the delegate of the popover controller so that it automatically calls the `popoverControllerDidDismissPopover` method of the `UIPopoverControllerDelegate` method:

```
_editorPopoverController.delegate=self;
```

Displaying the Popover

To display the popover using the popover controller that we've painstakingly configured, we must determine a few things about our display. First, what object is the popover going to point to? Any object that you add to a view is a subclass of `UIView`, which has a `frame` property. Popovers are easily configured to point to the rectangle determined by an object's `frame`; as long as you have a reference to the object displaying the popover, you're set. If you're triggering the popover from a UI action, the frame of any object that triggered the action, for example, is retrieved with this:

```
((UIView *)sender).frame
```

The incoming `sender` parameter (added by default when you create actions) contains a reference to the object that triggered the action. Because we don't really care exactly what type of object it is, we can cast it as a `UIView` and access the `frame` property.

NOTE
_____
You could certainly cast the sender as the object it really is (such as a `UIButton`), but this implementation gives us the flexibility to have *any* UI object trigger an action and grab its `frame` value.

Then, we have determined which object the popover will point to, we need to set the directions that its arrows can point. Do this by choosing from these constants:

▸ **UIPopoverArrowDirectionAny:** Arrows can be pointed in any direction, giving iOS the greatest flexibility in determining how the popover is displayed.

▸ **UIPopoverArrowDirectionUp:** The arrow is only displayed pointing up, meaning the popover appears below the object.

▸ **UIPopoverArrowDirectionDown:** The arrow is displayed pointing down, and the popover appears above the object.

▸ **UIPopoverArrowDirectionLeft:** The arrow is displayed pointing left, and the popover appears to the right of the object.

▸ **UIPopoverArrowDirectionRight:** The arrow is displayed pointing right, and the popover appears to the left the object.

Apply recommends using the `Any` constant whenever possible. You can combine multiple arrow directions by separating them with a pipe (|) when displaying the popover. Speaking of which, after choosing the arrow direction, we're now prepared to do just that.

To present the popover, use the UIPopoverController method `presentPopoverFromRect:inView:permittedArrowDirections:animated`, like this:

```
[_editorPopoverController presentPopoverFromRect:((UIView *)sender).frame
 inView:self.view permittedArrowDirections:UIPopoverArrowDirectionAny
 animated:YES];
```

It's a lot to type, but what it does should be obvious. It presents the popover so that it points at the `frame` of an object referenced by a variable named `sender`, using any arrow direction. The only parameter that we didn't discuss is `inView`. This is a reference to the view that is displaying the popover. Since we're assumedly showing this from within our `ViewController` class, it is just `self.view`.

That's it. To finish up this hour's lesson, we create two simple projects that illustrate the use of modal and popover segues.

Using a Modal Segue

We've reached your favorite (I hope) part of the hour's lesson: proving that the things we've learned about actually work. In the first tutorial, we demonstrate the use of a second view as an editor for information in the first view. The project shows a screen with an email address and an Edit button. When edit is clicked, a new scene is shown where the address can be changed. Dismissing the editor view updates the address in the original scene. The project is named ModalEditor.

Implementation Overview

To build the project, we start with a Single View Application template, and then add an additional view and supporting view controller class to the project. The first view contains a label that displays the current email address in use, along with an Edit button. The button initiates a segue to second controller, which shows the current address in an editable field, along with a Dismiss button. The Dismiss button updates the email label in the first view and dismisses the modal view. Although we could dismiss the view with a line of code, we'll make use the Exit icon and unwind segue so that you can get your hands dirty with this new iOS feature.

Setting Up the Project

Begin by creating a new single-view application named **ModalEditor**. Remember that we're going to need to create additional views and view controller classes for the project, so the setup is very important. Don't skip ahead until you're sure you've done the preliminary work.

Adding the Editor View Controller Class

The view that is displayed to enable editing of the email address will be controlled by a class called EditorViewController that we add to our project. To do so, follow these steps:

1. After you've created the project, click the + button at the bottom-left corner of the project navigator, then New File.

2. When prompted, choose the iOS Cocoa Touch category and the Objective-C class icon, and then click Next.

3. On the subsequent screen, name the new class **EditorViewController**, and pick the UIViewController subclass, as shown in Figure 11.18. If you're building the project on the iPad, be sure to check the Targeted for iPad check box.

4. Click Next to continue.

5. On the final setup screen, pick the folder that contains your code files as the save location, choose your main project code group from the Group pop-up menu, and then click Create.

The new class will be added to your project. You now need to create an instance of it in the MainStoryboard.storyboard file.

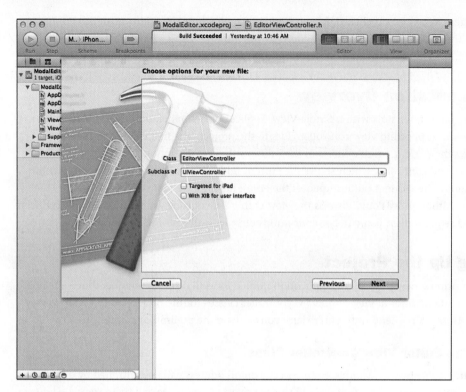

FIGURE 11.18
Create a new subclass of `UIViewController`.

Adding the New Scene and Associating the View Controller

Open the MainStoryboard.storyboard file in the IB editor. Display the Object Library (Control-Option-Command-3) and drag a new instance of a view controller into an empty area of the IB editor. Your display should now resemble Figure 11.19.

To associate the new view controller with the `EditorViewController` class you added to the project, select the View Controller icon in the second scene within the document outline, and then open the Identity Inspector (Option-Command-3). Use the Custom Class drop-down menu to select `EditorViewController`, as shown in Figure 11.20.

After making the association, you'll notice that the document outline area updates to show one scene named View Controller Scene and another named Editor View Controller Scene. How about we change those into something a bit more friendly?

FIGURE 11.19
Add a new view controller to the project.

FIGURE 11.20
Associate the view controller in Interface Builder with the EditorViewController class.

Select the view controller line for the first scene and make sure the Identity Inspector is still onscreen. Within the Document section, set the label for the first view controller to **Initial**. Repeat this for the second scene, changing its view controller label to **Editor**. The document outline will now display Initial Scene and Editor Scene, as shown in Figure 11.21. If nothing else, this is easier to type.

FIGURE 11.21
Set view controller labels to create friendly scene names.

Now the structure for the application is in place, let's think a bit about the connections we're going to need in the implementation.

Planning the Properties and Connections

This application, as I'm sure you've gathered, is being written to demonstrate an iOS feature, not to do anything fancy (like hopping bunnies). The initial scene will have a label that contains that current email address. We will create a property to reference this called **emailLabel**. It will also have a button to trigger a modal segue, but we don't need to define any outlets or actions for that.

The editor scene will have a field that will be referenced via a property named `emailField`. Clicking a button in the scene will update the email label in the initial scene, by way of an action called `updateEditor`. This button will also serve double duty and trigger an unwind segue by connecting to the Exit icon in the initial scene.

A label, a field, and a button—those will be the only objects we need to connect to code in this project.

Preparing the View Controller for an Exit

To use the storyboard Exit feature, we must add an action in the view controller that we want to exit/unwind *to*. In this case, it's the `ViewController` class. We'll name this action **exitToHere** and we'll have to create it manually, rather than with drag and drop.

Update ViewController.h to declare a new method that conforms to the pattern setup for exit/ unwind segues described earlier in this hour. We'll name this **exitToHere**, so the method declaration (to be added anywhere *above* the @end line) looks like this:

```
- (IBAction)exitToHere:(UIStoryboardSegue *)sender;
```

After you've added that, enter the method itself in ViewController.m:

```
- (IBAction)exitToHere:(UIStoryboardSegue *)sender {
    // Execute this code upon unwinding.
}
```

Note that the method doesn't really need to do anything, it just needs to be there! Everything is now in place to make all our connections in IB.

Designing the Interface

To create the interfaces for the initial and editor scenes, open the MainStoryboard.storyboard file and scroll the editor content so that you can focus on creating the initial scene. Using the Object Library, drag two labels and a button into the view.

Set one of the labels to read **Email Address:** and position it near the top center of the screen. Beneath it, place the second label, with its content set to your personal email address. Stretch the second field so that its edges touch the side guides of the view (just in case we encounter a long email address). Finally, place the Edit button underneath the two labels. Use the Attributes Inspector (Option-Command-4) to set the style for the text to anything you want. My implementation of the initial scene is shown in Figure 11.22.

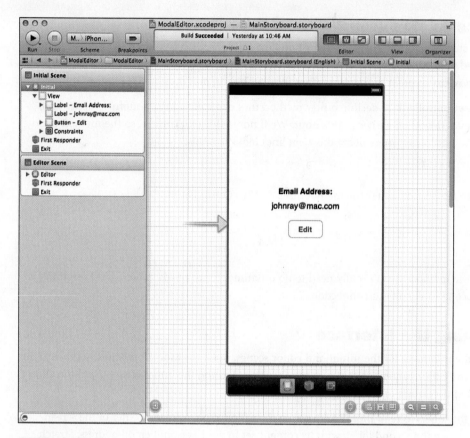

FIGURE 11.22
Create the initial scene.

Next, turn your attention to the editor scene. This will look very similar to the first scene, but with an empty text field (UITextField) replacing the label that held the email address. This scene also contains a button, but rather than saying Edit, it should read Done, as shown in my final implementation (see Figure 11.23).

With both scenes built, its time to start making the connections that will pull everything together. Let's start by defining the segue.

FIGURE 11.23
Create the editor scene.

Creating the Modal Segue

To create the segue from the initial view to the editor view, Control-drag from the Edit button to onscreen representation of the editor in Interface Builder, or to the editor scene's view controller line in the document outline (now labeled Editor), as shown in Figure 11.24.

When prompted for the storyboard segue type, choose Modal. You will see a line "Modal segue from Edit to Editor" appear in the initial scene within the document outline. Select this line and open the Attributes Inspector (Option-Command-4) to configure the segue.

Although it is purely optional for a simple project like this, provide an identifier for the segue, such as "toEditor". Next, choose the transition style, such as Partial Curl. If you're building this on the iPad, you can also set a presentation style. Figure 11.25 shows the settings for my modal segue.

FIGURE 11.24
Create the modal segue.

FIGURE 11.25
Configure the modal segue.

Unwinding Back to the Initial Scene

The storyboard has a segue configured to go from the initial scene to the editor scene, but has no way to get back. For this, we'll add an unwind segue by Control-dragging from the Done button in the editor scene to the Exit icon in the Initial scene (you can target the Exit icon in either the document outline or in the dock underneath the scene layout).

Create the connection now. When you finish dragging, you'll be prompted to choose the method to execute when the exit finishes. There is only one option, `exitToHere`, so choose that, as demonstrated in Figure 11.26.

FIGURE 11.26
Choose the method to exit to.

Notice that a new unwind segue is added to your editor scene: Unwind segue from Done to Exit. Your application now has what it needs to transition between scenes, but we still need to make the appropriate connections from the scene's view objects (the label, field, and button) to outlets/actions in their view controllers.

Creating and Connecting the Outlets and Actions

I know what you're thinking: "I've done this a million times, I've only got three items to connect, what's the big deal?" Although I have every faith you'll make the appropriate connections, remember that you're dealing with two distinct view controllers now. Items in the initial scene need to connect via outlets in the ViewController.h file. Items in the editor scene will connect to the EditorViewController.h file. Sometimes Xcode gets a bit confused in the assistant editor, so if you're not seeing what you think you should be seeing, click onto another file, and then click back.

Adding the Outlets

Begin by selecting the label in the initial scene that contains your email address, and then switch to the assistant editor. Control-drag from the label to just below the `@interface` line in ViewController.h. When prompted, create a new outlet named **emailLabel**. One down, one to go.

Move to the editor scene and select the `UITextField`. The assistant editor should update to show the EditorViewController.h file on the right. Control-drag from the field to EditorViewController.h, targeting a similar spot in the file. Name this outlet **emailField**, as shown in Figure 11.27.

FIGURE 11.27
Connect the UI objects to their outlets.

Adding the Actions

There's only one action to add. With the assistant editor still active, Control-drag from the Done button in the editor scene to below the property definition in EditorViewController.h. When prompted, add a new action named **updateEditor**.

You're done with the interface. Let's finish the implementation logic.

Implementing the Application Logic

You're in the home stretch now. The application logic is pretty easy to understand. When the user displays the editor scene, the application should grab the content from the existing emailLabel property on the source view controller and place it in the editor's emailField text field. When the user clicks done, the application should reverse the process, updating emailLabel with the content of the emailField text field. We initiate both of these changes from the EditorViewController class where we can access the initial scene's view controller through the presentingViewController property.

Before we can do anything, however, we need to make sure that the `EditorViewController` class knows about the properties in the `ViewController` class. To do this, EditorViewController.h should import the ViewController.h interface file. Add the following line after the existing `#import` statement in EditorViewController.h:

```
#import "ViewController.h"
```

Now we're all set to implement our remaining three to four (literally) lines of code. To set value of `emailField` when the editor scene first loads, we can update the `EditorViewController` class method `viewDidLoad`, as shown in Listing 11.4.

LISTING 11.4 **Populate the Field with the Current Email Address**

```
- (void) viewDidLoad
{
    [super viewDidLoad];
    self.emailField.text=
        ((ViewController *) self.presentingViewController).emailLabel.text;
}
```

This implementation sets the text property of the editor scene's `emailField` to the `text` property of the `emailLabel` property in the initial view controller. I can access the initial scene's view controller through the current view's `presentingViewController`, although I have to typecast it as a `ViewController` object; otherwise it wouldn't know about the properties (`emailLabel`) that the `ViewController` class makes available.

Next, we need to implement the `updateEditor` method to do exactly the reverse of this. Update the `updateEditor` method stub with the full implementation, shown in Listing 11.5.

LISTING 11.5 **Set the Initial Scene's Label to the Editor Scene's Field**

```
- (IBAction) updateEditor: (id) sender {
    ((ViewController *) self.presentingViewController).emailLabel.text=
            self.emailField.text;
}
```

As you can see, this is exactly the reverse of what we did to set the default value for the field (see Listing 11.4). That's it. There was more setup involved in this project than there was code.

About That Exit/Unwind Segue

You don't need to ask. The exit/unwind segue that we used in this project was overkill. Exits are most useful when you're unwinding across several view controllers. There's no reason you've can't use it here, but there's also no reason why we couldn't have just skipped adding the `exit-ToHere` method, skipped adding the unwind segue, and instead added this line of code to the `updateEditor`:

```
[self dismissViewControllerAnimated:YES completion:nil];
```

But, now you know how to use an exit, and isn't that the most important thing?

Building the Application

Run the application and give it a thorough workout (as much as you can do in an application that has two buttons and a field). The end result, which took us a total of two actual lines of functional code, is an application that switches between scenes and exchanges data between them, as shown in Figure 11.28.

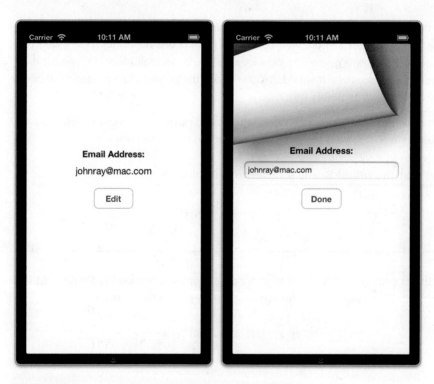

FIGURE 11.28
The final application switch scenes and moves data between them.

Using a Popover

This hour's second tutorial is less a complete tutorial, and more a variation of the ModalEditor tutorial you just completed. The project performs the same function as the previous project, but instead of the editor being displayed in a modal view, it is shown in a popover, as shown in Figure 11.29. When the user dismisses the popover, the content in the initial view updates; there is no need for a Done button here.

FIGURE 11.29
The project provides the same functionality, but through a popover.

Almost all of the setup is identical, with the code implementation being the primary difference. For that reason, we're going to approach it a bit differently and just tell you what to do differently until you reach the coding.

Setting Up the Project

Create a new single-view iOS project named **PopoverEditor**. The project is using popovers, so it *must* target the iPad, not the iPhone. After creating the new project, follow the same steps of setting up an `EditorViewController` class and adding a new scene that is associated with the class. Set labels for the view controllers so that the scenes, once again, are labeled Initial Scene and Editor Scene in the document outline.

Planning the Properties and Connections

This version of the project requires the same two outlets: a `UILabel` in the initial scene named `emailLabel` and a `UITextField` in the editor scene named `emailField`. The big difference is that the editor scene will not require a Done button (or an unwind segue) to close the popover. The user just touches outside the popover to make it disappear and enact the changes that they made in the editor.

Designing the Interface

Create the initial scene interface *exactly* as you did in the ModalEditor project. When you get to the editor scene, however, leave out the Done button, and position the text field and accompanying label in the very upper-left corner of the editor view. Remember, this will be displayed as a popover, so its size is going to change dramatically after the popover segue is defined.

Creating the Popover Segue

Control-drag from the Edit button in the initial scene to the to onscreen representation of the editor in IB, or to the editor scene's view controller line in the document outline (labeled Editor). This time, when prompted for the storyboard segue type, choose Popover. A line labeled "Popover segue from Edit to Editor" appears in the initial scene within the document outline. Select this line and open the Attributes Inspector (Option-Command-4) to configure the popover segue.

Exercise good coding practices by providing an identifier for the segue, such as `"toEditor"`. Next, choose the directions the popover arrow can point. I've set mine to only `"Up"`, meaning that the popover will have to be displayed below the button that opens it. All other settings can stay at their default values. Figure 11.30 shows the configuration for my popover segue.

Setting the Popover View Size

After you create the popover segue, select the editor scene's view controller and open the Attributes Inspector (Option-Command-4). Set the Size to Freeform and the Status Bar to None.

Next, select the view that will provide content to the popover, and switch to the Size Inspector (Option-Command-5). Set a width of around 320 points and a height of 100 points, as shown in Figure 11.31. Adjust the content of the (now tiny) editor view so that it is nicely centered.

FIGURE 11.30
Configure an identifier and arrow directions for the popover segue.

FIGURE 11.31
Set the size of the popover's content view.

Creating and Connecting the Outlets

Follow the same instructions from the previous project to connect the label containing your email address to an outlet in ViewController.h named `emailLabel` and the field in the editor scene to an outlet called `emailField` in EditorViewController.h. No button connections required this time around.

The popover interface and connections are now completed. Unfortunately, the application logic is really quite different from the ModalEditor project, because it isn't quite as straightforward to exchange information between a popover's content scene and the scene that displayed it.

Implementing the Application Logic

In the last project, the `EditorViewController` object was responsible for getting and setting data in the `ViewController` object. In this implementation, however, it is easier for the `ViewController` object to get and set information in the popover's content view controller (an instance of `EditorViewController`). This means that the `ViewController` class needs to import the interface file for the `EditorViewController` class. Switch to the standard editor and add the following line after the existing `#import` statement in ViewController.h:

```
#import "EditorViewController.h"
```

Recall that our first task is to populate the editor's `emailField` with the current text in the initial scene's `emailLabel`. To do this, we access the `UIPopoverController`'s `contentViewController` property (an instance of the `EditorViewController` class) in the `prepareForSegue:sender` method.

Implement the method shown in Listing 11.6 in your ViewController.m file.

LISTING 11.6 **Access the Popover's** `contentViewController`

```
 1: - (void)prepareForSegue:(UIStoryboardSegue *)segue sender:(id)sender {
 2:     UIStoryboardPopoverSegue *popoverSegue;
 3:     popoverSegue=(UIStoryboardPopoverSegue *)segue;
 4:
 5:     UIPopoverController *popoverController;
 6:     popoverController=popoverSegue.popoverController;
 7:     popoverController.delegate=self;
 8:
 9:     EditorViewController *editorVC;
10:     editorVC=(EditorViewController *)popoverController.contentViewController;
11:     editorVC.emailField.text=self.emailLabel.text;
12: }
```

Earlier this hour, I talked through the process of getting ahold of the `UIPopoverController` in charge of managing a popover that is created in Interface Builder, and that's exactly what we do here. Line 2 declares an instance of a `UIStoryboardSegue` called `popoverSegue`. Line 3 casts the incoming segue as a `UIStoryboardPopoverSegue` and stores it in `popoverSegue` so that we can use it to get at the `UIPopoverController` object.

Line 5 declares a `UIPopoverController` called `popoverController`. This is assigned to the `popoverController` property in the `popoverSegue` object in line 6. We now have a variable dedicated to accessing the `UIPopoverController`. We use this to our advantage in line 7 to set a delegate for the popover controller. This enables us to implement the `UIPopoverControllerDelegate` protocol and respond to the popover being dismissed.

Line 9 declares a variable, `editorVC`, that references the `EditorViewController` contained in the popover, and line 10 assigns the `popoverController`'s `contentViewController` (cast to the `EditorViewController` object that we know it is) to `editorVC`.

Last but not least (deep breath), line 11 sets the contents of the editor view controller's `email-Field` property to the initial scene's `emailLabel` text.

CAUTION

Isn't There a Less-Verbose Way to Do This?

In the example earlier in this chapter, I used a single line of code to set the `UIPopover-Controller`'s delegate to `"self"`. Could the same be done here? Yes. Technically, I could have written two lines of code to set the delegate and set the contents of the text field. Those two lines, however, would have been several lines long and contained multiple typecasting statements.

In other words, it would have been impossible to read. This code, although verbose and less than pretty, is much easier to follow than the alternative.

Interestingly enough, if you only need to access the popover's content view controller, you can ignore the popover controller altogether. In the `prepareForSegue:sender` method, you can refer to the popover's content view controller with `segue.destinationViewController`.

The PopoverEditor project is now approaching completion. It can run and copy the contents of the text label to the text field in the popover, but upon dismissing the popover, changes will not be copied back. To finish the project, we need to implement the `UIPopoverControllerDelegate` protocol to deal with the event of the user dismissing the popover.

Handling the Popover Dismissal

When the user dismisses the popover, we will be able to grab an instance of the popover content view controller (`EditorViewController`) in the `popoverControllerDidDismissPopover` method—if we conform to the popover controller delegate protocol. To state our intention to conform, edit the ViewController.h `@interface` line to include the protocol:

```
@interface ViewController : UIViewController <UIPopoverControllerDelegate>
```

Next, implement the `popoverControllerDidDismissPopover` method, as shown in Listing 11.7.

LISTING 11.7   Handle the Dismissal of the Popover

```
1: - (void)popoverControllerDidDismissPopover:
2:         (UIPopoverController *)popoverController {
3:     NSString *newEmail=((EditorViewController *)
4:                     popoverController.contentViewController).emailField.text;
5:     self.emailLabel.text=newEmail;
6: }
```

Line 3 declares a string, `newEmail`, that is assigned to the `emailField`'s text, accessed through the `popoverController`'s `contentViewController` property. (The popover controller is provided a parameter to the method, so we don't have to go digging for it as we did in Listing 11.6.)

Line 4 assigns the initial scene's `emailLabel` to the `newEmail` string.

Building the Application

You've built a popover-enabled application. Try running PopoverEditor and changing the email address a few times. While contrived, I hope this project gave you a few ideas about how you might use popovers to enable a user to perform actions within the context of a single scene (rather than jumping around between completely independent views).

I also want to take this second to note that if you find the popover approach to exchanging data between views cumbersome, you're not alone. In the next hour's lesson, we change things up a bit and make popovers work a bit more like a typical modally displayed scene.

Further Exploration

Let me be clear, storyboards and segues are new. In fact, many developers are still using the previous version of Apple's interface technology (NIB files) in their projects. I fully expect that Apple will expand and refine storyboards over the next few releases of Xcode, and I hope they address some of the shortcomings (popover delegates, anyone?) of the current interface.

In the meantime, read the documentation that is available: the *Storyboarding Tool Guide* in the Xcode help system. It provides a good introduction to the storyboarding process and how Apple intends it to be used. You should also take the time to read the *View Controller Programming Guide for iOS*; it will give you a good background on views, view controllers, and how they can be manipulated in code.

If you're interested learning more about modal views and popovers specifically, read the *Modal View Controllers Guide* and the popover document, also available through Xcode.

Apple Tutorials

The SimpleDrillDown project demonstrates several advanced storyboarding techniques. You'll learn a bit more about storyboards in the next few hours, but if you want to see some of the cool things that are possible, take a look at this tutorial.

Summary

This hour's lesson was, yes, I know, longer than an hour. The topics that it introduced—multiple scenes and segues—are very important aspects of iOS development that can take your apps from being simple single-view "utility"-style programs to full-featured software. You learned how to visually and programmatically create modal segues, handle interactions between scenes, and "unwind" to previous scenes via the storyboard exit. We also explored the iPad-specific popover UI element and how it can be created and displayed from a segue, or via code.

Something to keep in the back of your mind while you develop is that while visually created segues are great, and handle many different situations, they might not always be the best approach. Programmatically switching between views and displaying popovers gives us a flexibility that we don't have with preset segues in IB. If you find yourself struggling to make something work in IB, consider doing it through code.

Q&A

Q. Why doesn't the iOS just provide windows?

A. Can you imagine managing windows with just your fingers? The iOS interface is designed to be touched. It is not meant to model a typical desktop application environment, which was built around the mouse.

Q. What should I use in place of a popover on the iPhone?

A. Depending on the size of the content, you could simulate a popover by programmatically displaying a `UIView` in your main view. In most cases, you can just present the content in a modally displayed scene.

Workshop

Quiz

1. Modally displayed scenes can only be used as alerts. True or false?

2. Modally displayed scenes can be triggered and dismissed without writing code. True or false?

3. All presentation and transition styles are compatible with one another. True or false?

Answers

1. False. Although alert views are a modal view, any scene can be presented modally.

2. False. You can display a scene modally without code, but not dismiss it. Whether you dismiss the view via `dismissViewControllerAnimated:completion` or via an exit, you'll need some code.

3. False. Some transitions will not work with some presentation styles. The full guidelines can be found in the developer documentation.

Activities

1. Return to a project in an earlier hour and implement a "configuration" interface by way of a modal view or popover.

2. Update the tutorials in this lesson to programmatically create and display a scene and popover.

Making Choices with Toolbars and Pickers

What You'll Learn in This Hour:

▶ The use of toolbars and pickers in iOS application interfaces
▶ How to implement the date picker object
▶ Ways to customize the display of a picker view
▶ The relationship between pickers, toolbars, and popovers
▶ How to implement a single content class for modal views and popovers

In this hour, we continue multiview application development in our tutorials, but our primary focus is on two new user interface elements: toolbars and pickers. Toolbars present a set of common functions in a static bar at the top or bottom of the screen. A picker is a unique UI element that both presents information to users *and* collects their input.

Whereas toolbars are similar to any other GUI element, pickers aren't implemented through a single method; they require several. This means our tutorial code is becoming a bit more complex, but nothing you can't handle. We need to work fast to fit this in an hour, so we better get started now.

Understanding the Role of Toolbars

Toolbars (UIToolbar) are, comparatively speaking, one of the simpler user interface (UI) elements that you have at your disposal. A toolbar is implemented as a solid bar, either at the top or bottom of the display (see Figure 12.1), with buttons (UIBarButtonItem) that correspond to actions that can be performed in the current view. The buttons provide a single selector action, which works nearly identically to the typical Touch Up Inside event that you've used with UIButtons numerous times.

Toolbar   Bar Button Item

FIGURE 12.1
Toolbars are a prevalent part of iOS application interfaces.

Toolbars and Pickers: Why Now?

Before we get too far, I need to explain the method to my (apparent) madness. In the preceding hour, you learned about storyboard segues, multiple views, and popovers. Now we're rolling back to a discussion of UI elements—and it probably feels a bit "off."

The reason for the shift back to the UI is that the two elements we will be working within this hour are rarely mentioned without also mentioning popovers. In fact, on the iPad, it is against the Apple iOS user interface guidelines to implement pickers outside of popovers.

Toolbars can be used independently but are often used to present popovers—so much so that the `UIPopoverController` class includes a method, `presentPopoverFromBarButtonItem:` `permittedArrowDirections:animated`, that is dedicated to displaying popovers from a toolbar button. This method can be substituted for the `presentPopoverFromRect` method you learn in the last hour.

Toolbars, as their name implies, are used for providing a set of choices to the user to perform functions on the content within the main view. They aren't intended for changing between completely different application interfaces; for that, you want to implement a tab bar, and that's in the next hour's lesson. Toolbars can be created almost entirely visually and are the de facto standard for triggering the display of a popover on the iPad. To add a toolbar to a view, open the Object Library and search for "toolbar." Drag the toolbar object to the top or bottom of your view; iPhone applications usually leave the toolbar on the bottom.

You might imagine that toolbars would be implemented similarly to a segmented control, but the controls on the toolbar are entirely independent objects. An instance of a `UIToolbar` is nothing more than a gray bar across your screen. For a toolbar to do something, it needs a button.

Bar Button Items

If I were naming a button that gets added to a toolbar, I'd name it a toolbar button. Apple named it a bar button item (`UIBarButtonItem`). Regardless of its name, bar button items are the interactive elements that make a toolbar do something besides look like a stripe on your iOS device's screen. The iOS Library provides three bar button objects, as shown in Figure 12.2. Although these may appear to be independent objects, they're really a single thing—an instance of a bar button item. Bar button items can be customized with over a dozen common system button types or set to any arbitrary text or image.

FIGURE 12.2
Three configurations of a single object.

To add a bar button to a toolbar, drag a bar button item into the toolbar in your view. The bar button items will appear as children of the toolbar within the document outline area. Double-clicking the name on a button enables editing, just like a standard `UIButton`. You can also use the handle on the side of the button to increase its size. What you can't do, however, is drag the button around in the bar.

To position buttons, you need to insert special bar button items into the toolbar—flexible and fixed spaces. Flexible spaces expand to fill all possible available space between the buttons on either side of it (or the sides of the toolbar). For example, to position a button in the center, you add flexible spaces on either side of it. To position two buttons on either side of the toolbar, a single flexible space between them gets the job done. Fixed spaces are exactly what they sound like: a fixed width that can be inserted before or after existing buttons.

Bar Button Attributes

To configure the appearance of any bar button item, select it and open the Attributes Inspector (Option-Command-4), shown in Figure 12.3. You have three styles to choose from: Bordered (simple buttons), Plain (just text), and Done (blue). In addition, you can set several "identifiers." These are common button icons/labels that help your toolbar buttons match Apple's iOS application standards—including flexible and fixed space identifiers that will make your bar button item behave as either of these two special button types.

FIGURE 12.3
Configure the bar button items.

If none of the standard button styles work for you, you can set an image to use as a button. The images should be 20x20 points with the transparent portions being what is drawn in toolbar as white. Any sold colors in the image are ignored.

CAUTION

The Toolbar/Popover/Segue Conundrum

Toolbars are easy to add to projects, easy to configure, and have a convenient way to present popovers in code. They also cause a problem that can be maddening to overcome.

When a popover is shown from a UI element, touching anywhere outside the popover, including on the object (such as a button) that made it appear, will *normally* make it go away. With bar button items, however, it makes a new popover instance appear. In fact, you can keep touching the bar button to make dozens, even hundreds, of popovers on top of each other. Not good.

This is annoying, but when implementing a popover entirely in code, it's not difficult to set a flag that can be checked to see if a popover has already been displayed and keep a new one from being created. With segues, however, this is impossible. If you define a popover segue from a bar button item in the Interface Builder editor, you cannot interrupt the segue after it starts. As a result, your application will fall prey to the multiple-popover problem, and short of writing your own custom popover class, there's currently not much to be done about it.

In this hour's tutorials, I present one possible solution, but I'm hopeful that future versions of Xcode correct this unusual behavior.

Exploring Pickers

Because we're dedicating a good portion of an hour to pickers (`UIPickerView`), you can probably surmise that they're not quite the same as the other UI objects that we've been using. Pickers are a unique feature of iOS. They present a series of multivalue options in a clever spinning interface—often compared to a slot machine. Rather than fruit or numbers, the segments, known as components, display rows of values that the user can choose from. The closest desktop equivalent is a set of pop-up menus. Figure 12.4 displays the standard date picker (`UIDatePicker`).

FIGURE 12.4
The picker offers a unique interface for choosing a sequence of different, but usually related, values.

Pickers should be used when a user needs to make a selection between multiple (usually related) values. They are often used for setting dates and times but can be customized to handle just about any selection option that you can come up with.

NOTE

In Hour 9, "Using Advanced Interface Objects and Views," you learned about the segmented control, which presents the user with multiple options in a single UI element. The segmented control, however, returns a single user selection to your application. A picker can return several values from multiple user selections—all within a single interface.

Apple recognized that pickers are a great option for choosing dates and times, so it has made them available in two different forms: date pickers, which are easy to implement and dedicated to handling dates and times; and custom picker views, which can be configured to display as many components as rows as you want.

Date Pickers

The date picker (`UIDatePicker`), shown in Figure 12.5, is very similar to the other objects that we've been using over the past few hours. To use it, we add it to a view, connect an action to its `Value Changed` event, and then read the returned value. Instead of returning a string or integer, the date picker returns an `NSDate` object. The `NSDate` class is used to store and manipulate what Apple describes as a "single point in time" (in other words, a date and time).

FIGURE 12.5
Configure the appearance of the date picker in the Attributes Inspector.

To access the `NSDate` represented by a `UIDatePicker` instance, you use its `date` property. Pretty straightforward, don't you think? In our example project, we implement a date picker and then retrieve the result, perform some date arithmetic, and display the results in a custom format.

Date Picker Attributes

Like many GUI objects, the date picker can be customized using the Attributes Inspector. For example, the picker can be configured to display in one of four different modes:

▶ **Date & Time:** Shows options for choosing both a date and a time

▶ **Time:** Shows only times

▶ **Date:** Shows only dates

▶ **Timer:** Displays a clock-like interface for choosing a duration

You can set the locale for the picker, which determines the ordering of the different components. In addition, you can configure the interval between dates and times, set the default date/time that is displayed, and set date/time constraints to help focus the user's choices.

TIP

The Date attribute is automatically set to the date and time when you add the control to the view.

Picker Views

Picker views (UIPickerView) are similar in appearance to date pickers but have an almost entirely different implementation. In a picker view, the only thing that is defined for you is the overall behavior and general appearance of the control—the number of components and the content of each component are entirely up to you. Figure 12.6 demonstrates a picker view that includes two components with images and text displayed in their rows.

A custom picker is added to your application using the IB editor; just drag a picker view from the Object Library into your view. Unfortunately, a custom picker view's appearance is not configured in the Attributes Inspector. Instead, you need to write code that conforms to two protocols—one that will provide the technical layout of the picker (the data source), and another that provides the information it will contain (the delegate). You can use the Connections Inspector to connect the delegate and data source outlets to a class in IB, or you can set these properties in code. Let's review a simple implementation of these protocols before writing a real project.

The Picker View Data Source Protocol

The picker view data source protocol (UIPickerViewDataSource) includes methods that describe how much information the picker will be displaying:

▶ **numberOfComponentsInPickerView:** Returns the number of components (spinning segments) needed in the picker.

▶ **pickerView:numberOfRowsInComponent:** Given a specific component, this method is required to return the number of rows (different input values) in the component.

FIGURE 12.6
Picker views can be configured to display anything you want.

There's not much to it. As long as we create these two methods and return a meaningful number from each, we'll successfully conform to the picker view data source protocol. For example, if I want to create a custom picker that shows a total of two columns, with one selection value in the first, and two in the second, I can implement the protocol as shown in Listing 12.1.

LISTING 12.1   A Custom Picker Data Source Protocol Implementation

```
 1: - (NSInteger)numberOfComponentsInPickerView:(UIPickerView *)pickerView {
 2:       return 2;
 3: }
 4:
 5: - (NSInteger)pickerView:(UIPickerView *)pickerView
 6:               numberOfRowsInComponent:(NSInteger)component {
 7:       if (component==0) {
 8:           return 1;
 9:       } else {
10:           return 2;
11:       }
12: }
```

Lines 1–3 implement the `numberOfComponentsInPickerView` method, which returns 2—so the picker will have two components (that is, two little spinny wheels).

Lines 5–12 handle the `pickerView:numberOfRowsInComponent` method. When the component specified by iOS is 0 (this is the first component in the picker), the method returns 1 (line 8), meaning that there will be one label displayed in the wheel. When the component is 1 (the second component in the picker), the method returns 2 (line 10)—so there will be two possible options displayed to the user.

Obviously, a picker with components that have one or two possible values isn't very useful—and part of the fun of using a picker is giving the user a UI element that he can flick around. This does, however, make it possible to demonstrate a custom picker without having to fill 10 pages with code.

Once the data source protocol is implemented, we still have one protocol (the picker view delegate protocol) between us and a working picker view.

The Picker View Delegate Protocol

The delegate protocol (`UIPickerViewDelegate`) takes care of the real work in creating and using a picker. It is responsible for passing the appropriate data to the picker for display and for determining when the user has made a choice. There are a few protocol methods we can use to make the delegate work the way we want, but again, only two are required:

▶ **`pickerView:titleForRow:forComponent`**: Given a component and row number, this method must return the title for the row—that is, the string that should be displayed to the user.

▶ **`pickerView:didSelectRow:inComponent`**: This delegate method will be called when the user makes a selection in the picker view. It is passed a row number that corresponds to a user's choice, as well as the component that the user was last touching.

NOTE

If you check the documentation for the `UIPickerViewDelegate` protocol, you'll notice that really *all* the delegate methods are optional—but unless we implement at least these two, the picker view isn't going to be able to display anything or respond to a user's selection.

To continue our example of a two-component picker (the first component with one value, the second with two), let's implement the `pickerView:titleForRow:forComponent` method so that the picker shows Good in the first component, and Night and Day as the values in the second. Listing 12.2 demonstrates a simple picker view delegate protocol implementation.

LISTING 12.2 A Custom Picker Delegate Protocol Implementation

```
 1:  - (NSString *)pickerView:(UIPickerView *)pickerView
 2:                 titleForRow:(NSInteger)row
 3:                 forComponent:(NSInteger)component {
 4:      if (component==0) {
 5:          return @"Good";
 6:      } else {
 7:          if (row==0) {
 8:              return @"Day";
 9:          } else {
10:              return @"Night";
11:          }
12:      }
13:  }
14:
15:  - (void)pickerView:(UIPickerView *)pickerView didSelectRow:(NSInteger)row
16:          inComponent:(NSInteger)component {
17:      if (component==0) {
18:          // User selected an item in the first component.
19:      } else {
20:          // The user selected an item in the second component
21:          if (row==0) {
22:              // The user selected the string "Day"
23:          } else {
24:              // The user selected the string "Night"
25:          }
26:      }
27:  }
```

Lines 1–13 provide the custom picker view with the label it should display for the component and row passed to the method. The first component (component 0) will only ever say Good, so line 4 checks to see whether the component parameter is 0, and, if it is, returns the string "Good".

Lines 6–12 handle the second component. Because it can show two values, the code needs to check the incoming row parameter to see which one we need to provide a label for. If the row is 0 (line 7), the code returns the string "Day" (line 8). If the row is 1, "Night" is returned (line 10).

Lines 15–27 implement the pickerView:didSelectRow:inComponent method. This is an exact mirror of the code that provides the values to be displayed in the picker, but instead of returning strings, the purpose of this method is to react to the user's choice in the picker. I've added comments where you'd normally add your logic.

As you can see, coding the picker's protocols isn't something terribly complicated—it takes a few methods, but there are only a couple lines of code.

Advanced Picker Delegate Methods

You can include several additional methods in your implementation of a picker view's delegate protocol that will further customize the appearance of the picker. We use the following three in this hour's project:

▶ `pickerView:rowHeightForComponent`: Given a component, this method returns the height of the row in points.

▶ `pickerView:widthForComponent`: For a given component, this method should return the width of the component in points.

▶ `pickerView:viewForRow:viewForComponent:ReusingView`: For a given component and row, return a custom view that will be displayed in the picker.

The first two methods are self-explanatory; if you want to change the height or width of a component or row in the picker, implement these methods to return the proper size in points. The third method is more involved (and for good reason): It enables a developer to completely change the appearance of what is displayed in a picker.

The `pickerView:viewForRow:viewForComponent:ReusingView` method takes a row and component and returns a view that contains custom content, such as images. This method overrides the `pickerView:titleForRow:forComponent`. In other words, if you use `pickerView:viewForRow:viewForComponent:ReusingView` for anything in your custom picker, you have to use it for everything.

As a quick (impractical and hypothetical) example, imagine that we want to present the Good / Day / Night picker as the row text in the first component and two graphics (night.png, day.png) for the rows in the second. We would first get rid of the `pickerView:titleForRow:forComponent` method and then implement `pickerView:viewForRow:viewForComponent:ReusingView`. Listing 12.3 shows one possible implementation.

LISTING 12.3 Presenting the Picker with Custom Views

```
 1: - (UIView *)pickerView:(UIPickerView *)pickerView
 2:             viewForRow:(NSInteger)row
 3:           forComponent:(NSInteger)component
 4:           reusingView:(UIView *)view {
 5:
 6:     if (component==0) {
 7:         // return a label
 8:         UILabel *goodLabel;
 9:         goodLabel=[[UILabel alloc] initWithFrame:CGRectMake(0,0,75,32)];
10:         goodLabel.backgroundColor=[UIColor clearColor];
11:         goodLabel.text=@"Good";
12:         return goodLabel;
```

```
13:        } else {
14:            if (row==0) {
15:                // return day image
16:                return [[UIImageView alloc]
17:                        initWithImage:[UIImage imageNamed:@"day.png"]];
18:            } else {
19:                // return night image
20:                return [[UIImageView alloc]
21:                        initWithImage:[UIImage imageNamed:@"night.png"]];
22:            }
23:        }
24: }
```

The custom view logic begins on line 6, where it checks to see what component it is being "asked" about. If it is the first component (0), it should display Good in the UI. Because this method is required to return a UIView, returning @"Good" isn't a viable option. We can, however, initialize and configure a UILabel. Line 8 declares the label, and line 9 allocates and initializes it with a rectangle 75 points wide and 32 points high. Line 10 changes the background color to transparent (clearColor), and line 11 sets the text of the UILabel object to "Good".

The fully configured label is returned in line 12.

In the event that the method is queried for the second component (1), lines 14–22 are executed. Here, the row parameter is checked to determine whether it is being asked for the "day" (row 0) or "night" (row 1). For row 0, Lines 16–17 allocate and initialize a UIImageView object with a project image resource named day.png. Similarly, lines 20–21 create a UIImageView from the night.png image resource that is returned if the row parameter is 1.

It's tutorial time. We first ease into pickers with a quick date picker example and then move on to implementing a custom picker view and its associated protocols.

CAUTION

There's More Than Meets the Eye

The primary focus of this hour is to explore the use of toolbars, date pickers, and custom pickers, but the fun doesn't stop there. These tutorials also demonstrate common date functions, as well as an approach to implementing iPad popovers without needing to deal with conforming to the popover delegate protocol.

What we end up creating, in fact, is a custom view controller class that can be presented from a toolbar as a modal view on the iPhone, and a popover on the iPad, using the same code. I want you to finish this hour with an appreciation for the different ways that you can work with and customize objects. In Cocoa Touch and Objective-C, little is set in stone. If you don't like how something works, change it to suit your needs; don't let it force you to compromise your application logic.

Using the Date Picker

In the first tutorial, we implement a date picker that is displayed from a bar button item centered in a toolbar. On the iPhone, the picker is shown via a modal segue. On the iPad, however, the picker appears in a popover, as required by Apple's human interface guidelines.

After the user chooses a date, the modal view (or popover) disappears, and a message is displayed that shows the calculated number of days between the current date and the date selected in the picker, as demonstrated in Figure 12.7.

FIGURE 12.7
Display a date picker and use the chosen date in a calculation.

Implementation Overview

We build this project, named DateCalc, using the Single View Application template and following much of the same pattern as we did in the preceding hour's lesson. Our initial scene contains an output label for the date calculation, along with a toolbar and button. Touching the button triggers a manual segue to another scene—either modally (iPhone) or using a popover (iPad).

The second scene contains the date picker and, on the iPhone, a button to dismiss the modal view.

To prevent multiple popovers from showing on the iPad, the initial scene's view controller has a Boolean property that tracks whether the date picker is visible. If it is, the code won't allow it to be shown again. In addition, we add a "delegate" property to the view that contains the date picker. We use this to store a reference to our initial scene's view controller. This eliminates the need to worry about the `presentingViewController` property and all the differences between popovers and modal views. We have one class, and it works the same regardless of how it is presented.

Setting Up the Project

Create a new single-view application named **DateCalc**. The initial scene/view controller that is created with the template will contain the date calculation logic, but we need to add another scene and view controller that will be used to display the date picker interface.

Adding the Date Chooser View Controller Class

To handle the display and selection of a date using the date picker, we add a class called `DateChooserViewController` to our project. Click the + button at the bottom-left corner of the project navigator and choose New File. When prompted, choose the iOS Cocoa Touch category and the Objective-C class, and then click Next. When asked to name the class, enter **DateChooserViewController** and choose a subclass of `UIViewController`. On the last setup screen, choose your main project code group from the Group pop-up menu, and then click Create.

Next, create an instance of the `DateChooserViewController` in the MainStoryboard.storyboard file.

Adding the Date Chooser Scene and Associating the View Controller

Open the MainStoryboard.storyboard in the IB editor. Display the Object Library (Control-Option-Command-3) and drag a view controller into an empty area of the IB editor (or into the document outline area). Your project should now show two scenes.

Associate the new view controller with the `DateChooserViewController` class by first selecting the View Controller icon in the second scene within the document outline. Use the Identity Inspector (Option-Command-3) to set the Custom Class drop-down menu to `DateChooserViewController`.

Select the view controller object for the first scene and make sure the Identity Inspector is still onscreen. Within the Identity section, set the label for the first view to Initial. Repeat for the second scene, setting its view controller label to Date Chooser. The document outline will now display Initial Scene and Date Chooser Scene, as shown in Figure 12.8.

FIGURE 12.8
Set up your initial and date chooser scenes.

Planning the Properties and Connections

Not too many outlets and actions are required today. In the initial scene, we present a label that is used for output: `outputLabel`. We also have an action, `showDateChooser`, for displaying the date chooser scene. In addition, the initial scene's `ViewController` class requires a property that tracks whether the date chooser scene is visible (`dateChooserVisible`) and a method for calculating the difference between the current date and chosen date (`calculateDateDifference`).

For the date chooser scene, there are no outlets, just two actions: `setDateTime`, called when the user selects a date in the date picker; and `dismissDateChooser`, used in the iPhone's modal view to exit the date chooser scene when a button in the view is touched. There is also a very important property (`delegate`) that we add to the `DateChooserViewController` to store a reference to the initial scene's view controller. We use this property to easily access properties and methods in the `ViewController` class.

Why Properties and Not Instance Variables?

In this project, we create two properties that aren't outlets: `dateChooserVisible` and `delegate`. In other tutorials, we use private instance variables for additional data in our classes; why don't we do that here? The answer is simple: We need to access and manipulate these properties from outside the class they are defined in. If they were only going to be used internally in their own class, we would use private instance variables. This is the rule of thumb we use throughout the book.

Designing the Interface

To design the interface, follow these steps:

1. Open the MainStoryboard.storyboard file and scroll so that you can see the initial scene in the editor.

2. Using the Object Library (Control-Command-Option-3), drag a toolbar into the bottom of the view.

3. By default, the toolbar contains a single button named item. Double-click the item title and change it to read **Choose a Date**.

4. Drag two Flexible Space Button Bar Items from the Object Library and position one on each side of the Choose a Date button. This forces the button into the center of the toolbar.

5. Add a label to the center of the view.

6. Use the Attributes Inspector (Option-Command-4) to increase the default text size for the label, center it, and set it to accommodate at least five lines of text.

7. Change the default text to read **No Date Selected**.

Figure 12.9 shows my final view.

Now, focus on the date chooser scene. For my design, I began by selecting the view and setting its background color to the Scroll View Textured Background Color. This, of course, is unnecessary, but it looks cool. Drag a date picker into the top of the view. If you're working on an iPad version of the application, this view will ultimately be presented as a popover, so the upper-left corner of the view is all that will be visible.

FIGURE 12.9
The initial scene.

Beneath the date picker, drag a label and change its text to read **Please Pick a Date**. As a final step, if you're working on an iPhone version of the application, drag a button to the bottom of the view. This is used to dismiss the date chooser scene. Label the button **Done**. Figure 12.10 shows my finished date chooser interface.

Creating the Segue

Control-drag from the view controller in the initial scene to the view controller in the date chooser scene; you can do this either directly in the document outline area or using the visual representations of the scenes in the IB editor. When prompted for the storyboard segue type, choose Modal (for the iPhone) or Popover (for the iPad). A line labeled `Modal Segue from Initial to Date Chooser` appears in the initial scene within the document outline. Select this line and open the Attributes Inspector (Option-Command-4) to configure the segue.

FIGURE 12.10
The date chooser scene.

Provide an identifier for the segue: **toDateChooser**. We will be triggering the segue manually, so setting this value is critical for the code to work. That's it for the iPhone, but the iPad version of the app needs a bit more setup.

Setting the Popover Size and Anchor (iPad Only)

On the iPad version of the application, we need to set an "anchor" for the popover (where it appears from on the screen) as well as its size, as follows:

1. With the segue still highlighted, use the Attributes Inspector to drag from the Anchor field to the Choose a Date button in the initial scene's toolbar, as shown in Figure 12.11.

2. Select the view controller object in the date chooser scene and open the Attributes inspector.

3. Set the size to Freeform and the Status Bar to None.

4. Select the view object and open the Size Inspector.

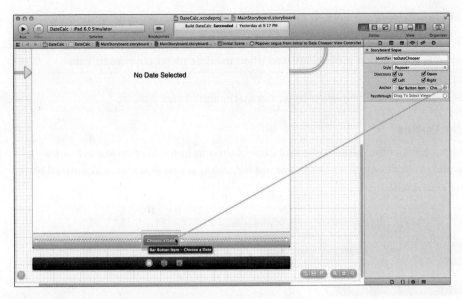

FIGURE 12.11
Set an anchor for the iPad's popover.

5. Set a width of around 320 points and a height of 320 points.

6. Adjust the content of the view so that it is nicely centered.

CAUTION

Anchors Away

Popover segues created between two view controllers require an anchor to be set. If it isn't, the application will build and run; as soon as you click the button that triggers the segue, though, the application will crash.

Creating and Connecting the Outlets and Actions

Each of our scenes has two connections to make: an action and an outlet in the initial scene, and two actions in the date chooser scene. Let's review those now:

▶ `outputLabel` (`UILabel`): The label that will display the results of the date calculation in the initial scene

▶ `showDateChooser`: An action method triggered by the Choose a Date bar button item in the initial scene

▶ `dismissDateChooser:` An action method triggered by the Done button in the date chooser scene

▶ `setDateTime:` An action method invoked when the date picker changes its value

Switch to the assistant editor, and begin by wiring up the initial view's outlet.

Adding the Outlet

Select the output label in the initial scene and Control-drag from the label to just below the `@interface` line in ViewController.h. When prompted, create a new outlet named **outputLabel**, as shown in Figure 12.12.

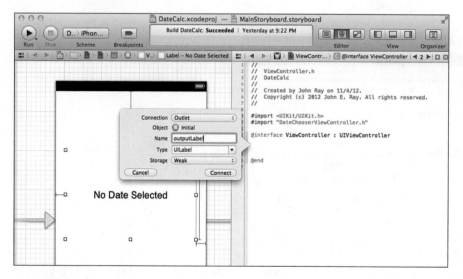

FIGURE 12.12
Connect to the output label.

Adding the Actions

Beyond the single outlet, every other connection in this project is an action. Within the initial scene, Control-drag from the Choose a Date button to below the property definition in ViewController.h. When prompted, add a new action named **showDateChooser**.

Move to the second (date chooser) scene and Control-drag from the date picker to the DateChooserViewController.h file, targeting below the `@interface` line. When prompted, create a new action named **setDateTime** that is triggered on the `Value Changed` event. If you're developing for the iPad, you're done; your users will just touch outside the popover to make it go away. If you're creating an iPhone app, however, you must Control-drag from the Done button to DateChooserViewController.h. Create a new action called **dismissDateChooser** that will be triggered from the button.

Implementing the Scene Segue Logic

We need to handle two primary tasks in the application logic. First, we need to handle the interactions between our initial scene's view controller and the date chooser view controller. Second, we need to be able to calculate and display a difference between dates. We start with the communications between the view controllers.

Importing the Interface Files

In the preceding hour's lesson, we had two view controllers, but only one of the two needed to access properties/methods inside the other. In this tutorial, the `ViewController` class needs to access properties in `DateChooserViewController` and vice versa.

Add the following line after the existing `#import` statement in ViewController.h:

```
#import "DateChooserViewController.h"
```

Similarly, in the DateChooserViewController.h, add an import line for ViewController.h:

```
#import "ViewController.h"
```

Once those lines are in place, our two classes can access the methods and properties defined in their interface (.h) files.

Creating and Setting a Delegate Property

In addition to the two classes being aware of the methods and properties each other provides, we require a convenient way for the date chooser view controller to access the initial scene's view controller object. It uses this property to trigger a date calculation in the initial scene's view controller and to indicate when it (the date chooser) has been removed from the display. Remember that for the popover version of this project, we need to make sure that the application tries to show us just one copy of the popover at a time.

If the project were using a modal segue only, we could use the `presentingViewController` property within `DateChooserViewController`, but this property doesn't work on popovers. To keep things consistent between modal and popover implementations, we add a `delegate` property to the `DateChooserViewController` class.

Edit DateChooserViewController.h and add the following line after the `@interface` directive:

```
@property (weak, nonatomic) id delegate;
```

This defines the new property with a type of `id`, meaning that it can reference any object we want—just like delegate properties that are built in to Apple's classes.

To set the `delegate` property, we can tie into the `prepareForSegue:sender` method that will automatically be called in ViewController.m when the segue between the initial scene and the date chooser scene takes place. Update ViewController.m to include the method shown in Listing 12.4.

LISTING 12.4   Set the Delegate During the Segue

```
- (void)prepareForSegue:(UIStoryboardSegue *)segue sender:(id)sender {
    ((DateChooserViewController *)segue.destinationViewController).delegate=self;
}
```

This line of code typecasts the segue's `destinationViewController` property to a `DateChooserViewController` object (which we know it is) and sets the `delegate` property we created in that class to `self` (that is, to the current instance of the initial scene's `ViewController` class).

NOTE

Particularly observant readers might be questioning whether we should instead be accessing the `contentViewController` property so that the code will work with a popover—as we did in the preceding hour. Good news. The `destinationViewController` property gives us the same reference as the `contentViewController` but takes less work to access it.

Now we're all set to communicate between the initial and date chooser scenes. Importing the interface files provided the foundation for referencing methods and properties between the scene's view controllers, and the delegate property provides a mechanism for exchanging information.

Our next step is to implement the segue between the scenes and to use the delegate (and another property we define shortly) to make sure that we don't try to execute the segue repeatedly and create multiple copies of the date chooser scene.

Handling the Segue to and from the Date Chooser Scene

In this app, the segue was created between view controllers rather than between an object and a view controller. This is what I've been referring to as a "manual" segue, because it will need to be triggered from code in the `showDateChooser` method. When triggering the segue, we first need to check whether the date chooser is already showing on the screen; we do this via a Boolean property (`dateChooserVisible`) that is added to the `ViewController` class. Update ViewController.h to include this property definition now:

```
@property (nonatomic) Boolean dateChooserVisible;
```

A Boolean value is not an object, so the `weak` keyboard isn't used when declaring the property.

Now, implement the `showDateChooser` method so that it first checks to make sure the `date-ChooserVisible` property isn't currently `YES`, uses `performSegueWithIdentifier:sender` to initiate the segue to the date chooser, and finally toggles the `dateChooserVisible` property to `YES` so that we know it is onscreen. Listing 12.5 shows my implementation in ViewController.m.

LISTING 12.5 Show the Date Chooser Scene, If Needed

```
- (IBAction)showDateChooser:(id)sender {
    if (self.dateChooserVisible!=YES) {
        [self performSegueWithIdentifier:@"toDateChooser" sender:sender];
        self.dateChooserVisible=YES;
    }
}
```

At this point, you can run the application and press the Choose a Date button to show the date chooser, but in the case of the iPad, you can show the chooser just one time because we haven't written code to set `dateChooserVisible` to `NO`. iPhone users won't be able to dismiss the modal date chooser scene because their Done button isn't wired up yet.

To address the first shortcoming, we can edit the DateChooserViewController.m class to include the `viewWillDisappear` method. This gives us a nice place to add the necessary code to set `dateChooserVisible` to `NO`, right as it is about to be removed from the device's screen. Because we're updating this property from the date chooser view controller, we use the `delegate` property we defined earlier to access `dateChooserVisible`. Implement `viewWillDisappear` in DateChooserViewController.m, as shown in Listing 12.6.

LISTING 12.6 Toggle the Date Chooser's Visibility Flag to `NO`

```
-(void)viewWillDisappear:(BOOL)animated {
    [super viewWillDisappear:animated];
    ((ViewController *)self.delegate).dateChooserVisible=NO;
}
```

The final method that we need for handling our segue is for the iPhone only: dismissing the modal segue when the user presses the Done button in the date chooser scene. You've already made the connection to `dismissDateChooser`; you just need to add a call to `dismissView-ControllerAnimated:completion`. Listing 12.7 shows the one-line implementation of `dismiss-DateChooser` in DateChooserViewController.m.

LISTING 12.7 Dismiss the Modal Scene

```
- (IBAction)dismissDateChooser:(id)sender {
    [self dismissViewControllerAnimated:YES completion:nil];
}
```

Everything is in place for hiding and showing the date chooser scene via a modal segue on the iPhone and a popover on the iPad. What isn't finished, however, is the logic for calculating the difference between the current day and the day the user chooses.

NOTE

In the preceding hour, we used the an exit/unwind segue to move back to the initial scene; it was meant as a learning exercise. In this implementation, we just use the `dismissViewController-Animated:completion` method, because it is easier and quicker for a two-scene project.

Implementing the Date Calculation Logic

The most difficult work that we still have in front of us with the date picker implementation is writing the `calculateDateDifference` logic. To do what we've set out to (show the difference between today's date and the date in the picker), we must complete several tasks:

▶ Get today's date

▶ Display a date and time

▶ Calculate the difference between two dates

Before writing the code, let's look at the different methods and data types that we need.

Getting the Date

To get the current date and store it in an `NSDate` object, all that we need to do is to initialize a new `NSDate` with the `date` method. When initialized, it automatically stores the current date. This means that a single line takes care of our first hurdle:

```
todaysDate=[NSDate date];
```

Displaying a Date and Time

Unfortunately, displaying a date and time is a bit more tricky than getting the current date. Because we're going to be displaying the output in a label, we already know how it is going to be shown on the screen, so the question is really, how do we format a string with an `NSDate` object?

Interestingly enough, there's a class to handle this for us. We'll create and initialize an `NSDateFormatter` object. Next, we use the object's `setDateFormat` to create a custom format using a pattern string. Finally, we apply that format to our date using another method of `NSDateFormatter`, `stringFromDate`—which, given an `NSDate`, returns a string in the format that we defined.

For example, if we assume that we've already stored an NSDate in a variable todaysDate, we can output in a format like Month, Day, Year Hour:Minute:Second(AM or PM) with these lines:

```
dateFormat = [[NSDateFormatter alloc] init];
[dateFormat setDateFormat:@"MMMM d, yyyy hh:mm:ssa"];
todaysDateString = [dateFormat stringFromDate:todaysDate];
```

First, the formatter object is allocated and initialized in a new object, dateFormat. Then the string @"MMMM d, YYYY hh:mm:ssa" is used as a formatting string to set the format internally in the object. Finally, a new string is returned and stored in todaysDateString by using the dateFormat object's instance method stringFromDate.

Where in the World Did That Date Format String Come From?

The strings that you can use to define date formats are defined by a Unicode standard that you can find here: http://unicode.org/reports/tr35/tr35-6.html#Date_Format_Patterns.

For this example, the patterns are interpreted as follows:

MMMM: The full name of the month

d: The day of the month, with no leading zero

YYYY: The full four-digit year

hh: A two-digit hour (with leading zero if needed)

mm: Two digits representing the minute

ss: Two digits representing the second

a: AM or PM

Determining the Difference Between Two Dates

The last thing that we need to understand is how to compute the difference between two dates. Instead of needing any complicated math, we can just use the timeIntervalSinceDate instance method in an NSDate object. This method returns the difference between two dates, in seconds. For example, if we have two NSDate objects, todaysDate and futureDate, we could calculate the time in seconds between them with this:

```
NSTimeInterval difference;
difference = [todaysDate timeIntervalSinceDate:futureDate];
```

NOTE

Notice that we store the result in a variable of type NSTimeInterval. This isn't an object. Internally, it is just a double-precision floating-point number. Typically, this is declared using the native C data type double, but Apple abstracts this from us by using a new type of NSTimeInterval so that we know exactly what to expect out of a date difference calculation.

Note that if the `timeIntervalSinceDate:` method is given a date *before* the object that is invoking the method (that is, if `futureDate` was *before* `todaysDate` in the example), the difference returned is negative; otherwise, it is positive. To get rid of the negative sign, we use the C function `fabs(<float>)` that, given a floating-point number, returns its absolute value.

Implementing the Date Calculation and Display

To calculate the difference and dates, we implement a method in ViewController.m called `calculateDateDifference` that receives a single parameter (`chosenDate`). After writing the method for the calculation, we add code to the date chooser view controller to call the calculation when the date picker is used.

First, add a prototype for the calculation in the ViewController.h file:

```
- (void)calculateDateDifference:(NSDate *)chosenDate;
```

Next, add the `calculateDateDifference` method from Listing 12.8 to your ViewController.m file.

LISTING 12.8   Calculate the Difference Between Two Dates

```
 1: - (void)calculateDateDifference:(NSDate *)chosenDate {
 2:     NSDate *todaysDate;
 3:     NSString *differenceOutput;
 4:     NSString *todaysDateString;
 5:     NSString *chosenDateString;
 6:     NSDateFormatter *dateFormat;
 7:     NSTimeInterval difference;
 8:
 9:     todaysDate=[NSDate date];
10:     difference = [todaysDate timeIntervalSinceDate:chosenDate] / 86400;
11:
12:     dateFormat = [[NSDateFormatter alloc] init];
13:     [dateFormat setDateFormat:@"MMMM d, yyyy hh:mm:ssa"];
14:     todaysDateString = [dateFormat stringFromDate:todaysDate];
15:     chosenDateString = [dateFormat stringFromDate:chosenDate];
16:
17:     differenceOutput=[[NSString alloc] initWithFormat:
18:         @"Difference between chosen date (%@) and today (%@) in days:%1.2f",
19:                 chosenDateString,todaysDateString,fabs(difference)];
20:     self.outputLabel.text=differenceOutput;
21: }
```

Much of this should look pretty familiar based on the preceding examples, but let's review the logic. First, in lines 2–6, we declare the variables we'll be using: `todaysDate` will store the current date, `differenceOutput` will be our final formatted string displayed to the user, and `todays-DateString` will contain the formatted version of the current day's date. `chosenDateString` will hold the formatted date that is passed to the method, `dateFormat` will be our date formatting object, and `difference` is the double-precision floating-point number used to store the number of seconds between two dates.

Lines 9 and 10 do most of the work we set out to accomplish. In line 9, we allocate and initialize `todaysDate` as a new `NSDate` object. This automatically stores the current date and time in the object.

In line 10, we use `timeIntervalSinceDate` to calculate the time, in seconds, between `todays-Date` and `[sender date]`. Remember that `sender` will be the date picker object, and the `date` method tells an instance of `UIDatePicker` to return its current date and time in an `NSDate` object, so this gives our method everything it needs to work with. The result is divided by 86400 and stored in the `difference` variable. Why 86400? This is the number of seconds in a day, so we will be able to display the number of days between dates, rather than seconds.

In lines 12–15, we create a new date formatter object (`NSDateFormatter`) and use it to format `todaysDate` and `chosenDate`, storing the results in `todaysDateString` and `chosenDateString`.

Lines 17–19 format the final output string by allocating a new string (`differenceOutput`) and then initializing it with `initWithFormat`. The format string provided includes the message to be displayed to the user as well as the placeholders `%@` and `%1.2f`—representing a string and a floating-point number with a leading zero and two decimal places. These placeholders are replaced with the `todaysDateString`, `chosenDateString`, and the absolute value of the difference between the dates, `fabs(difference)`.

In line 20, the label we added to the view, `differenceResult`, is updated to display `differenceOutput`.

Updating the Date Output

To finish the tutorial, we need to add code to call the `calculateDateDifference` method so that the display is updated when the user picks a date. There are actually two places we need to call the calculation: when the user picks a new date and when date chooser is first displayed. In the second case, the user hasn't picked a date and the current date is displayed in the picker.

Start with the most important use case: handling a user's action by calculating the date difference when the `setDateTime` method is called. Recall that this is triggered when the date picker value changes. Update the method stub in DateChooserViewController.m with the code in Listing 12.9.

LISTING 12.9 Calculate the Date Difference

```
- (IBAction)setDateTime:(id)sender {
    [(ViewController *)self.delegate
        calculateDateDifference:((UIDatePicker *)sender).date];
}
```

The `delegate` property is used to access the `calculateDateDifference` method in ViewController.m. We pass it the `date` property returned from the date picker, and we're done. Unfortunately, if the user exits the picker without explicitly making a choice, there won't be a date calculation displayed.

If the user exits the picker, we can assume that the current date is what the user wanted. To handle this implicit selection, add the `viewDidAppear` method in DateChooserViewController.m, as shown in Listing 12.10.

LISTING 12.10 Perform a Default Calculation When the Date Chooser Is First Displayed

```
- (void)viewDidAppear:(BOOL)animated {
    [super viewDidAppear:animated];
    [(ViewController *)self.delegate calculateDateDifference:[NSDate date]];
}
```

This is identical to the `setDateTime` method, but we pass it a new `date` object with the current date rather than querying the picker. This ensures that a calculated value is displayed, even if the user immediately dismisses the modal scene or popover.

Building the Application

The date picker application is complete. Run and test the app to get an idea for how the different pieces come together. Something to look for during your testing is the behavior of the iPad/ popover version of the application. You may have wondered why we update the initial scene's output label each time the user chooses a new date rather than waiting until the user dismisses the date chooser scene. The reason for this is because, in the iPad version, the initial scene remains visible while the date chooser is displayed in the popover. As a result, the user can actually see live feedback as he picks new dates.

You've just implemented a date picker, learned how to perform some basic date arithmetic, and even formatted dates for output using date formatting strings. What could be better? Creating your own custom picker with your own data, of course.

Using a Custom Picker

In the second project of this hour's lesson, you create a custom picker that presents two components, one with an image (an animal) and another with a text string (an animal sound). As with the previous project, the picker is displayed via a modal segue on the iPhone and a popover on the iPad, as shown in Figure 12.13.

FIGURE 12.13
Create a working custom picker.

When users choose an animal or sound from the custom picker view, their selection is displayed in an output label.

Implementation Overview

While the implementation of the custom picker requires that we have a class that conforms to the picker's delegate and data source protocols, many of the core processes in this application are identical to the last. An initial scene contains an output label and a toolbar with a single button. Touching the button triggers a segue to the custom chooser's scene. From there, the user can manipulate the custom picker and return to the initial scene by touching a Done button or, on the iPad, touching outside the popover that appears.

We also add the logic, using the same approach as earlier, to prevent multiple popovers from appearing. The property names will change a bit to better reflect their role in this application, but logic and implementation are nearly identical. Because of this similarity, we will work quickly and provide detailed instructions only where the projects differ.

Setting Up the Project

Create a new project named **CustomPicker** based on the Single View Application template. If you built the previous tutorial for the iPhone, I suggest that you build this project for the iPad (or vice versa). Even though developing for the two devices is almost identical, it's going to get a feel for using the design tools with the different hardware targets.

Adding the Image Resources

For the custom picker to show animal pictures, we need to add a few images to the project. Drag the Images folder to your main project code group and choose to copy files and create groups when prompted.

Open the Images group that appears and verify that you have seven images in your project: bear.png, cat.png, dog.png, goose.png, mouse.png, pig.png, and snake.png.

Adding the Animal Chooser View Controller Class

Like the DateChooserViewController class presented a scene with a date picker, the AnimalChooserViewController class will handle the display and selection of an animal and a sound. Click the + button at the bottom-left corner of the project navigator and choose New File. Create a new Objective-C class: a UIViewController subclass named AnimalChooserViewController. Place the new class files in your project's main code group.

Adding the Animal Chooser Scene and Associating the View Controller

Open the MainStoryboard.storyboard and display the Object Library (Control-Option-Command-3). Drag a view controller into an empty area of the IB editor or the document outline area.

Select the new scene's view controller icon, and then use the Identity Inspector (Option-Command-3) to set the Custom Class drop-down menu to AnimalChooserViewController. Use the Identity Inspector to set the label for the first view to Initial and the second scene to Animal Chooser. These changes should be reflected immediately in the document outline.

Planning the Properties, Variables, and Connections

The outlets and actions in this project mirror the last, with one exception. In the previous tutorial, we needed a method to be executed when the date picker changed its value. In this tutorial, we implement protocols for the custom picker that include a method that is called automatically when the picker is used.

The initial scene has a label for output (outputLabel) and an action (showAnimalChooser) for displaying the animal chooser scene. The scene's ViewController class tracks whether the animal chooser scene is visible through a property animalChooserVisible. The class shows the selected animal/sound using a method: displayAnimal:WithSound:FromComponent.

For the animal chooser scene, one action (dismissAnimalChooser) is tied to a button that is used to exit the animal chooser modal scene in the iPhone implementation. We also implement another delegate property that stores a reference to the initial scene's view controller. In addition, there are three private instance variables (_animalNames, _animalSounds, and _animalImages) added as NSArray objects. These contain the animal names that we are displaying, the sounds to display in the custom chooser components, and the image resource names that correspond to the animals.

Adding the Custom Picker Component Constants

When creating custom pickers, we have to implement a variety of protocol methods that refer to the various components (the spinny wheels) by number. To simplify a customer picker implementation, you can define constants for the components so that you can refer to them symbolically.

In this tutorial, we refer to component 0 as the animal component and component 1 as the sound component. By defining a few constants at the start of our implementation file, we easily refer to them by name. Edit AnimalChooserViewController.m and add these lines so that they follow the #import line:

```
#define kComponentCount 2
#define kAnimalComponent 0
#define kSoundComponent 1
```

The first constant, kComponentCount, is just the number of components that we want to display in the picker, whereas the other two constants, kAnimalComponent and kSoundComponent, can be used to refer to the different components in the picker without resorting to using their actual numbers.

What's Wrong with Referring to Something by Its Number?

Absolutely nothing. The reason that it is helpful to use constants, however, is that if your design changes and you decide to change the order of the components or add another component, you can just change the numbering within the constants rather than each place they're used in the code.

Designing the Interface

Open the MainStoryboard.storyboard file and scroll so that you can see the initial scene in the editor. Using the Object Library (Control-Command-Option-3), drag a toolbar into the bottom of the view. Change the default bar button item to read **Choose an Animal and Sound**. Use two Flexible Space Button Bar Items from the Object Library to center the button.

Next, add a label with the default text **Nothing Selected** to the center of the view. Use the Attributes Inspector to center the text, increase the font size, and set the label to display at least five lines of text. Figure 12.14 demonstrates my initial view layout.

FIGURE 12.14
The initial scene.

Configure the animal chooser scene as you did the date chooser scene, setting a background label that reads **Please Pick an Animal and Sound,** but this time drag a picker view object into the top of the scene. If you're working on an iPad version of the application, this view will ultimately be presented as a popover, so the upper-left corner of the view is all that will be visible.

If working on an iPhone version of the application, drag a button to the bottom of the view and label it **Done**. This, as before, is used to dismiss the animal chooser scene. Figure 12.15 shows my finished animal chooser interface.

FIGURE 12.15
The animal chooser scene.

Setting the Picker View Data Source and Delegate

In this project, we have the `AnimalChooserViewController` class serve double-duty and act as the picker view's data source and delegate. In other words, the `AnimalChooserViewController` class is responsible for implementing all the methods needed to make a custom picker view work.

To set the data source and delegate for the picker view, select it in the animal chooser scene or the document outline area, and then open the Connections Inspector (Option-Command-6). Drag from the `dataSource` outlet to the `Animal Chooser View Controller` line in the document outline. Do the same for the `delegate` outlet. Once finished, the Connections Inspector should resemble Figure 12.16.

FIGURE 12.16
Connect the picker view's `delegate` and `dataSource` outlets to the animal chooser view controller object.

Creating the Segue

It's time to make the segue between scenes. Control-drag from the view controller in the initial scene to the view controller in the animal chooser. Create a modal segue for the iPhone or popover for the iPad. A line labeled `Popover Segue from Initial to Animal Chooser` will show when the segue has been created. Open the Attributes Inspector (Option-Command-4) to configure the segue.

Provide an identifier for the segue: **toAnimalChooser**. We will use this ID to trigger the segue in our implementation code.

Setting the Popover Size and Anchor (iPad Only)

On the iPad version of the application, set an "anchor" for the popover by opening the Attributes Inspector and dragging from the Anchor field to the Choose an Animal and Sound button in the initial scene's toolbar.

Update the view controller for the animal chooser scene so that its size is freeform and its status bar is hidden. Use the Size Inspector to set the view's width and height to 320 points. Arrange your content so that it is attractively spaced in the scene.

Creating and Connecting the Outlets and Actions

A total of three connections are required (an action and an outlet in the initial scene, and a single action in the animal chooser scene):

▶ **outputLabel** (**UILabel**): The label in the initial scene that will display the results of the user's interactions with the picker view.

▶ **showAnimalChooser**: An action method triggered by the Choose an Animal and Sound bar button item in the initial scene.

▶ **dismissAnimalChooser**: An action method triggered by the Done button in the animal chooser scene. This is required only in the iPhone implementation.

Switch to the assistant editor and make the connections.

Adding the Outlet

Select the output label in the initial scene and Control-drag from the label to just below the @interface line in ViewController.h. When prompted, create a new outlet named outputLabel.

Adding the Actions

Again in the initial scene, Control-drag from the Choose an Animal and Sound button to below the property definition in ViewController.h. When prompted, add a new action named **showAnimalChooser**.

If you're working on an iPhone app, move to the second scene and Control-drag from the Done button to AnimalChooserViewController.h. Create a new action called **dismissAnimalChooser** that will be triggered from the button.

Implementing the Scene Segue Logic

As in the preceding previous tutorial, our implementation of the custom picker view requires some special attention. We need to make sure that in the popover version of the implementation the app doesn't end up displaying multiple overlapping copies of the animal chooser scene. The same process used in DateCalc is followed here.

Importing the Interface Files

Update the interface files for both of the view controller classes so that they import each other's interface. Add the following line after the existing #import statement in ViewController.h:

```
#import "AnimalChooserViewController.h"
```

In the AnimalChooserViewController.h, add an import line for ViewController.h:

```
#import "ViewController.h"
```

Creating and Setting a `delegate` Property

We will again use the delegate to access the view controller for the initial scene. Edit AnimalChooserViewController.h and add this line following the `@interface` line:

```
@property (weak, nonatomic) id delegate;
```

To set the new `delegate` property, update ViewController.m to include the method shown in Listing 12.11.

LISTING 12.11   Set the Delegate During the Segue

```
- (void)prepareForSegue:(UIStoryboardSegue *)segue sender:(id)sender {
    ((AnimalChooserViewController *)segue.destinationViewController).delegate=self;
}
```

Handling the Segue to and from the Animal Chooser Scene

In this tutorial, we use a property (`animalChooserVisible`) to store the current visibility of the animal chooser scene. Update ViewController.h to include this property definition now:

```
@property (nonatomic) Boolean animalChooserVisible;
```

Implement the `showAnimalChooser` method to call `performSegueWithIdentifier:sender` if the `animalChooserVisible` flag is set to NO. Listing 12.12 shows my implementation in ViewController.m.

LISTING 12.12   Show the Animal Chooser Scene, If Needed

```
- (IBAction)showAnimalChooser:(id)sender {
    if (self.animalChooserVisible!=YES) {
        [self performSegueWithIdentifier:@"toAnimalChooser" sender:sender];
        self.animalChooserVisible=YES;
    }
}
```

To toggle the `animalChooserVisible` flag to NO, we set it in the AnimalChooserViewController.m `viewWillDisappear` method, as shown in Listing 12.13.

LISTING 12.13   Toggle the Animal Chooser's Visibility Flag to NO

```
- (void)viewWillDisappear:(BOOL)animated {
    ((ViewController *)self.delegate).animalChooserVisible=NO;
}
```

The iPhone implementation requires that we manually dismiss the modal scene. If you're building the application for the iPhone platform, implement the `dismissAnimalChooser` method in AnimalChooserViewController.m (see Listing 12.14).

LISTING 12.14 Dismiss the Modal Scene

```
- (IBAction)dismissAnimalChooser:(id)sender {
    [self dismissViewControllerAnimated:YES completion:nil];
}
```

That finishes the handling of the popover/modal view segue and all the logic needed to make sure that it works as intended. This leaves us with the implementation of the custom picker view and display of the user's selection.

Implementing the Custom Picker View

Early in this hour, we presented a possible implementation of a very (very) limited custom picker view. Even though it didn't represent a real-world application, it is close to what we will need to do to finish this example and create a custom picker that displays images and text, side by side, in two components. We'll slow things down again and complete this hour's lesson with a full explanation of the creation of the custom picker view.

Loading the Picker Data

To present the picker, we need to supply it with data. We've loaded the image resources, but to provide the images to the picker, we need to be able to reference them by name. In addition, we need to be able to "translate" between the image of an animal and its real name. That is, if a user picks an image of a pig, we want the application to say Pig, not pig.png. To do this, we have an array of animal images (`_animalImages`) and an array of animal names (`_animal-Names`) that share the same index. For example, if the user picks an image that corresponds to the third element of `_animalImages`, we can get the name from the third element of `_animal-Names`. We also need the data for the list of animal sounds presented in the second picker view component. For that, we use a third array: `_animalSounds`.

Declare these three arrays as private instance variables in AnimalChooserViewController.m by updating the `@interface` block at the top of the file:

```
@interface AnimalChooserViewController () {
    NSArray *_animalNames;
    NSArray *_animalSounds;
    NSArray *_animalImages;
}
@end
```

Now, we need to allocate and initialize the data in each array. For the names and sounds arrays, we will just be storing strings. In the images array, however, we will be storing initialized `UIImageViews`. Implement the `viewDidLoad` method in AnimalChooserViewController.m as shown in Listing 12.15.

LISTING 12.15 Load the Data Required for the Picker View

```
 1: - (void)viewDidLoad
 2: {
 3:     [super viewDidLoad];
 4:
 5:     _animalNames=@[@"Mouse",@"Goose",@"Cat",@"Dog",@"Snake",@"Bear",@"Pig"];
 6:     _animalSounds=@[@"Oink",@"Rawr",@"Ssss",@"Roof",@"Meow",@"Honk",@"Squeak"];
 7:     _animalImages=@[
 8:         [[UIImageView alloc] initWithImage:[UIImage imageNamed:@"mouse.png"]],
 9:         [[UIImageView alloc] initWithImage:[UIImage imageNamed:@"goose.png"]],
10:         [[UIImageView alloc] initWithImage:[UIImage imageNamed:@"cat.png"]],
11:         [[UIImageView alloc] initWithImage:[UIImage imageNamed:@"dog.png"]],
12:         [[UIImageView alloc] initWithImage:[UIImage imageNamed:@"snake.png"]],
13:         [[UIImageView alloc] initWithImage:[UIImage imageNamed:@"bear.png"]],
14:         [[UIImageView alloc] initWithImage:[UIImage imageNamed:@"pig.png"]],
15:     ];
16: }
```

Line 5 creates the _animalNames array with seven animal names.

Line 6 initializes the _animalSounds array with seven animal sounds.

Lines 7–15 create the _animalImages array with seven `UIImageView` instances loaded from the images that were imported at the start of the project.

Implementing the Picker View Data Source Protocol

The next step is to begin implementing the protocols that the custom picker requires. The first, the data source protocol, provides information to the picker about the number of components it will be displaying and the number of elements within each of those components.

Declare that we will be conforming to the `UIPickerViewDataSource` by editing the AnimalChooserViewController.h and modifying the `@interface` line to read as follows:

```
@interface AnimalChooserViewController :
                UIViewController <UIPickerViewDataSource>
```

Next, implement the `numberOfComponentsInPickerView` method. This method returns the number of components the picker will display. Because we defined a constant for this (`kComponentCount`), all we need to do is return the constant, as shown in Listing 12.16.

LISTING 12.16   Return the Number of Components

```
- (NSInteger)numberOfComponentsInPickerView:(UIPickerView *)pickerView {
    return kComponentCount;
}
```

The other data source method required is the `pickerView:numberOfRowsInComponent`, which, given a component number, returns the number of elements that will be shown in that component. We can use the `kAnimalComponent` and `kSoundComponent` to simplify identifying which component is which, and the `NSArray` class method count to get the number of elements in an array. Using this, we can implement `pickerView:numberOfRowsInComponent` using the approach in Listing 12.17.

LISTING 12.17   Return the Number of Elements per Component

```
1: - (NSInteger)pickerView:(UIPickerView *)pickerView
2:              numberOfRowsInComponent:(NSInteger)component {
3:     if (component==kAnimalComponent) {
4:         return [_animalNames count];
5:     } else {
6:         return [_animalSounds count];
7:     }
8: }
```

Line 3 checks whether the component being queried is the animal component. If it is, line 4 returns a count of the number of animals in the _animalNames array. (The image array would work as well.)

If the component being checked isn't the animal component, we can assume it is the sound component (line 5) and return the count of elements in the _animalSounds array.

That's all the data source needs to do. The remainder of the picker view work is handled by the picker view delegate protocol: `UIPickerViewDelegate`.

Implementing the Picker View Delegate Protocol

The picker view delegate protocol handles customizing the display of the picker and reacting to a user's choice within the custom picker. Update AnimalChooserViewController.h to state our intention to conform to the delegate protocol:

```
@interface AnimalChooserViewController : UIViewController
                    <UIPickerViewDataSource, UIPickerViewDelegate>
```

Several delegate methods are needed to produce the picker we want, but the most important is `pickerView:viewForRow:forComponent:reusingView`. This method takes an incoming component and row and returns a custom view that will be displayed in the picker.

For our implementation, we want the animal images to be returned for the first component, and a label with the animal sounds returned for the second. Add the method, as written in Listing 12.18, to your project.

LISTING 12.18   Provide a Custom View for Each Possible Picker Element

```
 1: - (UIView *)pickerView:(UIPickerView *)pickerView viewForRow:(NSInteger)row
 2:          forComponent:(NSInteger)component reusingView:(UIView *)view {
 3:     if (component==kAnimalComponent) {
 4:         return _animalImages[row];
 5:     } else {
 6:         UILabel *soundLabel;
 7:         soundLabel=[[UILabel alloc] initWithFrame:CGRectMake(0,0,100,32)];
 8:         soundLabel.backgroundColor=[UIColor clearColor];
 9:         soundLabel.text=_animalSounds[row];
10:         return soundLabel;
11:     }
12: }
```

In lines 3–4, we check to see whether the component requested is the animal component, and if it is, we use the row parameter to return the appropriate UIImageView stored in the _animalImages array. If the component parameter isn't referring to the animal component, we need to return a UILabel with the appropriate referenced row from the _animalSounds array. This is handled in lines 5–11.

In line 6, we declare a UILabel named soundLabel. Line 7 allocates and initializes soundLabel with a frame using the initWithFrame method. Remember from earlier hours that views define a rectangular area for the content that is displayed on the screen. To create the label, we need to define the rectangle of its frame. The CGRectMake function takes starting x,y values and a width and height. In this example, we've defined a rectangle that starts at 0,0 and is 100 points wide and 32 points tall.

Line 8 sets the background color attribute of the label to be transparent. As you learned with web views, [UIColor clearColor] returns a color object configured as transparent. If we leave this line out, the rectangle will not blend in with the background of the picker view.

Line 9 sets the text of the label to the string of the specified row in _animalSounds.

Finally, line 10 returns the UILabel—ready for display.

Changing the Component and Row Sizes

If you were to run the application now, you'd see the custom picker, but it would look a bit squished. To adjust the size of components in the picker view, we can implement two more delegate methods: pickerView:rowHeightForComponent and pickerView:widthForComponent.

For this application example, some trial and error led me to determine that the animal component should be 75 points wide, while the sound component looks best at around 150 points.

Both components should use a constant row height of 55 points.

Translating this into code, implement both of these methods in AnimalChooserViewController.m, as shown in Listing 12.19.

LISTING 12.19 Set a Custom Height and Width for the Picker Components and Rows

```
- (CGFloat)pickerView:(UIPickerView *)pickerView
        rowHeightForComponent:(NSInteger)component {
    return 55.0;
}

- (CGFloat)pickerView:(UIPickerView *)pickerView
        widthForComponent:(NSInteger)component {
    if (component==kAnimalComponent) {
        return 75.0;
    } else {
        return 150.0;
    }
}
```

Reacting to a Selection in the Picker View

In the date picker example, you connected the picker to an action method and used the Value Changed event to capture when they modified the picker. Custom pickers, unfortunately, do not work this way. To grab a user's selection from a custom picker, you must implement yet another delegate method: `pickerView:didSelectRow:inComponent`. This method provides the component and row where a selection was made.

Notice anything strange about that method? It gives us the component and row the user selected but doesn't provide the status of the other components. To get the value of other components, we have to use the picker instance method `selectedRowInComponent` along with the component we're interested in checking.

In this project, when the user makes a selection, we call the method `displayAnimal:withSound:fromComponent` to display the selection in the initial scene's output label. We haven't yet implemented this method, so let's do so now. Update ViewController.h with this method prototype:

```
- (void)displayAnimal:(NSString *)chosenAnimal
        withSound:(NSString *)chosenSound
    fromComponent:(NSString *)chosenComponent;
```

The implementation of the method in ViewController.m should take the incoming parameter strings and display them in the output label. Nothing fancy is required. My implementation is provided in Listing 12.20.

LISTING 12.20   Create a Method to Display the User's Selection

```
- (void)displayAnimal:(NSString *)chosenAnimal
            withSound:(NSString *)chosenSound
        fromComponent:(NSString *)chosenComponent {

    NSString *animalSoundString;
    animalSoundString=[[NSString alloc]
                    initWithFormat:@"You changed %@ (%@ and the sound %@)",
                    chosenComponent,chosenAnimal,chosenSound];
    self.outputLabel.text=animalSoundString;

}
```

A string, `animalSoundString`, is created with the contents of the `chosenComponent`, `chosen-Animal`, and `chosenSound` strings. The output label is then set to display the new string.

Now that we have a mechanism for displaying the user's choice, we need to handle their selection. Implement `pickerView:didSelectRow:inComponent` in the AnimalChooserViewController.m file, as shown in Listing 12.21.

LISTING 12.21   React to a User's Selection

```
 1: - (void)pickerView:(UIPickerView *)pickerView didSelectRow:(NSInteger)row
 2:          inComponent:(NSInteger)component {
 3:
 4:      ViewController *initialView;
 5:      initialView=(ViewController *)self.delegate;
 6:
 7:      if (component==kAnimalComponent) {
 8:          int chosenSound=[pickerView selectedRowInComponent:kSoundComponent];
 9:          [initialView displayAnimal:_animalNames[row]
10:                    withSound:_animalSounds[chosenSound]
11:                fromComponent:@"the Animal"];
12:      } else {
13:          int chosenAnimal=[pickerView selectedRowInComponent:kAnimalComponent];
14:          [initialView displayAnimal:_animalNames[chosenAnimal]
15:                        withSound:_animalSounds[row]
16:                fromComponent:@"the Sound"];
17:      }
18:
19: }
```

The first thing that the method does is grab a handle to the initial scene's view controller in lines 4–5. We need this so we can display the user's selection within that scene.

Line 7 checks to see whether the selected component was the animal component. If it was, we still need to grab the currently selected sound (line 8). Lines 9–11 call the `displayAnimal:with Sound:fromComponent` method we just wrote, passing it the animal name, using the incoming row to select the right value from the array (line 9), the currently selected sound (line 10), and a string (the animal) to describe the component the user used (line 11).

In the event that the user chose a sound, lines 12–17 are executed instead. In this case, we need to look up the currently selected animal (line 13), and then, once again, pass all the relevant values to the display method to get them onscreen for the user.

Handling an Implicit Selection

As was the case with the date picker, the user can display the custom picker and then dismiss it without choosing anything. In this case, we should assume that the user wanted to choose the default animal and sound. To make sure this is accounted for, as soon as the animal chooser scene is displayed, we can update the output label in the initial scene with the default animal name, sound, and a message that nothing has been selected from a component ("nothing yet...").

As with the date picker, we can do this in the `viewDidAppear` method in AnimalChooserViewController.m. Implement the method as shown in Listing 12.22.

LISTING 12.22 Set a Default Selection

```
-(void)viewDidAppear:(BOOL)animated {
    [super viewDidAppear:animated];

    ViewController *initialView;
    initialView=(ViewController *)self.delegate;
    [initialView displayAnimal:_animalNames[0]
                  withSound:_animalSounds[0]
                fromComponent:@"nothing yet..."];
}
```

The implementation is simple. It grabs the initial view controller, and then it uses it to call the display method, passing the first element of the animal names and sounds arrays (because those are the elements displayed first in the picker). For the component, it passes a string to indicate that the user hasn't chosen anything from a component... yet.

Building the Application

Run the application and test your new custom picker view. The behavior of the animal chooser view controller should be nearly identical to the date picker despite the differences in implementation. The iPad version of the picker view (displayed in a popover) updates the output label as soon as a selection is made. The iPhone version does as well, but the view is obscured by the modal scene. Best of all, the project uses a single class and almost identical development to create a UI feature that follows best practices on both the iPhone and iPad. This is something you might want to revisit after learning about universal applications in Hour 23, "Building Universal Applications."

Further Exploration

As you learned in this lesson, `UIDatePicker` and `UIPickerView` objects are reasonably easy to use and quite flexible in what they can do. There are a few interesting aspects of using these controls that we haven't looked at that you may want to explore on your own. First, both classes implement a means of programmatically selecting a value and animating the picker components so that they "spin" to reach the values you're selecting: `setDate:animated` and `select Row:inComponent:animated`. If you've used applications that implement pickers, chances are, you've seen this in action.

Another popular approach to implementing pickers is to create components that appear to spin continuously (instead of reaching a start or stopping point). You may be surprised to learn that this is really just a programming trick. The most common way to implement this functionality is to use a picker view that simply repeats the same component rows over and over (thousands of times). This requires you to write the necessary logic in the delegate and data source protocol methods, but the overall effect is that the component rotates continuously.

Although these are certainly areas for exploration to expand your knowledge of pickers, you may also want to take a closer look at the documentation for toolbars (`UIToolbar`) and the `NSDate` class. Toolbars provide a clean way to create an unobtrusive user interface and save a great deal of space versus adding buttons everywhere in your views. The ability to manipulate dates can be a powerful capability in your applications.

Apple Tutorials

UIDatePicker, UIPickerView – UICatalog (accessible via the Xcode developer documentation): This great example code package includes samples of both the simple `UIDatePicker` and a full `UIPickerView` implementation.

Dates, Times, and Calendars – Date and Time Programming Guide (accessible via the Xcode developer documentation): This guide provides information on just about everything you could ever want to do with dates and times.

Summary

In this hour's lesson, you explored three UI elements—UIToolbar, UIDatePicker, and UIPickerView—that each present the user with a variety of options. Toolbars present a static list of buttons or icons at the top or bottom of the screen. Pickers present a "slot-machine" type of view where the user can spin components in the interface to create custom combinations of options. What ties these features together is that they are often employed with popovers. In fact, Apple requires that pickers be displayed in a popover.

Although toolbars and date pickers work like other UI elements you've experienced over the past few hours, the custom picker view is rather different. It requires us to write methods that conform to the UIPickerViewDelegate and UIPickerViewDataSource protocols.

In writing the sample picker applications, you also had a chance to make use of NSDate methods for calculating the interval between dates, as well as NSDateFormatter for creating user-friendly strings from an instance of NSDate. Although not the topic of this lesson, these are powerful tools for working with dates and times and interacting with your users.

Q&A

Q. Why didn't you cover the timer mode of the UIDatePicker?

A. The timer mode doesn't actually implement a timer; it's just a view that can display timer information. To implement a timer, you actually need to track the time and update the view accordingly—not something we can easily cover in the span of an hour.

Q. Where did you get the method names and parameters for the UIPickerView protocols?

A. The protocol methods that we implemented were taken directly from the Apple Xcode documentation for UIPickerViewDelegate and UIPickerViewDataSource. If you check the documentation, you can just copy and paste from the method definitions into your code.

Q. If we had to create a rectangle to define the frame of a UILabel, why didn't we do the same when creating the UIImageView objects?

A. When a UIImageView is initialized with an NSImage, its frame is set to the dimensions of the image.

Workshop

Quiz

1. An `NSDate` instance stores only a date. True or false?

2. The bar button item and flexible space item are two separate things. True or false?

3. Picker views can display images using the `pickerView:titleForRow:forComponent` method. True or false?

Answers

1. False. An instance of `NSDate` stores an "instant in time"—meaning a date and time.

2. False. The flexible space is just a special configuration of the bar button item.

3. False. The `pickerView:viewForRow:forComponent:reusingView` method must be implemented to display images within a picker.

Activities

1. Update the dateCalc project so that the program automatically sets the picker to the current date when it is loaded. You'll need to use the `setDate:animated` method to implement this change.

2. Update the CustomPicker project so that the user is rewarded for matching an animal to its sound. This was the original tutorial, but it had to be shortened for space. Here's a hint: The animal sounds are presented in the reverse order of the animals.

Advanced Storyboards Using Navigation and Tab Bar Controllers

What You'll Learn in This Hour:

▶ The purpose of navigation and tab bar controllers
▶ How to create navigation controller-based scenes with the storyboard
▶ How to build tab bar applications using the iOS tab bar template
▶ A way to share data between scenes using the navigation and tab bar controllers

Over the past few hours, you've become familiar with creating multiscene applications using modal scene segues and popovers. These are useful and common user interface (UI) features, but many iOS applications take a more "structured" approach to scene layout. Two of the most popular application layout methods involve the use of navigation controllers and tab bar controllers. Navigation controllers enable a user to drill down from one screen to another, exposing more detail as they go. You'll see this everywhere in iOS—from the settings app to bookmarks in Safari. The second approach, implementing a tab bar controller, is used for developing apps with multiple functional features, where each tab presents a different scene where the user can interact with a new set of controls.

In this hour, you learn about these two controllers and how they can provide a whole new world of interface options for your applications.

Advanced View Controllers

It is rare when an iOS (or any OS) update comes out that makes development simpler. Each release brings new features and new levels of complexity. Because of recent changes to Xcode and iOS, however, two common types of iOS view controllers have become much easier to integrate with your projects: navigation and tab bar controllers.

Previously relying on quite a bit of coding prowess, these advanced view controllers required multiple chapters just to cover basic implementation, and far more code than could be reasonably covered in a *24 Hours* book. Now, it's literally a matter of drag and drop.

Before we get started with looking at these new features, let's take a moment to review where we are in the book, and, specifically, what we've learned over the past few hours.

Multiscene Development

You've reached the second half of this book. Nicely done! You should now have a good sense of how to populate a scene and process a user's input.

We also started (in the past two hours) building apps with multiple scenes. This includes creating new view controller subclasses to handle each scene, adding segues, and, if necessary, writing code to manually trigger a segue. The key to being successful in creating multiscene applications is being able to easily exchange information between the different scenes so you can build a cohesive user experience. The more scenes you have, the more planning you need upfront to make sure that everything works the way you want it to.

In the preceding hour's lesson, you created a `delegate` attribute on one custom view controller subclass and used it to refer to the initial view controller object. Another approach is to create a brand-new class that does nothing but manage the information that needs to be shared across scenes. The two types of view controllers that we use in this hour include a "parent" view controller that manages multiple scenes that are presented to the user. This parent controller provides an excellent opportunity for exchanging information between scenes, since it is present regardless of which scene is visible. We put this to the test in our sample projects a bit later.

CAUTION
_____

Segues Where You Don't Want Them

If you need to directly reference one scene's view controller from another, you always can use an outlet to connect them. Just Control-drag from one view controller into the other view controller's interface file and add a property to reference it.

That said, if you attempt to add an outlet and then connect the view controller, Xcode prompts you to create a segue instead. Remember that if you want to create a connection and Xcode starts prompting you to make a segue, you can use the Connections Inspector to precisely target an outlet; no segue will get in the way.
_____

This hour is mostly visual—giving your typing fingers a break before kicking back in in the next hour. The Xcode storyboard feature makes what we're about to do possible in a *24 Hours* book and enables you to concentrate on coding application logic instead of worrying about getting the right scenes to display when you need them.

To Code or Not to Code, That Is the Question

Wherever it seems practical in this book, I provide instructions on how to perform actions through code. In the case of storyboard segues, the same code applies to any segue, so what you've learned over the past two hours to programmatically trigger a segue applies here as well.

Of course, there is still lower-level code than storyboard segues. In Hour 11, "Implementing Multiple Scenes and Popovers," for example, you learned how a popover can be created entirely in code and presented to a user. It wasn't difficult, but it also wasn't nearly as clean as presenting a popover via segue. It did, however, teach you how to instantiate and present view controllers programmatically.

In the case of navigation and tab bar controllers, the low-level code can get complex quickly, and, frankly, the utility of including it in the book is quite debatable; there isn't enough space to provide both working code examples and working storyboard examples. You may still need code for some advanced projects, but Apple has made it possible to create fully functional apps that don't require you to know all the inner details of implementing complex view controllers by hand.

To me, being able to pick up the book and create applications that work after only a few hours of reading is more important than a pedantic discussion of every iOS nuance, especially if you know where to look for more information. I write what I would want to read. If you have a different view, please let me know; I'm always striving to make the book more useful to the reader.

Exploring Navigation Controllers

The navigation controller (`UINavigationController`) class presents a series of scenes that represent hierarchical information. In other words, one scene presents a high-level view of a topic, a second scene drills down further, a third scene even further, and so on. For example, the iPhone version of the Contacts application presents a list of contact groups. Touching a group opens a list of contacts within that group. Touching an individual contact displays details on that person, as shown in Figure 13.1. At any point in time, a user can back out of a level of detail and return to the previous level or jump all the way to the starting point (called the root).

Managing this transition between scenes is the navigation controller. It creates a "stack" of view controllers. The root view controller is at the bottom. As a user navigates deeper into the scenes, each successive view controller is pushed on the stack, with the current scene's view controller at the very top. To return to a previous level, the navigation controller pops the topmost controller off the stack and returns to the one below it.

TIP

The terminology of `push` and `pop` is used to describe navigation controllers throughout the iOS documentation. You'll even be showing new scenes under a navigation controller by using the push segue. Be sure that you understand this concept before using it in your application.

FIGURE 13.1
Navigation controllers are prevalent in iOS.

Navigation Bars, Items, and Bar Button Items

In addition to managing the stack of view controllers, the navigation controller manages a navigation bar (UINavigationBar). Appearing similar to the toolbar you used in the preceding hour, a navigation bar is populated from an instance of a navigation item (UINavigationItem) that is added to each scene that falls under the navigation controller.

By default, the navigation item for a scene contains a title for that scene and a Back Button. The Back Button is added as a bar button item (UIBarButtonItem) within the navigation item (yes, just like the bar buttons you used in the last hour). You can even drag additional bar button items into the navigation item to add your own custom buttons to the navigation bar that is displayed for that scene.

I fully expect that if you've made it through that description you're getting a bit worried about having to manually handle all those different objects (and that's why doing this in code is not trivial!). Don't fear: Interface Builder makes it painless, and once you see how each scene is constructed, you'll have no problem working with all of these objects in your apps.

Using Navigation Controllers in Storyboard

Adding a navigation controller to a storyboard is very similar to adding a view controller, something you've done several times over the past two hours. It looks a bit different, but the process is the same. Let's assume you're starting with a Single View Application template.

First, you want to establish the code files for one or more view controller subclasses to handle the user's interactions within a given navigation controller scene. This is the same as any other scene. If you don't recall how to add new subclasses to your project, review Hours 11 and 12 to see how the modal scenes tutorials work.

Open your storyboard file in the IB editor. If you want your entire application to fall under the navigation controller, select the view controller in the default view and delete it. (You want to remove the corresponding ViewController.m and .h files, as well.) This removes the default scene. Next, you drag an instance of the navigation controller object from the Object Library into the document outline or the editor. This adds what appears to be two scenes to your project, as shown in Figure 13.2.

FIGURE 13.2
Add a navigation controller to your project.

The scene labeled Navigation Controller Scene represents the navigation controller. It is just a placeholder for the object that is going to control all the scenes that fall underneath it. Although you won't want to change much about the controller, you can use the Attributes Inspector to customize its appearance slightly (choosing a color scheme/tint, if desired).

The navigation controller is connected via a "relationship" to a scene titled with Root View Controller. By default, IB sets a table view controller as the root view controller. This can be removed, and the relationship to any custom view controller you'd like, created. We'll be doing that in one of today's tutorials.

The scenes under a navigation controller are exactly like any other scene; they just happen to have the navigation bar at the top and are able to use a push segue to transition to another scene. Development within these scenes is the same as developing in any other scene.

TIP
_____
I use the Single View Application template because it gives me an application with an associated storyboard file, and it gives me an initial view that I could, if needed, display before seguing into another view controller. If I don't want the initial scene, I delete it, and I delete the default ViewController.h and ViewController.m files. In my opinion, this is faster than using an empty application template and having to add a storyboard, and it is the best starting point for many applications.
_____

Setting the Navigation Bar Item Attributes

To change the title in the navigation bar, just double-click and start editing, or select the navigation item in the scene and open the Attributes Inspector (Option-Command-4), as shown in Figure 13.3.

FIGURE 13.3
Customize the navigation item for the scene.

There are three attributes you can change:

▶ **Title:** The title string that is shown at the top of the view

▶ **Prompt:** A line of text that provides instruction to the user (if needed) and is shown above the title

▶ **Back Button:** The text that appears in the Back button of the next scene

Now wait a minute. You can edit the text of the button that appears in a scene you don't even have yet? Yes. By default, when you transition from one navigation controller scene to another, the "title" of the previous scene shows up as the title of the Back Button in the next scene. Sometimes, however, the title may be long, or not necessarily appropriate. In these cases, you can set the Back Button attribute to whatever string you want, and if the user drills down to the next scene, that text will be displayed in the button that takes you back to the scene.

The Back Button text does one additional thing. Because iOS can no longer use its default behavior to create a Back Button, it creates a new custom bar button item within the navigation item that contains the title you wanted. You can customize this bar button item even more, changing its color and appearance using the Attributes Inspector.

So far, there is only a single scene under the navigation controller, so the Back button would never be displayed. Let's see how you can chain together multiple scenes to create the "drill-down" hierarchy that navigation controllers are known for.

NOTE
Remember, you can drag additional bar button items into a scene's navigation item to add toolbar-like controls to the scene.

Adding Additional Navigation Scenes with Push Segues

To add an additional scene to the navigation hierarchy, we follow the same process as adding a new modally presented scene to an application. Begin by creating a new scene that you want to be managed by the navigation view controller. Next, just Control-drag from the object that you want to trigger the segue to the new scene's view controller. When prompted, choose the push segue. You'll see a new segue line added to the originating scene, as well as a bunch of changes to the scene you just connected. The new scene shows the navigation bar and will automatically have its own navigation item added and displayed. You can customize the title and Back Button, add additional bar button items—the works.

What's even more important to realize here is that you can keep doing this. You can add additional push segues and even branch from multiple segues to follow different paths, as shown in Figure 13.4. Xcode keeps track of everything for you.

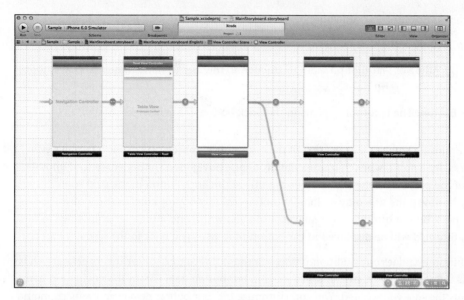

FIGURE 13.4
Create as many push segues as you need, even branches.

Keep in mind that these are just views, like any other, so you are welcome to add modal segues or popovers in your storyboard as well. One advantage that this hour's controllers have over modal segues is that transitioning to and from views is handled automatically. You don't need to add any code to use the Back Button within a navigation controller hierarchy, nor (as you learn shortly) any code to switch between scenes in a tab bar controller application.

Sharing Data Between Navigation Scenes

As I hinted early on, the navigation controller and tab bar controller classes, because they manage a series of views, give us a perfect place to share data. We can access these classes using the `parentViewController` attribute from any of the scenes we create—just like you used `presentingViewController` from a modal scene to access the view controller of the scene that presented it.

We can (and will) create a subclass of `UINavigationController` that does nothing but include properties we want to share between scenes, assign that as the identity class of the navigation controller that is managing all of our scenes, and then access those properties via `parentView-Controller` in any of the other views.

Understanding Tab Bar Controllers

The second type of view controller that we work with in this hour is the tab bar controller (`UITabBarController`). Tab bar controllers, like navigation controllers, are prominently featured in a wide range of iOS applications. As the name implies, a tab bar controller presents a series of "tabs" at the bottom of the screen, represented as icons and text, that can be touched to switch between scenes. Each scene represents a different function in the application or a unique way of viewing the application's information.

The Phone application on the iPhone, for example, presents different ways of sorting your calls using a tab bar controller, as shown in Figure 13.5.

FIGURE 13.5
A tab bar controller switches between unique scenes.

Like a navigation controller, the tab bar controller handles everything for you. When you touch a button to transition between scenes, it just works. You don't need to worry about programmatically handling tab bar events or manually switching between view controllers. The similarity doesn't end there.

Tab Bars and Tab Bar Items

The implementation of a tab bar within the storyboard is also very similar to a navigation controller. It contains a `UITabBar` that resembles a toolbar, but in appearance only. Any scene that is presented with the tab bar controller inherits this navigation bar within its scene.

The scenes presented by a tab bar controller must contain a tab bar item (`UITabBarItem`) that has a title, an image, and, if desired, a badge (a little red circle with a number in it).

TIP

If you're wondering why a tab might need a badge, imagine that you have a long-running calculation in one of the tab scenes in your application. If the user switches off of the tab, the calculation continues. You can have the scene's view controller update the badge in the tab, even when the user is viewing another tab's scene.

This gives an immediate visual indication that there is something to look at without the user needing to switch back and forth.

Using Tab Bar Controllers in Storyboard

Adding a tab bar controller to the storyboard is just as easy as adding a navigation controller. Let's walk through the steps of how to add the controller, configure the tab bar buttons, and add additional tab scenes to the storyboard.

CAUTION

We Don't Need No Stinkin' (Tabbed) Templates

Before you start building tab-based applications, I want to point out that Apple includes an iOS application template called the Tabbed Application. This template creates an application with two sample tabs already added and two view controller subclasses set up and associated with each tab. It also makes absolutely no sense (to me) to use.

This template may get you up and running a few seconds faster than adding a tab bar controller to a storyboard, but for production projects, it has a fatal flaw: Apple has associated two view controllers with the two default tabs in the application and named them `FirstViewController` and `SecondViewController`. There's nothing wrong with this for learning exercises, but in a real application, you want to name these in a way that reflects their actual use (`MovieListViewController`, `TheaterListViewController`, and so on). You could certainly rename all of their references in Xcode, but by the time you did that, it would have been faster to just add and associate your own tab bar controller and view controller subclasses.

To add a tab bar controller to an application, I recommend again starting with a Single View Application template. If you don't want the initial scene to segue into the tab bar controller, you just delete the initial scene by removing its view controller and then delete the corresponding `ViewController` interface and implementation files. Once your storyboard is in the state you want, drag an instance of the tab bar controller object from the Object Library into the document outline or the editor. This adds a controller and two sample tab bar scenes to the view, as shown in Figure 13.6.

FIGURE 13.6
Adding a tab bar controller adds two default scenes to the application.

The tab bar controller scene represents the `UITabBarController` object that coordinates all the scene transitions. Within it is a tab bar object that can be customized slightly with IB, changing the color.

From the tab bar controller are two "relationship" connections to the two scenes that the tab bar will display. The scenes can be differentiated by the name of the tab bar button that is added to them (Item 1 and Item 2, by default).

TIP

Even though all the tab bar item buttons are shown in the tab bar controller scene, they are actually part of the each individual scene. To change the tab bar buttons, you must edit the tab bar item added to a scene. The controller scene is left alone.

Setting the Tab Bar Item Attributes

To edit the tab bar item (`UITabBarItem`) that is displayed for any scene, open that scene's view controller and select the tab bar item within the document outline area, and then open the Attributes Inspector (Option-Command-4), as shown in Figure 13.7.

FIGURE 13.7
Customize each scene's tab bar item.

Using the Tab Bar Item section, you can set a value to be displayed in the tab bar item badge. Typically, you want to set this via tab bar item's `badgeValue` property (an `NSString`) in code. You can also use the Identifier pop-up menu to choose from over a dozen predefined tab bar icons and labels. If you choose to use a predefined icon/label, you cannot customize it further, because Apple wants these to remain constant throughout iOS.

To set your own image and title, use the Bar Item settings. The Title field sets the label for the tab bar item, and the Image drop-down associates an image resource from your project for the item.

TIP

Tab bar images are 32x32 points or smaller and are automatically styled by iOS to appear in a monochromatic color scheme (regardless of what colors you choose). Simple line drawings with a transparent background turn out the best when creating your tab bar interface art.

That's everything you need to configure a scene for a tab bar controller. But what if you want to add additional scenes to the tab bar? We tackle that now, and, as you'll see, it's even easier than adding a scene to a navigation controller.

Adding Additional Tab Bar Scenes

Unlike other segues that we've used, a tab bar has a clearly defined item (the tab bar item) that triggers a change in scene. The scene transition isn't even called a segue; it is a relationship between the tab bar controller and a scene. To create a new scene, tab bar item, and the relationship between the controller and scene, start by adding a new view controller to the storyboard.

Drag a new view controller instance into the document outline or editor. Next, Control-drag from the tab bar controller to the new scene's view controller in document outline. When prompted, choose Relationship Segue – View Controllers, as shown in Figure 13.8.

Creating the relationship does everything we need; it automatically adds a tab bar item to the new scene, ready to be configured. We can keep doing this to create as many tabs and scenes as we need in the tab bar.

NOTE

Let me repeat something I said earlier: The scenes that you're adding to the tab bar controller are the same as any other scene. You associate a view controller subclass using the Identity Inspector and then interact with the scene the same as you would any other.

To set the tab bar item's `badgeValue` property, for example, you can just create an outlet in your view controller to reference the tab bar item. It's exactly the same as if you had added a button or a label to a view and wanted to modify it programmatically.

FIGURE 13.8
Create a relationship between controllers.

Sharing Data Between Tab Bar Scenes

Like the navigation controller, a tab bar controller presents us with an easy opportunity to share information. Create a tab bar controller (UITabBarController) subclass that is assigned as the identity of the tab bar controller. Add properties to the subclass that represent the data we want to share, and then access those properties through the parentViewController property in each scene.

Now that you've seen how to add these new view controllers to your project, let's actually create a few examples that demonstrate these principles in action. As promised, these will be light on the typing, so don't expect a masterpiece. The beauty is that once you know see how easy it is to use these controllers, the possibilities for your applications will open up tremendously.

Using a Navigation Controller

In the first project, we create an application that presents a series of three scenes through a navigation controller. Within each scene, we show a Push button that increments a counter and then transitions to the next scene. The counter will be stored in a custom subclass of the navigation controller. In other words, this will provide both an example of building a navigation-based UI and of using the navigation controller to manage a property that all the scenes can access.

Figure 13.9 demonstrates what we want to accomplish.

FIGURE 13.9
Transition between scenes and manage shared information.

Implementation Overview

The implementation follows the process described earlier. We start with a Single View Application template, remove the initial scene and view controller, and then add a navigation controller and two custom classes: one a subclass of a navigation controller that will enable each scene in the application to share information, the other a subclass of a view controller that will handle user interactions in the scenes.

We remove the default table view controller that is used with the navigation controller and add three scenes, designating one as the root view scene for the controller. A Push button is included in each scene's view with an action method to increment a counter—as well as a segue from that button to the next scene.

NOTE

Doesn't each scene need its own view controller subclass? Yes and no. In most applications, you create a view controller for each scene. In this application, we're doing the same thing in each scene (so that a single view controller can be used, saving us time and code).

Setting Up the Project

Create a new single-view project called **LetsNavigate**. Before doing anything else, clean up the project so that we only have the things that we need. Start by selecting the `ViewController` class files (ViewController.h and ViewController.m) and pressing the Delete key. When prompted, choose to delete the files, not just the references.

Next, click the MainStoryboard.storyboard file and then select the View Controller line in the document outline area (Editor, Show Document Outline) and again press Delete. The scene will disappear. We now have the perfect starting point for our app.

Adding the Navigation Controller and Generic View Controller Classes

We need two additional classes added to the project. The first, a subclass of `UINavigationController`, manages our push count property and be named `CountingNavigationController`. The second, a subclass of `UIViewController`, is named **GenericViewController** and handles incrementing the push count as well as displaying the count in each scene.

Click the + button at the bottom-left corner of the project navigator and choose New File. Choose the iOS Cocoa Touch category and Objective-C class, and then click Next. Name the new class **CountingNavigationController**, set the subclass to **UINavigationController** (you will have to type in the class name), and, if you're building for iPad, click Targeted for iPad. Click Next. On the last setup screen, make sure that Xcode has chosen the code folder for your project (navigate to it, if not), choose your main project code group from the Group pop-up menu, and then click Create.

Repeat this process to create a new `UIViewController` subclass named `GenericViewController`. Make sure that you choose the right subclass for each of the new classes; otherwise, you'll have difficulty later on.

Adding the Navigation Controller

Open the MainStoryboard.storyboard in the IB editor. Display the Object Library (Control-Option-Command-3) and drag a navigation controller into an empty area of the IB editor (or into the document outline area). Your project will now show a navigation controller scene and a root view controller scene. For now, concentrate on the navigation controller scene.

We want to associate this controller with our `CountingNavigationController` class, so select the Navigation Controller line in the document outline, and then open the Identity Inspector (Option-Command-3). From the class drop-down menu, choose `CountingNavigationController`. Ta da! Done.

Now let's add the additional scenes we need and associate them with the generic view controller class we created.

Adding Additional Scenes and Associating the View Controller

With the storyboard still open, start by selecting the table view controller scene and pressing Delete. This gets rid of the default root view controller for the navigation controller. We want to associate our own (more flexible) `GenericViewController` class as the root view controller. To do this, drag a new view controller (`UIViewController`) from the Object Library into the IB editor. A new scene is created, and your document should resemble Figure 13.10. This will become your new root view.

FIGURE 13.10
Add a new view controller to use as a root view controller.

Control-drag from the navigation controller to the new view controller. When finished dragging, release your mouse button. You are prompted for the type of connection to make. Choose Relationship – Root View Controller. Your storyboard should now look like Figure 13.11.

FIGURE 13.11
The new root view controller is in place.

You're ready to add the other two scenes to the storyboard. Drag two more instances of the view controller object from the Object Library into the editor or the document outline. In a few minutes, these will be connected to the root view controller scene to form a series of scenes that are managed by the navigation controller.

After adding the additional scenes, we want to do two things to each of them (including the root view controller scene). First, we need to set the identity of each scene's view controller. In this case, one view controller class is handling all of them, so the identity will be set to GenericViewController. Next, it's a good idea to set a label for each view controller so that the scene has a friendlier name.

Start by selecting the root view controller scene's view controller object and opening the Identity Inspector (Option-Command-3). Use the Class drop-down menu to pick the GenericViewController. Still within the Identity Inspector, set the Label field (within the Document section) to **First**. Move to one of the new scenes you added, select its view controller line, set its class to GenericViewController, and the label to **Second**. Repeat the process for the last scene as well, setting its custom class and a label of **Third**. When finished, your document outline should look like Figure 13.12.

FIGURE 13.12
Your final document outline includes a navigation controller and three scenes (order is not important).

Planning the Properties and Connections

I'm intentionally trying to keep these projects light, so there isn't a great deal of information that needs to be stored or actions that will have to be defined. The CountingNavigationController will have a single property (pushCount) that contains the number of times we've pushed a new scene into view using the navigation controller.

The GenericViewController class will have a single property called countLabel that references a label in the UI displaying the current count of pushes. It will also have an action method named incrementCount that increases the pushCount property in the CountingNavigation Controller by one.

Why a Property Instead of an Instance Variable?

Remember, I've standardized on the approach of using a property for information that needs to be accessed from outside the class where it is defined. Instance variables are used for data that is only used inside the class where it is defined.

Does it really matter if you use properties for everything? Nope! You'll find Objective-C developers who will debate this to the world's end, but ultimately one implementation isn't any more "valid" than another (just as long as they work).

NOTE

The outlet and action in the `GenericViewController` class will be defined once, but, to be used in each scene, must be connected to the label and button individually in each scene.

Creating the Push Segues

Hey, isn't this the time when we work on the UI? In the past two hours, we created our UI and then we added the segue. What am I doing by switching things around? Good question. With applications that have only two scenes, it's easy to work on them separately and keep track of what is what. As soon as you start adding additional scenes, it becomes very helpful to lay them out in the storyboard, with segues, so that you can see how it all fits together before you create the interface. In addition, with the navigation controller and tab bar controllers, creating the connection actually adds objects to our scenes that we might want to configure when working on the interface; so, in my opinion, it just makes sense to create the segues first.

To build a segue for the navigation controller, we need something to trigger it. Within the storyboard editor, add a button (`UIButton`) labeled **Push** to the first and second scenes, but not the third. Why not the third? Because it is the last scene that can be displayed; there's nothing after it to segue to.

Next, Control-drag from the button in the first scene to the second scene's view controller line in the document outline, or target the scene directly in the editor. When prompted for the segue type, choose Push, as shown in Figure 13.13. A new segue line (push Segue from Push to Second) will be added to the first scene in the document outline, and the second scene will inherit the navigation controller's navigation bar, as well as gain a navigation item in its view.

Repeat this process, creating a push segue from the second scene's button to the third scene. Your IB editor should now contain a fully realized navigation controller sequence. Click and drag each scene in the view to arrange it in a way the makes sense to you. Figure 13.14 shows my interconnected views.

Designing the Interface

By adding the scenes and buttons, you've really just built most of the interface. The final steps will be customizing the title of the navigation item in each scene and adding an output label to display the push count.

Begin by going through each of the scenes (first, second, and third) and double-clicking the center of the navigation bar that now appears at the top of each view. Title the first view (in the root view controller) **First Scene**, the second **Second Scene**, and the third... wait for it... **Third Scene**.

FIGURE 13.13
Create a push segue.

FIGURE 13.14
Connect all of your views via segue.

Finally, to each of the scenes add a label (UILabel) near the top that reads **Push Count:** and a second label (the output label) with the default text of **0** (and a large, center aligned font, if you like) to the center of each view.

Figure 13.15 shows my final interface design.

FIGURE 13.15
The final layout of the navigation application.

Creating and Connecting the Outlets and Actions

There is only one outlet and one action that need to be defined in this project, but they need to be connected several times. The outlet (a connection to the label displaying the push count, countLabel) will be connected to each of the three scenes. The action (incrementCount) will need to be connected to the button only in the first and second scenes.

Position your display in the IB editor so that the first scene is visible (or just use the document outline), and click its push count label, and then switch to the assistant editor mode.

Adding the Outlet

Control-drag from the label in the center of the first scene to just below the `@interface` line in GenericViewController.h. When prompted, create a new outlet named `countLabel`.

That created the outlet and the connection from the first scene; now you need to connect it to the other two scenes. Control-drag from the second scene's push count label and target the `countLabel` property you just created. The entire line will highlight, as shown in Figure 13.16, showing you are making a connection to an existing outlet. Repeat this for the third scene, connecting its push count label to the same property.

FIGURE 13.16
Create the outlet, and then connect the other scenes' labels.

Adding the Action

Adding and connecting the action works in much the same way. Start by Control-dragging from the first scene's button to just below the property definition in GenericViewController.h. When prompted, create a new action named `incrementCount`.

Switch to the second view controller and Control-drag from its button to the existing `increment-Count` action. You've just made all the connections we need.

Implementing the Application Logic

Most of our work is now behind us. To finish the tutorial, we first need to set up the pushCount property in the CountingNavigationController class so that it can keep track of the number of times we've pushed a new scene in the application.

Adding the Push Count Property

Open the CountingNavigationController.h interface file and add a property definition for an integer named pushCount below the @interface line:

```
@property (nonatomic) int pushCount;
```

That's all we need to do to implement the custom CountingNavigationController class. Because it is a subclass of a UINavigationController, it already performs all the navigation controller tasks we need, and now it stores a pushCount property, too.

To access this property from the GenericViewController class that is handling the content for all the scenes in the application, we need to import the custom navigation controller's interface file in GenericViewController.h. Add this line following the existing #import statement:

```
#import "CountingNavigationController.h"
```

We're all set to finish our implementation, which is just a matter of adding the logic to GenericViewController that increments the counter and makes sure it is displayed on the screen when a new scene is pushed into view.

Incrementing and Displaying the Counter

To increment the counter in GenericViewController.m, we use the parentViewController property to access the pushCount property. The parentViewController, as you've learned, is automatically set to the navigation controller object within any scene managed by the navigation controller.

We need to typecast the parentViewController to our custom class of CountingNavigationController, but the full implementation is just a single line. Implement incrementCount, as shown in Listing 13.1.

LISTING 13.1   The incrementCount Implementation

```
- (IBAction)incrementCount:(id)sender {
    ((CountingNavigationController *)self.parentViewController).pushCount++;
}
```

The final step is to update the display to show the current count. Because pushing the button increments the push count and pushes a new scene into view, the incrementCount action isn't necessarily the best place for this logic to fall. In fact, it won't always be accurate, because the count could be updated in another view, and then the Back Button used to "pop" back to the original view, which would now be showing an invalid count.

To get around this, we just add the display logic to the viewWillAppear:animated method. This method is called right before a view is displayed onscreen (regardless of whether it is through a segue or by a user touching the Back Button), so it is a perfect place to update the label. Add the code in Listing 13.2 to the GenericViewController.m file.

LISTING 13.2   Update the Display in viewWillAppear:animated

```
1: -(void)viewWillAppear:(BOOL)animated {
2:     [super viewWillAppear:animated];
3:     NSString *pushText;
4:     pushText=[[NSString alloc] initWithFormat:@"%d",
5:         ((CountingNavigationController *)self.parentViewController).pushCount];
6:     self.countLabel.text=pushText;
7: }
```

Line 3 declares a new string, pushText, that will contain a string representation of the counter. Lines 4–5 allocate and initialize this string using the NSString initWithFormat method. The "%d" format string is replaced by the contents of the pushCount property, accessed using the same approach as in the incrementCount method.

In the last step, line 6, the countLabel is updated with the pushText string.

Building the Application

Run the application and test the navigation controller. Use the button to push new scenes on to the navigation controller stack, and then pop them back off with the Back Button functionality that we get for free. The push count stays in sync through all the different scenes because we now have a central class (CountingViewController) managing our shared property for us.

Using a Tab Bar Controller

In our second mini-project of the hour, we create an application with a tab bar controller that manages three individual scenes. As in the preceding project, each scene has a button to increment a counter, but these counters are unique for each scene (and visible in each scene's view). We even set the tab bar item's badge to that scene's counter. Again, we demonstrate the use of this custom controller and how scenes can share information through the controller class.

Figure 13.17 shows the result we want.

FIGURE 13.17
We will create a tab bar application with centrally stored properties.

Implementation Overview

We start with a cleaned-out Single View Application template. In this application, we add a tab bar controller and two custom classes: one a subclass of a tab bar controller to manage the application's properties, and the other a subclass of a view controller to manage the display of the other three views.

Each scene will again have a single button that calls a method to increment that scene's counter. Because the project calls for a unique counter for each scene, each button invokes a slightly different action method. This enables us to share all the code that is in common between the views (updating the badge and the count label) but have a slightly different increment action to target the right counter for that scene.

That's it; no segues needed this time around.

Setting Up the Project

Make a new single-view project called **LetsTab**. Clean out the project by removing the `ViewController` class files and the initial scene, just as you did in the previous tutorial. Your starting point should be a project with no view controller and an empty storyboard file.

Adding the Tab Bar Item Images

Each scene that is managed by the tab bar controller needs an icon to represent it in the tab bar UI element. The Images folder inside this hour's project folder contains three PNG files (1.png, 2.png, 3.png) that can be used for this example. Drag the folder into your main project code group now. Choose to create a new group, and copy the image resources when prompted.

Adding the Tab Bar Controller and Generic View Controller Classes

This project requires two custom classes. The first is a subclass of the UITabBarController that will hold three properties—counters for each of the scenes in the project. This custom controller class will be named **CountingTabBarController**. The second, a subclass of UIViewController, will be named **GenericViewController** and include an action to increment a scene-specific count of each button press that occurs.

Click the + button at the bottom-left corner of the project navigator and choose New File. Choose the iOS Cocoa Touch category and Objective-C class, and then click Next. Name the new class **CountingTarBarController** and configure the subclass to UITabBarController. If you're building for iPad, click Targeted for iPad, and then click Next. Be sure to create the class files inside your main project code group, or drag the files there later.

Repeat these steps, creating a new UIViewController subclass named **GenericViewController**. We did almost exactly this for the previous example, so if you're experiencing déjà vu, it's okay.

Adding the Tab Bar Controller

Open the project's storyboard, and drag a tab bar controller into an empty area of the IB editor (or into the document outline area). Your project will now show a tab bar controller scene with two scenes.

Associate the tab bar controller with the custom CountingTabBarController by selecting the Tab Bar Controller line in the document outline, and then open the Identity Inspector (Option-Command-3). From the class drop-down menu, choose CountingTabBarController.

Adding Additional Scenes and Associating the View Controller

The tab bar controller, by default, includes two scenes in your project. Why two? Because a tab bar controller only makes sense with more than one scene, so Apple chose to include two to start. This project, however, calls for three scenes to be managed by the tab bar controller, so drag an additional instance of the view controller object from the Object Library into the editor or the document outline.

After adding the additional scene, use the Identity Inspector to set each scene's custom class to be the GenericViewController and establish a label for easy identification.

Select the Item 1 scene that corresponds to the first tab in the tab bar. Using the Identity Inspector (Option-Command-3), set the Class drop-down menu to GenericViewController and the Label field to **First**. Move to the second scene and repeat, but set the label to **Second**. Finally, select the view controller line in the new scene you created. Set its class to GenericView Controller and the label to **Third**. Note that the third scene isn't yet connected to the tab bar controller; this is perfectly fine.

Planning the Properties and Connections

In this project, we need to track three different counts. The CountingTabBarController will have properties for each scene's counter: firstCount, secondCount, and thirdCount.

The GenericViewController class will have two properties. The first, outputLabel, references a UILabel that contains the current values of the counters for all three scenes. The second property, barItem, connects to each scene's tab bar item so that we can update its badge value.

Because there are three separate counters, the GenericViewController class requires three action methods: incrementCountFirst, incrementCountSecond, and incrementCountThird. A button in each scene invokes the method specific to that scene. Two additional instance methods (updateCounts and updateBadge) will also be added so that we can easily update the current count and badge value without having to rewrite the same code in each increment method.

Creating the Tab Bar Relationships

As with the navigation controller, it makes sense to connect the tab bar scenes to the tab bar controller before spending much time on the user interface. The act of making the connection will actually add the tab bar item object to each scene, which is something we need if we want to manipulate the item's badge value.

Control-drag from the Counting Tab Bar Controller line in the document outline to the additional scene you added (labeled Third). When prompted for the segue type, choose Relationship Segue – View Controllers, as shown in Figure 13.18. A new segue line (Relationship from "view controllers" to Third) will be added to the counting tab bar controller scene. In addition, the tab bar will become visible in the third scene, and a tab bar item will appear in the third scene's view.

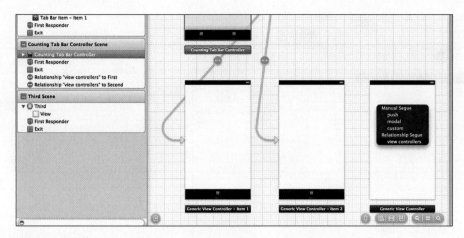

FIGURE 13.18
Create a relationship with the third scene.

Because all the other scenes are already connected to the tab bar controller, we're done making the segue connections. Now we can move on to creating the interface.

Designing the Interface

Visually, each scene in this project is identical, with the exception of the tab bar item and a label showing the scene's name.

Begin by adding a label (reading **Scene One**) to the first scene near the top of the view. Add a second label, to be used for output, to the center of the view. The output will span multiple lines, so use the Attributes Inspector (Option-Command-4) to set the number of lines for the label to 5. You can also center the text and adjust its size as desired.

Next, add a button labeled **Count** to the bottom center of the view. This will increment the counter for the view.

Then, click the tab bar item at the bottom of the view, and open the Attributes Inspector. Use the Bar Item settings to set the title to **Scene One** and the image to 1.png, as shown in Figure 13.19.

FIGURE 13.19
Configure the tab bar item for each scene.

Repeat these design steps for the other two scenes. The second scene should be labeled **Scene Two** and use the 2.png image file, and the third **Scene Three** with 3.png. Figure 13.20 shows my completed tab bar application design.

Creating and Connecting the Outlets and Actions

Two outlets and three actions need to be defined in this project. The outlets will be connected identically in each scene, but the actions will be unique for each. Let's review these connections now, starting with the outputs:

▶ **outputLabel (UILabel):** Used for displaying the results of each scene's counter, this label must be connected in each scene.

▶ **barItem (UITabBarItem):** References the tab bar item that was automatically added to each view by the tab bar controller. This connection must be made in each scene.

FIGURE 13.20
The final layout of the tab bar application.

And the actions:

- ▶ `incrementCountFirst`: Connected to the Count button in the first scene, this action method updates the first scene's counter.

- ▶ `incrementCountSecond`: Connected to the Count button in the second scene, this action method updates the second scene's counter.

- ▶ `incrementCountThird`: Connected to the Count button in the third scene, this action method updates the third scene's counter.

Make sure that the first scene is visible in IB (or just use the document outline), and then switch to the assistant editor mode.

Adding the Outlets

Control-drag from the label in the center of the first scene to just below the `@interface` line in GenericViewController.h. When prompted, create a new outlet named `outputLabel`.

Next, Control-drag from the tab bar item in the first scene to below the `outputLabel` property. Add another new outlet named `barItem`.

After creating the outlets for the first scene, connect them to the other two scenes. Control-drag from the second scene's output label and target the `outputLabel` property in GenericViewController.h. Do the same for the second scene's tab bar item.

Repeat this for the third scene, connecting its label and tab bar item to the defined outlets.

Adding the Actions

The actions are unique for each scene because each scene has a unique counter that needs to be updated. Start in the first scene and Control-drag from the Count button to below the property definitions in GenericViewController.h. When prompted, create a new action named `incrementCountFirst`.

Move to the second scene and Control-drag from its button to a line below the `incrementCount-First` action. Name this new action `incrementCountSecond`. Repeat this for the third scene, connecting to a new action named `incrementCountThird`.

Implementing the Application Logic

Only a little bit of development, and we have a fully functional tab bar application. It won't be particularly useful, but making useful content is your job! Switch back to the standard editor now.

We start by establishing the three properties to track the Count button presses in each of three scenes. These are going to be added in the `CountingTabBarController` class and will be named `firstCount`, `secondCount`, and `thirdCount`.

Adding the Push Count Property

Open the CountingTabBarController.h interface file and add three integer property definitions below the `@interface` line:

```
@property (nonatomic) int firstCount;
@property (nonatomic) int secondCount;
@property (nonatomic) int thirdCount;
```

To access these properties from the `GenericViewController` class, import the custom tab bar controller's interface file in GenericViewController.h. Add this line following the existing `#import` statement:

```
#import "CountingTabBarController.h"
```

To complete the implementation, we start by creating two methods to update the display within the scenes and then add the actions to increment the counters and call the update methods.

Implementing the Counter Display

Even though the counter differs between scenes, the logic to update the display of all three counter values is entirely the same and is simply an expanded version of the code we used in the previous tutorial. We implement this logic in a new method named updateCounts.

Edit the GenericViewController.h file to declare a method prototype for updateCounts. This isn't strictly necessary if we place the method at the top of the implementation file, but it is good practice and prevents warnings from Xcode. Add the following line after the existing action definitions in GenericViewController.h:

```
-(void)updateCounts;
```

Now, add the updateCounts method to the GenericViewController.m file, as shown in Listing 13.3.

LISTING 13.3   Update the Display Using the Counter Values

```
1: -(void)updateCounts {
2:     NSString *countString;
3:     countString=[[NSString alloc] initWithFormat:
4:               @"First: %d\nSecond: %d\nThird: %d",
5:           ((CountingTabBarController *)self.parentViewController).firstCount,
6:           ((CountingTabBarController *)self.parentViewController).secondCount,
7:           ((CountingTabBarController *)self.parentViewController).thirdCount];
8:     self.outputLabel.text=countString;
9: }
```

The code begins in line 2 by declaring a countString to hold the formatted version of the output string. Lines 3–7 create the string using the properties stored in the CountingTabBarController instance.

Line 8 outputs the formatted string in the outputLabel.

Incrementing the Tab Bar Item Badge

To increment a scene's tab bar item badge, we read the current value from the badge (badge Value), convert it to an integer, add 1, convert the new value to a string, and then set the badgeValue to the string. Why is all of that conversion necessary? Because the badgeValue is an NSString, not an integer, so we need to make sure we have a properly formatted string to change it.

Because we have added a uniform barItem property to all the scenes, we only need a single method in the GenericViewController class to handle incrementing the badge value. We'll call this method updateBadge.

Begin by adding a prototype for the new method to GenericViewController.h:

```
-(void)updateBadge;
```

Then add the code in Listing 13.4 to GenericViewController.m.

LISTING 13.4   Update the Tab Bar Item's Badge

```
1:  -(void)updateBadge {
2:      NSString *badgeCount;
3:      int     currentBadge;
4:      currentBadge=[self.barItem.badgeValue intValue];
5:      currentBadge++;
6:      badgeCount=[[NSString alloc] initWithFormat:@"%d",
7:                  currentBadge];
8:      self.barItem.badgeValue=badgeCount;
9:      }
```

Line 2 declares a new string, badgeCount, that will ultimately hold a formatted string to be assigned to the badgeValue property.

Line 3 declares an integer, currentBadge, that will hold the current badge in integer form.

In Line 4, the NSString instance method intValue is used to store the tab bar item's badgeValue, in integer form, in currentBadge.

Line 5 adds one to the current badge count.

Finally, line 6 allocates and initializes the badgeCount string with the value of currentBadge, and line 8 sets the tab bar item's badgeValue property to the new string.

Triggering the Counter Updates

The very last step of this project is to implement the incrementCountFirst, incrementCount-Second, and incrementCountThird methods. If that sounds like a lot, don't worry. Because the code to update the display and the badge is in a separate method, each of these methods is a total of three lines of code, and all of that code, with the exception of a single property, is the same in all three.

The purpose method must update the appropriate counter in the CountingTabBarController class and then call the updateCounts method and updateBadge method to update the interface appropriately. Listing 13.5 shows an implementation for the incrementCountFirst method.

LISTING 13.5   Add a Method in GenericViewController.m to Update Each Scene's Counter

```
- (IBAction)incrementCountFirst:(id)sender {
    ((CountingTabBarController *)self.parentViewController).firstCount++;
    [self updateBadge];
    [self updateCounts];
}
```

Add similar code for each of the other methods: `incrementCountSecond` and `incrementCount-Third`. The only difference will be the property you increment. Instead of `firstCount`, you use `secondCount` and `thirdCount`.

Building the Application

Run the application and switch between the different scenes. Use each scene's Count button to increment its unique counter. Thanks to the decision to store properties in the centrally shared class, `CountingTabBarController`, all three counts can be accessed and displayed by any scene.

The tab bar items should also show and increment their badges when the Count button is used, providing yet another form of visual feedback that you can give to the user.

You should now be comfortable creating projects based around the tab bar and navigation controllers—a dramatic improvement over just a single scene, don't you think? The next hour's lesson finishes up our look at custom view controllers by introducing another interesting UI element and an entirely new application template. Get your fingers ready for more typing!

Further Exploration

By now, you should have a good idea of how to implement multiple views and switch between them either manually or via segue. There was quite a bit of information covered in this past hour, so I recommend reviewing the topics that we covered and spending some time in the Apple documentation reviewing the classes, the properties, and their methods. Inspecting the UI elements in IB will give you additional insight into how they can be integrated into your apps.

The navigation controller (`UINavigationController`) is often combined with other types of views, such as the table view, to enable the viewing of structured information in a logical manner. You learn a bit more about this in the next hour, but a read of the `UINavigationController` class reference is highly recommended. Unlike many class references, the navigation controller documentation fully describes how navigation controllers can and should be used. You'll want to learn about the `UINavigationController` view hierarchy, as well as the `UINavigationControllerDelegate` protocol, which can help you respond to advanced user events within a navigation controller.

The tab bar controller (`UITabBarController`) also offers additional features beyond what we were able to cover here. If there are too many buttons to be displayed in a single tab bar, for example, the tab bar controller provides its own "more" view in the form of a navigation controller. This enables you to expand the user's options beyond the buttons immediately visible onscreen. The `UITabBarControllerDelegate` protocol and the `UITabBarDelegate` can even implement optional methods to enable the user to customize the tab bar within the application. You can see this level of functionality within Apple's Music application.

Apple Tutorials

Tabster (accessible via the Xcode developer documentation): This example demonstrates a complex multiview interface using a tab bar controller.

TheElements (accessible via the Xcode developer documentation): This project shows how to drill down to more detailed information using a navigation controller and the table of elements as its subject matter.

Summary

This hour's lesson introduced two new view controller classes to your iOS toolkit. The first, the navigation controller, displays a sequence of scenes that are displayed one after the other (and are often used to drill down into detailed information about something). Navigation controllers also provide an automatic way to back out of a scene and return to the previous scene. The process of moving to a new scene is called *pushing*, and returning to the previous scene is called *popping*.

The second view controller, the tab bar controller, is used to create applications with a single unifying bar at the bottom that can be used to switch between different scenes. Each scene, according to Apple's guidelines, should perform a unique function. Unlike the navigation controller, all the scenes managed by a tab bar controller are "random access," meaning that users can switch between whatever tabs they like; there is no preset order.

Both of these controllers present an opportunity for sharing information between the different scenes that they manage by implementing properties and methods on a custom subclass of the controller.

Finally, and possibly the best thing you learned in this hour's lesson, both of these controllers can be implemented almost entirely visually with the Xcode storyboard tools. This is a significant change from earlier releases where the code required to implement these features made them difficult to discuss.

Q&A

Q. What if I want to share information between objects that don't have a central controller class?

A. The fact that the tab bar controller and navigation controller have a nice place to implement shared properties is great, but not necessary. You can always create a custom class in your application and reference it in other classes that need to exchange data.

Q. Can I mix and match scenes and segues?

A. Yes and no. You can't use a push segue without a navigation controller or create a working tab bar application without a tab bar controller. You can, however, implement a navigation controller that is used in conjunction with a tab bar controller, display a modal segue that transitions to a navigation controller-managed series of scenes, and so forth.

Q. Are tab bar and toolbar objects interchangable?

A. Absolutely not. A tab bar is for switching between different functional areas of an application. A toolbar is for activating a feature within a single functional area of an app.

Workshop

Quiz

1. Navigation controllers and tab bar controllers require extensive coding with storyboard. True or false?

2. Tab bar item images are the same as toolbar images. True or false?

3. Attaching an action to an object that is performing a segue will cause the segue to be ignored. True or false?

Answers

1. False. The Xcode storyboard makes it possible to add these features almost entirely with drag-and-drop simplicity.

2. False. Tab bar images are 32x32 points and are not defined by the alpha channel. They should be created as simple line drawings.

3. False. Both the action and the segue will be executed.

Activities

1. Create a simple calculator application using the tab bar controller. Use one view, for example, for calculating the area of common shapes (circles, squares, and so on) and another for calculating volumes of their 3D equivalents (spheres, cubes, and so on). Use the central tab bar controller class to automatically populate dimensions that are entered in one view so that they can be reused in another.

2. Update the navigation controller example so that the navigation branches depending on a user's selection.

Navigating Information Using Table Views and Split View Controllers

---

What You'll Learn in This Hour:

▶ The types of table views

▶ How to implement a simple table view and controller

▶ Ways to add more structure and impact to a table with sections and cell images

▶ The purpose of split view controllers on the iPad

▶ How to use a Master-Detail Application template

So far, our exploration of iOS development has included typical interface elements that focus on getting information from the user, with little attention paid to output. What's missing is the ability to *present* categorized information in a structured manner. Everywhere you look (websites, books, applications on your computer), you see methods for displaying information in an attractive and orderly manner. The iOS has its own conventions for displaying this type of information.

First, the table view. This UI element is essentially a categorized list, like what you see when browsing your iOS contacts. Second, specific to the iPad, a SplitViewController object combines tables, a sliding panel (essentially a popover that slides in from the side), and a detail view into an experience very similar to using Apple's iPad Mail. In this hour, we explore how to implement a table view, and then we take that knowledge and apply it to a universal application that navigates information using a table/navigation controller combination on the iPhone and a split view controller on the iPad.

Understanding Tables

Like the other views you've seen in this book, a table view (UITable) holds information. A table view's appearance, however, is slightly counterintuitive. Instead of showing up as a true table (like an Excel worksheet), a table view displays a single list of cells onscreen. Each cell can be structured to contain multiple pieces of information but is still a single unit. In addition, the cells can be broken into sections so that the clusters of information can be communicated visually. You might, for example, list computer models by manufacturers, or models of the Macintosh by year.

Table views respond to touch events and enable the user to easily scroll up and down through long lists of information and select individual cells through the help of a table view controller (UITableViewController) and two protocols: UITableViewDataSource and UITableViewDelegate.

NOTE

A table view controller is just a standard view controller that displays only a table view. You can use this if a table view is going to be your entire view. That said, it offers no benefits over using a standard view controller and adding a table view except that its delegate and data source properties are set automatically. That's it!

In fact, by using a standard view controller and adding the two protocols, we can create tables that are sized any way we want within our views. We just need to connect the table's delegate and data source outlets to view controller class.

Because creating our own table view controller from a standard view controller offers the greatest flexibility, that's what we do in this lesson.

Table Appearance

There are two basic styles of table views: plain and grouped, as demonstrated in Figure 14.1. Plain tables lack the clear visual separation of sections of the grouped tables, but are often implemented with a touchable index (like the Contacts list of people). Because of this, they are sometimes called indexed tables. This text continues to refer to them by the names (plain/grouped) designated in Xcode.

Table Cells

Tables are only a container. To display content in a table, you must provide information to the table by configuring table view cells (UITableViewCell). By default, a cell can display a title, a detail label, an image, and an accessory—usually a disclosure arrow that indicates to the user that he can "drill down" to more information through a push segue and a navigation controller. Figure 14.2 shows a sample table cell layout with each of these features active.

In addition to its visual design, each table cell has a unique identifier called the reuse identifier. This is used to refer to the cell layout by name when we're coding and must be set when configuring the table.

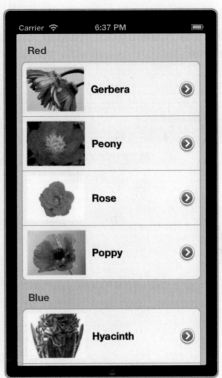

FIGURE 14.1
Plain tables look like simple lists, whereas grouped tables have more distinct divisions.

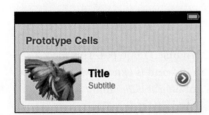

FIGURE 14.2
Table cells make up the content of a table.

Adding a Table View

To add a table to your view, drag the UITableView from the Object Library into one of your views. After adding the table, you can resize it to fill the view, or only a portion, if you prefer. If you drag a UITableViewController into the editor instead, you'll get a whole new scene in the storyboard with a table filling the entire view.

Setting Table Attributes

After adding the view, you can set its styling by selecting the table view and then opening Attributes Inspector (Option-Command-4) in the Interface Builder (IB) editor, demonstrated in Figure 14.3.

FIGURE 14.3
Set the attributes of the table.

The first thing you'll see is that the default table is set to use Dynamic Prototypes. This means that we can visually design the table and cell layout directly in IB—and is exactly what we want. The other option, Static Cells, is an older approach that does not offer the flexibility we now have in the latest versions of Xcode. You want to increase the Prototype Cells value to at least 1 (as is visible in Figure 14.3). This setting shows what the cells in the table will look like. You can update Prototype Cells to as many as you need; each one can take on a unique appearance and be accessed in code via its reuse identifier. (Just a minute and you'll see where that's set.)

Use the Style pop-up menu to choose between Plain and Grouped table styles, the Separator to choose the separator appearance between sections, and the Color pop-up to set the color of the lines that separate cells.

The Selection and Editing settings change the behavior of the table when it is touched. We won't be getting into table editing, so the default settings are sufficient (allowing only one row at a time to be touched and highlighting it when it is touched).

Once the setup of the table container is complete, you need to design the cell prototype.

Setting the Prototype Cell Attributes

To control the cells that are displayed in a table, you must configure the prototype cell (or cells) that you want to use in your application. By default, there are no prototype cells made available when adding a table, so make sure you add one; otherwise, you won't have anything to edit.

Begin editing the prototype by expanding the table view item within your view and selecting the table view cell (or just click the cell directly in the editor). Once the cell is highlighted, you can use its selection handle to increase the cell height. Everything else, however, needs the Attributes Inspector, as shown in Figure 14.4.

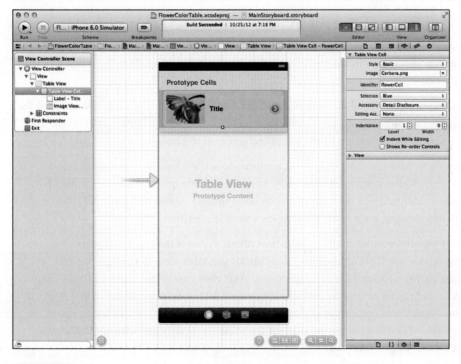

FIGURE 14.4
Configure your prototype cell.

At the top of the Attributes Inspector is a cell style. Custom cells require to you create a custom subclass for `UITableViewCell`, which is beyond the scope of this book. Thankfully, most tables use one of the standard styles:

▶ **Basic:** Only a cell title is visible.

▶ **Right Detail:** Title and detail labels are shown, detail on the right.

▶ **Left Detail:** Title and detail labels are shown, detail on the left.

▶ **Subtitle:** A detail label is displayed directly below the main cell title.

TIP

After setting a cell style, you can select the title and detail labels by clicking them within the prototype cell or the cell's view hierarchy in the document outline. Once selected, you can use the Attributes Inspector to customize the appearance of the label as you want.

Use the Image drop-down to add an image to the cell. You will, of course, need to have image resources in your project for anything to show up. Bear in mind that the image you set and the title/detail text you stylize in the prototype cell are just placeholders. They'll be replaced by actual data in code.

The selection and accessory drop-downs configure the color of the cell when it is selected and the accessory graphic (usually a disclosure arrow) that can be added to the right side of a cell. The other attributes, with the exception of the identifier, are used to configure editable table cells.

The identifier is probably the most important attribute to set. Without it, you cannot reference a prototype cell and display content in your code. You can use any arbitrary string for the identifier. Apple uses Cell in much of their sample code, for example. If you add multiple prototype cells with different designs, each must have its own unique identifier.

That covers the visual design of a table. Now, how about the code that makes it work? To populate a table, you use the Connections Inspector for the table view to connect the delegate and data source outlets to the class (probably your view controller) that will implement the `UITableViewDelegate` and `UITableViewDataSource` protocols, respectively. If you use a table view controller, these outlets are already connected, but you need to add a subclass of `UITableViewController` to your project and set the table view controller identity to the new class to have a place to put your code.

The Table View Data Source Protocol

The table view data source protocol (`UITableViewDataSource`) includes methods that describe how much information the table will be displaying, as well as provide the `UITableViewCell` objects to the application for display. This is a bit of a contrast to what we experienced with picker views, where the data source provided only the amount of information being displayed.

We focus on four of the most useful data source methods:

▶ **numberOfSectionsInTableView:** Returns the number of sections that the table will be divided into.

▶ **tableView:numberOfRowsInSection:** Returns the number of rows of information within a given section. Sections are numbered starting at 0.

▶ **tableView:titleForHeaderInSection:** Returns a string that represents the section number provided to the method.

▶ **tableView:cellForRowAtIndexPath:** Returns a properly configured cell object to display in the table.

For example, suppose that you want to create a table with two sections with the headings One and Two. The first section will have a single row, and the second will have two. This setup is handled by the first three methods, as demonstrated in Listing 14.1.

LISTING 14.1 **Configure the Sections and Row Count for the Table View**

```
 1: - (NSInteger)numberOfSectionsInTableView:(UITableView *)tableView {
 2:      return 2;
 3: }
 4:
 5: - (NSInteger)tableView:(UITableView *)tableView
 6:   numberOfRowsInSection:(NSInteger)section {
 7:      if (section==0) {
 8:          return 1;
 9:      } else {
10:          return 2;
11:      }
12: }
13:
14: - (NSString *)tableView:(UITableView *)tableView
15:      titleForHeaderInSection:(NSInteger)section {
16:      if (section==0) {
17:          return @"One";
18:      } else {
19:          return @"Two";
20:      }
21: }
```

Lines 1–3 implement the `numberOfSectionsInTableView` method, which returns 2; the table will have two sections.

Lines 5–12 handle the `tableView:numberOfRowsInSection` method. When the section number specified by iOS is 0 (the first section), the method returns 1 (line 10). When the section is 1 (the second table section), the method returns 2 (line 12).

Lines 14–21 implement the `tableView:titleForHeaderInSection` method, which is very similar to the previous method, except it returns a string to be used as a section's title. If the section is 0, the method returns `"One"` (line 20); otherwise, it returns `"Two"` (line 22).

These three methods set up the table's layout, but to provide content to a table cell, you must implement the `tableView:cellForRowAtIndexPath`. iOS passes an object called an `NSIndexPath` to the method. This includes a property called `section` and a property named `row` that identify the specific cell you should return. The method initializes a `UITableViewCell` and sets its `textLabel`, `detailTextLabel`, and `imageView` properties to change the information it displays.

Let's walk through a quick implementation of a method that could provide cell objects to a table view. This assumes that the table cell has the identifier `"Cell"`; that it has been configured to show an image, title, and detail label; and that we have an image file named generic.png that we want displayed in every cell. It's not a very realistic real-world example, but we'll save that for the exercises. Listing 14.2 shows a possible implementation of `tableView:cellForRow AtIndexPath`.

LISTING 14.2   A Silly Implementation of `tableView:cellForRowAtIndexPath`

```
 1: - (UITableViewCell *)tableView:(UITableView *)tableView
 2:           cellForRowAtIndexPath:(NSIndexPath *)indexPath {
 3:
 4:   UITableViewCell *cell = [tableView dequeueReusableCellWithIdentifier:@"Cell"];
 5:     UIImage *cellImage;
 6:     cellImage=[UIImage imageNamed:@"generic.png"];
 7:
 8:     if (indexPath.section==0) {
 9:         cell.textLabel.text=@"Section 0, Row 0";
10:         cell.detailTextLabel.text=@"Detail goes here.";
11:         cell.imageView.image=cellImage;
12:     } else {
13:         if (indexPath.row==0) {
14:             cell.textLabel.text=@"Section 1, Row 0";
15:             cell.detailTextLabel.text=@"Detail goes here.";
16:             cell.imageView.image=cellImage;
17:         } else {
18:             cell.textLabel.text=@"Section 1, Row 2";
```

```
19:                cell.detailTextLabel.text=@"Detail goes here.";
20:                cell.imageView.image=cellImage;
21:            }
22:        }
23:
24:    return cell;
25: }
```

The method starts on line 4 by declaring and initializing a cell object based on the prototype call with the identifier `"Cell"`. All implementations of this method should start with these lines.

Lines 5–6 declare and initialize a `UIImage` (`cellImage`) from a project resource named generic. png. In a real project, you'll likely want a different image for each cell.

Lines 8–12 configure the cell for the first section (`indexPath.section==0`). Because there is only a single row, we don't need to worry about which row is being requested.

The cell is populated with data by setting its `textLabel`, `detailTextLabel`, and `imageView` properties. These are just instances of `UILabel` and a `UIImageView`, so in the case of the labels, we need to assign the `text` property, and for the image view, we set the `image` property.

Lines 13–21 set up the cells for the second section (`1`). In the second section, however, the row matters (since it has two rows). So the row is checked to see if it is `0` or `1` (the first two rows), and then the contents of the cell are modified appropriately.

Line 24 returns the properly initialized cell.

That's all it takes to get a table view populated, but to react to a user's touch inside a table row, we need a method from the `UITableViewDelegate` protocol.

The Table View Data Source Protocol

The table view delegate protocol includes several methods for reacting to a user's interactions with a table—everything from selection rows to touching the disclosure arrow to editing the cells in the rows. For our purposes, we're only interested in when the user touches and highlights a row, so we will use the `tableView:didSelectRowAtIndexPath` method.

A table selection is provided to the `tableView:didSelectRowAtIndexPath` method using the `NSIndexPath` object. This means that you need to react to the section and row that the user touched. Listing 14.3 shows how we can react to a touch in the hypothetical table we've created.

LISTING 14.3   Reacting to a User's Touch

```
- (void)tableView:(UITableView *)tableView
        didSelectRowAtIndexPath:(NSIndexPath *)indexPath {
    if (indexPath.section==0) {
        // The user chose the first cell in the first section
```

```
    } else {
        if (indexPath.row==0) {
            // The user chose the first row in the second section
        } else {
            // The user chose the second row in the second section
        }
    }
}
```

Nothing to it, right? The comparison logic is the same as Listing 14.2, so refer back to it if you're wondering how the method determines which section/row is which.

That's all we need for tables! We'll now take a look at a special type of view controller and application template that pulls together navigation controllers, tables, and a universal iPad/iPhone application. You won't need any new coding knowledge for this, but you will need to call on several things you've learned over the past few hours.

TIP

If you want to make full use of tables in your applications, you should read Apple's documentation on `UITableView` and the `UITableViewDataSource` and `UITableViewDelegate` protocols. There's a great deal of information available that can help you create tables with far more features than we can fit in a single hour's lesson.

Exploring the Split View Controller (iPad Only)

The second interface element we look at in this lesson is the split view controller. Specific to the iPad, this controller isn't just a feature that you add to an application; it is a structure that you build entire applications around.

A split view controller enables you to display two distinct view controller scenes in a single iPad screen. In landscape mode, the left third of the screen is occupied by the "master" view controller's scene, while the right half contains the "detail" view controller scene. In portrait mode, the scene managed by detail view controller shifts to take up the entire screen. You can use any views and controls you want in either of these areas—tab bar controllers, navigation controllers, and so on.

As mentioned earlier, the split view controller pulls together tables, a sliding panel, and a number of views. It works like this: In landscape mode, a table is displayed on the left so that the user can make a selection. When an element from the table is touched, the detail area shows (guess what?) details about the selection. If the iPad is rotated to a portrait mode, the table disappears, and the detail fills the screen. To navigate between different items in portrait mode, the user can touch a toolbar button or swipe in from the left side of the sceen to display the detail table. This approach gives the user the flexibility to easily navigate a large amount of information and focus on a single item, if desired.

This application structure is widely used on the iPad in both Apple and third-party applications. Mail, for example, uses a split interface for showing the list of messages and the content of a selected message. Popular file management apps, like Dropbox, show a list of files on the left and the content of the selected file in the detail view, as shown in Figure 14.5.

FIGURE 14.5
A table on the left and details on the right.

Implementing the Split View Controller

You can add the split view controller to your project by dragging it from the Object Library to your storyboard. It must be set as the initial scene in the storyboard; you cannot transition to it from any other view. When first added, as shown in Figure 14.6, it automatically includes several default views that are associated with the master and detail view controllers.

FIGURE 14.6
Adding a split view controller includes a bit of cruft in your application interface.

These can be removed, new scenes added, and then the relationships between the split view controller and the master/detail scenes reestablished by Control-dragging from the split view controller object to the master scene and the detail scene and choosing Relationship – Master View Controller and relationship – Detail View Controller, respectively, when prompted.

TIP

The split view controller appears in the IB editor in portrait mode by default. This gives the appearance of only having a single scene (the detail scene) contained in it. To switch it to the landscape mode and see the division between the master/detail portions of the display, first select the split view controller object. Next open the Attributes Inspector (Option-Command-4) and change the Orientation pop-up menu to Landscape.

This is purely a visual change in the editor; it doesn't change how the application functions at all.

Once you've established a split view controller in your application, you build it out as you normally would, but you essentially have two unique "parts" that can work independently of one another (the master scene and the detail scene). To share information between them, each side's view controller can access the other side through the split view controller that manages them.

The master view controller, for example, can return the detail view controller using this:

```
[self.splitViewController.viewControllers lastObject]
```

And the detail view controller can get ahold of the master view controller with the following:

```
self.splitViewController.viewControllers[0]
```

The `splitViewController` property contains an array called `viewControllers`. Using the `NSArray` method `lastObject`, we can grab the last item in the view controller array (the detail view). Using an index `0`, we can get the first item in the array (the master view). From there, we're set; both view controllers can exchange information freely.

The Master-Detail Application Template

If it seems like I rushed through that, it's because I did. The split view controller can be whatever you want it to be; however, to be used as Apple intended, it needs a navigation controller and quite a few different views. Doing all the setup necessary to make it work like the iPad Mail app, for example, would take quite a few hours out of this book.

Thankfully, Apple has created an application template called the Master-Detail Application template that makes this easy. In fact, Apple recommends, in its documentation of the split view controller, that you use this template as a starting point instead of starting from scratch.

All the functionality is handled for you automatically. No need to deal with the sliding panel, no need to set up view controllers, no handling the swipe gesture, no manually rearranging the view after a user rotates the iPad. It just works. Your only job is to supply the content for the table, implemented in the template's `MasterViewController` class (a table) and the detail view, handled by the `DetailViewController` class.

It gets better! The Master-Detail Application template is set up so that you can easily create a universal application that works on the iPhone and iPad. On the iPhone, the application displays the `MasterViewController` in a scene with a scrolling table. Touching a row uses a navigation controller to display the `DetailViewController`-managed scene. The same code works for both iPad and iPhone, so you'll get your first taste of universal development in this exercise. Before we get to that, however, first we need to try our hand at creating a table.

A Simple Table View Application

To begin this hour's tutorials, we create a two-section table that lists the names of common red and blue flowers under a heading that describes their colors. Each table cell, in addition to a title, contains an image of the flower and a disclosure arrow. When the user touches an entry in the table, an alert appears showing the chosen flower name and color. The final application will look similar to Figure 14.7.

FIGURE 14.7
In our first application, we create a table that can react to a user's interactions.

Implementation Overview

The skills needed to add table views to your projects are very similar to what you learned when working with pickers. We add a table view to a Single View Application template and then implement the UITableView delegate and data source protocols.

We use two arrays to store the data for the table, but no additional outlets or actions are needed; everything is handled by conforming to the appropriate protocols.

Setting Up the Project

Begin by creating a new iOS single-view project named **FlowerColorTable**. We use the standard ViewController class to act as our table's view controller because this gives us the greatest flexibility in the implementation.

Adding the Image Resources

The table we create will display images for each flower it lists. To add the flower images, drag the Images folder to your main project code group and choose to copy files and create groups when prompted.

Planning the Variables and Connections

In this project, we need two arrays (_redFlowers and _blueFlowers) that, as their names imply, contain a list of the red flowers and blue flowers that we are going to display. These arrays will be added as private instance variables. The image file for each flower is titled after the flower's name; we can access each image by concatenating .png onto the flower name in the array.

The only connections required are from the data source and delegate outlets of the UITableView object back to ViewController. There will be *no* properties in our implementation.

Adding Table Section Constants

Instead of referring to table sections by number, it is helpful to work with them a bit more abstractly. To this end, we can add a few constants to the ViewController.m file so that, instead of needing to remember that "section 0" is the red flower, we can refer to it by something a bit friendlier.

Edit ViewController.m and add these lines so that they follow the #import line:

```
#define kSectionCount 2
#define kRedSection 0
#define kBlueSection 1
```

The first constant, kSectionCount, is the number of sections the table will display; the other two constants, kRedSection and kBlueSection, are used to refer to the individual sections within the table view.

That's all the setup that's required.

Designing the Interface

Open the MainStoryboard.storyboard file and drag an instance of a table view (UITableView) into your application's scene. Resize the table view to fit the entire scene.

CAUTION

Table View, Not Table View Controller

Remember, drag *just* a table view into the editor, not a table view controller. If you drag in a controller, it will add an entirely new scene. If you want to do that, no problem, but you'll need to delete the existing scene and set the table's view controller identity to the ViewController class.

Now, select the Table View and open the Attributes Inspector (Option-Command-4). Use the Content pop-up menu to choose Dynamic Prototypes (if it isn't already selected), and then update the Prototype Cells count to 1. Set the table style to Grouped if you want to exactly match my example, as shown in Figure 14.8.

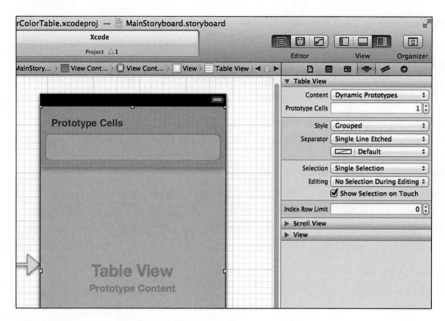

FIGURE 14.8
Set the table view attributes.

Congratulations, you've just completed 99% of the interface design! All that remains is configuring the prototype cell. Select the cell by clicking it in the editor or by expanding the table view object in the document outline and selecting the table cell object. Within the Attributes Inspector, begin by setting the cell identifier to `flowerCell`; if you leave this step out, your application won't work!

Next, set the style to Basic, and use the Image pop-up menu to pick one of the image resources you added earlier. Use the Accessory pop-up to add the Detail Disclosure accessory to the cell and finish its layout.

At this point, your cell will be ready, but it's probably looking a bit cramped. Click and drag the handle on the bottom of the cell to expand its height until it looks the way you want. Figure 14.9 shows my completed user interface (UI).

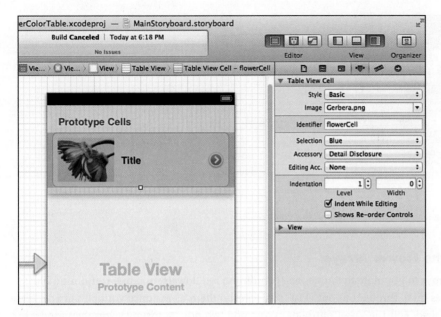

FIGURE 14.9
A completed prototype cell.

Connecting the Delegate and Data Source Outlets

Isn't it nice to work on a project that doesn't have a bazillion outlets and actions to define? I thought so. For our table to show information and react to a user's touch, it needs to know where it can find its delegate and data source prototype methods. We implement those in the `ViewController` class, so let's get it connected.

Select the table view object in the scene, and then open the Connections Inspector (Option-Command-6). In the Connections Inspector, drag from the `delegate` outlet to the `ViewController` object in the document outline. Do the same for the `dataSource` outlet. The Connections Inspector should now resemble Figure 14.10.

The UI is done and the connections are in place. All we need now is code.

Implementing the Application Logic

At the start of this hour, you learned about the two protocols that we must implement to populate a table view (`UITableViewDataSource`) and react to a user's selection of a cell (`UITableViewDelegate`). The difference between the earlier example and now is that we will be pulling data from an array. Because the array doesn't yet exist, creating it sounds like a good first implementation task, don't you think?

FIGURE 14.10
Connect the data source and delegate to the view controller

Populating the Flower Arrays

We need two arrays to populate the table: one containing red flowers, and one containing blue. We need to access these throughout our class, so declaring them as instance variables or properties is required. Edit the ViewController.m and add two private instance variables for _redFlowers and _blueFlowers, within the @interface block:

```
@interface ViewController () {
    NSArray *_redFlowers;
    NSArray *_blueFlowers;
}
@end
```

To fill the arrays with the names of flowers, allocate and initialize the arrays in the ViewController.m viewDidLoad method, as shown in Listing 14.4.

LISTING 14.4 Populate the Flower Arrays

```
- (void)viewDidLoad
{
    [super viewDidLoad];

    _redFlowers = @[@"Gerbera",@"Peony",@"Rose",@"Poppy"];
    _blueFlowers = @[@"Hyacinth",@"Hydrangea",@"Sea Holly",@"Phlox",@"Iris"];
}
```

We now have all the data we need for the table view data source protocol—the constants to determine the layout of the table and flower arrays to provide information.

Implementing the Table View Data Source Protocol

We need to implement a total of four data source methods to provide information to the table in our view: numberOfSectionsInTableView, tableView:numberOfRowsInSection, tableView:titleForHeaderInSection, and tableView:cellForRowAtIndexPath. We'll work through each of these, one at a time, but first we need to declare our intention to conform the ViewController class to the UITableViewDataSource protocol. Update the @interface line in ViewController.h to read as follows:

```
@interface ViewController : UIViewController <UITableViewDataSource>
```

Now, we add the methods, starting with numberOfSectionsInTableView. This method returns the number of sections the table will display, something we've conveniently stored in kSection-Count. Return this constant, and we're done. Implement this method as shown in Listing 14.5.

LISTING 14.5   Return the Number of Sections in the Table

```
- (NSInteger)numberOfSectionsInTableView:(UITableView *)tableView {
    return kSectionCount;
}
```

The next method, tableView:numberOfRowsInSection, returns the number of rows within a section (that is, the number of red flowers in the red section and the number of blue flowers in the blue section). By checking the provided section parameter against the red and blue section constants and then using the array method count to return a count of the items in the array, the implementation becomes trivial, as demonstrated in Listing 14.6.

LISTING 14.6   Return a Count of the Rows (Array Elements) in Each Section

```
- (NSInteger)tableView:(UITableView *)tableView
        numberOfRowsInSection:(NSInteger)section {
        switch (section) {
                case kRedSection:
                        return [_redFlowers count];
                case kBlueSection:
                        return [_blueFlowers count];
                default:
                        return 0;
        }
}
```

The only thing that might throw you off here is the switch statement. This looks at the incoming section parameter, and if it matches the kRedSection constant, it returns a count of the _redFlowers array and does the same for the blue flowers. The default case should be impossible to reach, so returning 0 is fine.

The `tableView:titleForHeaderInSection` method is even easier. It, again, must check the section against the red and blue flower constants, but it only needs to return a string (`"Red"` or `"Blue"`) to title each section. Add the implementation in Listing 14.7 to your project.

LISTING 14.7   Return a Heading for Each Section

```
- (NSString *)tableView:(UITableView *)tableView
        titleForHeaderInSection:(NSInteger)section {
    switch (section) {
        case kRedSection:
            return @"Red";
        case kBlueSection:
            return @"Blue";
        default:
            return @"Unknown";
    }
}
```

The last data source method is the most complicated and the most important. It provides the cell objects to the table view for display. In this method, we must create a new cell from the `flowerCell` identifier we configured in IB and then populate its `imageView` and `textLabel` attributes with the data we want displayed for each incoming `indexPath` parameter. Create this method in ViewController.m using Listing 14.8.

LISTING 14.8   Configure a Cell to Display in the Table View

```
 1: - (UITableViewCell *)tableView:(UITableView *)tableView
 2:         cellForRowAtIndexPath:(NSIndexPath *)indexPath
 3: {
 4:     UITableViewCell *cell = [tableView
 5:                         dequeueReusableCellWithIdentifier:@"flowerCell"];
 6:
 7:
 8:     switch (indexPath.section) {
 9:         case kRedSection:
10:             cell.textLabel.text=_redFlowers[indexPath.row];
11:             break;
12:         case kBlueSection:
13:             cell.textLabel.text=_blueFlowers[indexPath.row];
14:             break;
15:         default:
16:             cell.textLabel.text=@"Unknown";
17:     }
18:
19:     UIImage *flowerImage;
20:     flowerImage=[UIImage imageNamed:
```

```
21:                        [NSString stringWithFormat:@"%@%@",
22:                        cell.textLabel.text,@".png"]];
23:      cell.imageView.image=flowerImage;
24:
25:      return cell;
26: }
```

Lines 4–5 create a new `UITableViewCell` object named `cell` based on the prototype cell we created with the identifier `flowerCell`.

Lines 8–19 handle the majority of the logic. By looking at the `section` property of the incoming `indexPath` parameter, we can determine whether iOS is looking for something from the red or blue flower arrays. The `indexPath` `row` property, however, identifies the row number within the section whose cell we need to configure.

Line 10 uses the row to index into the red flower array, setting the `textLabel` of the cell to the string stored at that position in the array. Line 13 does the same for the blue array.

Lines 15–16 should never be reached.

To get and set the image of the flower, we can implement the logic in one place, rather than separately for red and blue flowers. How? Using the `textLabel` property that we've already configured for the cell, we can tack on `.png` and have the name of an image file!

Line 21 declares a new `UIImage` object, `flowerImage`, to hold the image we're looking for. Lines 22–24 return an image from the project's resources by concatenating the existing cell object `textLabel.text` string with the string `".png"`.

TIP

We've used `NSString`'s `stringWithFormat` method to create strings with integers and floating point numbers in earlier lessons. Here I'm using a format string of `"@%@%"` to represent two strings, one after the other, and providing the two string values we want concatenated to the method. The result is a new string containing the full image name.

Line 25 sets the cell `imageView` object's image property to the newly created `flowerImage`.

Finally, the fully configured cell is returned in line 27.

You should now be able to build the application and view a beautiful scrolling list of flowers, but touching a row won't do a thing. To react to a row's touch, we must implement one more method, this time in the `UITableViewDelegate` protocol.

Implementing the Table View Delegate Protocol

The table view delegate protocol handles a user's interactions with a table. To detect that a user has selected a cell in the table, we must implement the delegate method `tableView:didSelect` `RowAtIndexPath`. This method will automatically be called when the user makes a selection, and the incoming `IndexPath` parameter's section and row properties tell us exactly what the user touched.

Before writing the method, update the `@interface` line in ViewController.h one more time to show that we will be also conforming to the `UITableViewDelegate` protocol:

```
@interface ViewController : UIViewController
                      <UITableViewDataSource, UITableViewDelegate>
```

How you react to a row selection event is up to you, but for the sake of this example, we're going to use `UIAlertView` to display a message. The implementation, shown in Listing 14.9, should look very familiar by this point. Add this delegate method to the ViewController.m file.

LISTING 14.9 **Handle a Row Selection Event**

```
 1: - (void)tableView:(UITableView *)tableView
 2: didSelectRowAtIndexPath:(NSIndexPath *)indexPath {
 3:
 4:     UIAlertView *showSelection;
 5:     NSString    *flowerMessage;
 6:
 7:     switch (indexPath.section) {
 8:         case kRedSection:
 9:             flowerMessage=[[NSString alloc]
10:                           initWithFormat:
11:                           @"You chose the red flower - %@",
12:                           _redFlowers [indexPath.row]];
13:             break;
14:         case kBlueSection:
15:             flowerMessage=[[NSString alloc]
16:                           initWithFormat:
17:                           @"You chose the blue flower - %@",
18:                           _blueFlowers [indexPath.row]];
19:             break;
20:         default:
21:             flowerMessage=[[NSString alloc]
22:                           initWithFormat:
23:                           @"I have no idea what you chose!?"];
24:             break;
25:     }
26:
27:     showSelection = [[UIAlertView alloc]
28:                     initWithTitle: @"Flower Selected"
```

```
29:                     message:flowerMessage
30:                     delegate: nil
31:                     cancelButtonTitle: @"Ok"
32:                     otherButtonTitles: nil];
33:     [showSelection show];
34: }
```

Lines 4–5 declare `flowerMessage` and `showSelection` variables that will be used for the message string shown to the user and the `UIAlertView` instance that will display the message, respectively.

Lines 7–25 use a `switch` statement with `indexPath.section` to determine which flower array our selection comes from and the `indexPath.row` value to identify the specific element of the array that was chosen. A string (`flowerMessage`) is allocated and formatted to contain the value of the selection.

Lines 27–33 create and display an alert view instance (`showSelection`) containing the message string (`flowerMessage`).

Building the Application

After adding the delegate method to the implementation, build and run the application. You will now be able to scroll up and down through a list of flowers divided into section. Each cell in the table is configured with an image and a title string and shows a disclosure indicator (showing that touching it will do something).

Selecting a row displays an alert that identifies both the section where the touch occurred and the individual item the user selected. Of course, a "real" application would do something a bit more, so we will end this hour by doing something a bit more spectacular: creating a universal app that uses split view controllers, navigation controllers, tables, and web views.

Sounds difficult, but you'll find that the only real code required is what you just wrote while building a table.

Creating a Master-Detail Application

With a basic understanding of table controllers under our belt, we can move on to building an application that takes things to the next level by implementing a split view controller. Not only that, it will run on both the iPad and iPhone. Apple's Master-Detail Application template takes care of the tough stuff; we just need to provide content and handle a few loose ends that Apple left lying around.

This tutorial uses what we know about tables to create a list of flowers, by color, including images and a detail URL for each row. It also enables the user to touch a specific flower and show a detail view. The detail view loads the content of a Wikipedia article for the selected flower. The finished application will resemble Figure 14.11.

FIGURE 14.11
Our master-detail application will show flowers, including thumbnails, and details on specific flower types.

Implementation Overview

In the preceding example, we created a table view and went through all the steps of adding methods to display content. We need to repeat that process again, but UI is already provided. Unfortunately, Apple chose to set up the tables without dynamic prototypes, so we need to make a few changes to the storyboard before things will work.

To manage the data, we use a combination of NSDictionary and NSArray. In Hour 15, "Reading and Writing Application Data," you'll learn about persistent data storage, which will simplify the use of data even more in your future projects.

Possibly the biggest change in this project is that we will be building it as a universal application, meaning that it will run on the iPhone and iPad. You learn more about universal applications in Hour 23, "Building Universal Applications." For now, however, you need to know just one thing: The project will contain two storyboards, one for the iPhone (MainStoryboard_iPhone.storyboard) and one for the iPad (MainStoryboard_iPad.storyboard).

Setting Up the Project

Start Xcode and create a new project using the Master-Detail Application template. Name the project **FlowerDetail**. Be sure, when stepping through the project creation assistant, that you choose Universal from the device family selection and *do not* use Core Data.

The Master-Detail Application template does all the hard work of setting up scenes and view controllers for displaying a table (`MasterViewController`) and one for showing details (`DetailViewController`). This is the "heart and soul" of many applications and gives us a great starting point for adding functionality.

Adding the Image Resources

As in the previous tutorial, we want to display images of flowers within a table. Add the flower images by dragging the Images folder to your main project code group and choosing to copy files and create groups when prompted.

Understanding the Split View Controller Hierarchy

After creating the new project, explore the MainStoryboard_iPad.storyboard file. You'll notice an interesting hierarchy, as shown in Figure 14.12.

FIGURE 14.12
The iPad storyboard contains a split view controller, which connects to additional view controllers.

Connected to both the master and detail portions of the split controller are navigation controllers (`UINavigationController`). From the master navigation controller is another connection to a scene with a table view (`UITableView`); this is the master scene and corresponds to the `MasterViewController` class files.

From the detail navigation controller is a connection to a simple empty scene; this is the detail scene and is handled by the `DetailViewController` class. The navigation bar at the top of the detail scene includes a button for accessing the master view and making another selection.

Now, open the MainStoryboard_iPhone.storyboard file and take a look. It is much easier on the eyes. There is a navigation controller and two connected scenes. The first is the master scene (`MasterViewController`) and the second is the detail view (`DetailViewController`). You built something similar in the last hour's lesson.

Unfortunately, we need to make a few changes to these files, but we'll get back to that in a few minutes. Let's take a look at the variables and connections we need to power this monster.

Planning the Variables, Properties, and Connections

Apple already has a number of variables/properties and connections established in the project. You're welcome to review them and trace their function or just assume that Apple knows how to build software and focus on adding additional functionality. I choose the latter.

For our part, we will add two `NSArray` private instance variables to the `MasterViewController`: `_flowerData` and `_flowerSections`. The first holds dictionary objects that describe each flower, and the second holds the names of the sections within the table that we are creating. This structure makes it easy to interact with the table view data source and delegate methods.

In the `DetailViewController`, we add one outlet (`detailWebView`) for a `UIWebView` object that will be added to the interface and display details about a selected flower. That's the only additional object that we need to "talk" to.

Tweaking the iPad Interface

In this tutorial, we aren't determining the application interface so much as the template is providing it for us. That said, we still have a few changes that need to be made to both the iPad and iPhone storyboards. We start with the iPad storyboard. Select it in the project navigator to begin making edits.

Updating the Master Scene

To update the master scene, follow these steps:

1. Scroll to the upper-right corner of the iPad storyboard. There you should see the master scene's table view, currently titled Master in the navigation bar.

2. Double-click the title and change it to read **Flower Types**.

3. Select the table view in the master scene object hierarchy (it's best to use the document outline for this) and open the Attributes Inspector (Option-Command-4).

4. Use the inspector to change the table style to Grouped.

5. Turning your attention to the table cell itself, set the cell identifier to **flowerCell** and the style to Subtitle. This style includes a title label and a detail label displayed underneath the title (a subtitle); we use that to show a Wikipedia URL unique to each flower.

6. Choose one of the images from the resources you added to the project so that it is pre-viewed in the prototype cell.

7. Set a disclosure arrow using the Accessory pop-up menu, if you want. I chose not to because I think it looks a bit out of place in the iPad-version of the Master-Detail Application template.

8. Finish by selecting the subtitle label and changing its font size to 9 (or smaller). Then select the cell and use its handle expand it to a vertical size that is visually appealing.

Figure 14.13 shows my finished view.

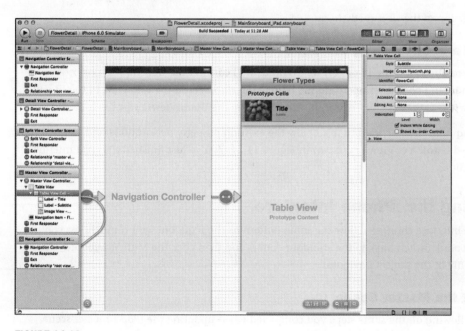

FIGURE 14.13
Tweak the master scene as shown here.

Updating the Detail Scene

To update the detail scene, follow these steps:

1. Scroll down from the master scene and you should find yourself staring at a big white scene with a label that reads `Detail View Content Goes Here.`

2. Update the label to say **Please Choose a Flower**, because it is the first thing the user will see on the iPad version of the app.

3. Drag a web view (`UIWebView`) from the Object Library into the scene.

4. Size it to fill the entire view; this is used to display a Wikipedia page describing the flower the user selected.

5. Position the "choose a flower" label on top of the web view by selecting the web view and using the Editor, Arrange, Send to Back menu option or by dragging the web view to the top of the view hierarchy in the document outline.

6. Finish the detail scene by updating its navigation bar title. Double-click the title and change it to read **Flower Detail**.

The iPad version of the UI is ready to go.

Creating and Connecting the Outlet (The First Time)

Because we're already in the IB editor, we might as well connect the web view to our code instead of jumping back after updating the iPhone interface. Select the web view in the IB editor, and then switch to the assistant editor; it should display the DetailViewController.h file.

Control-drag from the web view to just below the existing property declarations and create a new outlet named **detailWebView**, as shown in Figure 14.14. You've just finished the iPad interface and connections.

Tweaking the iPhone Interface

The iPhone interface changes follow the same pattern as the iPad, but with a much less complicated storyboard. Switch back to the standard editor, and then click the MainStoryboard_iPhone. storyboard file in the project navigator.

Updating the Master Scene

Begin by following all the same steps you completed when updating the iPad's master scene, and then complete these steps:

1. Set a new title for the scene.

2. Configure the table view with the Grouped style.

3. Update the prototype cell so that is using the Subtitle style with a 9-point font, has an image, and uses the `flowerCell` identifier.

The only difference from the iPad in my iPhone design is that I added the detail disclosure accessory. Everything else is completely identical.

FIGURE 14.14
Connect the new web view to an outlet in the detail view controller.

CAUTION

Don't Flip-Flop on Dynamic Prototypes!

By default, the Master-Detail Application template uses a table view with the Content setting set to Dynamic Prototypes. This is precisely what we want (and *wasn't* the default a year ago). If you happen to toggle this setting on and off, you will break the segues in place in the storyboard and the application won't work right.

If this happens to you, you can fix the connection by Control-dragging from the table cell (not the table) to the detail scene and choosing Push when prompted.

Updating the Detail Scene

Finish up the iPhone UI by adding a web view to the scene, sized to fill the entire display. Position the `detail view content goes here` label behind the web view this time. Why behind? The label will never be seen in the iPhone version, so there's no reason to change its content or worry about its display. Because the label is referenced in the Master-Detail

Application template, we can't simply delete it, so sending it to the back of the view is the next best thing.

As a final step, edit the title of the navigation bar in the detail scene to read **Flower Detail**. Figure 14.15 shows my final iPhone interface.

FIGURE 14.15
The completed iPhone interface in the master-detail application.

Connecting the Outlet (The Second, and Last, Time)

As with the iPad interface, we need a connection from the web view in the detail scene to the `webDetailView` outlet. This outlet was already created when we made the connection for the iPad interface, so all we need to do is hook up this instance of the web view to the same outlet.

Select the web view in the Interface Builder Editor and switch to the Assistant Editor. Control-drag from the web view to the existing `webDetailView` outlet; it highlights as you hover over it. Release your mouse button and you're done. Both of the interfaces and the connections are now complete.

Implementing the Application Data Source

In the previous table implementation project, we used multiple arrays and `switch` statements to differentiate between the different sections of flowers. This time around, however, we need to track the flower sections, names, image resources, and the detail URL that will be displayed.

Creating the Application Data Structures

What the application needs to store is quite a bit of data for simple arrays. Instead, we make use of an NSArray of NSDictionaries to hold the specific attributes of each flower and a separate NSArray to hold the names of each section. We'll index into each based on the current section/row being displayed, so no more switch statements.

To begin, edit MasterViewController.m to include private instance variable declarations for _flowerData and _flowerSections. Update the @interface block at the top of the file to read:

```
@interface MasterViewController () {
    NSMutableArray *_objects;
    NSArray *_flowerData;
    NSArray *_flowerSections;
}
@end
```

We've added two NSArrays: _flowerData and _flowerSections. These will hold our flower and section information, respectively. We also need to declare a method, createFlowerData, which is used to add the data to the arrays. Add this method prototype after the properties in MasterViewController.h:

```
- (void)createFlowerData;
```

Next step? Loading the data! Implement the createFlowerData method in MasterViewController.m, as shown in Listing 14.10. It will likely look a bit strange, but we cover the how's and why's in a minute.

LISTING 14.10   Populate the Flower Data Structures

```
 1: - (void)createFlowerData {
 2:
 3:     NSMutableArray *redFlowers;
 4:     NSMutableArray *blueFlowers;
 5:
 6:     _flowerSections=@[@"Red Flowers",@"Blue Flowers"];
 7:
 8:     redFlowers=[[NSMutableArray alloc] init];
 9:     blueFlowers=[[NSMutableArray alloc] init];
10:
11:     [redFlowers addObject:@{@"name":@"Poppy",
12:                             @"picture":@"Poppy.png",
13:                             @"url":@"http://en.wikipedia.org/wiki/Poppy"}];
14:     [redFlowers addObject:@{@"name":@"Tulip",
15:                             @"picture":@"Tulip.png",
16:                             @"url":@"http://en.wikipedia.org/wiki/Tulip"}];
```

```
17:        [redFlowers addObject:@{@"name":@"Gerbera",
18:                                 @"picture":@"Gerbera.png",
19:                                 @"url":@"http://en.wikipedia.org/wiki/Gerbera"}];
20:
21:
22:        [blueFlowers addObject:@{@"name":@"Phlox",
23:                                 @"picture":@"Phlox.png",
24:                                 @"url":@"http://en.wikipedia.org/wiki/Phlox"}];
25:        [blueFlowers addObject:@{@"name":@"Pin Cushion Flower",
26:                                 @"picture":@"Pincushion flower.png",
27:                                 @"url":@"http://en.wikipedia.org/wiki/Scabious"}];
28:        [blueFlowers addObject:@{@"name":@"Iris",
29:                                 @"picture":@"Iris.png",
30:                                 @"url":@"http://en.wikipedia.org/wiki/Iris_(plant)"}];
31:
32:        _flowerData=@[redFlowers,blueFlowers];
33:
34: }
```

The `createFlowerData` method creates two arrays: `_flowerData` and `_flowerSections`.

The `_flowerSections` array is allocated and initialized in line 6. The section names are added to the array so that their indexes can be referenced by section number. For example, `Red Flowers` is added first, so it is accessed by index (and section number) 0. `Blue Flowers` is added second and will be accessed through index 1. When we want to get the label for a section, we just reference it as `_flowerSections[section]`.

The `_flowerData` structure is a bit more complicated. As with the `_flowerSections` array, we want to be able to access information by section. We also want to be able to store multiple flowers per section, and multiple pieces of data per flower. So, how can we get this done?

First, let's concentrate on the individual flower data within each section. Lines 3 and 4 define two `NSMutableArrays`: `redFlowers` and `blueFlowers`. These need to be populated with each flower. Lines 11–30 do just that; the code allocates and initializes an `NSDictionary` with key/value pairs for the flower's name (`name`), image file (`picture`), and Wikipedia reference (`url`) and inserts it into each of the two arrays.

Wait a second. Doesn't this leave us with two arrays when we wanted to consolidate all the data into one? Yes, but we're not done. Lines 32 and 33 create the final `_flowerData` NSArray using the two `redFlowers` and `blueFlowers` arrays. What this means for our application is that we can reference the red flower array as `_flowerData[0]` and the blue flowers as `_flowerData[1]` (corresponding, as we wanted, to the appropriate table sections).

The end result will be a structure in memory that resembles Table 14.1.

TABLE 14.1 The `_flowerData` Structure

flowerData (NSMutableArray)			
Index	**NSMutableArray**		
0	**Red Flowers**		
	Index	**NSMutableDictionary**	
	0	**Name**	**Picture**	**URL**
		Gerbera	Gerbera.png	http://en.wikipedia.org/wiki/Gerbera
	1	**Name**	**Picture**	**URL**
		Peony	Peony.png	http://en.wikipedia.org/wiki/Peony
	2	**Name**	**Picture**	**URL**
		Rose	Rose.png	http://en.wikipedia.org/wiki/Rose
	3	**Name**	**Picture**	**URL**
		Hollyhock	Hollyhock.png	http://en.wikipedia.org/wiki/Hollyhock
	4	**Name**	**Picture**	**URL**
		Straw Flower	Strawflower.png	http://en.wikipedia.org/wiki/Strawflower
1	**Blue Flowers**		
	Index	**NSMutableDictionary**	
	0	**Name**	**Picture**	**URL**
		Sea Holly	Sea Holly.png	http://en.wikipedia.org/wiki/Sea_holly
	1	**Name**	**Picture**	**URL**
		'Grape Hyacinth	Grape Hyacinth.png	http://en.wikipedia.org/wiki/Grape_hyacinth
	2	**Name**	**Picture**	**URL**
		Phlox	Phlox.png	http://en.wikipedia.org/wiki/Phlox
	3	**Name**	**Picture**	**URL**
		Pin Cushion Flower	Pincushion flower.png	http://en.wikipedia.org/wiki/Scabious
	4	**Name**	**Picture**	**URL**
		Iris	Iris.png	http://en.wikipedia.org/wiki/Iris_(plant)

NOTE

The data that we included in the listing of the `createFlowerData` method is a small subset of what is used in the actual project files. If you would like to use the full dataset in your code, you can copy it from this hour's project files or add it manually to the method using these values:

Red Flowers

Name	Picture	URL
Gerbera	Gerbera.png	http://en.wikipedia.org/wiki/Gerbera
Peony	Peony.png	http://en.wikipedia.org/wiki/Peony
Rose	Rose.png	http://en.wikipedia.org/wiki/Rose
Hollyhock	Hollyhock.png	http://en.wikipedia.org/wiki/Hollyhock
Straw Flower	Strawflower.png	http://en.wikipedia.org/wiki/Strawflower

Blue Flowers

Name	Picture	URL
Sea Holly	Sea Holly.png	http://en.wikipedia.org/wiki/Sea_holly
Grape Hyacinth	Grape Hyacinth.png	http://en.wikipedia.org/wiki/Grape_hyacinth
Phlox	Phlox.png	http://en.wikipedia.org/wiki/Phlox
Pin Cushion Flower	Pincushion flower.png	http://en.wikipedia.org/wiki/Scabious
Iris	Iris.png	http://en.wikipedia.org/wiki/Iris_(plant)

Populating the Data Structures

The `createFlowerData` method is now ready for use. We can call it from within the `MasterViewController`'s `viewDidLoad` method. Update the method in MasterViewController.m by adding the following line at the end of its implementation:

```
[self createFlowerData];
```

CAUTION

Look, but Don't Touch

Unless you're positive of its purpose, be sure not to disturb any of the existing code in the project template files. Changing Apple's template code can render the project inoperable.

Implementing the Master View Controller

We've reached the point where we can build out our table view in the `MasterViewController` class. Very little changes between how we implemented our initial tutorial table controller and how we will be building this one. Once again, we need to satisfy the appropriate data source and delegate protocols to add an interface and event handling to our data.

The biggest change to the implementation is how we access our data. Because we've built a somewhat complex structure of arrays of dictionaries, we need to make absolutely sure we're referencing the data that we intend to be.

Creating the Table View Data Source Methods

Instead of completely rehashing the implementation details, let's just review how we can return the needed information to the various methods.

As with the previous tutorial, start by implementing the three basic data source methods within MasterViewController.m. Remember that these methods (`numberOfSectionsInTableView`, `tableView:numberOfRowsInSection`, and `tableView:titleforHeaderInSection`) must return the number of sections, the rows within each section, and the titles for the sections, respectively.

To return the number of sections, we just need to return the count of the elements in the `_flowerSections` array:

```
return [_flowerSections count];
```

Retrieving the number of rows within a given section is only slightly more difficult. Because the `_flowerData` array contains an array for each section, we must first access the appropriate array for the section, and then return its count:

```
return [_flowerData[section] count];
```

Finally, provide the label for a given section in the `tableView:titleforHeaderInSection` method (you'll need to add this method into MasterViewController.m). The application should index into the `_flowerSections` array by the section value and return the string at that location:

```
return _flowerSections[section];
```

Update the appropriate methods in MasterViewController.m so that they return these values. As you can see, each of these three method implementations is now a single line (hopefully making up for what seemed to be a complicated structure holding the data).

Creating the Table Cell

Now we're left with the most important method of the data source protocol: `tableView:cellForRowAtIndexPath`. Unlike the previous tutorial, we need to dig down into our data structures to retrieve the correct results. Let's review the different pieces of code required in the implementation.

First, we must declare and initialize a new cell object using the `flowerCell` identifier we established in the prototype cell:

```
UITableViewCell *cell = [tableView
                dequeueReusableCellWithIdentifier:@"flowerCell"];
```

Nothing new there, but that's where the similarities to what we've seen before end. To set a cell's title label, detail label (subtitle), and image, we need code like this:

```
cell.textLabel.text=@"Title String";
cell.detailTextLabel.text=@"Detail String";
cell.imageView.image=[UIImage imageNamed:@"MyPicture.png"];
```

Not too bad, right? We have all the information; we just need to get retrieve it. Let's quickly review the three-level hierarchy of our `_flowerData` structure:

`_flowerData(NSArray)` → NSArray → NSDictionary

The first level, the top `_flowerData` array, corresponds to the sections within the table. The second level, another array contained within the `_flowerData` array, corresponds to the rows within the section, and, finally, the NSDictionary provides the individual pieces of information about each row. Refer back to Table 14.1 if you're still having trouble picturing how information is organized.

So, how do we get to the individual pieces of data that are three layers deep? By first using the `indexPath.section` value to return the right array, and then from that, using the `indexPath. row` value to return the right dictionary, and then finally, using a key to return the correct value from the dictionary.

For example, to get the value that corresponds to the `"name"` key for a given section and row and assign it to a cell's main label, we can write the following:

```
cell.textLabel.text=_flowerData[indexPath.section][indexPath.row][@"name"];
```

Applying the same logic, we can assign a cell object's detail label to the value stored in the `"url"` key for a given section and row with this:

```
cell.detailTextLabel.text=_flowerData[indexPath.section][indexPath.row][@"url"];
```

Likewise, we can return and assign the image with the following:

```
cell.imageView.image=[UIImage imageNamed:
                 _flowerData[indexPath.section][indexPath.row][@"picture"]]
```

The only other step is to return the cell. Implement this code in your MasterViewController.m file now. Your master view should now be able to display a table, but we still need to be able to handle the selection of an item in the table and update the detail view accordingly. Before that, however, we should disable a feature we *don't* want: editing.

Disabling Editing

Apple has been kind enough to include the beginnings of some advanced features in the Master-Detail Application template, including the editing of the table view. This, however, isn't something that we want within our project, and is unfortunately outside the scope of what we can cram into this book. To disable editing within this project, edit the MasterViewController.m method `tableView:canEditRowAtIndexPath` to return NO, as shown in Listing 14.11.

LISTING 14.11 Disable Editing of Table Cells

```
- (BOOL)tableView:(UITableView *)tableView
          canEditRowAtIndexPath:(NSIndexPath *)indexPath
{
    // Return NO if you do not want the specified item to be editable.
    return NO;
}
```

Now, comment out (or remove) the lines related to buttons and button bars in the MasterViewController.m `viewDidLoad` method. This will keep the user interface from displaying buttons for editing the table items. The final version of viewDidLoad (including changes you made earlier) should resemble Listing 14.12.

LISTING 14.12 Disable the Editing User Interface

```
- (void)viewDidLoad
{
    [super viewDidLoad];

    self.detailViewController = (DetailViewController *)
            [[self.splitViewController.viewControllers lastObject]
                                              topViewController];

    [self createFlowerData];
}
```

Our project will now ignore attempts to edit the flower table; it's time to handle the actions we *do* want the user to perform.

Handling Navigation Events with the Delegate Protocol

In the previous tutorial application, we handled a touch event with the `tableView:didSelectRowAtIndexPath` UITableViewDelegate protocol method and displayed an alert to the user. This time, our implementation will need to tell the `DetailViewController` that it should update and display the contents of the URL in our data structure.

We'll be communicating with the `detailViewController` through one of its properties (of type id) called `detailItem`. Because `detailItem` can point to any object, we set it to the NSDictionary of the chosen flower; this will give us access to the `name`, `url`, and other keys directly within the detail view controller.

Implement `tableView:didSelectRowAtIndexPath` in MasterViewController.m, as shown in Listing 14.13.

LISTING 14.13 Set the Detail View Controller's `detailItem`

```
- (void)tableView:(UITableView *)aTableView
        didSelectRowAtIndexPath:(NSIndexPath *)indexPath {
    self.detailViewController.detailItem=
                        _flowerData[indexPath.section][indexPath.row];

}
```

When a flower is selected, it is passed to the `detailViewController`'s `detailItem` property.

Well now, that seems too easy, doesn't it? There's probably lots of work to be done trapping the event in the detail view controller and updating the view, right? Nope. To implement the detail view controller, we need to update a single method: `configureView`.

Implementing the Detail View Controller

We've already updated the detail view controller interface with a web view, and we know how it should work. When the user picks one of our flowers, the `UIWebView` instance (`detailWebView`) should be instructed to load the web address stored within the `detailItem` property. The method where we can implement this logic is `configureView`. It is automatically invoked whenever the detail view should update itself. Because `configureView` and `detailItem` are already in place, all that we need is a tiny bit of logic.

Displaying the Detail View

Because `detailItem` is a single `NSDictionary` for one of our flowers, we need to use the `"url"` key to access the URL string and turn that into a `NSURL` object. This is accomplished quite simply:

```
NSURL *detailURL;
detailURL=[[NSURL alloc] initWithString:[self.detailItem objectForKey:@"url"]];
```

First we declare the `NSURL` object `detailURL`, and then we allocate and initialize it using the URL stored in the dictionary.

You might remember from earlier lessons that loading a web page in a web view is accomplished with the `loadRequest` method. This method takes an `NSURLRequest` object as its input parameter. Because we only have an `NSURL` (`detailURL`), we also need to use the `NSURLRequest` class method `requestWithURL` to return the appropriate object type. One additional line of code takes care of all of this:

```
[self.detailWebView loadRequest:[NSURLRequest requestWithURL:detailURL]];
```

Now, remember that navigation item that we changed to read `Flower Detail` in the detail scene? Wouldn't it be nifty to set that to the name of the flower (`detailItem[@"name"]`)? We can! Using the `navigationItem.title` property, we can update the title in the navigation bar and set it to whatever we want. The code to set the title in the bar at the top of the detail view becomes the following:

```
self.navigationItem.title = self.detailItem[@"name"];
```

Finally, the label that displays the Choose a Flower message should be hidden after an initial selection is made. The property (already included in the template) for the label is detail DescriptionLabel. Setting its hidden property to YES hides the label:

```
self.detailDescriptionLabel.hidden=YES;
```

Pull all of this together into a single method by updating configureView in DetailViewController.m to read as shown in Listing 14.14.

LISTING 14.14   Configure the Detail View Using the detailItem

```
- (void)configureView
{
    // Update the user interface for the detail item.

    if (self.detailItem) {
        NSURL *detailURL;
        detailURL=[[NSURL alloc] initWithString:[self.detailItem
                                                objectForKey:@"url"]];
        [self.detailWebView loadRequest:[NSURLRequest requestWithURL:detailURL]];
        self.navigationItem.title = [self.detailItem objectForKey:@"name"];
        self.detailDescriptionLabel.hidden=YES;
    }
}
```

How Does Setting the detailItem Cause the configureView Method to Execute?

Remember that we access properties through getters and setters. Setting a property myObject.coolProperty=<something> is the same as executing [myObject setCoolProperty:<something>]. The DetailViewController implementation takes advantage of this and defines its own setter for detailItem (setDetailItem) that both assigns the detailItem value as needed and invokes the configureView method. This means that any time detailItem is set (even if it is using dot notation), the custom setter method is called.

Setting the Bar Button Title

We need to make one final tweak to the project to get things "just right." The panel that displays when the split view is in portrait mode reads Root List by default. We want to update it to say Flower Types.

Find the method splitViewController:willHideViewController:withBarButtonItem:for PopoverController in the DetailViewController.m file. Specifically, look for the one line that reads as follows:

```
barButtonItem.title = NSLocalizedString(@"Master", @"Master");
```

Update the line to this:

```
barButtonItem.title = NSLocalizedString(@"Flower List", @"Flower List");
```

Run the FlowerInfoViewer application. Try navigating through a few flowers. With a reasonably minor amount of coding, we've created what feels like a very complex iPad application!

Unless you run the app on the iPhone. Then... it doesn't work!

Fixing the Broken Detail View Controller Reference

Surprise! Thought you were done, didn't you? Nope. As it turns out, the application should work great on the iPad, but the iPhone has one teensy problem. The iPad version of the code takes advantage of the fact that the split view controller scenes can access one another's view controllers quite easily. This logic doesn't translate over to the iPhone implementation, so when it tries to set the `detailItem` for the detail view controller, it is actually setting a value on a nil (nonexistent) object. You don't get an error, but it doesn't work.

To fix the problem, we need to set the `detailItem` within the `prepareForSegue:sender` method. Apple already has a partial implemenation within the method, but it passes a date as the `detailItem` (just as an example). We just need to substitute the same `detailItem` from Listing 14.13 in place of the date. Update `prepareForSegue:sender` in MasterViewController.m as seen in Listing 14.15 and all will be well.

LISTING 14.15 Enable iPhone Access to the Detail View Controller

```
- (void)prepareForSegue:(UIStoryboardSegue *)segue sender:(id)sender
{
    if ([[segue identifier] isEqualToString:@"showDetail"]) {
        NSIndexPath *indexPath = [self.tableView indexPathForSelectedRow];
        [[segue destinationViewController] setDetailItem:
                           _flowerData[indexPath.section][indexPath.row]];
    }
}
```

Building the Application

Run and test the application on both the iPhone and iPad simulators. Try rotating the device on the iPad; the interface should update appropriately (and somewhat dramatically). The iPhone, however, uses the same code to provide the same functionality, but with a very different interface.

I know this is a somewhat unusual tutorial, but it's one that I consider important. The Master-Detail Application template is used very, very often and can jump-start your development of high-quality tablet and handheld applications.

Further Exploration

Although the most "dramatic" part of this hour was implementing the UISplitViewController, there is a wealth of additional features to be uncovered in the topic of tables. To continue your experience in working with tables, I suggest focusing on a few important enhancements.

The first is expanding what you can do with table cells. Review the property list for UITableViewCell. In addition to the TextLabel and ImageView properties, you can make numerous other customizations—including setting backgrounds, detail labels, and much, much more. In fact, if the default table cell options do not provide everything you need, Interface Builder supports visual customization of table cells by creating a completely custom cell prototype.

Once you have a handle on the presentation of the table views, you can increase their functionality by implementing a few additional methods in your table view controller. Read the reference for UITableViewController, UITableViewDataSource, and UITableViewDelegate. You can quickly enable editing functionality for your table by implementing a handful of additional methods. You'll need to spend some time thinking of what editing controls you want to use and what the intended result will be, but the basic functionality of deleting, reordering, and inserting rows (along with the associated graphic controls you're used to seeing in iPad applications) will come along "for free" as you implement the methods.

Apple Tutorials

Customizing table cells and views—TableViewSuite (accessible via the Xcode developer documentation): The TableViewSuite tutorial is an excellent look at how table views can be customized to suit a particular application.

Editing table cells—EditableDetailView (accessible via the Xcode developer documentation): The EditableDetailView tutorial implements row editing, including inserting, reordering, and deleting within a table view.

Summary

This hour introduced two of the most important iOS interface components: the table view and the split view controller. Table views enable users to sort through large amounts of information in an orderly manner. We covered how table cells are populated, including text and images, as well as the mechanism by which cell selection occurs.

We also explored the role of the split view controller in managing a master view and detail view and how it can be easily implemented by way of the Master-Detail Application template.

Coming away from this hour, you should feel comfortable working with tables in your applications and building basic apps using the new project template.

Q&A

Q. What is the most efficient way to provide data to a table?

A. You've almost certainly come to the conclusion that there has got to be a better way to provide data to complex views rather than manually defining all the data within the application itself. Starting in Hour 15, you learn about persistent data and how it can be used within applications. This will become the preferred way of working with large amounts of information as you move forward.

Q. Can a table row have more than a single cell?

A. No, but a customized cell can be defined that presents information in a more flexible manner than the default cell. As described in the "Further Exploration" section, custom cells can be defined in Interface Builder through the `UITableViewCell` class.

Q. Do split view controllers have to be implemented using the Apple Master-Detail Application template?

A. Absolutely not. The template, however, provides all the right methods for many split view applications and is a great starting place for beginners.

Workshop

Quiz

1. When working with the `NSIndexPath` object in the table view controller methods, which two properties will come in handy?

2. Which two protocols, both conformed to by the `UITableViewController` class, are required for a table view to be displayed and events to be handled?

Answers

1. The `section` property will identify the section within the table, and the `row` property refers to the specific cell inside of that section.

2. To display information, a table view requires methods defined within the `UITableViewDataSource` and `UITableViewDelegate` protocols.

Activities

1. Update the first tutorial to use a more expandable data structure that doesn't rely on constants to define the number of sections or the type of sections.

2. Use IB to create and customize an instance of the `UITableViewCell` class.

Reading and Writing Application Data

What You'll Learn in This Hour:

▶ Good design principles for using application preferences

▶ How to store application preferences and read them later

▶ How to expose your application's preferences to the Settings application

▶ How to store data from your applications

Most substantial applications, whether on a computer or mobile device, allow users to customize their operation to their own needs and desires. You have probably cursed an application before, only to later find a setting that removes the unholy annoyance, and you probably have a favorite application that you've customized to your exact needs so that it fits like a well-worn glove. In this hour, you learn how your iOS application can use preferences to allow the user to customize its behavior and how, in general, the user can store data on iDevices.

NOTE

Application preferences is Apple's chosen term, but you may be more familiar with other terms such as *settings*, *user defaults*, *user preferences*, or *options*. These are all essentially the same concept.

---

iOS Applications and Data Storage

The dominant design aesthetic of iOS applications is for simple single-purpose applications that start fast and do one task quickly and efficiently. Being fun, clever, and beautiful is an expected bonus. How do application preferences fit into this design view?

You want to limit the number of application preferences by creating opinionated software. There might be three valid ways to accomplish a task, but your application should have an opinion on the one best way to accomplish it and then should implement this one approach in such a polished and intuitive fashion that your users instantly agree it's the best way. Leave the other two approaches for someone else's application. It might seem counterintuitive, but there is a much bigger market for opinionated software than for applications that try to please everyone.

This might seem like odd advice to find in a chapter about application preferences, but I'm not suggesting that you avoid preferences altogether. There are some very important roles for application preferences. Use preferences for the choices your users must make, rather than for all the choices they could possibly make. For example, if you are connecting to the application programming interface (API) of a third-party web application on behalf of your user and the user must provide credentials to access the service, this is something the user must do, not just something users might want to do differently. So, it is a perfect case for storing as an application preference.

Another strong consideration for creating an application preference is when a preference can streamline the use of your application (for example, when users can record their default inputs or interests so that they don't have to make the same selections repeatedly). You want user preferences that reduce the amount of onscreen typing and taps that it takes to achieve the user's goal for using your application.

After you decide a preference is warranted, you have an additional decision to make. How will you expose the preference to the user? One option is to make the preference implicit based on what the user does while using the application. An example of an implicitly set preference is returning to the last state of the application. For example, suppose a user flips a toggle to see details. When the user next uses the application, the same toggle should be flipped and showing details.

Another option is to expose your application's preference in Apple's Settings application, shown in Figure 15.1. Settings is an application built in to iOS. It provides a single place to customize a device's operation. Everything from the hardware, built-in applications from Apple, and third-party applications can be customized from the Settings application.

A settings bundle lets you declare the user preferences of your application so that the Settings application can provide the user interface (UI) for editing those preferences. There is less coding for you to do if you let Settings handle your application's preferences, but less coding is not always the dominant consideration. A preference that is set once and rarely changes, such as the username and password for a web service, is ideal for configuring in Settings. In contrast, an option that the user might change with each use of your application, such as the difficulty level in a game, is not appropriate for Settings.

CAUTION

Simplicity Is Key

Users will be annoyed if they have to repeatedly exit your application, launch Settings to change the preference, and then relaunch your application. Decide whether each preference belongs in the Settings application or in your own application, but it's generally not a good idea to put them in both.

FIGURE 15.1
The Settings application.

Also keep in mind that the UI that Settings can provide for editing your application preferences is limited. If a preference requires a custom interface component or custom validation code, it can't be set in Settings, and it must be set from within your application.

State Preservation and Restoration: Pseudo Preferences

In iOS 6, Apple includes a new feature that enables you to (somewhat) easily restore portions of an application's interface to its previous condition when it starts. Your scrolling views would still be scrolled to the right places, your tab bars might still have the proper tabs selected, and so on. You pick and choose what gets restored.

So, how does this differ from implicit preferences that you store yourself?

State preservation can make it appear like your application is picking up where it left off—similar to what happens when you press the Home button and exit and then go back to an application. Unlike a suspended application, it works even if your application has exited (you reboot your phone, for example). State preservation, however, restores the *interface only*, not the state of the *logic*. What's more, if the user uses the task manager to force quit the application, the state preservation is deleted. The short story is that state preservation *shouldn't* be used in place of implicit preferences. It's useful for getting a user back into an application quickly, but you must still save relevant state/preference information on your own, in case the state preservation information is deleted by iOS.

To get started with state preservation, add these two methods to your application delegate (AppDelegate.m):

```
-(BOOL)application:(UIApplication *)application
    shouldRestoreApplicationState:(NSCoder *)coder
{
    return YES;
}

-(BOOL)application:(UIApplication *)application
     shouldSaveApplicationState:(NSCoder *)coder
{
    return YES;
}
```

You may then select the object (such as a text view) that you want to automatically restore, open the Identity Inspector (Option-Command-4) and enter a Restoration ID (an arbitrary string to identify the object). You should also do the same for the view controller object that contains the UI objects you're restoring. Make sure your restoration IDs are unique.

That's a quick and dirty way to play with this feature, but if you're interested in exploring more, begin by reading "State Preservation and Restoration" in the *iOS Programming Guide* in Xcode.

Data Storage Approaches

Once you decide that your application needs to store information, your next step is to decide how it is done. There are many, many ways for iOS applications to store information, but we focus on three approaches in this hour:

- ▶ **User defaults:** Settings that are stored on a per-application basis, typically without requiring user intervention

- ▶ **Settings bundles:** Provide an interface for configuring an application through the iOS settings application

- ▶ **Direct file system access:** Enables you to write and read files in your application's portion of the iOS file system

Each of these offers has its own pros and cons, and it's up to you to determine which is appropriate for your own applications. Before we get started using them, however, let's review a bit more detail on how they work and what they are typically used for.

User Defaults

Application preferences is Apple's name for the overall preference system by which applications can customize themselves for the user. The application preferences system takes care of the low-level tasks of persisting preferences to the device, keeping each application's preferences separate from other applications' preferences, and backing up application preferences to the computer via iTunes so that users won't lose their preferences in case the device needs to be restored. Your interaction with the application preferences system is through an easy-to-use API that consists mainly of the NSUserDefaults singleton class.

The NSUserDefaults class works similarly to the NSDictionary class. The main differences are that NSUserDefaults is a singleton and is more limited in the types of objects it can store. All the preferences for your application are stored as key/value pairs in the NSUserDefaults singleton.

NOTE
_____

A singleton is just an instance of the Singleton pattern, and a pattern in programming is just a common way of doing something. The Singleton pattern is fairly common in iOS, and it is a technique used to ensure that there is only one instance (object) of a particular class. Most often, it is used to represent a service provided to your program by the hardware or operating system.
_____

Writing and Reading User Defaults

All access to application preferences begins by getting a reference to your applications NSUserDefaults singleton:

```
NSUserDefaults *userDefaults = [NSUserDefaults standardUserDefaults];
```

Values can then be written and read from the defaults database by specifying the type of data being written and a key (an arbitrary string) that will be used to access it later. To specify the type, you use one of six different functions: setBool:forKey, setFloat:forKey, setInteger:forKey, setObject:forKey, setDouble:forKey, setURL:forKey (depending on the type of data you want to store). The setObject:forKey function can be used to store NSString objects, NSDates, NSArrays, and other common object types.

For example, to store an integer value under the key `"age"` and a string using the key `"name"`, you could use code that looks like this:

```
[userDefaults setInteger:10 forKey:@"age"];
[userDefaults setObject:@"John" forKey:@"name"];
```

When you write data to the defaults database, it isn't necessarily saved immediately. This can lead to issues if you assume your preferences are stored, but iOS hasn't gotten around to it yet. To ensure that all data is written to the user defaults, you use the `synchronize` method:

```
[userDefaults synchronize];
```

To read these values back into the application at a later time, you use a set of functions that read and return the value or object given their key. For example:

```
    float myAge = [userDefaults integerForKey:@"age"];
NSString *myName = [userDefaults stringForKey:@"name"];
```

Unlike the "set" storage methods, retrieving values requires specific methods for strings, arrays, and so on so that you can easily assign the stored objects to a particular type object when you need to access them. Choose from `arrayForKey`, `boolForKey`, `dataforKey`, `dictionaryForKey`, `floatForKey`, `integerForKey`, `objectForKey`, `stringArrayForKey`, `doubleForKey`, or `URLForKey` to retrieve your data into a usable object.

Settings Bundles

Another option for dealing with application preferences is through the use of settings bundles. Settings bundles use the underlying user defaults system that you just learned about, but they provide a UI that is managed through the iOS settings application.

What makes settings bundles attractive from the development standpoint is that they are created entirely in Xcode's plist editor. There is no UI design or coding—just defining the data you intend to store and the keys that it is stored under.

By default, applications do not include a settings bundle. You add them to your project by choosing File, New File and then picking Settings Bundle from the iOS Resource section, as shown in Figure 15.2.

The file that controls how an application's settings will appear in the Settings application is the Root.plist file in the settings bundle. Seven different preference types (see Table 15.1) can be read and interpreted by the Settings application to provide the UI to set our application's preferences.

FIGURE 15.2
Settings bundles must be added to projects manually.

TABLE 15.1   Preference Types

Type	Description
Text field	Editable text string
Toggle switch	On/off toggle button
Slider	Slider across a range of values
Multi value	Drop-down value picker
Title	Read-only text string
Group	Title for a logical group of preferences
Child pane	Child preferences page

Creating custom settings bundles is just a matter of creating rows in the Preference Items key within the Root.plist file. You will follow the simple schema in the Settings Application Schema Reference in the iOS Reference Library to set all the required properties, and some of the optional properties, of each preference, as shown in Figure 15.3.

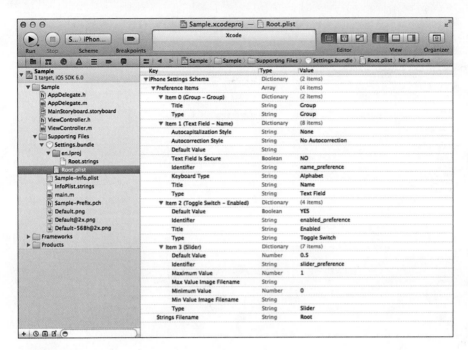

FIGURE 15.3
The settings UI is defined through the Root.plist file.

Once the settings bundle is complete, the user can alter user defaults through the settings application, and you, the developer, can access the settings through the same techniques described in the section "Writing and Reading User Defaults."

TIP
_____

The `identifier` attribute of a preference item within the settings bundle is the same as the `key` you use to retrieve a value from the user defaults.

_____

Direct File System Access

The final file access approach that we'll be looking at in this hour is direct file system access (the ability to open files and read or write their contents). This technique can be used to store any data you want—files you download off the Internet, files your app creates, and so on—but not anywhere you want.

In creating the iOS software development kit (SDK), Apple introduced a wide range of restrictions designed to protect users from malicious applications harming their devices. The restrictions are collectively known as the application sandbox. Any application you create with the SDK exists in a sandbox. There is no opting out of the sandbox and no way to get an exemption from the sandbox's restrictions.

Some of these restrictions affect how application data is stored and what data can be accessed. Each application is given a directory on the device's file system, and applications are restricted to reading and writing files in their own directory. This means a poorly behaved application can, at worst, wipe out its own data but not the data of any other application.

It also turns out that this restriction is not terribly limiting. The information from Apple's applications, such as contacts, calendars, and the photo and music libraries, is for the most part already exposed through APIs in the iOS SDK. (For more information, see Hour 19, "Working with Rich Media," and Hour 20, "Interacting with Other Applications.")

CAUTION
Play Within the Sandbox

With each version of the iOS SDK, Apple has been steadily ramping up what you can't do because of the application sandbox, but parts of the sandbox are still enforced via policy rather than as technical restrictions. Just because you find a location on the file system where it is possible to read or write files outside the application sandbox doesn't mean you should. Violating the application sandbox is one of the surest ways to get your application rejected from the iTunes Store.

Storage Locations for Application Data

Within an application's directory, four locations are provided specifically for storing the application's data: the Library/Preferences, Library/Caches, Documents, and tmp directories.

NOTE

When you run an application in the iOS simulator, the application's directory exists on your Mac in /Users/*<your username>*/Library/Application Support/iPhone Simulator/*<Device OS Version>*/ Applications. There are any number of applications in this directory, each with a directory named after a unique application ID (a series of characters with dashes) that is provided by Xcode. The easiest way to find the directory of the current application you are running in the iOS simulator is to look for the most recently modified application directory. Take a few minutes now to look through the directory of a couple applications from previous hours.

In OS X Lion (and later), the Library directory is hidden by default. You can access it by holding down Option and clicking the Finder's Go menu.

You encountered the Library/Preferences directory earlier in this hour. It's not typical to read and write to the Preferences directory directly. Instead, you use the NSUserDefaults API. The Library/ Caches, Documents, and tmp directories are, however, intended for direct file manipulation. The main difference between them is the intended lifetime of the files in each directory.

The Documents directory is the main location for storing application data. It is backed up to the computer when the device is synced with iTunes, so it is important to store any data users would be upset to lose in the Documents directory.

The Library/Caches directory is used to cache data retrieved from the network or from any computationally expensive calculation. Files in Library/Caches persist between launches of the application, and caching data in the Library/Caches directory can be an important technique used to improve the performance of an application.

Lastly, any data you want to store outside of the device's limited volatile memory, but that you do not need to persist between launches of the application, belongs in the tmp directory. The tmp directory is a more transient version of Library/Caches; think of it as a scratch pad for the application.

CAUTION
___

Space Concerns

Applications are responsible for cleaning up all the files they write, even those written to Library/ Caches or tmp. Applications are sharing the limited file system space (typically 16GB to 64GB) on the device. The space an application's files take up is not available for music, podcasts, photos, and other applications. Be judicious in what you choose to persistently store, and be sure to clean up any temporary files created during the lifetime of the application.
___

Getting a File Path

Every file on an iOS device has a path, which is the name of its exact location on the file system. For an application to read or write a file in its sandbox, it needs to specify the full path of the file.

Core Foundation provides a C function called NSSearchPathForDirectoriesInDomains that returns the path to the application's Documents or Library/Caches directory. Asking for other directories from this function can return multiple directories, so the result of the function call is an NSArray object. When this function is used to get the path to the Documents or Library/Caches directory, it returns exactly one NSString in the array, and the NSString of the path is extracted from the array using an index of 0.

NSString provides a method for joining two path fragments called stringByAppendingPath-Component. By putting the result of a call to NSSearchPathForDirectoriesInDomains with a specific filename, it is possible to get a string that represents a full path to a file in the application's Documents or Library/Caches directory.

Suppose, for example, your next blockbuster iOS application calculates the first 100,000 digits of pi, and you want the application to write the digits to a cache file so that they won't need to be calculated again. To get the full path to this file's location, you need to first get the path to the Library/Caches directory and then append the specific filename to it:

```
NSString *cacheDir =
        NSSearchPathForDirectoriesInDomains(NSCachesDirectory,
        NSUserDomainMask, YES)[0];
NSString *piFile = [cacheDir
                stringByAppendingPathComponent:@"American.pi"];
```

To get a path to a file in the Documents directory, use the same approach but with NSDocumentDirectory as the first argument to NSSearchPathForDirectoriesInDomains:

```
NSString *docDir =
        NSSearchPathForDirectoriesInDomains(NSDocumentDirectory,
        NSUserDomainMask, YES)[0];
NSString *scoreFile = [docDir stringByAppendingPathComponent:@"HighScores.txt"];
```

Core Foundation provides another C function called NSTemporaryDirectory that returns the path of the application's tmp directory. As before, this can be used to get a full path to a file:

```
NSString *scratchFile =
        [NSTemporaryDirectory() stringByAppendingPathComponent:@"Scratch.data"];
```

Reading and Writing Data

After creating a string that represents the path to the file that you want to use, reading and writing is rather straightforward. First, you'll likely want to check to see whether the file even exists. If it doesn't, your application will need to create it; otherwise, you'll need to present an error condition. To check for the presence of a file represented by the string myPath, you use the NSFileManager method fileExistsAtPath:

```
if ([[NSFileManager defaultManager] fileExistsAtPath:myPath]) {
    // file exists
}
```

Next, you use the NSFileHandle class methods fileHandleForWritingAtPath, fileHandleForReadingAtPath:, or fileHandleForUpdatingAtPath to grab a reference to the file for the purpose of writing, reading, or updating. For example, to create a file handle for writing, you could code the following:

```
NSFileHandle *fileHandle =
                [NSFileHandle fileHandleForWritingAtPath:myPath];
```

To write data to the file referenced by fileHandle, use the NSFileHandle method writeData. To write the string stringData to the file, you could use this:

```
[fileHandle writeData:[stringData dataUsingEncoding:NSUTF8StringEncoding]];
```

The NSString method dataUsingEncoding makes sure the data is in a standard Unicode format before it is written to the file. After you've finished writing to the file, you must close it:

```
[fileHandle closeFile];
```

Later, to read the contents of the file into a string, you must perform similar operations—but with "read" methods rather than "write". First get the file handle for reading, read the entire contents into a new string with the NSFileHandle instance method availableData, and then close the file:

```
NSFileHandle *fileHandle =
              [NSFileHandle fileHandleForReadingAtPath:myPath];
NSString *surveyResults=[[NSString alloc]
                    initWithData:[fileHandle availableData]
                    encoding:NSUTF8StringEncoding];
[fileHandle closeFile];
```

When you need to update the contents of a file, you can use other NSFileHandle methods such as seekToFileOffset or seekToEndOfFile to move to a specific location in the file. You use this approach in a tutorial later in this hour.

That concludes our introduction to data storage approaches in iOS. Now let's put them to practice in three short tutorial exercises.

Creating Implicit Preferences

In our first example, we create an admittedly ridiculous flashlight application. The application has an on/off switch and shines a light from the screen when it is on. A slider controls the brightness level of the light. We use preferences to return the flashlight to the last state the user left it in.

Implementation Overview

This project requires a total of three interface elements:

▶ A view that changes from black to white to provide light

▶ A switch to turn the poor-man's flashlight on and off

▶ A slider to change the brightness

These are connected to outlets so that they are accessible in the application. The on/off status and brightness, upon being changed, will be stored using user defaults. The stored values will automatically be restored when the application is restarted.

Setting Up the Project

Create a new single-view iOS application in Xcode and call it **Flashlight**. You're only going to be coding up one method and modifying another, so little setup is work needed.

Planning the Properties and Connections

We need a total of three outlets and one action. The switch connects to an outlet that we call `toggleSwitch`, the view to `lightSource`, and the slider to `brightnessSlider`. When the slider or switch changes values, it triggers an action method, `setLightSourceAlpha`.

NOTE
To control the brightness, you place a white view on top of a black background. To change the brightness, you adjust the `alpha` value of the view (its transparency). The less transparent it is, the brighter the view. The more transparent, the darker.

Adding Key Constants

As you learned at the start of this hour's lesson, accessing the user default preferences system requires that we define keys for whatever we want to store. These are strings that we need when storing or accessing any stored data. Because these are used in multiple places and are static values, they're a good candidate for constants. We'll define two constants for the project: `kOnOffToggle` for the key that refers to the current on/off state, and `kBrightnessLevel` for the brightness of our virtual flashlight.

Add these constants to the top of the ViewController.m interface file, following the `#import` line:

```
#define kOnOffToggle @"onOff"
#define kBrightnessLevel @"brightness"
```

Now, let's lay out the UI for the flashlight.

Designing the Interface

Open the MainStoryboard.storyboard file in the Interface Builder (IB) editor, making sure that the document outline and Utility areas are visible.

Select the empty view in the scene, and then open the Attributes Inspector (Option-Command-4). Using the inspector, set the background color of the view to black. (We want our flashlight to have a black background.)

Next, drag a `UISwitch` from the Object Library (View, Utilities, Show Object Library) onto the bottom left of the view. Drag a `UISlider` to the bottom right of the view. Size the slider to take up all the horizontal space not used by the switch.

Finally, add a UIView to the top portion of the view. Size it so that it is full width and takes up all the vertical space above the switch and slider. Your view should now look like Figure 15.4.

FIGURE 15.4
The Flashlight UI.

Creating and Connecting the Outlets and Actions

The code we will write to operate the flashlight and deal with the application preferences will need access to the switch, slider, and light source. We will also change the brightness of the flashlight based on the Value Changed event from the switch as well as the slider. In summary, you create and connect these outlets:

▶ **The on/off switch (UISwitch):** toggleSwitch

▶ **The Brightness slider (UISlider):** brightnessSlider

▶ **The view that provides the "light" (UIView):** lightSource

And the single action:

▶ **Changing the value of the switch or slider (`UISwitch`/`UISlider`):**
  `setLightSourceAlphaValue`

Switch to the assistant editor, hiding the project navigator and utility area if needed.

Adding the Outlets

Start by Control-dragging from the view that you added to the UI to just below the `@interface` line in ViewController.h. When prompted, create a new outlet named `lightSource`. Repeat this for the switch, connecting it to `toggleSwitch` and the slider to `brightnessSlider`.

In addition to being able to access the three controls, our code needs to respond to changes in the toggle state of the switch and changes in the position of the slider.

Adding the Actions

To create the action that, ultimately, both the switch and the slider will use, Control-drag from the slider to below the `@property` declarations. Define a new action, `setLightSource-AlphaValue`, that will be triggered on the `Value Changed` event, as shown in Figure 15.5.

FIGURE 15.5
Connect the switch and slider to the `setLightSourceAlphaValue` method.

To connect the switch to the same action, we can use the Connections Inspector (Option-Command-5) to drag from the Value Changed event of the switch to the newly added IBAction line, or we can rely on the fact that Control-dragging from the switch to the IBAction line will automatically select the Value Changed event. Whichever method you are comfortable with, complete it now.

Making sure that both the switch and slider are connected to the action ensures that immediate feedback is provided when the user adjusts the slider value or toggles the switch.

Implementing the Application Logic

What can I say? Flashlights don't have much logic!

When the user toggles the flashlight on or off and adjusts the brightness level, the application responds by adjusting the alpha property of the lightSource view. The alpha property of a view controls the transparency of the view, with 0.0 being completely transparent and 1.0 being completely translucent. The lightSource view is white and is on top of the black background. When the lightSource view is more transparent, more of the black shows through and the flashlight is darker. When we want to turn the light off, we just set the alpha property to 0.0 so that none of the white background of the lightSource view shows.

Update the setLightSourceAlphaValue method in ViewController.m, as shown in Listing 15.1.

LISTING 15.1   The Initial `setLightSourceAlphaValue` Implementation

```
- (IBAction)setLightSourceAlphaValue:(id)sender {
    if (self.toggleSwitch.on) {
        self.lightSource.alpha = self.brightnessSlider.value;
    } else {
        self.lightSource.alpha = 0.0;
    }
}
```

This simple method checks the on property of the toggleSwitch object, and, if it is true (that is, the switch is "on"), sets the alpha property of the lightSource UIView to the value property of the slider. The slider's value property returns a floating-point number between 0.0 and 100.0, so this is already enough code to make the flashlight work. You can run the project yourself and see.

Storing the Flashlight Preferences

We don't just want the flashlight to work; we want it to return to its last state when the user uses the flashlight application again later. We'll store the on/off state and the brightness level as implicit preferences. Recall that we've defined two constants, kOnOffToggle and kBrightness-Level, to use as the keys for our storage.

Update the `setLightSourceAlphaValue` method, adding the lines shown in Listing 15.2.

LISTING 15.2   The Final `setLightSourceAlphaValue` Implementation

```
 1: - (IBAction)setLightSourceAlphaValue:(id)sender {
 2:     NSUserDefaults *userDefaults = [NSUserDefaults standardUserDefaults];
 3:     [userDefaults setBool:self.toggleSwitch.on forKey:kOnOffToggle];
 4:     [userDefaults setFloat:self.brightnessSlider.value
 5:                     forKey:kBrightnessLevel];
 6:     [userDefaults synchronize];
 7:
 8:     if (self.toggleSwitch.on) {
 9:         self.lightSource.alpha = self.brightnessSlider.value;
10:     } else {
11:         self.lightSource.alpha = 0.0;
12:     }
13: }
```

In line 2, we get the `NSUserDefault` singleton using the `standardUserDefaults` method and then use the `setBool` and `setFloat` methods to store our preferences in line 3 and in lines 4–5. We wrap up in line 6 by using the `synchronize` method in `NSUserDefaults` to make sure that our settings are stored immediately.

NOTE

Our code now saves the values for our two keys, but where do they go? The idea here is that we don't have to know because we are using the `NSUserDefaults` API to shield us from this level of detail and to allow Apple to change how defaults are handled in future versions of the iOS.

It can still be useful to know, however, and the answer is that our preferences are stored in a plist file. If you are an experienced Mac user, you may already be familiar with plists, which are used for Mac applications, too. When running on a device, the plist will be local to the device, but when we run our application in the iOS simulator, the simulator uses our computer's hard drive for storage, making it easy for us to peek inside the plist.

Run the Flashlight application in the iOS simulator, and then use Finder to navigate to /Users/ *<your username>*/Library/Application Support/iPhone Simulator/*<Device OS Version>*/Applications. As you learned earlier, the directories in Applications are unique IDs, but it should be easy to find the directory for Flashlight by looking for the most recent data modified. You'll see Flashlight.app in the most recently modified directory, and you'll see the com.yourcompany.Flashlight.plist inside its Library/Preferences subdirectory. This is a regular Mac plist file, so when you double-click it, it will open with the Property List Editor application and show you the two preferences for Flashlight.

Reading the Flashlight Preferences

Now our application is writing out the state of the two controls anytime the user changes the flashlight settings. So, to complete the desired behavior, we need to read in and use the preferences for the state of the two controls anytime our application launches. For this, we use the viewDidLoad method and the floatForKey and boolForKey methods of NSUserDefaults. Edit viewDidLoad and get the NSUserDefaults singleton in the same way as before, but this time set the value of the controls from the value returned from the preference rather than the other way around.

In the ViewController.m file, update viewDidLoad, as shown in Listing 15.3.

LISTING 15.3   Handle the Settings in viewDidLoad

```
 1: - (void)viewDidLoad
 2: {
 3:     [super viewDidLoad];
 4:
 5:     NSUserDefaults *userDefaults = [NSUserDefaults standardUserDefaults];
 6:     self.brightnessSlider.value = [userDefaults floatForKey:kBrightnessLevel];
 7:     self.toggleSwitch.on = [userDefaults boolForKey:kOnOffToggle];
 8:     if ([userDefaults boolForKey: kOnOffToggle]) {
 9:         self.lightSource.alpha = [userDefaults floatForKey:kBrightnessLevel];
10:     } else {
11:         self.lightSource.alpha = 0.0;
12:     }
13: }
```

In line 5, we get the NSUserDefault singleton and use it to grab and set the Brightness Slider (line 6) and toggle switch (line 7). Lines 8–12 check to see whether the switch is on. If it is, the alpha value for the "light source" view is set to the stored value of the slider. If the switch is off, the alpha value is set to 0.0—or completely transparent—making the view appear completely black.

Building the Application

That's all there is to it. Run the application to verify its operation (see Figure 15.6). We, too, can make millions in the App Store.

TIP

If you're running the application and press the Home button, be aware that your application won't quit; it will be suspended in the background. To fully test the Flashlight app, be sure to stop the application using the Xcode Stop button. Then use the iOS task manager to force the application completely closed, and then verify that your settings are restored when it relaunches fresh.

FIGURE 15.6
Flashlight application in action.

But I Want to Make a *Real* Flashlight!

I'll admit it, this basis for this tutorial was created before the iPhone had an LED flash. Although I still think it is effective at demonstrating how to read and write implicit preferences, I know some of you are itching to create a *real* iPhone flashlight using the LED. I can't say that I understand why, but you have your reasons.

To turn on the iPhone LED, follow these steps. First, add the AVFoundation framework to your project, and make sure that you import the header in an appropriate place (like your ViewController.h file):

```
#import <AVFoundation/AVFoundation.h>
```

Next, add this code wherever you want the LED to turn on:

```
AVCaptureDevice *backCamera =
                [AVCaptureDevice defaultDeviceWithMediaType:AVMediaTypeVideo];
if ( [backCamera isTorchAvailable] &&
                [backCamera isTorchModeSupported:AVCaptureTorchModeOn]  ) {
     BOOL success = [backCamera lockForConfiguration:nil];
     if ( success )
```

```
        {
                [backCamera setTorchMode:AVCaptureTorchModeOn] ;
                [backCamera unlockForConfiguration] ;
        }

    }
```

This is code Apple provides in the AV Foundation release notes *specifically* for creating flashlight applications. If you want to turn the LED off, you'll write pretty much the same thing, but use the constant AVCaptureTorchModeOff with the setTorchMode method.

While we are waiting for the cash to pour in (it may be awhile), let's look at an application where the user takes more direct control of the application's preferences.

Implementing System Settings

A second option to consider for providing application preferences is to use the Settings application. You do this by creating and editing a settings bundle for your application in Xcode rather than by writing code and designing a UI, so this is a very fast and easy option—*once you get used to editing settings bundles*. Initially, you might have to take a few cracks at making all the plist changes you need; there is a learning curve for the process.

For our second application of the hour, we create an application that tells someone who finds a lost device how to return it to its owner. The Settings application is used to edit the contact information of the owner and to select a picture to evoke the finder's sympathy.

Implementation Overview

What you'll soon come to appreciate with settings bundles is that a great deal of tedious UI/ storage work happens "automagically," without needing to write any code. In this application, you create a settings bundle that defines several values that you can set within the iOS Settings application. These settings are read by the app and used to update the onscreen display when it is running. There will be no user inputs in the application itself, making our logic even simpler than the last tutorial.

Setting Up the Project

As we often do, begin by creating a new single-view iOS application in Xcode called **ReturnMe**.

We want to provide the finder of the lost device with a sympathy-invoking picture and the owner's name, email address, and phone number. Each of these items is configurable as an application preference, so we need outlets (but no actions) for these UI elements.

Planning the Properties and Connections

For the three text values that we want to display, we need to define labels (`UILabel`), which we'll call `name`, `email`, and `phone`. The image that we will be displaying will be contained within a `UIImageView` that will be named **picture**. That's it; we don't need any input controls because they will be managed through our settings bundle.

Adding Key Constants

As in the previous project, we are referencing stored user default values using a key. We need a total of four keys to each of the values we're working with. To keep things orderly, let's define constants that we can use to refer to the keys whenever we want. Edit the ViewController.m file and add the following lines after the existing `#import` line:

```
#define kName @"name"
#define kEmail @"email"
#define kPhone @"phone"
#define kPicture @"picture"
```

These should be self-explanatory; the names and string values are probably a dead giveaway.

Adding the Image Resources

As part of this project, we display an image that will help goad our Good Samaritan into return-ing the lost device rather than selling it to Gizmodo. Drag the Images folder into your main proj-ect code group. When you drag the folder into Xcode, make sure you click the option to copy the files and create groups where necessary.

TIP

Remember, to support Retina-class displays, all you need to do is create images with twice the horizontal and vertical resolution as your standard image resources, include a @2x suffix on the file-name, and add them to your project. The developer tools and iOS take care of the rest.

I've included @2x image resources with many of the projects in this book.

Designing the Interface

Now let's lay out the ReturnMe application's UI, as follows:

1. Open the IB editor by clicking the MainStoryboard.storyboard file.

2. Open the Object Library so that you can start adding components to the interface.

3. Drag three `UILabels` onto the view.

4. Set the text to a default value of your choosing for the name, email, and phone number.

5. Drag a UIImageView to the view.

6. Size the image view to take up the majority of the device's display area.

7. With the image view selected, use the Attributes Inspector to set the mode to be Aspect Fill, and pick one of the animal images you added to the Xcode project from the Image drop-down.

8. Add some additional UILabels to explain the purpose of the application and labels that explain each preference value (name, email, and phone number).

As long as you have the three labels and the image view in your UI, as shown in Figure 15.7, you can design the rest as you see fit. Have fun with it.

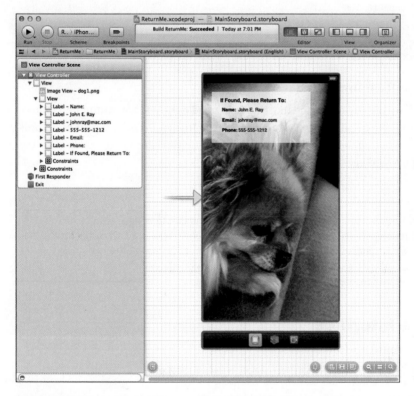

FIGURE 15.7
Create an interface with an image, labels, and anything else you want.

Creating and Connecting the Outlets

When you're finished building the interface, switch to the assistant editor and connect the
UIImageView and three UILabels to corresponding outlets: picture, name, email, and
phone. There aren't any actions to connect, so just Control-drag from each UI element to the
ViewController.h file, providing the appropriate name when prompted.

Now that the interface is built, we create the settings bundle, which will enable us to integrate
with the iOS Settings application.

Creating the Settings Bundle

Create a new settings bundle in Xcode by selecting File, New File from the menu bar and selecting Settings Bundle from the iOS Resource group in the sidebar, as shown in Figure 15.8. To
choose where the settings bundle is stored, click Next. When prompted, leave the default location
and name unchanged, but choose the Supporting Files group from the Group pop-up menu at
the bottom of the Save dialog box. If you forget to do this, you can drag the settings bundle into
your Supporting Files group later.

FIGURE 15.8
Settings bundle in Xcode's New File dialog.

The ReturnMe preferences are grouped into three groups: Sympathy Image, Contact Information, and About. The Sympathy Image group will contain a Multi Value preference to pick one of the images, the Contact Information group will contain three text fields, and the About group will link to a child page with three read-only titles.

CAUTION

Read Slowly and Practice

Before you start building your application preferences, be aware that the language of Apple's tools makes it difficult to describe the process without tying one's tongue in knots.

Here are a few important things to keep in mind:

▶ When I refer to a *property*, I am referring to a line within the plist file. Properties are defined by a key, a type, and one or more values.

▶ Properties can contain multiple other properties. I refer to these as being *within* an existing property—or *children* of the original property.

▶ The specific attributes that define a property (key, type, and value) are represented as columns within the plist editor. I refer to these by name where you need to make a change, when possible.

▶ You can accomplish the same thing in *many* different ways. Don't worry if you find a better way that accomplishes the same results.

Expand the Settings.bundle in Xcode and click the Root.plist file. You'll see a table of three columns: Key, Type, and Value. Expand the iPhone Settings Schema property, then Preference Items property within it; you'll see a series of four dictionary properties. These are provided by Xcode as samples, and each of them will be interpreted by Settings as a preference. You follow the simple schema in the Settings Application Schema Reference in the iOS Reference Library to set all the required properties, and some of the optional properties, of each preference.

Expand the first dictionary property under Preference Items called Item 0, and you'll see that it has a Type property with a value of Group. This is the correct type to define a preference group (which groups together a set of related preferences), but we will need to make some changes to reflect the settings we want. Change the Title property's value column to read **Sympathy Image** by clicking it and typing the new title. This provides a nice group heading in the Settings display.

The second preference item will contain multichoice settings for our Sympathy Image. Look at the value in parentheses to the right of the Item 1; note that it is currently set to be a Text Field. Our Sympathy Image will be selected as a multivalue, not a text field, so change it to Multi Value by clicking the Key column of the property and picking from the pop-up list that appears. Next, expand the property and edit its child properties. Change the Title to **Image Name**, the Identifier (what we will use to reference the value in our app) to **picture**, and the Default Value to **Dog**.

You can change the type for most properties by simply clicking the label in the key column; this opens a drop-down menu showing the available types. Unfortunately, not all types are represented in the menu. To access the full list of types, you need to expand the property and then set the underlying Type child property using the drop-down menu to the right of the Value column.

The choices for a multivalue picker come from two array properties: an array of item names and an array of item values. In our case, the name and value array properties will be the same, but we still must provide both of them. To add another property, click to select one of the existing properties (such as Default Value), and then click the + icon that appears (see Figure 15.9). This adds another property at the same level as the property you selected.

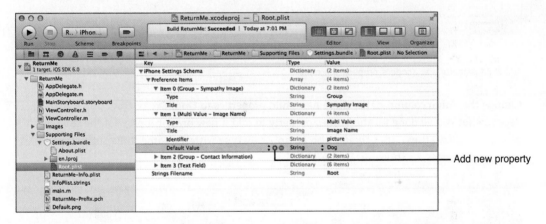

FIGURE 15.9
Add another property in Xcode's property list editor.

Set the name of the new property to **Values** and set the Type column to **Array**. Each of the three possible image names needs a property under Values. Expand the Values property to see what it contains (initially nothing). *With it expanded*, click the Values property and click the + icon three times to add new string properties as children: Item 0, Item 1, and Item 2, as shown in Figure 15.10.

The +/– icon we're using to add rows will add a row at the same level as the highlighted property, directly below the highlighted property. This holds true unless the property is a dictionary or array and is *also* expanded. In that case, it adds a new child property within the item.

In some cases, the +/– icons may not be visible (thanks a bunch Xcode!). If you want to add a row below a property and you don't see these icons, you can right-click a given property on the far-right side of its line and choose Add Row from the menu that appears.

FIGURE 15.10
Add child properties in Xcode's property list editor.

Change the Value column of the three new child properties to **Dog**, **Crazy Dog**, and **Coral**. Repeat what you've done for the Values property to add a new array property at the same level as Values called **Titles**. Titles should also be an Array type with the same three String type children properties, as shown in Figure 15.11.

FIGURE 15.11
The completed image selector preference in Xcode's property list editor.

The third property (Item 2) in our Preference Items should be the type Group with a title of **Contact Information**. Click the key column to change the Type; then expand the property and update the Title child property and remove all other items. The ultimate effect of this change will be that second group of settings with the title Contact Information appears within the Settings app.

The fourth property (Item 3) is the name preference. Click the Key column and change it to be a Text Field. Expand the property and configure the children properties as follows: set the Identifier property value to **name**, and the Default Value to **Your Name**. The type column should be set to String for both. Add three more children properties under Item 3. Set the Property keys to Keyboard Type, Autocapitalization Style, and Autocorrection Style, and the values to Alphabet, Words, and No Autocorrection, respectively. The Type column, again, should be set to String for all three child properties. You may have surmised, these are optional parameters that set up the keyboard for text entry.

You can test your settings so far by running the ReturnMe application in the iOS simulator, exiting the application with the Home button, and then running the Settings application in the simulator. You should see a Settings selection for the ReturnMe application and settings for the Sympathy Image and Name.

Add two more Text Field properties as children to the Preference Items property in the plist. The easiest way to do this so that the properties are added *below* Item 3 is to right-click on the far-right of the Item 3 line and choose "Add Row" from the pop-up menu that appears. After adding the properties, mirror what you set up for the name preference: one for email and one for phone number. Use the keys of **email** and **phone**, and change the values of child Keyboard Type property to Email Address and Number Pad, respectively. When you add the new properties, there may be more child properties than you are expecting. The Text Field properties you're adding now, for example, include a Title property that can be removed by selecting it and pressing Delete or clicking the – icon. They don't, however, contain the Keyboard Type, Autocapitalization Style, and so on. You can add these by adding a new row, and then use the pop-up menus in the Key, Type, and Value columns to configure the missing properties.

The final preference is About, and it opens a child preference pane; we'll add two more items to accomplish this. First, add a new property—Item 6—to the plist. Click the Key column for the property and set it to be a Group. Expand Item 6 and set the Title child property to a value **About ReturnMe** (configured with a Type column of String). As with the previous two groups, this creates a nicely titled division, About ReturnMe, within the Settings display.

Next, add Item 7; it can be any type you want, because the type property it contains needs to be adjusted a bit differently. Expand Item 7 and set the Type child property to **Child Pane**. Unlike other preference types, this is not available by clicking the property's Key column. Update the Title child property's value to **About**, and add a new child property with the key set to Filename, a type column of String, and a value column of **About**. Your completed Root.plist should resemble Figure 15.12. The child pane element assumes the value of the Filename identifier exists as another plist in the settings bundle. In our case, this is a file called About.plist.

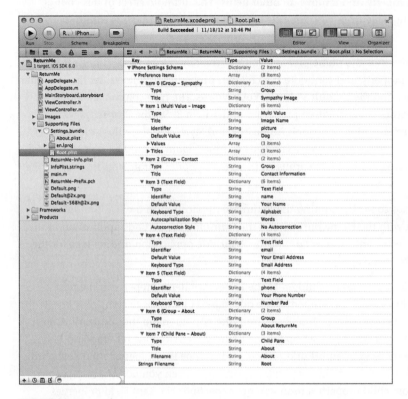

FIGURE 15.12
The completed Root.plist file.

The easiest way to create this second plist file in the settings bundle is by copying the Root.plist file we already have. Select the Root.plist file in the project navigator, and then choose File, Duplicate. Name the new file **About.plist**.

Select the About.plist file and right-click any property it contains. From the menu that appears, choose Property List Type, iPhone Settings plist. This tells Xcode what we intend to use the plist file for, which, in turn gives us property names in plain English.

Edit About.plist's Preference Items array to have four child properties. The first is a group property with a Title child property of **About ReturnMe**. The remaining three should be set to Title properties and are used for **Version**, **Copyright**, and **Website Information**. The Title properties contain three children properties by default: Type, Title, Identifier. Type should already be set to Title, and the Title property value set to the title strings for the information we want to display: Version, Copyright, or Website. The Identifier value doesn't matter because we won't be setting any of these in our code. Each of these three Title properties also need a new (fourth) child property with the key Default Value added to them. This will be of the type String, and the Value will be set to whatever text information you want displayed in the Settings app for the parent property. Figure 15.13 shows my finished About.plist file.

FIGURE 15.13
The About.plist file.

If you have any difficulties setting up your plist files, run the application, exit it, and then compare your preferences UI to Figure 15.14 and your plists to the plists in the settings bundle in the sample project's source code to see where you might have made a misstep.

CAUTION
_____

Value and Values, Types and Type Keys, Aarrrrgh!

The plist editor can be confusing to deal with because the UI and the terminology are convoluted. In this exercise, for example, we created a multivalue picker that requires an array named Values—the items in the array also have a value—so we have to work with values's Values. Fun, huh?

This is exacerbated by our need to add new properties of a certain type. Each property has an underlying data type (Array, Dictionary, String, and so on), but it may also have a child property with the identifier of Type that defines what that property (and its child properties) represents—like a text field. The result is a mishmash of terms that will drive you up the wall.

I recommend working through the exercise and changing keys and values to see the effect. It isn't difficult once you get the hang of it, but Apple has made it an absolute bear to describe.
_____

FIGURE 15.14
ReturnMe's settings in the Settings application.

Implementing the Application Logic

We have now bundled up our preferences so that they can be set by the Settings application, but our ReturnMe application also has to be modified to use the preferences. We do this in the ViewController.m file's `viewDidLoad` event. Here we will call a helper method we write called `setValuesFromPreferences`. Our code to use the preference values with the `NSUserDefaults` API looks no different from the Flashlight application. It doesn't matter if our application wrote the preference values or if the Settings application did; we can simply treat `NSUserDefaults` like a dictionary and ask for objects by their key.

We provided default values in the settings bundle, but it's possible the user just installed ReturnMe and has not run the Settings application. We should provide the same default settings programmatically to cover this case, and we can do that by providing a dictionary of default preference keys and values to the `NSUserDefaults` `registerDefaults` method. Start by adding a prototype for the `setValuesFromPreferences` method in ViewController.h file. Add this line following the property definitions:

```
-(void)setValuesFromPreferences;
```

Next, implement the method in ViewController.m. Listing 15.4 shows a completed implementation of `setValuesFromPreferences`.

LISTING 15.4   The `setValuesFromPreferences` Implementation

```
 1: - (void) setValuesFromPreferences {
 2:     NSUserDefaults *userDefaults = [NSUserDefaults standardUserDefaults];
 3:
 4:
 5:     NSDictionary *initialDefaults=@{kPicture:@"Dog",
 6:                                     kName:@"Your Name",
 7:                                     kEmail:@"you@yours.com",
 8:                                     kPhone:@"(555)555-1212"};
 9:
10:
11:     [userDefaults registerDefaults:initialDefaults];
12:     // [userDefaults synchronize];
13:
14:     NSString *picturePreference = [userDefaults stringForKey:kPicture];
15:     if ([picturePreference isEqualToString:@"Dog"]) {
16:         self.picture.image = [UIImage imageNamed:@"dog1.png"];
17:     } else if ([picturePreference isEqualToString:@"Crazy Dog"]) {
18:         self.picture.image = [UIImage imageNamed:@"dog2.png"];
19:     } else {
20:         self.picture.image = [UIImage imageNamed:@"coral.png"];
21:     }
22:
23:     self.name.text = [userDefaults stringForKey:kName];
24:     self.email.text = [userDefaults stringForKey:kEmail];
25:     self.phone.text = [userDefaults stringForKey:kPhone];
26: }
```

Things kick off in line 2, where we grab a reference to the NSUserDefaults singleton.

Lines 5–8 allocate and initialize an NSDictionary named initialDefaults that contains the default value/key pairs that our application should use if no preferences have been set in the Settings app yet. The pairs are added to the dictionary value first, followed by the key (represented by the constants we added to the project earlier).

In line 11, we use the NSUserDefaults method registerDefaults to register our sample default values. After that, the code should remind you of the previous tutorial. Lines 13–24 simply get the values stored for each of our keys and set the user interface elements accordingly.

We still, however, need to load the preferences when the application starts. Edit ReturnMe ViewController.m, implementing the viewDidLoad method to invoke setValuesFromPreferences, as shown in Listing 15.5.

LISTING 15.5   Load the Settings When the Initial View Loads

```
- (void) viewDidLoad
{
    [super viewDidLoad];
    [self setValuesFromPreferences];
}
```

Building the Application

Run the ReturnMe application, wait until it starts in the iOS simulator, and then click the Xcode Stop button. Using the iOS simulator's Settings app, change a few items for the ReturnMe application. Next, use the iOS application manager to terminate ReturnMe so that it isn't waiting in the background, and then relaunch it. Your new settings should be represented in the application display.

CAUTION

Use the Xcode Stop Button!

If you do not use the Xcode Stop button to exit your application and then stop and restart it manually in the iOS simulator, you will get an error in Xcode. The Xcode debugger will be upset because it can't connect to the application anymore. For that reason, when testing the app, be sure to use Xcode's Stop button and then run your tests of ReturnMe.

When we explore backgrounding in Hour 22, "Building Background-Aware Applications," you learn how to programmatically deal with applications that are starting, stopping, and moving to and from the background.

You can see that with very little code on our part, we were able to provide a sophisticated interface to configure our application. The Settings bundle plist schema provides a fairly complete way to describe the preference needs of an application.

Implementing File System Storage

In our final example for this hour, we create a simple survey application. The application collects a person's first name, last name, and email address and then stores them in a CSV file on the iOS device's file system. Touching another button retrieves and displays the contents of the file.

Implementation Overview

The survey application's user interface will be simple: three fields that collect data, a button to store the data, and another button to read all the accumulated results and display them in a scrolling text view. To store the information, we first generate a path to a new file in our application's Documents directory. We then create a file handle to that path and output our survey data as a formatted string. Reading the data back in will be much the same, except we grab the file handle and read the entire contents of the file into a string and then display that in a read-only text view.

Setting Up the Project

Create a new single-view iOS application in Xcode and call it **Survey**. We do have several UI elements that our code will need to interact with, so let's decide what they are and what they'll be called.

Planning the Properties and Connections

Because this is a survey and we'll be collecting information, obviously we need input areas for our data. In this case, these are text fields for collection first and last name and email address. We'll call these `firstName`, `lastName`, and `email`, respectively. To demonstrate that we've properly stored a CSV file, we'll read it in and output it in a text view that we will name `resultsView`.

We also need a total of three actions in this tutorial: two obvious and one less so. First, we need to store the data, so we add a button that triggers an action called `storeSurvey`. Next, we need to read the results and display them, so we have a second button that triggers an action called `showResults`. Unfortunately, there's a third action we want to add—our handy `hideKeyboard` implementation so that the user can touch the background of the view or the Done button on the mini keyboard to hide the onscreen keyboard.

Designing the Interface

To design the interface, follow these steps:

1. Shift into design mode by clicking the MainStoryboard.storyboard file and then opening the Object Library.

2. Drag three text fields (`UITextField`) into the view and position them near the top of the view. Add three labels beside the fields that read **First Name:**, **Last Name:**, and **Email:**.

3. Using the Attributes Inspector (Option-Command-4), select each field in turn, and then apply an appropriate Keyboard attribute (Email for the email field, for example), Return Key (such as Done), Capitalization, and any other features you think are appropriate. That completes our data entry form.

4. Drag a text view (`UITextView`) into the design and position it below the entry fields—this will display the contents of our survey results CSV file.

5. Add a label above it titled **Results**.

6. Using the Attributes Inspector, set the text view to be read-only, since a user won't be able to use it to edit the survey results being displayed.

7. Add two buttons (`UIButton`) below the text view—one titled **Store Survey** and the other **Show Results**. These trigger our two actions that interact with files.

8. To deal with hiding the keyboard when the background is tapped, add a single `UIButton` sized to cover the entire view. Use the Attributes Inspector to set the button type to Custom—this will make it invisible.

9. Use the Editor, Arrange menu to set the custom button to the back (behind the rest of the UI), or simply drag the custom button to the top of the list of objects in the view using the document outline.

Your final survey UI should resemble Figure 15.15.

FIGURE 15.15
The Survey application UI.

Creating and Connecting the Outlets and Actions

We need to wire up a number of connections in this project to interact with the user interface. Let's review what we'll be adding, starting with the outlets:

▶ **The first name field (UITextField):** firstName

▶ **The last name field (UITextField):** lastName

▶ **Email address (UITextField):** email

▶ **Text view results area (UITextView):** resultsView

And the actions:

▶ **Touching the Store Survey button (UIButton):** storeSurvey

▶ **Touching the Show Results button (UIButton):** showResults

▶ **Touching the background button (UIButton), or receiving the Did End on Exit event from any of the text fields:** hideKeyboard

Switch to the assistant editor to begin adding outlets and actions. Make sure that the document outline is available so that you can get an easy handle on the invisible custom button.

Adding the Outlets

Add each of the necessary outlets by Control-dragging from their representation in the view to the space following the @interface line in ViewController.h. Connect the field beside the First Name label to firstName, as shown in Figure 15.16. Repeat this for each of the other fields, as well as the text view, naming them with the conventions we've decided on. None of the other objects require an outlet.

FIGURE 15.16
Connect the fields and text view to their outlets.

Adding the Actions

Once the outlets are in place, begin adding the connections to the actions. Control-drag from the Store Survey button to below the @property definitions in the ViewController.h interface file, creating a new action named storeSurvey, as shown in Figure 15.17. Do the same for the Show Results button, creating a new action called showResults.

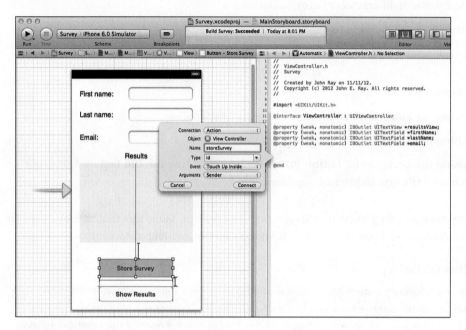

FIGURE 15.17
Connect the buttons to their actions.

As you probably remember, creating and connecting the hideKeyboard action isn't quite as straightforward. Begin by creating the action by Control-dragging from the custom button to the ViewController.h file. It may be easiest to use the Button line in the document outline rather than trying to target the button in the view. Name the new action hideKeyboard. That takes care of the user touching the background, but we still need to handle the user touching the onscreen keyboard's Done button.

Select the first of the text fields, and then open the Connections Inspector. You may need to hide the project navigator or document outline to make room in your workspace. From the Connections Inspector, drag from the Did End on Exit connection point to the hideKeyboard IBAction line in ViewController.h. Do the same for the other two fields.

We're done with the interface. Switch back to the standard editor and open the ViewController.m file to finish up the implementation.

Implementing the Application Logic

We need to implement three pieces of code to finish the application. First, we drop in the `hide-Keyboard` code, just to get it out of the way. Next, we add `storeSurvey` and `showResults` using the methods you learned at the beginning of this hour's lesson.

Hiding the Keyboard

To hide the keyboard, the object that currently has "control" of the keyboard must resign its first responder status using the method `resignFirstResponder`. In other words, our three text fields must each do this when `hideKeyboard` is invoked. Refer to Hour 7, "Working with Text, Keyboards, and Buttons," if you have any questions about how this works, and then implement `hideKeyboard` as shown in Listing 15.6.

LISTING 15.6   Hide the Keyboard When It Isn't Needed

```
- (IBAction)hideKeyboard:(id)sender {
    [self.lastName resignFirstResponder];
    [self.firstName resignFirstResponder];
    [self.email resignFirstResponder];
}
```

Storing the Survey Results

To store the survey fields, we format our incoming data, establish a path for the file that will contain the results, create a new file if needed, store the survey fields at the end of the file, and then close the file and clear out our survey form. Go ahead and enter the `storeSurvey` implementation in Listing 15.7, and then let's walk through the code.

LISTING 15.7   The `storeSurvey` Implementation

```
 1: - (IBAction)storeSurvey:(id)sender {
 2:
 3:     NSString *csvLine=[NSString stringWithFormat:@"%@,%@,%@\n",
 4:                     self.firstName.text,
 5:                     self.lastName.text,
 6:                     self.email.text];
 7:
 8:     NSString *docDir = NSSearchPathForDirectoriesInDomains(
 9:                                     NSDocumentDirectory,
10:                                     NSUserDomainMask, YES
11:                                     )[0];
12:     NSString *surveyFile = [docDir
13:                         stringByAppendingPathComponent:
14:                         @"surveyresults.csv"];
```

```
15:
16:      if  (![[NSFileManager defaultManager] fileExistsAtPath:surveyFile]) {
17:          [[NSFileManager defaultManager]
18:            createFileAtPath:surveyFile contents:nil attributes:nil];
19:      }
20:
21:      NSFileHandle *fileHandle = [NSFileHandle
22:                               fileHandleForUpdatingAtPath:surveyFile];
23:      [fileHandle seekToEndOfFile];
24:      [fileHandle writeData:[csvLine
25:                        dataUsingEncoding:NSUTF8StringEncoding]];
26:      [fileHandle closeFile];
27:
28:      self.firstName.text=@"";
29:      self.lastName.text=@"";
30:      self.email.text=@"";
31: }
```

The implementation begins by creating a new string (csvLine) in lines 3–6 that is formatted as a CSV line. Each %@ in the format string is replaced with the contents of one of our text entry fields. The \n at the end of the format string adds a newline—typically indicating a new record in a CSV file.

Lines 8–11 return the document directory for our application in the string docDir, which is then used to create the full survey path string, surveyPath, in lines 12–14 by appending the filename surveyresults.csv.

In lines 16–19, we check for the presence of the file represented by the path in surveyPath; if it does not exist, a new empty file with that name is created. After we've established that a file is present, we can write our data.

Lines 21–22 create a new file handle that points to our surveyPath file. The file handle is created using the method fileHandleForUpdatingAtPath since we want to update the existing contents of the file. Line 23 moves to the end of the existing file with seekToEndOfFile so that any data we write is written at the very end.

In line 24, our csvLine string is written to the file with the method writeData, and then the file is closed in line 26.

Lines 28–30 clean up the survey form by clearing the current values in the text fields.

Now that we've written to a file, let's see if we can get data back out.

Showing the Survey Results

To retrieve and display the survey results, we start by doing exactly what we did when storing them: establishing a path to the file. Next, we check for the existence of the file. If it is there, we have results we can read and display. If not, we don't need to do anything. Assuming there are results, we create a file handle using the NSFileHandle class method fileHandleForReading-AtPath and then read the contents of the file with the method availableData. The last step is just to set the text view's contents to the data we've read.

Implement the showResults method, as shown in Listing 15.8.

LISTING 15.8   The showResults Implementation

```
 1: - (IBAction)showResults:(id)sender {
 2:     NSString *docDir = NSSearchPathForDirectoriesInDomains(
 3:                         NSDocumentDirectory,
 4:                         NSUserDomainMask, YES
 5:                         )[0];
 6:     NSString *surveyFile = [docDir
 7:                         stringByAppendingPathComponent:
 8:                         @"surveyresults.csv"];
 9:
10:     if ([[NSFileManager defaultManager] fileExistsAtPath:surveyFile]) {
11:         NSFileHandle *fileHandle = [NSFileHandle
12:                             fileHandleForReadingAtPath:surveyFile];
13:         NSString *surveyResults=[[NSString alloc]
14:                             initWithData:[fileHandle availableData]
15:                             encoding:NSUTF8StringEncoding];
16:         [fileHandle closeFile];
17:         self.resultsView.text=surveyResults;
18:     }
19: }
```

Lines 2–8 create the surveyPath string, which is then used to check for the existence of the file in line 10.

If the file exists, it is opened for reading in lines 11–12, and the availableData method is used to retrieve the entire contents, which is stored in the string surveyResults.

Finally, the file is closed in line 16 and the results view in the UI is updated with the contents of the surveyResults string.

That's all there is to it. Run the application and give it a try. Store a few surveys, and then read and display the results, as shown in Figure 15.18. You now have the ability to write and read any data you want in the iOS file system.

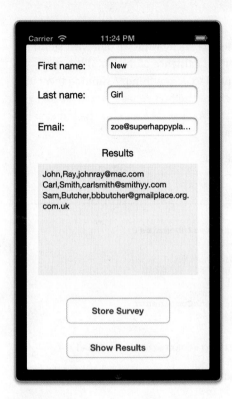

FIGURE 15.18
The Survey application stores and reads data.

TIP

I know I've been saying this a lot in this hour, but remember that iOS doesn't "quit" applications when you exit them; it suspends the app and moves it to the background. To verify that data is truly persisting between runs of your app, you can use the iOS task manager to force-quit your programs.

You'll learn more about application backgrounding in Hour 22. For now, be aware that there is a method called `applicationDidEnterBackground` in your application delegate class where you can put any application cleanup code that absolutely must be run before it quits.

Further Exploration

You have been exposed to most of what you need to know about preferences at this point. My main advice is to gain some more experience in working with preferences by going back to previous hours and adding sensible preferences to some of the example applications you have already worked on. The application preferences system is well documented by Apple, and you should take some time to read through it.

I also highly recommend that you read Apple's *Archives and Serializations Programming Guide for Cocoa*; this provides examples of not just how to save data, but also how to store objects in files and read and instantiate them at will. This can be used, for example, to create database applications with rich objects containing images, sound, and so forth. For even more complex data needs, you should begin reviewing the documentation on Core Data.

Core Data is a framework that provides management and persistence for in-memory application object graphs. Core Data attempts to solve many of the challenges that face other, simpler forms of object persistence such as object archiving. Some of the challenging areas Core Data focuses on are multilevel undo management, data validation, data consistency across independent data assessors, efficient (that is, indexed) filtering, sorting and searching of object graphs, and persistence to a variety of data repositories. In layman's terms, if you think your application might require a real database engine, you need Core Data.

Apple Tutorials

Application Preferences in iOS Application Programming is a tutorial-style guide to the various parts of the application preferences system.

Setting Application Schema References in the iOS Reference Library is an indispensable guide to the required and optional properties for the preferences in your plist files that will be edited by the Settings application.

Core Data Tutorial for iOS is an Apple tutorial for learning the basics of Core Data. This is a good place to start for an exploration of Core Data.

Summary

In this hour, you developed three iOS applications, and along the way you learned three different ways of storing the application's data. You captured the user's implicit preferences with the Flashlight application, allowed the ReturnMe application to be explicitly configured from the Settings application, and stored the Survey application's data through direct file system access. You also learned some important design principles that should keep you from getting carried away with too many preferences and should guide you in putting preferences in the right location.

This hour explored a lot of ground, and you have covered the topic of application data storage fairly exhaustively. At this point, you should be ready for most storage needs you encounter while developing your own applications.

Q&A

Q. What about games? How should game preferences be handled?

A. Games are about providing the player with an immersive experience. Leaving that experience to go to the Settings application or to interact with a stodgy table view is not going to keep the player immersed. You want users to set up the game to their liking while still remaining in the game's world, with the music and graphical style of the game as part of the customization experience. For games, feel free to use the NSUserDefaults API but provide a custom, in-game experience for the UI.

Q. I have more complex data requirements. Is there a database I can use?

A. Although the techniques discussed in this hour's lesson are suitable for most applications, larger apps may want to utilize Core Data. Core Data implements a high-level data model and helps developers manage complex data requirements. Although what happens behind the scenes is hidden from your application, Core Data uses SQLite to do its heavy lifting, so it is a database engine; you just don't need to worry about managing it.

Workshop

Quiz

1. What are user defaults?

2. What is a plist file?

Answers

1. The user defaults system provides a means of storing application preferences or other key/value data pairs without needing to manage files or file access. Think of it as an NSDictionary that persists between executions of your application.

2. A plist file is an XML property list file used to store the user's settings for a given application. Plist files can be edited from within Xcode, as you've discovered in this tutorial.

Activities

1. If you think through the life cycle of the Flashlight application, you may realize there is a circumstance we didn't account for. It's possible that the Flashlight application has never been run before and has no stored user preferences. To try this scenario, select Reset Content and Settings from the iOS Simulator menu, and then launch the Flashlight application in the simulator. With no prior settings, it defaults to off, with the brightness turned all

the way down. This is the exact opposite of what we would like to default to the first time Flashlight is run. Apply the technique we used in the ReturnMe application to fix this, and default the flashlight's initial state to on and 100% brightness.

2. Return to an earlier application, such as ImageHop, and use implicit preferences to save the state of the program (the hop rate and whether the bunnies are hopping) before it exits. When the user relaunches the application, restore the application to its original state. This is a key part of the iOS user experience and something you should strive for.

HOUR 16
Building Responsive User Interfaces

What You'll Learn in This Hour:

▶ How to make an application "responsive"
▶ Using Auto Layout to enable automatic resizing and rotation
▶ Creating UI elements programmatically for the ultimate control
▶ How to swap views for landscape and portrait viewing

You can use almost every iOS interface widget available, create multiple views and view controllers, add sounds and alerts, write files, and even manage application preferences, but until now, your applications have been missing a very important feature: responsive interfaces. The ability to create interfaces that display correctly regardless of your iDevice's screen size or orientation is one of the key features that users expect in an application—and the key goal of responsive interface design.

This hour's lesson explores the Xcode Auto Layout system and three different ways of adding rotatable and resizable interfaces to your apps. As you read this hour's lesson, an important fact to keep in mind is that there are *many* different ways to solve the problem of responsive interface design. What works best for you may be entirely different than what I describe here.

Responsive Interfaces

Years ago, when I had my first Windows Mobile smartphone, I longed for an easy way to look at web content in landscape mode. There was a method for triggering a landscape view, but it was glitchy and cumbersome to use. The iPhone introduced the first consumer phone with on-the-fly interface rotation that feels natural and doesn't get in the way of what you're trying to do.

The iPhone 5 shakes things up by introducing the first 4" iPhone screen with a different aspect ration and resolution than the traditional 3.5" models. Does this mean that you need to worry about iPhone 3.5" displays, 4" displays, iPad displays, and portrait and landscape orientations for each? Nope! The iOS Auto Layout system makes it easy to adapt to different resolution displays and change your interface layout as your device resolution changes.

TIP
_____

Using Auto Layout to adapt between 3.5" and 4" screens is no different from adapting to a device that rotates between portrait and landscape. The resolution changes on-the-fly in the case of rotation, but you'll use the same tools to compensate. The only difference is that you can control whether or not your application handles different orientations—you can't control whether or not your users buy a 4" iPhone screen.

Although you should definitely plan to accommodate all sizes of the iPhone screen in your iPhone apps, the decision to handle rotation is entirely up to you. Consider how the user will be interfacing with the app. Does it make sense to force a portrait-only view? Should the view rotate to accommodate any of the possible orientations the phone may assume? The more flexibility you give users to adapt to their own preferred working style, the happier they'll be. Best of all, enabling rotation is a simple process.

TIP
_____

Apple's user interface guidelines for the iPad strongly encourage the support of any orientation/ rotation: portrait, left landscape, right landscape, and upside-down.

Enabling Interface Rotation

The projects that you've built to-date have had supported limited interface rotation because of a single line of code in a single method in your view controller. This is added by default when you use one of Apple's iOS templates.

When an iOS device wants to check to see whether it should rotate your interface, it sends the `supportedInterfaceOrientations` message to your view controller. The implementation of `supportedInterfaceOrientations` just returns a value that describes the supported orientation. To cover more than one orientation, you just return the list of constants you want to use, separated by the | character.

There are seven screen orientation support constants, as listed here.

Orientation	Orientation Support Constant
Portrait	`UIInterfaceOrientationMaskPortrait`
Portrait upside-down	`UIInterfaceOrientationMaskPortraitUpsideDown`
Landscape left	`UIInterfaceOrientationMaskLandscapeLeft`

Orientation	Orientation Support Constant
Landscape right	`UIInterfaceOrientationMaskLandscapeRight`
Any Landscape	`UIInterfaceOrientationMaskLandscape`
Anything but upside-down	`UIInterfaceOrientationMaskAllButUpsideDown`
Anything	`UIInterfaceOrientationMaskAll`

For example, to allow your interface to rotate to either the portrait or landscape left orientations, you implement `supportedInterfaceOrientations` in your view controller with the code in Listing 16.1.

LISTING 16.1 This Method Activates Interface Rotation

```
- (NSUInteger)supportedInterfaceOrientations {
    return UIInterfaceOrientationMaskPortrait |
                UIInterfaceOrientationMaskLandscapeLeft;
}
```

The `return` statement handles everything. It returns the combination of the two constants that describe landscape left and portrait orientations.

NOTE

In addition to adding this method to your view controllers, you must also choose the orientations supported by your app by clicking the Supported Interface Orientation icons in the application summary. This is described in the section "Setting Supported Device Orientations" in Hour 2, "Introduction to Xcode and the iOS Simulator."

At this point, take a few minutes and go back to some of the earlier hours and modify this method in your view controller code to allow for different orientations. Test the applications in the iOS simulator or on your device. For iPhone apps, try switching between 3.5" and 4" displays.

Some of the applications will probably look just fine, but you'll notice that others, well, don't quite "work" in the different screen orientations and sizes, as shown in Figure 16.1 (ImageHop, from Hour 8, "Handling Images, Animation, Sliders, and Steppers").

Everything we've been building has defaulted to a portrait design and, for the iPhone, a 4" screen, so how can we create interfaces that look good regardless of the orientation and size of the screen? We obviously need to make some tweaks.

Add a View Controller.

FIGURE 16.1
Enabling an orientation doesn't mean it will look good.

Designing Rotatable and Resizable Interfaces

In the remainder of this hour, we explore several different techniques for building interfaces that rotate and resize themselves appropriately depending on the device, or when the user changes the device's screen orientation. Before we get started, let's quickly review the different approaches and when you'd want to use them.

Auto Layout

The Xcode Interface Builder (IB) editor provides tools for describing how your interface should react when it is rotated or when the size of the screen can be variable. It is possible to define a single view in IB that positions and sizes itself appropriately—no matter what the situation—without writing a single line of code. This bit of Apple magic is called *Auto Layout*. It will be your best friend and worst enemy in creating responsive interfaces.

Using Auto Layout should be the starting point for all interfaces. If you can successfully define portrait and landscape modes in a single view in the IB editor, your work is done.

Unfortunately, Auto Layout doesn't work well when there are many irregularly positioned interface elements. A single row of buttons? No problem. Half a dozen fields, switches, and images all mixed together? Probably not going to work.

Programming Interfaces

As you've learned, each UI element is defined by a rectangular area on the screen: its `frame` property. If we programmatically define an application interface, we can make it into anything we want. Although this might sound challenging, it's actually very simple and very effective for creating interfaces that vary dramatically between different sizes and orientations.

For example, to detect when the interface rotates, we can implement the method `didRotate-FromInterfaceOrientation` in our view controller. The view controller property `interfaceOrientation` will tell us the current orientation of the interface, by containing one of these four constants:

Orientation	Current Orientation Constant
Portrait	`UIInterfaceOrientationPortrait`
Portrait upside-down	`UIInterfaceOrientationPortraitUpsideDown`
Landscape left	`UIInterfaceOrientationLandscapeLeft`
Landscape right	`UIInterfaceOrientationLandscapeRight`

The drawback to doing everything in code is that you are doing *everything* in code. It becomes very difficult to prototype interface changes and visualize what your final interface will look like. In addition, it is harder to adapt to changes in the future. It's best, in my opinion, to use a combination of Auto Layout with hand-coded interfaces to provide the best flexibility and speed of development.

Swapping Views

A more dramatic approach to changing your view to accommodate different screen orientations is to use entirely different views for landscape and portrait layouts. When the user rotates the device, the current view is replaced by another view that is laid out properly for the orientation.

This means that you can define two views in a single scene that look exactly the way you want, but it also means that you must keep track of separate `IBOutlets` for each view. Although it is certainly possible for elements in the views to invoke the same `IBActions`, they cannot share the same outlets, so you'll potentially need to keep track of twice as many UI widgets within a single view controller.

NOTE

To know when to change frames or swap views, you will be implementing the method `didRotate-FromInterfaceOrientation` in your view controller. This message is sent to a view controller when the interface has finished changing orientation. If you want to react *prior* to the orientation change taking place, you could implement the `willRotateToInterfaceOrientation:duration` method.

Apple has implemented a screen-locking function so that users can lock the screen orientation without it changing if the device rotates. (This can be useful for reading while lying on your side.) When the lock is enabled, your application will not receive notifications about a change in orientation. In other words, to support the orientation lock, you don't need to do a thing.

Using Auto Layout

As already mentioned, Auto Layout enables us to build responsive interfaces without writing a line of code. Because of that, our first tutorial is a series of examples that you can follow along with, rather than a project that we build. I've included several sample storyboard files in this hour's Projects folder, but you should definitely get yourself into IB and attempt the examples on your own.

NOTE

You'll be making changes to the Empty.storyboard file in this example. I recommend copying this file and making changes to your copies. This will save you the time of having to create a new storyboard file (or deleing the contents of the current file) each time you want to try something new.

In addition, the examples in this section all target the iPhone. Why? Because the iPhone screen is the perfect place for practice. It can change between both portrait and landscape orientations *and* resize from 3.5" to 4" displays.

The Language and Tools of Auto Layout

When I see something with *Auto* in the name, I expect that it is going to do things for me: automatically. Auto Layout lives up to this, but not without a reasonably long "getting to know you" phase. To use Auto Layout effectively, you must understand the terminology and know where to look for the tools. We spend the next few minutes getting into details, and then walk through a few examples that should get you started on the way to mastery. (Perhaps of archery or speed skating. Auto Layout if you're lucky.)

Constraint Basics

Auto Layout works by building a series of *constraints* for your onscreen objects. Constraints define placement of objects, distances between objects, and how flexible these relationships are. A vertical constraint for a button, for example, might be along the lines of "keep X many points of space between this object and the top of the screen" or "keep object Y vertically centered in the view." Unfortunately, the language used for positioning can be a bit confusing; you may not be familiar with these terms:

▶ **Leading:** The "front" or left side of an object.

▶ **Trailing:** The "back" or right side of an object.

▶ **Superview:** The view that contains an object. In our examples, this is the "view" that makes up the scene itself.

NOTE

Xcode *must* always have enough constraints defined for an object that it can determine its horizontal and vertical position at any point in time (regardless of the screen orientation/size). This means that if you don't add constraints of your own (called user constraints and represented by a blue icon), Xcode will add system constraints automatically (represented by a purple icon).

For example, try adding a button to the window in the Empty.storyboard file; make sure is located toward the top-left side of the view and that you've resized the button slightly. Notice that parallel to the button in the document outline hierarchy a new Constraints entry shows up, as well as a Constraints item within the button object itself, as shown in Figure 16.2.

Navigating the Constraints Objects

Within the view's Constraints object are two constraints: horizontal space and vertical space constraint. The horizontal constraint states that the left side of the button will be a certain number of points from the left edge of the view. This is known as the *leading space* (versus the space between the right side and the edge of the view, which is called the *trailing space*). The vertical constraint is the distance from the top of the view to the top of the button.

What constraints are added depend on where the object is in relation to its containing view. Xcode does its best to choose what constraints make the most sense. If you position a button near the bottom of the view, for example, it will add a constraint for the distance between the bottom of the button and the bottom of the view.

Constraints, however, are more than just entries that tie an object to the view it is within. They can be flexible, ensuring that an object maintains *at least* or *at most* a certain distance from another object, or even that two objects, when resized, maintain the same distance between one another.

TIP

Alignment of objects is also a constraint, and is managed using the alignment tools you've already learned about. In other words, when you set vertical or horizontal alignments, you're actually configuring constraints that will be maintained regardless of the device's screen size or orientation!

FIGURE 16.2
The Constraints object represents the positioning relationships within a view, or Constraints on the UI elements themselves.

Constraints that set a specific size or distance between objects are called *pinning*. The flexibility (or inflexibility of a constraint) is managed by configuring a *relationship*.

This brings us to the second constraint object in the document outline: constraints on the object itself, not on its positioning. When you resize a user interface (UI) element or set constraints on how the content *within* it is positioned, Xcode adds (or modifies) a constraint object *within* the UI element itself. These constraints determine the width or height of the element. Not surprisingly, when you've got dozens of components in your UI, you'll have *lots* of constraints in your document outline.

Viewing and Editing Constraints via the Size Inspector

While sorting through constraints in the document outline can be a pain, you can quickly view *all* the constraints applied to an element (whether located in the Constraints object on the view the element is in, or within the UI element itself) within the Size Inspector (Option-Command-5). For example, if you've added a resized button to the storyboard, opening the Size Inspector should look something like Figure 16.3. Here horizontal and vertical positioning for the button are represented as constraints, as well as the width of the button.

FIGURE 16.3
Use the Size Inspector to view your constraints.

Using the gear menu to the right side of each constraint to do one of three things. First, you can select and edit a constraint. For example, if you pick a width constraint and choose Select and Edit, Xcode jumps you into the Attributes Inspector, where you can see and adjust the details of the constraint, as shown in Figure 16.4.

The Relation drop-down determines what the constraint is trying to do. Is it trying to keep a distance or size equal to a value? Greater than or equal to it? Less than or equal? You choose the relation that gives your interface the flexibility you need. With each relation, you can also set a constant. This is a measurement, in points, that the relationship will be maintaining.

FIGURE 16.4
Use the Attributes Inspector to edit constraints.

You'll also notice a Priority slider and a Standard check box (sometimes) appear in the editor. The Priority slider determines how "strong" the constraint relationship is. There may, for example, be instances when multiple constraints must be evaluated against one another. The priority setting determines the importance of any given constraint. A value of 1000 is a constraint that is required. If you move the Constraint slider, Xcode shows a description of what to expect at a given constraint priority.

The Standard check box lets Xcode use its internal database of spacing to set the recommended space between two objects. This, in many cases, is preferred because it ensures a consistent interface.

In a few minutes, we'll make use of the editor to configure a few relationships. Trust me, it makes more sense once you get started.

TIP

Constraints can also be edited by selecting them in the design view and opening the Attributes Inspector. If you're good at clicking on thin lines, you can do this without first going into the Size Inspector. I, personally, prefer starting by selecting the UI element, viewing the constraints in the Size Inspector, then jumping into editing from there.

The other options available in the gear menu in the Size Inspector are Promote to User Constraint and Delete. With Promote to User Constraint, you can select a constraint that you didn't add manually, turn it into a user constraint. The other option, Delete, removes the constraint from the Storyboard. Remember that there *must* be constraints to describe the object's position complete, so if you delete a constraint, don't be surprised to see Xcode add a new constraint back into the storyboard to fill in missing positioning details.

NOTE

You can edit system constraints *and* user constraints, so if the system constraints are serving your needs, there's no reason to turn it into a user constraint.

Content Hugging and Content Compression Resistance

When viewing an interface object with the Size Inspector, you probably noticed the settings Content Hugging Priority and Content Compression Resistance Priority. These features are related to Auto Layout, but what do they do?

When inspecting an object that is within an Auto Layout XIB, these settings control how closely the sides of an object "hug" the content in the object and how much the content can be compressed or clipped. Imagine a button that you want to expand horizontally, but not vertically. To allow horizontal expansion, you'd set horizontal hugging is a low priority. To keep it from growing vertically, you set vertical hugging to a high priority.

Similarly, the content (the button label) should not be compressed or clipped at all, so the content compression resistance settings for both horizontal and vertical compression should be very high priority.

You will not often need to adjust these settings beyond their defaults, which IB adds for you.

TIP

UI objects like buttons have *intrinsic* constraints that do not appear in the interface. These are the sizes that Xcode determines the object should have in order to display your content (such as a button label or button image). Xcode will automatically try to maintain these constraints unless you override them with your own user constraints and content compression/hugging settings. Other objects, such as switches, cannot resize at all, so there's no tweaking that will cause them to violate their intrinsic constraints. Text views, image views, and other "generic" content holders, however, will happily resize with no difficulty. You'll see this behavior in a few minutes.

I'm Beginning to See How This Works, But How Can You Create Complex Responsive Layouts with Just These Simple Tools?

There is no "one way" to build interfaces with Auto Layout, but there is a mindset that will be helpful as you build your own designs. Specifically, you should start by identifying the interface elements that you want to anchor somewhere on the screen, regardless of orientation or screen size. From there, begin looking for the relationships between those elements and the other objects that make up your interface. Building relationships between objects, rather than trying to tie each element to specific coordinates within a view, is a good tactic for successful UI design.

Example One: Centering Constraints

Let's look at a very simple example: a button that stays centered regardless of whether you use a 3.5" or 4" iPhone (or any iPad), or rotates between portrait and landscape orientations. To do this, begin by adding and positioning the button:

1. If you already have a push button added to a window in the Empty.storyboard file, you're in good shape. If not, open the file and add one now.

2. With the button highlighted, select Editor, Align, Vertical Center in Container.

3. Reselect the button, then choose Editor, Align, Horizontal Center in Container. The layout should now resemble Figure 16.5.

FIGURE 16.5
Align the button to the vertical and hortizontal centers.

The constraints that you've added show up as dark blue lines in the layout. Dark blue lines indicate user constraints; that is, *you* added the alignment constraints to the system.

TIP

If you don't add your own constraints Xcode will add some for you. In this example, had you dragged the button into the center of your view until both horizontal and vertical alignment guides appeared, Xcode would actually have created these same constraints for you! They would be system constraints, not user constraints, but they'd do the exact same thing.

Take a moment to view the constraints on the button via the Size Inspector. Select the button, then press Command-Option-5; the Size Inspector should show at least two constraints (more if you changed the size of the button), as shown in Figure 16.6.

Toggle between 3.5" and 4" iPhone screens.

FIGURE 16.6
Toggle the size of the screen.

Now try toggling the size of the screen between 3.5" and 4", using the toggle icon shown in Figure 16.6. The button should stay centered, regardless of the screen size. The final test is to try the interface in another orientation.

Make sure that the document outline is visible, select the view controller for the scene. Open the Attributes Inspector (Option-Command-4) and choose Landscape from the Orientation drop-down menu. IB updates to show the interface in landscape mode. Assuming your constraints are correct, the button should also properly center itself in the view, as demonstrated in Figure 16.7.

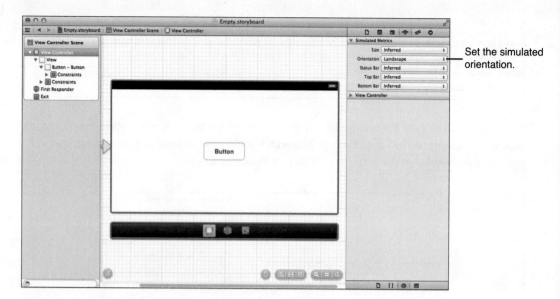

Set the simulated orientation.

FIGURE 16.7
The button centers itself, regardless of orientation and screen size.

That was pretty simple, wasn't it? Of course, not all your applications will consist of just a single button (only the best ones). For that reason, we cover a few more examples, starting with resizing controls.

Example Two: Expanding Controls

A common design problem is where you have a series of controls on the screen and they need to expand to fill the size of the screen (or, in the case of a 3.5" iPhone display, properly shrink to fit on the screen). For example, let's create an interface with two text views at the top and a button at the bottom. The button should always remain anchored at the bottom, but should grow horizontally to fill the width of the display. The text views should grow or shrink vertically, and expand horizontally to fill the screen.

Creating the Interface

Starting from a fresh copy of Empty.storyboard, follow these steps:

1. Drag a button to the storyboard, positioning it using the guide at the bottom of the view.

2. Resize each side of the button by dragging toward the side of the view, and then release when you see the blue guide appear.

By using the guides in steps 1 and 2, you've created three constraints that anchor to the side and bottom margins of the view, as shown in Figure 16.8.

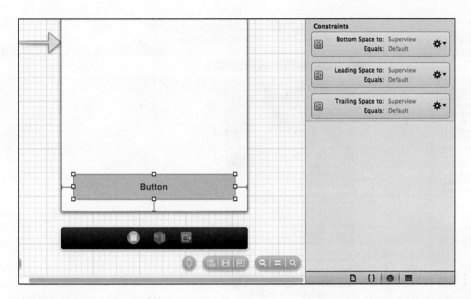

FIGURE 16.8
These three constraints make the button resize and stay anchored at the bottom, regardless of the screen size or orientation.

The constraints that have been automatically created are a good start for the button. These ensure that the sides of the button are always an equal distance from the sides of the view, regardless of the orientation. The same goes for the distance from the bottom of the view to the bottom of the button.

Next, add two text views to the scene:

1. Drag two text views to the scene, stacking one on top of the other.

2. Resize the text views to fill the scene horizontally, until the blue guides appear.

3. Size the text views vertically until the guides appear to keep the views from overlapping the button, one another, or the top margin of the scene.

4. Set the color of the text views to something other than white so that they are easier to see. Your finished view should look like Figure 16.9.

The top text view has constraints generated to attach it to the top of the view and the sides of the view. The bottom text view has constraints that keep it a set distance from the sides of the view and the button at the bottom. Between the two text views is a constraint that keeps them a set distance apart. Finally, one of the text views will have a height constraint applied.

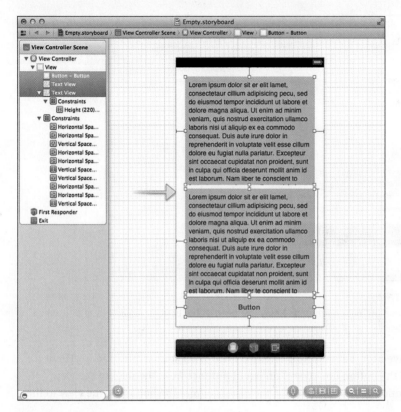

FIGURE 16.9
You've added three UI elements and quite a few system constraints.

Setting the Constraints

Try resizing and rotating the display. What you'll notice is that resizing it vertically (switching between 3.5" and 4" screens) likely works okay. What definitely doesn't is rotating to landscape. In landscape mode, one of the text views will shrink so much that it isn't even visible. To make the scene work right, you need to set some additional constraints.

Specifically, you need to accomplish these things:

1. Pin the height of the button so that at no point in time is it resized.

2. Pick one of the text views to be the first to shrink when the size changes. We set this view so that its height is greater than or equal to the smallest size we want it to reach. I will use the top view for this purpose and set its minimum height to 100 points or greater.

3. Set a fixed width on the bottom text view (I'll use 210 points) so that it doesn't change size. *But,* we need to set its priority to less than 1000 (the default). This lets the text view change

sizes in an extreme situation. That "extreme situation" would otherwise occur in landscape mode where the top view would try to maintain a height of 100 points but the bottom view's fixed height of 210 would force a condition where both can't hold.

Begin by selecting the button and choosing, Editor, Pin, Height from the menu bar. Simple enough!

Next, choose the top text view and choose Editor, Pin, Height (again). You've just created a height constraint, but it needs to be adjusted so that it is flexible. Select the height constraint within the design view (or within the size inspector), and then open the Attributes inspector.

Using the Relation drop-down, choose Greater Than or Equal. Set the constant to 100 (the text view must be 100 points in height or greater) and leave the priority alone. Your configuration should look like Figure 16.10.

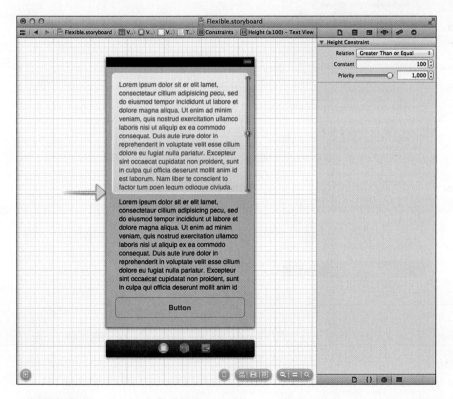

FIGURE 16.10
Set the relation for the height constraint.

Now the top text view will shrink when it needs to, but it can also grow; in fact, until a constraint is set on the bottom text view, it can grow *too large*, pushing the bottom text view until it is too small in any orientation.

Select the bottom text view and again add a height constraint (Editor, Pin, Height, yet again). Select the constraint and make sure that the relation is set to Equal with a constant around 210, as shown in Figure 16.11. This time, however, set the priority down to 999. This makes the constraint turn into a dotted line (visible in Figure 16.11) showing that the constraint will *try* to be maintained, but, if necessary, it can resize to avoid violating other constraints.

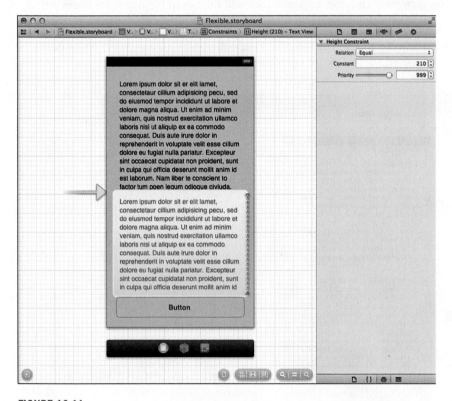

FIGURE 16.11
Set a height constraint with a priority lower than 1000 to enable the text view to change sizes if absolutely necessary.

Go ahead and try resizing the view between 3.5" and 4" iPhone screen sizes and rotating to landscape mode. Everything should work like a charm, with the top text view resizing when needed and the bottom text view resizing when it absolutely has to.

CAUTION

What If It Doesn't Work?

It's *really* easy to end up adding constraints you don't want by inadvertantly dragging things around in your view. If something doesn't appear to be working, it's likely because there are extra height constraints. Look for multiple height constraints (or any others that look out of place) and delete what you didn't intentionally add.

TIP

Combining multiple constraints with variable relationships, like this, is what you need to do to accommodate complex interfaces. Don't be shy about trying different relationships and priorities to see how they interact. There isn't a "recipe" for making effective Auto Layout designs. Spend a few hours playing with the tools—laying out interfaces in different ways. Hands-on is the only way you'll get the experience you need to be comfortable with Auto Layout.

Example Three: Variable and Matching Sizes (and Auto Layout Craziness!)

Okay, one more quick exercise to round things out. I promise this one is easier than the last. This time, we add three buttons in a horizontal line, and we add enough constraints to make the buttons all resize equally when we shift to a landscape mode.

CAUTION

They're *My* Constraints, Not Yours, Xcode!

When I say "Auto Layout craziness," I mean it. Even if you aren't building the example, be sure to read through this section to understand how Xcode can sometimes, without warning, start rewriting your Auto Layout constraints and wreaking havock on your work.

Let's make this happen! Create a new copy of the Empty.storyboard document, and then drag three buttons into the horizontal line on the screen. Label the buttons **Button A**, **Button B**, and **Button C**, as shown in Figure 16.12.

FIGURE 16.12
Add three buttons, nothing more.

You now know enough to make one of the buttons resize, but how could we constrain them so that *all* the buttons resize to fill in the screen in landscape mode? These are the constraints that I came up with:

1. Align all the buttons to the vertical center in the container. This keeps them centered vertically on the screen.

2. Pin the Leading Space of Button A to the superview (the edge of the view). This is unnecessary if you used a guide to align the left edge of the button and Xcode already added a constraint tying the edge of the button to the edge of the view.

3. Pin the Trailing Space of Button C to the superview. Like the first constraint, you don't technically need this one if you aligned the right side of the button to a guide and Xcode added a constraint for you.

4. Pin the Horizontal Spacing between Button A and Button B.

5. Pin the Horizontal Spacing between Button B and C. (If we stopped here, the center button (Button B) would stretch while the other buttons would stay the same size.)

6. Pin the buttons so that they all share the same width. (Select all the buttons, and then choose Editor, Pin, Widths Equally.)

Use the Editor menu to add these constraints to your project; you should know how to do it by now. There is no need to adjust the priority or relationships in this case. Your finished layout will hopefully be similar to Figure 16.13 (one of the = constraints may be on a different button. This is fine). *Save your work before continuing.*

FIGURE 16.13
Add these constraints to your scene.

Now, here's where it gets interesting (wake up!). When you rotate the view to landscape, all the buttons should resize equally and fill in the space across the screen, as shown in Figure 16.14.

FIGURE 16.14
The buttons' constraints force them to spread out across the screen and match sizes.

This is exactly what we want. *But*, what happens when you rotate back to a vertical position? Chances are that the buttons get all weird looking and overlap. Switch back and forth between horizontal and landscape orientations, and they may get even worse.

So, what's going on here? Xcode is being a pain, that's what. When you switch to landscape, it is rewriting the constraints as if you designed the view in landscape mode. You actually *lose* work and constraint logic depending on how the complex your interface is.

To deal with this bit of insanity, just use Command-Z to undo the switch to landscape orientation after validating that the interface looks okay. As long as it looks good in your original view and when it first switches to landscape, you're in good shape. The compiled view used in your actual application will work just fine (even if it switches back and forth between portrait and landscape orientations).

Wait, There's More

There is much more to the Auto Layout system than can be described in an hour. Be sure to explore the Pin menu to see the different types of constraints that you can put in place. Width/ height constraints enforce a given width or height on an object. Equal width/height constraints ensure multiple objects maintain an equal width or height. The leading/trailing space pinnings tie the left side of an object to the left side of its parent view (leading), or the right side of an object to the right side of its parent view (trailing).

Review Apple's documentation, starting with *Cocoa Auto Layout Guide*, for more information.

Programmatically Defined Interfaces

In the previous example, you learned how the IB editor can help quickly create interface layouts that look as good horizontally as they do vertically and that can resize between the 3.5" and 4" iPhone displays. Unfortunately, in plenty of situations, IB can't quite accommodate. Irregularly spaced controls and tightly packed layouts rarely work out the way you expect. You may also find yourself wanting to tweak the interface to look completely different—positioning objects that were at the top of the view down by the bottom and so on.

In cases like this, consider implementing the UI (or portions of it) completely in code. But, what about the nice and neat drag-and-drop approach? Well, using code isn't as convenient as drawing your interface in IB, but it *isn't* difficult. We're going to move to a project that is the exact opposite of our last few examples—rather than building a responsive interface without code, we're going to *only* use code to create an interface.

Implementation Overview

In this tutorial, we create a very simple application with three UI elements: two buttons (Button A and Button B) and a label. The buttons trigger a method to set the label to the title of the button. Most important, however, is that the interface reacts properly to orientation and size changes.

In the portrait orientation, the buttons are drawn with the label sandwiched between them. In landscape, the buttons move closer to the bottom, and the label repositions above them. The final output will resemble Figure 16.15.

Take note that the positioning of the buttons and the label cannot be handled in Auto Layout (at least not through any straightforward approach). When you encounter issues that can't be solved in Auto Layout, there's no harm in coding your way out of the forest.

To handle the rotation and resizing of the objects, we use the bounds property of the scene's view. This gives us the width and height of the device corresponding to whatever orientation it is in. We then use these values to position the UI elements on the screen. By basing the positioning on the bounds, the size of the device screen and orientation are largely irrelevant, as you'll soon see.

Setting Up the Project

Unlike the previous example, we can't rely pointing and clicking for the interface, so there is a bit of code in the project. Once again, create a new single-view iOS application project and name it **AllInCode**.

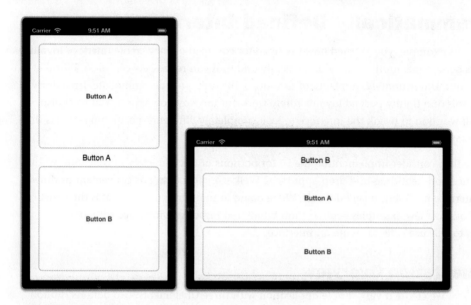

FIGURE 16.15
Buttons resize and reposition appropriately (all handled in code).

Planning the Properties and Connections

In this exercise, you manually resize and reposition three UI elements: two buttons (UIButton) and one label (UILabel). Although we aren't creating these with outlets, we define properties for them: buttonA, buttonB, and theLabel should suffice.

Why Aren't You Using Private Instance Variables?

Good question. You're welcome to do this, exactly as we have in some of our other projects. In this case, however, it might be useful for our view controller to expose these other elements so that they could be used by other classes. This also matches how IB itself handles UI elements. If you disagree with this approach, no worries; instance variables will work just fine.

We also implement a method: handleButton, which updates the onscreen label to show the title of a button that was tapped. Like the properties, this won't be declared using IB, but we'll be using it just like an IBAction. We also add two additional methods, initInterface and updateInterface, to handle setting up and updating the interface, respectively. These will be triggered by a change in orientation, so our next step is to set up the project to properly handle orientation changes.

Enabling Orientation Changes

For this project, enable support of all orientations. To do this, start by updating the project summary (click the blue project icon at the top of the project navigator) and select all the device orientations within the Supported Interface Orientations section. Next, add the supportedInterfaceOrientations method to ViewController.m and have it return the constant UIInterfaceOrientationMaskAll, as shown in Listing 16.2.

LISTING 16.2 Support All Interface Orientations

```
- (NSUInteger) supportedInterfaceOrientations {
    return UIInterfaceOrientationMaskAll;
}
```

Programming the Interface

We've now reached the point in the project where normally I'd say, "Let's design the interface." This time, however, there isn't going to be a visual design, just code. In fact, you've already seen the two screenshots that accompany this project, so if you're just skimming pictures, you'd better flip through a few more pages.

Defining Properties and Methods

We start by defining the properties and methods that the view controller will be using. Recall that we're adding three properties: buttonA, buttonB, and theLabel. We' also have three methods that we should prototype in ViewController.h: initInterface, updateInterface, and handleButton.

Edit ViewController.h, adding the properties and method prototypes, as shown in Listing 16.3.

LISTING 16.3   Add the Properties and Method Prototypes to ViewController.h

```
#import <UIKit/UIKit.h>

@interface ViewController : UIViewController

@property (weak,nonatomic) UIButton *buttonA;
@property (weak,nonatomic) UIButton *buttonB;
@property (strong,nonatomic) UILabel *theLabel;

- (void) initInterface;
- (void) updateInterface;
- (void) handleButton: (id) sender;

@end
```

Look closely and you'll notice that theLabel is set to use a strong property reference. Unfortunately, this is a result of overzealous memory cleanup by ARC. If we use weak instead, the label will actually be removed from memory before we can even get it onto the screen. Using strong ensures that the label sticks around as long as the ViewController object is active.

Everything else should look pretty straightforward. The initInterface and updateInterface methods don't take any arguments or return any values. The handleButton method is styled after a typical IBAction because it will behave exactly like a typical action; it's just being defined by hand rather than being built for us.

Initializing the Interface Properties

The next step is to add the initInterface method to ViewController.m. The purpose of this method is to configure all the interface elements (the two buttons and the label) so that they're ready to be added to the interface, but *not* display them just yet.

By keeping the display logic separated from the initialization logic, we can build a method that can be called at any time to update the interface. This method, aptly named updateInterface, is called at the end of the initInterface and anytime interface rotation is sensed.

Add the initInterface method from Listing 16.4 to ViewController.m.

LISTING 16.4   **Prepare the Interface But Don't Display It Yet**

```
 1: - (void)initInterface {
 2:     self.buttonA =[UIButton buttonWithType:UIButtonTypeRoundedRect];
 3:     [self.buttonA addTarget:self action:@selector(handleButton:)
 4:             forControlEvents:UIControlEventTouchUpInside];
 5:     [self.buttonA setTitle:@"Button A" forState:UIControlStateNormal];
 6:
 7:     self.buttonB =[UIButton buttonWithType:UIButtonTypeRoundedRect];
 8:     [self.buttonB addTarget:self action:@selector(handleButton:)
 9:             forControlEvents:UIControlEventTouchUpInside];
10:     [self.buttonB setTitle:@"Button B" forState:UIControlStateNormal];
11:
12:     self.theLabel=[[UILabel alloc] init];
13:     self.theLabel.text=@"Welcome";
14:     [self updateInterface];
15: }
```

This might be the first time we've manually created a number of UI elements, but because you've been working with these objects and adjusting their properties for hours, this code shouldn't seem completely foreign.

Line 2 initializes the `buttonA` property as a button of type `UIButtonTypeRoundedRect`—the standard button we use in our views. Lines 3–4 use the button's `addTarget:action:forControl Events` method to choose what will happen when the `Touch Up Inside` event occurs for the button. The `@selector` directive specifies which method will be called during the event—such as `handleButton`. This is exactly the same as connecting a button to an `IBAction` in IB.

Line 5 sets the title for the button to Button A.

Lines 7–10 repeat the same process for Button B (`buttonB`).

Lines 12–13 allocate and initialize a label (`theLabel`) with the default text Welcome.

Lastly, line 14 invokes the `updateInterface` method so that the newly defined user elements can be placed on the screen. So, what do we do now? Implement `updateInterface`.

Implementing the Interface Update Method

The `updateInterface` method does the heavy lifting for the application. It checks to see what the current orientation is, and then it draws content based on the view's `bounds` property. By basing the drawing on the height and width contained within `bounds`, you can scale to any screen size at all.

For example, consider this code snippet:

```
float screenWidth;
float screenHeight;
screenWidth=self.view.bounds.size.width;
screenHeight=self.view.bounds.size.height;
```

This grabs and stores the current screen width and height in the variables `screenWidth` and `screenHeight`. The dimensions and position of UI objects are determined by their `frame`, which is a property of type `CGRect`. To set the `frame` of a button property named `theButton` so that it filled the top half of the screen, I'd write the following:

```
self.theButton.frame=CGRectMake(0.0,0.0,screenWidth,screenHeight/2);
```

The first two values of `CGRectMake` (which create a `CGRect` data structure) set the origin point at 0,0. The second two parameters determine the width and height of the `CGRect`. Using `screenWidth` sets the button to the same width of the screen and `screenHeight/2` sets the height of the button to half the height of the screen. In an actual implementation, you want to include some margin around the edges. This is why you'll see +20 and other values tacked onto my coordinates. Speaking of which, go ahead and implement `updateInterface`, as shown in Listing 16.5. When you're done, we step through the code.

LISTING 16.5   The `updateInterface` Implementation

```
1: - (void)updateInterface {
2:      float screenWidth;
3:      float screenHeight;
4:      screenWidth=self.view.bounds.size.width;
5:      screenHeight=self.view.bounds.size.height;
6:
7:      if (self.interfaceOrientation==UIInterfaceOrientationPortrait ||
8:          self.interfaceOrientation==UIInterfaceOrientationPortraitUpsideDown) {
9:          self.buttonA.frame=CGRectMake(20.0,20.0,screenWidth-40.0,
10:                                        screenHeight/2-40.0);
11:          self.buttonB.frame=CGRectMake(20.0,screenHeight/2+20,
12:                                        screenWidth-40.0,screenHeight/2-40.0);
13:          self.theLabel.frame=CGRectMake(screenWidth/2-40,
14:                                         screenHeight/2-10,200.0,20.0);
15:      } else {
16:          self.buttonA.frame=CGRectMake(20.0,60.0,screenWidth-40.0,
17:                                        screenHeight/2-40.0);
18:          self.buttonB.frame=CGRectMake(20.0,screenHeight/2+30,
19:                                        screenWidth-40.0,screenHeight/2-40.0);
20:          self.theLabel.frame=CGRectMake(screenWidth/2-40,20.0,200.0,20.0);
21:      }
22:
23:      [self.view addSubview:self.buttonA];
24:      [self.view addSubview:self.buttonB];
25:      [self.view addSubview:self.theLabel];
26: }
```

Lines 2–5 grab and store the current screen size in `screenWidth` and `screenHeight`.

Lines 7–8 checks the `interfaceOrientation` property of the view controller, and, if it is in one of the portrait orientations, lines 8–14 are executed. Otherwise, lines 16–20 are evaluated. These blocks both have the same purpose: defining the `frame` properties for each of the UI elements (`buttonA`, `buttonB`, and `theLabel`).

Lines 8–14 define positions for the buttons so that there are margins on the edges of the screen and a space in the middle for the label. Lines 16–20 position the buttons lower on the screen and put the label at the top. The margins and spacing I used is completely arbitrary. You can try changing these values around to see what effect they have.

Finally, lines 23–25 add the buttons and label to the view so that they are visible onscreen.

Everything is now in place for the interface, but we need to take care of three small tasks before the project is complete. First, we need to make sure that the interface is drawn when the application first loads. Second, the interface must update when an orientation change occurs. Third, we need to implement `handleButton` to update the label when the buttons are pressed.

Drawing the Interface When the Application Launches

When the application first launches, there isn't an orientation change to trigger the interface to be drawn. To make sure there is something on the screen, we need to call `initInterface` when the application loads. Add this to `viewDidLoad`, as shown in Listing 16.6.

LISTING 16.6   Initialize the Interface When the Application Loads

```
- (void)viewDidLoad
{
    [super viewDidLoad];
    [self initInterface];
}
```

We're getting closer. The application will now initialize and display the interface, but it still can't adapt to a change in orientation.

Updating the Interface When Orientation Changes

To handle orientation changes, the application needs to call `updateInterface` within an implementation of `didRotateFromInterfaceOrientation`. We also need to remove the existing buttons, otherwise the old version of the interface will still be visible; this is surprisingly easy to do.

Add `didRotateFromInterfaceOrientation` to ViewController.m, as shown in Listing 16.7.

LISTING 16.7   Handle Rotation in `didRotateFromInterfaceOrientation`

```
1: - (void)didRotateFromInterfaceOrientation:
2:          (UIInterfaceOrientation)fromInterfaceOrientation {
3:      [[self.view subviews]
4:              makeObjectsPerformSelector:@selector(removeFromSuperview)];
5:      [self updateInterface];
6: }
```

Lines 3–4 use the very cool `makeObjectsPerformSelector` method on all the subviews in the scene's view (all of our UI elements) to send them the message `removeFromSuperview`. This, as expected, removes the buttons and label from the view.

Line 5 calls `updateInterface` and draws the appropriate version of the interface for whatever orientation we are currently in.

Handling the Button Touches

The last piece of the puzzle is implementing `handleButton` so that it updates the onscreen label with the label of the button being touched. This is just a single line, so add Listing 16.8 to the view controller, and you're done.

LISTING 16.8 Handle Button Touches

```
- (void)handleButton:(id)sender {
    self.theLabel.text=((UIButton *)sender).currentTitle;
}
```

The one line of the implementation uses the `sender` parameter (typecast as a `UIButton`) to grab the title of the button (`currentTitle`) that was pressed.

Building the Application

Build and run the application. It should rotate and resize with no problem. What's more, because all of the interface layout was based on the height and width of the view, this same code will work, without changes, in an iPad or iPhone project.

I hope this didn't scare you too much. The purpose of this exercise was to show that responsive and flexible interfaces can be accomplished in code without it being too much of a hassle. The biggest challenge is determining how the controls will be laid out and then coming up with the `CGRectMake` functions to define their locations.

Swapping Views on Rotation

Some applications display entirely different UIs depending on the device's orientation. The iPhone Music application, for example, displays a scrolling list of songs in portrait mode and a "flickable" Cover Flow view of albums when held in landscape. You, too, can create applications that dramatically alter their appearance by simply switching between views when the phone is rotated.

Our last tutorial in this hour is short and sweet and gives you the flexibility to manage your landscape and portrait views all within the comfort of the IB editor. What's more, you can still use Auto Layout within each of these views to position your interface objects to accommodate different screen sizes (like the 3.5" and 4" iPhone screens).

Implementation Overview

The previous examples used a single view and rearranged it (either through Auto Layout or code) to fit a different orientation. When the view is too different or complex for this to be feasible, however, you can use two individual views with a single view controller. This is precisely what we do in this application. We start by adding a second view to the traditional single-view application, and then we design both views and make sure we can easily access them through properties in our code.

Once that is complete, we write the code necessary to swap the views when the device rotates. There is a catch, which you'll learn about in a bit, but nothing that poses too much of a problem to coders as experienced as we are.

Setting Up the Project

Create a new project named **Swapper** using the Single View Application template. Although this includes a single view already (which we'll use for the default portrait display), we need to supplement it with a second landscape view.

Planning the Property and Connections

This application does not implement any real UI elements, but we need to access two UIView instances programmatically. One view is for portrait orientation (portraitView) and another for landscape orientation (landscapeView). We will implement a method to handle orientation changes, but it will not be triggered by any actions.

Adding a Degree to Radians Constant

Later in this exercise, we have to call a special Core Graphics method to define how to rotate views. The method requires a value to be passed in radians rather than degrees. In other words, instead of saying we want to rotate the view 90 degrees, we have to tell it we want to rotate 1.57 radians. To help us handle the conversion, we define a constant for the conversion factor. Multiplying degrees by the constant gets us the resulting value in radians.

To define the constant, add the following line after the #import line in ViewController.m:

```
#define kDeg2Rad (3.1415926/180.0)
```

Enabling Orientation Changes

As with the previous example, we need to ensure that the implementation of supportedInterfaceOrientations is behaving as we expect in our view controller. Unlike the previous implementation, however, this time we allow the device to rotate only between the two landscape modes and upright portrait.

Update ViewController.m to include the implementation in Listing 16.9.

LISTING 16.9 Disable the Upside-Down Orientation

```
- (NSUInteger)supportedInterfaceOrientations {
    return UIInterfaceOrientationMaskAllButUpsideDown;
}
```

Be sure to also go into the project summary and set the allowed orientations to everything but upside-down.

Designing the Interface

When you are swapping views, the sky is the limit for the design. You build them exactly as you would in any other application. The only difference is that if you have multiple views handled by a single view controller, you must define outlets that encompass all the interface elements.

This example demonstrates just how to swap views, so our work will be a piece of cake.

Creating the Views

Open the MainStoryboard.storyboard file and drag a new instance of the UIView object from the Object Library to the document outline, placing it at the same level in the hierarchy as the view controller, as shown in Figure 16.16. Don't put the UIView inside the existing view.

FIGURE 16.16
Add a second view to the scene.

TIP

It might seem counterintuitive, but there's no reason that a scene can't contain multiple views if they are going to be managed by the same view controller. Only the view nested within the view controller is displayed by default. Additional views have to be displayed manually.

Now, open the default view and add a label, such as **Portrait View**; make sure that it is selected. Use Editor, Align from the menu bar to set constraints so that it is aligned to the horizontal and vertical centers of the view. Now set a background color to differentiate the view. That finishes one view, but we still have another to do. Unfortunately, you can only edit a view that is assigned to a view controller in IB, so we have to be creative.

Drag the view you just created out of the view controller hierarchy in the document outline, placing it at the same level as the view controller. Drag the second view onto the view controller line in the document outline. You can now edit it by adding a unique background color and a label such as **Landscape View**. You may want to switch the view controller to simulate a landscape mode while making these edits. When the second view is done, rearrange the view hierarchy again, nesting the portrait view inside the view controller and the landscape view outside the view controller.

If you want to make this more interesting, you're welcome to add other controls and design the view as you see fit. Our finished landscape and portrait views are shown in Figure 16.17.

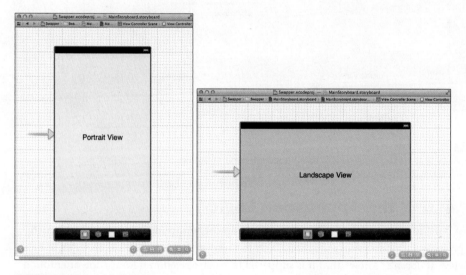

FIGURE 16.17
Edit the two views so that you can tell them apart.

Creating and Connecting the Outlets

To finish up our interface work, we need to connect the two views to two outlets. The default view (nested in the view controller) will be connected to `portraitView`. The second view will be connected to `landscapeView`. Switch to the assistant editor and make sure that the document outline is visible.

Because we're dealing with views rather than objects in our interface design, the easiest way to make these connections is to Control-drag from the respective lines in the document outline to the ViewController.h file. In addition, unlike with most of the projects in this book, we need to create outlets with the storage set to Strong; otherwise, ARC will conveniently get rid of the views when they aren't visible.

Control-drag from the default (nested) view to below the `@interface` line in ViewController.h. Create a new outlet for the view called `portraitView`, with the storage set as Strong. Repeat the process for the second view, naming the connection `landscapeView` as demonstrated in Figure 16.18.

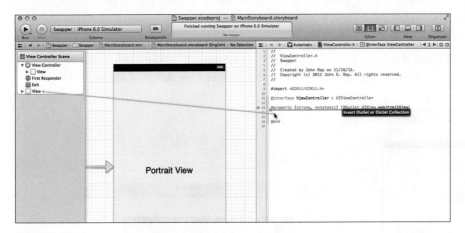

FIGURE 16.18
Connect the views to corresponding outlets using a storage type of Strong.

Implementing the Application Logic

For the most part, swapping views is actually easier than the reframing logic we implemented in the last project—with one small exception. Even though we designed one of the views to be in landscape view, it doesn't "know" that it is supposed to be displayed in a landscape orientation.

Understanding the View-Rotation Logic

For a landscape view to be successfully swapped onto the screen, we need to rotate it and define how big it is. The reason for this is that there is no inherent logic built in to a view that says "hey, I'm supposed to be sideways." As far as it knows, it is intended to be displayed in portrait mode but has UI elements that are pushed off the sides of display.

Each time we change orientation, we go through three steps: swapping the view, rotating the view to the proper orientation through the `transform` property, and setting the view's origin and size via the `bounds` property.

For example, assume we're rotating to landscape right orientation:

1. First, we can grab the current view size (after rotation) by accessing and storing `self.view.bounds`. This can be used later to make sure that the new view is set to the proper size:

```
currentBounds=self.view.bounds;
```

2. Second, we swap out the view by assigning `self.view`, which contains the current view of the view controller, to the `landscapeView` property. If we left things at that, the view would properly switch, but it wouldn't be rotated into the landscape orientation. A landscape view displayed in a portrait orientation isn't a pretty thing. For example:

```
self.view=self.landscapeView;
```

3. Next, to deal with the rotation, we define the `transform` property of the view. This property determines how the view will be altered before it is displayed. To meet our needs, we have to rotate the view 90 degrees to the right (for landscape right), –90 degrees to the left (for landscape left), and 0 degrees for portrait. As luck would have it, the Core Graphics C function, `CGAffineTransformMakeRotation()`, accepts a rotation value in radians and provides an appropriate structure to the `transform` property to handle the rotation. For example:

```
self.view.transform=CGAffineTransformMakeRotation(deg2rad*(90));
```

NOTE

Note that we multiply the rotation in degrees (90, –90, and 0) by the constant `kDeg2Rad` that we defined earlier so that `CGAffineTransformMakeRotation()` has the radian value it expects.

4. The final step is to set the `bounds` property of the view to the bounds that we stored in step 1. For example:

```
self.view.bounds=currentBounds;
```

Now that you understand the steps, let's take a look at the actual implementation.

Adding the View-Rotation Logic

All the rotation magic happens within a single method: `supportedInterfaceOrientations`.

Open the ViewController.m file and implement the method, as shown in Listing 16.7.

LISTING 16.10   Rotate the View into the Proper Orientation

```
 1: - (void)didRotateFromInterfaceOrientation:
 2:      (UIInterfaceOrientation)fromInterfaceOrientation {
 3:
 4:      CGRect currentBounds=self.view.bounds;
 5:
 6:      if (self.interfaceOrientation == UIInterfaceOrientationLandscapeRight) {
 7:          self.view=self.landscapeView;
 8:          self.view.transform=CGAffineTransformMakeRotation(kDeg2Rad*(90));
 9:      } else if (self.interfaceOrientation == UIInterfaceOrientationLandscapeLeft) {
10:          self.view=self.landscapeView;
11:          self.view.transform=CGAffineTransformMakeRotation(kDeg2Rad*(-90));
12:      } else {
13:          self.view=self.portraitView;
14:          self.view.transform=CGAffineTransformMakeRotation(0);
15:      }
16:      self.view.bounds=currentBounds;
17: }
```

Line 4 grabs the current bounds of the scene's view after the rotation has occurred, and stores it in currentBounds.

Lines 6–8 handle rotation to the right (landscape right). Lines 9–11 deal with rotation to the left (landscape left). Finally, lines 13–14 configure the view for the default orientation, portrait.

In the very last step, line 16, the bounds of the view we swapped in are set to the currentBounds that we stored when the method started.

NOTE

Although we used an if-then-else statement in this example, you could easily use a switch structure instead. The toInterfaceOrientation parameter and orientation constants are integer values, which means they can be evaluated directly in a switch statement.

TIP

In this hour's exercises, we used didRotateFromInterfaceOrientation to detect and react to a change in orientation. If you'd prefer to being reacting immediately *prior* to iOS adjusting the orientation, you can use the method willRotateToInterfaceOrientation:duration instead.

Building the Application

Save the implementation file, and then run and test the application. As you rotate the device or the iOS simulator, your views should be swapped in and out appropriately. This approach gives you a good combination of flexibility while keeping the benefits of Auto Layout. Unfortunately, it also means that you have to manage twice as many objects in your code.

When designing your own applications, you need to strike a balance between interface flexibility and code complexity. In some cases, it's just easier to design a different scene and use a second view and view controller to handle other orientations.

Further Exploration

Although we covered several different ways of working with rotation in the iPhone interface, you may want to explore additional features outside of this hour's lesson. Using the Xcode documentation tool, review the UIView instance methods. You'll see that there are additional methods that you can implement, such as willAnimateRotationToInterfaceOrientation:duration, which is used to set up a single-step animated rotation sequence. What's more, you can combine these methods with segues—programmatically triggering a segue to a new scene when an orientation event occurs.

In short, there are a number of ways to create interfaces that do anything you want. It's a good idea to practice the techniques discussed here to learn what will work best for your projects.

Summary

iDevices are all about the user experience—a touchable display, intuitive controls, and now, rotatable and resizable interfaces. Using the techniques described in this hour, you can adapt to almost any type of rotation scenario. To handle interface size changes without a line of code, for example, you can take advantage of the Auto Layout. For more complex changes, however, you might want to programmatically define your onscreen elements, giving you complete control over their size and placement. Finally, for a good balance in flexibility, you can create multiple different views and swap them as the device rotates.

By implementing rotation and size-aware applications, you give your users the ability to use their devices in the way that feels most comfortable to them.

Q&A

Q. Why don't many iPhone applications implement the upside-down portrait mode?

A. Although there is no problem implementing the upside-down portrait orientation using the approaches described in this hour, it isn't recommended. When the iPhone is upside-down, the Home button and sensors are not in the "normal" location. If a call comes in or the user needs to interact with the phone's controls, the user will need to rotate the phone 180 degrees—a somewhat complicated action to perform with one hand.

Q. **How do I get the controls in application XYZ to behave using Auto Layout?**

A. This is a difficult question with no clear answer because there may be dozens of ways of implementing constraints that have the desired effect. I have implemented Auto Layout constraints for 3.5" and 4" iPhone displays in all my sample projects. You may want to take a look at those to get an idea of how I solved resizing problems (landscape, however, is up to you!).

Workshop

Quiz

1. The iDevice interface can rotate through three different orientations. True or false?

2. How does an application communicate which rotation orientations it supports?

3. What was the purpose of the `kDeg2Rad` constant that we defined in the final exercise?

Answers

1. False. There are four primary interface orientations: landscape right, landscape left, portrait, and upside-down portrait.

2. As long as the the `supportedInterfaceOrientations` method is implemented in the view controller, the application identifies which of the four orientations it will operate in.

3. We defined the `kDeg2Rad` constant to give us an easy way of converting degrees to radians for the Core Graphics C function `CGAffineTransformMakeRotation()`.

Activities

1. Edit the Swapper example so that each view presents and processes user input. Keep in mind that because both views are handled by a single view controller, you must add all the outlets and actions for both views to the view controller interface and implementation files.

2. Return to an earlier lesson and revise the interface to support multiple different orientations and iPhone screen sizes. Use any of the techniques described in this hour's exercises for the implementation.

Using Advanced Touches and Gestures

What You'll Learn in This Hour:

▶ The multitouch gesture-recognition architecture

▶ How to detect taps

▶ How to detect swipes

▶ How to detect pinches

▶ How to detect rotations

▶ How to use the built-in shake gesture

A multitouch screen allows applications to use a wide variety of natural finger gestures for operations that would otherwise be hidden behind layers of menus, buttons, and text. From the very first time you use a pinch to zoom in and out on a photo, map, or web page, you realize that's exactly the right interface for zooming. Nothing is more human than manipulating the environment with your fingers.

iOS provides advanced gesture-recognition capabilities that you can easily implement within your applications. This hour shows you how.

GET YOUR IDEVICES READY

For most applications in this book, using the iOS simulator is perfectly acceptable, but the simulator cannot re-create all the gestures you can create with your fingers. For this hour, be sure to have a physical device provisioned for development. To run this hour's applications on your device, follow the steps in Hour 1, "Preparing Your System and iDevice for Development."

Multitouch Gesture Recognition

While working through this book's examples, you've gotten used to responding to events, such as `Touch Up Inside`, for onscreen buttons. Gesture recognition is a bit different. Consider a "simple" swipe. The swipe has direction, it has velocity, and it has a certain number of touch points (fingers) that are engaged. It is impractical for Apple to implement events for every combination of these variables; at the same time, it is extremely taxing on the system to just detect a "generic" swipe event and force you, the developer, to check the number of fingers, direction, and so on each time the event is triggered.

To make life simple, Apple has created "gesture-recognizer" classes for almost all the common gestures that you may want to implement in your applications, as follows:

- ▶ **Tapping** (`UITapGestureRecognizer`): Tapping one or more fingers on the screen

- ▶ **"Long" Pressing** (`UILongPressGestureRecognizer`): Pressing one or more fingers to the screen for a specific period of time

- ▶ **Pinching** (`UIPinchGestureRecognizer`): Pinching to close or expand something

- ▶ **Rotating** (`UIRotationGestureRecognizer`): Sliding two fingers in a circular motion

- ▶ **Swiping** (`UISwipeGestureRecognizer`): Swiping with one or more fingers in a specific direction

- ▶ **Panning** (`UIPanGestureRecognizer`): Touching and dragging

- ▶ **Shaking:** Physically shaking the iOS device

In earlier versions of iOS, developers had to read and recognize low-level touch events to determine whether, for example, a pinch was happening: Are there two points represented on the screen? Are they moving toward each other?

In iOS 4 and later, you define what type of recognizer you're looking for, add the recognizer to a view (`UIView`), and you automatically receive any multitouch events that are triggered. You even receive values such as velocity and scale for gestures such as "pinch." Let's see what this looks like translated into code.

TIP
_____
Shaking is not a multitouch gesture and requires a slightly different approach. Note that it doesn't have its own recognizer class.
_____

Adding Gesture Recognizers

You can add gesture recognizers to your projects in one of two ways: either through code or visually using the Interface Builder editor. While using the editor makes life much easier for us, it is still important to understand what is going on behind the scenes. Consider the code fragment in Listing 17.1.

LISTING 17.1 Example of the Tap Gesture Recognizer

```
1:    UITapGestureRecognizer *tapRecognizer;
2:    tapRecognizer=[[UITapGestureRecognizer alloc]
3:                  initWithTarget:self
4:                  action:@selector(foundTap:)];
5:    tapRecognizer.numberOfTapsRequired=1;
6:    tapRecognizer.numberOfTouchesRequired=1;
7:    [self.tapView addGestureRecognizer:tapRecognizer];
```

This example implements a "tap" gesture recognizer that will look for a single tap from a single finger within a view called `tapView`. If the gesture is seen, the method `foundTap` is called.

Line 1 kicks things off by declaring an instance of the `UITapGestureRecognizer` object, `tapRecognizer`. In line 2, `tapRecognizer` is allocated and initialized with `initWithTarget:action`. Working backward, the action is the method that will be called when the tap occurs. Using `@selector(foundTap:)`, we tell the recognizer that we want to use a method called `foundTap` to handle our taps. The target we specify, `self`, is the object where `foundTap` lives. In this case, it will be whatever object is implementing this code (probably a view controller).

Lines 5 and 6 set two properties of the tap gesture recognizer:

▶ **numberOfTapsRequired**: The number of times the object needs to be tapped before the gesture is recognized

▶ **numberOfTouchesRequired**: The number of fingers that need to be down on the screen before the gesture is recognized

Finally, line 7 uses the `UIView` method `addGestureRecognizer` to add the `tapRecognizer` to a view called `tapView`. As soon as this code is executed, the recognizer is active and ready for use, so a good place to implement the recognizer is in a view controller's `viewDidLoad` method.

Responding to the event is simple: Just implement the `foundTap` method. An appropriate method stub for the implementation looks like this:

```
- (void)foundTap:(UITapGestureRecognizer *)recognizer {
}
```

What happens when the gesture is found is entirely up to you. One could simply respond to the fact the gesture took place, use the parameter provided to the method to get additional details about where the tap happened on the screen, and so on.

All in all, not too bad, don't you think? What's even better? In most cases, you can do almost all of this setup entirely within Interface Builder. Beginning in Xcode 4.2, you can add and configure gesture recognizers with point-and-click simplicity, as shown in Figure 17.1. The tutorial in this hour shows how to do exactly that.

FIGURE 17.1
Gesture recognizers can be added through Interface Builder.

Using Gesture Recognizers

As people become more comfortable with touch devices, the use of gestures becomes almost natural—and expected. Applications that perform similar functions are often differentiated by their user experience, and a fully touch-enabled interface can be the deciding factor between a customer downloading your app and passing it by.

Perhaps the most surprising element of adding gestures to applications is just how *easy* it is. I know I say that often throughout the book, but gesture recognizers are one of those rare features that "just works." Follow along and find out what I mean.

Implementation Overview

In this hour's application, which we'll name **Gestures**, you implement five gesture recognizers (tap, swipe, pinch, rotate, and shake), along with the feedback those gestures prompt. Each gesture updates a text label with information about the gesture that has been detected. Pinch, rotate, and shake take things a step further by scaling, rotating, or resetting an image view in response to the gestures.

To provide room for gesture input, the application displays a screen with four embedded views (UIView), each assigned a different gesture recognizer directly within the storyboard scene. When you perform an action within one of the views, it calls a corresponding action method in our view controller to update a label with feedback about the gesture, and depending on the gesture type, updates an onscreen image view (UIImageView), too.

Figure 17.2 shows the final application.

FIGURE 17.2
The application detects and acts upon a variety of gestures.

CAUTION

Auto Layout—Our Frenemy

We have to be a bit clever in this application because image views that we add in Interface Builder are subject to Apple's constraint system. Ideally, we want to be able to take advantage of the Auto Layout system to position our image view in a nice default position, regardless of our screen size (exactly what you learned in the preceding hour). Once the application launches, however, we don't want any of the constraints enforced because we want to be able to resize and rotate the image view using our gestures.

You can take care of this in any number of ways, including programmatically finding and removing constraints with the removeConstraints NSLayoutConstraint method. The method we take, however, is to add an image view in Interface Builder so that we can position it visually and then replace it with our own constraint-free image view right after the application launches. It's a relatively simple way to take advantage of Auto Layout for the initial interface object layout and then gain the flexibility of working with a constraint-free object as the application executes.

Setting Up the Project

Start Xcode and create a new single-view iOS application called **Gestures**. This project requires quite a few outlets and actions, so be sure to follow the setup closely. You'll also be making connections directly between objects in Interface Builder, so even if you're used to the approach we've taken in other projects, you might want to slow down for this one.

Adding the Image Resource

Part of this application's interface is an image that can rotate or scale up and down. We use this to provide visual feedback to users based on their gestures. Included with this hour's project is an Images folder and a file named flower.png. Drag the Images folder into your main project code folder, choosing to copy the resources and create groups as needed.

Planning the Properties and Connections

For each touch gesture that we want to sense, we need a view where it can take place. Often, this would be your main view. For the purpose of demonstration, however, we will add four UIViews to our main view that will each have a different associated gesture recognizer. Surprisingly, none of these require outlets, because we'll connect the recognizers to them directly in Interface Builder.

We do, however, need two outlets and properties, `outputLabel` and `imageView`, of the classes `UILabel` and `UIImageView`, respectively. The label is used to provide text feedback to the user, while the image view shows visual feedback to the pinch and rotate gestures.

When the application senses a gesture within one of the four views, it needs to invoke an action method that can interact with the label and image. We will connect the gesture recognizers to methods called `foundTap`, `foundSwipe`, `foundPinch`, and `foundRotation`.

NOTE

Notice that we don't mention the shake gesture here? Even though we will eventually add shake recognition to this project, it will be added by implementing a very specific method in our view controller, not through an arbitrary action method that we define upfront.

Adding an Instance Variable for the Image View Size

When our gesture recognizers resize or rotate the image view in our UI, we want to be able to reset it to its default position and size. To make this happen, we need to "know" in our code what the default position for the image was. View positioning and sizing is described using a data structure (not an object) called a `CGRect` that contains four values: x and y coordinates (`origin.x` and `origin.y`), and width and height (`size.width` and `size.height`). We will add a private instance variable to the project that, when the application first launches, stores the size and location of the image view (the `CGRect` of the view) we added in Interface Builder. We'll name this variable **_originalRect**.

Open your ViewController.m file and update the `@interface` block following `#import` line so that it reads as follows:

```
@interface ViewController () {
    CGRect _originalRect;
}
@end
```

The `_originalRect` `CGRect` is declared and ready to be used in our implementation; but first, we need an interface.

Designing the Interface

Open the MainStoryboard.storyboard file and make room in your workspace. It's time to create our user interface (UI).

To build the interface, start by dragging four `UIView` instances to the main view. Size the first to a small rectangle in the upper-right portion of the screen; it will capture taps. Make the second a long rectangle beside the first (for detecting swipes). Size the other two views as large rectangles below the first two (for pinches and rotations). Use the Attributes Inspector (Option-Command-4) to set the background color of each view to be something unique.

Next, drag labels into each of the four views. The first label should read **Tap Me!**. The second should read **Swipe Me!**. The third label should read **Pinch Me!**. The fourth label should read **Rotate Me!**.

Drag a fifth `UILabel` instance to the main view, and center it at the top of the screen. Use the Attributes Inspector to set it to align center. This will be the label we use to provide feedback to the user. Change the label's default text to **Do something!**.

Finally, add a `UIImageView` layout, and then position it in an appropriately attractive location at the bottom center of the scene; use the Auto Layout constraints if you so desire (see Figure 17.3). Remember that we will not actually be using *this* image view to display gesture feedback; we want it solely for positioning. So, there is no need to set a default image for the image view.

FIGURE 17.3
Size and position the `UIImageView` similar to what is shown here.

With the view finished, in most projects, we start connecting our interface to our code through outlets and actions—but not this hour. Before we can create our connections, we need to add the gesture recognizers to the storyboard.

TIP

We're about to do a bunch of dragging and dropping of objects onto the `UIViews` that you just created. If you often use the document outline to refer to the objects in your view, you may want to use the `Label` field of the "Identity" group in the Identity Inspector (Option-Command-3) to give them more meaningful names than the default View label they appear with. Labels are arbitrary and do not affect the program's operation at all.

Adding Gesture Recognizers to Views

As you learned earlier, one way to add a gesture recognizer is through code. You initialize the recognizer you want to use, configure its parameters, and then add it to a view and provide a method it will invoke if a gesture is detected. Alternatively, you can drag and drop from the Interface Builder Object Library and barely write any code. We're going to do this now.

Make sure that MainStoryboard.storyboard is open and that the document outline is visible.

The Tap Recognizer

Our first step is to add an instance of the `UITapGestureRecognizer` object to our project. Search the Object Library for the tap gesture recognizer and drag and drop it onto the `UIView` instance in your project that is labeled Tap Me!, as shown in Figure 17.4. The recognizer will appear as an object at the bottom of the document outline, regardless of where you drop it.

FIGURE 17.4
Drag the recognizer onto the view that will use it.

CAUTION

Everything Is a View

Be careful not to drag the recognizer onto the label within the view. Remember that every onscreen object is a subclass of `UIView`, so you *could* potentially add a gesture recognizer to the label rather than to the intended view. You might find it easier to target the views in the document outline rather than in the visual layout.

Through the simple act of dragging the tap gesture recognizer into the view, you've created a gesture-recognizer object and added it to that view's gesture recognizers. (A view can have as many as you want.)

Next, you need to configure the recognizer so that it knows what type of gesture to look for. Tap gesture recognizers have two properties:

▶ **Taps:** The number of times the object needs to be tapped before the gesture is recognized

▶ **Touches:** The number of fingers that need to be down on the screen before the gesture is recognized

In this example, we're defining a *tap* as one finger tapping the screen once, so we define a single tap with a single touch. Select the tap gesture recognizer, and then open the Attributes Inspector (Option-Command-4), as shown in Figure 17.5.

Set both the Taps and Touches fields to 1—or go nuts; this is a perfect time to play with the recognizer properties as much as you like. Just like that, the first gesture recognizer is added to the project and configured. We still need to connect it to an action a bit later, but now we need to add the other recognizers.

TIP

If you look at the connections on the `UITapGestureRecognizer` object or the view that you dropped it onto, you'll see that the view references in an "outlet collection" called `gestureRecognizers`. An outlet collection is an array of outlets that make it easy to refer to multiple similar objects simultaneously. If you add more than one gesture recognizer to a view, the recognizer is referenced by the same outlet collection.

The Swipe Recognizer

You implement the swipe gesture recognizer in almost the same manner as the tap recognizer. Instead of being able to choose the number of taps, however, you can determine in which direction the swipes can be made—up, down, left, or right—as well as the number of fingers (touches) that must be down for the swipe to be recognized.

Taps

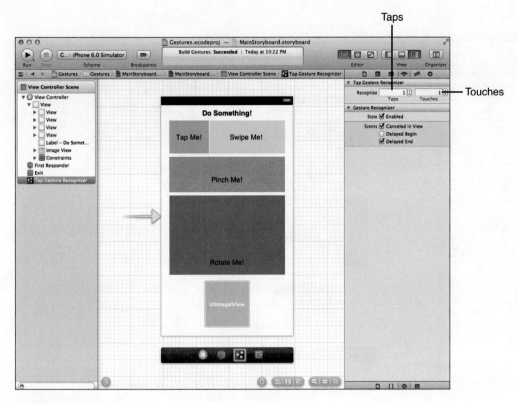

Touches

FIGURE 17.5
Use the Attributes Inspector to configure your gesture recognizers.

Again, use the Object Library to find the swipe gesture recognizer (UISwipeGestureRecognizer) and drag a copy of it in into your view, dropping it on top of the view that contains the Swipe Me! label. Next, select the recognizer and open the Attributes Inspector to configure it, as shown in Figure 17.6. For this tutorial, I configured the swipe gesture recognizer to look for swipes to the right that are made with a single finger.

NOTE

If you want to recognize and react to different swipe directions, you must implement multiple swipe gesture recognizers. It is possible, in code, to ask a single swipe gesture recognizer to respond to multiple swipe directions, but it cannot differentiate between the directions.

FIGURE 17.6
Configure the swipe direction and the number of touches required.

The Pinch Recognizer

A pinch gesture is triggered when two fingers move closer together or farther apart within a view, and it is often used to make something smaller or larger, respectively. Adding a pinch gesture recognizer requires even less configuration than taps or swipes because the gesture itself is already well defined. The implementation of the action that interprets a pinch, however, will be a bit more difficult because we are also interested in "how much" a user pinched (called the *scale* of the pinch) and how fast (the *velocity*), rather than just wanting to know that it happened. More on that in a few minutes.

Using the Object Library, find the pinch gesture recognizer (`UIPinchGestureRecognizer`) and drag it onto the view that contains the Pinch Me! label. No other configuration is necessary.

TIP
___

If you look at the Attributes Inspector for a pinch, you'll see that you can set a `scale` property. The `scale`, by default, starts at 1. Imagine you move your fingers apart to invoke a pinch gesture recognizer. If you move your fingers twice as far apart as they were, the scale property becomes 2 (1 x 2). If you repeat the gesture, moving them twice as far apart again, it becomes 4 (2 x 2). In other words, the `scale` value changes using its previous reading as a starting point.

Usually you want to leave the default `scale` value to 1, but be aware that you *can* reset the default in the Attributes Inspector if need be.

___

The Rotation Recognizer

A rotation gesture is triggered when two fingers move opposite one another as if rotating around a circle. Imagine turning a doorknob with two fingers on the top and bottom and you'll get the idea of what iOS considers a valid rotation gesture. As with a pinch, the rotation gesture recognizer requires no configuration; all the work occurs in interpreting the results—the rotation (in radians) and the speed (velocity) of the rotation.

Find the rotation gesture recognizer (`UIRotationGestureRecognizer`) and drag it onto the view that contains the Rotate Me! label. You've just added the final object to the storyboard.

TIP
___

Just like the pinch gesture recognizer's `scale` property, the rotation gesture recognizer has a `rotation` property that you can set in the Attributes Inspector. This value, representing the amount of rotation in radians, starts at 0 and changes with each successive rotation gesture. If you want, you can override the initial starting rotation of 0 radians with any value you choose. Subsequent rotation gestures start from the value you provide.

___

Creating and Connecting the Outlets and Actions

To respond to gestures and access our feedback objects from the main view controller, we need to establish the outlets and actions we defined earlier.

Let's review what we need, starting with the outlets:

- **The image view** (`UIImageView`): `imageView`
- **The label for providing feedback** (`UILabel`): `outputLabel`

And the actions:

- **Respond to a tap gesture:** `foundTap`
- **Respond to a swipe gesture:** `foundSwipe`

▸ **Respond to a pinch gesture:** `foundPinch`

▸ **Respond to a rotation gesture:** `foundRotation`

Prepare your workspace for making the connections. Open the MainStoryboard.storyboard file and switch to the assistant editor mode. Because you will be dragging from the gesture recognizers in your scene, make sure that the document outline is visible (Editor, Show Document Outline) or that you can tell the difference between them in the object dock below your view.

Adding the Outlets

Control-drag from the Do Something! label to just below the `@interface` line in the ViewController.h file. When prompted, create a new outlet called **outputLabel**, as shown in Figure 17.7. Repeat the process for the image view, naming it **imageView**.

FIGURE 17.7
Connect the label and image view.

Adding the Actions

Connecting the gesture recognizers to the action methods that we've identified works as you probably imagine, but with one difference. Usually when you connect an object to an action you're connecting a particular event on that object—such as `Touch Up Inside`, for buttons. In the case of a gesture recognizer, you are actually making a connection from the recognizer's "selector" to a method. Recall in the earlier code example that the selector is just the name of the method that should be invoked if a gesture is recognized.

TIP

Some gesture recognizers (tap, swipe, and long press) can also trigger segues to other storyboard scenes by using the Storyboard Segues section in the Connections Inspector. You learned about multiscene storyboards in Hour 11, "Implementing Multiple Scenes and Popovers."

To connect the gesture recognizer to an action method, just Control-drag from the gesture recognizer entry in the document outline to the ViewController.h file. Do this now with the tap gesture recognizer, targeting just below the properties you defined earlier. When prompted, configure the connection as an action with the name **foundTap**, as shown in Figure 17.8.

FIGURE 17.8
Connect the gesture recognizer to a new action.

Repeat this process for each of the other gesture recognizers—connecting the swipe recognizer to `foundSwipe`, the pinch recognizer to `foundPinch`, and the rotation recognizer to `foundRotation`. To verify your connections, select one of the recognizers (here, the tap recognizer) and view the Connections Inspector (Option-Command-6). You should see the action defined in Sent Actions and the view that uses the recognizer referenced in the Referencing Outlet Collections section, as shown in Figure 17.9.

FIGURE 17.9
Confirm your connections in the Connections Inspector.

TIP

Hover your mouse over a given connection in the Connection Inspector to see that item highlighted in your scene (shown in Figure 17.9). This is a quick way of verifying that your gestures are connected to the right views.

We're done with our interface and done adding gesture recognizers to our project; now let's make them do something.

Implementing the Application Logic

To begin the implementation, we address our image view problem: We need to replace the image view that gets added through Interface Builder with one we create programmatically. We also grab the position and size of the image view from its `frame` attribute (a `CGRect`) and store it in the `_originalRect` instance variable. Where will this happen? In a new view controller method `viewDidAppear`, which is called as soon as the interface comes up.

Replacing the Image View

Make sure the standard editor mode is selected, and then open the ViewController.m file and add the method in Listing 17.2.

LISTING 17.2 The `viewDidAppear` Implementation

```
 1: - (void)viewDidAppear:(BOOL)animated {
 2:      [super viewDidAppear:animated];
 3:
 4:      _originalRect=self.imageView.frame;
 5:
 6:      UIImageView *tempImageView;
 7:      tempImageView=[[UIImageView alloc]
 8:                      initWithImage:[UIImage imageNamed:@"flower.png"]];
 9:      tempImageView.frame=_originalRect;
10:      [self.view addSubview:tempImageView];
11:
12:      self.imageView=tempImageView;
13: }
```

Line 2 passes the `viewDidAppear` message up the to the parent class; this is a standard line in any `viewDidAppear` implementation.

Line 4 grabs the `frame` attribute from the image view that we added in Interface Builder. This is of the type `CGRect` and consists of four floating point values: `origin.x`, `origin.y`, `size.width`, and `size.height`. The original values are stored in the instance variable `_originalRect`.

Lines 6–8 declare, allocate, and initialize a new `UIImageView` (`tempImageView`) using the flower. png image that we added to our project earlier.

In Line 9, we set the `frame` of the new image view to the frame of the original image view, conveniently stored in `_originalRect`. That finishes up the configuration of the constraint-free image view; it is added to the view controller's main view (the scene) with the `addSubview` method in Line 10.

As a final step in swapping the image views, line 12 reassigns the `self.imageView` property to the new `tempImageView`. We can now access the new image view through the property that originally pointed to the image view added in Interface Builder.

Now, let's move on to the gesture recognizers, beginning with the tap recognizer. What you'll quickly discover is that after you've added one recognizer, the pattern is very, very similar for the others. The only difference is the shake gesture, which is why we're saving that for last.

Responding to the Tap Gesture Recognizer

Responding to the tap gesture recognizer is just a matter of implementing the `foundTap` method. Update the method stub in the view controller (ViewController.m) with the implementation shown in Listing 17.3.

LISTING 17.3   The `foundTap` Implementation

```
- (IBAction)foundTap:(id)sender {
    self.outputLabel.text=@"Tapped";
}
```

This method doesn't need to process input or do anything other than provide some indication that it has run. Setting the `outputLabel`'s `text` property to `"Tapped"` should suffice nicely.

Ta da! Your first gesture recognizer is done. We'll repeat this process for the other four, and we'll be finished before you know it.

TIP

If you want to get the coordinate where a tap gesture (or a swipe) takes place, you add code like this to the gesture handler (replacing `<the view>` with a reference to the recognizer's view):

`CGPoint location = [(UITapGestureRecognizer *)sender locationInView:<the view>];`

This creates a simple structure named `location`, with members `x` and `y`, accessible as `location.x` and `location.y`.

Responding to the Swipe Recognizer

We respond to the swipe recognizer in the same way we did with the tap recognizer, by updating the output label to show that the gesture was recognized. Implement the `foundSwipe` method as shown in Listing 17.4.

LISTING 17.4   The `foundSwipe` Implementation

```
- (IBAction)foundSwipe:(id)sender {
    self.outputLabel.text=@"Swiped";
}
```

So far, so good. Next up, the pinch gesture. This requires a bit more work because we're going to use the pinch to interact with our image view.

Responding to the Pinch Recognizer

Taps and swipes are simple gestures; they either happen or they don't. Pinches and rotations are slightly more complex, returning additional values to give you greater control over the user interface. A pinch, for example, includes a `velocity` property (how quickly the pinch happened) and `scale` (a fraction that is proportional to change in distance between your fingers). If you move your fingers 50% closer together, the scale is `.5`, for example. If you move them twice as far apart, it is `2`.

You've made it to the most complex piece of code in this hour's lesson. The `foundPinch` method accomplishes several things. It resets the `UIImageView`'s `rotation` (just in case it gets out of whack when we set up the `rotation` gesture), creates a feedback string with the scale and velocity values returned by the recognizer, and actually scales the image view so that the user receives immediate visual feedback.

Implement the `foundPinch` method as shown in Listing 17.5.

LISTING 17.5   The foundPinch Implementation

```
 1: - (IBAction)foundPinch:(id)sender {
 2:     UIPinchGestureRecognizer *recognizer;
 3:     NSString *feedback;
 4:     double scale;
 5:
 6:     recognizer=(UIPinchGestureRecognizer *)sender;
 7:     scale=recognizer.scale;
 8:     self.imageView.transform = CGAffineTransformMakeRotation(0.0);
 9:     feedback=[[NSString alloc]
10:                 initWithFormat:@"Pinched, Scale:%1.2f, Velocity:%1.2f",
11:                 recognizer.scale,recognizer.velocity];
12:     self.outputLabel.text=feedback;
13:     self.imageView.frame=CGRectMake(_originalRect.origin.x,
14:                                     _originalRect.origin.y,
15:                                     _originalRect.size.width*scale,
16:                                     _originalRect.size.height*scale);
17: }
```

Let's walk through this method to make sure we understand what's going on. Lines 2–4 declare a reference to a pinch gesture recognizer (`recognizer`), a string object (`feedback`), and a floating-point value (`scale`). These are used to interact with our pinch gesture recognizer, store feedback for the user, and hold the scaling value returned by the pinch gesture recognizer, respectively.

Line 6 takes the incoming sender object of the type `id` and casts it as a `UIPinchGestureRecognizer`, which can then be accessed through the recognizer variable. The reason we do this is simple. When you created the `foundPinch` action by dragging the gesture recognizer into your ViewController.h file, Xcode wrote the method with a parameter named `sender` of the generic "handles any object" type `id`. Xcode does this even though sender will always be, in this case, an object of type `UIPinchGestureRecognizer`. Line 6 just gives us a convenient way of accessing the object as the type it really is.

Line 7 sets `scale` to the recognizer's scale property.

Line 8 resets the `imageView` object to a rotation of `0.0` (no rotation at all) by setting its `transform` property to the transformation returned by the Core Graphics `CGAffineTransformMakeRotation` function. This function, when passed a value in radians, returns the necessary transformation to rotate a view.

Lines 9–11 allocate and initialize the feedback string to show that a pinch has taken place and output the values of the recognizer's scale and velocity properties. Line 12 sets the `outputLabel` in the UI to the feedback string.

For the scaling of the image view itself, lines 13–17 do the work. All that needs to happen is for the `imageView` object's `frame` to be redefined to the new size. To do this, we can use `CGRectMake` to return a new frame rectangle based on a scaled version of the `CGRect` stored in the original image view position: `_originalRect`. The top-left coordinates (`origin.x`, `origin.y`) stay the same, but we multiply `size.width` and `size.height` by the `scale` factor to increase or decrease the size of the frame according to the user's pinch.

Building and running the application will now let you enlarge (even beyond the boundaries of the screen) or shrink the image using the pinch gesture within the `pinchView` object, as shown in Figure 17.10.

NOTE

If you don't want to cast the `sender` variable to use it as a gesture recognizer, you can also edit Xcode's method declarations to include the exact type being passed. Just change the method declaration from

- (IBAction)foundPinch:(id)sender;

to

- (IBAction)foundPinch:(UIPinchGestureRecognizer *)sender;

If you do so, you'll be able to access `sender` directly as an instance of `UIPinchGestureRecognizer`.

Responding to the Rotation Recognizer

The last multitouch gesture recognizer that we'll add is the rotation gesture recognizer. Like the pinch gesture, rotation returns some useful information that we can apply visually to our onscreen objects, notably velocity and rotation. The rotation returned is the number of radians that the user has rotated his or her fingers, clockwise or counterclockwise.

FIGURE 17.10
Enlarge or shrink the image in a pinch (ha ha).

TIP

Most of us are comfortable talking about rotation in "degrees," but the Cocoa classes usually use radians. Don't worry. It's not a difficult translation to make. If you want, you can calculate degrees from radians using the following formula:

Degrees = Radians x 180 / Pi

There's not really any reason we need this now, but in your own applications, you might want to provide a degree reading to your users.

I'd love to tell you how difficult it is to rotate a view and about all the complex math involved, but I pretty much gave away the trick to rotation in the `foundPinch` method earlier. A single line of code will set the `UIImageView`'s transform property to a rotation transformation and visually rotate the view. Of course, we also need to provide a feedback string to the user, but that's not nearly as exciting, is it?

Add the `foundRotation` method in Listing 17.6 to your ViewController.m file.

LISTING 17.6   The `foundRotation` Implementation

```
 1: - (IBAction)foundRotation:(id)sender {
 2:      UIRotationGestureRecognizer *recognizer;
 3:      NSString *feedback;
 4:      double rotation;
 5:
 6:      recognizer=(UIRotationGestureRecognizer *)sender;
 7:      rotation=recognizer.rotation;
 8:      feedback=[[NSString alloc]
 9:              initWithFormat:@"Rotated, Radians:%1.2f, Velocity:%1.2f",
10:              recognizer.rotation,recognizer.velocity];
11:      self.outputLabel.text=feedback;
12:      self.imageView.transform = CGAffineTransformMakeRotation(rotation);
13: }
```

Again, we begin by declaring a reference to a gesture recognizer (`recognizer`), a string (`feedback`), and a floating-point value (`rotation`), in lines 2–4.

Line 6 takes the incoming sender object of the type `id` and casts it as a `UIRotationGesture Recognizer`, which can then be accessed through the `recognizer` variable.

Line 7 sets the rotation value to the recognizer's `rotation` property. This is the rotation in radians detected in the user's gesture.

Lines 8–10 create the `feedback` string showing the radians rotated and the velocity of the rotation, while line 11 sets the output label to the string.

Line 12 handles the rotation itself, creating a rotation transformation and applying it to the `imageView` object's `transform` property.

NOTE

The `foundPinch` method can also be implemented by updating the `transform` property for `imageView` and using the `CGAffineTransformMakeScale` method. In essence, you could replace lines 13-16 of `foundPinch` with a single line:

```
self.imageView.transform = CGAffineTransformMakeScale(scale,scale);
```

Why did we update the `frame` of the `imageView` instead? Two reasons. First, because it gives you experience with two approaches to manipulating a view. Second, because setting a transformation for the image view doesn't really change the view's underlying `frame`; it changes the appearance instead. If you really want to the view's size and location to change (not just the *appearance* of its size and location), applying a transformation isn't the way to go.

Run and test your application now. You should be able to freely spin the image view using a rotation gesture in the rotate view, as shown in Figure 17.11.

FIGURE 17.11
Spin the image view using the rotation gesture.

Although it might seem like we've finished, we still need to cover one more gesture: a shake.

Implementing the Shake Recognizer

Dealing with a shake is a bit different from the other gestures covered this hour. We must intercept a `UIEvent` of the type `UIEventTypeMotion`. To do this, our view controller or view must be the first responder in the responder chain and must implement the `motionEnded:withEvent` method.

Let's tackle these requirements one at a time.

Becoming First Responder

For our view controller to be a first responder, we have to allow it through a method called `canBecomeFirstResponder` that does nothing but return `YES`, and then ask for first responder status when the view controller loads its view. Start by adding the new method `canBecomeFirstResponder`, shown in Listing 17.7, to your ViewController.m implementation file.

LISTING 17.7   Enable the Ability to Be a First Responder

```
- (BOOL) canBecomeFirstResponder{
    return YES;
}
```

Next, we need our view controller to become the first responder by sending the message become-FirstResponder as soon as it has displayed its view. Update the ViewController.m viewDidAppear method to do this, as shown in Listing 17.8.

LISTING 17.8   Ask to Become a First Responder

```
- (void) viewDidAppear:(BOOL) animated {
    [super viewDidAppear:animated];
    [self becomeFirstResponder];

    _originalRect=self.imageView.frame;

    UIImageView *tempImageView;
    tempImageView=[[UIImageView alloc]
                  initWithImage:[UIImage imageNamed:@"flower.png"]];
    tempImageView.frame=_originalRect;
    [self.view addSubview:tempImageView];

    self.imageView=tempImageView;
}
```

Our view controller is now prepared to become the first responder and receive the shake event. All we need to do now is implement motionEnded:withEvent to trap and react to the shake gesture itself.

Responding to a Shake Gesture

To react to a shake, implement the motionEnded:withEvent method, as shown in Listing 17.9.

LISTING 17.9   Responding to a Shake Gesture

```
1: - (void)motionEnded:(UIEventSubtype)motion withEvent:(UIEvent *)event {
2:     if (motion==UIEventSubtypeMotionShake) {
3:         self.outputLabel.text=@"Shaking things up!";
4:         self.imageView.transform = CGAffineTransformIdentity;
5:         self.imageView.frame=_originalRect;
6:     }
7: }
```

First things first: In line 2, we check to make sure that the motion value we received (an object of type `UIEventSubtype`) is, indeed, a motion event. To do this, we just compare it to the constant `UIEventSubtypeMotionShake`. If they match, the user just finished shaking the device.

Lines 3–5 react to the shake by setting the output label, rotating the image view back to its default orientation, and setting the image view's frame back to the original size and location stored in our `_originalRect`. In other words, shaking the device will reset the image to its default state. Pretty nifty, huh?

Building the Application

You can now run the application and use all the gestures that we implemented this hour. Try scaling the image through a pinch gesture. Shake your device to reset it to the original size. Scale and rotate the image, tap, swipe—everything should work exactly as you'd expect and with a surprisingly minimal amount of coding. Although not a useful app in and of itself, this tutorial does illustrate many techniques that you can use in your own applications.

Gestures have become an integral part of applications and user expectations in iOS. Adding them to your applications will increase their viability and improve the overall user experience.

Further Exploration

In addition to the four gestures discussed this hour, there are two other recognizers that you should be able to immediately add to your apps: `UILongPressGestureRecognizer` and `UIPanGestureRecognizer`. The `UIGestureRecognizer` class is the parent to all the gesture recognizers that you've learned about in this lesson and offers additional base functionality for customizing gesture recognition.

We humans do a lot with our fingers, such as draw, write, play music, and more. Each of these possible gestures has been exploited to great effect in third-party applications. Explore the App Store to get a sense of what's been done with the iOS multitouch gestures.

You also might want to learn more about the lower-level handling of touches on iOS. See the "Event Handling" section of the Data Management iOS documentation for more information.

Be sure to look at the SimpleGestureRecognizers tutorial project, found within the Xcode documentation. This project provides many additional examples of implementing gestures on the iOS platform and demonstrates how gestures can be added through code. Although the Interface Builder approach to adding gesture recognizers can cover many common scenarios, it's still a good idea to know how to code them by hand.

Summary

In this hour, we've given the gesture recognizer architecture a good workout. Using the gesture recognizers provided through iOS, you can easily recognize and respond to taps, swipes, pinches, rotations, and more—without any complex math or programming logic.

You also learned how to make your applications respond to shaking: Just make them first responders and implement the `motionEnded:withEvent` method. Your ability to present your users with interactive interfaces just increased dramatically.

Q&A

Q. Why don't the rotation/pinch gestures include configuration options for the number of touches?

A. The gesture recognizers are meant to recognize common gestures. Although it is possible that you could manually implement a rotation or pinch gesture with multiple fingers, it wouldn't be consistent with how users expect their applications to work and isn't included as an option with these recognizers.

Workshop

Quiz

1. What gesture recognizer detects the user briefly touching the screen?

2. How can you respond to multiple swipe directions in a single gesture recognizer?

3. The rotation recognizer returns a rotation in degrees. True or false?

4. Adding shake sensing to your application is as simple as adding any other gesture recognizer.

Answers

1. The `UITapGestureRecognizer` is used to trap and react to one or more fingers tapping the screen.

2. You can't. You can trap multiple swipe directions in a single recognizer if you add it through code, but you should consider those directions to be combined into a *single* gesture. To react differently to different swipes, they should be implemented as different recognizers.

3. False. Most Cocoa classes dealing with rotation (including the rotation gesture recognizer) work with radians.

4. False. The shake gesture requires that your view or view controller become the first responder and trap motion `UIEvents`.

Activities

1. Expand the Gestures application to include panning and pressing gestures. These are configured almost identically to the gestures you used in this hour's tutorial.

2. Alter this project to use the image view that you added in Interface Builder rather than the one created programmatically. Practice using the constraints system to see the effect that constraints have on the image view as it changes size and rotates.

3. Improve on the user experience by adding the pinch and rotation gesture recognizers to the `UIImageView` object itself, enabling users to interact directly with the image rather than another view.

HOUR 18
Sensing Orientation and Motion

What You'll Learn in This Hour:

▶ What Core Motion is
▶ How to determine a device's orientation
▶ How to measure tilt and acceleration
▶ How to measure rotation

The Nintendo Wii introduced motion sensing as an effective input technique for mainstream consumer electronics. Apple applied this technology with great success to the iPhone, iPod touch, and iPad. Apple devices are equipped with an accelerometer that provides measurements of the orientation, movement, and tilt of the device. With the accelerometer, a user can control applications by simply adjusting the physical orientation of the device and moving it in space. In addition, Apple has introduced a gyroscope to the iDevice lineup (available in iPhone 4 or iPad 2 and all later models). This enables the device to sense rotation motions that aren't against the force of gravity. In short, if a user moves a gyroscope-enabled device, there are ways that your applications can detect and react to that movement.

The motion-input mechanism is exposed to third-party applications in iOS through a framework called Core Motion. In Hour 17, "Using Advanced Touches and Gestures," you saw how the accelerometer provides the shake gesture. Now you learn how to take direct readings from iOS for determining orientation, acceleration, and rotation. For all the magic that a motion-enabled application appears to exhibit, using these features is surprisingly simple.

Understanding Motion Hardware

All iOS devices, to date, can sense motion through the use of the accelerometer hardware. This capability is now supplemented with a gyroscope in all new iPhone and iPad models. To get a better sense for what this means to your applications, let's review what information each of these pieces of hardware can provide.

TIP

For most applications in this book, using the iOS simulator is perfectly acceptable, but the simulator does not simulate the accelerometer or gyroscope hardware. So for this chapter, be sure to have a physical device provisioned for development. To run this hour's applications on your device, follow the steps in Hour 1, "Preparing Your System and iDevice for Development."

Accelerometer

An accelerometer uses a unit of measure called a g, which is short for gravity. 1g is the force pulling down on something resting at sea level on Earth (9.8 meters per second squared). You don't normally notice the feeling of 1g (that is until you trip and fall, and then 1g hurts pretty bad). You are familiar with g-forces higher and lower than 1g if you've ever ridden on a roller coaster. The pull that pins you to your seat at the bottom of the roller coaster hill is a g-force greater than 1, and the feeling of floating up out of your seat at the top of a hill is negative g-force at work.

NOTE

An accelerometer measures acceleration relative to a free fall—meaning that if you drop your iDevice into a sustained free fall, say off the Empire State Building, its accelerometer will measure 0g on the way down. (Just trust me; don't try this out.) The accelerometer of a device sitting in your lap, however, measures 1g along the axis it is resting on.

The measurement of the 1g pull of Earth's gravity on the device while it's at rest is how the accelerometer can be used to measure the orientation of the device. The accelerometer provides a measurement along three axes, called x, y, and z (see Figure 18.1).

FIGURE 18.1
The three measurable axes.

Depending on how your device is resting, the 1g of gravity will be pulling differently on the three possible axes. If it is standing straight up on one of its edges or is flat on its back or on its screen, the entire 1g is measured on one axis. If the device is tilted at an angle, the 1g is spread across multiple axes (see Figure 18.2).

FIGURE 18.2
The 1g of force on a device at rest.

Gyroscope

Think about what you've just learned about the accelerometer hardware. Is there anything it can't do? It might seem, at first, that by using the measurements from the accelerometer, we can make a good guess as to what the user is doing, no matter what. Unfortunately, that's not quite the case.

The accelerometer measures the force of gravity distributed across your device. Imagine, however, that your iPhone or iPad is lying face up on a table. We can detect this with the accelerometer, but what we *cannot* detect is if you start spinning it around in a rousing game of "spin the bottle... err... iDevice." The accelerometer will still register the same value regardless of how the device is spinning.

The same goes for if the device is standing on one of its edges and rotates. The accelerometer can be used only if the device is changing orientation with respect to gravity; but the gyroscope can determine if, in any given orientation, the device is also rotating.

When querying a device's gyroscope, the hardware reports back with a rotation value along the x, y, and z axes. The value is a measurement, in radians, of the speed of rotation along that axis. If you don't remember your geometry, rotating 2 × pi radians is a complete circle, so a reading of 2 × pi (about 6.3) on any of the gyroscope's three axes indicates that the device is spinning once per second, along that axis, as shown in Figure 18.3.

FIGURE 18.3
A reading of roughly 6.3 from the gyroscope indicates that the device is rotating (spinning in a complete circle) at a rate of one revolution per second.

Accessing Orientation and Motion Data

To access orientation and motion information, we use two different approaches. First, to determine and react to distinct changes in orientation, we can request that our iOS device send notifications to our code as the orientation changes. We can then compare the messages we receive to constants representing all possible device orientations—including face up and face down—and determine what the user has done. Second, we take advantage of a framework called Core Motion to directly access the accelerometer and gyroscope data on scheduled intervals. Let's take a closer look before starting this hour's projects.

Requesting Orientation Notifications Through `UIDevice`

Although it *is* possible to read the accelerometer and use the values it returns to determine a device's orientation, Apple has made the process much simpler for developers. The singleton instance `UIDevice` (representing our device) includes a method `beginGeneratingDeviceOri-entationNotifications` that will tell iOS to begin sending orientation notifications to the notification center (`NSNotificationCenter`). Once the notifications start, we can register with an `NSNotificationCenter` instance to have a method of our choosing automatically be invoked with the device's orientation changes.

Besides just knowing that an orientation event occurred, we need some reading of what the orientation is. We get this via the `UIDevice` orientation property. This property, of type `UIDeviceOrientation`, can be one of six predefined values:

- ▶ `UIDeviceOrientationFaceUp`: The device is lying on its back, facing up.

- ▶ `UIDeviceOrientationFaceDown`: The device is lying on its front, with the back facing up.

- ▶ `UIDeviceOrientationPortrait`: The device is in the "normal" orientation, with the Home button at the bottom.

- ▶ `UIDeviceOrientationPortraitUpsideDown`: The device is in portrait orientation with the Home button at the top.

- ▶ `UIDeviceOrientationLandscapeLeft`: The device is lying on its left side.

- ▶ `UIDeviceOrientationLandscapeRight`: The device is lying on its right side.

By comparing the property to each of these values, we can determine the orientation and react accordingly.

How Is This Different from Adapting to Interface Rotation Events?

The interface-related events that you learned about in Hour 16, "Building Rotatable and Responsive User Interfaces," are just that: interface related. We first tell the device what orientations our interface supports, and then we can programmatically tell it what to do when the interface needs to change. The method we are using now is for getting instantaneous orientation changes regardless of what the interface supports. The constants `UIDeviceOrientationFaceUp` and `UIDeviceOrientationFaceDown` are also meaningless with regard to the interface-managing methods we covered.

Reading the Accelerometer and Gyroscope with Core Motion

You work with the accelerometer and gyroscope a bit differently. First, you need to add the Core Motion framework to your project.

Within your code, you create an instance of the Core Motion motion manager: CMMotionManager. The motion manager should be treated as a singleton—one instance can provide accelerometer and gyroscope motion services for your entire application.

NOTE

Recall that a singleton is a class that is instantiated once in the lifetime of your application. The readings of iDevice hardware are often provided as singletons because there is only one accelerometer and gyroscope in the device. Multiple instances of the CMMotionManager objects existing in your application wouldn't add any extra value and would have the added complexity of managing their memory and lifetime, both of which are avoided with a singleton.

Unlike orientation notifications, the Core Motion motion manager enables you to determine how often you receive updates (in seconds) from the accelerometer and gyroscope and allows you to directly define a *handler block* that executes each time an update is ready.

TIP

You need to decide how often your application can benefit from receiving motion updates. You should decide this by experimenting with different update values until you come up with an optimal frequency. Receiving more updates than your application can benefit from can have some negative consequences. Your application will use more system resources, which might negatively impact the performance of the other parts of your application and can certainly affect the battery life of the device. Because you'll probably want fairly frequent updates so that your application responds smoothly, you should take some time to optimize the performance of your CMMotionManager-related code.

Setting up your application to use CMMotionManager is a simple three-step process of initializing and allocating the motion manager, setting an updating interval, and then requesting that updates begin and be sent to a handler block via startAccelerometerUpdatesToQueue :withHandler.

Consider the code snippet in Listing 18.1.

LISTING 18.1   Using the Motion Manager

```
1: motionManager = [[CMMotionManager alloc] init];
2: motionManager.accelerometerUpdateInterval = .01;
3: [motionManager
```

```
4:      startAccelerometerUpdatesToQueue: [NSOperationQueue currentQueue]
5:      withHandler:^(CMAccelerometerData *accelData, NSError *error) {
6:          //Do something with the acceleration data here!
7:      }];
```

In line 1, the motion manager is allocated and initialized—you've seen code like this dozens of times.

Line 2 requests that the accelerometer send updates every .01 seconds—or 100 times per second.

Lines 3–7 start the accelerometer updates and define a handler block that is called for each update.

The handler block can be confusing looking, so I urge you to look at the CMMotionManager documentation to better understand the format. In essence, it's like a new method being defined within the startAccelerometerUpdatesToQueue:withHandler invocation.

The accelerometer handler is passed two parameters: accelData, an object of type CMAccelerometerData; and error, of type NSError. The accelData object includes an acceleration property of the type CMAcceleration. This will be the information we are interested in reading and includes acceleration values along x, y, and z axes. It is up to the code defined within the handler (currently just a comment in this snippet) to do something with this incoming data.

Gyroscope updates work *almost* the same way but require you to define a gyroUpdateInterval for the Core Motion motion manager and begin receiving updates with startGyroUpdatesToQue ue:withHandler. The gyroscope's handler receives an object, gyroData of type CMGyroData, and, like the accelerometer handler, an NSError object. We're interested in the rotation property of gyroData—data of the type CMRotationRate. The rotation property provides rotation rates along the x, y, and z axes.

TIP

Because only hardware built since 2010 supports the gyroscope, you may want to check for its presence using the CMMotionManager Boolean property gyroAvailable. If YES, it exists and can be used.

When you have finished processing accelerometer and gyroscope updates, you can stop receiving them with the CMMotionManager methods stopAccelerometerUpdates and stopGyroUpdates, respectively.

Feeling confused? Not to worry—it makes much more sense seeing the pieces come together in code.

Sensing Orientation

As our first introduction to detecting motion, we create the Orientation application. Orientation won't be wowing users; it's simply going to say which of six possible orientations the device is currently in. The Orientation application will detect these orientations: standing up, upside down, left side, right side, face down, and face up.

Implementation Overview

To create the Orientation application, we build an interface that contains a single label and then code up a method that executes whenever the orientation changes. For this method to be called, we must register with the `NSNotificationCenter` to receive notifications when appropriate.

Remember, this isn't the same as interface rotation and resizing; it doesn't necessitate a change in the interface, and it can handle upside-down and right-side-up orientations as well.

Setting Up the Project

As you've grown accustomed, begin by starting Xcode and creating a new project. We use our old standby, the Single View Application template, and name the new project **Orientation**.

Planning the Properties and Connections

In this project, we need a single label in our main application view that can be updated from code. This will be named **orientationLabel** and, as you might guess, will be set to a string containing the current device orientation.

Designing the Interface

Orientation's UI is simple (and very stylish); I've used a yellow text label in a field of gray. To create your interface, select the MainStoryboard.storyboard file to open the Interface Builder (IB) editor.

Next, open the Object Library (View, Utilities, Show Object Library) and drag a label into the view. Set the label's text to read **Face Up**.

Using the Attributes Inspector (Option-Command-4), set the color of the label, increase its size, and set its alignment to center. After configuring the attributes of your label, do the same for your view, setting an appropriate background color for the label.

TIP

Now is a good time to put into use the techniques you learned in Hour 16 to keep the text centered onscreen while the device rotates. It isn't necessary for the completion of the project, but it is good practice!

The finished view should look like Figure 18.4.

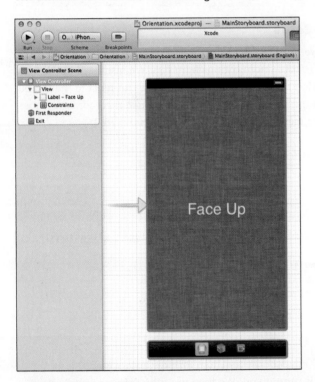

FIGURE 18.4
The Orientation application's UI.

Creating and Connecting the Outlet

Our application will need to be able to change the text of the label when the accelerometer indicates that the orientation of the device has changed. We need to create a connection for the label that we added. With the interface visible, switch to the assistant editor.

Control-drag from the label to just below the `@interface` line in ViewController.h. Name the new outlet **orientationLabel** when prompted. That's it for the bridge to our code: just a single outlet and no action.

Implementing the Application Logic

There are two pieces remaining in this puzzle. First, we must tell iOS that we are interested in receiving notifications when the device orientation changes. Second, we must react to those changes. Because this is your first encounter with the notification center, it might seem a bit unusual, but concentrate on the outcome. The code patterns for notifications aren't difficult to understand when you can see what the result is.

Registering for Orientation Updates

When our applications view is shown, we must register a method in our application to receive `UIDeviceOrientationDidChangeNotification` notifications from iOS. We also need to tell the device itself that it should begin generating these notifications so that we can react to them. You can accomplish all of this setup work in the ViewController.m `viewDidLoad` method. Let's implement that now. Update the `viewDidLoad` method to read as shown in Listing 18.2.

LISTING 18.2 Start Watching for Orientation Changes

```
 1: - (void)viewDidLoad
 2: {
 3:      [super viewDidLoad];
 4:
 5:      [[UIDevice currentDevice]beginGeneratingDeviceOrientationNotifications];
 6:
 7:      [[NSNotificationCenter defaultCenter]
 8:        addObserver:self selector:@selector(orientationChanged:)
 9:        name:@"UIDeviceOrientationDidChangeNotification"
10:        object:nil];
11: }
```

In line 5, we use the method [UIDevice currentDevice] to return an instance of UIDevice that refers to the device our application is running on. We then use the `beginGeneratingDeviceOrientationNotifications` to tell the device that we're interested in hearing about it if the user changes the orientation of his or her iPhone or iPad.

Lines 7–10 tell the NSNotificationCenter object that we are interested in subscribing to any notifications with the name UIDeviceOrientationDidChangeNotification that it may receive. They also tell that the class that is interested in the notifications is OrientationViewController by way of the addObserver:self message. We use the lines to say that we will be implementing a method called orientationChanged. In fact, coding up orientationChanged is the only thing left to do.

Determining Orientation

To determine the orientation of the device, we use the UIDevice property orientation. Unlike other values we've dealt with in the book, the orientation property is of the type UIDeviceOrientation (simple constant, not an object). Therefore, you can check each possible orientation via a simple switch statement and update the orientationLabel in the interface as needed.

Implement the orientationChanged method, as shown in Listing 18.3.

LISTING 18.3 Change the Label as the Orientation Changes

```
 1: - (void)orientationChanged:(NSNotification *)notification {
 2:
 3:     UIDeviceOrientation orientation;
 4:     orientation = [[UIDevice currentDevice] orientation];
 5:
 6:     switch (orientation) {
 7:         case UIDeviceOrientationFaceUp:
 8:             self.orientationLabel.text=@"Face Up";
 9:             break;
10:         case UIDeviceOrientationFaceDown:
11:             self.orientationLabel.text=@"Face Down";
12:             break;
13:         case UIDeviceOrientationPortrait:
14:             self.orientationLabel.text=@"Standing Up";
15:             break;
16:         case UIDeviceOrientationPortraitUpsideDown:
17:             self.orientationLabel.text=@"Upside Down";
18:             break;
19:         case UIDeviceOrientationLandscapeLeft:
20:             self.orientationLabel.text=@"Left Side";
21:             break;
22:         case UIDeviceOrientationLandscapeRight:
23:             self.orientationLabel.text=@"Right Side";
```

```
24:            break;
25:        default:
26:            self.orientationLabel.text=@"Unknown";
27:            break;
28:    }
29: }
```

The logic is straightforward. This method is called each time we have an update to the device's orientation. The notification is passed as a parameter, but we don't really need it for anything.

In line 3, we declare an `orientation` variable, and then we assign it with the `orientation` constant in line 4.

Lines 6–28 implement a `switch` statement (refer to Hour 3, "Discovering Objective-C: The Language of Apple Platforms," for details on `switch`) that compares each possible orientation constant to the value of the orientation variable. If they match, the `orientationLabel` text property is set appropriately.

TIP

Technically, the application is done; but when it runs, you'll notice that the iPhone *interface* doesn't support all orientations. The application runs as expected, but when you turn the phone upside down, the text will also be upside down. Remember that you can enable *all* possible orientations for your interface by adding this method to your view controller:

```
- (NSUInteger) supportedInterfaceOrientations
{
    return UIInterfaceOrientationMaskAll;
}
```

Adding this is purely optional—it corrects what you might consider a visual flaw, rather than a bug in functionality.

Building the Application

Save your files, and then run the application. Your results should resemble Figure 18.5. If you're running in the iOS simulator, rotating the virtual hardware (Hardware, Rotate Left/Right) will work, but you won't be able to view the face-up and face-down orientations.

FIGURE 18.5
Orientation in action.

Detecting Tilt and Rotation

In the Orientation application, we ignored the precise values coming from the accelerometer and instead just allowed iOS to make an all-or-nothing orientation decision. The gradations between these orientations, such as the device being somewhere between its left side and straight up and down, are often interesting to an application.

Imagine you are going to create a car racing game where the device acts as the steering wheel when tilted left and right and the gas and brake pedals when tilted forward and back. It is very helpful to know how far the player has turned the wheel and how hard the user is pushing the pedals to know how to make the game respond.

Likewise, consider the possibilities offered by the gyroscope's rotation measurements. Applications can now tell whether the device is rotating, even if there is no change in tilt. Imagine a turn-based game that switches between players just by rotating the iPhone or iPad around while it is lying on a table or sitting in a charging dock.

Implementation Overview

In our next application example, ColorTilt, we take a solid color and make it progressively more transparent as users tilt the device left or right or as they rotate the device faster. We add two toggle switches (UISwitch) to the view to enable/disable the accelerometer and gyroscope.

It's not as exciting as a car racing game, but it is something we can accomplish in an hour, and everything learned here will apply when you get down to writing a great iOS motion-enabled application.

Setting Up the Project

Open Xcode and begin by creating a new project based on the Single View Application template. Title this application **ColorTilt**.

We need to do a bit of extra setup on this project because the default template doesn't quite have everything we need. Specifically, we need to include the Core Motion framework.

Adding the Core Motion Framework

This project relies directly on Core Motion for accessing the accelerometer and gyroscope, so before we go any further, we must add the Core Motion framework to the project. Select the top-level project group for ColorTilt, and make sure that the Summary tab is highlighted in the editor area.

Next, scroll down the summary until you find the section called Linked Frameworks and Libraries. Click the + button below the list. Choose CoreMotion.framework from the list that appears, and then click the Add button, as shown in Figure 18.6.

NOTE
_____
When the Core Motion framework is added to the project, it will likely not fall within one of the project groups. To neaten things up, drag it to the Frameworks group. This isn't necessary, but it does keep things orderly.
_____

Planning the Properties and Connections

Our next step is to identify the properties and connections we need. Specifically, we want a view (UIView) that changes colors (colorView) and two UISwitch instances that indicate whether we should watch the accelerometer and gyroscope (toggleAccelerometer and toggleGyroscope). The switches also activate an action method called controlHardware that does the heavy lifting of turning on or off the hardware monitoring.

FIGURE 18.6
Add the Core Motion framework to the group.

We also need an instance variable for our CMMotionManager object, which we'll call **motion-Manager**. Because this is not directly related to an object in the storyboard and is part of enabling the functional logic, we add this in the implementation of the view controller logic.

Designing the Interface

Like the Orientation application, the ColorTilt application's interface is not a work of art. It requires a few switches, labels, and a view. Open the interface by selecting the MainStoryboard. storyboard file.

Lay out the user interface by dragging two UISwitch instances from the Object Library to the top-right of the view, one above the other. Use the Attributes Inspector (Option-Command-4) to set each switch's default to Off.

Next, add two labels (UILabel), titled **Accelerometer** and **Gyroscope**, to the view, positioned beside each switch.

Finally, drag a UIView instance into the view and size it to fit in the view below the switches and labels. Use the Attributes Inspector to change the view's background to green.

Your view should now resemble Figure 18.7. If you want to arrange the controls differently, feel free.

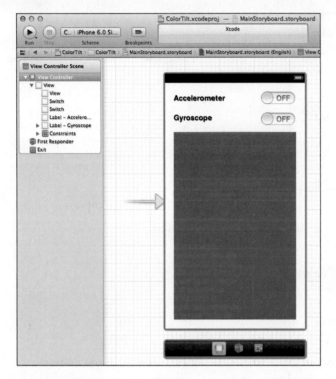

FIGURE 18.7
Create a layout that includes two switches, two labels, and a color view.

Creating and Connecting the Outlets and Actions

There are only a few outlets and actions in this project, but not all the connections are immediately obvious. Here's what we'll be using.

Starting with the outlets:

▶ **The view that will change colors (UIView):** colorView

▶ **Toggle switch that activates/deactivates the accelerometer (UISwitch):** toggle
Accelerometer

▶ **Toggle switch that activates/deactivates the gyroscope (UISwitch):** toggleGyroscope

And the action:

▶ **Toggle monitoring the accelerometer/gyroscope on and off from the switches:**
toggleAccelerometer

Make sure the MainStoryboard.storyboard file is selected, and then open the assistant editor.
Clear some room in your workspace if necessary.

Adding the Outlets

Begin by Control-dragging from the view to just below the @interface line in ViewController.h.
Name the outlet **colorView** when prompted, as shown in Figure 18.8. Repeat the process for the
two switches, connecting the switch beside the Accelerometer label to toggleAccelerometer and
the switch by the Gyroscope label to toggleGyroscope.

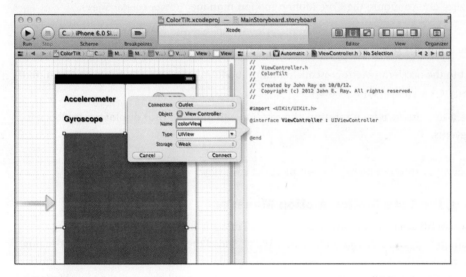

FIGURE 18.8
Connect the objects to the outlets.

Adding the Action

To finish the connections, the two switches need to be configured to invoke the control-
Hardware method when their Value Changed event occurs. Start by defining the action by
Control-dragging from the accelerometer switch to just below the last @property line in the
ViewController.h file.

When prompted, create a new action named controlHardware that responds to the switch's
Value Changed event. That takes care of the first switch, but in this particular case, we want
both switches connected to the same action. As you've learned in previous lessons, you can take
care of this in multiple ways.

The most precise way is to select the second switch and drag from the Value Changed outlet
in the Connections Inspector (Option-Command-6) onto the controlHardware IBAction line

that you just created in ViewController.h. That said, you can also Control-drag directly from the second switch onto the `IBAction` line, as well; this is because the IB editor defaults to using the `Value Changed` action when you make a connection from a switch. Choose an approach and make the connection.

Implementing the Application Logic

We need to take care of several different things to see our application work:

1. Initialize and configure the Core Motion motion manager (`CMMotionManager`).

2. Manage events to toggle the accelerometer/gyroscope on and off (controlHardware), registering a handler block when the hardware is turned on.

3. React to the accelerometer/gyroscope readings, updating the background color and alpha transparency values appropriately.

4. Prevent the interface from rotating; the rotation will interfere with displaying feedback to fast events.

Let's work our way through these different pieces of code now.

Initializing the Core Motion Motion Manager

When the ColorTilt application launches, we need to allocate and initialize a Core Motion motion manager (`CMMotionManager`) instance. We've added the Core Motion framework to our project, but none of the code knows about it yet. We need to include the Core Motion interface file in our ViewController.h file because that is the class where we'll be using the Core Motion methods. Add the following `#import` line to ViewController.h following the default `UIKit` import:

```
#import <CoreMotion/CoreMotion.h>
```

Next, we need to declare our motion manager. This persists for the life of the view, and is used only internally in the view controller class. This means it is a good candidate for being a private instance variable rather than a full-blown property. Declare a new instance variable, `_motion-Manager`, by updating the `@interface` block at the top of the ViewController.m implementation file to read as follows:

```
@interface ViewController () {
    CMMotionManager *_motionManager;
}
@end
```

Now we're prepared to use the Core Motion methods, and we have an instance variable that we can use to store and manipulate a motion manager object for the view controller class.

Next, we initialize the motion manager and set two properties, `accelerometerUpdateInterval` and `gyroUpdateInterval`, to match the frequency (in seconds) with which we want to get updates from the hardware. We'll update at 100 times a second, or an update value of .01. This is done in `viewDidLoad` so that monitoring begins as soon as our interface loads.

Update the `viewDidLoad` method, as shown in Listing 18.4.

LISTING 18.4   Initialize the Motion Manager

```
- (void)viewDidLoad
{
    [super viewDidLoad];

    _motionManager = [[CMMotionManager alloc] init];
    _motionManager.accelerometerUpdateInterval = .01;
    _motionManager.gyroUpdateInterval = .01;
}
```

The next step is to implement our action, `controlHardware`, so that when one of the `UISwitch` instances is turned on or off, it tells the motion manager to begin or end readings from the accelerometer/gyroscope.

Managing Accelerometer and Gyroscope Updates

The logic behind the `controlHardware` method is simple. If the accelerometer switch is toggled on, the `CMMotionManager` instance, `_motionManager`, is asked to start monitoring the accelerometer. Each update is processed by a handler block that, to make life simple, calls a new method `doAcceleration`. If the switch is toggled off, monitoring of the accelerometer stops.

The same pattern is implemented for the gyroscope, but our gyroscope handler block invokes a new method called `doGyroscope` whenever an update occurs.

Update the `controlHardware` method stub, as shown in Listing 18.5.

LISTING 18.5   The `controlHardware` Implementation

```
 1: - (IBAction)controlHardware:(id)sender {
 2:     if ([self.toggleAccelerometer isOn]) {
 3:         [_motionManager
 4:          startAccelerometerUpdatesToQueue:[NSOperationQueue currentQueue]
 5:          withHandler:^(CMAccelerometerData *accelData, NSError *error) {
 6:              [self doAcceleration:accelData.acceleration];
 7:          }];
 8:     } else {
 9:         [_motionManager stopAccelerometerUpdates];
10:     }
11:
```

```
12:      if ([self.toggleGyroscope isOn] && _motionManager.gyroAvailable) {
13:          [_motionManager
14:            startGyroUpdatesToQueue:[NSOperationQueue currentQueue]
15:            withHandler:^(CMGyroData *gyroData, NSError *error) {
16:                [self doRotation:gyroData.rotationRate];
17:            }];
18:      } else {
19:          [self.toggleGyroscope setOn:NO animated:YES];
20:          [_motionManager stopGyroUpdates];
21:      }
22: }
```

Let's step through this method to make sure we're all still on the same page.

Line 2 checks to see whether the toggle switch (UISwitch) is set to On for the accelerometer. If it is, lines 3–7 tell the motion manager to start sending updates for the accelerometer and define a code block to handle each update. The code block consists of a single line (line 6) that calls the doAcceleration method and sends it the acceleration property of the CMAccelerometerData object received by the handler. This is a simple structure with x, y, z components, each containing a reading of the acceleration on that axis.

Lines 8–10 handle the case of the accelerometer being toggled off, using the motion manager's stopAccelerometerUpdates method to end accelerometer readings.

In line 12, this same process begins for the gyroscope, with minor exceptions. In the conditional statement in line 12, we also check the _motionManager (CMMotionManager) gyroAvailable property. This is a Boolean value that indicates whether the device has a gyroscope at all. If it doesn't, we shouldn't try to read it; so, we toggle the switch back off in line 19.

Another difference from the accelerometer code is that when handling updates from the gyroscope (line 16) we call a method, doRotation, with the gyroscope's rotation data (available in a simple structure, rotationRate, with x, y, z components that indicate the rotation rate, in radians, along each axis).

Finally, when the gyroscope is toggled off, the motion manager's stopGyroUpdates method is called (line 20).

We now have the code in place to prepare our motion manager, start and stop updates, and invoke the doAccelerometer and doGyroscope methods with the appropriate data from our iOS hardware. The last step? Actually implementing doAccelerometer and doGyroscope.

TIP
___
If you know you're going to use both the accelerometer and gyroscope in your application, you can request updates from both simultaneously using the Core Motion motion manager (CMMotionManager) startDeviceMotionUpdatesToQueue:withHandler method. This incorporates both sensors into a single method with a single handler block.

Reacting to Accelerometer Updates

We start with `doAccelerometer` because it is the more complicated of the two. This method should do two things. First, it should change the color of `colorView` if the user moves the device suddenly. Next, if the user gently tilts the device along the x-axis, the method will progressively make the current color more solid.

To change colors, we need to sense motion. One way to do this is to look for g-forces greater than 1g along each of our x, y, and z axes. This is good for detecting quick, strong movements. A more subtle approach is to implement a filter to calculate the difference between gravity and the force the accelerometer is measuring. We'll go with the former for our implementation.

To set the alpha value as the device tilts, we pay attention to only the x-axis. The closer the x-axis is to being on edge (a reading of 1.0 or –1.0), the more solid (1.0 alpha) we'll make the color. The closer the x-axis reading is to 0 (the device standing upright), the more transparent (0.0 alpha) the color. We'll use the C function `fabs()` to get the absolute value of the reading because for this example, we don't care whether the device is tilting left edge or right.

Before implementing the full method in the ViewController.m implementation file, declare it in the ViewController.h interface file by adding this line following the action declaration:

```
- (void)doAcceleration:(CMAcceleration)acceleration;
```

This isn't absolutely necessary, but it tells other methods in the class (specifically the `control-Hardware` method that needs to use it) that it exists. If you don't do this, you must make sure that the implementation `doAccelerometer` is added before `controlHardware` in the implementation file.

Implement `doAcceleration`, as shown in Listing 18.6.

LISTING 18.6   The `doAcceleration` Implementation

```
 1: - (void)doAcceleration:(CMAcceleration)acceleration {
 2:     if (acceleration.x > 1.3) {
 3:         self.colorView.backgroundColor = [UIColor greenColor];
 4:     } else if (acceleration.x < -1.3) {
 5:         self.colorView.backgroundColor = [UIColor orangeColor];
 6:     } else if (acceleration.y > 1.3) {
 7:         self.colorView.backgroundColor = [UIColor redColor];
 8:     } else if (acceleration.y < -1.3) {
 9:         self.colorView.backgroundColor = [UIColor blueColor];
10:     } else if (acceleration.z > 1.3) {
11:         self.colorView.backgroundColor = [UIColor yellowColor];
12:     } else if (acceleration.z < -1.3) {
13:         self.colorView.backgroundColor = [UIColor purpleColor];
14:     }
15:
```

```
16:     double value = fabs(acceleration.x);
17:     if (value > 1.0) { value = 1.0;}
18:     self.colorView.alpha = value;
19: }
```

The logic is surprisingly simple. Lines 2–14 check the acceleration along each of the three axes to see whether it is greater (or less) than 1.3—that is, greater than the force of gravity on the device. If it is, the `colorView` `UIView`'s `backgroundColor` attribute is set to one of six different predefined colors. In other words, if you jerk the device in any direction, the color will differ.

TIP

A little experimentation shows that +/−1.3g is a good measure of an abrupt movement. Try it out yourself with a few different values, and you may decide another value is better.

Line 16 declares a double-precision floating-point variable value that stores the absolute value of the acceleration along the x-axis (`acceleration.x`). This is the measurement used to lighten or darken the color when the device tilts gently.

If `value` is greater than 1.0, it is reset to 1.0 in line 17.

Line 18 sets the `alpha` property of `colorView` to value to finish the implementation.

Not that bad, right? The gyroscope implementation is even easier.

Reacting to Gyroscope Updates

The gyroscope handling is even easier than the accelerometer because we don't need to change colors—only alter the `alpha` property of `colorView` as the user spins the device. Instead of forcing the user to rotate the device in one direction to get the alpha channel to change, we combine the rotation rates along all three axes. This is implemented in a new method called `doRotation`.

Again, before adding `doRotation`, declare it in your class's interface file; otherwise, you'll need to implement it above `controlHardware` in the ViewController.m file. Add the following line below the last method declaration in ViewController.h:

```
- (void)doRotation:(CMRotationRate)rotation;
```

Now, implement `doRotation` as shown in Listing 18.7.

LISTING 18.7 The `doRotation` Implementation

```
1: - (void)doRotation:(CMRotationRate)rotation {
2:     double value = (fabs(rotation.x)+fabs(rotation.y)+fabs(rotation.z))/12.5;
3:     if (value > 1.0) { value = 1.0;}
4:     self.colorView.alpha = value;
5: }
```

Line 2 declares value as a double-precision floating-point number and sets it to the sum of the absolute values of the three axis rotation rates (rotation.x, rotation.y, and rotation.z), divided by 12.5.

NOTE

Why are we dividing by 12.5? Because an alpha value of 1.0 is a solid color, and a rotation rate of 1.0 means that the device is rotating at about 1/6 of a rotation a second (1 radian × pi = 3.14; that is, half of a complete rotation). In practice, this is way too slow a rotation rate to get a good effect; barely turning the device at all gives us a solid color.

By dividing by 12.5, the rotation rate would have to be roughly two revolutions a second (2 revolutions × 2 radians × pi = 12.56) for value to reach 1, meaning it takes much more effort to make the view's background color solid.

In line 3, if value is greater than 1.0, it is set back to 1.0 because that is the maximum value the alpha property can accept.

Finally, in line 4, the alpha property of the colorView UIView is set to the calculated value.

Preventing Interface Orientation Changes

At this point, you can run the application, but you probably won't get very good visual feedback from the methods we've written. Apple's iOS templates include interface rotation settings that are turned on by default. The animation of the interface rotation will interfere with the quick color changes we need to see in the view.

To fix the problem, we need to disable support for rotation. Do this by adding the method in Listing 18.8 to ViewController.m.

LISTING 18.8   Disable Interface Rotation

```
- (NSUInteger)supportedInterfaceOrientations
{
    return UIInterfaceOrientationMaskPortrait;
}
```

This turns off interface orientation changes for all possible orientations except portrait—making our UI static.

Building the Application

You've just finished the application. Plug in your iDevice (this won't work in the simulator), choose your Device from the Xcode toolbar's Scheme pop-up menu, and then click Run. Experiment with the sudden motion, tilt, and rotation, as shown in Figure 18.9. Be sure to try activating both the accelerometer and gyroscope at once, and then one at a time.

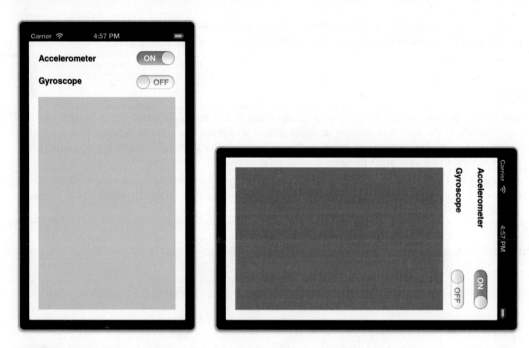

FIGURE 18.9
Tilt the device to change the opacity of the background color.

It's been a bit of a journey, but you can now tie directly into one of the core features of Apple's iOS device family: motion. Even better, you're doing so with one of Apple's latest-and-greatest frameworks: Core Motion.

Further Exploration

The Core Motion framework provides a great set of tools for dealing with all the iOS motion hardware in a similar manner. As a next step, I recommend reviewing the *Core Motion Framework Reference* and the *Event Handling Guide for iOS*, both available through the developer documentation system in Xcode. You also want to pay close attention to the CMAttitude class, which can give you a snapshot of a device's attitude at a given point in time. This includes pitch, roll, and yaw (rotation about the device's three axes) in one convenient structure.

Regardless of how you read motion data or what data you use, the biggest challenge is to use motion readings to implement subtler and more natural interfaces than those in the two applications we created in this hour. A good step toward building effective motion interfaces for your applications is to dust off your old math, physics, and electronics texts and take a quick refresher course.

The simplest and most basic equations from electronics and Newtonian physics are all that is needed to create compelling interfaces. In electronics, a low-pass filter removes abrupt signals over a cutoff value, providing smooth changes in the baseline signal. This is useful for detecting smooth movements and tilts of the device and ignoring bumps and the occasional odd, spiked reading from the accelerometer and gyroscope. A high-pass filter does the opposite and detects only abrupt changes; this can help in removing the effect of gravity and detecting only purposeful movements, even when they occur along the axes that gravity is acting upon.

When you have the right signal interpretation in place, there is one more requirement for your interface to feel natural to your users: It must react like the physical and analog world of mass, force, and momentum, and not like the digital and binary world of 1s and 0s. The key to simulating the physical world in the digital is just some basic seventeenth-century physics.

Wikipedia Entries

Low-pass filter: http://en.wikipedia.org/wiki/Low-pass_filter

High-pass filter: http://en.wikipedia.org/wiki/High-pass_filter

Momentum: http://en.wikipedia.org/wiki/Momentum

Newton's laws of motion: http://en.wikipedia.org/wiki/Newton's_laws_of_motion

Summary

At this point, you know all the mechanics of working with orientation, and with the accelerometer and gyroscope via Core Motion. You understand how to use the Core Motion motion manager (CMMotionManager) to take direct readings from the available sensors to interpret orientation, tilt, movement, and rotation of the device. You understand how to create an instance of CMMotionManager, how to tell the manager to start sending motion updates, and how to interpret the measurements that are provided.

Q&A

Q. Should I base my game's controls off of gyroscope and accelerometer readings?

A. I recommend that you offer more traditional touchscreen controls in addition to motion-based options. Although many users enjoy using motion controls, they require a certain amount of space and privacy that isn't always available.

Q. Are motion features only good for games?

A. Absolutely not! By combining the different sensor readings from the iPhone or iPad, you can learn a lot about how your users interact with your applications and adjust accordingly. Is your application sensing a face-down orientation? Your user is likely lying down and reading in bed. So, offering to switch to night colors may be appropriate. Are you getting frequent spikes in the accelerometer readings? If yes, your application is likely being used while the user is walking or riding in a vehicle. Allowing more time to react to interface events might be an appropriate adaptation under these circumstances.

Workshop

Quiz

1. What type of motion can't the accelerometer detect?

2. Should you drop your iDevice off the Empire State Building to test the accelerometer?

Answers

1. The accelerometer can only detect changes in how gravity is affecting the device. It cannot, for example, detect that a device is lying on a table and spinning because the force of gravity doesn't change. To detect rotation, a gyroscope is needed.

2. I don't recommend it.

Activities

1. When the Orientation application is in use, the label stays put and the text changes. This means that for three of the six orientations (upside down, left side, and right side), the text itself is also upside down or on its side. Fix this by changing not just the label text but also the orientation of the label so that the text always reads normally for the user looking at the screen. Be sure to adjust the label back to its original orientation when the orientation is standing up, face down, or face up.

2. In the final version of the ColorTilt application, sudden movement is used to change the view's color. You may have noticed that it can sometimes be difficult to get the desired color. This is because the accelerometer provides a reading for the deceleration of the device after your sudden movement. So, what often happens is that ColorTilt switches the color from the force of the deceleration immediately after switching it to the desired color from the force of the acceleration. Add a delay to the ColorTilt application so that the color can be switched at most once every second. This makes switching to the desired color easier because the acceleration will change the color but the deceleration will be ignored.

Working with Rich Media

What You'll Learn in This Hour:

▶ How to play full-motion video from local or remote (streaming) files

▶ Ways of recording and playing back audio files on your iDevice

▶ How to access the built-in music library from within your applications

▶ How to display and access images from the built-in photo library or camera

▶ The use of Core Image filters to easily manipulate images

▶ Methods of retrieving and displaying information about currently playing media items

Each year, new iPads and iPhones come out, and each year I find myself standing in line to snatch them up. Is it the new amazing features? Not so much. In fact, my primary motivation is to keep expanding my storage space to keep up with an ever-growing media library. Sounds, podcasts, movies, TV shows—I keep them all on my iDevices. When the original 8GB iPhone came out, I assumed that I'd never run out of space. Today, I've just started having to cut back on my sync list to fit everything under 64GB.

There's no denying that iOS is a compelling platform for rich media playback. To make things even better, Apple provides a dizzying array of Cocoa classes that will help you add media to your own applications—everything from video, to photos, to audio recording. This hour's lesson walks you through a few different features that you may want to consider, including in your development efforts.

Exploring Rich Media

Hour 10, "Getting the User's Attention," introduced you to System Sound Services for playing back short (30-second) sound files. This is great for alert sounds and similar applications, but it hardly taps the potential of iOS. This hour takes things a bit further, giving you full playback capabilities, and even audio recording, within your own applications.

In this hour, we use three new frameworks: Media Player, AV Foundation, and Core Image. These frameworks encompass more than a dozen new classes. Although we cannot cover everything in this hour, you will get a good idea of what's possible and how to get started.

In addition to these frameworks, we introduce the `UIImagePickerController` class. You can add this simple object to your applications to allow access to the photo library or camera from within your application.

CAUTION

Do as Appropriate, Not as I Do!

As I discuss these frameworks and classes, I provide code snippets that demonstrate their use. To keep the code as straightforward as possible, I treat everything as a variable within a method rather than a property or instance variable. In a production implementation, however, chances are, many of the objects I create would best be defined as instance variables or properties. You'll see this in the tutorial, but not in the tiny snippets of code used to describe a feature.

Media Player Framework

The Media Player framework is used for playing back video and audio from either local or remote resources. It can be used to call up a modal iPod interface from your application, select songs, and manage playback. This is the framework that provides integration with all the built-in media features that your device has to offer. We use five different classes in our tutorial later in this hour:

▶ **MPMoviePlayerController:** Allows playback of a piece of media, either located on the file system or through a remote URL. The player controller can provide a GUI for scrubbing through video, pausing, fast forwarding, rewinding, or sending to AirPlay.

▶ **MPMediaPickerController:** Presents the user with an interface for choosing media to play. You can filter the files displayed by the media picker or allow selection of any file from the media library.

▶ **MPMediaItem:** A single piece of media, such as a song.

▶ **MPMediaItemCollection:** Represents a collection of media items that will be used for playback. An instance of `MPMediaPickerController` returns an instance of `MPMediaItemCollection` that can be used directly with the next class—the music player controller.

▶ **MPMusicPlayerController:** Handles the playback of media items and media item collections. Unlike the movie player controller, the music player works "behind the scenes"—allowing playback from anywhere in your application, regardless of what is displayed on the screen.

To use any of the Media Player functionality, you must first import the Media Player framework and then import the interface file in the class where you intend to use it:

```
#import <MediaPlayer/MediaPlayer.h>
```

This prepares your application for a wide variety of media playback functions. Let's take a look at a few simple use cases for these media player classes.

Using the Movie Player

The `MPMoviePlayerController` class is used to present a movie file for playback. It can display video in both fullscreen and embedded views—and toggle between them with a simple method. It can also be used to enable AirPlay playback of any video that it is displaying.

To make use of the movie player, you declare and initialize an instance of the `MPMoviePlayerController`, typically using the `initWithContentURL` method to provide it with a file or URL where it can find a video.

For example, to create a movie player that will play a file named movie.m4v located inside my application, I could use the following:

```
NSString *movieFile = [[NSBundle mainBundle]
                         pathForResource:@"movie" ofType:@"m4v"];
MPMoviePlayerController *moviePlayer = [[MPMoviePlayerController alloc]
                                        initWithContentURL:
                                        [NSURL fileURLWithPath: movieFile]];
```

Adding AirPlay support is as simple as setting the movie player object's `allowsAirPlay` property to `true`:

```
moviePlayer.allowsAirPlay=YES;
```

To choose where the movie player is added to your screen, you must use the `CGRectMake` function to define a rectangle that it will occupy and then add the movie player to your view. Recall that the `CGRectMake` takes four values: x, y coordinates followed by a width and height in points. For example, to set the display of the movie player to a location of 50 points over and 50 points down (x,y) with a width of 100 points and a height of 75 points, I could use the following:

```
[moviePlayer.view setFrame:CGRectMake(50.0, 50.0, 100.0 , 75.0)];
[self.view addSubview:moviePlayer.view];
```

To transition to a fullscreen view, use the `setFullscreen:animated` method:

```
[moviePlayer setFullscreen:YES animated:YES];
```

Finally, to initiate playback, just send the `play` message to the movie player instance:

```
[moviePlayer play];
```

To pause playback, you can use the `pause` message, or to stop it altogether, the `stop` message.

What Are the Supported Formats?

Officially, Apple supports the following codecs: H.264 Baseline Profile 3, MPEG-4 Part 2 video in .mov, .m4v, .mpv, or .mp4 containers. On the audio side, AAC-LC, and MP3 formats are supported.

This is the complete list of audio formats supported by iOS:

AAC (16Kbps to 320Kbps)	MP3 VBR
AIFF	Audible (formats 2–4)
AAC Protected (MP4 from iTunes Store)	Apple Lossless
MP3 (16Kbps to 320Kbps)	WAV

Handling Movie Player Completion

When the movie player finishes playing a file, it's possible that we will need to do a bit of cleanup—including removing the media player from our view. To do this, we use the `NSNotificationCenter` class to register an "observer" that will watch for a specific notification message from the _moviePlayer object and then call a method of our choosing when it receives the notification. For example:

```
[[NSNotificationCenter defaultCenter]
                    addObserver:self
                    selector:@selector(playMovieFinished:)
                    name:MPMoviePlayerPlaybackDidFinishNotification
                    object:moviePlayer];
```

This statement adds an observer to our class that will watch for an event with the name `MPMoviePlayerPlaybackDidFinishNotification`. When it sees that event, it calls the method `playMovieFinished`.

In the implementation of `playMovieFinished`, we must remove the notification observer (because we're done waiting for a notification) and then perform any additional cleanup, such as removing the movie player from a view. Listing 19.1 shows a sample implementation.

LISTING 19.1   Handle the Notification of Playback Completion

```
-(void)playMovieFinished:(NSNotification*)theNotification
{
    MPMoviePlayerController *moviePlayer=[theNotification object];

    [[NSNotificationCenter defaultCenter]
                    removeObserver:self
                    name:MPMoviePlayerPlaybackDidFinishNotification
```

```
                  object:moviePlayer];

       [moviePlayer.view removeFromSuperview];
}
```

Note that we can retrieve a reference to the movie player using `[theNotification object]`. This gives us a simple way to reference the object that registered for a notification—in this case, the movie player.

Using the Media Picker

When Apple opened iOS for development, it didn't initially provide a method for accessing the iOS music library. This led to applications implementing their own libraries for background music and a less-than-ideal experience for the end user. Thankfully, this restriction is now a thing of the past.

To program a full music-playback function into your application, you need to implement a media picker controller (`MPMediaPickerController`) for choosing your media, along with a music player controller (`MPMusicPlayerController`) for playing it back.

The `MPMediaPickerController` class displays an interface for choosing media files from a user's device. The `initWithMediaTypes` method initializes the media picker and filters the files that are available to the user in the picker.

Before the media picker is displayed, we can tweak its behavior by setting the `prompt` property to a string that is displayed to the user when choosing media and enable or disable multiple pieces of media from being returned with the `allowsPickingMultipleItems` property.

The object's `delegate` property will also need to be set so that the application can react appropriately when a choice is made—more on that in a minute. Once configured, the media picker is displayed with the `presentViewController:animated:completion` method. Listing 19.2 displays the setup and display of a typical media picker.

LISTING 19.2 Typical Setup and Display of a Media Picker

```
MPMediaPickerController *mediaPicker;
mediaPicker = [[MPMediaPickerController alloc]
               initWithMediaTypes: MPMediaTypeMusic];

mediaPicker.prompt = @"Choose Songs";
mediaPicker.allowsPickingMultipleItems = YES;
mediaPicker.delegate = self;

[self presentViewController:mediaPicker animated:YES completion:nil];
```

Notice in this sample code that the value we provide for initWithMediaTypes is MPMediaTypeMusic. This is one of several types of filters that you can apply to the media picker, including the following:

▶ **MPMediaTypeMusic:** The music library

▶ **MPMediaTypePodcast:** Podcasts

▶ **MPMediaTypeAudioBook:** Audio books

▶ **MPMediaTypeAnyAudio:** Any type of audio file

When the media picker is displayed and songs are chosen (or not), that's where the delegate comes in. By conforming to the MPMediaPickerControllerDelegate protocol and implementing two new methods, we can handle the cases where a user has chosen media or canceled his selection entirely.

The Media Picker Controller Delegate

When a user displays the media picker and makes a selection, we need to do something—what that is, exactly, depends on conforming to the delegate protocol and implementation of two delegate methods. The first, mediaPickerDidCancel, is called if the user taps the Cancel button in the middle of choosing his media. The second, mediaPicker:didPickMediaItems, is invoked if the user made a valid selection from his media library.

In the case of a cancellation, a proper response is just to dismiss the view. Nothing was chosen, so there's nothing else to do, as shown in Listing 19.3.

LISTING 19.3   Handle Canceling Media Selection

```
- (void)mediaPickerDidCancel:(MPMediaPickerController *)mediaPicker {
        [self dismissViewControllerAnimated:YES completion:nil];
}
```

When media *is* selected, however, it is returned to the mediaPicker:didPickMediaItems delegate method by way of an instance of the class MPMediaItemCollection. This object contains a reference to all the chosen media items and can be used to queue up the songs in a music player. We haven't yet seen the music player object, so we'll come back to the handling of the MPMediaItemCollection shortly. In addition to providing the media item collection, this method should dismiss the view controller, because the user has finished making his selection. Listing 19.4 shows the beginnings of the method for handling media selection.

LISTING 19.4 Handle the Selection of Media Items

```
- (void)mediaPicker: (MPMediaPickerController *)mediaPicker
        didPickMediaItems:(MPMediaItemCollection *)mediaItemCollection {
    // Do something with the media item collection here
    [self dismissViewControllerAnimated:YES completion:nil];
}
```

That's it for the delegate methods. We can now configure and display a media picker, handle a user canceling the media selection, and receive a `MPMediaItemCollection` if the user decides to choose something. Now let's explore how to actually do something with that media collection.

Using the Music Player

Using the music player controller class (`MPMusicPlayerController`) is similar to using the movie player—but there are no onscreen controls, nor do you need to allocate or initialize the controller. Instead, you simply declare it, and then you choose whether it should be a controller that integrates with the iPod functionality or if it is localized to the application:

```
MPMusicPlayerController *musicPlayer;
musicPlayer=[MPMusicPlayerController iPodMusicPlayer];
```

Here, I've created an `iPodMusicPlayer`, which means that the songs I queue and the playback controls affect the system-level iPod controls. Had I chosen to create an `applicationMusicPlayer`, nothing I might do in my application would have any effect on the iPod playback outside of the program.

Next, to get audio into the player, I can use its method `setQueueWithItemCollection`. This is where the media item collection that was returned by the media picker comes in handy. We can use that collection to queue up the songs in the music player:

```
[musicPlayer setQueueWithItemCollection: mediaItemCollection];
```

After the media is queued in the player, we can control playback by sending the player messages such as `play`, `stop`, `skipToNextItem`, and `skipToPreviousItem`:

```
[musicPlayer play];
```

To verify that the music player is playing audio, we can check its `playbackState` property. The `playbackState` indicates what operation the player is currently performing. For example:

▶ **MPMusicPlaybackStateStopped**: Audio playback has been stopped.

▶ **MPMusicPlaybackStatePlaying**: Audio playback is underway.

▶ **MMPMusicPlaybackStatePaused**: Audio playback is paused.

In addition, we may want to access the audio file that is currently playing to provide some feedback to the user; we do this through the `MPMediaItem` class.

Accessing Media Items

A single piece of media in an `MPMediaItemCollection` is an `MPMediaItem`. To get the current `MPMediaItem` being accessed by the player, just reference its `nowPlayingItem` property:

```
MPMediaItem *currentSong;
currentSong=musicPlayer.nowPlayingItem;
```

The `MPMediaItem` can be used to access all the metadata stored for a media file by using the `valueForProperty` method, along with one of several predefined property names. For example, to get the title of the current song, you could use the following:

```
NSString *songTitle;
songTitle=[currentSong valueForProperty:MPMediaItemPropertyTitle];
```

Other properties include the following:

- ▶ **MPMediaItemPropertyArtist:** The artist of the media item

- ▶ **MPMediaItemPropertyGenre:** A string representing the genre of the item

- ▶ **MPMediaItemPropertyLyrics:** The lyrics, if available, for the item

- ▶ **MPMediaItemAlbumTitle:** The name of the album the media item comes from

These are just a few of the pieces of metadata available. You can even access the artwork, beats per minute (BPM), and other data using similar properties that you'll find documented in the `MPMediaItem` class reference.

The Media Player framework provides much more than we can cover in a single hour, let alone part of an hour; so I encourage you to use this as a starting point. You can add an amazing amount of additional functionality to your applications through this framework with only a limited amount of coding involved.

AV Foundation Framework

Although the Media Player framework is great for all your general media playback needs, Apple recommends the AV Foundation framework for most audio playback functions that exceed the 30 seconds allowed by System Sound Services. In addition, the AV Foundation framework offers audio recording features, making it possible to record new sound files directly in your application. This might sound like a complex programming task, but it takes only about four statements to prepare and begin recording to your iDevice.

You need just two new classes to add audio playback and recording to your apps:

▶ **AVAudioRecorder:** Records audio (in a variety of different formats) to memory or a local file on the device. The recording process can even continue while other functions are running in your application.

▶ **AVAudioPlayer:** Plays back audio files of any length. Using this class, you can implement game soundtracks or other complex audio applications. You have complete control over the playback, including the ability to layer multiple sounds on top of one another.

To use the AV Foundation framework, you must add it to your project's frameworks, and then import not one, but two, interface files:

```
#import <AVFoundation/AVFoundation.h>
#import <CoreAudio/CoreAudioTypes.h>
```

The CoreAudioTypes.h file defines several audio types that we want to be able to reference by name, so it is required for some operations in AV Foundation.

Using AV Audio Player

To play back an audio file in AV Audio Player, you follow the same steps as using the movie player described earlier. First, you create an NSURL instance that references a local or remote file, and then you allocate and initialize the player using the AVAudioPlayer method initWithContentsOfURL:error.

For example, to prepare the audio player to play back a sound file named sound.wav stored inside the current application, we write this:

```
NSString *soundFile = [[NSBundle mainBundle]
                  pathForResource:@"mysound" ofType:@"wav"];
AVAudioPlayer *audioPlayer = [[AVAudioPlayer alloc]
                  initWithContentsOfURL:[NSURL fileURLWithPath: soundFile]
                  error:nil];
```

To play the sound, we then send the player the play message:

```
[audioPlayer play];
```

Pausing or stopping the playback is just a matter of sending pause or stop. You'll find additional methods in the class reference for adjusting audio and jumping to specific points within the audio file.

Handling AV Audio Player Completion

If you have a need to react to the condition of your AV Audio Player finishing playing a sound, you can do this by conforming to the AVAudioPlayerDelegate protocol and setting the delegate property for the player to the class that will handle the completion state:

```
audioPlayer.delegate=self;
```

Then implement the method audioPlayerDidFinishPlaying:successfully, as shown in the method stub in Listing 19.5.

LISTING 19.5   Handle Playback Completion

```
- (void)audioPlayerDidFinishPlaying:(AVAudioPlayer *)player
                    successfully:(BOOL)flag {
    // Do something here, if needed.
}
```

No need to add a notification to the notification center (like the movie player). Just indicate that you're conforming to the protocol, set the delegate, and implement the method. In many cases, you won't even need to do this; you'll just play the file and walk away, so to speak.

Using AV Audio Recorder

Recording audio in your application is only marginally more difficult than playing it back. You identify a file (NSURL) where you can store the recording, configure the parameters of the sound file you want to create (an NSDictionary), and then allocate and initialize an instance of the AVAudioRecorder class with the file and settings.

First, prepare the sound file. If you're recording without the intention of keeping the sound file, you can record to the temp directory. Otherwise, you should target the documents directory. Refer to Hour 15, "Reading and Writing Application Data," for more details on accessing the file system. Here, I prepare an NSURL that references a file sound.caf in the temp directory:

```
NSURL *soundFileURL=[NSURL fileURLWithPath:
                [NSTemporaryDirectory()
                stringByAppendingString:@"sound.caf"]];
```

Next, I need to create an NSDictionary that contains the settings for my recorded audio:

```
NSDictionary *soundSetting = @{AVSampleRateKey:@44100.0F,
                AVFormatIDKey:@(kAudioFormatMPEG4AAC),
                AVNumberOfChannelsKey:@2,
                AVEncoderAudioQualityKey:@(AVAudioQualityHigh)
    };
```

This code creates an `NSDictionary` called `soundSetting` with keys and values that should be completely obvious, so I'll just move on. Just kidding. Unless you're familiar with audio recording, many of these might be pretty foreign sounding. Here's the 30-second summary:

- **`AVSampleRateKey`:** The number of audio samples the recorder will take per second.

- **`AVFormatIDKey`:** The recording format for the audio.

- **`AVNumberofChannelsKey`:** The number of audio channels in the recording. Stereo audio, for example, has two channels.

- **`AVEncoderAudioQualityKey`:** A quality setting for the encoder.

NOTE

To learn more about the different settings, what they mean, and what the possible options are, read the `AVAudioRecorder` Class Reference (scroll to the "Constants" section) in the Xcode Developer Documentation utility.

After getting the sound file and settings ready, we can finally prepare an instance of the AV Recorder by allocating it and initializing it with the `initWithURL:settings:error` method:

```
AVAudioRecorder *soundRecorder = [[AVAudioRecorder alloc]
                                initWithURL: soundFileURL
                                settings: soundSetting
                                error: nil];
```

We're now ready to record. To record, we send the recorder the `record` message; to stop, we send `stop`:

```
[soundRecorder record];
```

When recording is complete, we can play back the new sound file using the AV Audio Player.

The Image Picker

The image picker (`UIImagePickerController`) works like the `MPMediaPickerController`, but instead of presenting a view where songs can be selected, the user's photo library is displayed instead. When the user chooses a photo, the image picker hands us a `UIImage` object based on the user's selection.

Like the `MPMediaPickerController`, the image picker is presented within your application modally. The good news is that both of these objects implement their own view and view controller, so there's very little work that we need to do to get them to display—other than a quick call to `presentViewController:animated:completion`. On the iPad, the image picker is required to be displayed within a popover, so your code will need to change a bit for this; we cover that in the tutorial project a bit later.

Using the Image Picker

To display the image picker, allocate and initialize an instance of `UIImagePickerController`, and then set the sourceType to what the user should be allowed to pick from:

- ▶ **UIImagePickerControllerSourceTypeCamera:** A picture that will be taken from the device's camera

- ▶ **UIImagePickerControllerSourceTypePhotoLibrary:** A picture chosen from the device's photo library

- ▶ **UIImagePickerControllerSourceTypeSavedPhotosAlbum:** The device's camera roll

Next, the image picker's `delegate` should be set; this is the class that will handle doing something once the user picks a photo (or takes a picture), or taps the Cancel button. Finally, the image picker is displayed using the `presentViewController:animated:completion` method. Listing 19.6 shows a sample setup and display of an image picker that uses the camera as the source.

LISTING 19.6   Set Up and Display the Image Picker

```
UIImagePickerController *imagePicker;
imagePicker = [[UIImagePickerController alloc] init];
imagePicker.sourceType=UIImagePickerControllerSourceTypeCamera;
imagePicker.delegate=self;
[[UIApplication sharedApplication] setStatusBarHidden:YES];
[self presentViewController:imagePicker animated:YES completion:nil];
```

Notice that there is one "unusual" line in this implementation that calls the method setStatusBarHidden. This hides the application's status bar because the photo library and camera interfaces are meant to be viewed fullscreen. The statement [UIApplication sharedApplication] grabs our application object and then uses the application's setStatusBarHidden method to hide the bar.

NOTE

You may have encountered instances where you can choose an image and scale/crop it before using it. This functionality is "baked into" the image picker. To enable it, set the property allowsEditing to YES on the UIImagePickerController instance.

TIP

If you want to determine exactly what sort of camera devices are available on your system, you can test using the `UIImagePickerController` method `isCameraDeviceAvailable`, which returns a Boolean value: `[UIImagePickerController isCameraDeviceAvailable:<camera type>]`

Where the camera type is `UIImagePickerControllerCameraDeviceRear` or `UIImagePickerControllerCameraDeviceFront`

The UI Image Picker Controller Delegate

To handle the actions of when a user either cancels picking an image or picks one, you must conform your class to the `UIImagePickerControllerDelegate` protocol and implement the methods `imagePickerController:didFinishPickingMediaWithInfo` and `imagePickerControllerDidCancel`.

The first, `imagePickerController:didFinishPickingMediaWithInfo`, is called automatically when the user makes a selection in the image picker. The method is passed an `NSDictionary` object that can contain several things: the image itself, an edited version of the image (if cropping/scaling is allowed), or information about the image. We must provide the key value to retrieve the value we want. For example, to get back the chosen image, we would use the `UIImagePickerControllerOriginalImage` key, a `UIImage`. Listing 19.7 shows a sample implementation that retrieves the selected image, shows the status bar, and dismisses the image picker.

LISTING 19.7   Handle the Selection of an Image

```
- (void)imagePickerController:(UIImagePickerController *)picker
        didFinishPickingMediaWithInfo:(NSDictionary *)info {
  [[UIApplication sharedApplication] setStatusBarHidden:NO];
  [self dismissViewControllerAnimated:YES completion:nil];
  UIImage *chosenImage=
                  info[UIImagePickerControllerOriginalImage];
  // Do something with the image here
}
```

TIP

To learn more about the data that can be returned by the image picker, read the `UIImagePickerControllerDelegate` Protocol reference within the Apple developer documentation.

In the second delegate method, we react to the user canceling the image selection, show the status bar, and get rid of the image picker view. A sample implementation is shown in Listing 19.8.

LISTING 19.8   Handle Canceling Image Selection

```
- (void)imagePickerControllerDidCancel:(UIImagePickerController *)picker {
    [[UIApplication sharedApplication] setStatusBarHidden:NO];
    [self dismissViewControllerAnimated:YES completion:nil];
}
```

As you can see, there's more than a little similarity to the media picker controller; once you get the hang of one, using the other will be a piece of cake.

CAUTION

Using an Image Picker? Conform to the Navigation Controller Delegate

The navigation controller delegate (UINavigationControllerDelegate) is required whenever you use an image picker. The good news is that you won't need to implement any additional methods for it—just a reference in your interface file.

CAUTION

Popover Enforced on iPad

If you are building your application for the iPad, you'll need to display the media picker via a popover, as described in Hour 11, "Implementing Multiple Scenes and Popovers" (and in this hour's tutorial). If you don't, your application will encounter an error when it attempts to show the picker onscreen.

The Core Image Framework

Core Image provides nondestructive methods for applying filters to images and performing other types of image analysis (including face detection). If you've ever wondered how to add fancy image effects to an application without needing to understand the complex math behind image manipulation, Core Image can be your best friend.

To use Core Image in your application, first add the framework, and then import the Core Image interface file:

```
#import <CoreImage/CoreImage.h>
```

Using Core Image Filters

To get a feel of how Core Image works, let's examine its use to apply a "sepia tone" image filter (CIFilter) to an image in your application. Core Image defines a new "nondestructive" image type of CIImage, but we've been dealing exclusively with UIImages (frequently within UIImageViews) to this point. No worries—converting between these two types is not difficult.

For example, assume we have an image view called `myImageView`. To access its underlying `UIImage` and create a new `CIImage` called `imageToFilter` that we can manipulate, we could write the following:

```
CIImage *imageToFilter=[[CIImage alloc] initWithImage:myImageView.image];
```

To apply a filter, we must know the name of a filter and the names of the parameters that it requires. For example, the Core Image sepia tone filter is named `CISepiaTone`, and it takes a parameter called `inputIntensity` that is a number between 1.0 and 0.0. (1.0 is no sepia tone applied.) Armed with that information, we can create a new `CIFilter`, set its default values, perform any additional configuration, and then pass it the input image (`imageToFilter`) and get back the result in a new `CIImage`, as demonstrated in Listing 19.9. This is the process for applying *any* `CIFilter`.

LISTING 19.9   Process a `CIImage` with a `CIFilter`

```
1: CIFilter *activeFilter = [CIFilter filterWithName:@"CISepiaTone"];
2: [activeFilter setDefaults];
3: [activeFilter setValue: @0.5F
4:                 forKey: @"inputIntensity"];
5: [activeFilter setValue:imageToFilter forKey: @"inputImage"];
6: CIImage *filteredImage=[activeFilter valueForKey: @"outputImage"];
```

Line 1 declares and returns a new instance of the sepia `CIFilter`, and line 2 sets its defaults. In line 3, the `inputIntensity` parameter is configured to an `NSNumber` floating-point value of `0.5`.

Line 5 uses this same method to pass the input image (`imageToFilter`) to the filter. Line 6 returns the filtered image in `filteredImage` by accessing the `outputImage` key from the filter.

The `filteredImage` object is a `CIImage`, so chances are, to use it, we need to convert it back to a `UIImage`. The `UIImage` class method `imageWithCIImage` makes this a breeze:

```
UIImage *myNewImage = [UIImage imageWithCIImage:filteredImage];
```

The new `UIImage`, `myNewImage`, contains the final filtered image with sepia tone applied. To display it in a `UIImageView`, you can just set the `UIImageView`'s image property to the new image.

TIP

More than a dozen built-in Core Image filters are available for use in your applications. To learn the names of the filters and the parameters they require, be sure to read the developer document "Core Image Filter Reference" as well as the iOS release notes.

You've just learned the basics of working with quite a few of the iOS media frameworks; now it's time to put them to use in a media sandbox application.

I've Jumped Ahead and Written Some Code to Display Movies/ Record Audio/Play Audio, but It Doesn't Work. Why?

The transition to ARC has resulted in a few things that don't work exactly as you'd expect: movie players that come up as a black screen, audio recorders/players that don't seem to do a thing. The Apple discussion forums are filled with developers reporting these issues. Thankfully, there are plenty of workarounds.

The most straightforward workaround, in my opinion, is to make sure that if you're using one of these objects, it is referenced by an instance variable/property rather than just declaring, allocating/initializing, using, and crossing our fingers that ARC cleans everything up in the right place.

We follow this approach in the tutorial so that even if the problems don't go away in a future version of iOS, you'll be able to create code that works as you want.

The Media Playground Application

This hour's exercise is less about creating a real-world application and more about building a sandbox for testing out the rich media classes that we've introduced. The finished application shows embedded or fullscreen video, records and plays audio, browses and displays images from the photo library or camera, applies a filter to the images, and browses and selects music from the device's music library.

Implementation Overview

Because *so* much is going on in this application, be careful that you don't miss any of the connections or properties that we will be defining. We start by creating an application skeleton for all the different functionality, and then we fill them in to implement the features we've been discussing.

The application has five main components. First, a video player plays an MPEG-4 video file when a button is pressed; fullscreen presentation is controlled by a toggle switch. Second, we create an audio recorder with playback features. Third, we add a button that shows the photo library or camera and a `UIImageView` that displays the chosen photo. A toggle switch controls the image source. Fourth, after an image is chosen, the user will be able to apply a `CIFilter` to it. Finally, we enable the user to choose songs from the music library and start or pause playback. The title of the currently playing song is displayed onscreen in a label.

Setting Up the Project

Begin by creating a new single-view iOS application project in Xcode. Name the new project **MediaPlayground**. We need to define more than a few frameworks and properties, so follow along closely. If you experience any errors while building the application, it's likely that the frameworks, or a corresponding `#import` statement (or both), are missing.

Adding the Frameworks

This application requires that a total of three additional frameworks be added to accommodate media playback (MediaPlayer.framework), sound playback/recording (AVFoundation.framework and CoreAudio.framework), and image filtering (CoreImage.framework), as follows:

1. Select the MediaPlayground topmost project group and be sure that the default MediaPlayground target is selected.

2. Click the Summary tab in the editor area.

3. Scroll down the summary until you find the section called Linked Frameworks and Libraries.

4. Click the + button below the list.

5. Choose MediaPlayer.framework from the list that appears, and then click Add.

Repeat this process for AVFoundation.framework, CoreAudio.framework, and CoreImage. framework.

After adding the frameworks, drag them into the Frameworks group to keep them organized. Your final project code group should look similar to Figure 19.1.

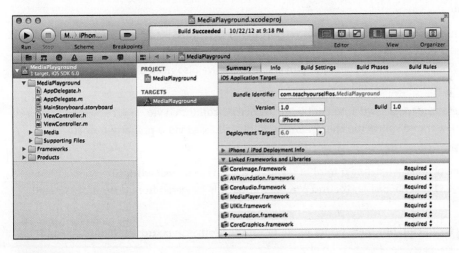

FIGURE 19.1
Make sure that you add the required frameworks.

Adding the Media Files

For this tutorial, we need to add two media files to our project: movie.m4v and norecording.wav. The first is used to demo the movie player, and the second is used as a default sound to play in our audio recorder if we haven't made a recording yet.

Locate the Media folder included in this hour's project folder, and drag it into your Xcode project code group so that we can access it directly in the application. Be sure to choose to copy the files and choose to create a new group, when prompted.

Planning the Properties and Connections

There's no way to sugarcoat this: We need a lot of stuff to make this application work. Let's start with the outlets/variables and then move on to the actions. For the media player, we need an outlet for the toggle switch that enables fullscreen mode: `toggleFullScreen`. We'll add a `UIView` as a placeholder for the media player itself; this is the same trick we used in Hour 17, "Using Advanced Touches and Gestures," for an image view. This view will be named `movieRegion`.

We also need a private instance variable for the `MPMoviePlayerController` instance itself: `_moviePlayer`. This won't be an outlet because we are creating it in code, not through the Interface Builder (IB) editor.

For the AV Foundation audio recording and playback, we want an outlet for the Record button so that we can toggle its title between record and stop; we'll name this `recordButton`. We also want an instance variable declared for both the audio recorder (`AVAudioRecorder`) and the audio player (`AVAudioPlayer`): `_audioRecorder` and `_audioPlayer`, respectively. Again, these do not need to be exposed as outlets, because there is nothing in the user interface (UI) to connect to them.

To implement music playback, we need a reference to a Play Music button that changes between Play and Pause (`musicPlayButton`) and a label that presents the name of the current track (`displayNowPlaying`). As with the other players/recorder, we also need an instance variable for the music player itself: `_musicPlayer`.

For the camera, the toggle switch to enable the camera is connected via `toggleCamera`. The image view that displays the chosen image will be accessed via a property named `displayImageView`.

Moving to the actions, we define a total of seven: `playMovie`, `recordAudio`, `playAudio`, `choose Image`, `applyFilter`, `chooseMusic`, and `playMusic`. Each is triggered from a similarly named button.

None of this is difficult, but there's a lot to do. Open the MainStoryboard.storyboard file and get started.

Designing the Interface

This application has a total of seven buttons (`UIButton`), two switches (`UISwitch`), three labels (`UILabel`), a `UIView`, and a `UIImageView`. The UIView acts as a placeholder for an embedded video player that is added programmatically. iPad developers will find this exercise much easier than those on the iPhone; we're really pushing the limits of what can fit in a view.

Figure 19.2 represents a potential design for the application. Feel free to use this approach with your layout, or modify it to suit your fancy, with a few minor exceptions. Be sure to title the button for recording audio **Record Audio** and the button for initiating music library playback as **Play Music**. We'll be changing those titles programmatically, so it's important to have a consistent starting point. Finally, make sure you add a label with the default text No Song Playing at the bottom of the view. This updates with the name of the song the user has chosen to play.

FIGURE 19.2
Create an interface for the different functions we'll be implementing.

TIP

You might want to consider using the Attributes Inspector (Option-Command-4) to set the UIImageView mode to Aspect Fill or Aspect Scale to make sure that your photos look right within the view.

Creating and Connecting the Outlets and Actions

When finished creating your view, switch to the assistant editor to get ready to start making connections. For your reference, the following list presents the required outlets, and then the actions, from top to bottom in my version of the interface:

▶ **The fullscreen toggle for movie playback (UISwitch):** `toggleFullscreen`

▶ **The view acting as a placeholder for the video player (UIView):** `movieRegion`

▶ **The Record Audio button (UIButton):** `recordButton`

▶ **The camera toggle switch (UISwitch):** `toggleCamera`

▶ **The image view (UIImageView):** `displayImageView`

▶ **The Play Music button (UIButton):** `musicPlayButton`

▶ **The default No Song Playing feedback label (UILabel):** `displayNowPlaying`

The actions:

▶ **The Play Movie button (UIButton):** `playMovie`

▶ **The Record Audio button (UIButton):** `recordAudio`

▶ **The Play Audio button (UIButton):** `playAudio`

▶ **The Choose Image button (UIButton):** `chooseImage`

▶ **The Apply Filter button (UIButton):** `applyFilter`

▶ **The Choose Music button (UIButton):** `chooseMusic`

▶ **The Play Music button (UIButton):** `playMusic`

Adding the Outlets

The bad news is that there are a bunch of outlets you need to add. The good news is that there isn't anything tricky about any of them. With the assistant editor open and the MainStoryboard. storyboard file selected, Control-drag from the fullscreen toggle switch to just below the `@interface` line in ViewController.h. When prompted, make a connection to `toggleFullscreen`, as shown in Figure 19.3.

Move through the rest of the outlets listed, repeating this process until each outlet has been added to the file. Time for the actions.

FIGURE 19.3
Work through the outlet list, adding each to ViewController.h.

Adding the Actions

Once all seven outlets are accounted for, move on to the actions. Begin by Control-dragging from the Play Movie button to below the last @property declaration you added. When prompted, create a new action named **playMovie**, as shown in Figure 19.4.

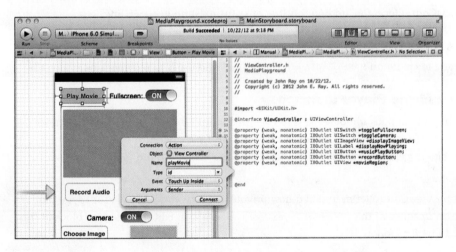

FIGURE 19.4
Connect the buttons to their actions.

Repeat this for each of the other buttons, until you've created a total of seven new actions in the ViewController.h file. Now pat yourself on the back; you've just finished the most tedious part of the project.

Implementing the Movie Player

In this exercise, we use the `MPMoviePlayerController` class that you learned about earlier this hour. Only three methods stand between us and movie-playback bliss:

▶ `initWithContentURL`: Provided with an `NSURL` object, this method initializes the movie player and prepares it for playback.

▶ `play`: Begins playing the selected movie file.

▶ `setFullscreen:animated`: Sets the movie playback to fullscreen.

Because the movie controller itself implements a graphical user interface (GUI) for controlling playback, we don't need to implement additional features ourselves. If we wanted to, however, there are many other methods, including `stop`, that we could call on to control playback.

TIP

Dozens of methods and properties are available for the movie player. You can get pointers to additional resources in the "Further Exploration" section at the end of this hour.

Preparing to Use the Media Player Frameworks

Before we can use the movie player, we must import the Media Player framework interface file. Modify the ViewController.h file, adding this line after the existing `#import` line:

```
#import <MediaPlayer/MediaPlayer.h>
```

Now we're ready to create an `MPMoviePlayerController` and use it to play back our video file.

Initializing a Movie Player Instance

The first step in playing back a movie file is to declare and initialize an instance of the movie player (`MPMoviePlayerController`) object. We will be setting up the movie player as an instance variable/property for our class and initializing the content in the `viewDidAppear` method.

Begin by editing ViewController.m to add a new private instance variable `_moviePlayer` that will reference an instance of the `MPMoviePlayerController` class. Edit the interface block at the top of the file to read as follows:

```
@interface ViewController () {
    MPMoviePlayerController *_moviePlayer;
}
@end
```

We now have a variable, _moviePlayer, that we can use throughout our class. Our next step is to initialize it with content. Add the viewDidAppear method to ViewController.m as shown in Listing 19.10.

LISTING 19.10   Initialize the Movie Player

```
 1: - (void)viewDidAppear:(BOOL)animated {
 2:      [super viewDidAppear:animated];
 3:      //Set up the movie player
 4:      NSString *movieFile = [[NSBundle mainBundle]
 5:                              pathForResource:@"movie" ofType:@"m4v"];
 6:      _moviePlayer = [[MPMoviePlayerController alloc]
 7:                      initWithContentURL: [NSURL
 8:                                          fileURLWithPath:
 9:                                          movieFile]];
10:      _moviePlayer.allowsAirPlay=YES;
11:      [_moviePlayer.view setFrame: self.movieRegion.frame];
12: }
```

Line 4 declares a string movieFile that will hold the path to the movie file (movie.m4v) we added to our project.

Next, lines 6–9 allocate and initialize _moviePlayer itself using an NSURL instance that contains the path from movieFile. Believe it or not, this is most of the "heavy lifting" of the movie playback method. After we've completed this line, we could (if we wanted) immediately call the play method on the _moviePlayer object and see the movie play.

Line 10 enables AirPlay for video playback.

Lines 11–12 sets the frame (size and location) of the movie player to the frame of the movie Region. This is our "trick" to use IB to lay out the location of the player, even though it isn't directly represented as an object in IB.

That handles preparing the movie player. We can now use it anywhere in our application to display the movie.m4v video file—but we know exactly where it needs to be displayed: in the playMovie method.

TIP

Wondering why we set up the movie player in viewDidAppear versus viewDidLoad where we normally do that sort of thing? The reason is that the iOS 6 Auto Layout system won't yet return a valid frame value for the movieRegion UIView that we're using as a placeholder. It isn't until we get to viewDidAppear that iOS knows the coordinates where the view is being displayed.

Implementing Movie Playback

For movie playback in the MediaPlayground application to work, we need to implement the playMovie method. This is invoked by the Play Movie button we added to the interface earlier. Let's add the method, and then walk through how it works.

Update the playMovie method in the ViewController.m file as shown in Listing 19.11.

LISTING 19.11   Initiate Movie Playback

```
 1: - (IBAction)playMovie:(id)sender {
 2:     [self.view addSubview:_moviePlayer.view];
 3:     [[NSNotificationCenter defaultCenter] addObserver:self
 4:                               selector:@selector(playMovieFinished:)
 5:                       name:MPMoviePlayerPlaybackDidFinishNotification
 6:                                        object:_moviePlayer];
 7:
 8:     if ([self.toggleFullscreen isOn]) {
 9:         [_moviePlayer setFullscreen:YES animated:YES];
10:     }
11:
12:     [_moviePlayer play];
13: }
```

Line 2 adds the _moviePlayer's view to our current view.

MPMoviePlayerController sends the MPMoviePlayerPlaybackDidFinishNotification when it has finished playing a piece of media. In lines 3–6, we register that notification for our _moviePlayer object and ask the notification center to invoke the playMovieFinished method when it receives the notification. Put simply, when the movie player is finished playing the movie (or the user stops playback), the playMovieFinished method is called.

Lines 8–10 check to see whether the toggle switch (toggleFullscreen) is turned "on" using the UISwitch instance method isOn. If the switch *is* on, we use the method setFullscreen:animated to expand the movie to fill the device's screen. If the switch is off, we do nothing, and the movie plays back within the confines of the frame we defined.

Finally, line 12 begins playback.

Handling Cleanup

To clean up after the movie playback has finished, we remove the _moviePlayer object from our view. You do not have to do so if you don't mind looking at the movie player block in the interface; but if we remove it, users can't distract themselves by interacting with it. To handle the cleanup, implement the `playMediaFinished:` method (triggered by the notification center) to the ViewController.m file, as shown in Listing 19.12.

LISTING 19.12   Clean Up After the Movie Player

```
1: -(void)playMovieFinished:(NSNotification*)theNotification
2: {
3:     [[NSNotificationCenter defaultCenter]
4:       removeObserver:self
5:       name:MPMoviePlayerPlaybackDidFinishNotification
6:       object:_moviePlayer];
7:
8:     [_moviePlayer.view removeFromSuperview];
9: }
```

Two things need to happen in this method. First, in lines 3–6, we tell the notification center that it can stop looking for the `MPMoviePlayerPlaybackDidFinishNotification` notification. Because we're done with playback from the movie player object, there's no point in keeping it around until we play the movie again. Second, Line 8 then removes the embedded movie player view from the main application view.

Movie playback is now available in the application, as demonstrated in Figure 19.5. Choose Run in the Xcode toolbar, press the Play Movie button, and sit back and enjoy the show.

Implementing Audio Recording and Playback

In the second part of the tutorial, we add audio recording and playback to the application. Unlike the movie player, we use classes within the AV Foundation framework to implement these features.

For the recorder, we use the `AVAudioRecorder` class and these methods:

▶ **initWithURL:settings:error:** Provided with an `NSURL` instance pointing to a local file and `NSDictionary` containing a few settings, this method returns an instance of a recorder, ready to use.

▶ **record:** Begins recording.

▶ **stop:** Ends the recording session.

FIGURE 19.5
The application will now play the video file when Play Movie is touched.

Not coincidentally, the playback feature, an instance of AVAudioPlayer, uses some very similar methods:

▶ **initWithContentsOfURL:error:** Creates an audio player object that can be used to play back the contents of the file pointed to by an NSURL object

▶ **play:** Plays back the audio

Preparing to Use the Media Player Frameworks

To use the AV Foundation framework fully, we must import the two sets of interface files: AVFoundation.h and CoreAudioTypes.h. Modify the ViewController.h file by adding these lines after the existing #import lines:

```
#import <AVFoundation/AVFoundation.h>
#import <CoreAudio/CoreAudioTypes.h>
```

NOTE

We do not implement the `AVAudioPlayerDelegate` protocol in this implementation because we don't really need to know when the audio player has finished; it can take as long as it needs.

Implementing Audio Recording

To add audio recording to the project, we need to create the `recordAudio:` method. Before we do, though, let's think through this a bit. What happens when we initiate a recording? In this application, recording continues until we press the button again.

To implement this functionality, the "recorder" object itself must persist between calls to the `recordAudio:` method. We make sure that this happens by adding an `_audioRecorder` instance variable in the ViewController.m file to hold the `AVAudioRecorder` object. Update ViewController.m with the new instance variable:

```
@interface ViewController () {
    MPMoviePlayerController *_moviePlayer;
    AVAudioRecorder *_audioRecorder;
}
@end
```

Next, we allocate and initialize the controller in the `viewDidLoad` method, making it available anywhere and anytime we need it. Edit ViewController.m and add the code in Listing 19.13 to `viewDidLoad`.

LISTING 19.13 Create and Initialize the Audio Recorder

```
 1: - (void)viewDidLoad
 2: {
 3:     [super viewDidLoad];
 4:
 5:     //Set up the audio recorder
 6:     NSURL *soundFileURL=[NSURL fileURLWithPath:
 7:                         [NSTemporaryDirectory()
 8:                             stringByAppendingString:@"sound.caf"]];
 9:
10:     NSDictionary *soundSetting;
11:     soundSetting = [NSDictionary dictionaryWithObjectsAndKeys:
12:     soundSetting = @{AVSampleRateKey:@44100.0F,
13:                     AVFormatIDKey:@(kAudioFormatMPEG4AAC),
14:                     AVNumberOfChannelsKey:@2,
15:                     AVEncoderAudioQualityKey:@(AVAudioQualityHigh)
16:     };
17:
18:     _audioRecorder = [[AVAudioRecorder alloc]
```

```
19:                              initWithURL: soundFileURL
20:                              settings: soundSetting
21:                              error: nil];
22:
23: }
```

The audio recorder implementation begins at line 5.

Starting with the basics, lines 6–8 declare and initialize a URL, soundFileURL, which points to the sound file we are going to record. We use the NSTemporaryDirectory() function to grab and the temporary directory path where your application can store its sound, and we concatenate on the name of the sound file itself: sound.caf.

Lines 10–16 create an NSDictionary object that contains keys and values for configuring the format of the sound being recorded. This is identical to the code introduced earlier in this hour.

In lines 18–21, the audio recorder, _audioRecorder, is initialized with soundFileURL and the settings stored in the soundSettings dictionary. We pass nil to the error parameter because we don't (for this example) care whether an error occurs. If we did experience an error, it would be returned in a value passed to this parameter.

Controlling Recording

With _audioRecorder allocated and initialized, all that we need to do is implement recordAudio so that the record and stop methods are invoked as needed. To make things interesting, we'll update the recordButton title to read Record Audio or Stop Recording when pressed.

Update the recordAudio method stub in ViewController.m with the code in Listing 19.14.

LISTING 19.14   The Initial recordAudio Method

```
 1: - (IBAction)recordAudio:(id)sender {
 2:     if ([self.recordButton.titleLabel.text
 3:         isEqualToString:@"Record Audio"]) {
 4:         [_audioRecorder record];
 5:         [self.recordButton setTitle:@"Stop Recording"
 6:                          forState:UIControlStateNormal];
 7:     } else {
 8:         [_audioRecorder stop];
 9:         [self.recordButton setTitle:@"Record Audio"
10:                          forState:UIControlStateNormal];
11:     }
12: }
```

Notice that I said this is in the initial implementation? We'll be modifying this slightly when implementing the audio playback because it serves as a lovely place to load up the audio we've recorded and prepare to play it.

For now, let's check out what this does.

In line 2, the method checks the title of the recordButton variable. If it is set to Record Audio, the method uses [_audioRecorder record] to start recording (line 4), and then in lines 5–6, it sets the recordButton title to Stop Recording. If the title *doesn't* read Record Audio, we're already in the process of making a recording. In this case, we use [_audioRecorder stop] in line 8 to end the recording and set the button title back to Record Audio in lines 9–10.

That's it for recording, Let's implement playback so that we can actually *hear* what we've recorded.

Implementing Audio Playback

To implement the audio player, we create an instance variable, _audioPlayer, that we can use throughout our application. We then initialize it to a default sound in viewDidLoad so that there is something to play back even if the user hasn't made a recording.

Begin by adding another new private instance variable in ViewController.m:

```
@interface ViewController () {
    MPMoviePlayerController *_moviePlayer;
    AVAudioRecorder *_audioRecorder;
    AVAudioPlayer *_audioPlayer;
}
@end
```

Now, allocate and initialize the player in the viewDidLoad method by adding the code in Listing 19.15.

LISTING 19.15 Prepare the Audio Player with a Default Sound

```
 1: - (void)viewDidLoad
 2: {
 3:     [super viewDidLoad];
 4:
 5:     //Set up the audio recorder
 6:     NSURL *soundFileURL=[NSURL fileURLWithPath:
 7:                          [NSTemporaryDirectory()
 8:                          stringByAppendingString:@"sound.caf"]];
 9:
10:     NSDictionary *soundSetting;
11:     soundSetting = [NSDictionary dictionaryWithObjectsAndKeys:
12:     soundSetting = @{AVSampleRateKey:@44100.0F,
13:                     AVFormatIDKey:@(kAudioFormatMPEG4AAC),
14:                     AVNumberOfChannelsKey:@2,
15:                     AVEncoderAudioQualityKey:@(AVAudioQualityHigh)
16:     };
17:
```

```
18:        _audioRecorder = [[AVAudioRecorder alloc]
19:                          initWithURL: soundFileURL
20:                          settings: soundSetting
21:                          error: nil];
22:
23:        //Set up the audio player
24:        NSURL *noSoundFileURL=[NSURL fileURLWithPath:
25:                          [[NSBundle mainBundle]
26:                          pathForResource:@"norecording" ofType:@"wav"]];
27:        _audioPlayer =  [[AVAudioPlayer alloc]
28:                          initWithContentsOfURL:noSoundFileURL error:nil];
29:
30: }
```

The setup of the audio player begins in line 24. Here, an NSURL, noSoundFileURL, is created to reference the file norecording.wav that was added to your project when you added the Media folder.

Line 37 allocates and initializes the audio player (_audioPlayer) with the contents of the noSoundFileURL. The _audioPlayer object can now be used to initiate playback of this default sound.

Controlling Playback

To start playing back the audio file that is referenced by _audioPlayer, all we need to do is send it the message play. Update the playAudio method to include to do just that. Listing 19.16 shows the full implementation of playAudio.

LISTING 19.16 The playAudio Method

```
- (IBAction)playAudio:(id)sender {
      [_audioPlayer play];
}
```

If you run the application now, you should be able to record sounds, but every time you press Play Audio, you'll hear the sound norecording.wav. This is because we never load the sound that has been recorded.

Loading the Recorded Sound

The perfect place to load the recording is after the user has clicked Stop Record in the record Audio method. Update recordAudio as shown in Listing 19.17.

LISTING 19.17   The Completed `recordAudio` Method

```
 1: - (IBAction)recordAudio:(id)sender {
 2:     if ([self.recordButton.titleLabel.text
 3:             isEqualToString:@"Record Audio"]) {
 4:         [_audioRecorder record];
 5:         [self.recordButton setTitle:@"Stop Recording"
 6:                              forState:UIControlStateNormal];
 7:     } else {
 8:         [_audioRecorder stop];
 9:         [self.recordButton setTitle:@"Record Audio"
10:                              forState:UIControlStateNormal];
11:         // Load the new sound in the _audioPlayer for playback
12:         NSURL *soundFileURL=[NSURL fileURLWithPath:
13:                             [NSTemporaryDirectory()
14:                                 stringByAppendingString:@"sound.caf"]];
15:         _audioPlayer =  [[AVAudioPlayer alloc]
16:                             initWithContentsOfURL:soundFileURL error:nil];
17:     }
18: }
```

Lines 12–14 should look familiar because, once again, they grab and store the temporary directory and use it to initialize an NSURL object, soundFileURL, that points to the sound.caf file we've recorded.

In lines 15–16, the audio player, _audioPlayer, is allocated and initialized with the contents of soundFileURL.

Try running the application again and see what happens. Now when you press the Play Audio button, you'll hear the default sound when no recording has been made; or, if the user has recorded audio, the recording will play.

CAUTION

Why Don't I Have to Clean Up After All the Audio Player Instances?

If you're filling the memory with audio players, you might be wondering: Each time a new sound is recorded, must a new audio player be allocated and initialized? The answer is no.

Each time a new audio player is created, the reference to the old player is removed, meaning that ARC automatically makes sure that the memory used is released. If you're really concerned, however, you can implement the AVAudioPlayer delegate method audioPlayerDidFinishPlaying: successfully to set the audio player object to nil.

It's time to move on to the next part of this hour's exercise: accessing and displaying photos from the photo library and camera.

Implementing the Photo Library and Camera

iDevices are great for storing pictures and, with the new high-quality camera in the iPhone, great for taking pictures, too. By integrating the photo library with your apps, you can directly access any image stored on the device or take a new picture and use it within your application. In this hour's tutorial, we interact with the library by implementing an instance of the UIImagePickerController class. We display the image picker interface using the method presentViewController:animated:completion within our main ViewController instance.

Preparing the Image Picker

To use the UIImagePickerController, we don't need to import any new interface files, but we do need to state that our class will conform to a few protocols, specifically the UIImagePickerControllerDelegate and UINavigationControllerDelegate protocols.

Update the @interface line in ViewController.h to include these new protocols:

```
@interface ViewController : UIViewController
        <UIImagePickerControllerDelegate,UINavigationControllerDelegate>
```

Now we're set to implement the UIImagePickerController using the methods described at the start of this hour. In fact, the code we use is very similar to what you've already seen.

Displaying the Image Picker

When a user touches the Choose Image button, our application triggers the method choose Image. Within this method, we will allocate the UIImagePickerController, configure the type of media (camera or library) that it will be browsing, set its delegate, and then display it.

Enter the chooseImage method shown in Listing 19.18.

LISTING 19.18   The chooseImage Implementation

```
 1: - (IBAction)chooseImage:(id)sender {
 2:     UIImagePickerController *imagePicker;
 3:     imagePicker = [[UIImagePickerController alloc] init];
 4:
 5:     if ([self.toggleCamera isOn]) {
 6:         imagePicker.sourceType=UIImagePickerControllerSourceTypeCamera;
 7:     } else {
 8:         imagePicker.sourceType=UIImagePickerControllerSourceTypePhotoLibrary;
 9:     }
10:     imagePicker.delegate=self;
11:
12:     [[UIApplication sharedApplication] setStatusBarHidden:YES];
13:     [self presentViewController:imagePicker animated:YES completion:nil];
14: }
```

In lines 2–3, imagePicker is allocated and initialized as an instance of UIImagePickerController.

Lines 5–9 set the sourceType property of the image picker to UIImagePickerControllerSourceTypeCamera if the toggleCamera switch is set to on or UIImagePickerControllerSourceTypePhotoLibrary if it isn't. In other words, the user can use the toggle switch to choose from photo library images or the camera.

Line 10 sets the image picker delegate to be the ViewController class. This means we need to implement some supporting methods to handle when the user is finished choosing a photo.

In Line 12, we hide the application's status bar. This is necessary because the Photo Library and camera interfaces are meant to be viewed fullscreen.

Line 13 adds the imagePicker view controller over the top of our existing view.

Displaying the Image Picker in a Popover (iPad Only)

If you've just implemented the code in the preceding section in an iPad version of this project, you'll find that it doesn't (or at least it shouldn't!) work. Apple explicitly prohibits the use of the image picker controller on the iPad without a popover.

To add a popover, we need a private instance variable to hold the popover controller and a few extra lines of code added to Listing 19.18. Update the ViewController.m file with a new instance variable, _popoverController. The @interface block should now read as follows:

```
@interface ViewController () {
    MPMoviePlayerController *_moviePlayer;
    AVAudioRecorder *_audioRecorder;
    AVAudioPlayer *_audioPlayer;
    UIPopoverController *_popoverController;
}
@end
```

Now, delete the last line of the existing chooseImage method and add the code you learned in Hour 11 to initialize the popover controller with the imagePicker content and present it. Listing 19.19 shows the final implementation for the iPad.

LISTING 19.19 The iPad's Popover-Enabled chooseImage Implementation

```
 1: - (IBAction)chooseImage:(id)sender {
 2:     UIImagePickerController *imagePicker;
 3:     imagePicker = [[UIImagePickerController alloc] init];
 4:
 5:     if ([self.toggleCamera isOn]) {
 6:         imagePicker.sourceType=UIImagePickerControllerSourceTypeCamera;
 7:     } else {
 8:         imagePicker.sourceType=UIImagePickerControllerSourceTypePhotoLibrary;
```

```
 9:        }
10:        imagePicker.delegate=self;
11:
12:
13:        _popoverController=[[UIPopoverController alloc]
14:                          initWithContentViewController:imagePicker];
15:        [_popoverController presentPopoverFromRect:((UIButton *)sender).frame
16:                                      inView:self.view
17:                        permittedArrowDirections:UIPopoverArrowDirectionAny
18:                                    animated:YES];
19: }
```

Notice that the line that hides the status bar has also been removed (previously line 12). Because we're displaying the information in a popover, hiding the status bar doesn't really make much sense.

Showing the Chosen Image

With what we've written so far, the user can now touch the Pick Image button, but not much is going to happen when he navigates to an image. To react to an image selection, we implement the delegate method imagePickerController:didFinishPickingMediaWithInfo.

Add the imagePickerController:didFinishPickingMediaWithInfo delegate method shown in Listing 19.20 to the ViewController.m file.

LISTING 19.20   Handle the User's Selection of an Image

```
1: - (void)imagePickerController:(UIImagePickerController *)picker
2:            didFinishPickingMediaWithInfo:(NSDictionary *)info {
3:      [[UIApplication sharedApplication] setStatusBarHidden:NO];
4:      [self dismissViewControllerAnimated:YES completion:nil];
5:      self.displayImageView.image=
6:              info[UIImagePickerControllerOriginalImage];
7: }
```

After the image is chosen, we can redisplay the status bar in line 3 and then dismiss the image picker using dismissViewControllerAnimated:completion in line 4.

Lines 5–6 do all the remaining work. We access the UIImage that the user has chosen by grabbing the object in the info dictionary that is referenced by the UIImagePickerControllerOriginalImage key. This is assigned to the image property of displayImageView, displaying the image, in all its glory, in the application's view.

If you are using an iPad and implementing the image picker as a popover, add one additional line after line 6:

```
[_popoverController dismissPopoverAnimated:YES];
```

This makes the popover disappear as soon as the user selects an image. Without it, they users must touch outside of the popover to dismiss it.

Cleaning Up After the Image Picker

There is still a scenario that must be accounted for before we can call the image-picking portion of our MediaPlayground application complete. A user can click a "cancel" button within the image picker, leaving the picker without choosing anything. The `imagePickerControllerDid-Cancel` delegate method was made for exactly this situation. Implement this method to reshow the status bar, and then dismiss the image picker by calling `dismissViewControllerAnimated:completion`.

Listing 19.21 shows the full implementation of this simple method.

LISTING 19.21   Handle Canceling Image Selection

```
- (void)imagePickerControllerDidCancel:(UIImagePickerController *)picker {
    [[UIApplication sharedApplication] setStatusBarHidden:NO];
    [self dismissViewControllerAnimated:YES completion:nil];
}
```

You should now run the application and use the Choose Image button to display photos from the photo library and camera, as shown in Figure 19.6.

CAUTION

Exercise Caution If Using the Simulator!

If you're using the iOS simulator, don't try picking an image with the camera active; you'll crash the app because we didn't check for the presence of a camera.

Our next step in this hour's lesson is implementing a Core Image filter. This is applied to the chosen image when the user presses the Apply Filter button.

Implementing a Core Image Filter

In my mind, manipulating an image *should* be one of the more difficult pieces of programming that you encounter. Core Image, however, makes it easy for developers to add advanced image features to their software. In fact, implementing a filter is the easiest thing you're going to do in this hour.

FIGURE 19.6
Choose (or capture) and display photos in your application.

First, update ViewController.h to include the Core Image framework's interface file. Add the following line after the myriad other #import statements:

```
#import <CoreImage/CoreImage.h>
```

Now we're ready to use Core Image to create a new filter, configure it, and apply it to the image being displayed in our application's UIImageView.

Preparing and Applying a Filter

Remember that applying a filter requires that we work with an instance of a CIImage, but all we have is a UIImageView. We have to do a bit of conversion to apply the filter and then to display the result. Because we covered this earlier, the code shouldn't be a surprise. Implement the applyFilter method, as shown in Listing 19.22.

LISTING 19.22   Apply a Filter to the Image in the UIImageView

```
 1: - (IBAction)applyFilter:(id)sender {
 2:     CIImage *imageToFilter;
 3:     imageToFilter=[[CIImage alloc]
 4:                     initWithImage:self.displayImageView.image];
 5:
 6:     CIFilter *activeFilter = [CIFilter filterWithName:@"CISepiaTone"];
 7:     [activeFilter setDefaults];
 8:     [activeFilter setValue: @0.75F
 9:                     forKey: @"inputIntensity"];
10:     [activeFilter setValue:imageToFilter forKey: @"inputImage"];
```

```
11:      CIImage *filteredImage=[activeFilter valueForKey: @"outputImage"];
12:
13:      UIImage *myNewImage = [UIImage imageWithCIImage:filteredImage];
14:      self.displayImageView.image = myNewImage;
15: }
```

Lines 2–3 declare a new `CIImage` called `imageToFilter` and then allocate and initialize it with the `UIImage` contained within the `displayImageView` object (`UIImageView`).

Line 6 declares and initializes a new Core Image filter: `"CISepiaTone"`.

Line 7 sets the filter's defaults. You want to do this for any filter that you use.

Lines 8–9 configure the filter's `"InputIntensity"` key, setting its value to an `NSNumber` floating-point value of `0.75`. Remember, these are documented in the Core Image Filter Reference in the Xcode documentation.

Line 10 uses the filter's `"inputImage"` key to set the image that the filter will work on (`imageToFilter`), while Line 11 grabs the filtered result in a new `CIImage` (`filteredImage`).

Finally, line 13 converts the filtered image to a new `UIImage` (`myNewImage`) using the `UIImage` class method `imageWithCIImage`. The filtered image is displayed by assigning the `display ImageView`'s `image` property to `myNewImage`.

Run the application, choose a photo, and then click the Apply Filter button. The sepia filter should remove most of the saturation from the original photo and make it look all "old timey," as shown in Figure 19.7.

FIGURE 19.7
Apply a filter to your photos.

Our final step in this hour's lesson is accessing the music library and playing content. You'll notice quite a few similarities to using the photo library in this implementation.

Accessing and Playing the Music Library

To finish off this hour's project, we implement access to the iDevice music library—both selecting sound files and playing them. First, you use the `MPMediaPickerController` class to choose the music to play. We call only a single method from this class:

▶ `initWithMediaTypes`: Initializes the media picker and filters the files that are available in the picker

We'll configure its behavior with a handful of properties that can be set on the object:

▶ `prompt`: A string that is displayed to the user when choosing songs

▶ `allowsPickingMultipleItems`: Configures whether the user can choose one or more sound files

We need to conform to the `MPMediaPickerControllerDelegate` protocol so that we can react when the user chooses a playlist. The method that we add as part of the protocol is `mediaPicker:didPickMediaItems`.

To play back the audio, we take advantage of the `MPMusicPlayerController` class, which can use the playlist returned by the media picker. To control starting and pausing the playback, we use four methods:

▶ `iPodMusicPlayer`: This class method initializes the music player as an "iPod" music player, capable of accessing the music library

▶ `setQueueWithItemCollection`: Sets the playback queue using a playlist (`MPMediaItemCollection`) object returned by the media picker

▶ `play`: Starts playing music

▶ `pause`: Pauses the music playback

As you can see, when you get the hang of one of the media classes, the others start to seem very "familiar," using similar initialization and playback control methods.

Preparing to Use the Media Picker

Because the media picker uses the same Media Player framework as the movie player, we're already halfway done with our preparation; there's no need to `#import` any additional files. What we do need to do, however, is state that we will be confirming to the

MPMediaPickerControllerDelegate, because this enables us to react to a user's selections. Update the ViewController.h file to include the new protocol in the @interface line:

```
@interface ViewController : UIViewController
    <MPMediaPickerControllerDelegate,UIImagePickerControllerDelegate,
    UINavigationControllerDelegate>
```

Preparing the Music Player

To react in a meaningful way to a selection in the media picker, we need to have a way of playing back music files. Like the movie player, audio recorder, and audio player, we want to create a new music player object that we can access from anywhere in the application.

Add a new private instance variable, _musicPlayer, that will hold an instance of the MPMusicPlayerController class. The @interface block at the top of your ViewController.m file should now look like this:

```
@interface ViewController () {
    MPMoviePlayerController *_moviePlayer;
    AVAudioRecorder *_audioRecorder;
    AVAudioPlayer *_audioPlayer;
    MPMusicPlayerController *_musicPlayer;
}
@end
```

NOTE

If you're building this project on the iPad, you should also have an instance variable for a popover controller.

That sets up the property to refer to the music player, but we still need to create an instance of it. As we did with the audio player and recorder, we'll initialize the music player in the viewDidLoad method. Update viewDidLoad one last time, using the MPMusicPlayerController class method iPodMusicPlayer to return a new instance of the music player, as demonstrated in Listing 19.23.

LISTING 19.23 The Final viewDidLoad Implementation

```
1: - (void)viewDidLoad
2: {
3:     [super viewDidLoad];
4:
5:     //Set up the audio recorder
6:     NSURL *soundFileURL=[NSURL fileURLWithPath:
7:                          [NSTemporaryDirectory()
```

```
 8:                            stringByAppendingString:@"sound.caf"]];
 9:
10:     NSDictionary *soundSetting;
11:
12:     soundSetting = @{AVSampleRateKey:@44100.0F,
13:                     AVFormatIDKey:@(kAudioFormatMPEG4AAC),
14:                     AVNumberOfChannelsKey:@2,
15:                     AVEncoderAudioQualityKey:@(AVAudioQualityHigh)
16:     };
17:
18:     _audioRecorder = [[AVAudioRecorder alloc]
19:                         initWithURL: soundFileURL
20:                         settings: soundSetting
21:                         error: nil];
22:
23:     //Set up the audio player
24:     NSURL *noSoundFileURL=[NSURL fileURLWithPath:
25:                     [[NSBundle mainBundle]
26:                         pathForResource:@"norecording" ofType:@"wav"]];
27:     _audioPlayer =  [[AVAudioPlayer alloc]
28:                         initWithContentsOfURL:noSoundFileURL error:nil];
29:
30:
31:     //Set up the music player
32:     _musicPlayer=[MPMusicPlayerController iPodMusicPlayer];
33:
34: }
```

The only new code is line 32, where the _musicPlayer instance is created and assigned. We now have everything we need to display the media picker and handle playing any music files that a user may select.

Displaying the Media Picker

The display of the media picker in our application is triggered by the user touching the Choose Music button, which, in turn, starts the action chooseMusic.

To use a media picker, we follow steps similar to the image picker: Initialize and configure the behavior of the picker, and then show the picker's view controller. When the user is done with the picker, we add the playlist it returns to the music player and dismiss the picker view controller. If users decide they don't want to pick anything, we can dismiss the picker and move on.

Update the ViewController implementation file with the chooseMusic method in Listing 19.24.

LISTING 19.24   Display the Media Picker

```
 1: - (IBAction)chooseMusic:(id)sender {
 2:     MPMediaPickerController *musicPicker;
 3:
 4:     [_musicPlayer stop];
 5:     self.displayNowPlaying.text=@"No Song Playing";
 6:     [self.musicPlayButton setTitle:@"Play Music"
 7:                         forState:UIControlStateNormal];
 8:
 9:     musicPicker = [[MPMediaPickerController alloc]
10:                 initWithMediaTypes: MPMediaTypeMusic];
11:
12:     soundSetting = @{AVSampleRateKey:@44100.0F,
13:                     AVFormatIDKey:@(kAudioFormatMPEG4AAC),
14:                     AVNumberOfChannelsKey:@2,
15:                     AVEncoderAudioQualityKey:@(AVAudioQualityHigh)
16:     };
17: }
```

First, line 2 declares the instance of MPMediaPickerController, musicPicker.

Next, lines 4–7 make sure that when the picker is called the music player will stop playing its current song, the nowPlaying label in the interface is set to the default string "No Song Playing", and the playback button is set to read Play Music. These lines aren't necessary, but they keep our interface from being out of sync with what is actually going on in the application.

Lines 9–10 allocate and initialize the media picker controller instance. It is initialized with a constant, MPMediaTypeMusic, that defines the type of files (music) the user will be allowed to choose with the picker. Line 12 sets a message that will display at the top of the music picker.

In line 13, we set the allowsPickingMultipleItems property to a Boolean value (YES or NO) to configure whether the user can select one or more media files.

Line 14 sets the delegate music picker's delegate. In other words, it tells the musicPicker object to look in the ViewController for the MPMediaPickerControllerDelegate protocol methods.

Line 16 uses the musicPicker view controller to display the music library over the top of our application's view.

Handling a User's Selection

To get the playlist that is returned by media picker (an object called MPMediaItemCollection) and clean up after ourselves, we add the mediaPicker:didPickMediaItems: protocol delegate method from Listing 19.25 to our growing implementation.

LISTING 19.25   Handle a User's Music Selection

```
- (void)mediaPicker: (MPMediaPickerController *)mediaPicker
          didPickMediaItems:(MPMediaItemCollection *)mediaItemCollection {
      [_musicPlayer setQueueWithItemCollection: mediaItemCollection];
      [self dismissViewControllerAnimated:YES completion:nil];
}
```

When the user is finished picking songs in the media picker, this method is called and passed the chosen items in an MPMediaItemCollection object, mediaItemCollection. For all intents and purposes, you can consider the mediaItemCollection object to be the equivalent of a media file playlist.

In the first line of this implementation, the music player instance, _musicPlayer, is configured with the playlist via the setQueueWithItemCollection: method.

To clean things up, the view is dismissed in the second line.

Handling an Empty Selection

We've got one more situation to account for before we can wrap up the media picker: the possibility of a user exiting the media picker without choosing anything (touching Done without picking any tracks). To cover this event, we add the delegate protocol method mediaPickerDid-Cancel. As with the image picker, we just need to dismiss view controller. Add this method to the ViewController.m file, as demonstrated in Listing 19.26.

LISTING 19.26   Handle Empty Selections in the Media Picker

```
- (void)mediaPickerDidCancel:(MPMediaPickerController *)mediaPicker {
      [self dismissViewControllerAnimated:YES completion:nil];
}
```

Congratulations! You're almost finished. The media picker feature is now implemented, so our only remaining task is to add the music player and make sure that the corresponding song titles are displayed.

Playing Music

Because the _musicPlayer object was created in the viewDidLoad method of the view controller (see the start of "Implementing the Media Picker") and the music player's playlist was set in mediaPicker:didPickMediaItems:, the only real work that the playMusic method must handle is starting and pausing playback.

To spice things up a bit, we'll try to be a bit clever—toggling the musicPlayButton title between Play Music (the default) and Pause Music as needed. As a final touch, we access a property of the _musicPlayer MPMusicPlayerController object called nowPlayingItem. This property is an object of type MPMediaItem, which, in turn, contains a string property called MPMediaItemPropertyTitle set to the name of the currently playing media file (if one is available).

Putting this all together, we get the implementation of playMusic in Listing 19.27.

LISTING 19.27   The playMusic Implementation

```
 1: - (IBAction)playMusic:(id)sender {
 2:        if ([self.musicPlayButton.titleLabel.text
 3:            isEqualToString:@"Play Music"]) {
 4:            [_musicPlayer play];
 5:            [self.musicPlayButton setTitle:@"Pause Music"
 6:                                   forState:UIControlStateNormal];
 7:            self.displayNowPlaying.text=[_musicPlayer.nowPlayingItem
 8:                                   valueForProperty:MPMediaItemPropertyTitle];
 9:
10:        } else {
11:
12:            [_musicPlayer pause];
13:            [self.musicPlayButton setTitle:@"Play Music"
14:                                   forState:UIControlStateNormal];
15:            self.displayNowPlaying.text=@"No Song Playing";
16:        }
17: }
```

Line 2 checks to see whether the musicPlayButton title is set to Play Music. If it is, line 4 starts playback, lines 5–6 reset the button to read Pause Music, and lines 7–8 set the displayNowPlaying label to the title of the current audio track.

If the musicPlayButton title is *not* Play Music (line 10), the music is paused, the button title is reset to Play Music, and the onscreen label is changed to display No Song Playing.

After completing the method implementation, run the application on your iDevice to test it. Pressing the Choose Music button opens a media picker, as shown in Figure 19.8.

After you've created a playlist, press the Done button in the media picker, and then touch Play Music to begin playing the songs you've chosen. The title of the current track is displayed at the bottom of the interface.

CAUTION

The Music Library Is Not Accessible on the iOS Simulator

If you're trying to test the music playback features on the simulator, they *will not* work. You need to use a real device for this portion of the tutorial.

FIGURE 19.8
The media picker enables browsing the device's music library.

This hour's lesson covered quite a bit, but consider the capabilities you've uncovered. Your projects can now tie into the same media capabilities that Apple uses in its own apps—delivering rich multimedia to your users with a relatively minimal amount of coding.

Further Exploration

We touched on only a few of the configuration options available for the `MPMoviePlayerController`, `MPMusicPlayerController`, `AVAudioPlayer`, `UIImagePickerController`, and `MPMediaPickerController` classes—but much more customization is possible if you dig through the documentation.

The `MPMoviePlayerController` class, for example, offers the `movieControlMode` property for configuring the onscreen controls for when the movie is playing. You can also programmatically "scrub" through the movie by setting the playback starting point with the `initialPlaybackTime` property. As mentioned (but not demonstrated) in this lesson, this class can even play back a media file hosted on a remote URL—including streaming media.

Custom settings on `AVAudioPlayer` can help you create background sounds and music with properties such as `numberOfLoops` to set looping of the audio playback and `volume` for controlling volume dynamically. You can even enable and control advanced audio metering, monitoring the audio power in decibels for a given sound channel.

On the image side of things, the `UIImagePickerController` includes properties such as `allowsEditing` to enable the user to trim video clips or scale and crop images directly within the image picker. Check out the capability of this class to further control a device's cameras (rear and front) and record video.

Core Image opens up new possibilities for image editing and manipulation in your apps that would have required an extensive amount of development previously. The *Core Image Programming Guide* is a great starting point for learning about Core Image, including filters, face detection, and more.

For those interested in going a step further, you may also want to review the documents "OpenGL ES Programming Guide for iOS," "Introduction to Core Animation Programming Guide," and "Core Audio Overview." These Apple tutorials introduce you to the 3D, animation, and advanced audio capabilities available in iOS.

As always, the Apple Xcode documentation utility provides an excellent place for exploring classes and finding associated sample code.

Apple Tutorials

Getting Started with Audio & Video (accessible through the Xcode documentation): This introduction to the iOS A/V capabilities will help you understand what classes to use for what purposes. It also links to a variety of sample applications demonstrating the media features.

AddMusic (accessible through the Xcode documentation): Demonstrates the use of the `MPMediaPickerController` and the `MPMediaPickerControllerDelegate` protocol and playback via the `MPMusicPlayerController` class.

MoviePlayer (accessible through the Xcode documentation): Explores the full range of features in the `MPMoviePlayerController` class, including custom overlaps, control customization, and loading movies over a network URL.

Summary

It's hard to believe, but in the span of an hour, you've learned about nine new media classes, three protocols, and a handful of class methods and properties. These provide much of the functionality you need to create applications that handle rich media. The AV Foundation framework gives us a simple method for recording and playing back high-quality audio streams. The Media Player framework handles streaming audio and video and can even tap into the existing resources stored in the music library. The easy-to-use `UIImagePickerController` class gives us surprisingly straightforward access to visual media and cameras on the device, while Core Image allows us to manipulate our images with ease.

Because many more methods are available in the Media Player and Core Image frameworks, I recommend spending additional time reviewing the Xcode documentation if you are at all interested in building multimedia applications using these technologies.

Q&A

Q. How do I make the decision between using `MPMusicPlayerController` versus `AVAudioPlayer` for sound playback in my applications?

A. Use the `AVAudioPlayer` for audio that you include in your application bundle. Use the `MPMusicPlayerController` for playing files from the music library. Although the `MPMusicPlayerController` is capable of playing back local files, its primary purpose is integrating with the existing music library media.

Q. I want to specifically control what camera a device is using to take a picture. How can I do this?

A. You'll want to take a look at the `cameraDevice` property of the `UIImagePickerController` class. Setting this property to `UIImagePickerControllerCameraDeviceFront` will use the iPhone/iPad's front-facing camera, for example.

Workshop

Quiz

1. What class can be used to implement a high-quality audio recorder?

2. What property and associated class represent the current piece of media being played by an instance of `MPMusicPlayerController`?

3. What do we take advantage of to determine whether an `MPMoviePlayerController` object has finished playing a file?

Answers

1. The `AVAudioRecorder` class enables developers to quickly and easily add audio recording capabilities to their applications.

2. The `nowPlaying` property of the `MPMusicPlayerController` is an instance of the `MPMediaItem` class. This class contains a number of read-only properties, including title, artist, and even album artwork.

3. To determine when a movie has finished playback, the `MPMoviePlayerPlaybackDidFinish Notification` notification can be registered and a custom method called. We use this approach to release the media player object cleanly in our sample code.

Activities

1. Return to an earlier application, adding an instance of `AVAudioPlayer` that plays a looping background soundtrack. You need to use the same classes and methods described in this hour's lesson, as well as the `numberOfLoops` property.

2. Implement image editing with the `UIImagePickerController` object. To do this, you need to set the `allowsImageEditing` property and use the `UIImagePickerControllerEdited Image` key to access the edited image when it is returned by the `UIImagePickerControllerDelegate` protocol.

3. Experiment with implementing additional Core Image filters in the `MediaPlayground` application. Provide a user interface for configuring the filter's parameters.

Interacting with Other Applications

In previous hours, you learned how your applications can interact with various parts of an iDevice's hardware and software. In the preceding hour, for example, you accessed the music library. In Hour 18, "Sensing Orientation and Motion," you used the accelerometer and gyroscope. It is typical of a full-featured application to leverage these unique capabilities of a device's hardware and software that Apple has made accessible through iOS. Beyond what you have learned already, the iOS applications you develop can take advantage of some additional built-in capabilities.

Extending Application Integration

In the previous hours, you've learned how to display photos that are stored on your device, take camera pictures, play iPod music, and even add web views (essentially mini Safari windows) to your apps. In this hour, you take your apps to the next level of integration by adding access to the Address Book, email, social networking sites Twitter and Facebook, and mapping capabilities.

Address Book

The Address Book is a shared database of contact information that is available to any iOS application. Having a common, shared set of contact information provides a better experience for the user than if every application manages its own separate list of contacts. With the shared Address

Book, there is no need to add contacts multiple times for different applications, and updating a contact in one application makes the update available instantly in all the other applications.

iOS provides comprehensive access to the Address Book database through two frameworks: the Address Book and the Address Book UI frameworks.

The Address Book UI Framework

The Address Book UI framework is a set of user interface classes that wrap around the Address Book framework and provide a standard way for users to work with their contacts, as shown in Figure 20.1.

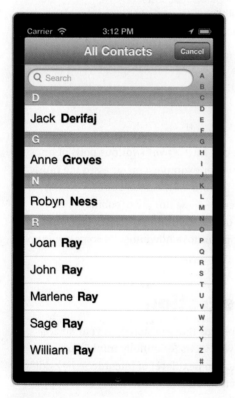

FIGURE 20.1
Access Address Book details from any application.

You can use the Address Book UI framework's interfaces to allow users to browse, search, and select contacts from the Address Book, display and edit a selected contact's information, and create new contacts. On the iPhone, the Address Book is displayed over top of your existing views in a modal view. You can choose to do the same on the iPad, or you can code it into a popover if you want.

To use the Address Book UI framework, you add it to your project and then import its interface file:

```
#import <AddressBookUI/AddressBookUI.h>
```

To display the UI for choosing a person from the Address Book, we must declare, initialize, and allocate an instance of the class ABPeoplePickerNavigationController. This class gives us a new view controller that displays our Address Book UI and enables us to "pick people." We must also set a delegate that will handle dealing with the person who is returned (if any). Finally, from our main application's view controller, we display the people picker with presentViewCont roller:animated:completion, like this:

```
ABPeoplePickerNavigationController *picker;
picker=[[ABPeoplePickerNavigationController alloc] init];
picker.peoplePickerDelegate = self;
[self presentViewController:picker animated:YES completion:nil];
```

Once the people picker is displayed, our application simply waits until the user does something. The people picker handles the UI and user interactions within the Address Book on its own. When the user does choose something, however, we must deal with it by way of the Address Book people picker navigation controller delegate. (That's a mouthful!)

People Picker Navigation Controller Delegate

The people picker delegate, as I call it, determines what happens when a user selects a person from the Address Book by implementing several methods (three to be exact). The class that is implementing these methods (such as your application's view controller class) must conform to the ABPeoplePickerNavigationControllerDelegate protocol.

The first delegate method that you need is peoplePickerNavigationControllerDidCancel. This is called if the user cancels his interactions with the people picker, so all it needs to do is use the dismissViewControllerAnimated:completion method to get rid of the display, as shown in Listing 20.1.

LISTING 20.1   Dismissing the People Picker

```
- (void)peoplePickerNavigationControllerDidCancel:
            (ABPeoplePickerNavigationController *)peoplePicker {
    [self dismissViewControllerAnimated:YES completion:nil];
}
```

In the case of a user actually touching a contact, we implement this delegate method: people PickerNavigationController:shouldContinueAfterSelectingPerson. This method serves two purposes. First, if provides us with a reference to the Address Book contact that the user touched. We can then use the Address Book framework (remember, this is all in the Address

Book *UI* framework) to work with the contact. Second, we can return YES if the user should be able to drill down further and choose individual properties from the user's Address Book entry, or we can return NO if selecting a person is as far as we want to go. Chances are, you will be implementing applications that follow the latter path. For example, consider the implementation in Listing 20.2.

LISTING 20.2 Handle the Selection of an Address Book Record

```
1: - (BOOL)peoplePickerNavigationController:
2:      (ABPeoplePickerNavigationController *)peoplePicker
3:       shouldContinueAfterSelectingPerson:(ABRecordRef)person
4:
5:      // work with the "person" address book record here
6:
7:      [self dismissViewControllerAnimated:YES completion:nil];
8:      return NO;
9: }
```

When a user touches a contact in the Address Book people picker, the method is called. All information about the individual is accessible through the person Address Book record reference, and we could work with it in the body of the method. When the method is done, we must dismiss the view (line 7) and return NO, indicating we don't want the Address Book to drill down any deeper.

The last method that we must implement for the delegate protocol requirements to be satisfied is peoplePickerNavigationController:shouldContinueAfterSelectingPerson:property: identifier. This is the method that *would* be called if we were to allow the user to drill down further than an individual contact. It returns the property of a contact record that a user touches. It must also return YES or NO depending on whether you want the user to be able to perform actions on the property the user touched. If the peoplePickerNavigationController :shouldContinueAfterSelectingPerson: returns NO, however, this method will never even be reached. Even so, we're still required to implement it, as shown in Listing 20.3.

LISTING 20.3 Handle Drilling Down to Individual Properties

```
- (BOOL)peoplePickerNavigationController:
     (ABPeoplePickerNavigationController *)peoplePicker
      shouldContinueAfterSelectingPerson:(ABRecordRef)perso
                             property:(ABPropertyID)property
                             identifier:(ABMultiValueIdentifier)identifier {
     //We won't get to this delegate method
     return NO;
}
```

This provides the basis for interacting with the Address Book UI, but it provides no facility for working with the actual data that is returned. To do that, we must turn to the Address Book framework.

The Address Book Framework

With the Address Book framework, your application can access the Address Book and retrieve and update contact data and create new contacts. You'll need it, for example, to work with the data returned by the Address Book UI framework. The Address Book framework is an older framework based on Core Foundation, which means the APIs and data structures of the Address Book framework are C rather than Objective-C. Don't let this scare you. As you'll see, the Address Book framework is still clean, simple, and easy to use, despite its C roots.

To use the Address Book framework, add it to your project, and then import the interface file:

```
#import <AddressBook/AddressBook.h>
```

Despite the somewhat unusual syntax provided by the C functions in the Address Book framework, it isn't difficult to use. For example, imagine that we're implementing the `peoplePicker NavigationController:shouldContinueAfterSelectingPerson:` method and have just received a variable, person (`ABRecordRef`), from the method. From this reference, we can access the contact's full Address Book entry using the function `ABRecordCopy(<ABRecordRef>,< requested property>)`.

To get the contact's first name, this looks like the following:

```
firstName=(__bridge NSString *)ABRecordCopyValue(person,
        kABPersonFirstNameProperty);
```

To access properties that might have multiple values (called an `ABMultiValueRef`), we can use the `ABMultiValueGetCount` function. For example, to check to see how many email addresses the contact has, we could write this:

```
ABMultiValueRef emailAddresses;
emailAddresses = ABRecordCopyValue(person, kABPersonEmailProperty);
int countOfAddresses=ABMultiValueGetCount(emailAddresses);
```

Then, to grab the first email address listed for the contact, we can use the function `ABMulti ValueCopyValueAtIndex(<ABMultiValueRef>,<index>)`:

```
firstEmail=(__bridge NSString *)ABMultiValueCopyValueAtIndex(emailAddresses, 0);
```

You get quite a bit of practice interacting with these methods (and a few others) in the tutorial in this hour. For a full list of all the properties that can be stored for a person (including whether they are multivalue properties), review the `ABPerson` reference for iOS in the developer documentation.

Email Messages

In the preceding hour, you learned how to enable a user to use Apple's image picker interfaces to select a photo for your application. Showing a system-supplied view controller is a common pattern in iOS, and the same approach is used in the Message UI framework to provide an interface for sending email, as demonstrated when sending a link from Mobile Safari (see Figure 20.2).

FIGURE 20.2
Present an email composition view to your users.

Your application provides the initial values for the email and then acts as a delegate while temporarily stepping out of the way and letting the user interact with the system-supplied interface for sending email. This is the same interface users use in the Mail application to send email, so they will find it familiar.

NOTE

Similar to how the previous hour's app did not include any of the details of working with the iOS database of photos or music, you do not need to include any of the details about the email server your user is using or how to interact with it to send an email. iOS takes care of the details of sending email at the expense of some lower-level control of the process. The trade-off makes it very easy to send email from your application.

To use the Message UI framework, you need to add the framework to your project and then update the class (probably your view controller) accessing the framework to include its interface file:

```
#import <MessageUI/MessageUI.h>
```

To display a Mail compose window, you must allocate and initialize a
`MFMailComposeViewController` object. This handles the display of the email message. Next, you need to create an array of email addresses that will be used as recipients and use the `set-ToRecipients` method to configure the Mail compose view controller with the addresses. Finally, a delegate for handling completion of sending the message is assigned, and the compose view controller is presented with `presentViewController:animated:completion`. Listing 20.4 shows a simple implementation of this process.

LISTING 20.4   **Preparing and Showing the Compose Dialog**

```
1:      MFMailComposeViewController *mailComposer;
2:      NSArray *emailAddresses;
3:
4:      mailComposer=[[MFMailComposeViewController alloc] init];
5:      emailAddresses=@[@"me@myemail.com"];
6:
7:      mailComposer.mailComposeDelegate=self;
8:      [mailComposer setToRecipients:emailAddresses];
9:      [self presentViewController:mailComposer animated:YES completion:nil];
```

Lines 1 and 2 declare the Mail compose view controller and an array of email addresses, respectively.

In line 4, the Mail compose view controller is allocated and initialized.

Line 5 initializes the array of addresses with a single address: `"my3@myemail.com"`.

Line 7 sets the delegate for the Mail compose view controller. The delegate is responsible for handling any tasks that need to happen after the message is sent or canceled.

Line 8 assigns the recipients to the Mail compose view controller, and line 9 displays the compose window.

The Mail Compose View Controller Delegate

Like the Address Book people picker, the Mail compose view controller requires that we conform to a protocol (`MFMailComposeViewControllerDelegate`) that implements a cleanup method that is called when the user finishes using the compose window. This method is `mailCompose Controller:didFinishWithResult:error`. In most cases, this method needs to do nothing more than dismiss the Mail Compose view controller, as shown in Listing 20.5.

LISTING 20.5 Handle the Composition Completion

```
- (void)mailComposeController:(MFMailComposeViewController*)controller
           didFinishWithResult:(MFMailComposeResult)result
                       error:(NSError*)error {
    [self dismissViewControllerAnimated:YES completion:nil];
}
```

If you're interested in what happened that resulted in the message composition view going away, however, you can look at the `MFMailComposeResult` result value, which may be one of these (self-explanatory) constants: `MFMailComposeResultCancelled`, `MFMailComposeResultSaved`, `MFMailComposeResultSent`, `MFMailComposeResultFailed`.

Posting to Social Networking Sites

Very similar to preparing email messages with iOS is the process of posting to social networking sites. Just include the Social framework, create a compose view controller for the service you want to use, and then display it modally. Figure 20.3 shows the iOS tweet compose view in action.

Unlike Mail, however, after you've presented the compose view, you don't need to deal with any cleanup. You simply display the view and you're done. Let's take a quick look at what this might look like in code.

First, after including the Social framework, you must include its interface file:

```
#import <Social/Social.h>
```

After that, you must create an instance of the `SLComposeViewController` using the class method `composeViewControllerForServiceType`. This specialized view controller provides the user interface can currently target three social networking websites: Twitter, Facebook, and Sina Weibo (Chinese) using the constants `SLServiceTypeTwitter`, `SLServiceTypeFacebook`, and `SLServiceTypeSinaWeibo`, respectively.

Before composing a post, it is important to use the `SLComposeViewController` class method `isAvailableForServiceType` to ensure that users have an active account configured for the service they're trying to use. Then, we can set the default text for the post, an image, and even a URL with the class methods setInitialText, addImage, and addURL. Finally, the controller is presented onscreen. Listing 20.6 shows an implementation example for Facebook.

FIGURE 20.3
Provide social networking integration in your applications.

LISTING 20.6 Prepare to Post to Facebook

```
SLComposeViewController *messageComposer;
messageComposer=[SLComposeViewController composeViewControllerForServiceType:
            SLServiceTypeFacebook];
if ([SLComposeViewController isAvailableForServiceType: SLServiceTypeFacebook]) {
    [messageComposer setInitialText:@"Hello Facebook Friends!"];
    [self presentViewController:messageComposer animated:YES completion:nil];
}
```

After presenting the view controller, there's nothing else to do. The user can use the interface to change the initial text, add personal images/locations/URLs, and, of course, post the message.

NOTE

This is just a simple example. Other methods are available to add additional functionality with multiple Twitter accounts, locations, and so on. You can also add a callback function if you want to be notified when the user is done posting. If you need more advanced social networking features, start with the Social Framework Reference in the Xcode documentation.

Mapping

The iOS implementation of Apple Maps puts a responsive and fun-to-use mapping application in your palm. Yes, the iOS 6 launch brought some controversy with the switch away from Google Maps, but Apple has been making rapid updates, and there is no denying that the new maps are *beautiful*. You can bring the Apple Maps experience to your apps using Map Kit.

Map Kit enables you to embed a map into a view and provides logic needed to display the map. It handles the scrolling, zooming, and loading of new map data as needed. Applications can use Map Kit to annotate locations on the map. Map Kit can also do reverse geocoding, which means getting place information (country, state, city, address) from coordinates.

You can start using Map Kit with no code at all, just by adding the Map Kit framework to your project and an `MKMapView` instance to one of your views in Interface Builder (IB). After adding a map view, you can set several properties within the Attributes Inspector to further customize the view (see Figure 20.4). You can select between map, satellite, and hybrid modes, you can determine whether the map should use Core Location (which you learn about in the next hour) to center on the user's location, and you can control whether the user should be allowed to interact with the map through swipes and pinches for scrolling and zooming.

If you want to control your map object (`MKMapView`) programmatically, you can do so through a variety of methods. Moving and sizing the map, for example, are common activities that you may want to do programmatically. First, however, you must import the Map Kit framework interface file:

```
#import <MapKit/MapKit.h>
```

In most cases where you manipulate a map, you also need to include the Core Location framework and its interface file:

```
#import <CoreLocation/CoreLocation.h>
```

We manage our map's view by defining a map "region" and then using the `setRegion:animated` method. A region is a simple structure (not an object) called a `MKCoordinateRegion`. It has members called `center`, which is another structure called a `CLLocationCoordinate2D` (coming from Core Location and containing `latitude` and `longitude`); and `span`, which denotes how many degrees to the east, west, north, and south of the center are displayed. A degree of latitude is 69 miles. A degree of longitude, at the equator, is 69 miles. By choosing small values for the span within the region (like 0.5), we narrow our display down to just a few miles around the center point. For example, if we want to define a region centered at 60.0 degrees latitude and 60.0 degrees longitude with a span of 0.5 degrees in each direction, we can write the following:

```
MKCoordinateRegion mapRegion;
mapRegion.center.latitude=60.0;
mapRegion.center.longitude=60.0;
mapRegion.span.latitudeDelta=0.5;
mapRegion.span.longitudeDelta=0.5;
```

FIGURE 20.4
A map view in the Attributes Inspector.

To center and zoom in on this region in a map object called map, we use the following:

```
[map setRegion:mapRegion animated:YES];
```

Another common map activity is the addition of annotations. Annotations enable us to display important points on top of the map.

Annotations

Annotations can be added to maps within your applications—just like they can in online mapping services. Using annotations usually involves implementing a new subclass of MKAnnotationView that describes how the annotation should appear and what information should be displayed.

For each annotation that we add to a map, we first need a "place mark" object, MKPlaceMark, that describes its location. For the tutorial in this hour, we need just one—to show the center of a chosen ZIP code.

To understand how these objects come together, let's work through a quick example. To add an annotation to a map called map, we must allocate and position an MKPlacemark object. Initializing the place mark requires an address (accessed with the property kABPersonAddress-Property from an Address Book contact) and a structure called CLLocationCoordinate2D that contains the latitude and longitude where the marker should be placed. Once initialized, the place mark is added to the map with the MKMapView method addAnnotation, as shown in the code fragment in Listing 20.7.

LISTING 20.7   Placing an Annotation

```
1:     CLLocationCoordinate2D myCoordinate;
2:     myCoordinate.latitude = 20.0;
3:     myCoordinate.longitude = 20.0;
4:
5:     MKPlacemark *myMarker;
6:     myMarker = [[MKPlacemark alloc]
7:                     initWithCoordinate:myCoordinate
8:                     addressDictionary:fullAddress];
9:     [map addAnnotation:myMarker];
```

In this example, Lines 1–3 declare and initialize a CLLocationCoordinate2D structure (myCoordinate) that holds a latitude of 20.0 and a longitude of 20.0.

Lines 5–8 declare, allocate, and initialize a new MKPlacemark (myMarker) using myCoordinate and fullAddress, which we must either access from an Address Book entry or create by hand using the definition of an Address property in the ABPerson reference documentation. Here, we assume it has been fetched from an Address Book entry.

Finally, Line 9 adds the annotation to the map.

TIP

To remove an existing annotation from a map view, just use `removeAnnotation` in place of `addAnnotation`; the parameters are the same.

When we add the annotation, iOS is being nice. Apple provides a subclass of the `MKAnnotationView` called `MKPinAnnotationView`. When you call `addAnnotation` on the map view object, iOS is automatically creating an instance of the `MKPinAnnotationView` for you (just a pin that is placed on the map). In many cases, this is all we need. To customize the pin drop, however, we must implement the map view's delegate method `mapView:viewForAnnotation`.

For example, consider this implementation (see Listing 20.8) of `mapView:viewForAnnotation` that allocates and configures a custom instance of `MKPinAnnotationView`.

LISTING 20.8   Customizing the Annotation View

```
 1: - (MKAnnotationView *)mapView:(MKMapView *)mapView
 2:             viewForAnnotation:(id <MKAnnotation>)annotation {
 3:
 4:      MKPinAnnotationView *pinDrop=[[MKPinAnnotationView alloc]
 5:             initWithAnnotation:annotation reuseIdentifier:@"myspot"];
 6:      pinDrop.animatesDrop=YES;
 7:      pinDrop.canShowCallout=YES;
 8:      pinDrop.pinColor=MKPinAnnotationColorPurple;
 9:      return pinDrop;
10: }
```

Line 4 declares, allocates, and initializes an instance of `MKPinAnnotationView` using the `annotation` parameter that iOS sends to the `mapView:viewForAnnotation` method (we don't touch this), along with a `reuseIdentifier` string. This `reuse` identifier is a unique identifying string that allows an allocated annotation to be reused in other places. For our purposes, this could be any string you want.

The new pin annotation view, `pinDrop`, is configured through three properties in lines 6–8. The `animatesDrop` Boolean property, when true, animates the pin dropping onto the map. The `canShowCallout` property sets the pin so that it displays additional information in a callout when touched, and the `pinColor` sets the color of the onscreen pin graphic.

Once properly configured, the new pin annotation view is returned to the map view in line 9.

Dropping this method into your code creates purple pins with callouts that are animated when added to a map. Your applications, however, can create entirely new annotation view types that don't necessary look like pins. We're just reusing Apple's `MKPinAnnotationView` and adjusting the properties only slightly beyond what we would get if this method were not included at all.

NOTE

If you're interested in doing more with location than just mapping, we take a close look at Core Location in Hour 21, "Implementing Location Services." Core Location gives you direct access to the GPS and compass capabilities of your device.

Using the Address Book, Email, Social Networking, and Maps

In this hour's example, we enable users to pick a contact as their best friend from their Address Book. After they have picked their best friend, we retrieve information from the Address Book about their friend and display it nicely on the screen—including their name, photo, and email address. We enable users to show their friend's home city in an interactive map and send that friend an email or post a tweet—all within a single app screen.

Implementation Overview

This project covers quite a bit of area, but you don't have to enter an extensive amount of code. We start by creating the interface, and then add Address Book, map, and finally, email and Twitter features. Each of these requires frameworks to be added and modifications to the #import lines in our view controller's interface file. In other words, if something doesn't seem to be working, make sure you didn't skip any steps on adding the frameworks or importing their headers.

Setting Up the Project

Start Xcode and create a new single-view iOS application called **BestFriend**. This tutorial has quite a bit of functionality, but most of the action happens in methods behind the scenes. We need to add several frameworks to accommodate this functionality, and we must add a handful of connections that we know we'll need from the start.

Adding the Frameworks

Start by adding the frameworks, as follows:

1. Select the BestFriend topmost project group and be sure that the default BestFriend target is selected.

2. Click the Summary tab in the editor area.

3. Scroll down the summary until you find the section called Linked Frameworks and Libraries.

4. Click the + button below the list.

5. Choose AddressBook.framework from the list that appears, and then click Add.

Repeat this process for AddressBookUI.framework, MapKit.framework, CoreLocation.framework, MessageUI.framework, and Social.framework. After you've finished adding the frameworks, drag them into the Frameworks group to keep them organized. Your final list of linked frameworks should look similar to Figure 20.5.

FIGURE 20.5
Add all the needed frameworks to the project.

Planning the Properties and Connections

Within our application, we allow users to select an Address Book contact, and we display a name, email address, and photo for the person they choose. We show the strings through two labels (UILabel) named name and email, and the image by way of a UIImageView named photo. Finally, we have an onscreen map (MKMapView) referenced through an outlet we name **map**, and a private instance variable of the type MKPlacemark, called _zipAnnotation. The latter references a point on the map where a special annotation is displayed.

The application also implements three actions: newBFF, which is called to enable the user to choose a new friend from the Address Book; sendEmail to send an email to your buddy; and sendTweet to post a tweet to your Twitter timeline.

Designing the Interface

Next, let's open the MainStoryboard.storyboard interface file and build the application UI. The BestFriend app is a sandbox of features; instead of trying to describe where everything goes, take a look at Figure 20.6 to see my approach to an interface.

FIGURE 20.6
Create the application interface to resemble this or use your own design.

Add two labels (UILabel): one (larger) for your friend's name, the other for his or her email address. In my UI, I've chosen to clear the contents of the email label. Next, add an image view (UIImageView) that will hold your buddy's photograph from the Address Book. Use the Attributes Inspector to change the image scaling to Aspect Fill.

Drag a new instance of a map view (MKMapView) into the interface. This is the map view that ultimately displays your location and the city your buddy is in.

Finally, add three buttons (UIButton): one to choose a buddy (titled **Choose a Buddy**), another to email your buddy (titled **Send Email**), and the last to post a tweet (**Send Tweet**) to your Twitter account.

Configuring the Map View

After adding the map view, select it and open the Attributes Inspector (Option-Command-4). Use the Type drop-down menu to pick which type of map to display (satellite, hybrid, and map), and then activate all the interaction options. This makes the map show the user's current location and enables the user to pan and zoom within the map view (just like in the iOS Maps application).

Creating and Connecting the Outlets and Actions

You've done this a thousand times (okay, maybe a few dozen), so this should be pretty familiar. You need to define a total of four outlets and three actions:

- ▶ **The label that will contain the contact's name (UILabel):** name

- ▶ **The "email" label (UILabel):** email

- ▶ **The image view for showing the contact's photo (UIImageView):** photo

- ▶ **The map view (MKMapView):** map

And three actions:

- ▶ **The Choose Buddy Button (UIButton):** newBFF

- ▶ **The Send Email Button (UIButton):** sendEmail

- ▶ **The Send Tweet Button (UIButton):** sendTweet

Switch to the assistant editor and open the MainStoryboard.storyboard file to begin making connections.

Adding the Outlets

Control-drag from the label that will display our chosen contact's name to just below the @ interface line in ViewController.h. When prompted, name the new outlet **name**. Repeat this for the email address label, connecting it to an outlet named (guess what) **email**. Do the same for the image view, connecting to an outlet named **photo**. Finally, Control-drag from the map view to ViewController.h, creating a new outlet named **map**.

Adding the Actions

Next, create the new actions. Control-drag from the Choose Buddy button to below the properties you've just created. When prompted, create a new action called newBFF. Following the same process, connect the Send Email button to an action named sendEmail, and the Send Tweet button to sendTweet.

As mentioned earlier, our map view implementation can include a delegate method (mapView:viewForAnnotation) for customizing the display of annotations. To set the map view's delegate to our view controller, we can write self.map.delegate=self in code, or we can connect the map view's delegate outlet to the view controller line in our IB document outline.

Select the map view and open the Connections Inspector (Option-Command-6). Drag from the delegate outlet to the view controller line in the document outline area, as shown in Figure 20.7.

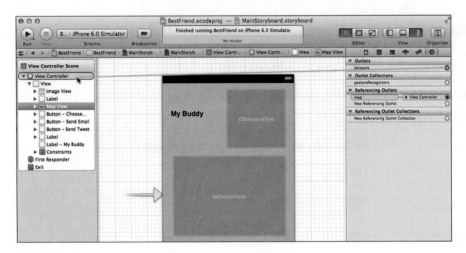

FIGURE 20.7
Set the delegate for the map view.

With those connections, you're done with the interface and its connections. Even though we will be presenting interfaces for email, Twitter, and Address Book, these elements are going to be generated entirely in code.

Implementing the Address Book Logic

There are two parts to accessing the Address Book: displaying a view that allows the user to choose a contact (an instance of the class ABPeoplePickerNavigationController) and reading the data that corresponds to that contact. Two steps... two frameworks that we need to use.

Preparing to Use the Address Book Frameworks

Before we access either the Address Book UI or the internal data, we must import the headers for the Address Book and Address Book UI frameworks and indicate that we implement the `ABPeoplePickerNavigation-ControllerDelegate` protocol.

Modify the ViewController.h file, adding these lines after the existing `#import` lines:

```
#import <AddressBook/AddressBook.h>
#import <AddressBookUI/AddressBookUI.h>
```

Next, update the `@interface` line, adding `<ABPeoplePickerNavigationControllerDelegate>` to show that we are conforming to the `ABPeoplePickerNavigationControllerDelegate` protocol:

```
@interface ViewController : UIViewController
                        <ABPeoplePickerNavigationControllerDelegate>
```

Displaying the Address Book People Picker

When the user presses the button to choose a buddy, we want to show the Address Book people picker view controller, which will provide the user with the familiar interface from the Contacts application.

Update the `newBFF` method in ViewController.m to allocate and present a picker, setting the picker's delegate to the view controller (`self`). The code, shown in Listing 20.9, should be very similar to what you saw earlier in this hour.

LISTING 20.9   The `newBFF` Implementation

```
1:  - (IBAction)newBFF:(id)sender {
2:      ABPeoplePickerNavigationController *picker;
3:      picker=[[ABPeoplePickerNavigationController alloc] init];
4:      picker.peoplePickerDelegate = self;
5:      [self presentViewController:picker animated:YES completion:nil];
6:  }
```

In line 2, we declare `picker` as an instance of `ABPeoplePickerNavigation-Controller`—a GUI object that displays the system's Address Book. Lines 3 and 4 allocate the object and set its delegate to our `ViewController` (`self`).

Line 5 displays the people picker as a view over top of our existing user interface.

Handling Cancellations and Drilldown

For the BestFriend application, we need to know only the friend the user has selected; we don't want the user to go on and select or edit the contact's properties. So, we need to implement the delegate method `peoplePickerNavigationContoller:peoplePicker:shouldContinueAfter SelectingPerson` to return `NO` when it is called—this will be our "workhorse" method. We also need our delegate methods to dismiss the person picker modal view and return control of the UI to our `ViewController`.

Before implementing this method, however, recall that there are two other methods required by the Address Book people picker delegate protocol: one to handle the conditions of the user canceling without picking someone (`peoplePickerNavigationControllerDidCancel`) and one to deal with a user drilling down further than a "person" to a specific attribute (`peoplePicker NavigationController:shouldContinueAfterSelectingPerson:property:identifier`). Because we're going to capture the user's selection before he or she even *can* drill down, this second method can just return `NO`; it is never going to get called anyway.

Implement the `peoplePickerNavigationControllerDidCancel` method in ViewController.m as shown in Listing 20.10.

LISTING 20.10   Handle Canceling the Display of the People Picker

```
- (void)peoplePickerNavigationControllerDidCancel:
                        (ABPeoplePickerNavigationController *)peoplePicker {
    [self dismissViewControllerAnimated:YES completion:nil];
}
```

Next, since drilldown to individual contact properties isn't required, add `peoplePicker NavigationController:shouldContinueAfterSelectingPerson:property:identifier` with an implementation that just returns `NO`, as shown in Listing 20.11.

LISTING 20.11   Disallow Drilldown Past an Individual Contact

```
- (BOOL)peoplePickerNavigationController:
    (ABPeoplePickerNavigationController *)peoplePicker
      shouldContinueAfterSelectingPerson:(ABRecordRef)person
                               property:(ABPropertyID)property
                             identifier:(ABMultiValueIdentifier)identifier {
    //We won't get to this delegate method
    return NO;
}
```

Choosing, Accessing, and Displaying Contact Information

If the user doesn't cancel the selection, the `peoplePickerNavigationContoller:shouldConti nueAfterSelectingPerson:` delegate method is called, and with it we are passed the selected person as an `ABRecordRef`. An `ABRecordRef` is part of the Address Book framework that we imported earlier.

We can use the C functions of the Address Book framework to read the data about this person from the Address Book. For this example, we read four things: the person's first name, picture, email address, and ZIP code. We check whether the person record has a picture before attempting to read it.

We don't access the person's attributes as the native Cocoa objects you might expect (namely, NSString and UIImage, respectively). Instead, the name string and the photo are returned as Core Foundation C data, and we convert it using the handy ABRecordCopyValue function from the Address Book framework and the imageWithData method of UIImage.

For the email address and ZIP code, we must deal with the possibility of multiple values being returned. For these pieces of data, we again use ABRecordCopyValue to grab a reference to the set of data, and the functions ABMultiValueGetCount to make sure that we actually have an email address or ZIP code stored with the contact, and ABMultiValueCopyValueAtIndex to copy the first value that we find.

Sounds complicated? It's not the prettiest code, but it's not difficult to understand.

Add the final delegate method peoplePickerNavigationController:shouldContinueAfter SelectingPerson to the ViewController.m file, as shown in Listing 20.12.

LISTING 20.12 Handle the Selection of a Contact

```
 1: - (BOOL)peoplePickerNavigationController:
 2:          (ABPeoplePickerNavigationController *)peoplePicker
 3:       shouldContinueAfterSelectingPerson:(ABRecordRef)person {
 4:
 5:      // Retrieve the friend's name from the address book person record
 6:      NSString *friendName;
 7:      NSString *friendEmail;
 8:      NSString *friendZip;
 9:
10:      friendName=(__bridge NSString *)ABRecordCopyValue
11:          (person, kABPersonFirstNameProperty);
12:      self.name.text = friendName;
13:
14:      ABMultiValueRef friendAddressSet;
15:      NSDictionary *friendFirstAddress;
16:      friendAddressSet = ABRecordCopyValue
17:          (person, kABPersonAddressProperty);
18:
19:      if (ABMultiValueGetCount(friendAddressSet)>0) {
20:          friendFirstAddress = (__bridge NSDictionary *)
21:              ABMultiValueCopyValueAtIndex(friendAddressSet,0);
22:          friendZip = friendFirstAddress[@"ZIP"];
23:      }
24:
```

```
25:     ABMultiValueRef friendEmailAddresses;
26:     friendEmailAddresses = ABRecordCopyValue
27:         (person, kABPersonEmailProperty);
28:
29:     if (ABMultiValueGetCount(friendEmailAddresses)>0) {
30:         friendEmail=(__bridge NSString *)
31:             ABMultiValueCopyValueAtIndex(friendEmailAddresses, 0);
32:         self.email.text = friendEmail;
33:     }
34:
35:     if (ABPersonHasImageData(person)) {
36:         self.photo.image = [UIImage imageWithData:
37:                             (__bridge NSData *)ABPersonCopyImageData(person)];
38:     }
39:
40:     [self dismissViewControllerAnimated:YES completion:nil];
41:     return NO;
42: }
```

Let's walk through the logic we've implemented here. First, note that when the method is called, it is passed a `person` variable of the type `ABRecordRef`. This is a reference to the person who was chosen and is used throughout the method.

Lines 6–8 declare variables that we use to temporarily store the name, email, and ZIP code strings that we retrieve from the Address Book.

Lines 10–11 use the `ABRecordCopyVal` method to copy the `kABPersonFirstNameProperty` property, as a string, to the `friendName` variable. Line 12 sets the `name` UILabel to this string.

Accessing an address is a bit more complicated. We must first get the set of addresses (each a dictionary) stored for the person, access the first address, and then access a specific field within that set. Within the Address Book, anything with multiple values is represented by a variable of type `ABMultiValueRef`. We declare a variable, `friendAddressSet`, of this type in line 14. This references *all* addresses of the `person`. Next, in line 15, we declare an `NSDictionary` called `friendFirstAddress`. We store the first address from the `friendAddressSet` in this dictionary, where we can easily access its different fields (such as city, state, ZIP, and so on). In lines 16–17, we populate `friendAddressSet` by again using the `ABRecordCopyVal` function on the `kABPersonAddressProperty` of person.

Lines 19–23 execute only if `ABMultiValueGetCount` returns a copy of greater than zero on the `friendAddressSet`. If it is zero, there are no addresses associated with the `person`, and we should move on. If there are addresses, we store the first address in `friendFirstAddress` by copying it from the `friendAddressSet` using the `ABMultiValueCopyValueAtIndex` method in lines 20–21. The index we use with this function is `0`, which is the first address in the set. The second address is `1`, third `2`, and so on.

Line 22 uses the NSDictionary to grab the ZIP code string. The key for the ZIP code is simply the string "ZIP". Review the Address Book documentation to find all the possible keys you may want to access.

Not Quite Done

In case you're wondering, the code here is not yet complete. We don't actually do anything with the ZIP code just yet. This ties into the map centering method we use later; so for now, we just get the value and ignore it.

This entire process is implemented again in lines 25–33 to grab the person's first email address. The only difference is that rather than email addresses being a set of dictionaries they're simply a set of strings. This means that after we verify that there are email addresses stored for the contact (line 29), we can just copy the first one in the set and use it immediately as a string (lines 30 and 31). Line 32 sets the email UILabel to the user's email address.

After all of that, you must be thinking to yourself, "Ugh, it's got to be a pain to deal with a person's photo." Wrong. That's actually the easy part. Using the ABPersonHasImageData function in line 35, we verify that person has an image stored. If he or she does, we copy it out of the Address Book using ABPersonCopyImageData and use that data along with the UIImage method imageWithData to return an image object and set the photo image within the interface. All of this occurs in lines 36–37.

Whew. A few new functions were introduced here, but once you get the pattern down, moving data out of Address Book becomes almost simple.

So, what about that ZIP code? What are we going to do with it? Let's find out now by implementing our interactive map.

Implementing the Map Logic

Earlier in the hour, we added two frameworks to the project: Core Location, which deals with locations; and Map Kit, which displays the embedded Apple Maps. To access the functions provided by these frameworks, we still need to import their interface files.

Preparing to Use Map Kit and Core Location

Update ViewController.h, adding two additional #import lines following the ones that are already in place:

```
#import <MapKit/MapKit.h>
#import <CoreLocation/CoreLocation.h>
```

We can now work with locations and programmatically control the map, but we still have one more piece of setup before we're home free: the annotation that we will be adding to the map. We need to create an instance variable/property to access it throughout our application.

Add a new private instance variable `_zipAnnotation` to ViewController.m, within the `@interface` block:

```
@interface ViewController () {
    MKPlacemark *_zipAnnotation;
}
@end
```

Controlling the Map Display

We already get the display of the map and the user's current location for "free" with the `MKMapView`, so the only thing we really need to do in this application is take the user's ZIP code, determine a latitude and longitude for it, and then center and zoom the map on that location. We will also drop a pushpin on the map at that location (thus, the `_zipAnnotation` place mark variable).

Unfortunately, neither Map Kit nor Core Location provides the ability to turn an address into a set of coordinates, but Google offers a service that does. By requesting the URL `http://maps.google.com/maps/geo?output=csv&q=<address>`, we get back a comma-separated list where the third and fourth values are latitude and longitude, respectively. The address that we send to Google is very flexible; it can be city, state, ZIP, street. Whatever information we provide, Google tries to translate it to coordinates. In the case of a ZIP code, it displays the center of the ZIP code's region on the map—exactly what we want.

Once we have the location, we need to use center and zoom the map. To keep things nice and neat in our application, we implement all this functionality in a nice new method called `centerMap:showAddress`. `centerMap:showAddress` takes two inputs: a string, `zipCode` (a ZIP code); and a dictionary, `fullAddress` (an address dictionary returned from the Address Book). The ZIP code is used to retrieve the latitude and longitude from Google and then adjust our `map` object to display it. The address dictionary is used by the annotation view to show a callout from the annotation pushpin.

Begin by adding a prototype for this new method to your ViewController.h file below the `IBActions` you've defined:

```
- (void)centerMap:(NSString*)zipCode showAddress:(NSDictionary*)fullAddress;
```

Now, open ViewController.m and enter the new `centerMap` method shown in Listing 20.13.

LISTING 20.13 **Center the Map and Add an Annotation**

```
 1: - (void) centerMap: (NSString*) zipCode
 2:       showAddress: (NSDictionary*) fullAddress {
 3:    NSString *queryURL;
 4:    NSString *queryResults;
 5:    NSArray *queryData;
 6:    double latitude;
 7:    double longitude;
 8:    MKCoordinateRegion mapRegion;
 9:
10:    queryURL = [[NSString alloc]
11:                initWithFormat:
12:                @"http://maps.google.com/maps/geo?output=csv&q=%@",
13:                zipCode];
14:
15:    queryResults = [[NSString alloc]
16:                initWithContentsOfURL: [NSURL URLWithString:queryURL]
17:                encoding: NSUTF8StringEncoding
18:                error: nil];
19:    queryData = [queryResults componentsSeparatedByString:@","];
20:
21:    if([queryData count]==4) {
22:        latitude=[queryData[2] doubleValue];
23:        longitude=[queryData[3] doubleValue];
24:        //      CLLocationCoordinate2D;
25:        mapRegion.center.latitude=latitude;
26:        mapRegion.center.longitude=longitude;
27:        mapRegion.span.latitudeDelta=0.2;
28:        mapRegion.span.longitudeDelta=0.2;
29:        [self.map setRegion:mapRegion animated:YES];
30:
31:        if (_zipAnnotation!=nil) {
32:            [self.map removeAnnotation: _zipAnnotation];
33:        }
34:        _zipAnnotation = [[MKPlacemark alloc]
35:                    initWithCoordinate:mapRegion.center
36:                    addressDictionary:fullAddress];
37:        [self.map addAnnotation: _zipAnnotation];
38:    }
39: }
```

Let's explore how this works. We start things off in lines 3–8 by declaring several variables we need: `queryURL`, `queryResults`, and `queryData` will hold the Google URL we need to request, the raw results of the request, and the parsed data, respectively. The latitude and longitude variables are double-precision floating-point numbers that are used to store the coordinate information gleaned from `queryData`. The last variable, `mapRegion`, is the properly formatted region that the map should display.

Lines 10–13 allocate and initialize `queryURL` with the Google URL, substituting in the `zipCode` string that was passed to the method. Lines 15–18 use the `NSString` method `initWithConten tsOfURL:encoding:error` to create a new string that contains the data located at the location defined in `queryURL`. We also make use of the `NSURL` method `URLWithString:` to turn the `que ryURL` string into a proper URL object. Any errors are disregarded.

TIP

The `initWithContentsOfURL:encoding:error` method expects an encoding type. The encoding is the manner in which the string passed to the remote server is formatted. For almost all web services, you want to use `NSUTF8StringEncoding`.

Line 19 uses the `NSString` method `componentsSeparatedByString`, which takes a string, a delimiter character, and returns an `NSArray` that breaks apart the string based on the delimiter. Google is going to hand back data that looks like this: <number>,<number>,<latitude>,<longit ude>. By invoking this method on the data using a comma delimiter (,), we get an array, `query Data`, where the third element contains the latitude and the fourth contains the longitude.

Line 21 does a *very* basic sanity check on the information we receive. If there are exactly four pieces of information found, we can assume the results are valid, and lines 22–37 are executed.

Lines 22 and 23 retrieve the strings at indices 2 and 3 of the `queryData` array and convert them to double-precision floating-point values, storing them in the `latitude` and `longitude` variables.

NOTE

Remember, an array's index starts at 0. We use an index of 2 to access the third piece of data in the array and an index of 3 to access the fourth.

Lines 25–29 define the region of the map to display and then use `setRegion:animated` to redraw the map accordingly.

Finally, lines 31–38 handle the annotation. In lines 31–33, we check to see whether an annotation has already been allocated. (This will happen if the person using the app chooses multiple addresses, resulting in the map being redrawn.) If `zipAnnotation` has already been used, we can call the `MKMapView` method `removeAnnotation` to remove the existing annotation. Once it is removed, we are free to add a new annotation to the map. Lines 34–36 allocate a new place mark, `MKPlaceMark`, using the point defined by the `map` object's `center` property and described by the address dictionary passed to the method, `fullAddress`.

With the `zipAnnotation` place mark defined, we can add it to the map using the `addAnnotation` method in line 37.

Customizing the Pin Annotation View

Earlier in the hour you learned that if you want to customize your annotation view you can do so by implementing the `mapView:viewForAnnotation` map view delegate method. We do that now, using the same code in Listing 20.8. The code is included again here (see Listing 20.14) for your reference.

LISTING 20.14   Customizing the Annotation View

```
 1: - (MKAnnotationView *)mapView:(MKMapView *)mapView
 2:             viewForAnnotation:(id <MKAnnotation>)annotation {
 3:     MKPinAnnotationView *pinDrop=[[MKPinAnnotationView alloc]
 4:                               initWithAnnotation:annotation
 5:                               reuseIdentifier:@"myspot"];
 6:     pinDrop.animatesDrop=YES;
 7:     pinDrop.canShowCallout=YES;
 8:     pinDrop.pinColor=MKPinAnnotationColorPurple;
 9:     return pinDrop;
10: }
```

Tying the Map Display to the Address Book Selection

Congratulations. Your code now has the smarts needed to locate a ZIP code on the map, zoom in, and add a pin annotation view. The last piece of magic we need to finish the mapping is to hook it into the Address Book selection so that the map is centered when a user picks a contact with an address.

Edit the `peoplePickerNavigationController:shouldContinueAfterSelectingPerson` method, adding the following line

```
[self centerMap:friendZip showAddress:friendFirstAddress];
```

immediately following this line:

```
friendZip = friendFirstAddress[@"ZIP"];
```

Our application is nearing completion. All that remains is adding the ability to email and tweet to our chosen buddy. Let the implementation begin.

Implementing the Email Logic

In our example of using the Message UI framework, we want to allow users to email a buddy by pressing the Send Mail button. We populate the To field of the email with the address that we located in the Address Book. The user can then use the interface provided by the `MFMailComposeViewController` to edit the email and send it.

Preparing to Use the Message UI Framework

As with our other examples, we need to import the Message UI interface file that corresponds to the framework we added earlier. Update ViewController.h to import the interface file by adding this line:

```
#import <MessageUI/MessageUI.h>
```

The class implementing the UI (in this case, `ViewController`) must also conform to the `MFMailComposeViewControllerDelegate`, which includes a method `mailComposeController:didFinishWithResult` that is called after the user is finished sending a message. Update the `@interface` line in ViewController.h to include this protocol:

```
@interface ViewController : UIViewController
    <ABPeoplePickerNavigationControllerDelegate,MFMailComposeViewControllerDelegate>
```

Displaying the Mail Compose View

To compose a message, we need to allocate and initialize an instance of `MFMailComposeViewController`. The recipients are configured with the `MFMailComposeViewController` method `setToRecipients`. One item of interest is that the method expects an array, so we need to take the email address for our buddy and create an array with a single element in it so that we can use the method. Once configured, the message composition view is displayed with `presentModalViewController:animated`.

Speaking of the email address, where will we access it? Glad you asked. Earlier we set the `email` `UILabel` to the address, so we just use `self.email.text` to get the address of our buddy.

Create the `sendEmail` method using Listing 20.15 as your guide.

LISTING 20.15   Configure and Display the Mail Compose View

```
 1: - (IBAction)sendEmail:(id)sender {
 2:     MFMailComposeViewController *mailComposer;
 3:     NSArray *emailAddresses;
 4:     emailAddresses=@[self.email.text];
 5:
 6:     mailComposer=[[MFMailComposeViewController alloc] init];
 7:     mailComposer.mailComposeDelegate=self;
 8:     [mailComposer setToRecipients:emailAddresses];
 9:     [self presentViewController:mailComposer animated:YES completion:nil];
10: }
```

Unlike some of the other methods we've written in this hour, there are few surprises here. Line 2 declares `mailComposer` as an instance of the `MFMailComposeViewController`—the object that displays and handles message composition. Lines 3–4 define an array, `emailAddresses`, that contains a single element grabbed from the `email UILabel`.

Lines 6–8 allocate and initialize the `MFMailComposeViewController` object, setting its delegate to `self` (`ViewController`) and the recipient list to the `emailAddresses` array. Line 9 presents the Mail compose window onscreen.

Handling Mail Completion

When a user is finished composing/sending a message, the modal composition window should be dismissed. To do this, we need to implement the `mailComposeController:didFinishWithRe` `sult` method defined in the `MFMailComposeViewControllerDelegate` protocol—exactly as demonstrated in Listing 20.5, re-created here for your reference (see Listing 20.16).

Add this to your ViewController.m implementation file.

LISTING 20.16   Dismiss the Mail Compose View

```
- (void)mailComposeController:(MFMailComposeViewController*)controller
         didFinishWithResult:(MFMailComposeResult)result
                       error:(NSError*)error {
    [self dismissViewControllerAnimated:YES completion:nil];
}
```

All that is needed is the single line to dismiss the view controller, and we're good to go. One more piece of functionality to add and our application is done.

Implementing the Social Networking Logic

The final piece of the BestFriend application is adding the logic behind the `sendTweet` method. When a user presses the Send Tweet button, we want to display a tweet compose window with the default text "I'm on my way!" This is the easiest part of this hour's lesson, so hang in there.

Preparing to Use the Social Framework

Import the Social interface file for the Social framework we added at the start of the project. Update ViewController.h one last time to import the interface file by adding this line at the bottom of your (very long) list of `#import` statements:

```
#import <Social/Social.h>
```

Using the basic social networking features doesn't require any delegate methods or protocols to be added, so this single `#import` addition is all we need to start tweeting.

Displaying the Compose View

To display a tweet compose window, we complete four tasks (one optional):

1. Declare, allocate, and initialize an instance of the SLComposeViewController.

2. Use the compose view controller class method isAvailableForServiceType to verify that we're even allowed to use Twitter.

3. (Optional) Create a default message to be displayed by calling the compose view controller instance method setInitialText.

4. Display the view with our old standby, presentViewController:animated:completion.

Open ViewController.m and implement our last method, sendTweet, as shown in Listing 20.17.

LISTING 20.17 A Simple Tweet Compose View Implementation

```
1: - (IBAction)sendTweet:(id)sender {
2:     SLComposeViewController *tweetComposer;
3:     tweetComposer=[SLComposeViewController composeViewControllerForServiceType:
4:                       SLServiceTypeTwitter];
5:     if ([SLComposeViewController isAvailableForServiceType: SLServiceTypeTwitter]) {
6:         [tweetComposer setInitialText:@"I'm on my way."];
7:         [self presentViewController:tweetComposer animated:YES completion:nil];
8:     }
9: }
```

Lines 2–4 declare and initialize tweetComposer, an instance of the social networking compose view controller of the type SLServiceTypeTwitter. Line 5 checks to make sure we are allowed to send tweets for that same service type. If we can, Line 6 sets the initial tweet text to I'm on my way, and Line 7 displays tweetComposer.

Building the Application

Use Run to test the application. Select a contact and watch as the map finds your friend's home location, zooms in, and then sets an annotation. Use the Email button to compose and send an email. Try tweeting. Fun and excitement for all.

In this project, shown in Figure 20.8, we've combined mapping, email, Twitter, and Address Book features in a single integrated application. You should now have some ideas about what is possible when you integrate existing iOS application features into your software.

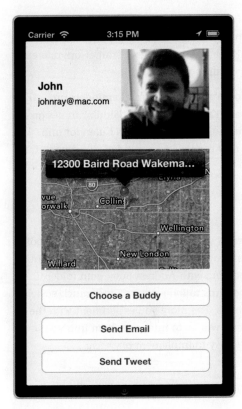

FIGURE 20.8
Mapping, email, Twitter, and Address Book integration—all in one app.

Further Exploration

Over the past few hours, you've learned much of what there is to know about accessing images, music, and sending email, but we haven't even scratched the surface of the Address Book and Address Book UI frameworks. In fact, the Address Book UI framework contains three additional modal view controllers. You can use the lower-level Address Book framework to create new contacts, set properties, and edit and delete contacts. Anything the Contacts application can do, you can do with the Address Book framework. For more detailed information about the use of these application programming interfaces (APIs), refer to the excellent guide from Apple iOS Dev Center called the *Address Book Programming Guide for iOS*.

In addition, review the Apple guide for Map Kit and complete the Core Location exercises in the next hour. Using these two frameworks, you can create complex map annotation views (MKAnnotationView) well beyond the simple pushpin annotations presented here. You can deploy these features in nearly any application that works with addresses or locations.

If your application presents a social networking opportunity, implementing Twitter and Facebook support is both fast and straightforward. What is shown here, however, is only scratching the surface of what the Social framework can do. Refer to Apple's Social Framework reference and "tweeting" source code for more examples of this exciting new tool.

Once you've mastered these integration topics, check out the Calendar and Reminders programming guide, which introduces you to Event Kit and Event Kit UI frameworks. Similar in design and function to the Address Book frameworks, these provide access to the iOS Calendar and Reminder information, including the ability to create new events and reminders directly in your application.

Summary

In this hour, you learned how to allow the user to interact with contacts from the Address Book, how to send email messages and tweets, and how to interact with the Map Kit and Core Location frameworks. Although there are some challenges to working with Address Book data (older C functions, for example), after you've established the patterns to follow, it becomes much easier. The same goes for the Map Kit and Core Location features. The more you experiment with the coordinates and mapping functions, the more intuitive it will be to integrate them into your own applications. As for email, there's not much to say: It's easy to implement *anywhere*.

Q&A

Q. Can I use the `MKMapView` when my device is offline?

A. No, the map view requires an Internet connection to fetch its data.

Q. Is there a way to differentiate between address (mailing or email) types in the Address Book data?

A. Yes. Although we did not use these features in our code, you can identify specific types (home, work, and so on) of addresses when reading Address Book data. Refer to the Address Book programming guide for a full description of working with Address Book data.

Workshop

Quiz

1. Map Kit implements discrete zoom levels for MKMapViews that you display. True or false?
2. You can avoid the older Address Book framework and use the new Address Book UI framework instead. True or false?

Answers

1. False. Map Kit requires you to define regions within your map that consist of a center point and a span. The scale of the map display is determined by the size of the span.

2. False. Although the Address Book UI framework provides user interfaces that save you a lot of time and provide familiarity to your users, you must still work with C functions and data structures from the Address Book framework when using the interfaces in your application.

Activities

1. Apply what you learned in Hour 15, "Reading and Writing Application Data," and make the BestFriend application persist the name and photo of the selected friend so that the user doesn't need to repeat the selection each time the application is run.

2. Enhance the BestFriend application to pinpoint your friend's address rather than just a ZIP code. Explore the annotation features of Map Kit to add a pushpin directly on your friend's home location.

3. Update the iPad version of the project so that the Person Picker is displayed in a popover rather than taking over the entire screen.

Implementing Location Services

What You'll Learn in This Hour:

▶ The available iOS location-sensing hardware

▶ How to read and display location information

▶ Detecting orientation with the compass

In the preceding hour's lesson, we looked briefly at the use of Map Kit to display map information in an application. In this lesson, we take the GPS capabilities of our devices a step further: We tie into the hardware capabilities of the iDevice lineup to accurately read location data and compass information.

In this hour, we work with Core Location and the electromagnetic compass. With location-enabled apps enhancing the user experience in areas such as Internet searches, gaming, and even productivity, you can add value and interest to your own offerings with these tools.

Understanding Core Location

Core Location is a framework in the iOS SDK that provides the location of the device. Depending on the device and its current state (within cell service, inside a building, and so forth), any of three technologies can be used: GPS, cellular, or WiFi. GPS is the most accurate of these technologies and will be used first by Core Location if GPS hardware is present. If the device does not have GPS hardware (WiFi iPads, for example), or if obtaining the current location with GPS fails, Core Location falls back to cellular and then to WiFi.

Getting Locations

Core Location is simple to understand and to use despite the powerful array of technologies behind it. (Some of it had to be launched into space on rockets.) Most of the functionality of Core Location is available from the location manager, which is an instance of the CLLocationManager class. You use the location manager to specify the frequency and accuracy of the location updates you are looking for and to turn on and off receiving those updates.

To use a location manager, you must first add the Core Location framework to your project and then import its interface file:

```
#import <CoreLocation/CoreLocation.h>
```

Next, you allocate and initialize an instance of the location manager, specify a delegate that will receive location updates, and start the updating, like this:

```
CLLocationManager *locManager = [[CLLocationManager alloc] init];
locManager.delegate = self;
[locManager startUpdatingLocation];
```

When the application has finished receiving updates (a single update is often sufficient), stop location updates with location manager's stopUpdatingLocation method.

Location Manager Delegate

The location manager delegate protocol defines the methods for receiving location updates. Whatever class we've designated as our delegate for receiving location updates must conform to the CLLocationManagerDelegate protocol.

There are two methods in the delegate relating to location: locationManager:didUpdateTo Location:fromLocation and locationManager:didFailWithError.

The locationManager:didUpdateToLocation:fromLocation method's arguments are the location manager object and two CLLocation objects (one for the new location and one for the previous location). The CLLocation instances provide a coordinate property that is a structure containing longitude and latitude expressed in CLLocationDegrees. CLLocationDegrees is just an alias for a floating-point number of type double.

As already mentioned, different approaches to geolocating have different inherit accuracies, and each approach may be more or less accurate depending on the number of points (satellites, cell towers, WiFi hot spots) it has available to use in its calculations. CLLocation passes this confidence measure along in the horizontalAccuracy property.

The location's accuracy is provided as a circle, and the true location could lie anywhere within that circle. The circle is defined by the coordinate property as the center of the circle and the horizontalAccuracy property as the radius of the circle in meters. The larger the horizontal Accuracy property, the larger the circle defined by it will be, so the less confidence there is in the accuracy of the location. A negative horizontalAccuracy property indicates that the coordinate is completely invalid and should be ignored.

In addition to longitude and latitude, each CLLocation provides altitude (in meters) above or below sea level. The altitude property is a CLLocationDistance, which is also just an alias for a floating-point number of type double. A positive number is an altitude above sea level, and a negative number is below sea level. Another confidence factor, this one called verticalAccuracy, indicates how accurate the altitude is. A positive `verticalAccuracy` indicates that the altitude could be off, plus or minus, by that many meters. A negative `vertical Accuracy` means the `altitude` is invalid.

Listing 21.1 shows an implementation of the location manager delegate's `locationManager:didUpdateToLocation:fromLocation` method that logs the longitude, latitude, and altitude is shown.

LISTING 21.1 Handle Location Updates

```
 1: - (void)locationManager:(CLLocationManager *)manager
 2:       didUpdateToLocation:(CLLocation *)newLocation
 3:            fromLocation:(CLLocation *)oldLocation {
 4:
 5:     NSString *coordinateDesc = @"Not Available";
 6:     NSString *altitudeDesc = @"Not Available";
 7:
 8:     if (newLocation.horizontalAccuracy >= 0) {
 9:         coordinateDesc = [NSString stringWithFormat:@"%f, %f +/- %f meters",
10:                         newLocation.coordinate.latitude,
11:                         newLocation.coordinate.longitude,
12:                         newLocation.horizontalAccuracy];
13:     }
14:
15:     if (newLocation.verticalAccuracy >= 0) {
16:         altitudeDesc = [NSString stringWithFormat:@"%f +/- %f meters",
17:                     newLocation.altitude, newLocation.verticalAccuracy];
18:     }
19:
20:     NSLog(@"Latitude/Longitude:%@   Altitude: %@", coordinateDesc,
21:             altitudeDesc);
22: }
```

The key statements to pay attention to in this implementation are the references to the accuracy measurements in lines 8 and 15, and accessing the latitude, longitude, and altitude in lines 10, 11, and 17. These are just properties, something you've grown accustomed to working with over the past 20 hours.

One element in this example that you might not be familiar with is line 20's NSLog function. NSLog, which you learn to use in Hour 24, "Application Tracing and Debugging," provides a convenient way to output information (often debugging information) without having to design a view.

The resulting output looks like this:

```
Latitude/Longitude: 35.904392, -79.055735 +/- 76.356886 meters    Altitude:
28.000000 +/- 113.175757 meters
```

Watch Your Speed

`CLLocation` also provides a property `speed`, which is based on comparing the current location with the prior location and comparing the time and distance variance between them. Given the rate at which Core Location updates, the `speed` property is not very accurate unless the rate of travel is fairly constant.

Handling Location Errors

When your application begins tracking the user's location, a warning displays on the user's screen, as shown in Figure 21.1.

FIGURE 21.1
Core Location asks permission to provide an application with location data.

If the user chooses to disallow location services, iOS does not prevent your application from running, but instead generates errors from the location manager.

When an error occurs, the location manager delegate's `locationManager:didFailWithError` method is called, letting you know the device cannot return location updates. A distinction is made as to the cause of the failure. If the user denies permission to the application, the error argument is `kCLErrorDenied`; if Core Location tries but cannot determine the location, the error is `kCLErrorLocationUnknown`; and if no source of trying to retrieve the location is available, the error is `kCLErrorNetwork`. Usually Core Location continues to try to determine the location after an error. After a user denial, however, it doesn't, and it is good form to stop the location manager with location manager's `stopUpdatingLocation` method and set its instance variable (if you used one in your implementation) to `nil` so that the object's memory can be freed. Listing 21.2 shows a simple implementation of `locationManager:didFailWithError`.

LISTING 21.2   Handle Core Location Errors

```
 1: - (void)locationManager:(CLLocationManager *)manager
 2:          didFailWithError:(NSError *)error {
 3:
 4:     if (error.code == kCLErrorLocationUnknown) {
 5:         NSLog(@"Currently unable to retrieve location.");
 6:     } else if (error.code == kCLErrorNetwork) {
 7:         NSLog(@"Network used to retrieve location is unavailable.");
 8:     } else if (error.code == kCLErrorDenied) {
 9:         NSLog(@"Permission to retrieve location is denied.");
10:         [manager stopUpdatingLocation];
11:     }
12: }
```

As with the previous example implementation of handling location manager updates, in the error handler we also work solely with properties on the objects the method receives. In lines 4, 6, and 8, we check the incoming `NSError` object's code property against the possible error conditions and react accordingly.

CAUTION

Please Wait While I Get My Bearings

It is important to keep in mind that the location manager delegate will not immediately receive a location; it usually takes a number of seconds for the device to pinpoint the location, and the first time it is used by an application, Core Location first asks the user's permission. You should have a design in place for what the application will do while waiting for an initial location and what to do if location information is unavailable because the user didn't grant permission or the geolocation process failed. A common strategy that works for many applications is to fall back to a user-entered ZIP code.

Location Accuracy and Update Filter

It is possible to tailor the accuracy of the location to the needs of the application. An application that needs only the user's country, for example, does not need 10-meter accuracy from Core Location and will get a much faster answer by asking for a more approximate location. You do this, by setting the location manager's `desiredAccuracy` property, before you start the location updates. `desiredAccuracy` is an enumerated type, `CLLocationAccuracy`. Five constants are available with varying levels of precision (with current consumer technology, the first two are the same): `kCLLocation AccuracyBest`, `kCLLocationAccuracyNearestTenMeters`, `kCLLocationNearest HundredMeters`, `kCLLocationKilometer`, and `kCLLocationAccuracyThreeKilometers`.

After updates on a location manager are started, updates continue to come into the location manager delegate until they are stopped. You cannot control the frequency of these updates directly, but you can control it indirectly with location manager's `distanceFilter` property. The `distanceFilter` property is set before starting updates and specifies the distance in meters the device must travel (horizontally, not vertically) before another update is sent to the delegate.

For example, starting the location manager with settings suitable for following a walker's progress on a long hike might look like this:

```
CLLocationManager *locManager = [[CLLocationManager alloc] init];
locManager.delegate = self;
locManager.desiredAccuracy = kCLLocationAccuracyHundredMeters;
locManager.distanceFilter = 200;
[locManager startUpdatingLocation];
```

CAUTION

Location Comes with a Cost

Each of the three methods of locating the device (GPS, cellular, and WiFi) can put a serious drain on the device's battery. The more accurate an application asks the device to be in determining location, and the shorter the distance filter, the more battery the application will use. Be aware of the device's battery life and only request as accurate and as frequent location updates as the application needs. Stop location manager updates whenever possible to preserve the battery life of the device.

Getting Headings

The location manager includes a `headingAvailable` property that indicates whether the device is equipped with a magnetic compass. If the value is `YES`, you can use Core Location to retrieve heading information. Receiving heading events works similarly to receiving location update events. To start receiving heading events, assign a location manager delegate, assign the `head-ingFilter` property for how frequently you want to receive updates (measured in degrees of change in heading), and call the `startUpdatingHeading` method on the location manager object:

```
locManager.delegate = self;
locManager.headingFilter = 10
[locManager startUpdatingHeading];
```

CAUTION

North Isn't Just "Up"

There isn't one true north. Geographic north is fixed at the North Pole, and magnetic north is located hundreds of miles away and moves every day. A magnetic compass always points to magnetic north; but some electronic compasses, like the one in the iPhone and iPad, can be programmed to point to geographic north instead. Usually, when we deal with maps and compasses together, geographic north is more useful. Make sure that you understand the difference between geographic and magnetic north and know which one you need for your application. If you are going to use the heading relative to geographic north (the `trueHeading` property), request location updates as well as heading updates from the location manager; otherwise, the `trueHeading` property won't be properly set.

The location manager delegate protocol defines the methods for receiving heading updates. There are two methods in the delegate relating to headings: `locationManager:didUpdate Heading` and `locationManager:ShouldDisplayHeadingCalibration`.

The `locationManager:didUpdateHeading` method's argument is a `CLHeading` object. The `CLHeading` object makes the heading reading available with a set of properties: the `magnetic Heading` and the `trueHeading`. (See the relevant Watch Out!) These values are in degrees, and are of type `CLLocationDirection`, which is just a double-precision floating-point number. In plain English, this means that

- ▶ If the heading is 0.0, we're going north.
- ▶ When the heading reads 90.0, we're headed due east.
- ▶ If the heading is 180.0, we're going south.
- ▶ Finally, if the heading reads 270.0, we're going west.

The `CLHeading` object also contains a `headingAccuracy` confidence measure, a `timestamp` of when the reading occurred, and an English language description that is more suitable for logging than showing to a user. Listing 21.3 shows an implementation example of the `location Manager:didUpdateHeading` method.

LISTING 21.3 Handle Heading Updates

```
 1: - (void)locationManager:(CLLocationManager *)manager
 2:        didUpdateHeading:(CLHeading *)newHeading {
 3:
 4:     NSString *headingDesc = @"Not Available";
 5:
 6:     if (newHeading.headingAccuracy >= 0) {
 7:         CLLocationDirection trueHeading = newHeading.trueHeading;
 8:         CLLocationDirection magneticHeading = newHeading.magneticHeading;
 9:
10:         headingDesc = [NSString stringWithFormat:
11:                         @"%f degrees (true), %f degrees (magnetic)",
12:                         trueHeading,magneticHeading];
13:
14:         NSLog(headingDesc);
15:     }
16: }
```

This implementation looks very similar to handling location updates. We check to make sure there is valid data (line 6), and then we grab the true and magnetic headings from the `true-Heading` and `magneticHeading` properties passed to us in the `CLHeading` object (lines 7–8). The output generated looks a bit like this:

```
180.9564392 degrees (true), 182.684822 degrees (magnetic)
```

The other delegate method, `locationManager:ShouldDisplayHeadingCalibration`, literally consists of a line returning YES or NO. This indicates whether the location manager can display a calibration prompt to the user. The prompt asks the user to step away from any source of interference and to rotate the device 360 degrees. The compass is always self-calibrating, and this prompt is just to help that process along after the compass receives wildly fluctuating readings. It is reasonable to implement this method to return NO if the calibration prompt would be annoying or distracting to the user at that point in the application (in the middle of data entry or game play, for example).

NOTE

The iOS simulator reports that headings are available, and it provides just one heading update.

Creating a Location-Aware Application

Many iOS and Mac users have a, shall we say, "heightened" interest in Apple Computer; visiting Apple's campus in Cupertino, California, can be a life-changing experience. For these special users, we're going to create a Core Location-powered application that keeps you informed of just how far away you are.

Implementation Overview

The application is created in two parts: The first introduces Core Location and displays the number of miles from the current location to Cupertino. In the second section, we use the device's compass to display an arrow that points users in the right direction, should they get off track.

In this first installment, we create an instance of a location manager and then use its methods to calculate the distance between our current location and Cupertino, California. While the distance is being determined, we display a Please Wait message. In cases where we happen to be *in* Cupertino, we congratulate the user. Otherwise, a display of the distance, in miles, is shown.

Setting Up the Project

For the rest of this hour, we work on a new application that uses the Core Location framework. Create a new single-view iOS application in Xcode and call it **Cupertino**.

Adding the Core Location Framework

The Core Location framework isn't linked into our project by default, so we need to add it. Select the top-level project group for Cupertino, and make sure that the Summary tab is highlighted in the editor area.

Next, scroll down the summary until you find the section called Linked Libraries and Frameworks. Click the + button below the list. Choose CoreLocation.framework from the list that appears, and then click the Add button, as shown in Figure 21.2. If it doesn't add directly to the Frameworks group, drag the CoreLocation.framework icon into the group to keep the project tidy.

Adding Background Image Resources

To ensure that the user remembers where we're going, we have a nice picture of an apple as the application's background image. Drag the Images folder, which contains apple.png, into your main code group in the project navigator. Be sure to choose to copy items and create groups when prompted.

Planning the Properties and Connections

The view controller serves as the location manager delegate, receiving location updates and updating the user interface to reflect the new locations. Within the view controller, we need a private instance variable (a property is overkill) for an instance of the location manager. We will name this `_locMan`.

FIGURE 21.2
Add the Core Location framework to the project.

Within the interface itself, we need a label with the distance to Cupertino (`distanceLabel`) and two subviews (`distanceView` and `waitView`). The `distanceView` contains the `distanceLabel` and is shown only after we've collected our location data and completed our calculations. The `waitView` is shown while our iDevice gets its bearings.

Adding Location Constants

To calculate the distance to Cupertino, we obviously need a location in Cupertino that we can compare to the user's current location. According to http://gpsvisualizer.com/geocode, the center of Cupertino, California, is at 37.3229978 latitude, –122.0321823 longitude. Add two constants for these values (`kCupertinoLatitude` and `kCupertinoLongitude`) after the `#import` line in the ViewController.m implementation file:

```
#define kCupertinoLatitude 37.3229978
#define kCupertinoLongitude -122.0321823
```

Designing the View

The user interface for this hour's lesson is simple: We can't perform any actions to change our location (teleportation isn't yet possible), so all we need to do is update the screen to show information about where we are.

Open the MainStoryboard.storyboard file, open the Object Library (View, Utilities, Show Object Library), and commence design:

1. Start by adding an image view (UIImageView) onto the view and position it so that it covers the entire view. This serves as the background image for the application.

2. With the image view selected, open the Attributes Inspector (Option-Command-4). Select apple.png from the Image drop-down menu.

3. Drag a new view (UIView) on top of the image view. Size it to fit in the bottom of the view; it serves as our primary information readout, so it needs to be sized to hold about two lines of text.

4. Use the Attributes Inspector to set the background to black. Change the Alpha to 0.75, and check the Hidden check box.

5. Add a label (UILabel) to the information view. Size the label up to all four edge guidelines and change the text to read **Lots of miles to the Mothership**. Use the Attributes Inspector to change the text color to white, aligned center, and sized as you want. Figure 21.3 shows my view.

FIGURE 21.3
The beginnings of the Cupertino Locator UI.

6. Create a second semitransparent view with the same attributes as the first, but *not* hidden, and with a height of about an inch.

7. Drag the second view to vertically center it on the background. This view will contain the `Please Wait` message while the device is finding our location.

8. Add a new label to the view that reads **Checking the Distance**. Resize the label so that it takes up approximately the right two thirds of the view.

9. Drag an activity indicator (`UIActivityIndicatorView`) to the new view and align it to the left side of the label. The indicator shows a "spinner" graphic to go along with our Checking the Distance label. Use the Attributes Inspector to set the Animated attribute; it makes the spinner spin.

The final view should resemble Figure 21.4.

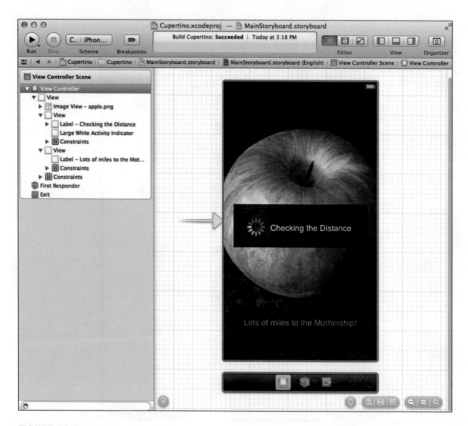

FIGURE 21.4
The final Cupertino Locator UI.

Creating and Connecting the Outlets

In this exercise, all we do is update the user interface (UI) based on information from the location manager. In other words, there are no actions to connect (hurray). We need connections from the two views we added as well as the label for displaying the distance to Cupertino.

Switch to the assistant editor. Control-drag from the Lots of Miles label to below the @interface line in ViewController.h. Create a new outlet named **distanceLabel** when prompted. Do the same for the two views, connecting the view with the activity indicator to a waitView outlet and the view that contains the distance estimate to a distanceView outlet.

Implementing the Application Logic

Based on the interface we just laid out, the application starts up with a message and a spinner that let the user know that we are waiting on the initial location reading from Core Location. We'll request this reading as soon as the view loads in the view controller's viewDidLoad method. When the location manager delegate gets a reading, we calculate the distance to Cupertino, update the label, hide the activity indicator view, and unhide the distance view.

Preparing the Location Manager

To use Core Location and create a location manager, we need to make a few changes to our setup to accommodate the framework. First, update ViewController.h by importing the Core Location interface file, and then add the CLLocationManagerDelegate protocol to the @interface line. Your ViewController.h file, after you make these additions, should look like Listing 21.4.

LISTING 21.4   The Final ViewController.h

```
#import <CoreLocation/CoreLocation.h>

@interface ViewController : UIViewController <CLLocationManagerDelegate>

@property (weak, nonatomic) IBOutlet UILabel *distanceLabel;
@property (weak, nonatomic) IBOutlet UIView *waitView;
@property (weak, nonatomic) IBOutlet UIView *distanceView;

@end
```

Our project is now prepared to use the location manager, but we still need to add the private instance variable that we'll use to reference it (_locMan). Update the @interface block at the top of your ViewController.m file so that it reads as follows:

```
@interface ViewController () {
    CLLocationManager *_locMan;
}
@end
```

It's time to implement the location manager and distance calculation code.

Creating the Location Manager Instance

To use the location manager, we need to make one. Update the `viewDidLoad` method in ViewController.m, and instantiate a location manager with the view controller itself as the delegate, a `desiredAccuracy` of `kCLLocationAccuracyThreeKilometers`, and a `distanceFilter` of 1,609 meters (1 mile). Start the updates with the `startUpdatingLocation` method. The implementation should resemble Listing 21.5.

LISTING 21.5   Create the Location Manager Instance

```
- (void)viewDidLoad
{
    [super viewDidLoad];

    _locMan = [[CLLocationManager alloc] init];
    _locMan.delegate = self;
    _locMan.desiredAccuracy = kCLLocationAccuracyThreeKilometers;
    _locMan.distanceFilter = 1609; // a mile
    [_locMan startUpdatingLocation];
}
```

If you have any questions about this code, refer to the introduction to location manager at the start of this hour's lesson. This code mirrors the examples from earlier, with some slightly changed numbers and, because it isn't just a code fragment, the use of an actual property for accessing the location manager.

Implementing the Location Manager Delegate

Now we need to implement the two methods of the location manager delegate protocol. We start with the error condition: `locationManager:didFailWithError`. In the case of an error getting the current location, we already have a default message in place in the `distanceLabel`, so we just remove the `waitView` with the activity monitor and show the `distanceView`. If the user denied access to Core Location updates, we also clean up the location manager instance variable. Implement `locationManager:didFailWithError` in ViewController.m as shown in Listing 21.6.

LISTING 21.6   Handle Location Manager Errors

```
 1: - (void)locationManager:(CLLocationManager *)manager
 2:         didFailWithError:(NSError *)error {
 3:
 4:     if (error.code == kCLErrorDenied) {
 5:         // Turn off the location manager updates
 6:         [_locMan stopUpdatingLocation];
 7:         _locMan=nil;
 8:     }
 9:     self.waitView.hidden = YES;
10:     self.distanceView.hidden = NO;
11: }
```

In this error handler, we're only worried about the case of the location manger not being able to provide us with any data. In line 4, we check the error code to make sure access wasn't denied. If it was, the location manager is stopped (line 6) and we get rid of it by setting it to `nil` in line 7.

In line 9, the wait view is hidden and the distance view, with the default text of `Lots of miles to the Mothership`, is shown.

NOTE

In this example, I use the `_locMan` instance variable to access the location manager. I could have used the `manager` variable provided to the method; there really wouldn't have been a difference in the outcome. Because we have the private instance variable, however, using it consistently makes sense from the perspective of code readability.

Our final method (`locationManager:didUpdateLocation:fromLocation`) does the dirty work of calculating the distance to Cupertino. This brings us to one more hidden gem in `CLLocation`. We don't need to write our own longitude/latitude distance calculations because we can compare two `CLLocation` instances with the `distanceFromLocation` method. In our implementation of `locationManager:didUpdateLocation:fromLocation`, we create a `CLLocation` instance for Cupertino and compare it to the instance we get from Core Location to get the distance in meters. We then convert the distance to miles, and if it's more than 3 miles, we show the distance with an `NSNumberFormatter` used to add a comma if more than 1,000 miles. If the distance is less than 3 miles, we stop updating the location and congratulate the user on his or her reaching "the Mothership." Listing 21.7 provides the complete implementation of `location Manager:didUpdateLocation:fromLocation`.

LISTING 21.7   Calculating the Distance When the Location Updates

```
 1: - (void)locationManager:(CLLocationManager *)manager
 2:      didUpdateToLocation:(CLLocation *)newLocation
 3:             fromLocation:(CLLocation *)oldLocation {
```

```
 4:
 5:        if (newLocation.horizontalAccuracy >= 0) {
 6:            CLLocation *Cupertino = [[CLLocation alloc]
 7:                                     initWithLatitude:kCupertinoLatitude
 8:                                     longitude:kCupertinoLongitude];
 9:            CLLocationDistance delta = [Cupertino
10:                                     distanceFromLocation:newLocation];
11:            long miles = (delta * 0.000621371) + 0.5; // meters to rounded miles
12:            if (miles < 3) {
13:                // Stop updating the location
14:                [_locMan stopUpdatingLocation];
15:                // Congratulate the user
16:                self.distanceLabel.text = @"Enjoy the\nMothership!";
17:            } else {
18:                NSNumberFormatter *commaDelimited = [[NSNumberFormatter alloc]
19:                                                     init];
20:                [commaDelimited setNumberStyle:NSNumberFormatterDecimalStyle];
21:                self.distanceLabel.text = [NSString stringWithFormat:
22:                                     @"%@ miles to the\nMothership",
23:                                     [commaDelimited stringFromNumber:
24:                                     [NSNumber numberWithLong:miles]]];
25:            }
26:            self.waitView.hidden = YES;
27:            self.distanceView.hidden = NO;
28:        }
29: }
```

The method starts off in line 5 by checking that the new location received by the method is useful information (an accuracy greater than zero). If it is, the rest of the method is executed; otherwise, we're done.

Lines 6–7 create a CLLocation object (Cupertino) with the latitude and longitude of Cupertino.

Lines 9–10 create a CLLocationDistance variable named delta. Remember that CLLocationDistance isn't an object; it is a double-precision floating-point number, which makes using it quite straightforward. The number is the distance between the CLLocation (Cupertino) object we just made and the new location received by the method.

In Line 11, an integer representing the conversion of the distance from meters to miles is calculated and stored in miles.

Lines 12–16 check to see whether the distance calculated is less than 3 miles. If it is, the location manager is stopped and the message Enjoy the Mothership is added to the distance label.

If the distance is greater than or equal to 3 miles, we allocate and initialize a number formatter object called commaDelimited in lines 18–19. Line 20 sets the style for the formatter.

Number formatters work by first setting a style for the object with the `setNumberStyle` method (in this case, `NSNumberFormatterDecimalStyle`). The `NSNumberFormatterDecimalStyle` setting defines decimal numbers with properly placed commas (for example, 1,500).

Once configured, the formatter can use the method `stringFromNumber` to output a nicely formatted number as a string. Unfortunately, a catch applies: The formatter accepts `NSNumber` objects for formatting, not simple C data types. To satisfy this requirement, you must use one of the `NSNumber` convenience methods, such as `numberWithLong` or `numberWithInt`, to convert from a simple data type to an `NSNumber` object.

Lines 21–24 set the distance label to show the number of miles (as a nicely formatted number).

Lines 26 and 27 hide the "wait" view and show the distance view, respectively.

Building the Application

Choose Run and take a look at the result. Your application should, after determining your location, display the distance to Cupertino, California, as shown in Figure 21.5.

FIGURE 21.5
The Cupertino application in action showing the distance to Cupertino, California.

TIP

You can set simulated locations when your app is running. To do this, start the application, and then choose View, Debug Area, Show Debug Area (or click the center button in Xcode's View area of the toolbar). You will see the standard iOS "location" icon at the top of the debug area. Click it to choose from a number of preset locations.

Another option is to use the Debug, Location menu in the iOS simulator itself. There, you can easily configure a custom latitude and longitude for testing.

Note that you must set a location before responding to the app's request to use your current location; otherwise, it assumes that no locations are available as soon as you click OK. If you make this mistake, stop the application's execution in Xcode, uninstall the app from the iOS simulator, and then run it again. This forces it to prompt for location information again.

Using the Magnetic Compass

The iPhone 3GS was the first iOS device to include a magnetic compass. Since its introduction, the compass has been added to the iPad. It is used in Apple's Compass application and in the Maps application (to orient the map to the direction you are facing). The compass can also be accessed programmatically within iOS, which is what we look at now.

Implementation Overview

As an example of using the compass, we are going to enhance the Cupertino application and provide the users with a left, right, or straight-ahead arrow to get them pointed toward Cupertino. As with the distance indicator, this is a limited look at the potential applications for the digital compass. As you work through these steps, keep in mind that the compass provides information much more accurate than what we're indicating with three arrows.

Setting Up the Project

Depending on your comfort level with the project steps we've already completed this hour, you can continue building this directly off the existing Cupertino application or create a copy. You'll find a copy of Cupertino Compass, which includes the additional compass functionality for comparison, in this hour's projects folder.

Open the Cupertino application project, and let's begin by making some additions to support the use of the compass.

Adding the Direction Image Resources

The Images folder in the Cupertino project contains three arrow images: arrow_up.png, arrow_right.png, and arrow_left.png. If you copied the entire Images directory to the Cupertino project, you already have these PNGs in your project's Images group. If not, add them now.

Planning the Properties and Outlets

To implement our new visual direction indicator, the view controller requires an outlet to an image view (`UIImageView`) to show the appropriate arrow. We'll name this **directionArrow**.

We also need the *last* location that we were at, so we create another private instance variable called **_recentLocation**. We need to store this because we'll be doing a calculation on each heading update that uses the current location. We implement this calculation in a new method called `headingToLocation:current`.

Adding Radian/Degree Conversion Constants

Calculating a relative direction requires some rather complicated math. The good news is that someone has already written the formulas we need. To use them, however, we need to be able to convert between radians and degrees.

Add two constants to ViewController.m, following the latitude and longitude for Cupertino. Multiplying by these constants allows us to easily perform our conversions:

```
#define kDeg2Rad 0.0174532925
#define kRad2Deg 57.2957795
```

Updating the User Interface

To update our application for the compass, we need to add a new image view to the interface. Open the MainStoryboard.storyboard file and the Object Library.

Drag an image view (`UIImageView`) onto the interface, positioning it above the waiting view. Using the Attributes Inspector (Option-Command-4), set the image for the view to up_arrow.png. We'll be setting this dynamically in code, but choosing a default image helps with designing the view. Next, use the Attributes Inspector to configure the image view as hidden; you can find this in the Drawing settings of the View section of the attributes. We don't want to show a direction until we've calculated one.

Now, using the Size Inspector (Option-Command-5), set the width and height of the image view to be 150 points x 150 points. As a final step, adjust the view so that it is centered nicely on the screen and not overlapping the waiting view. You can feel free to shift things around as you see fit.

My final UI resembles Figure 21.6.

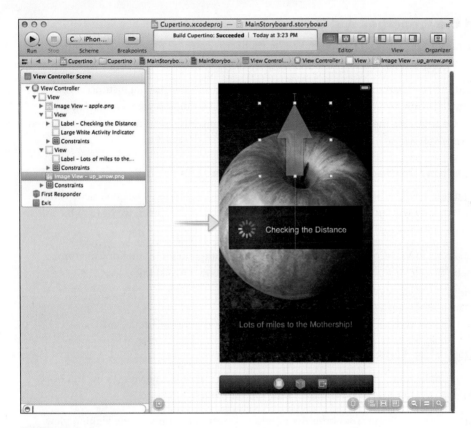

FIGURE 21.6
The updated Cupertino application UI.

Creating and Connecting the Outlet

When finished with your interface, switch to the assistant editor. We need to make a single connection for the image view we just added. Control-drag from the image view to just below the last @property line in ViewController.h. When prompted, create a new outlet named **directionArrow**.

We can now wrap up our app by implementing heading updates. Switch back to the standard editor and open the ViewController.m implementation file.

Updating the Application Logic

To finish the project, we must do four things:

▶ First, we need to ask our location manager instance to start updating us whenever it receives a change in heading.

▶ Second, we need to store the current location whenever we get an updated location from Core Location so that we can use the most recent location in the heading calculations.

▶ Third, we must implement logic to get a heading between our current location and Cupertino.

▶ And fourth, when we have a heading update, we need to compare it to the calculated heading toward Cupertino and change the arrow in the UI if any course adjustments need to be made.

Starting Heading Updates

Before asking for heading updates, we should check with the location manager to see whether heading updates are available via the class method headingAvailable. If heading updates aren't available, the arrow images are never shown, and the Cupertino application works just as before. If headingAvailable returns YES, set the heading filter to 10 degrees of precision and start the updates with startUpdatingHeading. Update the viewDidLoad method of the ViewController.m file, as shown in Listing 21.8.

LISTING 21.8   Request Heading Updates

```
1: - (void)viewDidLoad
2: {
3:     [super viewDidLoad];
4:
5:     _locMan = [[CLLocationManager alloc] init];
6:     _locMan.delegate = self;
7:     _locMan.desiredAccuracy = kCLLocationAccuracyThreeKilometers;
8:     _locMan.distanceFilter = 1609; // a mile
9:     [_locMan startUpdatingLocation];
10:
11:     if ([CLLocationManager headingAvailable]) {
12:         _locMan.headingFilter = 10; // 10 degrees
13:         [_locMan startUpdatingHeading];
14:     }
15: }
```

The squeaky-clean new code just takes up four lines. In line 11, we check to see whether a heading is available. If one is, we ask to be updated only if a change in heading is 10 degrees or more (line 12). In line 13, the location manager instance is asked to start updating us when there are heading changes. If you're wondering why we didn't just set a delegate, it's because the location manager already has one set from our earlier code in line 6. This means that our class must handle both location updates and heading updates.

Storing the Recent Location

To store the recent location, we need to declare a new instance variable that we can use in our methods; this, like the location manager, can be another private instance variable. Locations are managed as objects of type CLLocation; we'll name ours **_recentLocation**. Update the @interface block at the top of ViewController.m to read as follows:

```
@interface ViewController () {
    CLLocationManager *_locMan;
    CLLocation *_recentLocation;
}
@end
```

Next, we need to add a line to set the _recentLocation to the value of newLocation in the locationManager:didUpdateLocation:fromLocation method. We should also stop updating the heading if we are within 3 miles of the destination, just as we stopped updating the location. Listing 21.9 shows these two changes to the locationManager:didUpdateLocation:from Location method.

LISTING 21.9 Store the Recently Received Location for Later Use

```
 1: - (void)locationManager:(CLLocationManager *)manager
 2:     didUpdateToLocation:(CLLocation *)newLocation
 3:            fromLocation:(CLLocation *)oldLocation {
 4:
 5:     if (newLocation.horizontalAccuracy >= 0) {
 6:
 7:         // Store the location for use during heading updates
 8:         _recentLocation = newLocation;
 9:
10:         CLLocation *Cupertino = [[CLLocation alloc]
11:                                  initWithLatitude:kCupertinoLatitude
12:                                  longitude:kCupertinoLongitude];
13:         CLLocationDistance delta = [Cupertino
14:                                     distanceFromLocation:newLocation];
15:         long miles = (delta * 0.000621371) + 0.5; // meters to rounded miles
16:         if (miles < 3) {
17:             // Stop updating the location and heading
18:             [_locMan stopUpdatingLocation];
19:             [_locMan stopUpdatingHeading];
20:             // Congratulate the user
21:             self.distanceLabel.text = @"Enjoy the\nMothership!";
22:         } else {
23:             NSNumberFormatter *commaDelimited = [[NSNumberFormatter alloc]
24:                                                  init];
25:             [commaDelimited setNumberStyle:NSNumberFormatterDecimalStyle];
26:             self.distanceLabel.text = [NSString stringWithFormat:
```

```
27:                                      @"%@ miles to the\nMothership",
28:                                      [commaDelimited stringFromNumber:
29:                                      [NSNumber numberWithLong:miles]]];
30:          }
31:          self.waitView.hidden = YES;
32:          self.distanceView.hidden = NO;
33:      }
34: }
```

The only changes from the previous tutorial are the addition of line 8, which stores the incoming location in _recentLocation, and line 19, which stops heading updates if we are sitting in Cupertino.

Calculate the Heading to Cupertino

In the previous two sections, we avoided doing calculations with latitude and longitude. This time, it requires just a bit of computation on our part to get a heading to Cupertino and then to decide whether that heading is straight ahead or requires the user to spin to the right or to the left.

Given two locations such as the user's current location and the location of Cupertino, it is possible to use some basic geometry of the sphere to calculate the initial heading the user would need to use to reach Cupertino. A search of the Internet quickly finds the formula in JavaScript (copied here in the comment), and from that we can easily implement the algorithm in Objective-C and provide the heading. We add this as a new method, headingToLocation:current, that takes two locations and returns a heading that can be used to reach the destination from the current location.

Start by adding a prototype of the method to ViewController.h. This isn't strictly necessary, but it is good form and will help you avoid warnings in Xcode. Add the following lines below the properties:

```
-(double)headingToLocation:(CLLocationCoordinate2D)desired
                   current:(CLLocationCoordinate2D)current;
```

Next, add the headingToLocation:current method in the ViewController.m file as in Listing 21.10.

LISTING 21.10   Calculating a Heading to a Destination

```
/*
 * According to Movable Type Scripts
 * http://mathforum.org/library/drmath/view/55417.html
 *
 *   Javascript:
 *
```

```
 * var y = Math.sin(dLon) * Math.cos(lat2);
 * var x = Math.cos(lat1)*Math.sin(lat2) -
 * Math.sin(lat1)*Math.cos(lat2)*Math.cos(dLon);
 * var brng = Math.atan2(y, x).toDeg();
 */


-(double)headingToLocation:(CLLocationCoordinate2D)desired
                  current:(CLLocationCoordinate2D)current {

    // Gather the variables needed by the heading algorithm
    double lat1 = current.latitude*kDeg2Rad;
    double lat2 = desired.latitude*kDeg2Rad;
    double lon1 = current.longitude;
    double lon2 = desired.longitude;
    double dlon = (lon2-lon1)*kDeg2Rad;

    double y = sin(dlon)*cos(lat2);
    double x = cos(lat1)*sin(lat2) - sin(lat1)*cos(lat2)*cos(dlon);

    double heading=atan2(y,x);
    heading=heading*kRad2Deg;
    heading=heading+360.0;
    heading=fmod(heading,360.0);
    return heading;
}
```

Don't worry about the math here. I didn't make it up, and there's no reason you need to understand it. What you do need to know is that, given two locations—one current and one desired (the destination)—this method returns a floating-point number in degrees. If the returned value is 0, we need to head north to get where we're going. If it's 180, we need to go south (and so on).

If you're interested in the history of the process and how it works, look up "great circle navigation" on your search engine of choice.

Handling Heading Updates

The last piece of our implementation is handling heading updates. The `ViewController` class implements the `CLLocationManagerDelegate` protocol, and as you learned earlier, one of the optional methods of this protocol, `locationManager:didUpdateHeading`, provides heading updates anytime the heading changes by more degrees than the `headingFilter` amount.

For each heading update our delegate receives, we should use the user's current location to calculate the heading to Cupertino, compare the desired heading to the user's current heading, and then display the correct arrow image: left, right, or straight ahead.

For these heading calculations to be meaningful, we need to have the current location and some confidence in the accuracy of the reading of the user's current heading. We check these two conditions in an if statement before performing the heading calculations. If this sanity check does not pass, we hide the directionArrow.

Because this heading feature is more of a novelty than a true source of directions (unless you happen to be a bird or in an airplane), there is no need to be overly precise. Using +/–10 degrees from the true heading to Cupertino as close enough to display the straight-ahead arrow. If the difference is greater than 10 degrees, we display the left or right arrow based on whichever way would result in a shorter turn to get to the desired heading. Implement the locationManager: didUpdateHeading method in the ViewController.m file, as shown in Listing 21.11.

LISTING 21.11 Handle the Heading Updates

```
 1: - (void)locationManager:(CLLocationManager *)manager
 2:        didUpdateHeading:(CLHeading *)newHeading {
 3:
 4:    if (_recentLocation != nil && newHeading.headingAccuracy >= 0) {
 5:        CLLocation *cupertino = [[CLLocation alloc]
 6:                                initWithLatitude:kCupertinoLatitude
 7:                                       longitude:kCupertinoLongitude];
 8:        double course = [self headingToLocation:cupertino.coordinate
 9:                                         current:_recentLocation.coordinate];
10:        double delta = newHeading.trueHeading - course;
11:        if (abs(delta) <= 10) {
12:            self.directionArrow.image = [UIImage imageNamed:
13:                                        @"up_arrow.png"];
14:        }
15:        else
16:        {
17:            if (delta > 180) {
18:                self.directionArrow.image = [UIImage imageNamed:
19:                                            @"right_arrow.png"];
20:            }
21:            else if (delta > 0) {
22:                self.directionArrow.image = [UIImage imageNamed:
23:                                            @"left_arrow.png"];
24:            }
25:            else if (delta > -180) {
26:                self.directionArrow.image = [UIImage imageNamed:
27:                                            @"right_arrow.png"];
28:            }
29:            else {
30:                self.directionArrow.image = [UIImage imageNamed:
31:                                            @"left_arrow.png"];
32:            }
```

```
33:         }
34:             self.directionArrow.hidden = NO;
35:         } else {
36:             self.directionArrow.hidden = YES;
37:         }
38: }
```

We begin in line 4 by checking to see whether we have valid information stored for our _recentLocation and a meaningful heading accuracy. If these conditions aren't true, the method hides the directionArrow image view in line 36.

Lines 5–7 create a new CLLocation object that contains the location for Cupertino. We use this for getting a heading from our current location (stored in _recentLocation) in Lines 8–9. The heading that would get us to our destination is stored as a floating-point value in course.

Line 10 is a simple subtraction, but it is the magic of the entire method. Here we subtract the course heading we calculated from the one we've received from core location (newHeading.trueHeading). This is stored as a floating-point number in the variable delta.

Let's think this through for a second. If the course we should be going in is north (heading 0) and the heading we're actually going in is also north (heading 0), the delta is 0, meaning that we do not need to make a course correction. However, if the course we want to take is east (a heading of 90), and the direction we are going in is north (a heading of 0), the delta value is –90. Need to be headed west but are traveling east? The delta is –270, and we should turn toward the left. By looking at the different conditions, we can come up with ranges of delta values that apply to the different directions. This is exactly what happens in lines 11–33. You can try the math yourself if you need convincing. Line 11 is a bit different; it checks the absolute value of delta to see whether we're off by more than 10 degrees. If we aren't, the arrow keeps pointing forward.

NOTE

We don't have a backward-pointing arrow here, so any course correction needs to be made by turning left or right. Understanding this can be helpful in seeing why we compare the delta value to greater than 180 and greater than –180 rather than greater than or equal to. 180/–180 is *exactly* in the opposite direction we're going, so left or right is ambiguous. Up until we reach 180/–180, however, we can provide a turn direction. At exactly 180, the else clause in line 29 kicks in and we turn left. Just because.

Building the Application

Run the project. If you have a device equipped with an electromagnetic compass, you can now spin around in your office chair and see the arrow images change to show you the heading to

Cupertino (see Figure 21.7). If you run the updated Cupertino application in the iOS simulator, you might not see the arrow; heading updates seem to be hit or miss in the simulator. Usually miss.

FIGURE 21.7
The completed Cupertino application with compass.

Further Exploration

In the span of an hour, you covered a great deal of what Core Location has to offer. I recommend that you spend time reviewing the Core Location framework reference as well as the guide *Making Your Application Location-Aware*, both of which are accessible through the Xcode documentation.

In addition, I greatly recommend reviewing Movable Type Scripts documentation on latitude and longitude functions (http://www.movable-type.co.uk/scripts/latlong.html). Although Core

Location provides a great deal of functionality, there are things (such as calculate a heading/bearing) that it can't currently do. The Movable Type Scripts library should give you the base equations for many common location-related activities.

Apple Tutorials

LocateMe (accessible through the Xcode documentation interface): A simple Xcode project to demonstrate the primary functions of Core Location.

Summary

In this hour, you worked with the powerful Core Location toolkit. As you saw in the application example, this framework can provide detailed information from an iDevice's GPS and magnetic compass systems. Many modern applications use this information to provide data about the world around the user or to store information about where the user was physically located when an event took place.

You can combine these techniques with the Map Kit from the previous hour to create detailed mapping and touring applications.

Q&A

Q. Should I start receiving heading and location updates as soon as my application launches?

A. You can, as we did in the tutorial, but be mindful that the hardware's GPS features consume quite a bit of battery power. After you establish your location, turn off the location/heading updates.

Q. Why do I need that ugly equation to calculate a heading? It seems overly complicated.

A. If you imagine two locations as two points on a flat grid, the math is easier. Unfortunately, the Earth is not flat but a sphere. Because of this difference, you must calculate distances and headings using the great circle (that is, the shortest distance between two points on a curved surface).

Q. Can I use Core Location and Map Kit to provide turn-by-turn directions in my application?

A. Yes and no. You can use Core Location and Map Kit as part of a solution for turn-by-turn directions, and some developers do this, but they are not sufficiently functional on their own. In short, you have to license some additional data to provide this type of capability.

Workshop

Quiz

1. True north and magnetic north are the same thing. True or false?

2. What can be done to limit the drain on battery life when using Core Location?

3. Explain the role of these important classes: `CLLocationManager`, `CLLocationManagerDelegate`, and `CLLocation`.

Answers

1. False. Magnetic fields vary and are not exactly aligned with true (geographic) north. The error between the two is called *declination*.

2. Use the `distanceFilter` and `headingFilter` properties of `CLLocationManager` to get updates only as frequently as your application can benefit from them. Use the `stopUpdatingLocation` and `stopUpdatingHeading` methods of `CLLocationManager` to stop receiving the updates as soon as you no longer need them.

3. A `CLLocationManager` instance provides the basis of the interaction with Core Location services. A location manager delegate, implementing the `CLLocationManegerDelegate` protocol, is set on the `CLLocationManager` instance, and that delegate receives location/heading updates. Location updates come in the form of a pair of `CLLocation` objects, one providing the coordinates of the previous location, and the other providing the coordinates of the new location.

Activities

1. Adopt the Cupertino application to be a guide for your favorite spot in the world. Add a map to the view that displays your current location.

2. Identify opportunities to use the location features of core location. How can you enhance games, utilities, or other applications with location-aware features?

Building Background-Aware Applications

What You'll Learn in This Hour:

▶ How iOS supports background tasks
▶ What types of background tasks are supported
▶ How to disable backgrounding
▶ How to suspend applications
▶ How to execute code in the background

"Real multitasking" claims the commercial for a competitor's tablet. "Unlike Apple, you can run multiple things at once," chides another ad. As a developer and a fan of iOS, I've found these threads amusing in their naiveté and somewhat confusing. iDevices have always run multiple applications simultaneously in the background, but they were limited to Apple's applications. This restriction has been to preserve the user experience of the device instead of letting it bog down to the point of being unusable. Rather than an "anything goes" approach, Apple has taken steps to ensure that iOS devices remain responsive at all times.

In iOS 4, Apple opened up background processing to third-party applications. Unlike the competitors, however, Apple has been cautious in its backgrounding approach—opening it up to a specific set of tasks that users commonly encounter. In this hour's lesson, you learn several of the multitasking techniques that you can implement in your applications.

Understanding iOS Backgrounding

As you've built the tutorials in this book, you might have noticed that when you quit the applications on your device or in the iOS simulator, they still show up in the iOS task manager, and unless you manually stop them, they tend to pick up right where they left off. The reason for this is that projects are background ready as soon as you click the Run button. That doesn't mean that they will run in the background, just that they're aware of the background features and will take advantage with a little bit of help.

Before we examine how to enable backgrounding (also called multitasking) in our projects, let's first identify exactly what it means to be a background-aware application, starting with the types of backgrounding supported and then the application life cycle methods.

Types of Backgrounding

We explore four primary types of backgrounding in iOS: application suspension, local notifications, task-specific background processing, and task completion.

Suspension

When an application is suspended, it ceases executing code but is preserved exactly as the user left it. When the user returns to the application, it appears to have been running the whole time. In reality, all tasks are stopped, keeping the app from using up your device's resources. Any application that you compile will, by default, support background suspension. You should still handle cleanup in the application if it is about to be suspended (see the "Background-Aware Application Life Cycle Methods" section, later in this hour), but beyond that, it "just works."

In addition to performing cleanup as an application is being suspended, it is your responsibility to recover from a background suspended state and update anything in the application that should have changed while it was suspended (time/date changes and so on).

Local Notifications

The second type of background processing is the scheduling of local notifications (UILocalNotification). If you've ever experienced a push notification, local notifications are the same but are generated by the applications that you write. An application, while running, can schedule notifications to appear onscreen at a point in time in the future. For example, the following code initializes a notification (UILocationNotification), configures it to appear in five minutes, and then uses the application's scheduleLocalNotification method to complete the scheduling:

```
UILocalNotification *futureAlert;
futureAlert = [[UILocalNotification alloc] init];
futureAlert.fireDate = [NSDate dateWithTimeIntervalSinceNow:300];
futureAlert.timeZone = [NSTimeZone defaultTimeZone];
[[UIApplication sharedApplication] scheduleLocalNotification:futureAlert];
```

These notifications, when invoked by iOS, can show a message, play a sound, and even update your application's notification badge. They cannot, however, execute arbitrary application code. In fact, it is likely that you will simply allow iOS to suspend your application after registering your local notifications. A user who receives a notification can click the View button in the notification window to return to your application.

Task-Specific Background Processing

Before Apple decided to implement background processing, it did some research on how users worked with their handhelds. What Apple found was that people needed specific types of background processing. First, they needed audio to continue playing in the background; this is necessary for applications like Pandora. Next, location-aware software needed to update itself in the background so that users continued to receive navigation feedback. Finally, VoIP applications like Skype needed to operate in the background to handle incoming calls.

These three types of tasks are handled uniquely and elegantly in iOS. By declaring that your application requires one of these types of background processing, you can, in many cases, enable your application to continue running with little alteration. To declare your application capable of supporting any (or all) of these tasks, you will add the Required Background Modes (UIBackgroundModes) key to the project's plist file and then add values of App Plays Audio (Audio), App Registers for Location Updates (Location), or App Provides Voice over IP Services (VoIP).

Task Completion for Long-Running Tasks

The fourth type of backgrounding that we'll use is task completion. Using task-completion methods, you can "mark" the tasks in your application that will need to finish before the application can be safely suspended (file upload/downloads, massive calculations, and so on).

For example, to mark the beginning of a long-running task, first declare an identifier for the specific task:

```
UIBackgroundTaskIdentifier myLongTask;
```

Then use the application's beginBackgroundTaskWithExpirationHandler method to tell iOS that you're starting a piece of code that can continue to run in the background:

```
myLongTask = [[UIApplication sharedApplication]
          beginBackgroundTaskWithExpirationHandler:^{
              // If you're worried about exceeding 10 minutes, handle it here
          }];
```

And finally, mark the end of the long-running task with the application endBackgroundTask method:

```
[[UIApplication sharedApplication] endBackgroundTask:myLongTask];
```

Each task you mark will have roughly 10 minutes (total) to complete its actions, which is plenty of time for most uses. After the time completes, the application is suspended and treated like any other suspended application.

Background-Aware Application Life Cycle Methods

In Hour 4, "Inside Cocoa Touch," you started learning about the application life cycle, shown in Figure 22.1. You learned that applications should clean up after themselves in the `application-DidEnterBackground` delegate method. This replaces `applicationWillTerminate` in earlier versions of the OS, or as you'll learn shortly, in applications that you've specifically marked as not capable (or necessary) to run in the background.

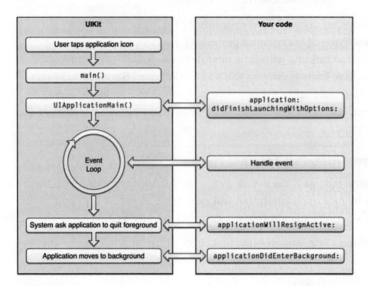

FIGURE 22.1
The iOS application life cycle.

In addition to `applicationDidEnterBackground`, you should implement several other methods to be a proper background-aware iOS citizen. For many small applications, you do not need to do anything with these other than leave them as is in the application delegate. As your projects increase in complexity, however, make sure that your apps move cleanly from the foreground to background (and vice versa), avoiding potential data corruption and creating a seamless user experience.

CAUTION
_____

Your Application Can Terminate at Any Time

It is important to understand that iOS can terminate your applications, even if they're backgrounded, if it decides that the device is running low on resources. You can expect that your applications will be fine, but plan for a scenario where they are forced to quit unexpectedly.
_____

Apple expects to see the following methods in your background-aware apps:

▸ **application:didFinishLaunchingWithOptions**: Called when your application first launches. If your application is terminated while suspended or purged from memory, it needs to restore its previous state manually. (You did save it to your user's preferences, right?)

▸ **applicationDidBecomeActive**: Called when an application launches or returns to the foreground from the background. This method can be used to restart processes and update the user interface, if needed.

▸ **applicationWillResignActive**: Invoked when the application is requested to move to the background or to quit. This method should be used to prepare the application for moving into a background state, if needed.

▸ **applicationDidEnterBackground**: Called when the application has become a background application. This largely replaces applicationWillTerminate, which was used when an application quit. You should handle all final cleanup work in this method. You may also use it to start long-running tasks and use task-completion backgrounding to finish them.

▸ **applicationWillEnterForeground**: Called when an application returns to an active state after being backgrounded.

▸ **applicationWillTerminate**: Invoked when an application on a nonmultitasking version of iOS is asked to quit or when iOS determines that it needs to shut down an actively running background application.

Method stubs for all of these exist in your application delegate implementation files. If your application needs additional setup or teardown work, just add the code to the existing methods. As you'll see shortly, many applications, such as the majority of those in this book, require few changes.

CAUTION

Targeting Older Devices and iOS Versions

The assumption in this hour's lesson is that you are using iOS 4 or later. If you are not, using background-related methods and properties on earlier versions of the OS will result in errors. To successfully target both current and earlier devices, check to see whether backgrounding is available, and then react accordingly in your apps.

Apple provides the following code snippet in the *iOS Application Programming Guide* for checking to see (regardless of OS version) whether multitasking support is available:

```
UIDevice* device = [UIDevice currentDevice];
BOOL backgroundSupported = NO;
if ([device respondsToSelector:@selector(isMultitaskingSupported)])
    backgroundSupported = device.multitaskingSupported;
```

If the resulting backgroundSupported Boolean is YES, you're safe to use background-specific code.

Now that you have an understanding of the background-related methods and types of background processing available to you, let's look at how they can be implemented. To do this, we reuse tutorials that we've built throughout the book (with one exception). We do not cover how these tutorials were built, so be sure to refer to the earlier hours if you have questions on the core functionality of the applications.

Disabling Backgrounding

We start with the exact opposite of enabling backgrounding: disabling it. If you think about it, there are many different "diversion" apps that don't need to support background suspension or processing. These are apps that you use and then quit. They don't need to hang around in your task manager afterward.

For example, consider the HelloNoun application in Hour 6, "Model-View-Controller Application Design." There's no reason that the user experience would be negatively affected if the application started from scratch each time you ran it. To implement this change in the project, follow these steps:

1. Open the project in which you want to disable backgrounding (such as HelloNoun).

2. Choose the main project group and click the HelloNoun target, and then expand the Custom iOS Target Properties under the Info tab. Or open the project's plist file in the Supporting Files group (HelloNoun-Info.plist).

3. Add an additional row to the displayed property list (right-click the list, choose Add Row), selecting Application Does Not Run in Background (`UIApplicationExitsOnSuspend`) from the Key pop-up menu.

4. Choose Yes from the pop-up menu at the right side of the Value column, as shown in Figure 22.2.

NOTE
By default, the plist editor shows the "developer friendly" names for plist entries. To see the underlying keys/values, right-click on the list and choose Show Raw Keys & Values from the menu.

Run the application on your device or in the iOS simulator. When you exit the application with the Home button, it will not be suspended, and it will restart fresh when you launch it the next time.

FIGURE 22.2
Add the Application Does Not Run in Background (`UIApplicationExitsOnSuspend`) key to the project.

Handling Background Suspension

In the second tutorial, we handle background suspension. As previously noted, you don't have to do anything to support this other than build your project with the iOS development tools. That said, we use this example as an opportunity to prompt users when they return to the application after it was backgrounded.

For this example, we update the ImageHop application from Hour 8, "Handling Images, Animation, Sliders, and Steppers." It is conceivable (work with me here, folks) that a user will want to start the bunny hopping, exit the application, and then return to exactly where it was at some time in the future.

To alert the user when the application returns from suspension, we edit the application delegate method `applicationWillEnterForeground`. Recall that this method is invoked only when an application is returning from a backgrounded state. Open AppDelegate.m and implement the method, as shown in Listing 22.1.

LISTING 22.1   Implement the `applicationWillEnterForeground` Method

```
1: - (void)applicationWillEnterForeground:(UIApplication *)application
2: {
3:     UIAlertView *alertDialog;
4:     alertDialog = [[UIAlertView alloc]
5:                     initWithTitle: @"Yawn!"
```

```
 6:                            message:@"Was I asleep?"
 7:                            delegate: nil
 8:                            cancelButtonTitle: @"Welcome Back"
 9:                            otherButtonTitles: nil];
10:        [alertDialog show];
11: }
```

Within the method, we declare, initialize, show, and release an alert view, exactly as we did in the Getting Attention tutorial in Hour 10, "Getting the User's Attention." After updating the code, run the application. Start the ImageHop animation, and then use the Home button to background the app.

After waiting a few seconds (just for good measure), open ImageHop again using the task manager or its application icon (not with Xcode's Run). When the application returns to the foreground, it should pick up exactly where it left off and present you with the alert shown in Figure 22.3.

FIGURE 22.3
The applicationWillEnterForeground method is used to display an alert upon returning from the background.

Implementing Local Notifications

Earlier in this lesson, you saw a short snippet of the code necessary to generate a local notification (UILocalNotification). As it turns out, there's not much more you need beyond those few lines. To demonstrate the use of local notifications, we update Hour 10's doAlert method. Instead of just displaying an alert, it also shows a notification 5 minutes later and then schedules local notifications to occur every day thereafter.

Common Notification Properties

You want to configure several properties when creating notifications. A few of the more interesting of these include the following:

▶ **applicationIconBadgeNumber:** An integer that is displayed on the application icon when the notification is triggered.

▶ **fireDate:** An NSDate object that provides a time in the future for the notification to be triggered.

▶ **timeZone:** The time zone to use for scheduling the notification.

▶ **repeatInterval:** How frequently, if ever, the notification should be repeated.

▶ **soundName:** A string (NSString) containing the name of a sound resource to play when the notification is triggered.

▶ **alertBody:** A string (NSString) containing the message to be displayed to the user.

Creating and Scheduling a Notification

Open the GettingAttention application and edit the doAlert method so that it resembles Listing 22.2. (Bolded lines are additions to the existing method.) Once the code is in place, we walk through it together.

LISTING 22.2 Update doAlert to Register a Local Notification

```
1: - (IBAction)doAlert:(id)sender {
2:     UIAlertView *alertDialog;
3:     UILocalNotification *scheduledAlert;
4:
5:     alertDialog = [[UIAlertView alloc]
6:                     initWithTitle: @"Alert Button Selected"
7:                     message:@"I need your attention NOW (and in a little bit)!"
8:                     delegate: nil
9:                     cancelButtonTitle: @"Ok"
```

```
10:                    otherButtonTitles: nil];
11:        [alertDialog show];
12:
13:        [[UIApplication sharedApplication] cancelAllLocalNotifications];
14:        scheduledAlert = [[UILocalNotification alloc] init];
15:        scheduledAlert.applicationIconBadgeNumber=1;
16:        scheduledAlert.fireDate = [NSDate dateWithTimeIntervalSinceNow:300];
17:        scheduledAlert.timeZone = [NSTimeZone defaultTimeZone];
18:        scheduledAlert.repeatInterval =  NSDayCalendarUnit;
19:        scheduledAlert.soundName=@"soundeffect.wav";
20:        scheduledAlert.alertBody = @"I'd like to get your attention again!";
21:
22:        [[UIApplication sharedApplication]
23:         scheduleLocalNotification:scheduledAlert];
24: }
```

First, in line 3, we declare scheduledAlert as an object of type UILocalNotification. This local notification object is what we set up with our desired message, sound, and so on and then pass off to the application to display sometime in the future.

In line 13, we use [UIApplication sharedApplication] to grab our application object and then call the UIApplication method cancelAllLocalNotifications. This cancels any previously scheduled notifications that this application may have made, giving us a clean slate.

Line 14 allocates and initializes the local notification object scheduledAlert.

In line 15, we configure the notification's applicationIconBadgeNumber property so that when the notification is triggered, the application's badge number is set to 1 to show that a notification has occurred.

Line 16 uses the fireDate property along with the NSDate class method DateWithTimeInterval SinceNow to set the notification to be triggered 300 seconds in the future.

Line 17 sets the timeZone for the notification. This should almost always be set to the local time zone, as returned by [NSTimeZone defaultTimeZone].

Line 18 sets the repeatInterval property for the notification. This can be chosen from a variety of constants, such as NSDayCalendarUnit (daily), NSHourCalendarUnit (hourly), and NSMinuteCalendarUnit (every minute). You can find the full list in the NSCalendar class reference in the Xcode developer documentation.

In Line 19, we set a sound to be played along with the notification. The soundName property is configured with a string (NSString) with the name of a sound resource. Because we already have soundeffect.wav available in the project, we can use that without further additions.

Line 20 finishes the notification configuration by setting the `alertBody` of the notification to the message we want the user to see.

When the notification object is fully configured, we schedule it using the `UIApplication` method `scheduleLocalNotification` (lines 22–23). This finishes the implementation.

Choose Run to compile and start the application on your device or in the iOS simulator. After GettingAttention is up and running, click the Alert Me! button. After the initial alert is displayed, click the Home button to exit the application. Go get a drink, and come back in about 4 minutes and 59 seconds. At exactly 5 minutes later, you'll receive a local notification, as shown in Figure 22.4.

FIGURE 22.4
Local notifications are displayed onscreen even when the application isn't running.

Using Task-Specific Background Processing

So far, we haven't actually done any real background processing. We've suspended an application and generated local notifications, but in each of these cases, the application hasn't been doing any processing. Let's change that. In our final two examples, we execute *real* code behind the scenes while the application is in the background. Although it is well beyond the scope of this book to generate a VoIP application, we can use our Cupertino application from the preceding hour's lesson, with some minor modifications, to show background processing of location and audio.

Preparing the Cupertino Application for Audio

When we finished off the Cupertino application in the preceding hour, it told us how far away Cupertino was and presented straight, left, and right arrows on the screen to indicate the direction the user should be traveling to reach the mothership. We can update the application to audio using SystemSoundServices, just as we did in Hour 10's GettingAttention application.

The only tricky thing about our changes is that we won't want to hear a sound repeated if it was the same as the last sound we heard. To handle this requirement, we use a constant for each sound: 1 for straight, 2 for right, and 3 for left, and store this in a variable called lastSound each time a sound is played. We can then use this as a point of comparison to make sure that what we're about to play isn't the same thing we did just play.

Adding the AudioToolbox Framework

To use System Sound Services, we need to first add the AudioToolbox framework. Open the Cupertino (with compass implementation) project in Xcode. Select the top-level project group for Cupertino, and make sure that Summary tab is highlighted in the editor area.

Scroll down the summary until you find the section called Linked Libraries and Frameworks. Click the + button below the list. Choose AudioToolbox.framework from the list that appears, and then click Add, as shown in Figure 22.5. Move it to the Frameworks group if needed.

FIGURE 22.5
Add the Audio-Toolbox framework to the project.

Adding the Audio Files

Within the Cupertino Audio Compass project folder included with this hour's lesson, you'll find an Audio folder containing simple direction sounds: straight.wav, right.wav, and left.wav. Drag the audio folder to the main project code group within the Xcode project. Choose to copy the files and create groups when prompted.

Adding Audio Instance Variables and Constants

Now that the necessary files are added to the project, we need to update the ViewController.h file. Add the new `#import` directive to the interface file so that the top of the file now includes UIKit, CoreLocation, and AudioToolbox:

```
#import <UIKit/UIKit.h>
#import <CoreLocation/CoreLocation.h>
#import <AudioToolbox/AudioToolbox.h>
```

Next, we need to update the `@interface` block in ViewController.m to declare three new private instance variables for three `SystemSoundID`s (`_soundStraight`, `_soundLeft`, and `_soundRight`) and an integer (`_lastSound`) to hold the last sound we played. Add these to ViewController.m now. The finished block should read similar to this:

```
@interface ViewController () {
    CLLocationManager *_locMan;
    CLLocation *_recentLocation;
    SystemSoundID _soundStraight;
    SystemSoundID _soundRight;
    SystemSoundID _soundLeft;
    int _lastSound;
}
@end
```

To help keep track of which sound we last played, we declared the `_lastSound` instance variable. Our intention is to use this to hold an integer representing each of our three possible sounds. Rather than remembering that 2 = right, 3 = left, and so on, let's add some constants to the ViewController.m file to keep these straight.

Insert these three lines following the existing constants we defined for the project:

```
#define kStraight 1
#define kRight 2
#define kLeft 3
```

The setup is complete; we're ready to implement the code to generate the audio directions for the application.

Implementing the Cupertino Audio Directions

To add sound playback to the Cupertino application, we need to modify two of our existing `ViewController` methods. The `viewDidLoad` method will give us a good place to load all three of our sound files and set the `_soundStraight`, `_soundRight`, and `_soundLeft` references appropriately. We also use it to initialize the `_lastSound` variable to `0`, which doesn't match any of our sound constants. This ensures that whatever the first sound is, it will play.

Edit ViewController.m and update the first half of `viewDidLoad` to match Listing 22.3.

LISTING 22.3   Initialize the Sound File References in `viewDidLoad`

```
- (void)viewDidLoad
{
    [super viewDidLoad];

    NSString *soundFile;

    soundFile = [[NSBundle mainBundle] pathForResource:@"straight"
                                        ofType:@"wav"];
    AudioServicesCreateSystemSoundID((__bridge CFURLRef)
                            [NSURL fileURLWithPath:soundFile]
                            ,&_soundStraight);

    soundFile = [[NSBundle mainBundle] pathForResource:@"right"
                                        ofType:@"wav"];
    AudioServicesCreateSystemSoundID((__bridge CFURLRef)
                            [NSURL fileURLWithPath:soundFile]
                            ,&_soundRight);

    soundFile = [[NSBundle mainBundle] pathForResource:@"left"
                                        ofType:@"wav"];
    AudioServicesCreateSystemSoundID((__bridge CFURLRef)
                            [NSURL fileURLWithPath:soundFile]
                            ,&_soundLeft);

    _lastSound=0;

    // Nothing changes below this line.
    _locMan = [[CLLocationManager alloc] init];
    _locMan.delegate = self;
    _locMan.desiredAccuracy = kCLLocationAccuracyThreeKilometers;
    _locMan.distanceFilter = 1609; // a mile
    [_locMan startUpdatingLocation];
```

```
if ([CLLocationManager headingAvailable]) {
    _locMan.headingFilter = 10; // 10 degrees
    [_locMan startUpdatingHeading];
    }
}
```

TIP

Remember, this is all code we've used before. If you are having difficulties understanding the sound playback process, refer back to the Hour 10 tutorial.

The final logic that we need to implement is to play each sound when there is a heading update. The ViewController.m method that implements this is locationManager:didUpdateHeading. Each time the arrow graphic is updated in this method, we prepare to play the corresponding sound with the AudioServicesPlaySystemSound function. Before we do that, however, we check to make sure it isn't the same sound as _lastSound; this helps prevent a Max Headroom stuttering effect as one sound file is played repeatedly over top of itself. If _lastSound doesn't match the current sound, we play it and update _lastSound with a new value. For the left arrow, for example, we might use this code fragment to play the sound and set the _lastSound variable:

```
if (_lastSound!=kLeft) {
    AudioServicesPlaySystemSound(_soundLeft);
    _lastSound=kLeft;
}
```

Edit the locationManager:didUpdateHeading method as described. Your final result should look similar to Listing 22.4.

LISTING 22.4   Add Audio Feedback When the Heading Updates

```
- (void)locationManager:(CLLocationManager *)manager
      didUpdateHeading:(CLHeading *)newHeading {

    if (_recentLocation != nil && newHeading.headingAccuracy >= 0) {
        CLLocation *cupertino = [[CLLocation alloc]
                            initWithLatitude:kCupertinoLatitude
                            longitude:kCupertinoLongitude];
        double course = [self headingToLocation:cupertino.coordinate
                                    current:_recentLocation.coordinate];
        double delta = newHeading.trueHeading - course;
        if (abs(delta) <= 10) {
            self.directionArrow.image = [UIImage imageNamed:
                                    @"up_arrow.png"];
```

```
        if (_lastSound!=kStraight) {
            AudioServicesPlaySystemSound(_soundStraight);
            _lastSound=kStraight;
        }
    }
    else
    {
        if (delta > 180) {
            self.directionArrow.image = [UIImage imageNamed:
                                        @"right_arrow.png"];
            if (_lastSound!=kRight) {
                AudioServicesPlaySystemSound(_soundRight);
                _lastSound=kRight;
            }
        }
        else if (delta > 0) {
            self.directionArrow.image = [UIImage imageNamed:
                                        @"left_arrow.png"];
            if (_lastSound!=kLeft) {
                AudioServicesPlaySystemSound(_soundLeft);
                _lastSound=kLeft;
            }
        }
        else if (delta > -180) {
            self.directionArrow.image = [UIImage imageNamed:
                                        @"right_arrow.png"];
            if (_lastSound!=kRight) {
                AudioServicesPlaySystemSound(_soundRight);
                _lastSound=kRight;
            }
        }
        else {
            self.directionArrow.image = [UIImage imageNamed:
                                        @"left_arrow.png"];
            if (_lastSound!=kLeft) {
                AudioServicesPlaySystemSound(_soundLeft);
                _lastSound=kLeft;
            }
        }
    }
    self.directionArrow.hidden = NO;
} else {
    self.directionArrow.hidden = YES;
}
}
```

The application is now ready for testing. Click Run to install the updated Cupertino application on your device, and then try moving around. As you move, it will speak "Right," "Left," and "Straight" to correspond to the onscreen arrows. Try exiting the applications and see what happens. Surprise. It won't work. That's because we haven't yet updated the project's plist file to contain the Required Background Modes (`UIBackgroundModes`) key.

TIP

If, while you're testing the application, it still seems a bit "chatty" (playing the sounds too often), you might want to update `_locMan.headingFilter` to a larger value (like 15 or 20) in the `view-DidLoad` method. This will help cut down on the number of heading updates.

Adding the Background Modes Key

Our application performs two tasks that should remain active when in a background state. First, it tracks our location. Second, it plays audio to give us a general heading. We need to add both audio and location background mode designations to the application for it to work properly. Update the Cupertino project plist by following these steps:

1. Choose the main project group and click the Cupertino target, and then expand the Custom iOS Target Properties under the Info tab. Or open the project's plist file in the Supporting Files group (Cupertino-Info.plist).

2. Add an additional row to the property list, selecting Required Background Modes (`UIBackgroundModes`) from the Key pop-up menu.

3. Expand the key and add two values within it: App Plays Audio (Audio) and App Registers for Location Updates (Location), as shown in Figure 22.6. Both values will be selectable from the pop-up menu in the Value field.

FIGURE 22.6
Add the background modes that are required by your application.

After updating the plist, install the updated application on your device and try again. This time, when you exit the application, it will continue to run. As you move around, you'll hear spoken directions as Cupertino continues to track your position behind the scenes.

By declaring the location and audio background modes, your application is able to use the full services of Location Manager and iOS's many audio playback mechanisms when it is in the background.

Completing a Long-Running Background Task

In our final tutorial of the hour, we need to create a project from scratch. Our book isn't about building applications that require a great deal of background processing. Sure, we could demonstrate how to add code to an existing project and allow a method to run in the background, but we don't have any long-running methods that could make use of it.

Implementation Overview

To demonstrate how we can tell iOS to allow something to run in the background, we create a new application, **SlowCount**, that does nothing but count to 1,000—slowly. We use the task-completion method of background to make sure that, even when the application is in the background, it continues to count until it reaches 1,000 (as shown in Figure 22.7).

Setting Up the Project

Create a new single-view application named **SlowCount**. We move through development fairly quickly because, as you can imagine, this application is pretty simple.

Planning the Properties and Connections

The application has a single outlet, a `UILabel` named `theCount`, which we use to present the counter onscreen. In addition, it needs several private instance variables: an integer to use as a counter (`_count`), an `NSTimer` object that triggers the counting at a steady interval (`_theTimer`), and a `UIBackgroundTaskIdentifier` variable (not an object) that we use to reference the task we have running in the background (`_counterTask`).

NOTE
***

Every task that you want to enable for background task completion needs its own `UIBackground`
`TaskIdentifier`. This is used along with the `UIApplication` method `endBackgroundTask` to
identify which background task has just ended.

***

FIGURE 22.7
To simulate a long-running task, our application will count slowly.

Designing the Interface

It's a bit of a stretch to claim that this application has a "user interface" (UI), but we still need to prepare the MainStoryboard.storyboard to show the theCount label on the screen.

Open the initial scene, and drag a label (UILabel) into the center of the view. Set the label's text to read 0. With the label selected, use the Attributes Inspector (Option-Command-4) to set the label alignment to center and the font size to something a bit bigger. Finally, align the right and left sides of the label with the right and left sizing guides. You've just created a UI masterpiece, as shown in Figure 22.8.

Creating and Connecting the Outlet

We've got one UI object to connect to a single outlet. Switch to the assistant editor, and then Control-drag from the label to below the @interface line in ViewController.h. Name the outlet **theCount** when prompted to make the connection.

FIGURE 22.8
Add a `UILabel` to the view to hold the current count.

Implementing the Application Logic

To finish our application's core functionality (counting), we need to declare and deal with the additional variables/properties: the counter (_count), the NSTimer to give us a nice delay while counting (_theTimer), and a UIBackgroundTaskIdentifier to track the task (_counterTask).

In addition, we implement a method that does the counting (and nothing else) called countUp. To avoid any Xcode warnings, we should add a method prototype for this in the ViewController.h interface file.

Begin by updating ViewController.h to include the method prototype, as shown in Listing 22.5.

LISTING 22.5 Add the Instance Variables and Property

```
#import <UIKit/UIKit.h>

@interface ViewController : UIViewController

@property (weak, nonatomic) IBOutlet UILabel *theCount;

- (void) countUp;

@end
```

Next, update the ViewController.m file's `@interface` block to declare the private instance variable's we need:

```
@interface ViewController () {
    int _count;
    UIBackgroundTaskIdentifier _counterTask;
    NSTimer *_theTimer;
}
@end
```

With most of the prep work done, there are two more things left to complete. First, we need to set the counter (_count) to 0 and allocate and initialize NSTimer to fire at a regular interval. Second, when the timer fires, we ask it to invoke a second method, countUp. In the countUp method, we check to see whether _count is 1000. If it is, we turn off the timer and we're done; if not, we update _count and display it in our UILabel theCount.

Initializing the Timer and Counter

Let's start with initializing the counter and timer. What better place to do this than in SlowCount.m's viewDidLoad method? Implement viewDidLoad as shown in Listing 22.6.

LISTING 22.6   Schedule a Timer When the Application Starts

```
 1: - (void)viewDidLoad
 2: {
 3:     [super viewDidLoad];
 4:     _count=0;
 5:     _theTimer=[NSTimer scheduledTimerWithTimeInterval:0.1
 6:                                     target:self
 7:                                     selector:@selector(countUp)
 8:                                     userInfo:nil
 9:                                     repeats:YES];
10: }
```

Line 4 initializes our integer counter, _count, to 0.

Lines 5–9 initialize and allocate the _theTimer NSTimer object with an interval of 0.1 seconds. The selector is set to use the method countUp, which we write next. The timer is set to keep repeating with repeats:YES.

All that remains is to implement countUp so that it increments the counter and displays the result.

Updating the Counter and Display

Add the countUp method, as shown in Listing 22.7, in ViewController.m. This should be quite straightforward: If the count equals 1000, we're done and it's time to clean up (we can set the timer object to nil); otherwise, we count.

LISTING 22.7   Updating the Counter

```
 1:  - (void) countUp {
 2:      if (_count==1000) {
 3:          [_theTimer invalidate];
 4:          _theTimer=nil;
 5:      } else {
 6:          _count++;
 7:          NSString *currentCount;
 8:          currentCount=[[NSString alloc] initWithFormat:@"%d",_count];
 9:          self.theCount.text=currentCount;
10:      }
11:  }
```

Lines 2–4 handle the case that we've reached the limit of our counting (_count==1000). If it has, we use the timer's invalidate method to stop it and then set it to nil because it isn't needed anymore.

Lines 6–9 handle the actual counting and display. Line 6 updates the _count variable. Line 7 declares the currentCount string, which is then allocated and populated in line 8. Line 9 updates our theCount label with the currentCount string. Line 10 releases the string object.

Run the application. It should do exactly what you expect: count slowly until it reaches 1,000. Unfortunately, if you background the application, it will suspend. The counting will cease until the application returns to the foreground.

Enabling the Background Task Processing

To enable the counter to run in the background, we need to mark it as a background task. We use this code snippet to mark the beginning of the code we want to execute in the background:

```
_counterTask = [[UIApplication sharedApplication]
            beginBackgroundTaskWithExpirationHandler:^{
                // If you're worried about exceeding 10 minutes, handle it here
            }];
```

And we use this code snippet to mark the end:

```
[[UIApplication sharedApplication] endBackgroundTask:_counterTask];
```

NOTE

If you are worried about the application not finishing the background task before it is forced to end (roughly 10 minutes), you could implement the optional code in the `beginBackgroundTaskWithExpirationHandler` block. You can always check to see how much time is remaining by checking the `UIApplication` property `backgroundTimeRemaining`.

Let's update our `viewDidLoad` and `countUp` methods to include these code additions. In `viewDidLoad`, we start the background task right before we initialize the counter. In `countUp`, we end the background task after `_count==1000` and the timer is invalidated and cleared out.

Update `viewDidLoad` as shown in Listing 22.8 (lines 4–7).

LISTING 22.8 Set the Start of Background Processing

```
 1: - (void)viewDidLoad
 2: {
 3:     [super viewDidLoad];
 4:     _counterTask = [[UIApplication sharedApplication]
 5:                   beginBackgroundTaskWithExpirationHandler:^{
 6:             // If you're worried about exceeding 10 minutes, handle it here
 7:                   }];
 8:     _count=0;
 9:     _theTimer=[NSTimer scheduledTimerWithTimeInterval:0.1
10:                                         target:self
11:                                       selector:@selector(countUp)
12:                                       userInfo:nil
13:                                        repeats:YES];
14: }
```

Then make the corresponding additions to `countUp` (line 5), demonstrated in Listing 22.9.

LISTING 22.9 Set the End of Background Processing

```
 1: - (void)countUp {
 2:     if (_count==1000) {
 3:         [_theTimer invalidate];
 4:         _theTimer=nil;
 5:         [[UIApplication sharedApplication] endBackgroundTask:_counterTask];
 6:     } else {
 7:         _count++;
 8:         NSString *currentCount;
 9:         currentCount=[[NSString alloc] initWithFormat:@"%d",_count];
10:         self.theCount.text=currentCount;
11:     }
12: }
```

That's all it takes. Your project should now be able to run in the background.

Building the Application

Save your project files and then run the application on your device or in the simulator. After the counter starts counting, press the Home button to move the application to the background. Wait a minute or so, and then reopen the application through the task manager or the application icon. The counter will have continued to run in the background.

Obviously, this isn't a very compelling project itself, but the implications for what can be achieved in real-world apps is definitely exciting.

Further Exploration

When I sat down to write this lesson, I was torn. Background tasks/multitasking is definitely the "must have" feature of iOS, but it's a challenge to demonstrate anything meaningful in the span of a dozen or two pages. What I hope we've achieved is a better understanding of how iOS multitasking works and how you might implement it in your own applications. Keep in mind that this is not a comprehensive guide to background processing; there are many more features available and many ways that you can optimize your background-enabled apps to maximize battery life and speed.

As a next step, you should read the following sections in Apple's *iOS Application Programming Guide* (available through the Xcode documentation): "Executing Code in the Background," "Preparing Your Application to Execute in the Background," and "Initiating Background Tasks."

As you review Apple's documentation, pay close attention to the tasks that your application should be completing as it enters the background. There are implications for games and graphic-intensive applications that are well beyond the scope of what we can discuss here. How well you adhere to these guidelines will determine whether Apple accepts your application or kicks it back to you for optimization.

Summary

Background applications on iOS devices are not the same as background applications on your Macintosh. There are well-defined rules that background-enabled applications must follow to be considered "good citizens" of iOS. In this hour's lesson, you learned about the different types of backgrounding available and the methods available to support background tasks. Over the course of five tutorial applications, you put these techniques to the test, creating everything from notifications triggered when an application isn't running to a simple navigation app that provides background voice prompting.

You should now be well prepared to create your own background-aware apps and take full advantage of the powerful hardware in your iPhone, iPad, or iPod.

Q&A

Q. Why can't I run any code I want in the background?

A. Someday, I suspect you will, but for now the platform is constrained to the specific types of background processing we discussed. The security and performance implications of running anything and everything on a device that is always connected to the Internet are enormous. Apple intends to ensure that your device remains operational in any conditions, unlike the competitors, where anything goes.

Q. What about timeline-based background processing, like IM clients?

A. Timeline-based processing (reacting to events that occur over time) is currently not allowed in iOS. This is a disappointment but ensures that there aren't dozens of apps sitting around, eating up resources, waiting for something to happen.

Workshop

Quiz

1. Background tasks can be anything you want in iOS. True or false?

2. Any application you compile for iOS will continue to run when the user exits it. True or false?

3. Only a single long-running background task can be marked background completion. True or false?

Answers

1. False. Apple has a well-defined set of rules for implementing background processing.

2. False. Applications will suspend in the background by default. To continue processing, you must implement background tasks as described in this hour's lesson.

3. False. You can mark as many long-running tasks as you'd like, but all of them must complete within a set period of time (around 10 minutes).

Activities

1. Return to a project in an earlier hour and properly enable it for background processing.

2. Test to see what happens when an application with background processing attempts to run longer than 10 minutes. Is it suspended? Terminated? How do you recover from this if your application does not finish its task?

Building Universal Applications

What You'll Learn in This Hour:

▶ What makes a universal application *universal*

▶ How to use the universal application template

▶ Ways of designing universal applications

▶ How to detect the device an application is running on

▶ Tools for migrating to a universal architecture

The iPhone and iPod touch represent Apple's first entry into touch-based computing, but they aren't the only game in town. The venerable iPad has been an undeniable success and extends the iOS platform to a much larger screen. Throughout this book, we've been targeting one platform or another. But you know what's even better? Targeting both.

In this hour's lesson, you learn how to create an application that runs on both the iPhone and the iPad—termed a *universal application* by Apple. You also learn, firsthand, some of the problems that come with supporting an application that works on both platforms and some tips for overcoming them. You're an iOS developer now, and there's no reason you can't extend your efforts to the entire iDevice lineup.

Universal Application Development

A universal application is one that contains the necessary resources to run on the iPhone and the iPad. Although the iPad already supports running iPhone applications, they don't look so great. To build a truly unique iPad experience, you need different storyboards, images, and maybe even completely different classes. Your code may even need to make decisions on-the-fly about the type of device it is running on.

If this is starting to sound like a bit of a pain, that's because it can be. The iPhone and iPad are not the same device. Users expect a different experience from each of them; so, although an app may have the same functionality, it will likely need to look and work differently depending on where it is running. Depending on how you approach a universal application design, you might end up with duplicate classes, methods, resources, and so on that you must support for each device. The good news is that, from your users' perspective, they get a single application that they can run on either their iPhone, iPad, or both, and you get to reach a much larger audience than targeting a single device.

Not all developers have decided that a universal application is the best approach for their projects. Many have created separate "HD" versions of their apps that are sold at a slightly higher price than an iPhone version. If your application is going to be substantially different on the two platforms, this might be the route you want to take, too. Even if it is, you can consolidate development into a single project that builds two different executables, called *targets*. Later in the hour, we look at the tools available in Xcode that can set this up for you.

If you know upfront that you want to create an application that works on any device, you'll likely begin development by setting your template's device family to Universal, rather than iPhone or iPad. We look at the universal version of the Single View Application template, but the other template types follow this same approach.

Where Am I Running?

To detect what device an application is running on, you can use the `UIDevice` class method `currentDevice` to get an object that refers to the active device and then access its `model` property. The `model` is an `NSString` that describes the device (such as `"iPhone"`, `"iPad Simulator"`, and so on). The code fragment to return this string is just this:

```
[UIDevice currentDevice].model
```

No instantiation or setup is required. Just check the contents of model. If it contains iPhone, you're on an iPhone; iPod, you're on an iPod touch; and iPad, you're on an iPad device.

Understanding Universal Templates

To aid you in creating a universal application, Apple has provided the ability to create universal versions of the templates you've used throughout the book. When creating a new project in

Xcode, you can set the device family to Universal, as shown in Figure 23.1. This creates a new project that will target both the iPhone and iPad devices.

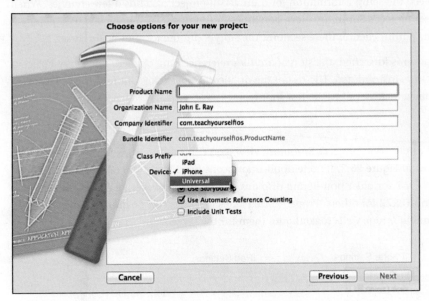

FIGURE 23.1
Begin your universal applications with the Universal template.

Universal templates are identical to device-specific templates, but with a key difference. Rather than a single MainStoryboard.storybord file, there are targeted storyboards: MainStoryboard_iPhone.storyboard and MainStoryboard_iPad.storyboard, as demonstrated in Figure 23.2. As the names suggest, the files with the suffix iPad are used when the application executes on the iPad and iPhone when it is running on the iPhone. The application classes remain the same.

FIGURE 23.2
A universal application includes distinct storyboard files for the iPad and iPhone platforms.

Universal Application Setup Changes

As you might expect, the setup information for a universal project also has a few changes. When viewing a universal project's Summary view, you'll notice that it shows iPhone *and* iPad deployment information. Within each of these sections, the storyboard file for that device is set.

When the application is launched, the storyboard files referenced are opened, and every object in their initial scene is instantiated. The rest of the application branches out from these important starting points, a fact we put to the test shortly.

Icon Files

Using a universal application project's Summary view, you can set app icons for both iPhone and iPad, as shown in Figure 23.3. iPhone application icons are 114x114 pixels for Retina display devices and 57x57 for older non-Retina displays. iPad icons, however, are 144x144 for Retina displays and 72x72 for others. Properly sized icons graphics can be dragged and dropped into the corresponding image wells to configure them for the project.

FIGURE 23.3
Add icon files for iPhone and iPad in the Summary area.

NOTE
When you drag and drop an image into one of the Xcode image wells (such as adding an icon), the file is copied to your project folder and appears in the project navigator. To keep things neat, you may want to drag it into the Supporting Files group in the project.

Launch Images

Recall that the launch image is the picture that is displayed as an application loads on your device. Because the iPhone, iPhone 5, and iPad have different screen sizes, they require multiple types of launch images. Use the image wells to set the launch images for each platform, just as you did the icons.

Beyond those minor setup changes, the universal application template is very much ready to go. I could, at this point, just say "use it," but this hour wouldn't be very useful if I did. Let's go ahead and take the universal version of the Single View Application template to a place where it becomes useful. We'll build out an application that launches and displays different views and executes a simple line of code on both the iPad and iPhone platforms.

TIP
On the iPhone, launch images should be created with the dimensions 640x1136 pixels for the iPhone 5, 640x960 for 3.5" Retina display devices (iPhone 4/4s) and 320x480 for older devices. If the device operates in landscape mode only, those numbers are flipped to 1136x640, 960x640, and 480x320. If you are leaving the status bar visible, subtract 40 pixels from the vertical resolution for Retina devices or 20 pixels for non-Retina displays. Because the iPad's status bar is never supposed to be hidden, its launch images should always have 40 or 20 pixels removed from the vertical dimension—that is, 1536x2008 (portrait, Retina-display) or 2048x1496 (landscape, Retina-display). Non-Retina iPads should use 768x1004 pixels (portrait) or 1004x748 (landscape).

Creating a Universal Application (Take 1)

We're going to go through the process of building two universal applications. Both examples have the same purpose: to launch, instantiate a view controller, load a device specific view, and then display a string that identifies the type of device the code is running on. It's not the most exciting thing we've done in the book, but it should give you the background you need to build your apps for all of Apple's iDevices. Figure 23.4 shows the outcome we hope to achieve.

I'm an iPad App!

iPad Simulator

I'm an iPhone App!

iPhone Simulator

FIGURE 23.4
We will create an application that runs and displays information on iPhone and iPad devices.

Implementation Overview

Our first approach to a universal application is to use the vanilla Apple universal templates. This sets us up to use a single-view controller for managing both the iPad and iPhone views. It is a straightforward approach, but one that may not be practical in large projects where the iPhone and iPad interface will differ greatly.

We will create two identical (except for size) views, one for each device, with a label that can be changed. The labels are then connected back to the same view controller. Within that controller, we make the determination of whether we're running on an iPhone or iPad and output an appropriate message to the device.

Setting Up the Project

Begin by creating a new Single View Application template with a Device Family setting of Universal. Name the application **Universal**, in case there's any question of what we're trying to do. The application skeleton will look exactly like what you've seen before, but this time there will be a storyboard for each of our devices.

Planning the Properties and Connections

There will only be a single connection required in this project: a UILabel that we will call
deviceType. We use it to dynamically output the type of device the application is running on
when the view is loaded. That's all we need.

Designing the Interface

You have two storyboards to work on in this tutorial: MainStoryboard_iPad.storyboard and
MainStoryboard_iPhone.storyboard. Open each of the storyboard files in turn and add a static
label proclaiming the type of application that it should represent. In other words, in the iPhone
view, place the text **I'm an iPhone App!**, and in the iPad view, **I'm an iPad App!**.

If you want, you've now done enough work that you can run the app in the iOS simulator and
use the Hardware, Device menu to change between iPhone and iPad implementations. When
running the app as an iPad, you'll see the view you created in the iPad storyboard, and the
iPhone equivalent on the iPhone. This, however, is just static text; we need to make sure that a
single view controller can, indeed, control both views.

Edit each of the views so that below the exclamatory text, you include a UILabel with the
default text set to **Device**. Your views should resemble Figure 23.5.

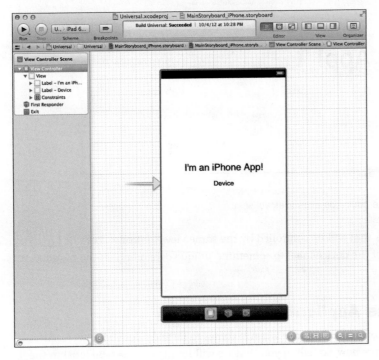

FIGURE 23.5
Design two views, each with static text and a device label.

Creating and Connecting the Outlet

There is a single dynamic element in the views you created; it needs to be connected to an outlet named `deviceType`. Because two views connect to a single outlet in a single view controller, they need to share.

Begin by switching to the assistant editor and hiding the navigator area or utilities area if you need space. Select one of the two storyboard files; it doesn't matter which. With the ViewController.h file visible on the right, Control-drag from the Device label to just below the `@interface` line. Name the outlet `deviceType` when prompted.

Now you need to create the same connection for the second view, but because the outlet has already been added for `deviceType`, you don't need to define a new outlet. Open the second storyboard and Control-drag from the second device label until you are just on top of the `@property` declaration for `deviceType` in ViewController.h, as shown in Figure 23.6.

FIGURE 23.6
Connect the second label to the outlet you already established.

You've just set up two views that will be controlled by the same view controller. Let's finish up by adding the code that will set the device label to something unique depending on the platform it is running on.

Implementing the Application Logic

There is no logic that you don't already know when it comes to setting a label. You've been doing this for almost 24 hours now, so telling you that we will set the `deviceType` label in the `viewDidLoad` method of the ViewController.m is pretty obvious. What isn't so obvious, however, is how we can change the label depending on the type of device we're running on. Remember, this is one piece of code serving both user interfaces (UIs). How can we possibly change the output depending on the device? We'll find out the answer in the UIDevice class.

Detecting and Displaying the Active Device

Our goal for our application is to get and display the name of the device that it is running on. To do this, we'll use the string returned by the following:

```
[UIDevice currentDevice].model
```

To display this in our views, we set the text property of the deviceType label to the model string. Switch to the standard editor, and then implement the change to viewDidLoad, as shown in Listing 23.1.

LISTING 23.1 Detecting and Displaying the Active Device

```
- (void)viewDidLoad
{
    [super viewDidLoad];
    self.deviceType.text=[UIDevice currentDevice].model;
}
```

Nicely done. That's it. Each view now displays a different label depending on the model provided by UIDevice. You can use this to make code execute conditionally depending on what hardware it is running on, even altering its operation if it is running in the iOS simulator.

Building the Application

At this point, you can run the app and finally see the results on the iPhone or iPad. So, what have you learned? Hopefully, you've learned that universal application development, if interfaces are similar, can be quite simple. You can have a single-view controller handle interactions from two storyboards and make decisions, if needed, to differentiate between them.

TIP

The easiest way to target a specific platform in the iOS simulator is to use the right side of the Scheme menu on Xcode's toolbar. Choose iPad Simulator to force the application to run on the iPad or choose iPhone Simulator to force it to the iPhone.

Unfortunately, this approach can get overwhelming if you are producing an app with radically different interfaces for iPhones and iPads. In these cases, it might make more sense to have a separate view controller managing each interface. In our second project, we do exactly that: create an application that looks identical to this one but that has a unique view controller handling interactions depending on the device it is running on.

Creating a Universal Application (Take 2)

Our second pass at building a universal application will work similarly to what we just built, but with one distinct difference. Instead of using the default universal template as is, we create a view controller called `iPadViewController` that is dedicated to managing the iPad's views. We continue to use the default `ViewController` class for the iPhone.

By structuring the project this way, we end up with two unique controllers that can implement interfaces as alike or dissimilar as we want. In addition, we do not need to check to see what type of device we're running on because the correct view controller class for the correct device is automatically instantiated when the storyboard is chosen at launch.

Setting Up the Project

Start the second tutorial the same way as the first: Use the Single View Application with a Device Family setting of Universal to create a new application. Name the new application **UniversalToo**. Next, we need to create the iPad view controller class that will contain all of our iPad-specific UI management.

Adding an iPad View Controller

Our application already has a single view controller subclass (`ViewController`), but we need another. To create a new `UIViewController` subclass, choose File, New File from the menu. When prompted, navigate to the iOS Cocoa Touch category and choose the Objective-C class icon, and then click Next. Name the new class **iPadViewController** and set the subclass to `UIViewController`, as shown in Figure 23.7.

Make sure the Targeted for iPad check box is checked, and then click Next to choose where the class files will be created.

Finally, when prompted, choose the location for storing your new view controller class files. You should pick the same directory (inside your project folder) where the default ViewController.h and ViewController.m files are stored, and then click Create.

You should see the new implementation and interface files for the `iPadViewController` class in the project navigator. Drag them into the main project code group to keep things organized.

Associating the `iPadViewController` with the iPad View

Your project now has a view controller class for the iPad, but if you code everything up, the initial view in the MainStoryboard_iPad.storyboard file still uses the `ViewController` class to manage its view. To fix this, we must set the identity of the view controller object that is represented in the initial scene in the iPad's storyboard.

FIGURE 23.7
Add a new UIViewController subclass to target iPad development.

Click the MainStoryboard_iPad.storyboard file in the project navigator. When it opens, select the view controller object within the Document Outline, and then open the Identity Inspector (Option-Command-3). To set the view controller to the `iPadViewController` class, select it in the Class drop-down menu at the top of the inspector, as shown in Figure 23.8.

With the identity set, our work is essentially done. We can proceed to develop the application as if it were two separate apps; both our views and our view controllers are separate.

NOTE

Just because views and view controllers are managed separately doesn't mean that *no* code can be shared. You could, for example, create additional utility classes to implement application logic and core functionality that is shared between the iPad and iPhone.

Designing the Interface

The rest of the application development follows very closely to the last app. Create two views: one in MainStoryboard_iPhone.storyboard and one in MainStoryboard_iPad.storyboard. Each view should include a label that identifies the device it is running on and a label with the text

`Device` that will be set dynamically in code. You can even open up the storyboards in the original universal app tutorial and copy and paste the UI elements into this project.

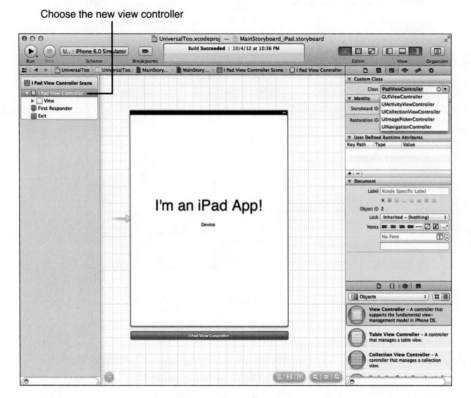

FIGURE 23.8
Set the class that implements the initial view's view controller.

Once the views are in place, switch to the assistant editor mode. We need to make connections from the `Device` label in both interfaces to their corresponding view controllers.

Creating and Connecting the Outlets

Unlike the other example, this tutorial requires us to make new connections for the device label in both the iPad and iPhone views. Starting with the MainStoryboard_iPhone.storyboard, Control-drag from the `Device` label to just below the `@interface` line in ViewController.h. Name the outlet **deviceType**.

Switching to the MainStoryboard_iPad.storyboard file, verify that the assistant editor has loaded the iPadViewController.h file, not ViewController.h. Complete the same setup to connect this view's `Device` label to another new outlet named `deviceType`.

You can now switch back to the standard editor to finish up this (almost complete) project.

Implementing the Application Logic

The only logic that we need to implement is setting the `deviceType` label to the name of the device that the application is running on. You can do this in exactly the same way as the first tutorial (see Listing 23.1), but you will need to implement it in *both* ViewController.m and iPadViewController.m.

However, *and this is a big however*, because we already know that ViewController.m is executing on an iPhone and iPadViewController.m is running on an iPad, we can add lines like these to each class's `viewDidLoad` method:

```
self.deviceType.text=@"iPhone";
```

Or (for the iPad):

```
self.deviceType.text=@"iPad";
```

Like I said, for all intents and purposes, using this approach you can develop your iPad and iPhone applications as if they were completely independent, sharing code where it makes sense and staying separate elsewhere.

CAUTION

Not All Subclasses Are Created Equal

When you add the new `UIViewController` subclass (`iPadViewController`) to the project, don't expect the contents to look exactly like the view controller files that are part of your iOS templates. In the case of the iPad view controller, you may need to uncomment the `viewDidLoad` method, because it is disabled by default.

Building the Application

If you run the UniversalToo application, it should appear exactly the same as the first application. The takeaway from this exercise is that there are two general approaches to building universal apps, both with their positives and negatives.

Applications that share a view controller require less code and setup. On the one hand, your iPad and iPhone interfaces are similar; this makes maintenance simpler. On the other hand, if you have dissimilar UIs or want to implement features in one device's version of the app and not in the other, separating out the code may be a smarter path.

It's up to you, and you now have the tools to make it happen.

Using Multiple Targets

To close out the chapter, I want to mention a third possibility for creating universal projects that, although they do not result in a single universal application, can be compiled for either the iPhone or iPad platforms.

To do this, you must define multiple targets for your app. A target defines the platform that your app will be compiled for (the iPhone or iPad). Remember how the Summary view of your project can be used to configure the Storyboard that is loaded when your app starts? By adding a new target to your project, you'll be able to configure a completely different setup that can be pointed to a new storyboard file. In turn, that storyboard can invoke the project's existing view controller or a new one, just like the exercises we completed in this hour's tutorials.

To add a target to a project, the easiest approach is to duplicate the existing one. Open your project file in Xcode and select the topmost project group. To the right of the project navigator is a list of targets. Usually just one is shown: your iPhone or iPad target. Right-click the target and choose Duplicate.

iPhone to iPad Targets

If you are duplicating the target on an iPhone project, you are prompted to transition to the iPad, as shown in Figure 23.9. Choose Duplicate and Transition to iPad and you're done. Xcode creates iPad resources for your app, but they are segregated from the iPhone application. Your project will have two targets: the original iPhone target and an iPad target. Although you can share resources and classes, you choose between the targets when building, thus creating distinct executables for both platforms.

Duplicate iPhone Target

The selected target is an iPhone target, you can duplicate and transition it to an iPad target at the same time. The user interface used for running on iPhone can be used as a starting point for iPad development. Would you like to duplicate the iPhone target and transition the new target for running on iPad?

[Duplicate Only]   [Cancel]   [**Duplicate and Transition to iPad**]

FIGURE 23.9
Xcode can help you upgrade your iPhone apps to run on the iPad.

To select between targets when running/building your app, click the left side of the scheme pop-up menu on the Xcode toolbar. All your targets are listed, with submenus for choosing whether to run them on a device or the iOS simulator.

The Duplicate and Transition to iPad option automatically names your new target with the suffix `iPad`. The duplicate comment usually just appends `copy` to the existing target name. You can rename a target by clicking its name, just as you would rename an icon in the Finder.

iPad to iPhone Targets

If you're duplicating your target on an iPad template, the duplication command completes silently and creates another identical iPad target. You must do a bit more manipulation to get to the same place that the Duplicate and Transition to iPad option gets us on iPhone projects, as follows:

1. Create a new storyboard that is targeted for the iPhone using File, New File from the menu bar.

2. Use the User Interface category in the iOS category to choose a new storyboard file, and then click Next.

3. When prompted, choose the device family for the new storyboard file (presumably the iPhone) and click Next.

4. In the File Creation dialog box, provide a meaningful name for the new storyboard (MainStoryboard_iPhone.storyboard seems strangely appropriate, don't you think?) and navigate to the same place in your project where the original storyboard is located.

5. Then click Create.

6. Drag the new storyboard into your project code group within the project navigator if it doesn't appear there on its own.

7. Select the top-level group in your project and be sure the Summary tab is selected in the editor area.

8. Click the newly created target in the column to the right of the project navigator. (The summary refreshes to show the configuration for the selected target.)

9. Switch the Devices pop-up menu to target the iPhone, and then use the Main Storyboard pop-up menu to choose the iPhone storyboard file you created, as shown in Figure 23.10.

New target   New target's device   New target's storyboard

FIGURE 23.10
Configure the new target.

You can now proceed to develop the project exactly as you would a universal application. When you want to build, remember to click the right side of the Scheme pop-up menu to select the appropriate target.

CAUTION
_____

Remember, Using Multiple Targets Does Not Make Your Application Universal

An application with multiple targets is not universal. The target defines a platform for an executable. If you have a target for the iPhone and a different target for the iPad, you must create two executables to cover both platforms.
_____

Further Exploration

The best way to learn more about universal applications is to start building them. Apple's developer documentation "iPad Human Interface Guidelines" and "iPhone Human Interface Guidelines" will help you understand how your application's interface can be presented on each device.

These documents are also important because what is "acceptable" on one platform (according to Apple) might not be acceptable on the other. iPhone UI classes such as `UIPickerView` and `UIActionSheet`, for example, cannot be displayed directly within a view on the iPad. These features require the use of a popover (`UIPopoverController`) to meet Apple's guidelines. In fact, this UI feature is probably one of the largest differences between developing interfaces for the platforms. Be sure to read up on `UIPopoverController` before just converting your interface to the iPad.

Summary

This hour's lesson covered the process of building universal applications on the iPhone and iPad platforms. Using the universal iOS application templates, you can quickly create an application that is customized to the device that it is running on. As you learned, there are multiple ways to structure a universal app. You can use the default approach, as we did in the first tutorial, and share a view controller between the different interfaces. Alternatively, you can use entirely different code for managing the interfaces. This was demonstrated in the second tutorial.

The lesson ended with a quick look at how defining targets can enable you to create projects that produce both iPhone and iPad applications depending on the scheme you choose when compiling.

Q&A

Q. Why isn't everyone building universal applications?

A. Surprisingly, many people are creating versions of their iPhone applications that run only on the iPad. In my opinion, this is being driven by two things. First, many applications, when expanded for the iPad, are "different" enough that a separate application is warranted. Second, I think that many developers see the potential for higher profits by selling multiple copies of their apps.

Q. I want to share code, but my views are too different to share a controller. What do I do?

A. Look for opportunities to create other shared classes. View controllers aren't the only opportunity for shared code. Any application logic that is shared between the iPhone and iPad could potentially be placed in its own class.

Workshop

Quiz

1. Universal apps run on the Mac, iPhone, and iPad. True or false?

2. Apple requires that any app available for both the iPhone and iPad be submitted as a universal application. True or false?

3. Only a single icon is required for universal applications. True or false?

Answers

1. False. Universal apps run only on the iPhone and iPad platforms (not including the iOS simulator on the Mac).

2. False. You can create separate applications for iPad and iPhone platforms, or a universal app. Apple does not take this into account during evaluation.

3. False. You must configure the deployment information summary for both the iPad and iPhone.

Activities

1. Review the App Store to see the current trends in Universal versus individual iPhone/iPad apps. What are the pricing differences between the approaches?

2. Return to a project in an earlier hour and create an iPad-ready or iPhone-ready version.

HOUR 24
Application Tracing and Debugging

What You'll Learn in This Hour:

- ▶ Using the NSLog function
- ▶ Navigating the Xcode debugger
- ▶ Setting breakpoints and watchpoints
- ▶ Modifying variable values on-the-fly
- ▶ Tracing iOS program execution

Despite our best efforts, no application is ever bug-free. As we end our 24-hour exploration of iOS development, we look at techniques for finding and fixing issues in our applications. The ability to find and eliminate bugs quickly is an essential skill.

Xcode brings together the five basic tools of the software developer's trade into a single application: the text editor, compiler, linker, debugger, and reference documentation. Xcode has debugging tools integrated within it, so all your debugging activities can take place from within the now-familiar confines of Xcode.

This hour covers the debugging and tracing tools included in Xcode. You learn how to use the NSLog function to output debugging information to the Xcode console. You also use Xcode's debugger to find and correct errors. This will give you a good start toward finding and solving problems that might otherwise lead to hours of head scratching, tears, and extreme frustration.

With the term *debugging*, it is assumed your project builds with no errors but then encounters an error or otherwise fails to work as designed when it's executed. If there is an error in your code that prevents it from building, you are still coding, not debugging. The tools in this hour are for improving applications that build but then have logic errors during execution.

Instant Feedback with NSLog

As you've developed applications throughout this book, one that has likely become clear is that producing output in an iOS application is more than just saying "print 'Hello World'." We must deal with view controllers, scenes, storyboards, labels, outlets, connections, and so on, just to get a bit of text on the screen. This makes the traditional approach of debugging (outputting internal values and messages as a program executes) quite cumbersome. Even if we want to jump through all the hoops of building code and connections to output debugging information, we still have to make sure that none of it appears or interferes with our final production-ready app.

Thankfully, there is a way to quickly generate output from a running application that doesn't interfere with your interface or your application logic. Enter the humble NSLog function. Many a gnarly bug has been slain with just this function alone. At any point in your application, you can embed a call to NSLog to confirm the flow of your application into and out of methods or to check the current value of a variable. Any statement you log with NSLog is echoed to Xcode's debugger console.

Using NSLog

The NSLog function takes an NSString argument that can optionally contain string format specifiers. You've used these throughout the book to create formatted NSString objects and can get the full list of string format specifiers from the "String Format Specifier" section of the *String Programming Guide for Cocoa* in Xcode's Help.

The three string format specifiers you'll likely need while debugging are %d for integers (often used to debug loop counters and array indices), %f for floating-point numbers, and %@ for any Objective-C object, including NSString objects.

Consider the code fragment in Listing 24.1.

LISTING 24.1   Calling the NSLog Function

```
NSLog(@"Entering method");
int foo = 42;
float bar = 99.9;
NSLog(@"Value of foo: %d, Value of bar: %f", foo, bar);

NSString *name = [[NSString alloc] initWithString:@"Klaus"];
NSDate *date = [NSDate distantPast];
NSLog(@"Value of name: %@, Value of date:.%@", name, date);
```

In this example, the NSLog function is used to output a string, integer, floating-point value, and two objects (a string and a date). The output looks like this:

```
2012-10-15 16:16:22.329 Sample[4160:f803] Entering method
2012-10-15 16:16:22.331 Sample[4160:f803] Value of foo: 42, Value of bar: 99.9
2012-10-15 16:16:22.333 Sample[4160:f803] Value of name: Klaus, Value of date:
                                           0001-12-30 00:00:00 +0000
```

So, where does this output appear? If it isn't on the iOS device screen, where can you see the results of using NSLog? The answer is the Xcode debugger console, but rather than just telling you where, let's see this in action.

NOTE

When the %@ string format specifier is used with an Objective-C object, the object's description method is called; this can provide additional information about the object within the debugging output. Many of Apple's classes include an implementation of description that is useful for debugging. If you need to debug your own objects with NSLog, you can implement description, which returns an NSString value.

Viewing the Output

Open the project Counting in this hour's projects folder. Click Run to start running the application in the iOS simulator. You'll see... nothing... just a blank screen with some static text (nothing at all changing on the screen). Behind the scenes, however, the application ran a counter in the view controller's viewDidLoad method.

To view the output of the counter, choose View, Debug Area, Activate Console (or press Shift-Command-C). This displays the console and any output your application has generated with NSLog, as shown in Figure 24.1.

TIP

To hide/show the console area, use the middle button in the Xcode toolbar's view controls, choose an option from the View, Debug Area menu, or click the hide/show icon (an arrow in a box) at the left side of the debug area.

As you build more projects, NSLog will become a powerful tool in determining that your applications are executing as you expect. It isn't, however, the most powerful method of debugging an app. For instances where the size or complexity of the application doesn't lend itself to using NSLog, you'll want to turn to the Xcode debugging tools, which enable you to view your application as it executes without having to change your code.

CAUTION

Don't Go NSLog Crazy

As its name implies, the NSLog function is actually intended for logging, not debugging. In addition to printing the statements to Xcode's console, the statements are written out to a file on the file system. Logging to the file system is not what you're intending; it's just a side effect of using NSLog for debugging. It's easy to accidentally leave old NSLog statements in your code after you've finished debugging, which means your application is taking time to write out statements to the file system and is wasting space on the user's device. Search through your project and remove or comment old NSLog statements in your application before you build a release to distribute.

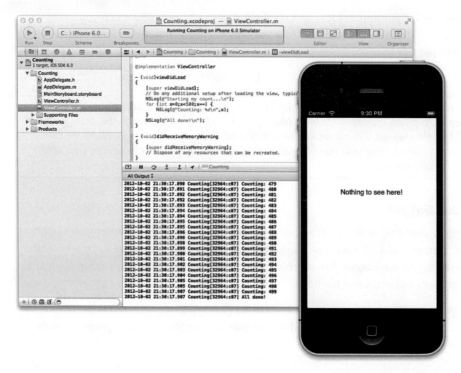

FIGURE 24.1
View the output of NSLog in the console area.

Using the Xcode Debugger

NSLog is a good quick-and-dirty approach to debugging, but it is not the best tool for debugging more complex issues. It's often more productive to use a debugger, which is a tool that lets you examine a running program and inspect its state. It's been said that what separates true software development professionals from weekend hackers is the ability to proficiently use a debugger. If this statement is true, you are in luck, because using Xcode's debugger is not hard.

Normally an application executes at computer speeds, which on an iDevice is millions of instructions per second. A debugger acts like the developer's brake, slowing down the progress of the application to human speeds and letting the developer control the progress of the program from one instruction to the next. At each step in the program, the developer can use the debugger to examine the values of the variables in the program to help determine what's gone wrong.

Debuggers work on the machine instructions that are compiled from an application's source code. With a source-level debugger, however, the compiler provides data to the debugger about which lines of source code generated which instructions. Using this data, the source-level debugger insulates the developer from the machine instructions generated by the compiler and lets the developer work with the source code he has written.

Xcode's iOS debugger, called lldb, is a source-level debugger. The compiler doesn't always generate the data needed for source-level debugging. It can amount to a lot of data, and it provides no benefit to an application's users, so the data is not generated in a release build configuration. Before you can benefit from source-level debugging, you need to build your application in a debug build configuration that will generate the debug symbols.

By default, a new Xcode project comes with two build configurations: Debug and Release. The Debug build configuration includes debug symbols, whereas the Release build configuration does not. Whenever you are working on developing your application, you use the Debug configuration so that you can drop into the debugger whenever you need to. Because Debug is usually the build configuration you want to work with, it's the default configuration, too. To switch to a release configuration, you must build for an iOS device instead of the simulator, and you must use the Product, Edit Scheme menu to switch to a Release configuration. In Figure 24.2, for example, I've set my Scheme so that when I run my app I will be running it on an iOS device in a Release configuration.

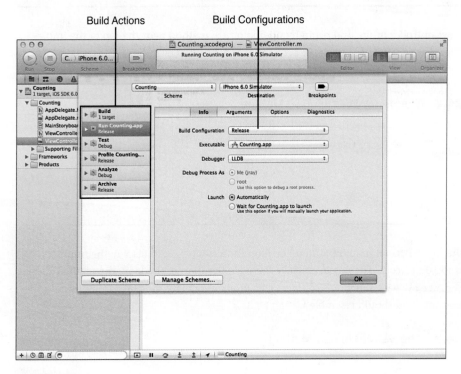

FIGURE 24.2
Set the configuration using the Product, Edit Scheme menu.

NOTE

Make sure that you remember to use the Release build configuration when you create a version of your application for distribution.

Setting Breakpoints and Stepping Through Code

To use the debugger, you must have something to debug. For the rest of this hour, we work through building and debugging a simple application.

Create a new Xcode project with the Single View iOS Application template and call it **DebuggerPractice**. There is no user interface (UI); therefore, no outlets and actions are required in this exercise.

TIP

The debugger often references source code line numbers, and it is helpful to have these displayed in the gutter. Turn on line numbers by opening the Xcode preferences and activating the Line Numbers option under the Text Editing settings.

Open the ViewController.m file and begin by adding a new method near the top of the implementation file. This method, `describeInteger`, returns a string of even if an integer passed to it is divisible by 2, or odd if it isn't. Listing 24.2 contains my implementation of this method.

LISTING 24.2 The `describeInteger` Method

```
-(NSString *)describeInteger:(int)i {
    if (i % 2 == 0) {
        return @"even";
    } else {
        return @"odd";
    }
}
```

Next, edit the `viewDidLoad` method. Add a `for` loop that uses `NSLog` to display the numbers between 1 and 10 in Xcode's debugger console. For each iteration of the loop, the method should call `describeInteger` with the loop's counter. This provides activity that we can monitor in the debugger. Your method should resemble Listing 24.3.

LISTING 24.3 The `viewDidLoad` Method

```
- (void)viewDidLoad
{
    [super viewDidLoad];
    // Do any additional setup after loading the view, typically from a nib.
```

```
NSString *description;

NSLog(@"Start");
for (int i = 1;i <= 10;i++) {
    description = [self describeInteger:i];
    NSLog(@"Variables: i - %d and description - %@", i, description);
    NSLog(@"----");
}
NSLog(@"Done");
}
```

After entering the code, take a moment to look at the editor. Notice the light-gray area (essentially a margin) located to the left of your code. This is called the *gutter* and is where you configure many of Xcode's debugging features. Figure 24.3 shows the gutter.

The Gutter

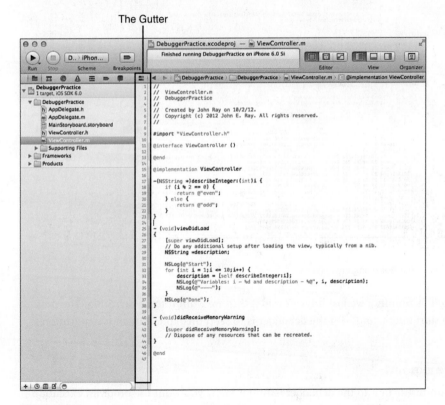

FIGURE 24.3
Xcode's gutter is used for debugging.

Click the Breakpoints button on the Xcode toolbar, and then click Run. The program starts up and brings us to our application's empty view. Use the center button in the Xcode toolbar's

View settings to show the debug area, and then click the button in the upper-right corner of the debug area to show the console. Alternatively, choose View, Debug Area, Activate Console (Shift-Command-C) from the menu bar.

The output from our NSLog statements are in the debugger console, but nothing else, as shown in Figure 24.4.

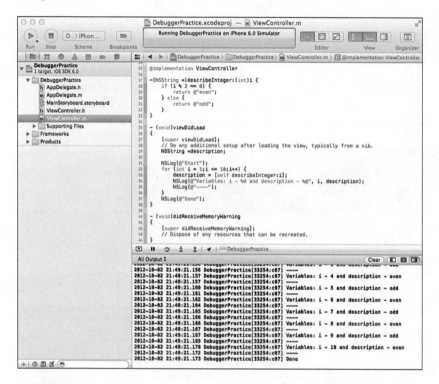

FIGURE 24.4
The debugger is running but not doing anything.

The lldb debugger is running; we just haven't told it that we want it to do anything. The most common way to start interacting with the debugger is to set a breakpoint in your application's source code.

Setting a Breakpoint

A breakpoint is an instruction to the debugger letting it know you want the program execution to pause at that point. To set a breakpoint, click once in the gutter next to the line where you want the application to pause. A breakpoint will appear as a blue arrow, as demonstrated in Figure 24.5. Click the arrow to toggle the breakpoint off and on. When the breakpoint is on, it is displayed as a solid blue color. When it is off, it is light transparent gray, and the debugger ignores it. To remove a breakpoint, simply drag it out of the Xcode gutter and it will disappear. While a program is executing, a green arrow in the gutter indicates the current line of source that is active.

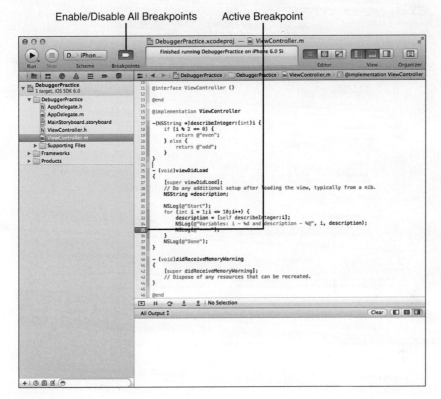

FIGURE 24.5
Set a breakpoint by clicking in the gutter.

Let's create and use a breakpoint. Quit the execution of the application by clicking the Xcode Stop button, and then click the gutter to set a breakpoint next to this line in the viewDidLoad method of ViewController.m:

```
NSLog(@"----");
```

Make sure the breakpoints icon is highlighted in the toolbar (this enables/disables debugging breakpoints), and then click the Run button. Notice that the application stops after printing just one of the inner loop statements to the debugger console:

```
2012-10-02 21:52:30.643 DebuggerPractice[33283:c07] Start
2012-10-02 21:52:30.645 DebuggerPractice[33283:c07] Variables: i - 1 and
description - odd
(lldb)
```

The debugger has paused the execution of the application at our breakpoint and is awaiting further direction, as shown in Figure 24.6.

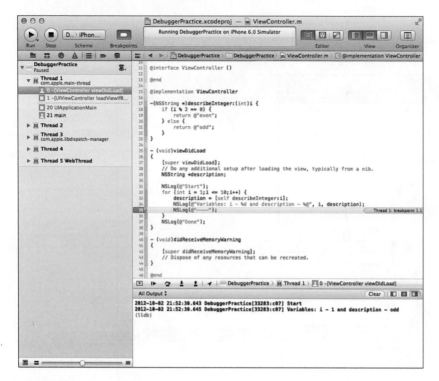

FIGURE 24.6
The debugger pauses at breakpoints.

NOTE

The Xcode debugger pauses when it reaches a line with a breakpoint, but it does not execute that line. You must manually continue execution for the line with the breakpoint to be run. You'll see how this works shortly.

Examining and Changing Variable States

Now that the execution of the program is paused in the debugger, we can look at the value of any variables that are in scope. One of the easiest ways Xcode provides to examine variables is the debugger *datatip*. Just hover over a variable in the source code of the paused method and Xcode will display a cascading pop-up menu, visible in Figure 24.7. The type, name, memory address, and value of the variable are displayed. Hover over the i loop counter in the for statement and then the description variable. Notice that the datatip for i is just one level, but the datatip for the more complex NSString object has multiple levels. (Hover over the disclosure triangles to see the additional levels.)

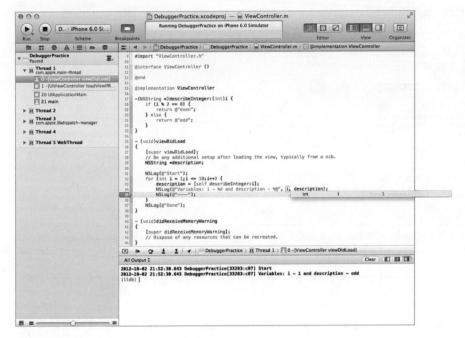

FIGURE 24.7
You can display the datatip for the i variable by hovering over the variable.

Datatips can also be used to change the value of a variable. Again, hover over the i variable in the for loop statement and click the value in the datatip. It is currently 1, but you can change it to 4 by typing 4 and pressing Enter. The value in the running program is immediately changed, so the next trip through the loop logs to the console with a value of 5, and there won't be a logged statement with a value of 2, 3, or 4. To confirm that the program does execute as if the i variable has a value of 4, we need to continue the execution of the program.

Stepping Through Code

By far, the most common debugging activity is watching the flow of your application and following what it does while it's running. To do this, you need to be able to control the flow of execution, pausing at the interesting parts and skipping over the mundane.

The debugger provides four icons for controlling program execution (see Figure 24.8):

▶ **Continue:** Resumes execution of the paused program, pausing again at the next error or active breakpoint.

▶ **Step Over:** Steps to the next line of code in the same method.

▶ **Step Into:** Steps into the method that is being called. If a method isn't being called on the current line of code, it acts like Step Over.

▶ **Step Out:** Steps out of the current method back to the caller of the current method.

FIGURE 24.8
Program execution control icons.

NOTE

You'll notice a fifth icon beside the Step Out control. You use this to set a simulated location for location services. I'm not sure why Apple chose to place it there, but they did. It does not affect day-to-day debugging.

Whereas the global breakpoint control is obvious (and *useful*), the other options might not be so clear. Let's take a look at how each of these works to control the flow of our application. First click the Continue icon a couple of times. Control returns back to the same breakpoint each time you continue, but if you hover over the i and description variables, you'll see that i is incrementing and description is switching between even and odd.

Add a breakpoint to this line of code by clicking the gutter:

```
description = [self describeInteger:i];
```

Click the Continue icon again, and this time you'll see the program stops at the new breakpoint because it's the next breakpoint the program encounters. This breakpoint is on a line of source where we are calling the describeInteger method. If we want to see what's going on inside that method, we need to step into it. Click the Step Into icon, and the program stops on the first line of the describeInteger method, demonstrated in Figure 24.9.

To step line by line through a method without entering any of the methods that might be called, use the Step Over task. Click the Step Over icon three times to step through the describeInteger method and return to the viewDidLoad method.

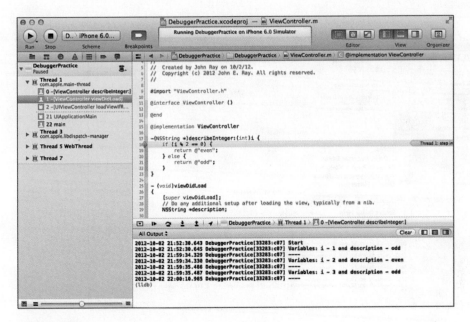

FIGURE 24.9
Program execution after stepping into the describeInteger method.

Click the Continue icon until you return to the breakpoint on the describeInteger method, and click the Step Into icon to step into the method a second time. This time, instead of stepping all the way through describeInteger, click the Step Out icon and you'll be stopped back at the line where the describeInteger method was called. The rest of the describeInteger method still executed; you just didn't watch each step of it. You are stopped where the program flow has just exited the describeInteger method.

In addition to these program control tasks, another important option is hidden in the gutter. It's called Continue to Here. Continue to Here works on the line of code you select it on, and it works like a combination of the continue task and a temporary breakpoint. Program flow continues until it reaches an error or an active breakpoint or it reaches the line of code you continued to.

To try this, make sure you're stopped at a breakpoint in viewDidLoad, and then right-click in the gutter next to this line:

```
NSLog(@"Done");
```

Click Continue to Here in the contextual menu, as shown in Figure 24.10. Notice that we didn't make it to the line of code we continued to; we stopped on one of the two existing breakpoints inside the for loop.

FIGURE 24.10
The Continue to Here option of the gutter context menu.

NOTE

You can also access the Continue to Here function by hovering your mouse near the right side of the gutter and clicking the green circle with arrow icon that appears next to the code line in the editor. Unfortunately, Xcode is very touchy about when it shows the icon while hovering, so you may find the contextual menu approach the most reliable.

Click each breakpoint once to make it inactive, and click Continue to Here on the gutter next to the final line of the method one more time. This time we make it to the end of the method. Inspect the i and description variables with the hover datatip and notice that description's value is even, but i is no longer in scope and can't be inspected. The i variable was scoped only to the for loop, and now that we have exited the for loop, it no longer exists. You can now stop the iOS application.

Setting a Watchpoint

Let's suppose now that there is a tricky bug in your application that only occurs on the 1,000th time through the loop. You wouldn't want to put a breakpoint in the loop and have to click the continue icon 1,000 times. That's where a watchpoint comes in handy. A watchpoint is a conditional breakpoint; it doesn't stop execution every time, it stops only when a condition you define is true.

To test this out, update the `for` loop to execute 2,000 times rather than 10 times. Your `viewDid-Load` method should now resemble Listing 24.4.

LISTING 24.4   Update `viewDidLoad` to Loop 2,000 Times

```
- (void)viewDidLoad
{
    [super viewDidLoad];
        // Do any additional setup after loading the view, typically from a nib.
    NSString *description;

    NSLog(@"Start");
    for (int i = 1;i <= 2000;i++) {
        description = [self describeInteger:i];
        NSLog(@"Variables: i - %d and description - %@", i, description);
        NSLog(@"----");
    }
    NSLog(@"Done");
}
```

Now let's set a watchpoint that stops execution when the loop counter equals 1,000. First, remove the existing breakpoints by dragging them out of the gutter. Next, add a normal breakpoint by clicking in the gutter next to this line:

```
NSLog(@"Start");
```

Click the gutter next to this line to add a breakpoint:

```
NSLog(@"Variables: i - %d and description - %@", i, description);
```

Then right-click the breakpoint and choose Edit from the contextual menu. The Breakpoints dialog then opens, as shown in Figure 24.11. Here you can use the Condition field to specify when the breakpoint becomes active. Set the condition to `i == 1000`.

Click the Run button to execute the application. The program stops at the first breakpoint. Click the Continue icon, and the application will go through the loop 999 times before stopping on the watchpoint on the 1,000th trip through the loop when the loop counter `i` is equal to 1,000. You can confirm this by looking at the 999 log messages in the debugger console or by hovering over the `i` variable in the source and looking at its value in the datatip.

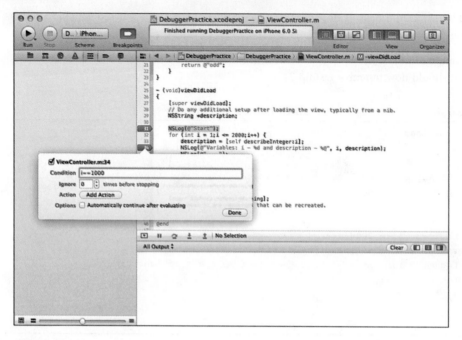

FIGURE 24.11
Program execution stops on the 1,000th iteration.

Accessing the Variable List

If, at any time, you want to access a list of all variables that are active in your current method, you can do so by switching the debugger area to the Variables view using the three icons in the upper-right corner of the Debug area. These switch between the Variable view (left), a Split Variable/Console view (middle), and the Console view (right). To this point, we've been focusing solely on the Console view.

Click to display the Variable List, and you'll see that both the i and description variables (and their values) that we've been inspecting with datatips are shown prefixed with an *L* icon, as shown in Figure 24.12. This means these variables are declared locally in the method that is currently executing. You'll also see *A* icons for Arguments scope variables that have been passed into the current method as arguments. A pop-up menu at the upper-left corner of the Variable List enables you to show All variables, Local variables only, or Auto—to let Xcode choose what it thinks is relevant.

TIP
Double-clicking a variable line in the Variable List enables you to change its value, just as you could through the datatips.

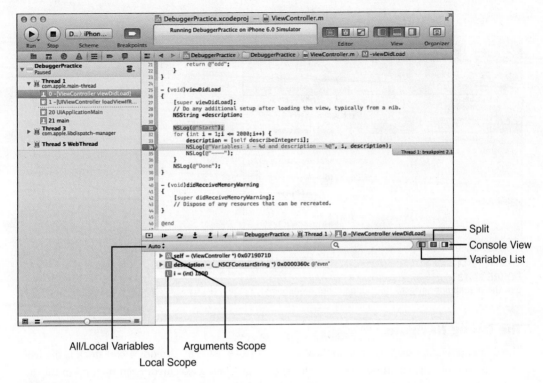

FIGURE 24.12
Use the Variable List to inspect and change the value of active variables in your application.

Using the Debugger Navigators

We first looked at the debugger by examining console output, and since then we've focused on debugging in that area alone. There are also two navigator area displays—the debug navigator and the breakpoint navigator—that have some helpful benefits. You may have noticed these appearing on the left side of the Xcode workspace while working with the debugger. You can jump either at any time by selecting them from the View, Navigators menu.

The Breakpoint Navigator

Large projects with hundreds of breakpoints can get out of hand quickly. Where are all the breakpoints? How do you selective enable/disable/edit/remove them? The breakpoint navigator, shown in Figure 24.13, is your one-stop shop for managing breakpoints in your project.

All breakpoints are listed by the file where they are located. You can click any breakpoint to jump to that spot in your code or right-click any listed breakpoint to manage it (including setting conditions, disabling it, and so on).

Debug Navigator

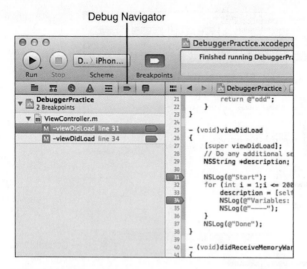

FIGURE 24.13
Use the breakpoint navigator to manage your breakpoints.

The Debug Navigator

The debug navigator displays the application's call stack listed by thread. A call stack is the list of all the subroutines (methods and functions) currently being executed. Each method in the call stack has been called by the method below it. To better understand this, it is best to see it in action.

Remove the existing breakpoints from your code, and then add a new breakpoint at the start of `describeInteger` by clicking in front of this line:

```
if (i % 2 == 0) {
```

Now, execute your code and let the breakpoint take effect. After execution has stopped, open the debug navigator by choosing View, Navigators, Show Debug Navigator or by clicking the navigator area toolbar icon (two solid lines with a dashed line in the middle).

Notice that the `describeInteger` method of our view controller is at the top of the stack and was called by the `viewDidLoad` method, exactly as we'd expect. The call stack entries listed with a blue icon are code that we have implemented in our project; clicking one of these entries shows a green cursor where the program execution is currently "waiting." The `describeInteger` method is waiting on our breakpoint, while the `viewDidLoad` method waits on the `describeInteger` method (and so on). Figure 24.14 shows an example of a call stack.

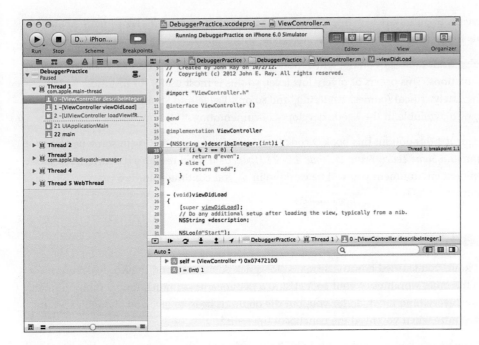

FIGURE 24.14
View the call stack in the debug navigator.

The rows in the call stack that are not in blue are for methods where the debugger only has assembly language available. Click one to see some Assembly code. (Doesn't that make you thankful that we have a source-level debugger?)

You've done enough now to start getting the hang of using the debugger. With just these few simple steps for controlling program flow and inspecting and changing program state, you can debug many of the issues you may run into.

Further Exploration

Invest some time into becoming proficient with Xcode debugging. When you're approaching the launch date for your application, you'll want to check and double-check your code. In these cases, time is short and the stress level is high, so it's not the ideal circumstances to be learning application debugging for the first time. Become comfortable with these tools now, and they'll provide a significant productivity boost when you need it the most.

Xcode offers many other tools for testing and optimizing your applications, but each could take a book in its own right. The Instruments system, for example, allows you to stress-test your application under a number of conditions and identify potential problems. You can even use Instruments to automate user interaction with your apps to test them. Learn more about Instruments in the *Instruments User Guide*, accessible within the Xcode developer documentation.

You may also want to look at Shark, which analyzes your code for performance issues and recommends solutions. This occurs at a very low level, so this is most useful for instances where speed is absolutely critical (games, rendering, and so on). Delve into Shark by reading the *Shark User Guide*, also available in the Xcode developer documentation.

As you've learned throughout this book, Xcode is a large, *large* product. I (with some personal bias) recommend *Sams Teach Yourself Xcode 4 in 24 Hours* as a good resource to learn more about the development environment you will be working in as you continue your iOS development.

Summary

In this last hour, you learned how to use `NSLog` for quick debugging and the Xcode debugger for examining the inner workings of your code. Using a debugger takes much longer than an hour to understand everything it can do for you, but the goal has been to give you enough exposure that you recognize when you need the benefits of the tools.

With that, you've reached the end of this book. I sincerely hope that you've enjoyed yourself and are ready to write some apps. Remember to visit the support website http://teachyourselfios.com for additional materials and corrections.

Q&A

Q. **Why is using a debugger easier or better than just using NSLog?**

A. `NSLog` is a great place for beginning developers to start. It gives a degree of insight into what is going on in the code, without having to change the development process. Using the full-blown Xcode debugger, however, will enable you to view and modify values in your code as it is running. In addition, it doesn't require any changes directly to your code, so there isn't a need to remove debugger statements when the code is clean. Using a debugger takes awhile to get used to, but for large projects, it is a must.

Workshop

Quiz

1. What is a breakpoint? What is a watchpoint?

2. What is a call stack?

3. You can use the Xcode debugging tools to change the value of a variable while your program is executing. True or false?

Answers

1. A breakpoint tells the debugger to stop execution at the start of a particular line of source code so that the developer can inspect and possibly change the state of the running application and control and monitor the application's progress. A watchpoint is a conditional breakpoint that stops execution only if a specified condition is true.

2. A call stack is the list of all the subroutines (methods and functions) currently being executed.

3. True. The Xcode debugger enables you to modify your variables as the code runs. This can be useful for testing a variety of conditions, but be aware that the debugger will allow you to set variables to values that couldn't possibly be generated by your code. It's that flexible.

Activities

1. Try breaking applications by using the debugger to set values outside their bounds—text in numeric fields, loops that extend beyond their endpoint, and so on. How does Xcode react?

2. Use the debugging tools to monitor the inner workings of the applications you built earlier in this book. Then take a break.

Index

B

back button attribute, 415

background-aware apps

adding background modes key, 753-754

backgrounding

disabling, 742

types of, 739

completing long-running background tasks, 739, 754-760

handling background suspension, 743-744

implementing directions for audio in, 750-753

life cycle methods, 739-742

task-specific background processing, 739, 747-753

background image resources, adding to location-aware apps, 715

background modes key, adding to apps, 753-754

background processing, task-specific, 739, 747-753

background suspension, 743-744

background tasks, long-running, 739, 754-760

background touch, hiding keyboards with, 214-215

backgrounds

buttons, customizing, 206

changing colors of, 201

hiding keyboards by touching, 214-215

setting for looped animations, 232-233

badges, tab bar item, 441-443

bar button attributes, 366

bar button items, 365, 412

bar button titles, setting, 485-486

barItem outlet, 438

bars

navigation, 412

tab, 418

Basic table style, 452

battery life, 712

beginGeneratingDeviceOrientation-Notifications method, 603

BestFriend app

building, 702

creating and connecting outlets and actions, 689-690

designing the interface, 688-689

implementing logic in

address books, 690-695

email, 700-701

maps, 695-699

social networking, 701-702

setting up the project, 686-688

beta versions

access to, 8

Xcode, 13

blocks

functional building. See classes

in methods, 86-87

Bluetooth, 7

brackets, in protocols, 72

breakpoint navigator, 797

breakpoints, setting, 786-796

build schemes, choosing, 46

building apps

BestFriend, 702

with custom pickers, 406

with the date picker, 390

detecting tilt and rotation, 621-622

flashlight, 506

FlowerWeb, 268

with gestures, 595

location-aware, 723-724

long-running background tasks, 739, 754-760

looped animations, 243

with magnetic compass, 733

with Master-Detail Application templates, 486

with navigation controllers, 433

with orientation sensing, 610

with popovers, 360

programmatically defined interfaces, 562

scrolling views, 276

Settings, 520

with Single View Application templates, 184-185

story creators, 217

swapping views on rotation, 569

with tab bar controllers, 443

with table views, 469

universal, 771, 775-776

in Xcode, 46-50

bundle identifiers, 29

bundles, settings, 494-496, 511-517

button attributes, editing, 204-205

constraints in Size Inspector, 541-543

text in buttons, 415

titles in navigation bars, 414-415

user interfaces

disabling, 482

Interface Builder, 135-139

variable states, 791

viewDidLoad method, 786-787

editor area, 31

editor scene field, setting initial scene label to, 353

EditorViewController class, 331

email

BestFriend app

building, 702

creating and connecting outlets and actions, 689

designing the interface, 688-689

implementing logic in, 700-701

setting up the project, 686-688

integrating with apps, 678-680

email addresses, populating fields with current, 353

Empty Application template, 29

empty categories, 78

empty files, adding to projects manually, 34

empty selections, media picker, 666

enterprise developer program, 8

errors

correcting, 48-50

location, 710-711

in older device versions, 741

esoteric conditions, simulating, 60-61

Event Kit framework, 103

Event Kit UI framework, 100

events

detecting outside fields, 214

interface rotation, 603

low-memory, simulating, 61

multitouch, generating in iOS Simulator, 59

Touch Up Inside, 153, 189

Exit icon, 129

exit segues, 324-325, 353

exiting

apps, 184

Xcode, 14

exits

described, 313

preparing view controllers for, 325, 347

expressions

described, 87-88

making decisions with, 88-89

extensions for files, xcodeproj, 31

External Accessory framework, 104

F

Facebook, integrating with other apps, 680-682

feedback

app tracing and debugging, 782-783

audio, 751

iOS devices, 7

fees, Apple Developer Program, 8

fields

alert views, 301

detecting events outside, 214

editor scene, setting initial scene label to, 353

populating with current email addresses, 353

text

adding to user interfaces, 193-194

alert view, 302-303

attributed, 196

editing attributes of, 194-196

plain, 196

purpose of, 115, 190

text entry, alertViewStyle property, 283

treating as passwords, 198

file extensions, xcodeproj, 31

file paths, data storage, 498-499

file system storage, implementing, 520-528

File Template library, 133

files

AppDelegate, 170

class, 170-171

R

radian conversion constants, **725**

radians constant, adding degrees to, **563**

RAM (random access memory), iPhones, **6**

random access memory (RAM), iPhones, **6**

recognizers, gestures. *See* gesture recognizers

recordAudio method, **652, 655**

recorders, AV audio, **634-635**

recording, audio, **649-655**

references

circular, 75

to objects, 82

removing from projects, 35-36

registration

development devices, 17, 18

iOS developer, 9

orientation updates, 608-609

relationships

creating between controllers, 414, 421

described, 313

tab bar, creating, 436-437

release message, **67-68**

remote content, loading, **250-251**

removeConstraints NSLayoutConstraint method, **575**

removing

connections, 154

constraints from image views, 575

files and resources from projects, 35-36

installed apps from iOS Simulator, 58

repeatInterval property, **745**

repetition, with loops, **89-91**

replace option, segues, **321**

replacing, image views, **587**

requestWithURL class, **250-251**

@required directive, **80-81**

resetting iOS Simulator to defaults, **58**

resignFirstResponder method, **212**

resistance, content compression, **543**

resolutions, iOS devices, **4-5**

resources

adding to projects, 34-35

animation, adding to looped animations, 225

image

adding to gestures, 576

adding to Settings app, 509

background, 715

direction, 724

Master-Detail Application templates, 471

table views, 461

removing from projects, 35-36

sound, adding to apps, 291

See also files

Resources group, **33**

responders, described, **108**

responsive interfaces, programmatically defined, **555-562**

responsive user interfaces

described, 533-534

designing rotatable and resizable interfaces, 536-538

enabling interface rotation, 534-535

See also Auto Layout system

restoration, **492**

retain message, **91-92**

Retina displays

app icons for, 53

image views, 223

launch images for, 54-55

locating high-resolution images for, 228

resolution of, 4

Return Key trait, **198**

rich media

AV Foundation framework, 632-635

creating MediaPlayground app

accessing and playing the music library, 662-668

creating and connecting outlets and actions, 644-645

designing the interface, 642-643

implementing audio recording and playback, 649-655

implementing Core Image filter, 659-662

implementing movie player, 646-650

implementing the photo library and camera, 656-659

setting up the project, 640-642

reusing in other applications, 162

simulating, 145

simulating rotations of, 60

Xcode, tour of, 31-32

See also apps; projects

utility area, 31-32

V

valueForProperty method, 632

values

in CGRectMake function, 49

floating-point

float data type, 111

initializing strings with, 109

height, 276

initializing strings with, 109

inputting on iPads, 7

media picker filters, 630

MFMailComposeResult, 680

nil, 85, 110

numbers, referring by, 393

playbackState property, 631

property, 172

retrieving and setting, 73

setValuesFromPreferences, 518-519

UIDeviceOrientation property, 603

width, 276

working with, 111

variable lists, accessing, 796

variable sizes, 551-554

variable states, examining and changing, 791

variables

assignments with, 82

audio, adding to apps, 749

declaring as pointers, 82-83

described, 68

instance. *See* instance variables

mathematical operations with, 82

myLabel, 165

planning

in apps with Master-Detail Application templates, 472

in apps with table views, 461

as pointers to objects, 82

private, 77-78

private instance, 556

sender, 212-213

soundID, 307

states of, examining and changing, 791

version control, snapshots as, 46

versions

devices, simulating apps on each, 61

iOS, checking for multitasking support in, 739-741

vertical constraints, 141

vibrations, 288, 290, 308

videos

capturing on iOS devices, 7

playing, 639

supported file formats for, 628

View Controller icon, 128

view controller subclasses, 316-319

view controllers

associating with projects, 344-346

associating with scenes

date picker, 376-377

navigation controller, 425-426

tab bar controller, 435-436

becoming first responders, 593-594

changing simulated size of, 271-272

Cocoa Touch, 106

described, 164-166, 313

displaying, 329

generic, classes of, 424

instantiating, 326

iPad, setting up in universal apps, 772-773

preparing for exits, 325, 347

referencing one scene's view controller from another, 410

setting identifiers for, 326-328

stacks of, 411

View icon, 128

view-rotation logic, 567-568

ViewController class, 108, 171-173, 331

ViewController file, 237

ViewController files, 170, 174-175

viewDidAppear method, 276, 587

viewDidLoad method, 209-210, 653, 663, 750, 786-787